ORGANIZATIONAL BEHAVIOR

AN EXPERIENTIAL APPROACH
SIXTH EDITION

DAVID A. KOLB
Case Western Reserve University

JOYCE S. OSLAND
University of Portland

IRWIN M. RUBIN
Temenos, Inc.

PRENTICE HALL
Englewood Cliffs, NJ 07632

Kolb, David A., 1939–
    Organizational behavior : an experiential approach / David A.
Kolb, Joyce S. Osland, Irwin M. Rubin. -- 6th ed.
        p.   cm.
    Includes bibliographical references.
    ISBN 0-13-151010-X
    1. Psychology, Industrial.   2. Organizational behavior.
I. Osland, Joyce. II. Rubin, Irwin M., 1939–   . III. Title.
HF5548.8K552   1995   94-42475
158.7--dc20   CIP

Production Editor: Pencil Point Studio: Suzanne Visco
In-house Project Manager: Alana Zdinak
Acquisitions Editor: Natalie Anderson
Interior Design: Pencil Point Studio
Cover Design: Pencil Point Studio
Proofreader: Pencil Point Studio/Helen Ambrosio
Permissions Editor: Pencil Point Studio: Suzanne Visco
Manufacturing Buyer: Vincent Scelta
Assistant Editor: Lisamarie Brassini
Editorial Assistant: Nancy Proyect

Cover Art: Marles Najaka

ISBN 0-13-151010-X

Prentice-Hall International (UK) Limited, *London*
Prentice-Hall of Australia Pty. Limited, *Sydney*
Prentice-Hall Canada Inc., *Toronto*
Prentice-Hall Hispanoamericana, S.A., *Mexico*
Prentice-Hall of India Private Limited, *New Delhi*
Prentice-Hall of Japan, Inc., *Tokyo*
Simon & Schuster Asia Pte. Ltd., *Singapore*
Editoria Prentice-Hall do Brazil, Ltda., *Rio de Janeiro*

To Jonathan

Asbjorn, Jessica,
Michael, Katrina, Bergit, and Ellie

Beth, Steven, and Corey

CONTENTS

Chapter 3
Individual and Organizational Learning   41

Chapter 4
Individual Motivation and Organizational Behavior   71

Chapter 5
Values and Ethics   101

Chapter 6
Personal Growth, Career Development, and Work Stress   125

PART II
CREATING EFFECTIVE WORK GROUPS   161

Chapter 7
Interpersonal Communication   162

PART III
LEADERSHIP AND MANAGEMENT   325

Chapter 13
Leadership   326

Chapter 14
Leadership and Organizational Culture   343

Foreword

This book–or better, the body of experiences it proposes–seeks to communicate some knowledge of general psychological principles, and some skills in applying that knowledge to social and organizational situations. Science tries to illuminate concrete reality by disclosing the general laws and principles that make the reality what it is. The generalization gives meaning to the concrete instance, but the instance carries the generalization into the real world–makes it usable. Experiencing social situations and then analyzing that experience brings generalization and concrete reality into effective union.

In teaching undergraduate and graduate management courses, I have frequently encountered students who hold a magical belief in a real world, somehow entirely different from any world they had hitherto experienced, and different, too, from the world of their textbooks. In teaching experienced executives, I have as frequently encountered men who balked at the proposal to apply general psychological principles to the concrete experiences of their everyday world. If there are skeptics of either variety in a group that undertakes one of these exercises, they can conduct their own tests of the relevance of theory to experience and vice versa. That is what the exercises are about.

But are the exercise themselves "real"? Can you really simulate social or organizational phenomena in a laboratory? The answer hangs on what we know of people–of their readiness to take roles, or, more accurately, their *inability not* to take roles when they find themselves in appropriate social situations, but this in itself is a psychological generalization: Man is a role-taker. Like any generalization, it should be tested empirically; and the exercises do just that. Each participant can be his own witness to the reality–or lack of it–of what has gone on.

But the purpose of the exercises is not just to increase understanding of principles, or understanding of concrete situations in terms of principles. They can be useful also as a means of developing skills for group situations: skills of observing, skills of self-insight, skills of understanding the behaviors and motives of others, skills of adapting behavior to the requirements of a task and the needs of groups and persons.

There is no magic to it. Learning here, like all learning, derives from time and attention directed to relevant material. The exercises provide the material. The time, attention, and active participation must be supplied by those who take part in them.

Herbert A. Simon

Preface

This sixth edition of *Organizational Behavior: An Experiential Approach* is the latest improvement on an experiment that began over 20 years ago. The first edition of this book was developed at MIT in the late 1960s and was the first application of the principles of experience-based learning to teaching in the field of organizational psychology. Since then the field has changed, the practice of experience-based learning has grown in acceptance and sophistication, and we, the authors, have changed.

The field of organizational behavior has grown rapidly in this time period and is today a complex tapestry of historical trends, contemporary trends, and new emerging trends. In the Introduction that follows we will describe these trends in more detail.

In comparison with previous editions, more emphasis has been placed upon cross-cultural and diversity issues throughout the entire book. We included new chapters on ethics, coaching and empowerment, and leadership and made substantial revisions in the remaining chapters. As always, our objective was not to overwhelm students with a comprehensive array of theories and findings, but to provide them with the essential material and experiences they need to become effective managers and good employees.

Since the publication of our first edition, a number of other experience-based texts have been published in organizational behavior and other management specialties, and experiential-learning approaches have become widely accepted in higher education, particularly in programs for adult learners. The value of educational approaches that link the concepts and techniques of academia with learners' personal experiences in the real world is no longer questioned. In this latest edition we have attempted to reflect the state of the art in the practice of experiential learning and to bring these approaches to bear on the latest thinking and research in the field of organizational behavior.

This book is intended for students and managers who wish to explore the personal relevance and conceptual bases of the phenomena of organizational behavior. There are two goals in the experiential learning process. One is to learn the specifics of a particular subject matter. The other is to learn about one's own strengths and weaknesses as a learner (i.e., learning how to learn from experience). Thus, the book is focused upon exercises, self-analysis techniques, and role plays to make the insights of behavioral science meaningful and relevant to practicing managers and students. Each chapter is designed as an educational intervention that facilitates each stage of the experience-based learning process. Exercises and simulations are designed to produce experiences that create the phenomena of organizational behavior. Observation schemes and methods are introduced to facilitate understanding of these experiences. Theories and models are added to aid in forming generalizations. And finally, the intervention is structured in a way that encourages learners to experiment with and test what they have learned either in class or other areas of their lives. Our purpose is to teach students how to learn so that they will become continuous learners, capable of responding to demands for change and new skills throughout their career. Learning is no longer a special activity reserved for the classroom, but an integral and explicit part of work itself.

In addition to teaching students to be life-long learners, the exercises and the order of the chapters are designed to facilitate self-knowledge and team work. Students should leave this course with a much clearer understanding of themselves and the effect their behavior has on others. Students work in the same learning groups throughout the course. In these groups, members share their experiences and provide support, advice, feedback, and friendship to each other. A by-product of this group approach is the creation of a class environment that facilitates learning.

A companion readings book, *The Organizational Behavior: Reader, Sixth Edition*, is also published by Prentice Hall. Many footnotes in this sixth volume make reference to articles that have been reprinted there. These are simply cited as *"Reader"* in the footnote entries.

A preface is a place to publicly thank the many people who have helped us. Our feelings of pride in our product are tempered by the great indebtedness we feel to many others whose ideas and insights preceded ours. It is a tribute to the spirit of collaboration that pervades our field that the origin of many of the exercises recorded here is unknown. We have tried throughout the manuscript to trace the origins of those exercises we know about and in the process we may, in many areas, fall short of the original insight. For that we can only apologize. The major unnamed contributors are our students. In a very real sense, this book could never have been completed without their active participation in our explorations.

We wish to thank James McIntyre, our co-author in the first four editions of this book, for his generous and creative contributions. While much has changed and will continue to change through successive editions of this book, Jim's presence will always be there.

The many instructors who, as users of previous editions of our text, have shared their experiences, resources, insights and criticisms have been invaluable guides in the revision process.

Anthony Buono, Barbara Gayle, Howard Feldman, Leslie Hickcox, Asbjorn Osland, and Judith White were especially helpful, as were the reviewers of the last edition. Bruce Drake deserves a special mention for selflessly contributing his formidable editorial skills to this project. The chapter "Managing Diversity" was jointly developed by a Case Western Reserve University project team consisting of David Akinussi, Lynda Benroth, Rafael Estevez, Elizabeth Fisher, Mary Ann Hazen, David Kolb, Dennis O'Connor, and Michelle Spain.

Natalie Anderson and Lisamarie Brassini, our Prentice Hall Editors, have been patient, persistent, and supportive throughout the revision process. Gene Garone and Suzanne Visco of Pencil Point Studio were a joy to work with on the production of the book. We owe a special debt of gratitude to Nichole Wilson, who cheerfully and efficiently tackled the endless details of preparing the manuscript.

David A. Kolb
Joyce S. Osland
Irwin M. Rubin

REVIEWERS

Robert Bontempo, Columbia University, New York, NY
Anthony Buono, Bentley College, Waltham, MA
Jared Jay Look, University of Connecticut at Waterbury, Waterbury, CT
Peter Poole, Lehigh University, Bethlehem, PA
Bruce Johnson, Gustavus Adolphus College, Saint Peter, MN

Introduction to the Workbook

I hear and I forget
I see and I remember
I do and I understand
CONFUCIUS

As teachers responsible for helping people learn about the field of organizational behavior, we have grappled with a number of basic educational dilemmas. Some of these dilemmas revolve around the issue of *how* to teach about this most important and intensely personal subject. The key concepts in organizational behavior (indeed, in social science in general) are rather abstract. It is difficult through the traditional lecture method to bring these ideas meaningfully to life. Other problems concern issues of what to teach, since the field of organizational behavior is large and continues to grow. Relevant concepts and theories come from a variety of disciplines, and no single course could begin to scratch the surface. Another dilemma is one of control. Who should be in control of the learning process? Who should decide what material is important to learn? Who should decide the pace at which learning should occur? Indeed, who should decide what constitutes learning? Our resolution of these and related dilemmas is contained within this book. The learning materials in this book are an application of the theory of experiential learning to the teaching and learning of organizational behavior. In this method, primary emphasis is placed upon learning from your own experience. Each of the chapters in the workbook begins with an introduction that raises key questions and provides a framework for your experiences in the unit. The core of each unit is an action-oriented behavioral simulation. The purpose of these exercises is to allow you to generate your own data about each of the key concepts to be studied. A format is provided to facilitate your ability to observe and share the personal reactions you have experienced, while the summaries at the end of each unit help to integrate the unit experiences and stimulate further questions and issues to be explored. If there is an overriding objective of the book, it is that you learn how to learn from all your experiences.

LEARNING ABOUT ORGANIZATIONAL BEHAVIOR

It has been over 20 years since we first began developing and testing the feasibility of experiential learning methods for teaching organizational behavior. Our initial attempts to substitute exercises, games, and role plays for more traditional educational approaches were met in many quarters by polite skepticism and resistance. Today experiential learning approaches are an integral part of management school curricula and management training programs everywhere. During these years, the subject matter of organizational behavior has undergone much change as well. Some of this change has been subtle and quiet, involving the consolidation and implementation of trends that began years ago. Other changes have been more dramatic. New vital perspectives have come alive, reorganizing and redirecting research, theory, and teaching in the field. Still other trends loom on the horizon the way toward the future shape of the field.

As we began to work on this sixth edition, v ck of these changes so that we might faithfully, in ne ential exercises, portray the field of organizational be f vital themes enduring from the past, alive in the pres Such a stocktaking is difficult to achieve objectively. t field with indefinite boundaries overlapping sister disciplines of social psychology, sociology, and anthropology, and management fields such as operations research, business policy, and industrial relations. One could convincingly argue that any patterns one sees in such diversity and complexity lie more in the eye of the beholder than in objective reality. At the very least, where one stands in defining organizational behavior is greatly influenced by where one sits, by one's particular experience and orientation to the field. Recognizing that any organization of the field is constructed from a combination of objective reality and subjective preference, we nonetheless felt that there is value in making explicit our view of the field, since it was on the basis of that view that choices of topics and exercises were made. By understanding our view, you, as learners, may be better able to articulate your own agreements and disagreements, thereby helping to sort the actual state of the field from our individual viewpoints.

Table I-1 summarizes the changes we have seen in the field in the last 50 years in six general areas: the way organizational behavioral is defined, the way management education is conducted, the field's perspective on the nature of persons, its view as to how human resources are to be managed, its perspective on organizations, and the nature of the change/improvement process. In each of these areas there are three kinds of trends: *historical foundations of trends*, previous historical development that is now widely influential in shaping the field; *contemporary trends*, current research and development that is capturing the excitement and imagination of scholars and practitioners; and *emerging trends*, new issues and concerns that seem destined to shape the future of organizational behavior in research and practice.

Definition of the Field

Paul Lawrence[1] traces the origin of the field of organizational behavior back to the early 1940s. He cites as the first key contribution to the field the group climate experiments of Kurt Lewin and his associates in 1943. Early scholars in the field came from industrial and social psychology and later from sociology. Organizational behavior departments were housed administratively in business schools, but in general they maintained their separate identity from the profession of management. Today we see major changes in the orientation as organizational behavior departments have become more integrated units within professional business schools. Most new faculty today have Ph.D.s in management as opposed to basic disciplines, and interdisciplinary research around the managerial task has burgeoned. Concepts are now more often defined in managerial terms (e.g., work team development) as opposed to behavioral science terms (group dynamics).

Active developments in organizational behavior today involve the expansion of the field from an industrial-business focus to a wider application of behavioral science knowledge in other professional fields-health care management, law, public administration, education, and international development. Perhaps because of this expansion into more complex social and political institutions, an emerging trend is toward a focus on sociological and political concepts that increase our understanding of management in complex organizational environments. In recent years the issue of environmental determinism has been raised, an even more "macro" approach to organizations. The population ecologists study the rise and fall of organizations within an entire industry and maintain that it is the environment, rather than actions by humans, that influences organizations. There is an active intellectual debate in the field between those who see strategic leadership and choice as the determinant of organizational success and those who subscribe to the environmental determinist position.

---

[1]Paul Lawrence, "Historical Development of Organizational Behavior," in Jay Lorsch (Ed.), *Handbook of Organizational Behavior* (Englewood Cliffs, N.J.: Prentice Hall, 1987)

TABLE I-1

Thematic Trends in Organizational Behavior, 1940–1990

	HISTORICAL TRENDS			CONTEMPORARY TRENDS			EMERGING TRENDS	
1. Definition of the field	Behavioral science discipline orientation	to	Professional orientation	Industrial business focus	to	Management focus	Micro psychological emphasis	to	Balance of macro and micro views; systems focus and environmental determinism
2. Perspective on organizations	Job satisfaction human fulfillment	to	Organization productivity	Internal organizational functioning	to	Organization, environment adaptation	Organizations as dominant, stable structures	to	Organizations as symbolic entities networked with industries, institutions, careers in a global economy; boundaryless organizations
3. Perspective on persons	Tender (communication, intimacy, growth)	to	Tough (power and influence)	Socioemotional factors	to	Cognitive problem-solving factors	Deficiency orientation (adjustment)	to	Appreciation orientation (development); self-efficacy
4. Human resource management	Human Relations	to	Human resources	Management of people	to	Management of work	Organization development	to	Career development; management of diversity
5. Change processes	Expert, content consultation	to	Process consultation	Change created by change agents; Simple, global technologies	to	Management of change by the system; Highly differentiated problem-specific technologies	Change via change intervention, action research	to	Change via vision-based strategic transformation; learning organizations; self-directed work teams and empowerment
6. Management education	Academic	to	Experiential	Creating awareness	to	Skill building	Performance orientation	to	Learning to learn orientation; team focus

Early work in organizational behavior took a somewhat limited view of organizations, being primarily concerned with job satisfaction and human fulfillment in work. The recent past has included much research aimed at organizational productivity as well. But until recently the primary focus on the study of organizations has been on internal functioning. Some of the most vital research activity in the field stems from what is known as the open systems view of organizations. This view states that since organizations, to survive, must adapt to their environment, organizational functioning cannot be understood without examining organization-environment relationships. This led to the contingency theory of organizations, which states that there is no one best way to organize and manage; it depends on the environmental demands and corresponding tasks for the organization.

The open systems view of organizations leads to an important emerging trend in the study of organizations. In most research to date, the organization is the focal point of study, conceived as the dominant stable structure around which the environment revolves. Yet in many cases the organization is but a part of a more pervasive and dominant industry, institutional, or professional career structure. Utilities, for example, cannot be understood without understanding the impact of their relationship with governmental regulatory institutions, and medical organizations such as hospitals are dominated by the medical profession as a whole and particularly by the socialization and training of M.D.s. Improvements in the effectiveness of these organizations can be achieved only by consideration of the system of relationships among the organization and the institutions and professions that shape it.

Interorganizational networks are replacing the traditional view of the organization as the primary entity. Quasi-firms, such as construction jobs, which consist of subcontracted work teams, are becoming more common. Now we talk about boundaryless organizations that work at eliminating or diminishing boundaries between both internal and external groups and constituencies. The influence of the global economy is felt everywhere. Current research portrays organizations as symbolic systems in which members interpret their shared social reality. In this approach, reality is what is agreed upon, rather than an objective fact. The importance of organizational culture and shared values has also become an important trend.

Perspective on Persons

In their perspective on persons and human personality, organizational behavior scholars have added an emphasis on power and influence processes to an earlier concern with the more "tender" aspects of socioemotional behavior (e.g., communication, intimacy, and human growth). These concerns with the social-motivational aspects of human behavior are currently being expanded by many researchers to consider cognitive processes—learning, problem solving, decision making, and planning—thus contributing to a more holistic view of human behavior. A most promising future perspective on human functioning is emerging from the work of adult development psychologists in personality development, ego development, moral development, and cognitive development. Researchers in these fields are providing frameworks for human functioning in organizations that emphasize developmental-appreciative processes as opposed to the deficiency-adjustment perspective that has dominated much work on human behavior in organizations in the past. Recent research focuses upon self-efficacy and self-management.

The changes in perspectives on the person, which we have just discussed, have been mirrored in changes in philosophy about how human beings are to be managed. From our current historical vantage point, early approaches to management in organizational psychology seem defensive and vaguely paternalistic. People were involved in work decisions and attention was paid to "human relations" to keep workers happy and to avoid resistance to change initiated by management. Recently participative management has come to be viewed more as a positive tool for improving organizational functioning. People are involved in decision making not only to make them feel more satisfied, but also because the improved information and problem-solving capability resulting from a a participative process is more productive and effective.

Current research takes a more systematic approach to human resource management, shifting the perspective from management of people and the social-motivational techniques of management style, organizational climate, management by objectives (MBO), and so on, to a management of work perspective. This perspective considers the whole person as he or she adapts to the work environment. Work is seen as a sociotechnical system, considering the content of jobs as well as the management process. Managing work involves designing technological systems, organizational arrangements, and jobs themselves to obtain effective organizational adaptation to the environment and maximum utilization of human resources and talents.

An important emerging trend in human resource management involves the addition of a career development perspective to the organization development perspective we have outlined. A host of trends are occurring in the labor market, including an older population, a more balanced male-female work force, a more culturally and racially diverse work force, and increasing career mobility and change among workers through their work lives.

There is an emergent trend that encourages greater responsibility on the part of workers to develop their own careers. As a result of downsizing to leaner structures and the clog of baby boomers, some companies are making it clear to employees that they can no longer guarantee a lifelong career within the company. While many companies still manage the careers of those in the "fast track," career responsibility belongs primarily to workers themselves. At present, the topic of managing diversity, both the domestic and international variety, is receiving a good deal of attention.

Change Processes

Concern with change and organization improvement has been central to organizational behavior from its inception. Kurt Lewin's research methodology has been a dominant approach to integrating knowledge generation and practical application following his dictum: "If you want to understand something, try to change it." In the last decade the specialized field of organization development (OD) has emerged from the Lewinian tradition as a powerful practical approach for using behavioral science knowledge to improve organizational effectiveness and human fulfillment in work. A major contribution of OD has been an understanding of the process of introducing change. Process consultation, an approach that helps the organization to solve its own problems by improving the problem-solving, communication, and relationship processes in the organization, has emerged as an alternative to expert consultation, the approach where outside consultants generate problem solutions and present them for consideration by the organization. Currently the technologies for introducing and managing change are expanding and becoming more sophisticated and problem-specific as OD programs are being initiated in organizations or all types. As change becomes a way of life in most organizations, there is a shift of focus from change as something created and managed by external consultants to a concern with the manager as change agent, managing the change process as part of his or her job function. As a result there is less concern today with training OD professionals and greater concern with improving managers' OD skills.

With greater change and complexity in organizational systems, the dialectic in Lewin's action research model seems to be shifting from an emphasis on action to an emphasis on research. Policy development and strategy planning techniques are being developed to assist organizations in their adaptation to increasingly complex and turbulent environments. These approaches seem to be reversing Lewin's dictum—"If you want to change something, try to understand it."

Management Education

From the beginning, the field of organizational behavior has been concerned with educational innovations, particularly those aimed at communicating abstract academic knowledge in a way that is helpful and meaningful to pragmatically oriented professional managers and management students. The two dominant innovative traditions in this respect have been the development of the case method, particularly at the Harvard Business School, and the experiential learning approaches that have grown from Kurt Lewin's early work on group dynamics and the sensitivity training movement that followed. Both these traditions have developed educational technologies that are sophisticated in their application of theory to practice. Today, most management schools offer a mix of educational approaches-the traditional lecture, the case discussion, and experiential exercises, sometimes combining them in new and innovative ways, such as in computer-based business simulations. With these new educational technologies, management educators have begun to raise their aspirations from increasing student awareness and understanding to improving skills in interpersonal relations, decision making, managing change, and other key managerial functions. These new aspirations create new challenges for the design of management education and training programs, where the criteria for success are based on performance rather than cognitive comprehension. Yet the future poses an even greater challenge. The rapid growth of knowledge and increasing rate of social and technological change are making specific skill training more and more vulnerable to obsolescence. The answer seems to lie not in learning new skills, but in learning how to learn and adapt throughout one's career. An emerging concern in management education and research is, therefore, how individuals and organizations learn.

In many ways, organizational behavior is a mature field with concepts that have been fairly thoroughly researched (although with controversial results in some areas, like leadership) and widely disseminated. The Total Quality movement accelerated the acceptance of many aspects of group skills and participative management. At present there is a trend towards self-management and empowerment. With the diminished number of middle managers, self directed work teams are now expected to develop analytical, team-building, problem-solving,and leadership skills. Responsibility and control are being pushed to lower levels in organizations, requiring more training for a different group of employees.

THE PLAN OF THIS BOOK

In choosing topics and exercises for this book, we have attempted to represent all three trends in organizational behavior: those that are mature and established, those that are the focus of current research excitement, and new ideas that suggest the future shape of the field. The book is organized into four parts progressing from a focus on the individual to the group, organization, and the organization-environment interface.

Part I examines the individual in the organization and presents some of the different mental maps that individuals possess. Chapters 1 and 6 consider the individual's relationship with the organization over time through the concepts of the psychological contract and organizational socialization and career development. Chapter 2 reviews the principal theories of management and managerial functions. Chapters 3 and 4 focus, respectively, on the learning process and motivational determinants of human behavior in organizations. Chapter 5 centers upon individual values and their effect upon ethical decision-making.

Whereas the primary focus of Part I is self-awareness and the appreciation of individual differences, in Part II there is more emphasis upon the skill-building needed to develop effective work relationships and teams. It begins with a grounding in interpersonal communication (Chapter 7) and progresses to interpersonal perception and attribution in Chapter 8. Chapter 9 focuses on group dynamics and self-managed work teams, while Chapter 10 deals with problem management. Managing multigroup relations, conflict, and negotiation are addressed in Chapter 11. Managing diversity, both in the U.S. and abroad, is the topic of Chapter 12.

Part III focuses upon the skills needed for leadership (Chapter 13) and the critical leadership functions in the managerial role—creating, maintaining, and changing organizational culture (Chapter 14), decision making (Chapter 15), power and influence (Chapter 16), coaching and empowerment (Chapter 17), and performance appraisal (Chapter 18).

Part IV is concerned with managing effective organizations. Chapter 19 examines the organization-environment relationship via the concept of open system analysis. Chapter 20 looks at the key issues of organization structure, communication and design, and Chapter 21 is concerned with the sociotechnical design of work and its impact on worker motivation. Chapter 22 describes processes of planned change and organization development.

YOUR ROLE AS A LEARNER

You will find as you work with book that a new role is being asked of you as a learner. Whereas in many of your prior learning experiences you were in the role of a passive recipient, here you are given the opportunity to become an active creator of your own learning. This is an opportunity for you to develop new and different relationships with faculty members responsible for this course. As you many already have sensed, the experiential learning approach provides numerous opportunities for shared leadership in the learning process.

PART 1

UNDERSTANDING YOURSELF AND OTHER PEOPLE AT WORK

Chapter

THE PSYCHOLOGICAL CONTRACT AND ORGANIZATIONAL SOCIALIZATION

OBJECTIVES   After completing Chapter 1, you should be able to:

A. Define the terms "psychological contract" and the "self-fulfilling prophecy" and explain their importance.

B. Describe the external influences that affect expectations.

C. Describe predictions about the workplace in the year 2000.

D. Explain the "pinch model."

E. Make a psychological contract with your professor.

F. List the characteristics of the field of organizational behavior.

A Cold Slap in the Face... Past Graduates, Corporate Managers Explain Why You Probably Can't 'Have it All'

Douglas A. Campbell

Kreig Smith believed he knew what to expect in the business world after earning a master's degree from Brigham Young University last year. Successful internships, including four months with IBM Corp. in Rochester, Minn., had prepared him for the rigors of life after college, he thought.

Kreig's confidence was buoyed when he met the chief executive of the small computer concern that had recruited him. The man spoke of team effort, hard work and family. "He used to refer to himself as the father of the company, and he was proud to be a father," recalls Kreig, who says his ideals are as important to him as career success.

Source: Reprinted from *Managing Your Career*, Fall 1987, Dow Jones & Co., Inc., pp. 6,9.

The job lasted one year. By the time Kreig left, he was calling management in American business a sham and was totally disillusioned with the man to whom he had looked for leadership.

Marie Robard, a recent University of Denver graduate, took a sales job with an electronics industry giant when she graduated two years ago. She worked hard enough in college to get decent grades, but no more. So the demands of her new job, where she spent from 7:00 A.M. until after the dinner hour, were unexpected. Still, Marie dived into her work, and soon she was outperforming her peers and exceeding her sales quota by a remarkable margin.

Then Marie (not her real name) discovered the reward for her effort: Her quota was doubled, and the big bonuses that once fell into her pocketbook each month now had to be chased.

Like many new college graduates, Marie and Kreig were surprised newcomers to business. Although many graduates manage smooth transitions into their chosen careers, the road from the classroom to the conference room can be riddled with unexpected hazards.

"It's a complete change of cultures," says Victor R. Lindquist, director of placement at Northwestern University.

"Most people get a perception in their minds (of what work will be like)," adds Robert K. Armstrong, manager of professional staffing at DuPont Co. "All too frequently, it turns out not to be that way," resulting in a high degree of turnover at most companies in the first five years of employment, says Mr. Armstrong.

Professionals who work with recent graduates report that they're often surprised at the level of pay they receive, the hours they're required to work, the effect of those hours on their social lives and on their expectations for developing a family. They're also unprepared for office politics and for the need to seek–and accept–the help of those with more experience.

Hedwin Naimark, a social psychologist, conducted a study of college seniors in 1985 and 1986 to find out what they expected from the workplace. "They seemed to focus on what it's like to be a student," Ms. Naimark says. "You go to class, you do your work and you receive a good grade if you do what you're supposed to do. The concept that there are other things involved when you go to the workplace was missing," she says.

"Their concept of how they are going to live their lives is deeply affected by the whole aura of the country, which right now is (that) everybody is going to do everything and everybody is going to have everything," Ms. Naimark says.

If you have been lured by the beer commercial asking, "Who says you can't have it all?" consider the experience of Marie Robard.

"I found that to be good at what I was doing, (the job) had to be the number one priority in my life," says Marie, who describes her college experience as "a whole lot of fun."

"I would say my first year out of college, I didn't have a social life," she says.

That didn't bother Marie, because she was establishing herself as a star salesperson and because she was being rewarded with early promotions. What did bother her were the office politics ("It's really frustrating. It's constantly going on, and you have to learn to play it.") and what she saw as a lack of cooperation between corporate departments ("It's like you're fighting against somebody instead of everybody working together").

And then there was the matter of quotas. "I was penalized for being successful," says Marie, who still works for the same company.

For Kreig Smith, it was the human interplay that drove him from his corporate job. With a degree in organizational behavior, Kreig took a job as an internal management consultant. After interviewing workers to determine what motivated them, he was convinced they were seeking "respect and dignity" as much as anything. And so when the

CEO talked "about quality, quality that extended beyond the product to how we dealt with everyone," that hit a responsive chord in Kreig.

Then the company's business took a nosedive.

"When things get tough, (the CEO's) tune changed. I talked with him personally. He would say, 'I'm tired of being the father. They're a bunch of crying babies.'

"I heard him say, 'As president, I have to compromise my integrity. If I didn't compromise , I couldn't interact with the board of directors.'"

The reality of the workplace eventually drove Kreig to start his own business, a consulting firm where he and a partner call the shots and set the standards.

TOO MUCH TIME

One of the most common and unexpected realities for recent graduates is the time a job demands, according to Elizabeth A. Meyer, director of Stanford University's Career Management Center. Employers attempt to make time demands clear, Ms. Meyers says, "but it's still sometimes a shock."

"It's often lifestyle issues that are troubling–things they (recent graduates) hadn't anticipated or thought wouldn't be important, the location or hours of the job," Ms. Meyers explains. "Many of our people are on the job 80 hours a week, and they think I can handle it. And then they see their marriages or social lives falling apart."

In some industries–computer concerns and financial houses in particular–recent graduates often find room for rapid advancement. But industries with slower growth paths offer less chance for promotion–and more frustration.

"A number one ticket item (among recent graduates) is the expectation...that advancement's going to take place quickly with a very well-defined path," says DuPont's Mr. Armstrong. But for that to happen, he says, there has to be a combination of a well-qualified employee and a company with a need.

"In becoming more competitive, more productive, companies have had to come to grips with how they can do business...with fewer people," Mr. Armstrong says. As corporations pare management levels, new recruits have fewer positions into which they can rise. At DuPont, for example, an engineer who once could expect a management post after five years now may find himself on the engineering bench for 10 years or more before advancement, Mr. Armstrong says.

"I have five engineers who have been here for a while. Business is so-so, so we really don't have a need to promote them," says Mr. Armstrong. "Yet they have a feeling there should be advancement."

LEARNING THE ROPES

On any new job, recent graduates will find it necessary to learn the ropes–the peculiarities of the particular company and its expectations of new workers. To do that, Mr. Lindquist suggests that on visits to prospective employers, job seekers should spend time with potential new colleagues "to see whether this is a group of people with whom you would like to work."

A big mistake is failing to ask questions. "You can expedite the learning process by asking the right questions," Mr. Lindquist advises. New hires also should be wary of "the person who offers all kinds of counsel gratuitously as to what's in and what's not, who's good and who's bad. Very often, this is a discontented employee who hasn't figured out the system and isn't likely to be moving on," Mr. Lindquist says.

Ms. Naimark, the psychologist who studied undergraduates for Catalyst, a nonprofit New York City organization that specializes in women's career development issues, says among the 1,000 students she surveyed, "both men and women think they're going to have demanding and exciting careers. They think they're going to increase their salaries, be married and have children and be good parents."

After dealing with the realities of the workplace, she says the students' attitudes change. "What you see is a great growth...of the understanding that there are options and trade-offs."

In other words, the experts say, you can't have it all.

 # Premeeting Preparation

A. Read "A Cold Slap in the Face."

B. Read the Topic Introduction.

 # Topic Introduction

All the recent graduates in Campbell's article, "A Cold Slap in the Face" had one thing in common: In each case the psychological contract between the employee and the employer had broken down. When individuals join an organization, they form an unwritten, implicit or (less frequently) explicit, psychological contract with the organization. This contract consists of the mutual expectation employees and employers have of each other. The psychological contract is based upon the perception of both the employee and employer that their contributions obligate the other party to reciprocate. If a new employee is given the impression that hard work will be rewarded with a promotion and raise in the near future and neither are forthcoming, the psychological contract is broken because the organization has failed to meet the employee's expectations about both advancement and credibility. On the other hand, if an organization agrees to pay the cost of an employee's MBA program, her boss may expect her to work harder or be more loyal because the company is contributing more to her than to other employees.

Even though such expectations may never formally be stated, they do exist and they have a tangible impact on the relationship between employee and employer. When the expectations of either side are not fulfilled or when the contract is violated, intense emotional reactions such as outrage, shock, resentment and anger, result.[1] The trust and good faith of the employer-employee relationship is destroyed and cannot easily be rebuilt. The disillusionment over broken psychological contracts affects employee job satisfaction, productivity, and desire to continue with the organization.[2] A company staffed by employees who feel cheated or betrayed cannot expect to be a high performance company.

Psychological contracts differ from employment contracts because they focus upon a dynamic relationship that defines the employees' psychological involvement with their employer. The actions of both parties mutually influence the psychological contract. For example, high company expectations about what employees should contribute to the company can produce increased individual performance; when individuals perform at a high level, they come to expect more than just a paycheck. They may also expect job security, respectful treatment, and challenging jobs and training that will help them develop and grow. From the company's perspective, the key questions are, "How can we manage our human resources so that we can maximize individual contributions?" and "How can we socialize our members to accept our expectations and norms as legitimate?" For the individual, the questions are, "How can I get the satisfaction and rewards that I want from this organization?", "How can I manage my own career so that my socialization takes place in organizational settings that encourage my personal growth and development?" and "How can I fulfill the expectations of the organization and still have time for my personal life?"

One way for business students to avoid disillusionment with their first jobs is to gain a more realistic idea about what to expect from organizations by participating in internships. Campbell suggested that "the cold slap in the face" might be avoided by asking more questions during the job interview process. Certainly both prospective employees and employers would be better off if their expectations were made explicit from the beginning. But often we are not aware of our expectations until they have been disappointed. That's why mechanisms or forums that allow for continued discussions and renegotiations of the contract are so crucial throughout the term of employment. Effective managers understand that the psychological contract is important because it links the individual to the organization. They ensure that the mutual expectations that comprise the contract are both understood and fulfilled so the employee-employer relationship is carefully maintained.

Another important concept that relates to expectations and new employees is the self-fulfilling prophecy. This occurs when expectations for an employee cause a manager to treat the employee differently; therefore the employee responds in a way that confirms the manager's initial expectations. We have Rosenthal and his albino rats to thank for this particular contribution to organizational behavior. In an experiment, he gave the same strain of rats to different groups of students at Harvard.[3] The students' task was to teach their rats to run a maze. However, one group of students was told their rats were bright; the other group was told their rats were dull. Although there were no inherent differences between the two groups of rats, the so-called "bright" rats learned to run mazes better than the "dull" rats. Further inquiry revealed that the students found the "bright" rats more likeable and therefore had treated them differently. Intrigued, Rosenthal and Jacobson tried the same experiment with school children.[4] They randomly chose one child out of every five and told teachers that these children were "academic spurters." At the year's end, the "academic spurters" had improved their IQ by an average of 22 points. The teachers' expectations about these students affected the way they treated the children. The children's response to that treatment was to become "academic spurters." The critical variable in these examples is the teacher's (or rat handler's) expectation: higher expectations were associated with higher learning. The children (and the rats) became what the teachers thought they were, which is a perfect example of self-fulfilling prophecy.

We find the same self-fulfilling prophecy at work with newly hired people. Studies indicate that new hires who are immediately given challenging jobs are more likely to show high performance later on in their careers.[5] Today, many large corporations formally label those employees for whom they have high expectations as "fast-trackers." As part of their succession management programs, companies pay special attention to this group and provide them with the experiences and opportunities that will prepare them to take a top leadership role in the future. Such programs can be very effective, but one of their by-products may be resentment and complaints (both valid and invalid) by "nonfast trackers" who feel that they too could shine if they received the special treatment that goes along with higher expectations of one's performance.

What is the practical significance in the workplace of understanding the self-fulfilling prophecy?

- Employees who are expected to do well will likely perform better than those who are not when, in fact, there may be no differences between them.
- Supervisors who have high expectations of their employees will be more likely to have their expectations met.

EXTERNAL INFLUENCES AND CHANGING EXPECTATIONS

The tremendous rate of change that businesses undergo as they try to adapt to a global economy and changing economic conditions has resulted in marked changes in workplace expectations and psychological contracts. We can observe the dynamic nature of psychological contracts in the change that has occurred with employer-employee loyalty in the last 15 years. In the U.S., massive terminations resulting from mergers, acquisitions, and downsizing in previously stable companies and the increased percentage of people who remain unemployed for a longer period of time has caused people to question the American Dream itself.[6] Previously, the terms of the psychological contract between many Americans and their corporate employers were relatively simple. Employees were willing to work their way slowly up the corporate ladder in return for the promise of a sufficiently high promotion in their middle age to allow them to live comfortably during their retirement years. This contract was always somewhat unbalanced because while the company was expected to be loyal to employees, the employees could resign whenever they wished. Today, even IBM (as well as a growing number of Japanese and West German companies) can no longer guarantee lifelong job security. How do employees react to the broken psychological contracts that accompany corporate restructuring? Some employees are modifying their expectations and making whatever sacrifices are necessary to retain their jobs in a difficult economy, while others are giving more importance to family and non-work interests. Still others are placing more emphasis on developing their reputational capital (i.e., building their resumes so they are more attractive to other companies) than on institution-building activities that would benefit their current employer. Employee loyalty is further eroded by companies that 1) promise employees more than they intend to deliver, 2) hire overqualified people with the expectation of "getting more out of them" for less money, 3) save money by overworking employees who survive major lay-offs, and 4) manipulate employees with vague promises of early salary reviews and job possibilities that never materialize.[7]

Key questions for managers and human resource professionals are, "How do organizations promote commitment on the part of employees who no longer trust in job security? How do companies satisfy employees who expect rapid promotions in an economy that is not expanding enough to create as many jobs at the top?"

According to one HR expert, the new employment contract with employees will change from long-term employment relationships and paternalism to employment that is based upon business needs. Employees will be rewarded for skills and performance, not tenure. Loyalty and commitment "become focused on maintaining the employment relationship, on what the company and employee must do to keep the relationship (and presumably the company) going. In turn, the company shares more power and control with the employees to make them more self-reliant, self-directed and responsible for their own career management." [8]

Another answer to this question of how do we encourage commitment in unstable times may come from research on "healthy companies." The seven values found in such organizations are 1) commitment to self-knowledge and development (continuous learning); 2) firm belief in decency (fair treatment, equity); 3) respect for individual differences (celebration of diversity); 4) spirit of partnership (strong belief in community, shared effort, teamwork, widespread participation); 5) high priority for health and well-being; 6) appreciation for flexibility and resilience (change is managed well); and 7) a passion for products and process (concern for both what is produced and how that happens, balancing stakeholder interests–family support, community responsibility, and environmental protection). Not all organizations believe in these dimensions or put them into practice, but they reflect the growing belief that the contribution of the workforce is the ultimate key to the success of any company and provides an idea of what many employees are coming to expect from their employer.

Another example of changing expectations concerns the way we do business.[10] Examples of new thinking and expectations in U.S. business are identified in a book entitled, **Workforce 2000**. [11]

1. The traditional U.S. workplace was, for most people, characterized by limited demands. Coming on time, following orders, and meeting minimum demands was enough to keep a job. This is no longer true.

2. "Just okay" quality is no longer good enough; survival depends upon excellence.

3. Superior customer service is critical.

4. Companies must learn to innovate fast and make do with less of everything.

This same book makes the following predictions about what the workplace will look like at the turn of the century. We can expect flatter, leaner, more aggressive organizations capable of responding quickly to changing customer demands. The middle management layer that has been sacrificed in downsizing efforts will not return. Instead, the processing, analyzing, and decision-making performed by middle mangers will be moved to lower-level employees who will be aided by more sophisticated software. Because there will be fewer promotion opportunities in flat organizations, more people will turn to entrepreneurship as a means to get ahead.

The trend towards decreased job security will continue. The "just in time" workforce[12] consists of a larger percentage of flexible, part-time, temporary or contract workers that buffer companies from the uncertainties of rapidly changing demand. People can expect to have ten or more different types of jobs and work for at least five different companies during their career. Employees will be responsible for managing their own career. They will need to invest in education and retraining and should plan on being continuous learners. The requisite skills for employee success will be flexibility, creativity, analytical ability, computer literacy, and a rudimentary grasp of statistics.

Companies will demand more of employees and will instill a "cult of performance excellence." Employees will be asked to "buy in, join up, or leave" and be expected to become a member of the team. Simply putting in one's time will not be acceptable. As a result, finding the right "fit" with a company will be critical for potential employees.

There will be a move from managerial control to more self control. Supervisors will assume the role of enablers-facilitators and technical support managers. Teams will be responsible for planning, scheduling, organizing, directing, and controlling their own work process. Companies will share more information with employees. There will be more constant performance feedback to each employee and more peer pressure to perform. Most rewards will be for team rather than individual performance. Status perks will be replaced with recognition for good performance.

Last but not least, the complexion of the workforce will be very different. According to predictions about the year 2000, white males will comprise only 39% of the total workforce.[13] By the end of the century only 15% of new hires will be white males; the remaining 85% of new hires will be composed of women, African-Americans, Hispanics, Asians, and Native Americans.[14] Many companies are already trying to take advantage of a diverse workgroup by learning to 1) appreciate and understand differences, 2) communicate and work with diverse groups, and 3) develop an organizational culture that welcomes all groups and their unique contributions.

An equally powerful set of expectational shifts can be deduced from changing value trends.[15] In addition to differences in the values held by various generations, changing societal norms also affect our psychological contracts at work and home. For example, at present only 12% of U.S. families consist of a working husband and a stay-at-home wife who cares for the children.[16] This departure from what used to be the norm forces us to rethink our expectations of what it means to be a good employee, spouse, and parent and to adapt our psychological contracts accordingly. For example, flexible hours and company day care programs help dual career parents and single parents combine working and parenting.

A MODEL FOR MANAGING PSYCHOLOGICAL CONTRACTS

Working with people from other cultures forces the realization that psychological contracts have a cultural flavor to them. The Japanese concept of lifetime employment is one of many examples of cultural differences. The European expectation that worker councils will participate in company decisions is another example. Yet another is the Latin American expectation that bosses will attend the family celebrations–baptisms, first communions, marriages, and funerals–of their employees. In multicultural settings it quickly becomes apparent that different cultures utilize different psychological contracts, and it is critical to understand these differences. However, given the changing expectations within our society and the varying expectations of different generations and groups in the workplace, we may do well to follow the cross-cultural model where in one proceeds on the assumption that other people's expectations are not necessarily the same as our own. Therefore, in order to avoid misunderstandings and disillusionment, it is crucial to identify and share mutual expectations in an on-going process.

Sherwood and Glidewell have developed a simple but powerful model, the Pinch Model, that 1) describes the dynamic quality of psychological contracts and 2) suggests ways of minimizing the potentially dysfunctional consequences of shifting expectations (Figure 1-1). It provides a framework for the continuous management of the psychological contract in the day-to-day work setting. The first stage of any relationship between two individuals and/or an individual and an organization is characterized by a *sharing of information and a negotiating of expectations.* Suppose that a manager interviewing job candidates informs them that they will be expected to attend frequent company social events after hours and on weekends. If this does not appear to be a reasonable expectation to some candidates, they will deselect themselves, the equivalent of a *planned termination* in the model below.

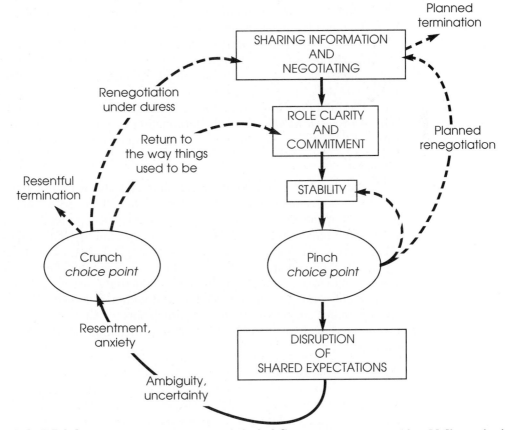

FIGURE 1-1   **Model for Managing Psychological Contracts** Source: Adapted from J.J. Sherwood and J.C. Glidewell, *"Planned Renegotiation: A Norm Setting OD Intervention,"* in Contemporary Organization Development: Orientations and Interventions, *edited by W.W. Burke (Washington DC:NTL Institute, 1972), pp. 35-46.*

Assuming that both parties accept the other's expectations, they enter a stage of *role clarity* and *joint commitment*. In other words, both the new employees and the manager understand and accept the role the other party expects them to play and are motivated to meet those expectations. The employee and employer both expect to move into a period of *stability* and productivity. It is time to get down to work.

Even with the best of intentions and full sharing of initial expectations, changes are likely to occur over time. One or both of the parties begin to feel a "pinch" as Sherwood and Glidewell term it. For example, an employee may have been more than willing to put in heavy overtime and cover weekend shifts when he or she was single and new in town. But a marriage involving certain expectations about the time a couple should spend together might change the employee's attitude toward demanding hours and the automatic assumption that this particular employee will work them. Sherwood and Glidewell suggest that a pinch like this can be used as an early warning sign to manage the psychological contract process before situations become disruptive. Discussing and renegotiating expectations at this point will lead to either a return to stability or, if the differences cannot be resolved, to a planned departure. Employees sometimes respond to pinches by saying, "I don't have time to test this issue with him" or "If I raise this issue with my boss, she'll think I'm just complaining so I'll ignore it." But pinches have a habit of growing into larger problems if they are not handled in a planned manner rather than in the heat of emotion that accompanies the next stage, a *disruption of shared expectations*.

Since the "rules" that were accepted initially have been upset, one or both parties experience heightened *ambiguity and uncertainty*, which invariably results in *resentment and anxiety*. The situation may reach a crisis point, or *crunch*. People often refer to crunches as the straw that broke the camel's back, e.g., the boss who unfairly accuses a dedicated employee of not working hard because the boss is misinformed, or a job promotion that goes to another employee who is clearly less qualified. Crunches force the participants to choose among three alternative actions. A common outcome is an effort to *return to the way things used to be*. The parties apologize for the misunderstanding, smooth over the conflict, and attempt to renew their commitment to one another under the terms of the old contract. Another possibility is that the two parties *renegotiate under duress* by again sharing information and negotiating their expectations. The final possibility is that little or no discussion occurs and the result is some form of *resentful termination*. The termination may be either psychological ("I'll be darned if I'm going to do any more than I'm required to on this job" or "That's the last thing I ever do for that employee") or physical (absenteeism, tardiness, quitting or firing).

In the classroom, the psychological contract is also very important. Generally only one of the parties makes their expectations explicit. Teachers begin a course by stating their requirements of students. Students are rarely asked to reciprocate, but woe to the teacher who fails to meet students' unstated expectations! The purpose of this unit is to introduce you to the concept of the psychological contract as it exists in the learning organization you are about to enter. In this way you will be able to move as quickly as possible to a period of stability and productivity (learning) and set in motion the processes of communication needed to deal with any subsequent "pinches" that may develop. In this course we encourage participants to state their expectations in the following exercise because it is the first step in taking responsibility for one's own learning.

Procedure for Group Meeting:
Instructor/Participant Interviews

Preparation

The goal in this part of this exercise is for the instructor to learn from the group members *their* expectations for the course regarding what they hope to learn. In addition, the instructor will try to learn what members feel they can contribute to the achievement of their expectations and to the learning process. In this part, the instructor will interview participants in the course via representatives.

STEP 1. The total group should divide into small discussion groups, four or five people per group, and introduce themselves.

STEP 2. Each group should select a representative of the team who will be interviewed by the instructor.

STEP 3. Using the guide provided in the accompanying Instructor's Interview of Participants: A Question Guide, each group should discuss the general question areas.

Note: The instructor may add at this point any specific issues of concern not covered in this guide.

STEP 4. All representatives must understand their group's position on each of these questions so they can accurately represent their views in response to the questions the instructor will pose during the interview. You may want to jot these down on the guide provided. (time allotted for steps 1-4: 30 minutes)

Instructor's Interview of Participants:
A Question Guide

Few instructors ask group members to articulate their expectations for a class. During the ensuing interview, the instructor will try to gain an understanding of your views in the following general areas:

1. What are your goals for this course? To increase self-awareness? To learn theories? To fulfill a requirement? To get a grade? To apply learning in your job? Something else?

2. How can the instructor best help you achieve your goals? Lectures, examinations, seminar discussions? (Think back to excellent professors/courses you've experienced.)

3. What, if anything, have you heard about this textbook and/or this course from others?

4. What reservations, if any, do you have about this course?

5. What is the best thing that could happen in this course? What is the worst thing?

6. What are your resources for this course (prior work experience, courses in psychology, etc.)?

7. What norms of behavior or ground rules should we set to ensure that the course is successful? (Mutual respect, only one person talks at a time, punctuality, etc.)

Instructor's Interview

STEP 5. The representatives, one from each team, meet with the instructor. The instructor will interview them (using the Instructor's Interview of Participants: A Question Guide) to understand their expectations for the course. The remainder of the class acts as observers, paying particular attention to the instructor's questions and the areas that seem most salient. You might find it helpful to jot down on the upcoming Participants' Interview of Instructor: A Suggested Question Guide the observations that you feel will help you prepare for the second round of interviewing. (time allotted for step 5: 20 minutes)

PARTICIPANTS' INTERVIEW OF INSTRUCTOR

Preparation

The goal in this part of the exercise is for the course participants to find out what the instructor's expectations are for the course. What does the instructor hope they will learn from the course? What can the instructor contribute to the learning process? In this part, the participants will interview the instructor via representatives.

STEP 6. The class should form into the same small discussion groups used in Part A.

STEP 7. Each group should select a member (other than the person they selected in step 2) as their team representative who will interview the instructor.

STEP 8. Using the guide provided as a starting point (Participants' Interview of Instructor: A Suggested Question Guide), each group should discuss any questions that they would like their representatives to pose to the instructor. Please feel free to ask questions that do not appear in this guide.

STEP 9. Representatives should make certain that they understand the group's concerns so that they can accurately translate these concerns into questions to be posed to the instructor. (You may want to jot these down on the guide provided.) (time allotted for steps 6-9: 30 minutes)

Participants' Interview of Instructor:
A Suggested Question Guide

You will have the opportunity to ask the instructor any questions you feel are relevant to effective learning during this course. (Note: It is important that you ask questions that are of real concern to you at this point. Only in this way can potentially important problems or conflicts be identified and managed.) You probably have many ideas of your own and the questions asked by the instructor during the first interview should suggest others to you.

Some areas you may want to discuss are the following:

1. The instructor's objectives for the course–what does he or she hope to accomplish?

2. The instructor's theory of learning (i.e. how do people learn?)

3. The instructor's opinion on the question of evaluation

4. The instructor's expectations of you

5. The instructor's role in the class

6. Anything else you think is important

Be sure to ask specific questions. Think about the assumptions that may underlie some of your questions, for example, why you feel this is important. Test these assumptions by asking the instructor's opinion if you feel it will be helpful.

Participants' Interview

STEP 10. Representatives interview instructor to understand the instructor's expectations for them and the course. The remainder of the group acts as observers, paying particular attention to the following areas:

    a. In what ways do your (groups') expectations agree or disagree with the contributions the instructor feels he or she can make?

    b. In what ways do the instructor's expectations agree or disagree with the contributions you feel you can make?

    c. In looking back over your group discussions, how much diversity was there within the group concerning expectations?

    (time allotted for step 10: 30 minutes)

COMPARISON OF INTERVIEWS AND IDENTIFICATION OF POTENTIAL PINCHES

STEP 11. The total group should develop a list of 1) areas of difference that become apparent during the previous two interviews and 2) possible future conflicts–pinches–that will be important to watch for.

    a. To the extent possible, differences that will influence the learning process should be discussed further, with an eye toward a mutually acceptable negotiated resolution.

    b. With respect to potential future pinches, the group should discuss their expectations concerning

       (1) Whose responsibility it will be or should be to raise a pinch if and when it develops.

       (2) The mechanisms to be used for raising pinches (e.g., written comments, informal discussions at the end of meetings).

STEP 12. Instructor and participants should discuss their feelings about beginning a course in this fashion and assess the value of this method. What differences do you see when you compare this method to the traditional way other courses begin? (time allotted for steps 11 and 12: 30-40 minutes)

Follow-Up

Although we do not often view the processes in the same terms, entering a classroom environment the first time is very much like the first day on a new job. The typical orientation program in a company is usually very one-sided. Most company communication flows from the organization to the individual, "These are our policies, procedures, expectations."

One effect of this one-sided process is to cause "new employees" to feel that the organization is much more powerful than they are as individuals. This feeling of powerlessness often creates a situation in which new employees, when asked their expectations, try to second-guess the company's expectations. Instead of trying to formulate and articulate their own expectations, the new employees (participants) often repeat what they *think* the organization (instructor) wants to hear. Another effect is the organization's tendency to oversocialize new members. This can result in a feeling of powerlessness and even greater passivity on the part of the employee.

Recall your last job interview. Remember how you tried to "look good" to the organization–to guess what it wanted. How much time did you spend telling the interviewer what your expectations were and asking what the organization could contribute to your needs? Probably very little and then very cautiously. Our studies on individuals' entries into organizations and our work with orientation and training programs has led to the conclusion that upon entering an organization, nearly everyone experiences a feeling of helplessness and dependency on the organization. From a functional point of view, this dependency seems necessary so that the organization can begin to socialize the incoming member to meet its norms and values, its way of doing things. Yet our observations have led us to conclude that most organizations overdo this–they tend to oversocialize their members. For example, placing too much emphasis upon the organization's expectations of newcomers may result in conformity. The phase of entry into an organization seems to be a critical period for the new members. Individuals who are overpowered and overcontrolled by organizational constraints become listless, passive members. In contrast, those who are challenged by the tasks they face and are encouraged toward responsibility can move toward success and mastery.

The organization often reads passivity as a sign that new employees want and need more direction and control—they want to be told exactly what to do. This situation can create a feedback cycle that, in the long run, operates to the detriment of both the individual and the organization. The organization needs people who are innovative, creative, and independent thinkers to survive and remain productive in a rapidly changing environment. Individual growth and satisfaction also demand these same kinds of behavior. Often, however, the new employee's (participant's) first contact with the organization sets in motion a cycle that acts in direct opposition to these long-range goals and needs.

There is another way in which we can view the process of organizational socialization and the notion of the psychological contract. In approaching any new organization, an individual makes two classes of decisions: a decision to join and a decision to participate.[17] In some cases, such as being drafted into the military or taking required courses, individuals have no control over their own decision to join.

The process by which we join an organization has implications for the second class of decisions–the decision to participate. This particular decision refers to whether or not a person chooses to play an active role in the organization or is content with merely being physically present. At work, employees who have made a decision to participate are involved and working hard to contribute. Those who have decided not to participate are simply marking time, putting in their hours. In the classroom, those who choose to participate take an active role in the course and become involved in their own learning process. In contrast, those who decide not to participate either sit passively or don't attend and work just enough to get by and fulfill the organization's requirements for a grade. Their own expectations for learning, involvement, and stimulation go unsatisfied because they never made such expectations explicit when they joined.

Our purpose in encouraging students to participate in a joint expectation-setting exercise is to provide you with an opportunity to decide whether you want to join and participate in this course. Some educational systems and programs often unwittingly encourage passivity in students when learners are not expected to take responsibility for their own learning. They are much more accustomed to the instructor's assuming full responsibility. Thus, when confronted with a genuine opportunity to participate in the learning process, they often became confused ("What kind of way is this to start a class?") or suspicious ("I wonder what the instructor is trying to do?")

When asked to articulate expectations, learners tend to be very vague and general which is frustrating to everyone involved. Expectations are much more likely to be satisfied when a set of realistic, concrete goals can be developed. Instructors must realize that learners who are unused to controlling their own education will have to learn to accept that responsibility. The point is that *both* participants and instructor have a share of the responsibility for the learning process.

This point is an important one to reemphasize. (Confusion often develops as a result of this initial contracting session, along the lines of: "Why all this talk about our expectations and stuff? You [the instructor] already have the course laid out, the syllabus typed, and the schedule planned!" As is true in any organization, the general thrust or goals are given. This is not a course in art or home economics. It is a course in organizational behavior, but there are many areas of flexibility: what *specific* goals you as a participating learner set within the general objectives, how you relate to peers and staff, who takes what responsibility for *how* goals are achieved. Differences might exist around those issues, and they need to be explored during the initial socialization process.

Clearly, within the context of a first class session of a few hours, all the possible conflicts that can arise will not be anticipated nor can all those identified be solved. More important than any concrete conclusions that may come out of this expectation-setting exercise is a series of norms for dealing with conflicts. As a result of this contract exploration process, the legitimacy of conflict or differences can be established, the right to question each other and particularly the instructor can be demonstrated, and a decision-making process of shared responsibility to resolve conflicts can be introduced.

The next two sections focus on what we mean by organizational behavior and the authors' objectives in designing this course.

CHARACTERISTICS OF ORGANIZATIONAL BEHAVIOR

One of the criticisms sometimes leveled at organizational behavior is that it is just "common sense." In fact, many common-sense truisms are actually paradoxical—for example, "Nothing ventured, nothing gained" as opposed to "Better safe than sorry" or "Two heads are better than one" and "Too many cooks spoil the broth." The interesting question is, "If so much of organizational behavior is common sense, why is it not common practice?" One of the aims of this course is to find answers to the question, "What does it take to get common sense into common practice?"

Organizational behavior is characterized by the following traits. It is a relatively young *multidisciplinary field* that pulls from the disciplines of psychology, sociology, anthropology, political science, and economics. It consists of *three levels of analysis: individual, group, and organizational.* Figure 2-1 on page 31 presents a broad sample of the topics that fall within the realm of organizational behavior. One of the basic tenants of organizational behavior is that behavior is a function of the person and the environment, B=f(P) (E)[18]. For didactic purposes, the following equation is perhaps more helpful. Behavior is a function of the person (P), the group to which he or she belongs (G), and the organization (O) with its own unique culture, and the external environment (E), or B=f (P) (G) (O) (E). *Environmental forces* have a major impact on behavior within organizations. The external changes (global economy, industrial and economic conditions, and societal change) that affect our expectations and psychological contracts are examples of environmental impact.

Knowledge in the field is accumulated by using the *scientific method*, which means that theories and relationships are tested to see whether they can actually predict behavior. Much of the research looks at *performance* at all three levels of analysis. Researchers are constantly trying to determine what makes for success in organizations and what's the most effective way to do things. Therefore, organizational behavior is an *applied science*—its purpose is to develop knowledge that is useful to managers and employees. Because of the emphasis upon performance and application, it comes as no surprise that OB is a *change oriented discipline*. Strategies for improving performance or modifying behavior have always been important to the field, particularly the subfield of OD, organizational development.

Because of the variety and complexity of human behavior, there are few simple answers to questions about organizations. Organizational behavior scholars and consultants usually respond to questions with an "It depends," followed up by many questions about the particular situation and maybe even a request to observe what's going on. To managers looking for quick answers, such a response may seem evasive. However, the management literature abounds with examples of companies that made policy and management decisions based upon a small fragment of the entire picture and lived to regret it. That's why this course is designed to broaden your appreciation of the complexity of organizational behavior.

COURSE OBJECTIVES

We hope that you will not only learn the basic organizational behavior theories and concepts, but that you will be able to use them to understand human behavior. As a result of the course, we'd like you to perceive organizations through new lenses with a much greater appreciation of their complexity. Organizations are like puzzles that need to be decoded.

We study organizational behavior because it helps us function more effectively in organizations. Regardless of our position in the company, it helps us understand what is occurring around us. It also teaches us the necessary skills to be a good employee, team member or manager. Many people reach a plateau in their careers because they have risen as far as their technical skills allow. Good "people skills" are usually a prerequisite for higher management jobs. As one professor stated in an attempt to sell his OB course to students, "The difference between understanding organizational behavior and not understanding it is the difference between a six-figure and a five-figure salary." We can't promise you a six-figure salary if you master everything in this course. But, if you do your part, you should finish the course with a greater understanding about who you are, more people and group skills, and a new way of looking at organizations.

Learning Points

1. Psychological contracts are the unwritten, implicit or explicit agreements on mutual expectations between employees and employers that reflect the dynamic relationship between the two parties.

2. Psychological contracts are important because they are the link between the individual and the organization. If the contract is broken, disillusionment can affect employee satisfaction, productivity, and their desire to continue with the company.

3. The self-fulfilling prophecy occurs in business when a manager's expectations for an employee causes the manager to treat the employee differently; therefore the employee responds in a way that confirms the manager's initial expectations. If managers have high expectations of their employees, they are more likely to have their expectations met.

4. External influences, such as adapting to a global economy, economic conditions, and societal change, affect workplace expectations and psychological contracts.

5. Changes in the way we think about business are: 1) companies must expect and get higher levels of productivity from their employees; 2) "just okay" quality is not good enough; 3) superior customer service is critical; and 4) companies must learn to innovate faster and make do with less.

6. Predictions for Workplace 2000 include leaner, flatter, more flexible organizations and more empowered employee teams performing functions previously done by a greatly diminished middle management level. Employees will have ten or more jobs in at least five different companies; they will be responsible for managing their own career and should focus on continuous learning. Companies will focus on excellence and expect employees to become active members of the team. Employees will receive more information on the company and feedback on their own performance.

7. The composition of the workforce by the year 2000 will be much more diverse. Only 39% of the workforce will be white males.

8. The Pinch Model is a way to avoid major disruptions by heeding early warning signs that expectations about the psychological contract have changed and need to be reconsidered.

9. In approaching any new organization, an individual makes two classes of decisions: a decision to join and a decision to participate.

10. Organizational behavior has the following characteristics:
    a. Multidisciplinary nature
    b. Three levels of analysis: individual, group, organizational
    c. Acknowledgement of environmental forces
    d. Grounded in the scientific method
    e. Performance orientation
    f. Applied orientation
    g. Change orientation

for Managers

- Set aside time to establish and discuss expectations early.
- Remember that psychological contracts are very likely to change over time. Therefore, make opportunities to check out whether the contract is still viable and renegotiate if necessary. Managers or leaders who take the initiative to do this checking are greatly appreciated because it is sometimes difficult for subordinates to bring "pinches" to their boss' attention.
- "Pinches" are easier to handle than full-blown breakdowns in expectations.
- Sample questions for checking out expectations are:
  - What do you like/dislike about your job (or this relationship)?
  - Why do you continue with it?
  - Is there one thing that, if it were changed, would make you quit your job?
  - What are your expectations of me?
  - Do you think I am meeting them?
  - Is there any way I can help you do your job better?
  - What kind of supervision do you like best, or (for employees) what type of supervision do you prefer to use with employees?
  - Does the organization or do I hinder you in completing your work?
  - Is there anything you would like to see changed?
- Some people use the following matrix to judge whether mutual expectations are fairly balanced and reasonable. The contributions that a person or organization gives should be balanced, more or less, by what they get. This matrix can be a good basis for discussion, but bear in mind that good human relationships are not based upon a tit-for-tat mentality, but upon a flexible give-and-take approach.

INDIVIDUAL (YOU)		ORGANIZATION OR GROUP	
Expect to Get	Expect to Contribute	Expect to Get	Expect to Contribute

 Personal Application Assignment

The following assignment is modeled after Kolb's adult learning cycle that appears in Chapter 3. Please respond to the questions and submit them at next week's class. Each section of the assignment is worth 4 points that will be assigned according to the criteria that follow. [19]

The topic of this assignment is to think back on a significant incident when you experienced a "pinch" in a psychological contract. Pick an experience about which you are motivated to learn more; that is, there is something about it that you do not totally understand, that intrigues you, that makes you realize you lack certain skills, that is problematical or very significant for you. It could have taken place in a work relationship or a social one (with a club or group) or within a personal relationship.

A. *Concrete Experience*

1. *Objectively* describe the experience ("who," "what," "when," "where," "how" type information–up to 2 points).

2. *Subjectively* describe your feelings, perceptions, and thoughts that occurred *during* (not after) the experience (up to 2 points). Does this section have too much detail? (If so, delete 1 point.)

B. *Reflective Observation*

1. Look at the experience from different points of view. How many points of view did you include that are *relevant* (up to 2 points)?

2. Use these perspectives to add more meaning to the incident (up to 2 points).

C. *Abstract Conceptualization*

1. Relate concepts from the assigned readings and the lecture to the experience (i.e., what theories that you heard in the lecture or read in the Reader relate to your understanding of this incident?). (up to 2 points)

2. Make reference to at least two sources. Use standard referencing format and include the page number to which you are referring. How many sources did you use and how clearly did you explain their theories? (up to 2 points)

3. You can also create an original model or theory, but it should not replace course concepts.

D. *Active Experimentation*
1. Write about what you will do in the future that will improve your effectiveness. Use rules of thumb or action resolutions.
2. Are they described specifically, thoroughly, and in detail. (up to 4 points)

[1]Rousseau, Denise M., "The Impact of Psychological and Implied Contracts on Behavior in Organizations," Kellogg Graduate School of Management, Northwestern University, Evanston, Illinois, 1987. See also Denise M. Rousseau and Judi McLean Parks, "The Contracts of Individuals and Organizations," *Research in Organizational Behavior*, Vol. 15 pp. 111–194.

[2]Walter W. Tornow, "Contract Redesign," *Personnel Administrator*, October 1988, p. 97-101.

[3]Robert Rosenthal and K.L. Fode, "The Effect of Experimenter Bias on the Performance of the Albino Rat," *Behavioral Science*, Vol. 8, 1968, pp. 183-189.

[4]Robert Rosenthal and L.F. Jacobson, "Teacher Expectations for the Disadvantaged," *Scientific American*, Vol. 218, 1968, pp. 19-23.

[5]Douglas W. Bray, Richard J. Campbell, and Donald L. Grant, *Formative Years in Business: A Long-Term AT&T Study of Managerial Lives* (New York: John Wiley, 1974) and David E. Berlew and Douglas T. Hall, "The Socialization of Managers: The Effects of Expectations on Performance," *Administrative Science Quarterly*, Vol.11, no. 2 (September 1966), pp. 207-233.

[6]Oxford Analytica, *America in Perspective* (Boston: Houghton Mifflin, 1986).

[7]Donald L. Kanter and Philip H. Mirvis, *The Cynical Americans: Living and Working in an Age of Discontent and Disillusion* (San Francisco: Jossey Bass, 1989).

[8]Tornow, "Contract Redesign," p. 100

[9]Robert H. Rosen with Lisa Berger, *The Healthy Company: Eight Strategies to Develop People, Productivity, and Profits.* (New York: Tarcher/Perigee) 1992.

[10]Jack Stack, The Great Game of Business. (New York: Doubleday Currency, 1992) describes how one company has revolutionized the way they operate.

[11]William B. Johnston and Arnold E. Packer, *Workforce 2000: Work & Workers for the Twenty-First Century.* Hudson Institute, 1987 and William B. Johnston, "Global Workforce 2000: The New Labor Market." *Harvard Business Review*, March-April 1991, pp. 115-129.

[12]Tornow, "Contract Redesign," p. 99.

[13]S. Pedigo, "Diversity in the Workforce: Riding the Tide of Change," *The Wyatt Communicator*, (The Wyatt company, Winter 1991), p.9.

[14]Nancy B. Songer, "Work Force Diversity," *Business & Economic Review* (April-June 1991), pp. 3-6; and Jim Kennedy and Anna Everest, "Put Diversity in Context," *Personnel Journal* (September 1991), 50-54. See also *HR Focus*, Vol. 70, (6), June 1993, p. 3-4.

[15]See "The Impact of Changing Values on Organizational Life—the Latest Update" by Richard E. Boyatzis and Florence R. Skelly, *Reader*, 1994.

[16]*Population Today*, Vol. 20, no. 4, April, 1992, p. 5.

[17]See James G. March and Herbert A. Simon, *Organization* (New York: John Wiley, 1963), especially Chapter 4, for a fuller discussion of this conceptual scheme.

[18]Kurt Lewin, *A Dynamic Theory of Personality* (New York: McGraw-Hill, 1935).

[19]This guideline was developed by Don McCormick, Ph.D., Antioch University, Los Angeles.

Chapter

2

THEORIES OF MANAGING PEOPLE

OBJECTIVES By the end of this chapter, you should be able to:

A. Describe six theories of management and their "ideal" manager.

B. Explain why it's important to identify your personal theories about management and organizational behavior.

C. Describe your personal theory of management.

D. Identify the managerial skills you need in today's environment.

The Education of a Modern International Manager

Jacques G. Maisonrouge

The novelist Gore Vidal once said that it is not enough to succeed; your friends must also fail. It is cleverly phrased–a true bon mot that speaks volumes about human psychology. But I do not agree, because success is not a zero-sum game in which there must be a loser for every winner.

This sentiment must sound odd coming from someone who has spent his adult life in the business world where the law of the jungle is supposed to prevail. But those of us who actually inhabit that world know that the modern business enterprise is too complex and too far-flung to be anything but a vast, cooperative effort with many interdependent parts. A multitude of skills and talents must mesh to make a large enterprise work. It is therefore in the common interest that as many people as possible succeed in what they do every single day. Toward that end, we learn from each other as much as we can.

Source: Excerpt from a speech by Mr. Maisonrouge, senior vice president, IBM Corporation, and chairman of the board, IBM Word Trade Corporation, when he received the International Business Leader of the Year Award from the Academy of International Business in 1982. Reprinted in *Journal of International Business Studies*, Spring-Summer, 1983, pp. 141-146.

Businesses have also learned to learn from each other–for example, through associations, through industry conferences, through consultants–and they have learned from universities. It is in this spirit that I am happy to share with you some thoughts on management education for an international career.

Throughout my career, I have met people with the same ambition, the same drive, even the same formal education–be they MBAs, graduate engineers, whatever–who did not achieve the same results at all. Those who are not successful—and I define success here as either rising on the hierarchical ladder or attaining professional distinction— share certain traits. First, they exhibit a lack of sensitivity in their relations with others. They become so mesmerized by the process of management or the demands of their discipline that they lose sight of the human element. They forget that people are the sine qua non of working, planning, and decision making—in short, the ultimate resource of their operations.

Given these facts, it follows that the managers' quintessential responsibility is to help their people realize their highest potential. They don't do this by intimidating them, or taking them for granted, or making them feel like "hired hands." They do it by inspiring them, recognizing their unique contributions to the general effort, and making them feel like valued members of a team. Certainly, a major reason for Japan's famous "economic miracle" has been its recognition that its chief resource– almost its only resource–is its people.

The second trait shared by the unsuccessful is a habit acquired first in school. Having chosen to study only the subjects they liked, they continue that self-indulgence in business. What they like to do, they do well and neglect the rest. But to be successful in management, you must try to do well whatever needs doing.

Third, those who are unsuccessful never discard their youthful prejudices. To this day, they mistrust foreigners, members of the opposite sex, people who come from different regions of the country–anyone, in short, who differs from them. In the process, they miss the opportunity and benefits of learning from those who have another perspective.

So much for what the manager ought not to be or do.

Business has become subject to very rapid change. Alvin Toffler, the futurist, has dramatized this by translating the last 50,000 years into 800 lifetimes, then observing that of those 800 lifetimes, only 70 could communicate with their descendants through writing, only the last 8 ever saw a printed word, only the last 4 were able to measure time with any precision, only the last 2 used an electric motor, most of the material goods we use in our daily lives were developed within the 800th lifetime, and more technological progress will be made during the 801st lifetime than during the previous 800 combined.

Clearly, in a fast-changing environment the ability to plan for change becomes a managerial imperative. Consequently, tomorrow's managers will have to demonstrate more awareness of the world around them, more flexibility of mind, more "technological literacy" than ever before. In a world where new knowledge continues to accumulate rapidly, the most valuable managers of all will be those who have learned how to learn.

The two qualities I consider most essential to a manager's success in today's business world are a true global perspective and the ability to manage human resources. We in business look to the colleges and universities to impart the basic skills on which these qualities depend to the men and women who will someday take our places. In turn, we will do our best to translate what is being taught in the classroom into solid achievement.

Premeeting Preparation

A. Read "The Education of a Modern International Manager."

B. Fill out and score the questionnaire on the following page.

C. Answer the following questions.

1. How would you describe the ideal manager?

2. How did you arrive at this ideal–previous experiences, values, role models, education, training, reading, and so on?

3. What values underly your picture of the ideal manager?

4. What were the significant learning points from the reading?

D. Read the Topic Introduction that follows.

LEADERSHIP STYLES QUESTIONNAIRE*

This instrument is designed to help you better understand the assumptions you make about people and human nature. There are ten pairs of statements. Assign a weight from 0—10 to each statement to show the relative strength of your belief in the statements in each pair. The points assigned for each pair must total ten in each case. Be as honest with yourself as you can and resist the natural tendency to respond as you would "like to think things are." This instrument is not a "test." There are no right or wrong answers. It is designed to be a stimulus for personal reflection and discussion.

1. It's only human nature for people to do as little work as they can get away with. _____ (a)

   When people avoid work, it's usually because their work has been deprived of its meaning. _____ (b)

   10

2. If employees have access to any information they want, they tend to have better attitudes and behave more responsibly. _____ (c)

   If employees have access to more information than they need to do their immediate tasks, they will usually misuse it. _____ (d)

   10

3. One problem in asking for the ideas of employees is that their perspective is too limited for their suggestions to be of much practical value. _____ (e)

   Asking employees for their ideas broadens their perspective and results in the development of useful suggestions. _____ (f)

   10

4. If people don't use much imagination and ingenuity on the job, it's probably because relatively few people have much of either. _____ (g)

   Most people are imaginative and creative but may not show it because of limitations imposed by supervision and the job. _____ (h)

   10

5. People tend to raise their standards if they are accountable for their own behavior and for correcting their own mistakes. _____ (i)

   People tend to lower their standards if they are not punished for their misbehavior and mistakes. _____ (J)

   10

6. It's better to give people both good and bad news because most employees want the whole story, no matter how painful. _____ (k)

   It's better to withhold unfavorable news about business because most employees really want to hear only the good news. _____ (l)

   10

*Adapted from M. Scott Myers, *Every Employee a Manager*. New York: McGraw-Hill Book Company, 1970.

7. Because a supervisor is entitled to more respect than those below him in the organization, it weakens his prestige to admit that a subordinate was right and he was wrong.

_____ (m)

Because people at all levels are entitled to equal respect, a supervisor's prestige is increased when he supports this principle by admitting that a subordinate was right and he was wrong.

_____ (n)
10

8. If you give people enough money, they are less likely to be concerned with such intangibles as responsibility and recognition.

_____ (o)

If you give people interesting and challenging work, they are less likely to complain about such things as pay and supplemental benefits.

_____ (p)
10

9. If people are allowed to set their own goals and standards of performance, they tend to set them higher than the boss would.

_____ (q)

If people are allowed to set their own goals and standards of performance, they tend to set them lower than the boss would.

_____ (r)
10

10. The more knowledge and freedom a person has regarding his job, the more controls are needed to keep him in line.

_____ (s)

The more knowledge and freedom a person has regarding his job, the fewer controls are needed to insure satisfactory job performance.

_____ (t)
10

SCORING INSTRUCTIONS

Record the number you assign to each of the following letters in the space provided and then total each column.

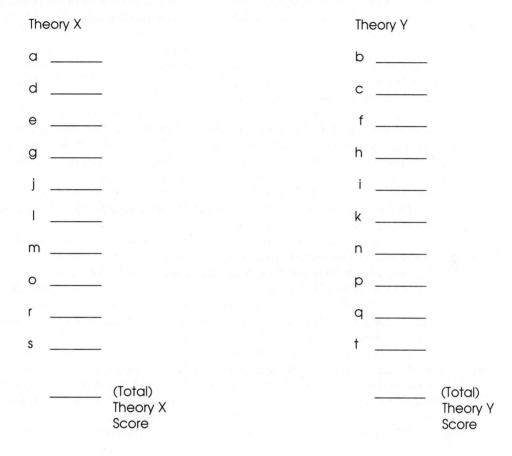

Theory X

a _____

d _____

e _____

g _____

j _____

l _____

m _____

o _____

r _____

s _____

_____ (Total)
Theory X
Score

Theory Y

b _____

c _____

f _____

h _____

i _____

k _____

n _____

p _____

q _____

t _____

_____ (Total)
Theory Y
Score

Topic Introduction

Just like Jacques Maisonrouge, whose speech was excerpted in the opening vignette, we all have our theories about what makes for successful managers and organizations. Over the years, there have been numerous and varied contributions to our knowledge about organizations. Each reflected the theorists' model of what made for excellent organizations and managers within their socio-historical context. Some of the major theories or schools of thought will be touched upon in the following paragraphs to set the stage for the study of organizational behavior.

Frederick Taylor's *scientific management*[1] the "one best way" of doing a job, which emerged in the late 1800s, emphasized the efficient division of labor into small, specialized, standardized jobs that were carefully matched with the capacities of workers. For the first time, Taylorism made it possible for engineers to research the most efficient way to do jobs. Taylor's goal was to develop workers to the best of their abilities and to convey the message that it was *cooperation* between capital and labor that resulted in success. By increasing profits, rather than arguing over their distribution, both labor and owners would prosper.

Taylor's name is often mistakenly associated with time-and-motion studies run amok and an inhumane emphasis upon output. In fact, Taylor was concerned about both the proper design of the job *and* the worker. In Taylor's eyes, the ideal manager (perhaps with the aid of an engineer) scientifically determined the goals that needed to be accomplished, divided the work up in the most efficient way, trained workers to do the job, and rewarded them by wage incentives such as piecework. However, since foremen were cast as the "brains" who did planning rather than actual operations, workers came to be seen as little more than "a pair of hands." While that sounds pejorative, it was a perspective more easily understood when placed within the context of a country just beginning to industrialize. The labor force quite naturally consisted primarily of people from rural areas without prior factory experience. In that era, workers were viewed as one more resource, much like machines.

The next phase in management history was termed *administrative theory*. At that time, beginning about the late 1920s, managers were grappling with the problems of organizing larger and larger organizations and defining the emerging role of the professional manager. Administrative theory came up with answers to both issues. Fayol defined the functions of a manager as planning, controlling, organizing, and commanding and advocated the study of management as a discipline.[2] Weber contributed greatly to our understanding of the "ideal" bureaucracy and the different types of authority that were appropriate for it.[3] In those days, bureaucracy did not have the negative connotations it does today. Indeed, bureaucracy was then viewed as a solution to the nepotism, favoritism, and unprofessional behavior found in organizations of the day. During this era, people believed that if managers designed the organization correctly and followed the proven principles of management (e.g., having a limited number of people report to each supervisor, having only one boss for each worker, and engaging in merit-based selection of employees), the organization would succeed.

However, this formula for success was further complicated by the famous Hawthorne studies[4] that took place in the late 1920s and 1930s. It was a time when the credibility of business people was low due to the stock market crash, and feelings of exploitation fueled the union movement. Decreased immigration had made labor scarce, and, as a result, the needs of workers began to receive attention. The Hawthorne studies contributed the idea that worker output was affected by numerous, heretofore ignored, variables: how they were treated; how they felt about their work, co-workers, and boss; and what happened to them outside of work.

The attention the workers received in the experiment, rather than the varied work conditions, caused them to work harder. This phenomenon has come to be known as the Hawthorne effect. The *human relations school* grew out of this research and acknowledged that workers had to be considered as more than "hands"; workers also had "hearts," i.e., feelings and attitudes that affected productivity. And the norms or implicit rules of the work groups to which they belonged also affected productivity. Therefore, the effective manager was expected to pay attention to people's social needs and elicit their ideas about work issues.

March and Simon[5], writing in the late 1950s, were proponents of the *decision-making school*. They added yet another layer of complexity to our understanding of organizations with their description of organizations as social systems in which individual decisions are the basis of human behavior. As mentioned in the previous chapter, employees make the decision to join an organization, but once hired, they also have another decision to make–whether or not to participate and work as hard as they can. The outcome of this decision depends upon the employee's rational analysis of the situation and the rewards involved. Now managers also had to take into account workers' "minds." The effective manager set the premises for employee decisions and relied upon their rationality to make choices that would be best for both themselves and the organization. For example, if a CEO of a company in which marketing was seen as the springboard into top management decided that more emphasis needed to be placed upon operations, he or she would promote more rapidly from operations positions. Employees would then realize that operations was the area receiving top-level attention and ambitious workers would elect to work in that area. Manipulating the decision premises is an unobtrusive form of controlling the organization.

However, March and Simon also made the sobering observation that our decisions are limited by the number of variables our brains can handle, the time available, our reasoning powers, and so on; they called this bounded rationality. It means that we often "satisfice" (choose a solution that is merely good enough) rather than maximize or optimize (search and consider all the available information) when we make decisions. Routine work drives out nonroutine work, which explains why it seems so much harder to launch important new projects than it is to maintain routine tasks. For theorists of this school, managerial effectiveness consisted of a thorough understanding of decision making.

By the middle of the century, managers and scholars had identified many variables that were thought to be related to success such as job specialization, managerial principles, worker attitudes and human relations, and rational decisions made by workers. In the 1960s, many scholars converged on the idea that there was no "one best way" to manage. Instead, they tried to identify which variables would be successful for particular situations.

This is still the dominant perspective in the field of organizational behavior and is referred to as *contingency theory*.[6] The gist of this theory is that effectiveness varies according to the particular situation. We know now that individuals, groups, cultural groups, occupational subgroups, industries, types of technology, managerial styles, organizations, and external environments can all vary enormously. There are many examples of successful organizations that do things quite differently. For example, ITT under Harold Geneen and Matsushita under Konosuke Matsushita are examples of extremely well-managed, but exceedingly diverse, companies.[7] As long as the various aspects of the organization *fit* together, organizations seem to work. The building blocks of organizations are popularly referred to as the 7 S's: strategy, structure, systems, staff, style, skills, and superordinate goals.[8]

Procter and Gamble[9] is an example of a company that has good "fit." Their management values about staffing are (1) to hire good people of high character, (2) treat them as individuals and develop their individual talents, and (3) provide a work environment that rewards individual achievement. The company is well-known for its training programs and promotion from within. General managers are evaluated and rewarded for their success in terms of volume, profit, and people. P&G has developed systems (sometimes cumbersome) and skills (marketing, marketing research and R&D) that reinforce their strategic goals. They have been very responsive to changing market conditions and demographics. Marketing strategies are customized for different ethnic groups, and they have made a major effort to integrate employees from diverse ethnic and cultural backgrounds. P&G has also experimented with various structures to help them compete more effectively both domestically and globally. Their success is due, in large part, to their ability to keep the 7 Ss in alignment and maintain the fit with their environment.

Being an effective manager now meant having an understanding of organizations as *open systems*. Systems theory maintains that organizations and all the subdivisions within them take in resources and transform them into a service or product that is purchased or utilized by a larger system. Acknowledging the interdependence among different parts of the systems and seeing organizations as embedded in the larger environment allowed us to see that dealing with external entities is a crucial role for many managers. In this view, organization effectiveness is governed by three major factors: the individuals who make up the organization, the organization itself, and the environment in which the organization exists. Effective management of the interfaces between these factors–between the individual and the organization and between the organization and its environment–is central to organizational success. The relationship between the individual and the organization is often mediated or linked by a work group. Figure 2-1 illustrates a systems model of organizations.

Looking back upon these theories of organization, one is reminded of the parable of the blind men who each touched a different part of the elephant and assumed that they understood the entire animal. How is it that previous theorists only touched upon one part of organizing? One answer lies in the bounded rationality of their social context; most popular theories reflect ideas whose time has come, along with the personal predispositions and biases of the theorists themselves. Another answer is the increasing popularity of the concept of "paradox" regarding the process of organizing. Previous theories emphasized only one side of the equation (change versus stability, production versus social needs, Theory X versus Theory Y, etc.) rather than the balancing act that managers actually perform between them.

One of the most recent theories of organizing concerns the importance of mastering the paradoxes and competing demands of high performance. Quinn[10] maintains that parts of the different schools of management theory described in this chapter are still appropriate to modern organizations. Organizational success comes from the ability to utilize the contradictory logic of all these theories. Each theory appears to be the opposite of the one it faces diagonally in Figure 2-2. Both the expectations and the value assumptions of opposite theories seem to be in competition. For example, maximizing output (rational goal model) is at odds with developing human resources (human relations model); growth and expansion (open systems model) looks like the opposite of consolidation and continuity (internal process model).

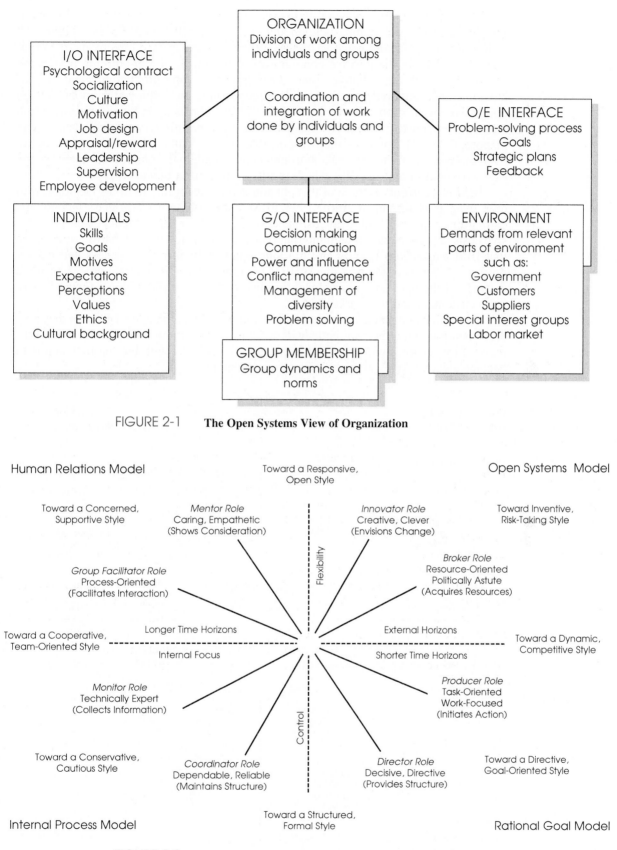

FIGURE 2-1   **The Open Systems View of Organization**

FIGURE 2-2   **Competing Values Framework of Leadership Roles**
Source: Robert E. Quinn, Beyond Rational Management (San Francisco: Jossey-Bass, 1988), p.86.

According to Quinn, none of these models is the one best way to organize or manage; in fact, too much emphasis upon any one model will lead to failure. Figure 2-3 shows both positive and negative zones. When a model is used effectively, the organization will lie in the positive zone; however, too much of a good thing pushes the organization into the negative zone. Overemphasis upon productivity and lack of attention and sensitivity to human resources results in employee burnout and an oppressive sweat shop culture. In contrast, overemphasis upon human resources and lack of attention to productivity results in extreme permissiveness, irrelevance, and inappropriate participation—the irresponsible country club. The other two poles are overemphasis upon the external environment and change–the tumultuous anarchy–and excessive control and stability, which results in the frozen bureaucracy.

IBM is a current example of this phenomenon. According to Louis Gerstner, who took over as chairman in April, 1993, IBM's strengths are world-class technology, extraordinary people, and loyal customers. He identified IBM's weaknesses as excessive costs, a preoccupation with internal processes, and slowness.[11] Most critics agree that IBM banked too heavily and too long upon its mainframe business and market position. In terms of Quinn's theory, IBM overemphasized its internal processes at the expense of the open systems values. In other words, they should have focused more upon customers and the market.

How can managers learn to deal with paradox and be effective? How can they predict when following their strengths will result in success rather than failure? The summary of this chapter will go into this question in greater detail, but the first step is to become aware of one's own theories of management.

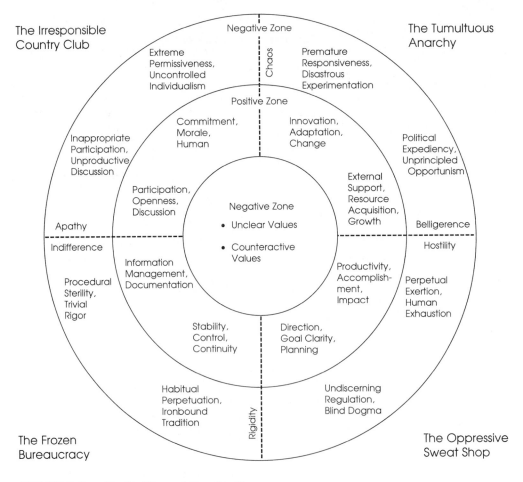

FIGURE 2-3   **The Positive and Negative Zones**
Source: Robert E. Quinn, Beyond Rational Management (San Francisco: Jossey-Bass, 1988), p.7.

All of us have these theories, and it is these models that guide our behavior. For example, if manager A holds the belief that people are motivated primarily by money, he will see increased salary as a solution to low productivity. He may then see his role as little more than laying out the work that needs to be done and seeing that employees are well paid for doing it. In contrast, if manager B believes that people's attitudes affect their productivity, she will try to improve morale and see her managerial role as including mentoring and coaching. These examples indicate more than the ubiquitous presence of theories or models of behavior. They also show that our theories determine what we actually see in situations. Manager A may never consider the possibility that morale issues may be involved, while manager B may overlook the role of pay equity. Thus, our mental maps determine what we perceive when we look at situations and what role we are likely to take as a result of our theories.

Figure 2-2 also shows the different managerial roles that grow out of each theory. These are placed in the inner ring. The outer ring shows eight leadership styles that differ along three axes: flexibility-control, internal focus-external focus, and longer time horizons-shorter time horizons. One's theories about management determine the roles and leadership style one assumes.

The prework for today's lesson was assigned to help you clarify your personal theory about the role of effective managers.

Procedure for Group Meeting:
Manager of the Year Acceptance Speech

STEP 1.   Divide into groups of five to seven participants.

STEP 2.   One of you (in each group) is about to receive the Manager of the Year Award. Your group can determine which member will receive this honor and the privilege of making a 5-minute acceptance speech, just as Jacques Maisonrouge did. The entire group should help to craft the speech, which should come close to representing all your views. You can draw ideas from your prework assignment. The speech should include two subjects:

a. A brief description of today's business environment;

b. The qualities and skills essential to a manager's success in today's business world.
(40 minutes)

STEP 3.   The award winner from each group presents a 5-minute speech to the entire class.
(40 minutes)

STEP 4.   **a.** Listen for common themes in the speeches.

b. As you are listening to the speeches, try to categorize the qualities and skills mentioned in the appropriate quadrant of Quinn's theory in Figure 2-2. For example, communication would fit under the Human Relations Model, while setting clear goals would fall into Rational Goal Model. Keep track (using hatch marks) of how many times each quality or skill is mentioned. Below we'll use the term "competencies" because it encompasses both qualities and skills.

STEP 5.   Discuss as a class the following questions:

a. What were the common themes you heard in the speeches?

b. What competencies did you place in the Human Relations quadrant?
Open Systems? Rational Goal? Internal Process?

c. Which quadrant(s) had the most competencies? The most frequently mentioned
competencies? Were there any quadrants that were not mentioned at all?
What implications can we draw from this?

d. Was anything mentioned that did not fit into the four quadrants?
What can we learn from this?

ANALYSIS OF THE SPEECHES

Write the values and skills that you hear in the appropriate category below and mark
how many times the same item is mentioned.

HUMAN RELATIONS MODEL	OPEN SYSTEMS MODEL
INTERNAL PROCESS MODEL	RATIONAL GOAL MODEL

Items that cannot be categorized:

Follow-Up

Another example of mental maps that people have concerning management is McGregor's Theory X and Theory Y concept.[10] McGregor described two ends of a continuum of assumptions about people and human nature. These assumptions appear in Figure 2-4. The Leadership Style Questionnaire that you filled out as part of the pre-meeting preparation is designed to help you assess the extent of your own Theory X versus Theory Y assumptions about people. Understanding these assumptions is of crucial importance because of the potential that exists for self-fulfilling prophecies. In other words, if you believe people are lazy and irresponsible (Theory X assumptions), you will manage them in a way that is consistent with these assumptions (e.g., watch over their shoulders all the time). This behavior can cause your subordinates to feel that they really have no responsibility in their job, which could lead them to work hard only when you are watching them closely. A self-fulfilling prophecy has thus begun and will be continually reinforced.

In some cultures, we find a stronger tendency towards a Theory X or Y orientation. One of the dimensions anthropologists use to differentiate cultures is their view of human nature. Is human nature good, evil, or neutral? Cultures that perceive humankind as innately evil tend towards a Theory X orientation (e.g. Latin countries). Cultures that perceive humankind as good are more likely to be characterized by a Theory Y orientation (e.g., Scandinavia). These generalizations do not mean that all managers in these cultures are similar, but that we will find more aspects of Theory X or Y in their organizations and managerial style.

The purpose of the group exercise was to identify still more of your own theories about managing and organizing. This is the first step to being able to evaluate when your theories are adequate and when you need to learn or borrow other theories that may be more appropriate to specific situations. Quinn argued that master managers are capable of utilizing competing theories, either sequentially or simultaneously, to master the paradoxes found in organizations. Numerous management writers have written about the importance of managers' mental maps. Yankelovich and Immerwahr claim that the American work ethic has not disappeared, it is merely mismanaged by older managers who do not understand the values (and the mental maps related to them) of the younger generation.[12] Streufert and Swezey claim that there is a correlation between reaching the executive suite and high "cognitive complexity."[13] Cognitive complexity refers to the extent to which people are multidimensional in their thinking and to the number of different relationships they can make between different dimensions or concepts. A manager with high cognitive complexity can see Quinn's four theory models and shuffle them around to choose the one that is most appropriate for a given situation. A manager with high cognitive complexity can be summed up as a person who possesses a variety of maps in his or her cognitive bank and who has the flexibility to play with them until an accurate combination is reached.

To be effective, today's managers must possess the capacity to analyze complex situations accurately and to choose appropriate responses. For example, do the individuals you supervise have a Theory X or a Theory Y orientation? Does this vary according to the tasks they are performing? What's the best way to manage them? Answering these questions successfully may mean introducing a different theory or going against one's natural way of doing things. Perhaps when life was less complex, it was sufficient for managers to espouse a "one best way" for managing and have a knee-jerk response to all situations. Today's environment, however, is too turbulent for routine responses. How do you handle a joint venture with China or the issue of AIDS in the workplace?

What managers need now is a broad behavioral repertoire and the analytical skill to know what behaviors are most appropriate for each situation. Effectiveness also requires the self-control and self-discipline to do something other than "what comes naturally" when one's natural style would not work. The key then is learning–learning as many models or theories as possible, learning what's involved in different or changing situations, learning about different people and what makes them tick, and learning what works and what doesn't.

 # Learning Points

1. Everyone has his or her personal theories about management and the role of managers.

2. Taylor's scientific management emphasized the efficient division of labor into small, standardized jobs that were matched to the capabilities of trained workers who received wage incentives.

3. Administrative theory focused upon understanding the basic tasks of management and developed guidelines or principles for managing effectively.

4. The human relations school acknowledged the effect of the informal social system with its norms and individual attitudes and feelings upon organizational functioning. This theory underlined the importance of employee morale and participation.

5. The decision-making school described organizations as social systems based upon individual decisions and contributed the idea of bounded rationality. Managers could control employee behavior by controlling the premises of decision making.

6. Contingency theory contends that there is no one best way to manage in every situation. Managers must find the appropriate method to match a given situation.

7. Successful organizations are characterized by good "fit" among strategy, structure, systems, staff, style, skills, and superordinate goals.

8. Open systems theory maintains that organizations and all the subdivisions within them take in resources and transform them into a service or product that is purchased or utilized by a larger system. All parts are interdependent, including the larger environment in which the organization is embedded.

9. Quinn's theory consists of a competing value approach and proposes that, to be successful, managers need to manage the paradoxes of the four different theories or quadrants: open systems model, rational goal model, internal process model, and the human relations model.

10. Too much emphasis upon any one model will lead to failure. Master managers are balanced in their ability to function in each of these quadrants and know when "more of the same" would not be warranted.

11. The first step in managing the paradoxes of organizational effectiveness is understanding one's own theories of management.

12. Our theories or mental maps determine what we see when we look at situations and determine the roles we perform.

13. Today's managers need to learn:

    a. How to analyze complex situations using a variety of models or theories;

    b. A repertoire of behaviors and the knowledge of when to use them; and

    c. How to adapt to rapidly changing environments.

- People often look down upon those whose theories are dissimilar to their own. One way to develop yourself is to seek out and work with people who have different beliefs. Doing so may involve a cost to you, but the payoff should be greater cognitive complexity and understanding of different mental maps.
- Gathering as many perspectives as possible about situations is helpful. Just as there is no one best way of managing, there is no one best way to see a situation. Managers who can count on others to help them "see" what's going on and give their opinions on what could be done are fortunate. If, however, you give the impression that you don't like to hear a different perspective or receive advice, you won't–until it's too late to do much about it.
  - Quinn made the following suggestions about developing oneself as a manager.[14]
    - Learn about yourself.
    - Develop a change strategy:
      - Keep a journal.
      - Identify specific areas in need of improvement.
      - Identify role models for your weak areas; read appropriate books on management skills.
    - Implement the change strategy:
      - Be honest about the costs of improvement (it may be high).
      - Develop a social support system (who will help you change or at least support your efforts?).
      - Constantly evaluate and modify your strategy.

- One way to better understand yourself and your mental maps is to take assessment instruments like the one at the beginning of this chapter. Having other people evaluate you is also valuable because it provides another perspective. If you are surprised by their evaluations, discuss any differences in perception with an honest coworker or friend.

- The interdependence aspect of open systems theory means that changes in one part of the system will have repercussions elsewhere. Try to determine these consequences *before* making decisions and implementing changes.

The interdependence aspect of open systems theory means that problems are often rooted in other parts of the system. Train yourself to take a systems approach when looking at problems. At a minimum, ask yourself, "Have I thought about what's taking place on the individual, group, organizational, and environmental level with regard to this particular situation?"

Personal Application Assignment

A. What is your own theory of management? You can describe it in words or draw it as a model. (Keep a copy for yourself so that you can modify it as the course proceeds.)

B. Based upon your theory of management and today's environment, answer the following questions.

    1. What blind spots could your theory lead you to have?

2. What personal values seem to underlie your theory, that is, "people, managers, or organizations should/should not _____ (what?)."

3. What implicit assumptions, if any, are you making about human nature or human motivation?

4. What skills do you think are necessary to be a "master" manager?

5. Which of these do you already possess?

6. What skills would you like to work on during this course?

7. Write up an action plan for learning these skills. How will you work on them? How will you know when they have improved?

[1]Frederick A. Taylor, *The Principles of Scientific Management* (New York: W.W. Norton, 1911).

[2]Henri Fayol, *General and Industrial Management*, trans. C. Storrs (London: Sir Isaac Pitman, 1949).

[3]Max Weber, *The Theory of Social and Economic Organization,* trans. T. Parsons (New York: Free Press, 1947).

[4]Felix J. Roethlisberger and W.J. Dickson, *Management and the Worker* (Cambridge, MA: Harvard University Press, 1939).

[5]James March and Herbert Simon, *Organizations* (New York: John Wiley, 1958).

[6]See David A. Nadler and Michael Tushman, "A Congruence Model for Diagnosing Organizational Behavior," *Reader*. For a famous example of research on contingency theory, see P. R. Lawrence and J. W. Lorsch, *Organization and Environment: Managing Differentiation and Integration* (Homewood, IL: Richard D. Irwin, 1969).

[7]Richard Tanner Pascale and Anthony G. Athos, *The Art of Japanese Management* (New York: Simon & Schuster, 1981).

[8]The 7S scheme, based upon the work of other organizational writers, was joined by Pascale and Athos and consultants of the McKenzie Company. It appears in *The Art of Japanese Management*, by Pascale and Athos (ibid.), and in the Waterman, et al, article, "Structure is not Organization," *Reader*.

[9]Christopher A. Bartlett and Sumantra Ghoshal. *Transnational Management*. (Homewood, Illinois: Irwin, 1992).

[10]Robert E. Quinn, *Beyond Rational Management* (San Francisco: Jossey-Bass, 1988).

[11]Judith H. Dobrzynski, "Rethinking IBM," *Business Week*, pp. 86-97, October 4, 1993. No. 3339.

[12]Daniel Yankelovich and John Immerwahr, "Management and the Work Ethic," *Directors and Boards*, Fall 1983.

[13]Sigmund Streufert and R. W. Swezey, *Complexity, Managers, and Organizations* (Orlando, FL: Academic Press, 1986).

[14]Quinn, *Beyond Rational Management*, p. 121.

Chapter

3

INDIVIDUAL AND ORGANIZATIONAL LEARNING

OBJECTIVES   By the end of this chapter, you should be able to:

A. Describe the model of adult learning.

B. Identify individual learning styles.

C. Improve the learning organization in this course by sharing learning objectives, available resources for learning, and learning environment preferences.

D. Understand the importance of continuous learning.

Planning as Learning...At Shell, Planning Means Changing Minds, Not Making Plans

Arie P. DeGeus

Some years ago, the planning group at Shell surveyed 30 companies that has been in business for more than 75 years. What impressed us most was their ability to live in harmony with the business environment, to switch from a survival mode when times were turbulent to a self-development mode when the pace of change was slow.

Outcomes like these don't happen automatically. On the contrary, they depend on the ability of a company's senior managers to absorb what is going on in the business environment and to act on that information with appropriate business moves. In other words, they depend on learning. Or, more precisely, on institutional learning, which is the process whereby management teams change their shared mental models of their company, their markets, and their competitors. For this reason, we think of planning as learning and of corporate planning as institutional learning.

Because high-level, effective, and continuous institutional learning and ensuing corporate change are the prerequisites for corporate success, we at Shell[1] have asked ourselves two questions. How does a company learn and adapt? And, what is planning's role in corporate learning?

My answer to the first question, "how does a company learn and adapt," is that many do not or, at least, not very quickly. A full one-third of the Fortune "500" industrials listed in 1970 had vanished by 1983. And W. Stewart Howe has pointed out in his 1986 book *Corporate Strategy* that for every successful turnaround there are two ailing companies that fail to recover. Yet some companies obviously do learn and can adapt. In fact, our survey identified several that were still vigorous at 200, 300, and even 700 years of age. What made the difference? Why are some companies better able to adapt?

Sociologists and psychologists tell us it is pain that makes people and living systems change. But crisis management–pain management–is a dangerous way to manage for change. The problem is that you usually have little time and few options. The deeper into the crisis you are, the fewer options remain. Crisis management, by necessity, becomes autocratic management. The challenge, therefore, is to recognize and react to environmental change before the pain of a crisis. Not surprisingly, this is what the long-lived companies in our study were so well able to do. All these companies had a striking capacity to institutionalize change. They never stood still. Moreover, they seemed to recognize that they had internal strengths that could be developed as environmental conditions changed.

Changes like these grow out of a company's knowledge of itself and its environment. All managers have such knowledge and they develop it further all the time, since every living person–and system–is continuously engaged in learning. In fact, the normal decision process in corporations is a learning process, because people change their own mental models and build up a joint model as they talk. The problem is that the speed of that process is slow–too slow for a world in which the ability to learn faster than competitors may be the only sustainable competitive advantage.

Some five years ago, we had a good example of the time it takes for a message to be heard. One way in which we in Shell trigger institutional learning is through scenarios.[2] A certain set of scenarios gave our planners a clear signal that the oil industry, which had always been highly integrated, was so no longer. That contradicted all our existing models. High integration means that you are more or less in control of all the facets of your industry, so you can start optimizing. Optimization was the driving managerial model in Shell. What these scenarios essentially were saying was that we had to look for other management methods.

The first reaction from the organization was at best polite. There were few questions and no discussion. Some managers reacted critically: the scenarios were "basic theory that everyone already knew"; they had "little relevance to the realities of today's business." The message had been listened to but it had not yet been heard.

After a hiatus of some three months, people began asking lots of questions; a discussion started. The intervening months had provided time for the message to settle and for management's mental models to develop a few new hooks. Absorption, phase one of the learning process, had taken place.

During the next nine months,we moved through the other phases of the learning process. Operating executives at Shell incorporated this new information into their mental models of the business. They drew conclusions from the revised models and tested them against experience. Then, finally, they acted on the basis of the altered model. Hearing, digestion, confirmation, action: each step took time, its own sweet time.

In my experience this time span is typical. It will likely take 12 to 18 months from the moment a signal is received until it is acted on. The issue is not whether a company will learn, therefore, but whether it will learn fast and early. The critical question becomes, **"Can we accelerate institutional learning?"**

I am more and more persuaded that the answer to this question is yes. But before explaining why, I want to emphasize an important point about learning and the planner's role. The only relevant learning in a company is the learning done by those people who have the power to act (at Shell, the operating company management teams). So the real purpose of effective planning is not to make plans but to change the microcosm, the mental models that these decision makers carry in their heads. And this is what we at Shell and others elsewhere try to do.

Fortified with this understanding of planning and its role, we looked for ways to accelerate institutional learning. Curiously enough, we learned in two cases that changing the rules, or suspending them, could be a spur to learning. Rules in a corporation are extremely important. Nobody likes them but everybody obeys them because they are recognized as the glue of the organization. And yet, we have all known extraordinary managers who got their organizations out of a rut by changing the rules. Intuitively they changed the organization and the way it looked at matters, and so, as a consequence, accelerated learning.

Several years ago one of our work groups introduced, out of the blue, a new rule into the corporate rain dance: "Thou shall plan strategically in the first half of the calendar year." (We already had a so-called business planning cycle that dealt with capital budgets in the second half of the calendar year.) In the first year the results of this new game were scanty, mostly a rehash of the previous year's business plans. But in the second year the plans were fresher and each year the quality of thinking that went into strategic planning improved.

A similar thing happened when we tried suspending the rules. In 1984, we had a scenario that talked about $15 a barrel oil. (Bear in mind that in 1984 the price of a barrel of oil was $28 and $15 was the end of the world to oil people.) We thought it important that, as early in 1985 as possible, senior managers throughout Shell start learning about a world of $15 oil. But the response to this scenario was essentially, "If you want us to think about this world, first tell us when the price is going to fall, how far it will fall, and how long the drop will last."

A deadlock ensued which we broke by writing a case study with a preface that was really a license to play. "We don't know the future," it said. "But neither do you. And though none of us knows whenever the price is going to fall, we can agree that it would be pretty serious if it did. So we have written a case showing one of many possible ways by which the price of oil could fall." We then described a case in which the price plummeted at the end of 1985 and concluded by saying: "And now it is April 1986 and you are staring at a price of $16 a barrel. Will you please meet and give your views on these three questions: What do you think your government will do? What do you think your competition will do? And what, if anything, will you do?"

Since at that point the price was still $28 and rising, the case was only a game. But that game started off serious work throughout Shell, not on answering the question "What will happen?" but rather exploring the question, "What will we do if it happens?" The acceleration of the institutional learning process had been set in motion.

As it turned out, the price of oil was still $27 in early January of 1986. But on February 1 it was $17 and in April it was $10. The fact that Shell had already visited the world of $15 oil helped a great deal in that panicky spring of 1986.

By now, we knew we were on to something: games could significantly accelerate institutional learning. That's not so strange when you think of it. Some of the most difficult and complex tasks in our lives were learned by playing: cycling, tennis, playing an instrument. We did it, we experimented, we played. But how were we going to make it OK to play?

One characteristic of play, as the Tavistock Institute in London has shown, is the presence of a transitional object. For the person playing, the transitional object is a representation of the real world. A child who is playing with a doll learns a great deal about the real world at a very fast pace.

Successful consultants let themselves be treated as transitional objects. The process begins when the consultant says something like this to a management team: "We know from experience that many good strategies are largely implicit. If you let us interview people at various levels in your organization, we'll see whether we can get your strategy out on paper. Then we'll come back and check whether we've understood it."

Some weeks later the consultant goes back to the team and says: "Well, we've looked at your strategy and we've played it through a number of likely possibilities, and here is what we think will be the outcome. Do you like it?" The management team will almost certainly say no. So the consultant will say: "All right, let's see how we can change it. Let's go back to your original model and see what was built in there that produced this result." This process is likely to go through a number of iterations, during which the team's original model will change considerably. Those changes constitute the learning that is taking place among the team's members.

Like consultants, computer models can be used to play back and forth management's view of its market, the environment, or the competition. The starting point, however, must be the mental model that the audience has at the moment. If a planner walks into the room with a model on his computer that he has made up himself, the chances are slim that his audience will recognize this particular microworld.

But why go to all this trouble? Why not rely on the natural learning process that occurs whenever a management team meets? For us at Shell, there are three compelling reasons. First, although the models in the human mind are complex, most people can deal with only three or four variables at a time and do so through only one or two time iterations.

The second reason for putting mental models into computers is that in working with dynamic models, people discover that in complex systems (like markets or companies) cause and effect are separated in time and place. To many people such insight is also counter-intuitive. Most of us, particularly if we are engaged in the process of planning, focus on the effect we want to create and then look for the most immediate cause to create that effect. The use of dynamic models helps us discover other trigger points, separated in time and place from the desired effect.

Lastly, by using computer models we learn what constitutes relevant information. For only when we start playing with these microworlds do we find out what information we really need to know.

When people play with models this way, they are actually creating a new language among themselves that expresses the knowledge they have acquired. And here we come to the most important aspect of institutional learning, whether it be achieved through teaching or through play as we have defined it: the institutional learning process is a process of language development. As the implicit knowledge of each learner becomes explicit, his or her mental model becomes a building block of the institutional model. How much and how fast this model changes will depend on the culture and structure of the organization. Teams that have to cope with rigid procedures and information systems will learn more slowly than those with flexible, open communication channels. Autocratic institutions will learn faster or not at all–the ability of one or a few leaders being a risky institutional bet.

Human beings aren't the only ones whose learning ability is directly related to their ability to convey information. As a species, birds have great potential to learn, but there are important differences among them. Titmice, for example, move in flocks and mix freely, while robins live in well-defined parts of the garden and for the most part communicate antagonistically across the borders of their territories. Virtually all the titmice in the U.K. quickly learned how to pierce the seals of milk bottles left at doorsteps. But robins as a group will never learn to do this (though individual birds may) because their capacity for institutional learning is low; one bird's knowledge does not spread.[3] The same phenomenon occurs in management teams that work by mandate. The best learning takes place in teams that accept that the whole is larger than the sum of the parts, that there is a good that transcends the individual.

What about managers who find themselves in a robin culture? Clearly, their chances of accelerating institutional learning are reduced. Nevertheless, they can take a significant step toward opening up communication and thus the learning process by keeping one fact in mind: institutional learning begins with the calibration of existing mental models.

We are continuing to explore other ways to improve and speed up our institutional learning process. Our exploration into learning play via a transitional object (a consultant or a computer) looks promising enough at this point to push on in that direction. And while we are navigating in poorly charted waters, we are not out there alone.[4]

Our exploration into this area is not a luxury. We understand that the only competitive advantage the company of the future will have is its managers' ability to learn faster than their competitors. So the companies that succeed will be those that continually nudge their managers towards revising their views of the world. The challenges for the planner are considerable. So are the rewards.

 # Premeeting Preparation

(Time Allotted: 1 1/2 Hours)

A. Read "Planning Is Learning."

B. Respond to this problem and answer the questions that follow:
Identify a real learning situation that you have recently faced or are currently facing (e.g., learning to use a computer, play an instrument, understand the new income tax laws, master a new management technique, give a speech, play a new sport).

1. Describe what you were (or are) trying to learn.

2. How did you go about learning to do it? What sequence of steps did you follow?

3. What was the outcome?

4. What was the best group learning experience you ever had? What was good about it?

5. What was your worst group learning experience? What made it that way?

6. In your opinion, what conditions promote adult learning?

7. What are the significant learning points from the readings?

C. Complete the Learning Style Inventory that follows.

D. Score the Learning Style Inventory.

E. Read the entire unit after completing A, B, and C.

The Learning Style Inventory

This survey is designed to help you describe how you learn–the way you find out about and deal with ideas and situations in your life. Different people learn best in different ways. The different ways of learning described in the survey are equally good. The aim is to describe how you learn, not to evaluate your learning ability. You might find it hard to choose the descriptions that best characterize your learning style. Keep in mind that there are no right or wrong answers–all the choices are equally acceptable.

There are nine sets of four descriptions listed in this inventory. Mark the words in each set that are most like you, second most like you, third most like you, and least like you.

Put a numeral "4" next to the description that is most like you, a "3" next to the description that is second most like you, a "2" next to the description that is third most like you, and a "1" next to the description that is least like you (4 = most like you; 1 = least like you). Be sure to assign a different rank number to each of the four words in each set; do not make ties.

EXAMPLE

<u>4</u> happy   <u>3</u> fast   <u>1</u> angry   <u>2</u> careful

Some people find it easiest to decide first which word best describes them (4 happy) and then to decide the word that is least like them (1 angry). Then you can give a 3 to that word in the remaining pair that is most like you (3 fast) and a 2 to the word that is left over (2 careful).

1. __ discriminating   __ tentative   __ involved   __ practical
2. __ receptive   __ relevant   __ analytical   __ impartial
3. __ feeling   __ watching   __ thinking   __ doing
4. __ accepting   __ risk taker   __ evaluative   __ aware
5. __ intuitive   __ productive   __ logical   __ questioning
6. __ abstract   __ observing   __ concrete   __ active
7. __ present-oriented __ reflecting   __ future-oriented   __ pragmatic
8. __ experience   __ observation   __ conceptualization __ experimentation
9. __ intense   __ reserved   __ rational   __ responsible

SCORING INSTRUCTIONS

The four columns of words corresponding to the four learning style scales: concrete experience (CE), reflective observation (RO), abstract conceptualization (AC), and active experimentation (AE). To compute your scale scores, write your rank numbers in the boxes below only for the designated items. For example, in the third column (AC), you would fill in the rank numbers you have assigned to items 2, 3, 4, 5, 8, and 9. Compute your scale scores by adding the rank numbers for each set of boxes.

First Column   Second Column   Third Column   Fourth Column
Score items: Score items: Score items: Score items:
2 3 4 5 7 8   1 3 6 7 8 9   2 3 4 5 8 9   1 3 6 7 8 9
[ ][ ][ ][ ][ ][ ]   [ ][ ][ ][ ][ ][ ]   [ ][ ][ ][ ][ ][ ]   [ ][ ][ ][ ][ ][ ]
CE = _____   RO = _____   AC = _____   AE = _____

To compute the two combination scores, subtract CE from AC and subtract RO from AE. Preserve negative signs if they appear.

$$\text{AC-CE:} \quad \boxed{} - \boxed{} =$$ $$\text{AE-RO:} \quad \boxed{} - \boxed{} =$$

AC   CE   AE   RO

To interpret the meaning of these scores, read the topic introduction.

Topic Introduction

For most of us, the first associations we have with the word "learning" are teacher, classroom, and textbook. These associations reflect some implicit assumptions that we tend to make about the nature of the learning process. Our years in school, particularly in secondary and higher education, may have trained us to think that the primary responsibility for learning lies with teachers. Their training and experience make them experts; we are more passive participants in the learning process. As students, our job is to observe, read, and memorize what the teacher assigns, and then to repeat "what we have learned" in examinations. Teachers have the responsibility of evaluating our performance and telling us what we should learn next. They set requirements and objectives for learning since it is often assumed that students do not yet have the experience to know what is best for themselves.

The textbook symbolizes the assumption that learning is primarily concerned with abstract ideas and concepts. Learning is the process of acquiring and remembering ideas and concepts. The more remembered, the more you have learned. The relevance and application of these concepts to your own job will come later. Concepts come before experience.

The classroom symbolizes the assumption that learning is a special activity cut off from the real world and unrelated to one's life. Learning and doing are separate and antithetical activities. Many students at graduation feel, "Now I am finished with learning, I can begin living." The belief that learning occurs only in the classroom is so strong that academic credentials are assigned great importance in hiring and promotions, in spite of the fact that psychological research has had little success in establishing correlations between performance in the classroom (grades) and success in later life.

As a result of these assumptions, the concept of learning seldom seems relevant to us in our daily lives and work. And yet a moment of deeper reflection says that this cannot be so.

Peter Vaill is credited with a metaphor that has quickly gained popularity. He maintains that today's business environment is like "white water." In the past, managers could paddle their canoes wherever they wanted on calm, still lakes. Now they are forced to learn to deal with a seemingly endless run of "white water," the rock-strewn, turbulent, fast-moving water in which canoeists struggle to stay afloat and unharmed. White water is exhilarating, but only if you possess the necessary skills. In a world where the rate of change is increasing rapidly every year and where people are expected to hold ten or more different jobs and work in at least five different companies during their career[5]. The ability to learn seems an important, if not *the* most important, skill.

This book is designed to create the learning environment that is most responsive to the unique needs of adult learners by addressing five characteristics of that environment. First, it is based on a *psychological contract of reciprocity*, a basic building block of human interaction. It is well documented that relationships that are based on a mutual and equal balance of giving and getting thrive and grow; those based on unequal exchange very quickly decay. This process of reciprocity is particularly important for creating an effective learning environment because many initial assumptions about learning run counter to it. Learning is most often considered a process of getting rather than giving. This is most evident in conceptions of traditional student/teacher roles: teachers give and students get. Yet in adult learning both giving and getting are critical. In getting, there is the opportunity to incorporate new ideas and perspectives. In giving, there is the opportunity to integrate and apply these new perspectives and to practice their use.

A second characteristic of an adult learning environment is that it is *experienced based*. Ideally the motivation for learning comes not from the instructor's dispensation of rewards and grades, but from problems and opportunities arising from the learner's own life experience. Experience show adults what they need to learn, but their experience also allows them to contribute to the learning of others.

Third, the adult learning environment emphasizes *personal application*. Since adults' learning needs arise from their own experience, the main goal of learning is to apply new knowledge, skills, and attitudes to the solution of the individual's practical problems.

Fourth, the learning environment is *individualized and self-directed*. Just as every individual's experience is different, so are each person's learning goals and learning style. A major concern in the management of an adult learning environment is to organize program resources in such a way that they are maximally responsive to what each learner wants to learn and how he or she learns it. Essential to achievement of this kind of learning environment is the learners' willingness to take responsibility for the achievement of their learning objectives. Perhaps the most important of the learners' responsibilities is that of evaluating how well they are getting the learning resources needed to achieve their goals and alerting the community to problems when they arise since they are in the best position to make this judgment.

A final characteristic of an adult learning environment is that it *integrates learning and living*. There are two goals in the learning process. One is to learn the specifics of a particular subject matter. The other is to learn about one's own strengths and weaknesses as a learner (i.e., learning how to learn from experience). When the process works well, individuals finish their educational experience not only with new intellectual insights, but also with an understanding of their own learning style. This understanding of learning strengths and weaknesses helps in "back-home" application of what has been learned and provides a framework for continuing learning on the job. Learning is no longer a special activity reserved for the classroom; it becomes an integral and explicit part of life itself.

A MODEL OF THE LEARNING PROCESS

By examining the learning process we can come closer to understanding how it is that people generate from their experience the concepts, rules, and principles that guide their behavior in new situations, and how they modify these concepts to improve their effectiveness. This process is both active and passive, concrete, and abstract. It can be conceived of as a four-stage cycle: 1) concrete experience is followed by 2) observation and reflection, which lead to 3) the formation of abstract concepts and generalizations, which lead to 4) hypotheses to be tested in future action, which in turn lead to new experiences.

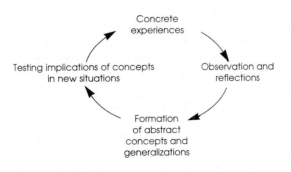

There are several observations to be made about this model of the learning process. First, this learning cycle is continuously recurring. We continuously test our concepts in experience and modify them as a result of our observation of the experience. In a very important sense, all learning is relearning and all education is reeducation.

Second, the direction that learning takes is governed by one's felt needs and goals. We seek experiences that are related to our goals, interpret them in the light of our goals, and form concepts and test implications of these concepts that are relevant to these felt needs and goals. The implication of this fact is that the process of learning is erratic and inefficient when personal objectives are not clear.

Third, since the learning process is directed by individual needs and goals, learning styles become highly individual in both direction and process. For example, a mathematician may come to place great emphasis on abstract concepts, whereas a poet may value concrete experience more highly. A manager may be primarily concerned with active application of concepts, whereas a naturalist may develop exceptional observational skills. Each of us in a more personal way develops a learning style that has some weak points and strong points. We may jump into experiences but fail to observe the lessons to be derived from these experiences; we may form concepts but fail to test their validity. In some areas our objectives and needs may be clear guides to learning; in others, we wander aimlessly.

INTERPRETATION OF YOUR SCORES ON THE LEARNING STYLE INVENTORY

The Learning Style Inventory (LSI)[6] is a simple self-description test, based on experiential learning theory, that is designed to measure your strengths and weaknesses as a learner in the four stages of the learning process. Effective learners rely on four different learning modes: *concrete experience (CE), reflective observation (RO), abstract conceptualization (AC), and active experimentation (AE)*. That is, they must be able to involve themselves fully and openly, and without bias in new experiences (CE); they must be able to reflect on and observe these experiences from many perspectives (RO); they must be able to create concepts that integrate their observations into logically sound theories (AC); and they must be able to use these theories to make decisions and solve problems (AE).

The LSI measures your relative emphasis on the four learning modes by asking you to rank order a series of four words that describes these different abilities. For example, one set of four words is *feeling* (CE), *watching* (RO), *thinking* (AC), *doing* (AE). Combination scores indicate the extent to which you emphasize abstractness over concreteness (AC-CE) and the extent to which you emphasize active experimentation over reflection (AE-RO).

One way to understand better the meaning of your scores on the LSI is to compare them with the scores of others. The "target" in Figure 3-1 gives norms on the four basic scales (CE, RO, AC, AE) for 1,933 adults ranging from 18 to 60 years of age. About two-thirds of the group are men and the group as a whole is highly educated (two-thirds have college degrees or higher). A wide range of occupations and educational backgrounds are represented, including teachers, counselors, engineers, salespersons, managers, doctors, and lawyers.

The raw scores for each of the four basic scales are listed on the crossed lines of the target. **By circling your raw scores on the four scales and connecting them with straight lines you can create a graphic representation of your learning style profile.** The concentric circles on the target represent percentile scores for the normative

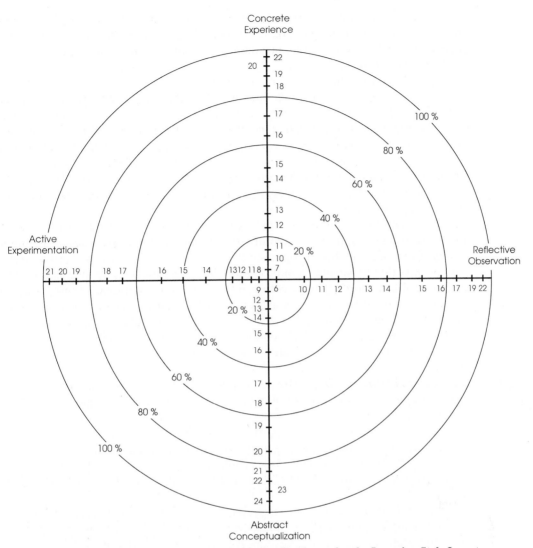

FIGURE 3-1   **The Learning Style Profile Norms for the Learning Style Inventory**
(Copyright 1976 by David A. Kolb)

group. For example, if your raw score on *concrete experience* was 15, you scored higher on this scale than about 55 percent of the people in the normative group. If your CE score was 22 or higher, you scored higher than 99 percent of the normative group. Therefore, in comparison with the normative group, the shape of your profile indicates which of the four basic modes you tend to emphasize and which are less emphasized.

It should be emphasized that the LSI does not measure your learning style with 100 percent accuracy. Rather, it is simply an indication of how you see yourself as a learner. You will need data from other sources if you wish to pinpoint your learning style more exactly (e.g., how you make decisions on the job, how others see you, and what kinds of problems you solve best). Be aware of stereotyping yourself and others with your LSI scores. Your scores indicate which learning modes you emphasize in general. It may change from time to time and situation to situation.

The Learning Style Inventory was designed as an aid for helping you to identify your own learning style. The four learning modes–concrete experience, reflective observation, abstract conceptualization, and active experimentation–represent the four stages of the learning process. The inventory is designed to assess the relative importance of each of these stages to you so that you can get some indication of which learning modes you tend to emphasize. No individual mode is better or worse than any other. Even a totally balanced profile is not necessarily best. The key to effective learning is being competent in each mode when it is appropriate. A high score on one mode may mean a tendency to overemphasize that aspect of the learning process at the expense of others. A low score on a mode may indicate a tendency to avoid that aspect of the learning process.

An *orientation toward concrete experience* focuses on being involved in experiences and dealing with immediate human situations in a personal way. It emphasizes the perception of feeling, focusing on the uniqueness and complexity of present reality as opposed to theories and generalizations, an intuitive, "artistic" approach as opposed to the systematic, scientific approach to problems. People with a concrete experience orientation enjoy and are good at relating to others. They are often good intuitive decision makers and function well in unstructured situations. People with this orientation value relating to people, being involved in real situations, and an open-minded approach to life.

An *orientation toward reflective observation* focuses on understanding the meaning of ideas and situations by carefully observing and impartially describing them. It emphasizes understanding as opposed to practical application, a concern with what is true or how things happen as opposed to what is practical, an emphasis on reflection as opposed to action. People with a reflective orientation enjoy thinking about the meaning of situations and ideas and are good at seeing their implications. They are good at looking at things from different perspectives and at appreciating different points of view. They like to rely on their own thoughts and feelings to form opinions. People with this orientation value patience, impartiality, and considered, thoughtful judgment.

An *orientation toward abstract conceptualization* focuses on using logic, ideas, and concepts. It emphasizes thinking as opposed to feeling, a concern with building general theories as opposed to understanding intuitively unique, specific areas, a scientific as opposed to an artistic approach to problems. A person with an abstract conceptual orientation enjoys and is good at systematic planning, manipulation of abstract symbols, and quantitative analysis. People with this orientation value precision, the rigor and discipline of analyzing ideas, and the aesthetic quality of a neat, conceptual system.

An *orientation toward active experimentation* focuses on actively influencing people and changing situations. It emphasizes practical applications as opposed to reflective understanding, a pragmatic concern with what works as opposed to what is absolute truth, an emphasis on doing as opposed to observing. People with an active experimentation orientation enjoy and are good at getting things accomplished. They are willing to take some risk to achieve their objectives. They also value having an impact and influence on the environment around them and like to see results.

IDENTIFYING YOUR LEARNING STYLE TYPE

It is unlikely that your learning style will be described accurately by just one of the four preceding paragraphs. This is because each person's learning style is a combination of the four basic learning modes. It is therefore useful to describe your learning style by a single data point that combines your scores on the four basic modes. This is accomplished by using the two combination scores, AC-CE and AE-RO. These scales indicate the degree to which you emphasize abstractness over concreteness and action over reflection, respectively.

The grid in Figure 3-2 shows the raw scores for these two scales on the crossed lines (AC-CE on the vertical and AE-RO on the horizontal) and percentile scores based on the normative group on the sides. By marking your raw scores on the two lines and

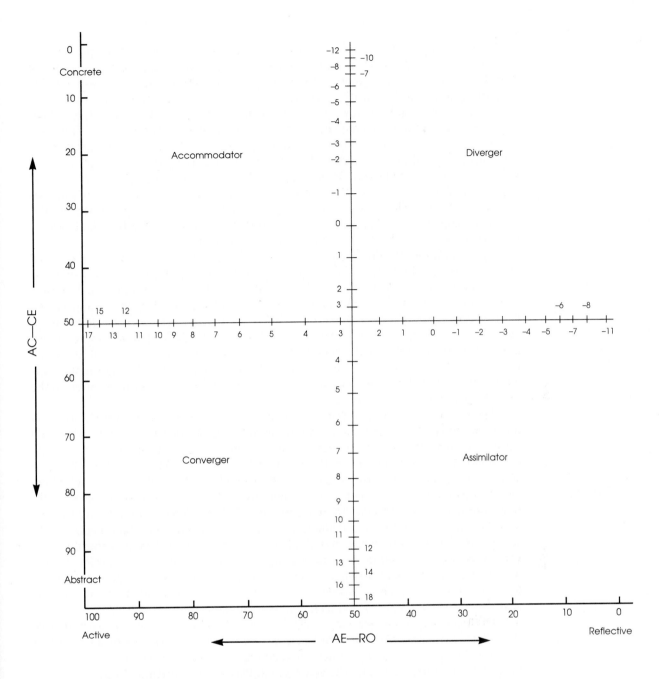

FIGURE 3-2   **Learning Style Type Grid**   (Copyright 1976 by David A. Kolb)

plotting their point of interception, you can find which of the four learning style quadrants you occupy. These four quadrants, labeled *accommodator, diverger, converger, and assimilator*, represent the four dominant learning styles. If your AC-CE score were -4 and your AE-RO score were +8, you would definitely occupy the accommodator quadrant. An AC-CE score of +4 and an AE-RO score of +3 would put you only slightly in the converger quadrant. The closer your data point is to the point where the lines cross, the more balanced is your learning style. If your data point is close to any of the four corners, this indicates that you rely heavily on one particular learning style.

The following is a description of the characteristics of the four basic learning styles based both on research and clinical observation of these patterns of LSI scores.

The *divergent* learning style has the opposite strengths of the convergent style and emphasizes concrete experience and reflective observation. The greatest strength of this orientation lies in imaginative ability and awareness of meaning and values. The primary adaptive ability in this style is to view concrete situations from many perspectives and to organize many relationships into a meaningful "Gestalt." The emphasis in this orientation is on adaptation by observation rather than by action. This style is called "diverger" because a person of this type performs better in situations that call for generation of alternative ideas and implications such as a "brainstorming" idea session. Persons oriented toward divergence are interested in people and tend to be imaginative and feeling oriented. Divergers have broad cultural interests and tend to specialize in the arts. This style is characteristic of individuals from humanities and liberal arts backgrounds. Counselors, organization development specialists, and personnel managers tend to be characterized by this learning style.

In *assimilation*, the dominant learning abilities are abstract conceptualization and reflective observation. The greatest strength of this orientation lies in inductive reasoning, in the ability to create theoretical models and in assimilating disparate observations into an integrated explanation. As in convergence, this orientation is less focused on people and more concerned with ideas and abstract concepts. Ideas, however, are judged less in this orientation by their practical value. Here it is more important that the theory be logically sound and precise. This learning style is more characteristic of individuals in the basic sciences and mathematics rather than the applied sciences. In organizations, persons with this learning style are found most often in the research and planning departments.

The *convergent* learning style has the opposite strength of the diverger style. It relies primarily on the dominant learning abilities of abstract conceptualization and active experimentation. The greatest strength of this approach lies in problem solving, decision making, and the practical application of ideas. We have called this learning style the "converger" because a person with this style seems to do best in such situations as conventional intelligence tests where there is a single correct answer or solution to a question or problem. In this learning style, knowledge is organized in such a way that, through hypothetical-deductive reasoning, it can be focused on specific problems. Liam Hudson's research on individuals with this style of learning show that convergent persons are controlled in their expression of emotion.[7] They prefer dealing with technical tasks and problems rather than with social and interpersonal issues. Convergers often have specialized in the physical sciences. This learning style is characteristic of many engineers and technical specialists.

The *accommodative* learning style has the opposite strengths of assimilation, emphasizing concrete experience and active experimentation. The greatest strength of this orientation lies in doing things, in carrying out plans and tasks, and in getting involved in new experiences. The adaptive emphasis of this orientation is on opportunity seeking, risk taking, and action. This style is called "accommodation" because it is best suited for those situations in which one must adapt oneself to changing immediate circumstances. In situations where the theory or plans do not fit the facts, those with an accommodative style will most likely discard the plan or theory. (With the opposite learning style, assimilation, one would be more likely to disregard or reexamine the facts.) People with an accommodative orientation tend to solve problems in an intuitive trial and error manner, relying on other people for information rather than on their own analytic ability. Individuals with accommodative learning styles are at ease with people but are sometimes seen as impatient and "pushy." This person's educational background is often in technical or practical fields such as business. In organizations, people with this learning style are found in "action-oriented" jobs, often in marketing, sales, or management.

Reprinted courtesy of Mell Lazarus and Field Newspaper Syndicate.

LEARNING STYLES AND MANAGEMENT EDUCATION

Differences in learning styles need to be managed in management education. For example, managers who return to the university in mid-career experience something of a "culture shock." Fresh from a world of time deadlines and concrete specific problems that they must solve, they are suddenly immersed in a strange slow-paced world of generalities, where the elegant solution to problems is sought even when workable solutions have been found. One gets rewarded here for reflection and analysis rather than concrete goal-directed action. Managers who "act before they think–if they ever think" meet the scientists who "think before they act–if they ever act." Research on learning styles has shown that managers on the whole are distinguished by very strong active experimentation skills and are very weak on reflective observation skills. Business school faculty members usually have the reverse profile. To bridge this gap in learning styles, the management educator must somehow respond to pragmatic demands for relevance and the application of knowledge, while encouraging the reflective examination of experience that is necessary to refine old theories and to build new ones. In encouraging reflective observation, the teacher often is seen as an interrupter of action–as a passive "ivory tower" thinker. Indeed, this is a critical role to be played in the learning process. Yet if the reflective observer role is not internalized by the learners themselves, the learning process can degenerate into a value conflict between teacher and student, each maintaining that theirs is the right perspective for learning.

Neither the faculty nor student perspective alone is valid. Managerial education will not be improved by eliminating theoretical analysis or relevant case problems. Improvement will come through the *integration* of the scholarly and practical learning styles. One approach to achieving this integration is to apply the experiential learning model directly in the classroom. This workbook provides games, role plays, and exercises (concrete experiences) that focus on central concepts in organizational behavior. These simulations provide a common experiential starting point for participants and faculty to explore the relevance of behavioral concepts for their work. In traditional management education methods, the conflict between scholar and practitioner learning styles is exaggerated because the material to be taught is filtered through the learning style of faculty members in their lectures or presentation and analysis of cases. Students are "one down" in their own analysis because the data are secondhand and already biased. In the experiential learning approach, this filtering process does not take place because both teacher and student are observers of immediate experiences which they both interpret according to their own learning style. In this approach to learning, the teachers' role is that of facilitator of a learning process that is basically self-directed. They help students to experience in a personal and immediate way the phenomena in their field of specialization. They provide observational schemes and perspectives from which to observe these experiences. They stand ready with alternative theories and concepts as students attempt to assimilate their observations into their own conception of reality. They assist in deducing the implications of the student's concepts and in designing new "experiments" to test these implications through practical "real-world" experience.

LEARNING AND CULTURE

Another learning style difference that must be managed in the classroom relates to cultural diversity. For example, in some cultures professors are perceived as experts with all the answers. They dispense their knowledge to students who are socialized not to interrupt or question, but to act respectfully with teachers in or out of class. In many U.S. classrooms (but not all), students are encouraged, expected, or even forced to participate in class. Asking questions that may reflect badly on the professor's expertise, while not necessarily politic, is not taboo in the American milieu. Students in Asian classrooms are seldom expected to speak and would never say anything to embarrass a professor in public. In general, Latin American students are less comfortable with unstructured, participative classes, and they expect professors to be more dramatic and expressive. Experiential learning may come as a shock to students who have been socialized to have more traditional expectations about learning and classroom roles. There is no question that some people will be more comfortable, at least in the beginning, than others in an experiential course. As a group, we should seek to understand and discuss the differences in our expectations and, when possible, make allowances for them.

There are two goals in the experiential learning process. One is to learn the specifics of a particular subject matter. The other is to learn about one's own strengths and weaknesses as a learner (i.e., learning how to learn from experience). This understanding of learning strengths and weaknesses helps in the back-home application of what has been learned and provides a framework for continuing learning on the job. Day-to-day experience becomes a focus for testing and exploring new ideas.

THE ORGANIZATION AS A LEARNING SYSTEM

Organizations learn and develop distinctive learning styles. Like individuals, they do so through their transactions with the environment and through their choice of how to relate to that environment. This has come to be known as the open systems view of organizations. Since many organizations are large and complex, the environment they relate to becomes highly differentiated and diverse. The way the organization usually adapts to this external environment is to differentiate itself into units, each of which deals with just one part of the firm's external conditions. Marketing and sales face problems associated with the market, customers, and competitors; research deals with the academic and technological worlds; production deals with production equipment and raw materials sources; personnel and labor relations deal with the labor market; and so on.

Because of this need to relate to different aspects of the environment, the different units of the firm develop characteristic ways of thinking and working together–different styles of decision making and problem solving. These units select and shape managers to solve problems and make decisions in the way their environment demands. In fact, Lawrence and Lorsch define organizational differentiation as "the difference in cognitive and emotional orientation among managers in different functional departments."[8]

If we think of organizations as learning systems, each of the differentiated units that is charged with adapting to the challenges of one segment of the environment will have a characteristic learning style that is best suited to meet those environmental demands. The Learning Style Inventory should be a useful tool for measuring this organizational differentiation among the functional units of a firm. To test this, we studied about 20 managers from each of five functional groups in a Midwestern division of a large American industrial corporation.[9] The five functional groups are described, followed by our hypothesis about the learning style that should characterize each group given the environments to which they relate.

1. Marketing ($n = 20$). This group is made up primarily of former salespersons who have a nonquantitative "intuitive" approach to their work. Because of their practical sales orientation in meeting customer demands, they should have accommodative learning styles (i.e., concrete and active).

2. Research ($n = 22$). The work of this group is split about 50:50 between pioneer research and applied research projects. The emphasis is on basic research. Researchers should be the most assimilative group (i.e,. abstract and reflective, a style fitted to the world of knowledge and ideas).

3. Personnel-labor relations ($n = 20$). In this company, workers from this department serve two primary functions: interpreting personnel policy and promoting interaction among groups to reduce conflict and disagreement. Because of their " people orientation," these people should be predominantly divergers, concrete and reflective.

4. Engineering ($n = 18$). This group is made up primarily of design engineers who are quite production oriented. They should be the most convergent sub-group (i.e., abstract and active), although they should be less abstract than the research group. They represent a bridge between thought and action.

5. Finance ($n = 20$). This group has a strong computer information systems bias. Financial personnel, given their orientation toward the mathematical task of information system design, should be highly abstract. Their crucial role in organizational survival should produce an active orientation. Thus, finance group members should have a convergent learning style.

Figure 3-3 shows the average scores on the active-reflective (AE-RO) and abstract-concrete (AC-CE) learning dimensions for the five functional groups. These results are consistent with the predictions with the exception of the finance group, whose scores are less active than predicted and thus fall between the assimilative and convergent quadrants. The LSI clearly differentiates the learning styles that characterize the functional units of at least this one company. Managers in each of these units apparently use very different styles in doing their jobs.

But differentiation is only part of the story of organizational adaptation and effectiveness. The result of the differentiation necessary to adapt to the external environment is the creation of a corresponding internal need to integrate and coordinate the different units. This necessitates resolving in some way the conflicts inherent in these different learning styles. In actual practice, this conflict gets resolved in many ways. Sometimes it is resolved through confrontation and integration of the different learning styles. More often, however, it is resolved through dominance by one unit over the other units, resulting in an unbalanced organizational learning style. We all know of organizations that are controlled by the marketing department, or are heavily engineering oriented, and so on. This imbalance may be effective if it matches environmental demands in a stable environment, but it can be costly if the organization is called upon to learn to respond to changing environmental demands and opportunities.

One important question concerns the extent to which the conflict between units is a function of managers' learning styles rather than merely a matter of conflicting job and role demands. To get at this question, we asked the managers in each of the five functional units in the study to rate how difficult they found it to communicate with each of the other four units. We hypothesized that there should be a correspondence between how similar two units are in their learning style and how easy they find it to

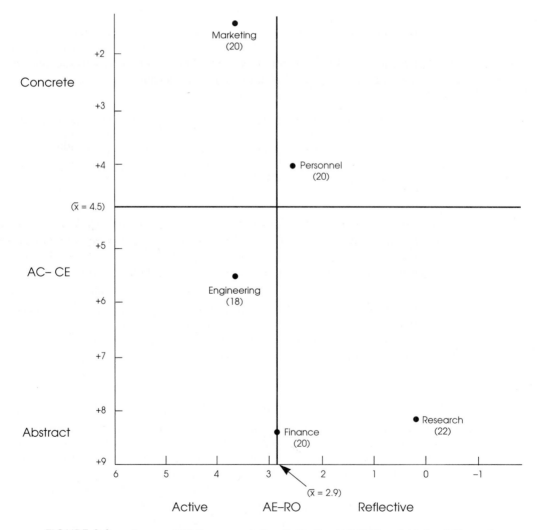

FIGURE 3-3   **Average LSI Scores on Active-Reflective (AE-RO) and Abstract-Concrete (AC-CE) by Organizational Function**

communicate. When the average communication difficulty ratings among the five units are compared with differences in unit learning styles, we find that in most cases this hypothesis is confirmed (i.e., those units that are most different in learning style have most difficulty communicating with one another). To test this notion more rigorously, we did a more intensive study of communication between the two units who were most different in learning styles, marketing and research. To ascertain whether it was a manager's learning style that accounted for communication difficulty, we divided managers in the marketing unit into two groups. One group had learning styles that were similar to those managers in research (i.e., assimilators), while the other group had accommodative learning styles typical of the marketing function. The research group was divided similarly. The results of this analysis showed that when managers have learning styles similar to those of another group, they have little trouble communicating with that group. When style differences are great, communication difficulty rises. These results suggest that managers' learning styles are an important factor to consider in achieving integration among functional units.

Procedure for Group Meeting: The Learning Style Inventory

SHARING INDIVIDUAL LEARNING STYLES, OBJECTIVES, AND RESOURCES

(Time Allotted: 1 Hour)

STEP 1. Individual self-assessment. (5 minutes) Group members should individually review their Learning Style Inventory scores in the light of what they now know about learning styles and their own personal experiences in learning (e.g., their educational background, current job function, and positive and negative learning experiences).

a. With this broader perspective, individuals should alter their position on the learning style type grid (Figure 3-2) to reflect their current best judgment as to the learning style that best describes them. *Do this by placing an "X" on the grid spot that best defines your learning style.* You may agree with the position indicated by your LSI score. If so, place the "X" on top of the point of intersection you calculated earlier with the AC-CE and AE-RO scores. Or you may feel you are really farther away from or closer to the center. If so, move the "X" accordingly.

STEP 2. Portraying the learning style of class members. (10 minutes)

a. Using masking tape, a learning style type grid (see Figure 3-2) large enough for the entire class to stand on should be laid out on the floor of an open area.

b. Individual group members should stand on this floor grid in the position corresponding to their X as positioned in step 1.

STEP 3.   Individuals with similar learning styles join together in small groups of three to six.
(20 minutes)

    a. Once the group members have positioned themselves on the spot that best indicates their learning style, they should form small groups (four to six persons with their closest neighbors (i.e., those with similar learning styles).

    b. When this is completed, all members of these groups, in turn, should share with the group their thoughts on the following three topics. (The questions listed under these topics are suggestions only. Each person should speak about what he or she thinks is relevant.)

        1. Do your learning profile scores seem valid to you? How do you characterize the way in which you learn? Does your learning style profile relate to the way you went about the recent learning situation you described in the pre-work assignment earlier?

        2. What do you think is your greatest strength as a learner?

        3. What is your greatest weakness?

    Other members of the group may ask questions as each person speaks; however, the group should budget its time so that all participants get a chance to share their thoughts on these questions.

STEP 4.   Reports to the total group. (25 minutes)   A representative of each small group should briefly report to the total group:

    a. Where they stood on the grid.

    b. The main points of their discussion –the *content* of the meeting.

    c. Observations about the process of their group meeting. How did it feel to be in a group of individuals who had learning styles similar to yours? Was the group's learning style reflected in the way the meeting ran? Do you prefer being in a group with similar or mixed learning styles?

    d. What connection can you make between this exercise and the readings for today's class?

CREATING A LEARNING COMMUNITY

(Time allotted: 1 Hour)

Form learning groups of approximately six members. Diversity should be the criterion for group composition because this will maximize your learning. Try to have at least one person from each of the four learning styles and people of different ages, sexes, races, occupations, and majors.

STEP 1.   In your learning group discuss your answers to the premeeting question. (20 minutes)

a. What was your best group learning experience?
What was good about it?

b. What was your worst group learning experience? What made it that way?

c. In your opinion, what conditions promote adult learning?

STEP 2.   Prepare two lists on flipchart paper– a GIVE list and a GET list. (20 minutes)

a. The GIVE list should record what individuals and/or the group as a whole are prepared to contribute to meet the learning needs of the class. These can be arranged in two categories:

1. Contributions to course content such as specific areas of expertise, relevant work experience, books, or other learning materials.

2. Contributions to the course learning process such as willingness to listen, willingness to share successes and failures candidly, and willingness to help manage time constraints.

b. The GET list should record what individuals and /or the group as a whole want from the learning experiences. This list can also be arranged in two categories:

1. Content (specific knowledge, skills, or attitudes needed). Your answers to the last chapter's questions about managerial skills you want to work on during the course fit in here.

2. Process (the kind of learning environment characteristics individuals feel they need to learn most effectively).

STEP 3.   The group should choose a spokesperson to report the results of the group's work and answer questions about the charts. The two lists for each group should be posted for viewing by the entire community. The spokesperson for each group should briefly describe his or her group's list. (20 minutes)

Follow-Up

Today's highly successful managers and administrators are distinguished not so much by any single set of knowledge or skills but by their ability to adapt to and master the changing demands of their job and career, that is, by their ability to learn. The same is true for successful organizations. Continuing success in a changing world requires an ability to explore new opportunities and learn from past successes and failures. So stated, these ideas are neither new nor particularly controversial. Yet it is surprising that this ability to learn, which is so widely regarded as important, receives little explicit attention by managers and their organizations. There is a kind of fatalism about learning; one either learns or one does not. The ability consciously to control and manage the learning process is usually limited to such childhood maxims as "Study hard" and "Do your homework."

Part of the reason for this fatalism lies in a lack of understanding about the learning process itself. If managers and administrators had a model about how individuals and organizations learn, they would better be able to enhance their own and their organization's ability to learn. This unit described such a model and attempted to show some of the ways in which the learning process and individual learning styles affect management education, managerial decision making and problem solving, and organizational learning. As we saw in the opening vignette, survival depends upon our ability to create learning organizations.

ADAPTIVE AND GENERATIVE LEARNING

For years Chris Argyris[10] has studied the reasoning that underlies our actions and the relationship that exists with learning. He concluded that we have two types of theories: *"espoused theories"* that we profess to believe (Do as I say, not as I do) and *"theories in action"* that actually guide our behavior. We seldom examine the assumptions upon which these theories are based. Indeed, we insulate them in defensive routines that prevent us from questioning their validity. An example of a defensive routine is "smoothing over" the conflict that arises on a team without ever looking carefully at the reasons for the conflict, thereby perpetuating the status quo.

This discovery led Argyris to describe two types of learning. Single loop learning is like tracking the temperature on a gauge and responding to the feedback that it is too high or too low. An example of single loop learning, now commonly referred to as *adaptive* learning, can be taken from the fast food industry a few years back. Some chains looked at a flat market and stiff competition and reacted by cutting costs and designing new promotional ideas to attract more customers, thereby sparking more price wars. They took a coping approach and measured what they were currently doing and tried to improve upon it.

They did not, however, question their theories or mental models about the fast food business. This is what distinguishes single and double loop learning. In double loop learning, people question the assumptions that underly their theories and ask themselves hard questions. Double loop learning is currently known as *generative* learning. Generative learning consists of continuous experimentation and feedback in an on-going analysis of how organizations define and solve problems.[11] As a result, it is a creative response, rather than a coping response.

Let's return to the fast food business for an example of double loop, generative learning. Taco Bell looked at the same environment, but reacted differently because they used a different learning process. Rather than making incremental improvements to their previous strategy, management defined a new theory: customers value food, service, and the physical appearance of the restaurant. Most chains would agree with this analysis but not all chains turn this "espoused theory" into a "theory in action" as Taco Bell did. They changed their selection and recruitment policies to hire store managers with positive attitudes toward responsibility, teamwork, customer service, and sharing. Because such people are value-driven to serve the customer, they require less supervision. The span of control went from one regional supervisor for every five stores in 1988 to one for every twenty stores four years later. The supervisors' role changed from providing direction and control to coaching and support. Store managers were trained and supported in the skill areas they needed to implement a customer-oriented approach –communication, performance management, team building, coaching and empowerment. Furthermore, Taco Bell instituted new computer systems that liberated store managers from paperwork and, at the same time, provided the necessary data for managerial decisions. Taco Bell switched from a manufacturing to an assembly operations by outsourcing much of their vegetable prep work. This freed up employees to focus more on customers and their needs. The results of this generative learning were 60% growth in sales in company owned stores, 25% growth in profits (compared with less than 6% at McDonald's), and a 25% decrease in prices.[12]

Taco Bell was successful because the mental map they held about their business did in fact reflect reality. Mental maps are "deeply ingrained assumptions, generalizations, or even pictures or images that influence how we understand the world and how we take action."[13]

Organizations must be careful not to rely much on "old programming," obsolete mental maps, and adaptive learning. Companies that are unlikely to survive in a rapidly changing environment not only limit themselves to adaptive learning; they may even punish generative learning. There are numerous examples of employees who leave large, unresponsive corporations to form successful, competing companies where they can put their knowledge and ideas to work. Organizational cultures that stifle creativity and innovation are sometimes accused of playing the "whack the gopher game."[14] People who stick their necks out by asking questions that threaten defensive routines or by making radical suggestions get "whacked." Extensive suggestions and guidance for companies that want to encourage generative learning are found in the articles by Peter Senge and David Garvin in the Reader.[15]

MANAGING THE LEARNING PROCESS

Some organizations employ parallel learning structures. These are defined as part of the organization that operates alongside the normal bureaucracy with the purpose of increasing organizational learning by creating and/or implementing new thoughts and behaviors. Parallel learning structures consist of "a steering committee and a number of small groups with norms and operating procedures that promote a climate conducive to innovation, learning, and group problem-solving" that is not possible within the larger bureaucracy.[16] For example, one fast-growing semiconductor company created a parallel learning structure that focused upon organizational adaptation to a competitive and stagnant market. The parallel structure came up with solutions that the larger organization then implemented.

To conclude, let us examine how managers and organizations can explicitly manage their learning process. We have seen that the experiential learning model is useful not only for examining the educational process, but also for understanding managerial problem solving and organizational adaptation. But how can an awareness of the experiential learning model and our own individual learning style help improve individual and organizational learning? Two recommendations seem important.

First, learning should be an explicit objective that is pursued as consciously and deliberately as profit or productivity. Managers and organizations should budget time to learn from their experiences. When important meetings are held or important decisions are made, time should be set aside to critique and learn from these events. All too few organizations have a climate that allows for free exploration of such questions as, "What have we learned from this venture?" Usually, active experimentation norms dictate: "We don't have time; let's move on."

This leads to the second recommendation. The nature of the learning process is such that opposing perspectives–action and reflection, concrete involvement, and analytical detachment–are all essential for optimal learning. When one perspective comes to dominate others, learning effectiveness is reduced. From this we can conclude that the most effective learning systems are those that can tolerate differences in perspective. This point can be illustrated by the case of an electronics firm that we have worked with over the years. The firm was started by a group of engineers with a unique product. For several years they had no competitors, and when some competition entered the market, they continued to dominate and do well because of their superior engineering quality. Today it is a different story. They are now faced with stiff competition in their original product area, and, in addition, their very success has caused new problems. They are no longer a small intimate company but a large organization with several plants in the United States and Europe. The company has had great difficulty in responding to these changes because it still responds to problems primarily from an engineering point of view. Most of the top executives in the company are former engineers with no formal management training. Many of the specialists in marketing, finance, and personnel who have been brought in to help the organization solve its new problems feel like "second-class citizens." Their ideas just don't seem to carry much weight. What was once the organization's strength, its engineering expertise, has become to some extent its weakness. Because engineering has flourished at the expense of the development of other organizational functions such as marketing and the management of human resources, the firm is today struggling with, rather than mastering, its environment.

The following chart (Figure 3-4) shows the strengths of the four learning styles and the steps people can take to develop each style. It also describes what tends to occur when there is too little or too much of a particular learning style in an organization or work unit.

Concrete Experience

Accommodator

Strengths: Getting things done
Leadership
Risk taking

Excess: Trivial improvements
Meaningless activity

Deficiency: Work not completed on time
Impractical plans
Not directed to goals

To develop Accommodator learning skills,
practice:

- Committing yourself to objectives
- Seeking new opportunities
- Influencing and leading others
- Being personally involved
- Dealing with people

Diverger

Strengths: Imaginative ability
Understanding people
Recognizing problems
Brainstorming

Excess: Paralyzed by alternatives
Can't make decisions

Deficiency: Idea poor
Can't recognize problems and
opportunities

To develop Diverger learning skills, practice:

- Being sensitive to people's feelings
- Being sensitive to values
- Listening with an open mind
- Gathering information
- Imagining the implications of uncertain
situations

Active
Experimentation _____ Reflective
Observation

Converger

Strengths: Problem solving
Decision making
Deductive reasoning
Defining problems

Excess: Solving the wrong problems
Hasty decision making

Deficiency: Lack of focus
No testing of ideas or theories
Scattered thoughts

To develop Converger learning skills, practice:

- Creating new ways of thinking and doing
- Experimenting with new ideas
- Choosing the best solution
- Setting goals
- Making decisions

Assimilator

Strengths: Planning
Creating models
Defining problems
Developing theories

Excess: Castles in the air
No practical application

Deficiency: Unable to learn from mistakes
No sound basis for work
No systematic approach

To develop Assimilator learning skills, practice:

- Organizing information
- Building conceptual models
- Testing theories and ideas
- Designing experiments
- Analyzing quantitative data

Abstract Conceptualization

FIGURE 3-4 **Characteristics of the Four Learning Styles**

Learning Points

1. The rapid degree of change present in today's business environment makes a necessity of continuous learning for both individuals and organizations.

2. Adult learning
    a. Is based on reciprocity.
    b. Is based on experience.
    c. Has a problem-solving orientation.
    d. Is individualized and self-directed.
    e. Integrates learning and living.
    f. Needs to be applied.

3. The adult learning process is a cycle composed of the following components: concrete experience, reflective observation, abstract conceptualization, and active experimentation.

4. The four learning styles differ along two dimensions. The first dimension represents the concrete experiencing of events at one end and the abstract conceptualization at the other (feeling versus thinking). The second dimension has active experimentation at one extreme and reflective observation at the other (doing versus watching).

5. Individuals usually see themselves as having a predisposition or a learned facility for one of the four stages in the learning model: divergence, assimilation, convergence, and accommodation.

6. Learning communities and organizations profit from having members with different learning styles because each style has its particular strengths and weaknesses.

7. Argyris claims we have two types of theories: "espoused theories" that we profess to believe and "theories in action" that actually guide our behavior.

8. People develop defensive routines that prevent them from questioning the validity of the assumptions underlying espoused theories and theories in action.

9. Adaptive learning (single loop learning) focuses on *coping*–solving problems in the current way of doing business.

10. Generative learning (double loop learning) focuses on *creating*–continuous experimentation and feedback in an ongoing analysis of how organizations define and solve problems. This involves questioning our assumptions about the way we work.

11. Parallel learning structures are part of the organization that operates alongside the normal bureaucracy with the purpose of increasing organizational learning by creating and/or implementing new thoughts and behaviors.

for Managers

- Be aware of your personal learning style so that you understand how you approach work issues and how you react to others who have different styles.

- When you are training others (even if it's only breaking in a replacement), remember that people have a tendency to assume that everyone learns the same way they do. Since this is not true, find out how the trainee learns best and adapt your instruction accordingly.

- Ensure that people with different learning styles are valued for their strengths. If you find yourself in a situation where this is not the case, you may want to give the work team or the management group the Learning Style Inventory so that the differences can be understood in a positive manner. The LSI is often used as an opening exercise in team-building efforts.

- In order to create a learning organization, managers should:[17]

  - Make time to reflect upon work events and assume the stance, "What can we learn from this?" for both yourself and your employees.

  - Perceive failure as a feedback loop in the learning process so people are not afraid to experiment and fail.

  - Avoid allowing an elite group or single point of view to dominate organizational decision making.

  - Create a climate of openness and supportiveness so that employees feel enough psychological safety to raise questions and new ideas.

  - Reward generative thinking.

  - Encourage the expression of conflicting ideas and train employees in conflict resolution.

- Make available to all members data on performance, quality, consumer satisfaction and competitiveness so more people can make informed decisions and reflect upon the company situation.

- Use cross-functional teams to benefit from different approaches and expertise.

- Create norms that encourage people to question assumptions and challenge the status quo.

- Focus on systems thinking by looking for interrelationships, examining entire work processes, and looking beyond symptoms for root causes.

 Personal Application Assignment

Please respond to the following question in the upcoming week. Each section of the assignment is worth 4 points which will be assigned according to the criteria shown.

The topic of this assignment is to think back on a previous learning experience that was significant to you. Choose an experience about which you are motivated to learn more; that is, there was something about it that you do not totally understand, that intrigues you, that made you realize that you lack certain skills, or that was problematical or significant for you. It may have been an academic one or a nonformal educational experience (e.g., tennis camp, a seminar, on-the-job training program).

A. *Concrete Experience*

    1. *Objectively* describe the experience ("who," "what," "when," "where," "how," information–up to 2 points).

    2. *Subjectively* describe your feelings, perceptions, and thoughts that occurred *during* (not after) the experience (up to 2 points). Does this section have too much detail? (If so, delete 1 point.)

B. *Reflective Observation*

    1. Look at the experience from different points of view. How many points of view did you include that are *relevant* (up to 2 points)?

    2. Use these perspectives to add more meaning to the incident (up to 2 points).

C. *Abstract Conceptualization*

   1. Relate concepts from the assigned readings and the lecture to the experience (i.e., what theories that you heard in the lecture or read in the Reader relate to your understanding of this incident?).

   2. Make reference to at least two sources. Use standard referencing format and include the page number to which you are referring. How many sources did you use and how clearly did you explain their theories (up to 4 points)?

   3. You can also create an original model or theory, but it should not replace course concepts.

D. *Active Experimentation*

   1. Write about what you will do in the future that will improve your effectiveness. Use rules of thumb or action resolutions.

   2. Are they described specifically, thoroughly, and in detail (up to 4 points)?

E. *Integration, Synthesis, and Writing*

   1. Did you write about something personally important to you (up to 1 point)?

   2. Was it well written (up to 2 points)?

   3. Did you integrate and synthesize the different sections (up to 1 point)?

[1]Author's note: I use the collective expression "Shell" for convenience when referring to the companies of the Royal dutch/Shell Group in general, or when no purpose is served by identifying the particular Shell company or companies.

[2]Pierre Wach wrote about our system in "Scenarios: Uncharted Waters Ahead," HBR September-October 1985, p. 72 and in "Scenarios: Shooting the Rapids," *HBR* November-December 1985, p. 139.

[3]Jeff S. Wyles, Joseph G. Kunkel, and Allan C. Wilson, "Birds, Behavior and Anatomical Evolution," *Proceedings of th National Academy of Sciences, USA*, July 1983.

[4]Through MIT's Program in Systems Thinking and the New Management Style, a group of senior executives are looking at this and other issues.

[5]William B. Johnston and Arnold E. Packer, Workforce 2000: Work & Workers for the Twenty-first Century. Hudson Institute, 1987 and William B. Johnston, "Global Workforce 2000: The New Labor Market." *Harvard Business Review*, March-April 1991, pp. 115-128.

[6]The Learning Style Inventory is copyrighted by David A. Kolb (1976) and distributed by McBer and Co. 137 Newbury St., Boston, Mass. 02116. Further information on theory, construction, reliability, and validity of the inventory is reported in *The Learning Style Inventory: Technical Manual,* available from McBer and Co. The theory and its implications are found in Kolb's book, *Experiential Learning: Experience as the Source of Learning and Development* (Englewood Cliffs, NJ: Prentice-Hall, 1984).

[7]Hudson Liam, *Contrary Imaginations* (New York: Schocken Books, 1966).

[8]Paul Lawrence and Jay Lorsch, *Organization and Environment* (Boston: Division of Research, Graduate School of Business Administration, Harvard University, 1967).

[9]These data were collected by Frank Weisner as part of his Sloan School of Management M.S. thesis (1971). We have reanalyzed his data for presentation here.

[10]Chris Argyris, *Reasoning, Learning, and Action* (San Francisco: Jossey-Bass, 1982).

[11]Michael E. McGill, John W. Slocum, Jr., and David Lei, "Management Practices in Learning Organizations," *Organizational Dynamics*, Summer 1992, pp. 5-17.

[12]McGill et al, *Management Practices*, p. 9.

[13]Peter M. Senge, *The Fifth Discipline*, (New York: Doubleday, 1990) p. 8.

[14]This metaphor is attributed to Peter DeLisi of Digital Equipment Corporation in Edgar H. Schein's article, "How Can Organizations Learn Faster? The Challenge of Entering the Green Room," *Sloan Management Review* (Winter 1993) pp. 85-94.

[15]Peter M. Senge, "The Leader's New Work: Building Learning Organizations" and David A. Garvin, "Building a Learning Organization" in the *Reader*.

[16]Gervase R. Bushe and A.B. Rami Shani, *Parallel Learning Structures: Increasing Innovation in Bureaucracies* (Reading, MA: Addison-Wesley, 1991), pp. 9-10.

[17]These suggestions are taken primarily from Richard Tanner Pascale, *Managing on the Edge* (New York, NY: Simon & Schuster, 1991), pp. 236-37 and the works cited in this chapter: Senge's *The Fifth Discipline*; McGill's et al, *"Management Practices;"* Schein's *"Organizations Learn Faster;"* and Garvin's *"Building a Learning Organization."*

INDIVIDUAL MOTIVATION AND ORGANIZATIONAL BEHAVIOR

OBJECTIVES By the end of this chapter, you should be able to:

A. Explain several theories of motivation.

B. Understand McClelland's three basic social motives and how they are defined.

C. Gain insight into your own motive patterns.

D. Explain how managers can direct individual motivation and behavior in organizations.

*N*o Contest

Joyce Osland

Once upon a time a new hotel sales manager, whose staff was responsible for selling banquets and hotel packages, was highly motivated to take advantage of a year-end bonus program for managers. In order to win the bonus, he needed to bring in new business so he decided to initiate a contest for his sales agents. He announced that he would pay $100 to the agent who had brought in the most new clients by the end of the month. Then he sat back in his chair to await the results and decide how he would spend his bonus money.

While visions of Porsches danced through his head, his sales agents were busily belly-aching for the following reasons:

1. They were used to working as a team and resented being encouraged to compete against close friends.

2. In the manager's last contest, a new sales agent had reportedly cheated and "stole" new clients from the old-timers.

3. The winner of the last contest was paid the prize money several months late, only after she had "shaken" it out of the sales manager.

4. One sales agent position had not been filled so the others felt they were already operating beyond full capacity and working extra hours because the new sales manager made them attend evening functions for clients, something they had never done in the past.

5. The sales manager had neglected to endear himself to the agents, and they felt he was just using them to get his bonus.

6. The sales agents felt as if they were being manipulated and perceived the $100 as an insult.

As a result, the sales agents decided to ignore the contest. The sales manager was angry when he saw the low level of new business at the end of the month and concluded that the agents were lazy. He told them they were unprofessional and complained about them at staff meetings so that soon everyone in the organization had heard about their "laziness." Old-timers-in-the-know scratched their heads because they remembered how hard the sales agents used to work before the new sales manager was hired. And everyone lived unhappily ever after (except for a few agents who quit and went to work for a competitor) until the sales manager went back to school and learned about theories of motivation.

 Premeeting Preparation

A. Read "No Contest"

B. Read the Instructions for the Test of Imagination.[1]

C. Write stories on four pictures of your choice on the pages following those pictures. Do not take more than 5 minutes per story. Do this before reading the Topic Introduction.

D. Read the Topic Introduction and the Procedure for Group Meeting: TAT Motive Analysis.

E. What were the significant learning points from the readings?

Please read the following instructions carefully before turning the page.

An important asset in the world is imagination. This test gives you an opportunity to use your imagination to show how you can create ideas and situations by yourself. In other words, instead of presenting you with ready-made answers from which you choose one, it gives you the chance to show how you can think things up on your own. On the following pages, write out four stories that you make up. To help you get started, there is a series of pictures that you can interpret and around which you can build your stories. When you have finished reading these instructions, turn the page, look at the first picture briefly, then turn the page again and write a story suggested by the picture. To help you cover all the elements of a story plot in the time allowed, you will find four questions spaced out over the page:

1. What is happening? Who are the people?

2. What has led up to this situation? That is, what has happened in the past?

3. What is being thought? What is wanted? By whom?

4. What will happen? What will be done?

Please remember that the questions are only guides for your thinking and need not be answered specifically in so many words. That is, your story should be *continuous and not just a set of answers to these questions.* If you limit yourself to brief answers, there will not be enough material to analyze. Please write a story that fills up the entire page. Do not take more than 5 minutes per story. You should complete the whole test 20 minutes after you begin, although you may finish in less time if you like (i.e., 4 stories at about 5 minutes each).

There are no right or wrong stories. In fact, any kind of story is all right. You have a chance to show how quickly you can imagine and write a story on your own. Do not simply describe the pictures; write a story about them. They are vague and suggestive of many things on purpose, and are just to help give you an idea to write about. Try to make your stories interesting and dramatic. Show that you have an understanding of people and can make up stories about human relationships.

If you have read these instructions carefully and understand them, turn the page, look at the picture, and then write your story. Then choose another picture, write out the story it suggests, and so on through the booklet.

Just look at the picture briefly (10 to 15 seconds) and write the story it suggests.

Work rapidly, do not spend more than 5 minutes on this story.

1. What is happening? Who are the people?

2. What has led up to this situation? That is, what has happened in the past?

3. What is being thought? What is wanted? By whom?

4. What will happen? What will be done?

When you have finished your story or your time is up, turn to the next picture.

Just look at the picture briefly (10 to 15 seconds) and write the story it suggests.

Work rapidly, do not spend more than 5 minutes on this story.

1. What is happening? Who are the people?

2. What has led up to this situation? That is, what has happened in the past?

3. What is being thought? What is wanted? By whom?

4. What will happen? What will be done?

When you have finished your story or your time is up, turn to the next picture.

Just look at the picture briefly (10 to 15 seconds) and write the story it suggests.

Work rapidly, do not spend more than 5 minutes on this story.

1. What is happening? Who are the people?

2. What has led up to this situation? That is, what has happened in the past?

3. What is being thought? What is wanted? By whom?

4. What will happen? What will be done?

When you have finished your story or your time is up, turn to the next picture.

Just look at the picture briefly (10 to 15 seconds) and write the story it suggests.

Work rapidly, do not spend more than 5 minutes on this story.

1. What is happening? Who are the people?

2. What has led up to this situation? That is, what has happened in the past?

3. What is being thought? What is wanted? By whom?

4. What will happen? What will be done?

When you have finished your story or your time is up, turn to the next picture.

Just look at the picture briefly (10 to 15 seconds) and write the story it suggests.

Work rapidly, do not spend more than 5 minutes on this story.

1. What is happening? Who are the people?

2. What has led up to this situation? That is, what has happened in the past?

3. What is being thought? What is wanted? By whom?

4. What will happen? What will be done?

When you have finished your story or your time is up, turn to the next picture.

Just look at the picture briefly (10 to 15 seconds) and write the story it suggests.

Work rapidly, do not spend more than 5 minutes on this story.

1. What is happening? Who are the people?

2. What has led up to this situation? That is, what has happened in the past?

3. What is being thought? What is wanted? By whom?

4. What will happen? What will be done?

When you have finished your story or your time is up, turn to the next picture.

Topic Introduction

Concern over productivity levels in the United States raises the question of how well companies can compete in both the domestic or global marketplace. One of the many factors that affect productivity is motivation. Motivation has always been an issue of concern for managers; it has long been recognized as one of the classic managerial functions–planning, motivating, coordinating, controlling, and organizing. There persist, however, some common sense notions about motivation that are misleading and just plain wrong. First among these notions is the idea that there are persons who are not motivated. This is incorrect. Every living human being is motivated. What managers really mean when they say that a worker is not motivated is that the worker is not motivated to do what the manager wants the worker to do. The same "lazy" employee who just goes through the motions at work may stay up all night working with great intensity on a sports car or devote many hours outside of work to the Girl Scouts. While it is true that some people are more energetic than others, the most important factor to consider is how this energy is directed–toward what goals and objectives. The prime task for managing motivation, therefore, is channeling and directing human energy toward the activities, tasks, and objectives that further the organization's mission.

A second erroneous idea about motivation is that managers "motivate" workers and that motivation is something you do *to* someone else. Motivation is an *internal* state that directs individuals toward certain goals and objectives. Managers cannot directly influence this *internal* state; they can only create expectations on the part of employees that their motives will be satisfied by doing the organization's work and provide the rewards that satisfy the employee's needs.

This distinction may appear subtle, but it is important because failure to understand it often leads managers to attempt to use motivation to manipulate employees. The opening vignette, "No Contest," is an example of such manipulation. The sales manager did not understand either his employees or theories of motivation well enough to realize that a contest of this sort contained more demotivators than motivators for this particular group of sales agents. Manipulation is a very inefficient way of managing motivation because it requires that you as a manager maintain control of the carrot and stick. As a result you must spend time scheming about how you will motivate those you supervise on a day-to-day basis. And you must do it alone. A more effective way of managing motivation is through understanding. If you understand the needs and objectives of those you supervise, you can work with them to develop an equitable psychological contract that recognizes their particular desires and creates conditions where these motives can be satisfied in the work setting. The same is true of your own motivation. By becoming more aware of your own motives and desires, you can better organize your work and life activities to achieve satisfaction and productivity.

Motive is a word often used in mystery stories and among actors. All of us have some intuitive understanding of the meaning of the term in those contexts. For instance, detectives looking for the culprit will always seek someone with a "motive," a *reason* for committing the murder. An actor or actress, in like manner, wants to understand the motivation of some character. In both instances the search for motive is the search for a process of thinking and feeling that causes a person to act in specific ways.

Our understanding of human motivation has increased substantially over the past few decades. Simplistic theories arguing that people worked primarily for money or primarily for social gratification have been replaced with more complex theories of human nature. Some of these theories are called *content* theories because they attempt to identify the factors within the individual that energize, direct, sustain, and stop behavior. They focus upon the specific internal needs that motivate people. Maslow's work, for example, provided two important postulates concerning human motivation.[2] One is that human needs can be viewed in an hierarchical fashion. Lower-order needs–physical needs and security–must be satisfied to some extent before higher-order needs–needs for social belonging, self-esteem, and self-actualization–become activated. Second is the notion that a satisfied need is no longer a motivator of behavior. The order of these needs varies from culture to culture. For example, the security need is more important than self-actualization in Greece and Japan. Social needs are more important in collectivist African countries than the self-esteem and self-actualization needs that are more figural in an individualistic culture like the U.S.

Maslow's insight that a satisfied need no longer motivates behavior helps us to understand why beyond a certain point, salary increases may be of marginal motivational value. Individuals can be at different levels in the motivational hierarchy at different times, causing different needs to be aroused. Herzberg suggests a two-factor theory of motivation that is based on Maslow's hierarchy.[3] *Hygiene factors*–extrinsic factors such as the attractiveness of the physical facilities, salary, company policy and administration, working conditions, and interpersonal relations–create dissatisfaction if they do not exist. Their presence, however, does not create positive motivation. A second set of intrinsic factors–*motivators* such as the work itself, challenge, responsibility, advancement, and recognition–are necessary to stimulate positive motivation. Once we have met a person's hygiene needs, "more of the same" yields marginal benefits. Some studies indicate that providing extrinsic rewards actually takes the intrinsic pleasure out of performing a task.[4]

Psychologists, most notably David McClelland, have made a great deal of progress over the past 30 years in scientifically measuring and defining human motive.[5] McClelland began by looking not at external action but at the way a person thinks and feels. He used the Thematic Apperception Test (TAT), which you completed in the premeeting preparation section, to record thought samples that could then be studied and grouped according to the dominant concerns, or themes, expressed in the stories. He and his coworkers were able to group the responses into three broad categories, each representing an identifiable human motive: need for affiliation (n-Aff), need for power (n-Pow), and need for achievement (n-Ach).

Most people, McClelland found, have a degree of each of these motives in their thoughts, but seldom in the same strength. A person may be high in the need for affiliation, low in the need for achievement, and moderate in the need for power. Such people would tend to think more about friendship than about doing a good job or controlling others. Their motivation to work will be of a different order than that of the employee who is high in achievement motivation and low in affiliation and power motivations. The needs identified in McClelland's framework are similar to Malow's higher-order needs and Herzberg's motivation factors. McClelland states that these motives are learned from our parents and our culture. He discovered different motive patterns for different cultures, which is an important fact to bear in mind when engaged in international business. The power motive in Latin America is very pronounced because power and control are dominant cultural themes. McClelland and his colleagues successfully taught Indian entrepreneurs to become more achievement-oriented.

Because of its projective nature, the TAT test can be readily used with people from different cultures. However, Hofstede notes that the word achievement does not exist in many languages and therefore he questions whether this theory applies to all cultures.[6]

We can sharpen our understanding of these motives in management settings by examining the motive patterns of some "typical" managers.

The need for power is defined as "the need to influence and lead others, and be in control of one's environment." A high need for power is very common among middle-and upper-level managers because, by definition, their job is to influence people and organizations. A strong need for power can be satisfied by working in professions that allow people to influence others, such as executives, politicians, labor leaders, police officers, military officers, and lawyers. There are two faces of n-Power. The positive face is *socialized power* which is used for the good of others. People motivated by this need seek power to make their club, department, or organization function better so that others (members, customers, and employees) benefit. Characteristic actions that allow this group to satisfy their need for power are playing competitive sports as an adult, and occupying officer roles in the organizations to which they belong. They tend to be more emotionally mature than people with a need for personalized power and are more hesitant to use their power in a manipulative fashion. They are less defensive and selfish, are more willing to take advice from experts, have a longer range view, and accumulate fewer material possessions. They are more likely to use a participative coaching style; rather than creating dependence in their followers, they empower them.[7]

The negative face is *personalized power*, an unsocialized concern for personal dominance. People with a personalized power concern have little inhibition or self-control and they exercise power impulsively. According to McClelland and Burnham, U.S. subjects with a high need for personalized power tend to drink too much and become nasty drunks, engage in casual sexual exploitation (scoring), and collect prestige symbols like expensive cars and large offices. They satisfy their needs vicariously by watching contact sports or violent TV shows or films, and using alcohol, drugs, or mystical rituals in a way that makes them feel more powerful.[8] Dictators and people who establish fiefdoms at work are motivated by this type of n-Power.

A manager's effectiveness depends not only on his or her need for power but also on the other values they bring to their job. John Andrew's study of two Mexican companies is striking in this regard.[9] Both companies had presidents who scored high in n-Power, but one firm was stagnating whereas the other was growing rapidly. The manager of the growing company, although high in n-Power, was also high in n-Achievement and was dedicated to letting others in the organization satisfy their own needs for achievement by introducing improvements and making decisions on their own. The stagnant company, although well capitalized and enjoying a favorable market, was constantly in turmoil and experienced a high rate of turnover, particularly among its executives. In this company, the president's high n-Power, coupled with highly authoritarian values, led him to make all the decisions himself, leaving no room for individual responsibility on the part of his personnel. A comparison of motivation scores of upper-level managers of the two companies showed that the dynamic company's managers were significantly higher in n-Achievement than were those of the stagnant company, who tended to be more concerned with power and compliance than with individual responsibility and decision making.

The results of research have shown that a manager needs a reasonably high n-Power to function as a leader.[10] Whether he or she uses it well depends in large part on the other values and motives the individual holds. Being high in n-Power does not automatically make one autocratic or authoritarian. Good leadership may indeed be a function of the manager's ability to understand his or her need for power and to use it in creative, satisfying ways.

N-AFFILIATION

The need for affiliation (n-Aff) is "the desire for friendly and close interpersonal relationships." People high in n-Affiliation prefer cooperative situations to competitive situations, and they seek relationships involving a high degree of mutual understanding. As with the power motive, there are two faces of this need. The positive face of n-Affiliation, *affiliative interest*, is a concern for interpersonal relationships but not at the expense of goal-oriented behavior. People with this need value good relationships and work at maintaining them, but their concern with relationships does not prevent them from giving negative feedback or making tough decision.

The negative face of n-Affiliation is *affiliative assurance*, a concern with obtaining assurance about the security and strength of one's relationships and avoiding rejection. According to Boyatzis,[11] managers with a strong need for affiliative assurance look for proof that others are committed to them and avoid issues and conflicts that might threaten the stability of the relationship. They seek approval from others and devote more energy to maintaining relationships than to achieving work goals. They worry about being disliked.

Although a high need for affiliation is found more often in supervisors than high-level leaders, people with a need for affiliative interest make a valuable contribution by creating a friendly, cooperative atmosphere at work. High n-Affiliation managers spend more time communicating with others than do managers high in either n-Power or n-Achievement[12] and are good at creating the networks that are crucial for success in many organization.[13]

N-ACHIEVEMENT

The need for achievement (n-Ach) is "a need to accomplish goals, excel, and strive continually to do things better." Whereas a high need for achievement seems absolutely necessary for entrepreneurs, it is not always functional for managers to be extremely high in this motive. Executives high in n-Achievement tend to have fewer meetings than other executives and tend to want to work alone, despite the fact that many organizational problems would be better solved by collaborative effort.[14] As with executives high in n-Power, their effectiveness as managers depends more on their other values than on their motivation alone.

Persons high in n-Achievement want to take personal responsibility for their success or failure, like to take calculated (moderate) risks, and like situations in which they get immediate, concrete feedback on how well they are doing. Their need for feedback keeps them from getting too involved in open-ended exploratory situations with no concrete goal and no benchmarks along the way. Their sense of personal responsibility will keep them from delegating authority unless they value developing subordinates. They will be task oriented, but the kind of climate they create in an organization will be healthier if their strong n-Achievement is balanced by moderate needs for power and affiliation.

The need profile of effective top-level managers in large organizations is high in n-Power and low in n-Affiliation.[15] These managers use their power to achieve organizational goals, practice a participative coaching style when they interact with subordinates, and do not concentrate on developing close relationships with others.[16] However, a high need for both power and achievement has been found in effective low- and middle-level managers.[17]

Procedure for Group Meeting: TAT Motive Analysis

MOTIVE ANALYSIS AND SCORING

(Time Allotted: 1 Hour)

The purpose of this exercise is to help you identify (but not score in detail) the motivational themes you expressed in your TAT stories.

Divide the group into trios for the scoring and have one trio member read their first story to the other two. Using the criteria that follow, score the imagery in the story and enter it on the individual scoring form provided. Repeat until all stories of each trio member have been scored and entered.

The following criteria, taken from the empirical scoring systems, will help you to decide which of the three motives, if any, is present in your stories. Record on the form provided those motives present in each story plus any other motivational concerns that you and your group may notice. It is possible for a story to contain none or all three of these motives as well as other motivational concerns, such as sex, aggression, hunger, or security.

In approaching the task, you should keep several things in mind. The TAT pictures and your responses are meant to be stimuli for reflection and discussion, not necessarily an absolute measure of your motives. In addition, you are not expected to become expert scorers, but to become familiar with general patterns. Finally, be wary of the pressure to reach consensus in your trio meetings. Each listener will, in fact, hear another's story through his or her own motivational filter. For example, a person high in the need for affiliation may well "see" considerable affiliation imagery in someone else's story.

The point of this exercise is that people do have different needs and that they do consequently see the world in different ways. A manager's task is to become aware of and effectively integrate these real differences.

Achievement motivation is present in a story when any one of the following occurs:

1. Someone in the story is concerned about a *standard of excellence*. The individual wants to win or to do well in a competition. The person has self-imposed standards for a good performance or is emotionally involved in attaining an achievement goal. Standards of excellence can be inferred by the use of words such as good or better or similar words when used to evaluate performance.

2. Someone in the story is involved in a *unique accomplishment*, such as an invention or an artistic creation. Here the standard of excellence can be inferred and need not be explicitly stated.

3. Someone in the story is involved in a *long-term goal*, such as an invention or an artistic creation. Here the standard of excellence can be inferred and need not be explicitly stated.

Power motivation is present in a story when any of the following occurs.[18]

1. People describe actions in which they express their power. For example, strong forceful actions which affect others, such as assaults, attacks, chasing or catching, verbal insults, threats, accusations, reprimands, crimes, sexual exploitation, and gaining the upper hand all indicate the presence of the power motive.

2. There are statements about someone giving help, assistance, advice, or support that has not been solicited by the other person.

3. There are statements which indicate that someone is trying to control another person through regulating his or her behavior, or through searching for information that would affect another person's life or actions. Examples of the last category are searching, investigating, and checking up on someone.

4. Someone is trying to persuade, influence, convince, bribe, make a point, or argue with another person, but not with the motive of reaching agreement or understanding. Mention of a disagreement is not sufficient to score the power motive here; there must be action or a desire for action that has the objective of changing another's opinion.

5. Someone is trying to impress another person or the world at large. Or someone in the story is described as being concerned about his or her reputation or position. Creative writing, publicity, trying to win an election or identifying closely with another person running for office, seeking fame and notoriety are all scorable for power.

6. Someone does something that arouses strong positive or negative emotions in others, such as pleasure, delight, awe, gratitude, fear, respect, jealousy and so forth.

Affiliation motivation is present when any of the following occurs:

1. Someone in the story is concerned about establishing, maintaining, or restoring a *positive emotional relationship* with another person. Friendship is the most basic kind of positive emotional relationship, and to mention that two characters in the story are friends would be a minimum basis for scoring imagery. Other relationships, such as father-son or lover-lover, should be scored *only* if they have the warm, compassionate quality implied in the definition given.

2. There is a statement that *one person likes or wants to be liked* by someone else or that someone has some similar feeling about another. Moreover, if a close interpersonal relationship has been disrupted or broken, imagery can be scored if someone feels sorrow or grief or takes action to restore the relationship.

3. Also, score if the story mentions such *affiliative activities* as parties, reunions, visits, or relaxed small talk as in a bull session. However, if the affiliative nature of the situation is explicitly denied in the story, such as by describing it as a busi-

ness meeting or an angry debate, imagery is not scored. Friendly actions such as consoling or being concerned about the well-being or happiness of another person are scored, except when these actions are culturally prescribed by the relationship (e.g., father-son). In other words, there must be evidence that the nurturant activity is not motivated solely by a sense of obligation.

Discussion of Motive Scores

When a trio has finished scoring their stories, they should join with the other trios from your learning group and discuss the following questions:

1. How much similarity or difference was there in your group concerning the dominant motivational concerns expressed in the stories? Of what significance is this similarity or difference?

2. In what ways did the motivational concerns you expressed in the stories agree or disagree with the image you held of yourself *before* you took the test? Of what significance are any differences?

3. What kinds of things cause one person to express affiliation concerns, another person to express power concerns, and a third to express achievement concerns in response to the same picture? Consider immediate (e.g., "He hadn't had anything to eat all day.") as well as historical (e.g., "She flunked math in high school.") factors.

4. Were there any particular reasons that you chose the four pictures you did? In other words, you chose not to respond to two pictures in particular–why? Did others choose the same pictures as you?

5. What motives do you think are relevant or important within the context of a job?

6. Of what value, if any, do you feel are projective techniques such as the TAT in assessing human motivation? What other alternatives might be feasible or better?

7. What connections can you make between this exercise and the readings?

INDIVIDUAL SCORING FORM FOR TEST OF IMAGINATION

Circle the motives present in each story and indicate other motivational concerns in the space provided.

	PERSON A	PERSON B	PERSON C	OTHER MOTIVES PRESENTED IN STORY
Story 1	Achievement Power Affiliation	Achievement Power Affiliation	Achievement Power Affiliation	
Story 2	Achievement Power Affiliation	Achievement Power Affiliation	Achievement Power Affiliation	
Story 3	Achievement Power Affiliation	Achievement Power Affiliation	Achievement Power Affiliation	
Story 4	Achievement Power Affiliation	Achievement Power Affiliation	Achievement Power Affiliation	
Story 5	Achievement Power Affiliation	Achievement Power Affiliation	Achievement Power Affiliation	
Story 6	Achievement Power Affiliation	Achievement Power Affiliation	Achievement Power Affiliation	
Summary	Number of stories with: Achievement ____ Power ____ Affiliation ____	Number of stories with: Achievement ____ Power ____ Affiliation ____	Number of stories with: Achievement ____ Power ____ Affiliation ____	Other major concerns:

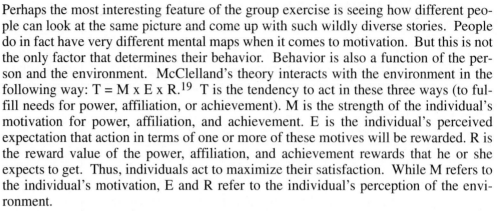

Follow-Up

Perhaps the most interesting feature of the group exercise is seeing how different people can look at the same picture and come up with such wildly diverse stories. People do in fact have very different mental maps when it comes to motivation. But this is not the only factor that determines their behavior. Behavior is also a function of the person and the environment. McClelland's theory interacts with the environment in the following way: $T = M \times E \times R$.[19] T is the tendency to act in these three ways (to fulfill needs for power, affiliation, or achievement). M is the strength of the individual's motivation for power, affiliation, and achievement. E is the individual's perceived expectation that action in terms of one or more of these motives will be rewarded. R is the reward value of the power, affiliation, and achievement rewards that he or she expects to get. Thus, individuals act to maximize their satisfaction. While M refers to the individual's motivation, E and R refer to the individual's perception of the environment.

The equation in the preceding paragraph is based upon the assumption that employees make conscious choices about their behavior at work. They calculate whether a certain level of effort will result in a particular goal; they determine whether the reward is worth the effort, and they also compare whether their efforts and rewards are comparable to those of other people. These decisions, which are based upon employees' perception of the environment and previous experiences, affect their behavior and level of productivity.

These are the assumptions that underlie the second category of motivation theories, *process* theories that attempt to describe how personal factors and environmental factors interact and influence each other to produce certain kinds of behavior. Examples of these theories, some of which are described in the *Reader*, are expectancy theory, equity theory, reinforcement theory, and goal setting. Equity theory and reinforcement theory are described below.

The equity that people perceive in their situation also influences motivation. If they discover that another employee who does the same job or produces the same results is paid more highly, they are likely to reduce their effort. According to equity theory,[20] employees perceive what they receive from a job (outputs like pay, bonuses, job security, promotions, recognition, etc.) in relation to what they contribute (inputs such as time, skills, creativity, effort, etc.). They compare their own input-output ratio with 1) relevant others, 2) system policies and precedents, and 3) criteria related to the "self," such as previous jobs or family commitments. When inequity exists and they are either over-rewarded or under-rewarded, people will attempt to correct this situation. Those who are over-rewarded will increase production or the quality of their work; those who are under-rewarded will decrease production or quality, increase absenteeism and perhaps even resign. When compensation systems are perceived as equitable, employees report greater levels of job satisfaction, organizational commitment, and trust in their supervisors.

Social reinforcement theory is another process theory that is useful for managers. This theory ignores internal reasons for behavior and focuses upon learned behavior. People learn to continue behavior that is rewarded and to suppress behavior that is punished. It is important for managers to understand the effect of their behavior and policies upon subordinates and to know whether it is perceived as a reward or a punishment. For example, highly productive employees are sometimes "rewarded" only by being assigned extra work that less responsible employees are not completing. When this occurs, the productive employee may perceive this as working more for the same salary, (i.e., a punishment) while irresponsible employees are "rewarded" by having less work to do. As a result, managers sometimes lose their high performers due to burn-out or equity complaints. (See the article in the Reader, "On the Folly of Rewarding A while Hoping for B," for an interesting slant on rewards.) The main tenets of reinforcement theory are that managers should reinforce desired behavior and extinguish (by ignoring) or punish undesirable behavior.[21]

While individuals come to organizations with previously learned motive patterns and unique needs, managers can affect how employees perceive their environment. They shape and direct motivation by establishing expectations and rewards that tap into employee motives and further the organization's goals. The manager's task is to make sure there is a fit and a direct link–between employee needs and rewards, between performance and rewards, and between employees and jobs. The better the fit, the higher employee motivation.

Managers cannot influence employee motivation unless they understand what motivates the individual employees. This is easier said than done. One study asked workers and supervisors to rank ten job factors in order of their importance to the workers. Those factors that the workers ranked first, second, and third–appreciation for their work, being in on things, and sympathy for personal problems–were ranked eighth, ninth, and tenth by their supervisors! The supervisors mistakenly assumed that good wages, job security, and promotion were most important to the workers.[22] People often hold mistaken assumptions about what motivates others.

If we return to the sales manager and his contest in the opening vignette, we see that he was not only mistaken about his employees' needs but also about what constituted incentives for them. If he had possessed a better understanding of motivation theories, what might he have done differently? First, the sales manager could have explained the need for increased business and sought the agents' commitment and participation concerning this goal. This might have prevented the agents' feelings of being manipulated. Second, he could have investigated and attempted to remedy, if possible, any factors that were preventing the agents from bringing in new business. The understaffing issue, employee feelings about the previous contest, and maybe even work design concerns might have been raised. Perhaps as a team they could have looked for alternatives–ways to work smarter rather than harder.

Third, had the sales manager spent more time talking with the agents, he would have discovered that, since the agents already perceived themselves to be understaffed and overworked, $100 was not an equitable reward for the extra work required to generate new business. By knowing his employees better and discussing such matters with them, the sales manager could have discovered both what their individual needs were and what they saw as an equitable reward for increased effort.

And, finally, knowing that the agents were a tightly knit group who had worked as a team for several years should have told the manager that an individual prize in a contest that encouraged competition among peers would be a negative incentive. Had the manager set both a team goal and team incentive (after consulting the agents to discover what they would consider to be a positive incentive), he would have been more likely to connect with their needs for both affiliation and achievement. Competing against their own previous record or competing against other sales groups in the corporation would have been more motivating and appropriate for this particular group of sales agents.

Learning Points

1. Motivation is not something that is "done" to other people. It is an internal state that directs individuals toward certain goals.

2. Individuals are motivated by different needs. Managers sometimes have false assumptions about what motivates their employees.

3. The manager's job is to understand and channel the motivation employees already possess and direct it toward tasks that further the organization's objectives.

4. Maslow developed a hierarchy of needs–physical safety, security, affiliation, self-esteem, and self-actualization. Lower-order needs must be satisfied before higher-order needs become motivators. Once a need is satisfied, it no longer motivates behavior.

5. Herzberg identified extrinsic factors as hygiene factors and stated that they create dissatisfaction if they are not present. Once hygiene factors are present, intrinsic factors motivate people.

6. McClelland's theory of motivation focuses upon three needs that are learned from the culture and the family: affiliation, achievement, and power. Almost everyone has these needs but in varying degrees.

7. We can measure need strength and motive pattern (scores for affiliation, power, and achievement) with the Thematic Apperception Test (TAT). Job performance is affected by people's motive pattern as well as by the values that individuals hold.

8. There are two faces, positive and negative, to n-Power (socialized and personalized) and n-Affiliation (interest and assurance).

9. According to McClelland, high achievers
   a. Like to set their own goals.
   b. Tend to avoid either extremely difficult or extremely easy goals.
   c. Prefer tasks that provide immediate feedback on their performance.

10. In addition to internal need states, motivation is also affected by the environment. $T = M \times E \times R$, where T = tendency to act, M = strength of motive, E = expectation that motive will be rewarded, and R = reward value.

11. Equity theory maintains that employee motivation is affected by the perceived fairness of what people contribute and receive.

12. According to social reinforcement theory, people learn to use behaviors that are rewarded and to suppress behaviors that are punished or ignored.

13. Managers can create an environment in which goal-oriented behavior is encouraged and rewarded by making sure there are fits between employee needs and rewards, between performance and rewards, and between employees and jobs.

for Managers

- Managers often misdiagnose employees' motives for the following reasons:

  - They assume that everyone is motivated by the same factors that motivate them.

  - They hold stereotyped views of types of employees or make attributions about individual employees that prevent them from actually investigating motive patterns.

  - They overlook the individual differences in employee motive patterns.

  - They fail to comprehend that employee motives change over time.

- Figuring out what motivates employees is not always a simple matter of asking them. Finding out about employees' nonwork activities, observing what they do with discretionary time at work, and determining what type of work or projects they enjoy are indirect methods of gauging their motive patterns. The yearly performance appraisal provides a good opportunity to check whether the manager's assumptions about what motivates an employee are accurate. There is a close relationship between understanding what motivates your workers and negotiating and renegotiating an effective psychological contract with them.

- Set challenging but attainable goals, establish clear work objectives and standards of good performance, and provide appropriate feedback to encourage achievement among employees.

- Link rewards to performance and ensure that rewards are equitably distributed; people who produce more should receive greater rewards. Reward employees for behaviors that promote the organization's goals. Be sure that the reward is one that the individual employee finds valuable or motivating.

- Whenever you are contemplating changes in the organization, make sure you have taken motivation patterns into consideration. For example, a secretary with a very boring job that is redeemed only by a central location that allows her to satisfy a high need for affiliation will not be as excited as you are about a new work station placed in a remote location. The easiest way to avoid making errors of this sort is to understand what makes the job challenging or at least palatable for each employee and discuss possible changes with him or her before they are made.

- Put people in jobs they will find rewarding and recognize their contributions. Managers who always have their eyes on the next step of the career ladder often disparage workers who are content to remain in "dead-end" jobs. Doing a boring job well is just as great a contribution to an organization as doing any other job well.

- Organizations need to find ways to harness, channel, and stimulate higher levels of achievement motivation. One way of approaching this challenge is the concept of intrapreneuring. Internal entrepreneurs, according to Pinchot,[23] are individuals whose high need to achieve does not result in their leaving their organizations to start their own businesses. Rather, the organization strives to create the climate, conditions, structures, and procedures that allow and reward these budding entrepreneurs for staying, for becoming intrapreneurs. They are given the freedom and incentive to create and market their own ideas for their own profit and for the company's. Intrapreneurs, Pinchot is quick to point out, are much more than inventors: "Intrapreneurs need team-building skills and a firm grasp of business and marketplace reality."[24] Like their entrepreneurial colleagues, they also have little understanding of the word "no." They are driven by their vision and are more than willing to take personal responsibility for their own success or failure. The challenge to the organization is to capture this innovative spirit.

 # Personal Application Assignment

The topic of this assignment is to think back on a motivation experience that was significant for you. Choose an experience about which you were motivated to learn more; that is, there was something about it that you did not totally understand, that intrigued you, that made you realize that you lack certain skills, that was problematical for you, and so on. It may have been an academic one or a nonformal education experience (tennis camp, a seminar, on-the-job training program, etc.).

A. *Concrete Experience*

1. *Objectively* describe the experience ("who," "what," "when," "where," "how," type information–up to 2 points).

2. *Subjectively* describe your feelings, perceptions, and thoughts that occurred during (not after) the experience (up to 2 points). Does this section have too much detail? (If so, delete 1 point.)

B. *Reflective Observation*

1. Look at the experience from different points of view. How many points of view did you include that are *relevant* (up to 2 points)?

2. Use these perspectives to add more meaning to the incident (up to 2 points).

C. *Abstract Conceptualization*

1. Relate concepts from the assigned readings and the lecture to the experience (i.e., what theories that you heard in the lecture or read in the Reader relate to your understanding of this incident?). Make reference to at least two sources. Use standard referencing format and include the page number to which you are referring. How many sources did you use and how clearly did you explain their theories (up to 4 points)?

2. You can also create an original model or theory, but it should not replace course concepts.

D. *Active Experimentation*

1. Write about what you will do in the future that will improve your effectiveness. Use rules of thumb or action resolutions.

2. Are they described specifically, thoroughly, and in detail (up to 4 points).

E. *Integration, Synthesis, and Writing*

1. Did you write about something personally important to you (up to 1 point)?

2. Was it well written (up to 2 points)?

3. Did you integrate and synthesize the different sections (up to 1 point)?

[1]This test is a variation of the standard six-picture Thematic Apperception Test cited in John Atkinson, ed., *Motives in Fantasy, Action, and Society* (Princeton, NJ: D. Van Nostrand, 1958).

[2]Abraham Maslow, *Motivation and Personality* (New York: Harper & Row, 1970).

[3]Frederic Herzberg, B. Mausner, and B. Snyderman, *The Motivation to Work* (New York: John Wiley, 1959).

[4]Alfie Kohn, "Why Incentive Plans Cannot Work," *Harvard Business Review*, September-October 1993, p. 54-63.

[5]See John Atkinson, *Motives in Fantasy, Action, and Society* (Princeton, NJ: D. Van Nostrand, 1958), David C. McClelland, *The Achieving Society* (Princeton, NJ: D. Van Mostrand, 1961), and David C. McClelland, *Human Motivation* (Glenview, IL: Scott, Foresman, 1985).

[6]Geert Hofstede, Culture's Consequences, (Beverly Hills: Sage, 1980). See also "Motivation, Leadership, and Organization: Do American Theories Apply Abroad?," *Reader*, for Hofstede's critique of the major theories mentioned in this chapter.

[7]McClelland, *Human Motivation*.

[8]McClelland, *Human Motivation*.

[9]John D. Andrews, "The Achievement Motive in Two Types of Organizations," *Journal of Personality and Social Psychology*, Vol. 6 (1967), pp. 163-168.

[10]Herbert A. Wainer and Irwin M. Rubin, "Motivation of Research and Development Entrepreneurs: Determinants of Company Success," *Journal of Applied Psychology*, Vol. 53, no. 3 (1969), pp. 178-184.

[11]Richard E. Boyatzis, "The Need for Close Relationships and the Manager's Job", *Reader*, 1991.

[12]Khalil Noujaim, "Some Motivational Determinants of Effort Allocation and Performance" (Ph.D. thesis. Sloan School of Management, Massachusetts Institute of Technology, 1968).

[13]Gary A. Yukl, *Leadership in Organizations* (Englewood Cliffs, NJ: Prentice-Hall, 1994).

[14]Noujaim, *Motivational Determinants*.

[15]David C. McClelland, Power: *The Inner Experience*, (New York: Irvington, 1975). and Boyatzis "The Need for Close Relationships and the Manager's Job".

[16]David C, McClelland and David H. Burnham, "Power is the Great Motivator," *Harvard Business Review*, March-April 1976, pp. 100-110; the "Good Guys Make Bum Bosses" article in the *Reader*.

[17]Adrian M. Harrell and Michael J. Stahl, "A Behavioral Decision Theory Approach for Measuring McClelland's Trichotomy of Needs" *Journal of Applied Psychology*, April 1981, p. 242-247; Michael J. Stahl and Adrian M. Harrell, "Evolution and Validation of a Behavioral Theory Measurement Approach to Achievement, Power, and Affiliation," *Journal of Applied Psychology*, December, 1982, pp. 744-51; and Michael J. Stahl, "Achievement, Power, and Managerial Motivation: Selecting Managerial Talent with the Job Choice Exercise," *Personnel Psychology*, Winter 1983, pp. 775-89.

[18]These categories were developed by David G. Winter, *The Power Motive* (New York: Free Press, 1973), pp. 251-255.

[19]J. Atkinson, *An Introduction to Motivation* (Princeton, NJ: D. Van Nostrand, 1964), and J. Atkinson and N.T. Feather, *A Theory of Achievement Motivation* (New York: John Wiley, 1966).

[20]J. Stacy Adams, "Inequity in Social Exchanges," in L. Berkowitz (ed.), *Advances in Experimental Social Psychology* (New York: Academic Press, 1965) p. 16-23.

[21]Fred Luthans and Robert Kreitner, *Organizational Behavior Modification and Beyond: An Operant and Social Learning Approach* (Glenview, IL: Scott, Foresman, 1985). For excellent compilations of the research on this theory, see Frank Andrasik, "Organizational Behavior Modification on Business Settings: A Methodological and Content Review," *Journal of Organizational Behavior Management*, no. 1, 1989, pp. 59-77; and Gerald A. Merwi, Jr., John A. Thomason, and Eleanor E. Sanford, "A Methodology and Content Review of Organizational Behavior Management in the Private Sector: 1978-1986," *Journal of Organizational Behavior Management*, no. 1, 1989, pp. 39-57.

[22]Paul Hersey and Kenneth J. Blanchard, *Management of Organizational Behavior: Utilizing Human Resources* (Englewood Cliffs, NJ: Prentice-Hall, 1977), p. 47.

[23]G. Pinchot III, *Intrapreneuring* (New York: Harper & Row, 1965).

[24]Ibid., p. 33.

Chapter

5

VALUES AND ETHICS

NOTE: This chapter was co-authored by Judith White. Special thanks to James Weber and Bruce Drake for sharing their expertise and materials.

OBJECTIVES By the end of this chapter, you should be able to:

A. Describe how organizations foster unethical behavior.

B. Explain how organizations can promote ethical behavior.

C. Define ethics and values.

D. Better articulate your own values.

E. Distinguish between ethical and non-ethical values.

F. Explain and recognize the stages of moral reasoning.

G. Describe four different ethical models.

*T*he Double Bottom Line*

Hanna Andersson attributes its business success to a concern for the "double bottom line," both financial and social objectives. This children's clothing catalog company developed a $40 million business in ten years due to high quality merchandise, excellent customer service, and a unique returned merchandise program called Hannadowns, a play on the word "hand-me-downs." The company accepts clothing that customers' children have outgrown, which demonstrates the durability of their product. Customers receive a 20% credit towards their next purchase, and Hanna Andersson donates the used clothing to local and national charities. The company receives 2,700-3,000 items of used clothing each month, and CEO Gun Denhart credits the Hannadowns program with their 15% growth rate, which compares to less than 7% for the rest of the catalog industry. Employees take pride in the Hannadowns program because it allows them to serve the community. Hanna Andersson also pays half the child care costs for both full-time and part-time employees, which Ms. Denhart believes has resulted in a more motivated work force with a very low turnover rate. Not surprisingly, Ms. Denhart was a 1992 recipient of the Business Enterprise Award for combining business success with social contributions.

* This vignette is based upon Kevin Gudridge, "High Prices Wear Well for Cataloger," *Advertising Age*, August 23, 1993. p. 10; Stephanie Weiss, "Social Entrepreneurship: The Story of Gun Denhart, Hanna Andersson." (Stanford, CA: The Business Enterprise Trust, 1992).

Premeeting Preparation

A. Read "The Double Bottom Line."

B. Fill out the Rokeach Values Survey and score it.

C. Complete the Moral Judgment Interview.

D. Read the Topic Introduction.

Rokeach Values Survey

Please rate each value in terms of its importance to you, by circling the appropriate number (1=of lesser importance, 7=of greater importance). Think about each value *in terms of its importance to you, as a guiding principle in your life.* Is it of greater importance to you, or of lesser importance, or somewhere in between? As you work, *consider each value in relation to all the other values listed on that page.* Work slowly and think carefully about the importance you assign to all the values listed there.

TERMINAL VALUES

	OF LESSER IMPORTANCE				OF GREATER IMPORTANCE			WEIGHT
A comfortable life	1	2	3	4	5	6	7	x 5 =_____
An exciting life	1	2	3	4	5	6	7	x 4 =_____
A sense of accomplishment	1	2	3	4	5	6	7	x 4 =_____
A world at peace	1	2	3	4	5	6	7	x 5 = _____
A world of beauty	1	2	3	4	5	6	7	x 3 = _____
Equality	1	2	3	4	5	6	7	x 5 = _____
Family security	1	2	3	4	5	6	7	x 1 =_____
Freedom	1	2	3	4	5	6	7	x 1 =_____

Happiness	1	2	3	4	5	6	7	x 4 =_____
Inner harmony	1	2	3	4	5	6	7	x 5 =____
Mature love	1	2	3	4	5	6	7	x 4 =____
National security	1	2	3	4	5	6	7	x 5 = ____
Pleasure	1	2	3	4	5	6	7	x 5 =____
Salvation	1	2	3	4	5	6	7	x 3 =____
Self-respect	1	2	3	4	5	6	7	x 5 =____
Social recognition	1	2	3	4	5	6	7	x 3 =_____
True friendship	1	2	3	4	5	6	7	x 4 =____
Wisdom	1	2	3	4	5	6	7	x 5 =____

$$\frac{\quad}{P} \quad \frac{\quad}{S}$$
Total   Total

$$P \ - \ S \ = \ T$$
$$\underline{\quad} - \underline{\quad} = \underline{\quad}$$

SCORING INSTRUCTIONS

1. Multiply the number you circled by the weighted value that appears under the heading "Weight" and write it down in the blank to the right.

2. Sum the numbers in the first column and write the total below where it says P Total. P stands for Personal Values.

3. Sum the numbers in the second column and write the total below where it says S Total. S stands for Social Values.

4. Subtract S Total from P Total to find your Terminal Values score. A positive sum indicates a "personal" orientation while a negative sum indicates a "social" orientation.

INSTRUMENTAL VALUES

	OF LESSER IMPORTANCE				OF GREATER IMPORTANCE			WEIGHT	
Ambitious	1	2	3	4	5	6	7	x 5 =_____	
Broadminded	1	2	3	4	5	6	7	x 2 =_____	
Capable	1	2	3	4	5	6	7	x 5 =_____	
Cheerful	1	2	3	4	5	6	7	x 4 =	_____
Clean	1	2	3	4	5	6	7	x 3 =	_____
Courageous	1	2	3	4	5	6	7	x 2 =	_____
Forgiving	1	2	3	4	5	6	7	x 5 =	_____
Helpful	1	2	3	4	5	6	7	x 5 =	_____
Honest	1	2	3	4	5	6	7	x 2 =	_____
Imaginative	1	2	3	4	5	6	7	x 5 =_____	
Independent	1	2	3	4	5	6	7	x 5 =_____	
Intellectual	1	2	3	4	5	6	7	x 5 =_____	
Logical	1	2	3	4	5	6	7	x 5 =_____	
Loving	1	2	3	4	5	6	7	x 5 =	_____
Obedient	1	2	3	4	5	6	7	x 1 =	_____
Polite	1	2	3	4	5	6	7	x 3 =	_____
Responsible	1	2	3	4	5	6	7	x 4 =_____	
Self-controlled*	1	2	3	4	5	6	7		

_____ _____
 C   M
Total Total

C – M = I

___ – ___ = ___

* This value cannot be neatly categorized, so it is not calculated in your total scores.

SCORING INSTRUCTIONS

1. Multiply the number you circled by the weighted value that appears under the heading "Weight" and write it down in the blank to the right.

2. Sum the numbers in the first column and write the total below where it says C Total. C stands for Competence Values.

3. Sum the numbers in the second column and write the total below where it says M Total. M stands for Moral Values.

4. Subtract M Total from C Total to find your Instrumental Values score. A positive sum indicates a "competence" orientation while a negative sum indicates a "moral" orientation.

5. Depending upon your scores, mark the appropriate quadrant in the following chart. For example, if you have a personal orientation in your terminal values and a competence orientation in your instrumental values, mark the upper left quadrant.

		Terminal Values	
		Personal	Social
Instrumental Values	Competence	Preference for Personal-Competence Values	Preference for Social-Competence Values
	Moral	Preference for Personal-Moral Values	Preference for Social-Moral Values

Figure 5-1   **Personal Values Orientation Typology**

NOTE: The instructions for scoring this version of the Rokeach Value Survey were developed by James Weber, "Managerial Value Orientations: A Typology and Assessment," *International Journal of Value Based Management*, Vol. 3(2), 1990, pp. 37-54.

MORAL JUDGMENT INTERVIEW[1]

Roger worked for a small accounting firm and was conducting an annual audit of a machinery manufacturer when he found that the firm had received a large loan from the local savings and loan association. It is illegal for savings and loan associations to lend money to a manufacturing firm; they are restricted by law to mortgages based upon residential real estate.

Roger took his working papers and a copy of the ledger showing the loan to his boss, the partner in charge of the office. His boss listened to Roger, and then told Roger, "I will take care of this privately. We simply cannot afford to lose a client of this status. You put the papers you have through the shredder."

Roger wonders what he should do.

Please answer the following questions as if you were Roger. Put yourself in his shoes and express your own personal opinion. There are no "correct" answers. Please explain why you might choose one action over another. Very short answers cannot be coded so be sure to elaborate fully. Even if you give a long description of what you think is right or what you think should be done, it is of no help if you do not explain why you think it is right or why you think it should be done.

1. Should Roger shred the papers? _____ (yes or no)
   Why or why not?

   _____

   _____

   _____

   _____

2. Does the illegality of the loan and Roger's duty as an auditor make a difference in Roger's decision to shred the papers? Explain.

   _____

   _____

   _____

   _____

3. If Roger had been advised by one of his peers to shred his papers, should Roger shred his papers? Why, or why not?

   _____

   _____

   _____

   _____

4. Is it important for people to do everything they can to follow their conscience? Explain.

_____

_____

_____

_____

5. Shredding papers is against the AICPA Code and covers up an illegally made loan. Is Roger morally wrong if he shreds his papers? Explain.

_____

_____

_____

_____

6. If Roger's career was threatened if he refused to shred his papers, should Roger shred them? Why or why not?

_____

_____

_____

_____

7. Should people do everything they can to further their own careers? Explain.

_____

_____

_____

_____

Topic Introduction

Although business has always occupied a central role in U. S. society, Americans have often been ambivalent about business, money and success.[2] In books and movies, business people are usually portrayed in a negative light. As a profession, business has experienced alternating stages of low prestige and high prestige. Unethical trading on Wall Street and the Savings & Loan debacle are merely the latest in a long history of scandals. However, the very nature of business means that managers may be confronted with more ethical questions than most other professions. Companies confront internal issues such as employee safety, discrimination and sexual harassment, theft of company property, and irregular accounting practices. In addition, companies have struggled with a host of external ethical dilemmas such as balancing profit with environmental protection and consumer safety and doing business in cultures where bribes are commonplace.

Ethics refers to *"standards of conduct that indicate how one should behave based on moral duties and virtues arising from principles about right and wrong."*[3] There is a perception that firms that act ethically have lower profits.[4] This may be true in the short term, but companies that engage in unethical practices make themselves vulnerable to lawsuits, boycotts, governmental restrictions and regulations, and loss of reputation—all of which can endanger profits. There is a strong argument that ethical practices pay off in the long-run since trusting relationships with employees, stockholders, and well-satisfied customers are the basis of business success. Hartley contends that:

> *"The interests of a firm are best served by scrupulous attention to the public interest and by seeking a <u>trusting relationship</u> with the various publics with which a firm is involved. In the process, society also is best served....Such a trusting relationship suggests concern for customer satisfaction and fair dealings. The objective is loyalty and repeat business, a durable and mutually beneficial relationship, which is contrary to the philosophy of short-term profit maximization, corporate self-interest, and coercive practices with employees and dependent suppliers."*[5]

There are many ethical business people who prosper in large part because of their integrity. In recent years, we have seen an increase in companies who define themselves as socially responsible companies in their mission statement. Organizations like Anita Rodick's Body Shop and Ben and Jerry's Ice Cream donate part of their profits to "good works," such as human rights, community development projects, environmental groups, and peace programs.

Nevertheless, there have always been and always will be unethical people for whom money and power takes precedence over all else. The key question is whether they are perceived as heroes or villains.[6] This is determined by societal values and by the ethical climate and norms created by each organization. Many companies place employees in positions that force them to choose between their careers and their personal sense of ethics.

Factors that lead to questionable practices in business are:

1. Overemphasis on both individual and firm performance;

2. Mission statements, evaluation systems and organizational cultures that focus on profit as the organization's sole objective;

3. Intense competition between firms, departments or individuals;

4. Management concern for the letter of the law rather than the spirit;

5. Ambiguous policies that employees interpret as "window dressing" for outsiders rather than clear expectations for ethical behavior;

6. Inadequate controls so that managers get away with violating standards, allowing them to pursue greater sales and profits for personal benefit;

7. Expediency and indifference to the customers' best interest;

8. Management's failure to comprehend the public's ethical concerns;

9. Custom ("Let the buyer beware"); and

10. A "groupthink" mentality that fosters group decisions that individual members would not countenance.[7]

Companies that want to encourage ethical behavior need to 1) communicate their expectations that employees will act in an ethical manner, which they define for employees; 2) hire top executives who set an example of moral behavior; 3) reward ethical behavior and punish unethical behavior; 4) teach employees the basic tools of ethical decision making; and 5) encourage the discussion of ethical issues.[8]

One of the factors that inhibits the discussion of ethics in the work force is a reluctance on the part of managers to discuss the moral aspects of their decision making, even when they are acting for moral reasons.[9] Managers give several reasons for avoiding moral talk. 1) People do not like to appear judgmental or intrusive, or lay themselves open to counter-charges of wrong-doing. As a result, they often avoid confronting others who are not behaving ethically. 2) Moral talk threatens efficiency when it simply muddies the waters and distracts attention from problem solving. Managers worry that it may be self-serving, simplistic, inflexible, or inexact. 3) Some managers fear that the esoteric and idealistic nature of moral talk is not in keeping with the image they want to convey, and they are leery about exposing their lack of training in ethics. Therefore, we find a norm in many businesses to justify decisions on the basis of organizational interests, practicality, and sound economic sense, even when moral considerations play an important role. Although managers struggle individually with ethical problems, they seldom discuss them in groups of managers, which gives rise to the term "the moral muteness" of managers. The purpose of this chapter is to provide you with a rudimentary understanding of ethical terms and principles so you can take part in ethical discussions.

VALUES

Both individuals and organizations have codes of ethics that are based upon their values. One of the first steps in teaching ethics is to help people identify and articulate their own values. Values are "*core beliefs or desires that guide or motivate attitudes and actions.*" Whereas the study of ethics is concerned with how a moral person *should* behave, values concern the various beliefs and attitudes that determine how a person *actually* behaves. People do not always act in accordance with their espoused values. Our values are fixed early in life; we learn them from our parents, friends, teachers, church, and the culture that surrounds us. As adults, we often seek environments that are compatible with the values we learned as children. For example, values help determine what companies we are attracted to and how long we stay with them. They also affect how motivated we are at work; people who share the same values as the organization are more committed to the organization than those who do not. Whenever people make decisions or talk about what constitutes appropriate behavior at work, we can observe the impact of values, or even conflicts between different values. For example, when companies consider whether to employ temporary or permanent employees, which values are more important—saving money for the company or providing benefits and job security to employees?

Within our personal value system, some values are more important than others. The exercise in the premeeting preparation allows you to see which of the most common American values have the greatest significance for you. In the following chapter on Career Development, you can see the link between values and career planning in the premeeting preparation exercise.

Rokeach[10], who developed the list of values that you rated, believes that people possess a relatively small number of values which they hold to varying degrees. He classified these key values into two types. Terminal values are desirable end states of existence or the goals that a person would like to achieve during his or her lifetime. Terminal values can be subdivided further into two categories: *personal* values (a comfortable life, freedom, happiness, salvation) and *social* values (world peace, equality, national security).

Instrumental values are preferable modes of behavior or the means to achieving one's terminal values. There are two types of instrumental values: *moral* values and *competence* values. Moral values (cheerful, courageous, helpful, honest) tend to have an interpersonal focus; when they are violated, we feel pangs of conscience or guilt. Competence values (ambitious, capable, intellectual, responsible) have a personal focus. When they are violated, we feel ashamed of our personal inadequacy, rather than guilt about wrongdoing.

Rokeach looked for a relationship between terminal and instrumental values and found that all combinations are possible, as shown in Figure 5-1 on page 105. The personal-competence value orientation is most commonly preferred by managers. The personal-moral and social-moral value orientations are the least common for managers and much of the total U. S. population.[11] When we compare individual values of managers with those of the population at large, we find that "sense of accomplishment," "self-respect," "a comfortable life," and "independence" are more highly valued by managers.[12]

ETHICAL VERSUS NON ETHICAL VALUES

When ethical issues arise, we have to distinguish between *ethical* and *non ethical* values. The former are values that directly relate to beliefs concerning what is right and proper (as opposed to what is simply correct or effective) or which motivate a sense of moral duty. Core ethical values that transcend cultural, ethnic, and socio-economic differences in the U. S. are 1) trustworthiness, 2) respect, 3) responsibility, 4) justice and fairness, 5) caring and 6) civic virtue and citizenship.[13] The effort to identify these values is part of a trend towards character building as a remedy for the breakdown in societal values that is taking place in many countries. It is difficult for adults to act ethically if they have not been inculcated with ethical values when they were growing up.

Non ethical values simply deal with things we like, desire or find personally important. Examples of non ethical values are money, fame, status, happiness, fulfillment, pleasure, personal freedom, and being liked. They are ethically neutral. One of the guides to ethical decision making is that *ethical values should always take precedence over non ethical values.*

MORAL REASONING

Values alone do not determine our actions. Our behavior is also influenced by our moral reasoning, organizational culture, the influence of significant others, the type of harm that could result from a decision involving ethics, and who might be harmed.[14] The first factor, moral reasoning, is the process by which we transform our values and beliefs into action. This reasoning affects the way managers make decisions.[15]

Kohlberg[16] conducted a longitudinal study of the moral reasoning reported by male subjects at various ages. He identified three different levels of moral development which we will call: *self-centered, conformity, and principled*. Kohlberg uses different labels here (*preconventional, conventional,* and *postconventional*), but we think it is easier for you to remember titles that describe the major characteristic of each level.[17] The progression through these levels can be summarized as moving from 1) a self-centered conception of right and wrong to 2) an understanding of the importance of social contracts and 3) universal principles of justice and rights. As shown in Figure 5-2, each level has two stages, the second of which is more advanced.[18]

Self-Centered Level (Preconventional)   This level of moral reasoning has a personal focus and an emphasis upon consequences. It is usually found among children who see moral issues in the black and white terms of "good and bad" and "right and wrong." Actions are judged either by their consequences (punishment, reward, exchange of favors), or in terms of the physical power of those who lay down the rules.

Figure 5-2   **Three Levels of Moral Development According to Kohlberg**

Stage	What is considered to be right
Level One–Self-centered (Preconventional)	
Stage One—Obedience and Punishment Orientation	Sticking to rules to avoid physical punishment. Obedience for its own sake.
Stage Two–Instrumental Purpose and Exchange	Following rules only when it is in one's immediate interest. Right is an equal exchange, a fair deal
Level Two–Conformity (Conventional)	
Stage Three-Interpersonal Accord, Conformity, Mutual Expectations	Stereotypical "good" behavior. Living up to what is expected by peers and people close to you.
Stage Four-Social Accord and System Maintenance	Fulfilling duties and obligations of social system. Upholding laws except in extreme cases where they conflict with fixed social duties. Contributing to the society, group.
Level Three–Principled (Postconventional)	
Stage Five-Social Contract Individual Rights	Being aware that people hold a variety of values; that rules are relative to the group. Upholding rules because they are the social contract. Upholding nonrelative values and rights regardless of majority opinion.
Stage Six-Universal Ethical Principles	Following self-chosen ethical principles of justice and rights. When laws violate principles, act in accord with principles.

Source: Adapted from Kohlberg by Linda K Trevino, "A Cultural Perspective on Changing and Developing Organizational Ethics," in Research in Organizational Change and Development (Eds.) W.A. Pasmore and R.W.Woodman, (Greenwich, CT: JAI Press, 1990) p.198.

This level is divided into two stages:

Stage 1: The Obedience and Punishment Orientation. The physical consequences of an action determine its goodness or badness. An avoidance of punishment and unquestioning deference to power are valued, but not because the individual believes in the importance of a moral order supported by punishment and authority.

Stage 2: Instrumental Purpose and Exchange (Instrumental Relativist Orientation). Interest in satisfying one's own needs is the most important consideration. Elements of fairness, reciprocity, and equal sharing are present, but they are always interpreted in a physical or pragmatic way. For example, reciprocity is a matter of "you scratch my back, and I'll scratch yours," rather than loyalty, gratitude, or justice.

Conformity Level (Conventional)   At this level, there is a group focus and an emphasis upon social harmony. People are concerned with meeting the expectations of their family, group, or nation. They have moved beyond a preoccupation with consequences to focus upon conformity and loyalty to the social order. They support, justify, and identify with the existing social order or with the people or group(s) involved in it. Like the self-centered individuals, this group also sees rules and laws as outside themselves but they obey them because they have accepted them. At this level, we find the following two stages.

Stage 3: Interpersonal Accord, Conformity, Mutual Expectations (The "Good Boy-Nice Girl" Orientation). Good behavior is defined as behavior that pleases or helps others and is approved by them. Conformity to stereotypical images of what is "natural" behavior (in other words, behavior that is characteristic of the majority of people) is a common guide. People are concerned with maintaining mutually trusting relationships with people. The Golden Rule, "Do unto others as you would have others do unto you," is common at this stage of moral reasoning. Judging behavior by its intention, for example, "she meant well," is also found for the first time at this stage.

Stage 4: Social Accord and System Maintenance (The Law and Order Orientation). At stage 4, the individual takes the perspective of a member of society. The individual perceives the social system as a consistent set of codes and procedures (legal, religious, societal) that apply impartially to all members in a society. There is an emphasis upon "doing one's duty" and showing respect for authority and maintaining the social order for its own sake.

Principled level (Postconventional)   At this level, individuals have a more universal focus that emphasizes internalized ethical standards, rights or duties. Individuals at this level examine society's rules and laws and then develop their own set of internal principles. These internalized principles take precedence over rules and laws.

Stage 5: Social Contract, Individual Rights (The Social-Contract Legalistic Orientation). At this stage, the individual realizes that there is an arbitrary element to rules and the law. Right is relative and perceived as a matter of personal values and opinion. For the sake of agreement, the individual agrees to procedural rules like respect for contracts and the rights of others, majority will, and the general good.

Stage 6: The Universal Ethical Principles Orientation. Right is defined by decisions of conscience, in accord with self-chosen ethical principles that are logically comprehensive, universal, and consistent. These principles are abstract and ethical, like justice, the reciprocity and equality of human rights, and respect for the dignity of human beings.

The research of Kohlberg and others concluded that:[19]

1. People's reasoning tends to reflect one dominant stage, although they may occasionally be either one stage lower or higher than the dominant stage.
2. Most adults in Western urban societies reason at stages 3, 4, and 5. Stage 4 reasoning is the most common. Development can stop at any stage. Many prison inmates never get beyond stage two reasoning.
3. People develop moral maturity gradually, moving from step to step; they do not skip stages.
4. Development is not governed by age. Some young people reason at a higher stage than their elders. However, cognitive development (which normally occurs during adolescence) is a necessary condition for abstract reasoning, but it does not guarantee moral maturity.
5. Empathy, the capacity to feel what others are feeling, is also a necessary, but not sufficient condition for moral development.
6. Managers whose values are categorized as social-moral in Figure 5.1 demonstrated a higher level of moral reasoning.[20]
7. Ethical decision making and intended ethical behavior generally increase as individuals utilize higher stages of moral reasoning.[21]

Although Kohlberg's theory of moral development has been the target of various criticisms over the past twenty years,[22] it has been refined and clarified in response and is still the most widely accepted model of moral development.

Both personal values and moral reasoning affect the way people make decisions. The group exercise provides an opportunity to discuss an ethical dilemma and identify different types of moral reasoning and value considerations.

Procedure for Group Meeting:
The Roger Worsham Case [23]

STEP 1.   Read the extended version of the Roger Worsham Case individually. (10 minutes)

ACTION RECOMMENDED

Shred the Papers	Do Not Shred the Papers
Stage	
1 There is no reason for Roger to be a hero and risk losing everything.	Roger can avoid the worst penalty of all which would be a criminal charge against him.
2 This would enable Roger to acquire the two years of auditing experience needed to get his CPA.	Shredding the papers could ruin Roger's credibility and stand in the way of a promotion or a future job.
3 Roger would be acting as a "team player" within the firm and his boss would appreciate that.	This course of action is the best for Roger, the firm and the stockholders of the savings and loan.
4 There is an obligation for every employee to be loyal to the employer. This is essential for the operation of any firm.	If we ignore accepted written laws within our society, there would be a breakdown of the system.
5 The partner has a right to run his office in the manner he deems necessary. He may have other information which may justify his actions for the greater good of all involved.	Roger should not compromise his perceived ethical code for a business.

Figure 5-3   **Representative examples of reasoning at each stage.**

Source: James Weber and Sharon Green, "Principled Moral Reasoning: Is it a Viable Approach to Promote Ethical Integrity?" *Journal of Business Ethics*, 10 (1991), p. 328.

Arnold Abramson and Company is a regional accounting firm, with offices in Michigan and northern Wisconsin. It was founded in 1934 to provide auditing and tax services and, despite the depression, was immediately successful due to the economic growth of the area. The southern offices of Arnold Abramson and Company, in Flint and Detroit, competed directly with the large, national CPA firms, the "Big-Six." They were able to operate successfully until the mid-1960's by providing more personalized services and by charging somewhat lower rates. However, competition sharply increased in the late 1960's and early 1970's as the tax laws became more complex, the auditing procedures more rigorous and the bookkeeping more automated. The "Big-Six" firms were able, through their extensive training programs and their continual staff additions, to provide more extensive help and assistance to their clients on tax changes and data processing procedures. Many of the small and medium sized companies that had been customers of Arnold Abramson for years switched to one of the national firms. It was eventually necessary to close the Detroit office and to reduce the size of the staff at Flint.

Some of the partners of the company recommended a merger with one of the national CPA firms, but the founder, Mr. Arnold Abramson, was not only still living but was still active, and he and his two sons were uncompromising in their opposition to any sale or merger.

> *The old gentleman was 84 when I joined the firm, and he simply was not going to surrender to Arthur Andersen or Price Waterhouse. And, you know, he had a point; there is room left in the world for the more personal approach, even in auditing. The old man was adamant about this. I understand that at the partners' dinner this year he laid it right on the line to the other members of the firm. "You are to keep the local banks, retail stores and manufacturers as your clients; if you lose your clients to those people from Detroit, we'll shut down your office." He always referred to representatives of the Big-Six firms as "those people from Detroit" even though they might be from offices in Lansing, Grand Rapids or Milwaukee. (statement of Roger Worsham)*

Roger Worsham was 32-years-old when he graduated from the MBA program at the University of Michigan. He had majored in accounting, but had found it difficult to obtain employment at the large national CPA firms. He had interviewed with eight of the largest companies, and had been rejected by all eight. The Director of Placement at the School of Business Administration had explained that this was due to his age, and that the Big Six firms were exceedingly hesitant to hire anyone over 28 to 30 years of age since they felt that the older entrants were unlikely to stay with the firm over the first few years of auditing, which some people found to be dull and tedious.

Roger, however, felt that perhaps his personality was more at fault than his age. He found it difficult to converse easily in the interviews, and he was afraid that he projected himself as a hesitant, uncertain individual. He had worked for six years as a science teacher in a primary grade school after graduating from college. Interviewers always asked about his decision to change professions, and always seemed to imply that he was not certain about his objectives in life or his commitment to accounting.

At the suggestion of a faculty member who taught the small business management course at the Business School, Roger applied to some of the smaller CPA firms in the state, and was almost immediately accepted by Arnold Abramson and Company.

> *I met Mr. Abramson, Jr. and he talked about what I wanted to do in accounting, not what I had done in teaching. That interview went really well, and I knew when he asked me if my wife and I would mind living in a small town that he was going to offer me a job. It does not pay as much as working for some of the other firms, but I can get my CPA (in Michigan, two years of auditing experience is required after passing the written examinations) and then I assume they'll pay me more, or I can move into industry. (statement of Roger Worsham).*

Roger was assigned to one of the northern offices, and he moved his wife and two children to the area and started work immediately after graduation. He had interesting, enjoyable work and his family enjoyed the area in which they were living. He felt that his life was beginning to take on a direction and purpose. But then he found clear evidence of fraud, and encountered a situation that threatened his newly-found security and employment.

We were doing the annual audit for the machinery manufacturer. This company had not been doing well. Sales had been declining for four or five years, losses had been reported for each of those years, and the financial position of the company had steadily deteriorated. I was going through the notes payable, and found that they had a loan, and a large one, from the savings and loan association in our town.

Now, in the first place, it is illegal for a savings and loan association to make a loan to a manufacturing firm. They are restricted by law to mortgages based upon residential real estate. But, even more, I knew this loan was not on the books of the savings and loan since I had been the one to audit the loan portfolio there. I had looked at every loan in the file. I had not statistically sampled from the file (which is the usual practice), but had checked each loan to see that it was supported by a properly assigned mortgage and a currently valid appraisal. The only thing I had not done was to add up the total for the file to check with the reported total, since the usual way is to sample, and you don't get a total when you sample. I still had my working papers back at our office, of course, so I went back and ran the total. Sure enough, it was off by the amount of the loan to the manufacturing company.

It was obvious what had happened. Someone had taken the folder covering the illegal loan out of the file prior to our audit. It became obvious who had done it: the president of the savings and loan association was a lawyer in the town who, I found by checking the stockholder lists, was the largest owner of the manufacturing company. He was also on the board of directors of the local bank, and reputedly was a wealthy, powerful person in the community.

I took my working papers and a Xerox copy of the ledger showing the loan, and went to see the partner in charge of our office the next morning. He listened to me, without saying a word. When I finished, he told me, "I will take care of this privately. We simply cannot afford to lose a client of the status of (the name of the lawyer). You put the papers you have through the shredder."

I was astonished, The AICPA Code of Ethics and generally accepted auditing standards both require that you either resign from the engagement or issue an adverse opinion when you find irregularities. This was not a small amount. The loan was not only illegal, it was in default, and would adversely affect the savings and loan association.

I hesitated because I was surprised and shocked. He told me, "I will not tell you again. You put those papers through the shredder or I'll guarantee that you'll never get a CPA in Michigan or work in an accounting office in this state for the rest of your life.

I didn't know what to do. (statement of Roger Worsham)

STEP 2.   In your learning group, discuss what Roger should do and why he should take this action.

STEP 3.   If possible, come to a group consensus. What values can you identify in this discussion?

STEP 4.   Using Figure 5-3 on page 114, what stage of moral development is reflected in the reasoning behind your group decision? What stage of reasoning is reflected in your individual decision in the premeeting preparation? (Steps 2-4: 30 minutes)

STEP 5.   General Debriefing Questions. (30-40 minutes)

1. What was your group decision? Describe the reasoning it was based upon.
2. Did having more information change your individual reasoning about the case? Why or why not?
3. What values were evident in your group discussion? Was anyone thinking of different values when you made your individual decision prior to class? Which values took precedence–ethical or non ethical?
4. Do your decisions pass the Ethics Warning System i.e., Does it fit the Golden Rule? Would you care if the newspaper published your decision? Would you be happy with the decision if your children were watching perched on your shoulder?
5. What would you have said to the partner if you were in Roger's shoes?
6. Who are the stakeholders in this decision? What harm could come to them as a result of Roger's decision?
7. Quickly read the descriptions of the four ethical models in the beginning of the Follow-Up section. Which of these approaches–utilitarian, rights, justice, or caring ethics–did you and your group utilize in your discussion?

Follow-Up

Another conceptual framework that helps us understand the different ways we look at ethical issues are models of ethics, most of which come to us from the study of philosophy. The four basic approaches to ethics that people use to make decisions are shown below.

1. *Utilitarian approaches.*   In utilitarian ethics, behavior is judged in terms of its effects on the welfare of everyone. A moral act produces the greatest good for the greatest number. Therefore, the good of the group takes precedence over consideration for individuals. Actions, plans and policies are judged by their consequences. This approach is quite common in business decisions. For example, when managers maximize profit, or opt for efficiency and productivity, they can argue that they are obtaining the greatest good for the greatest number. A disadvantage of this approach is that the rights of minority groups can be easily overlooked. The utilitarian orientation is often used with environmental issues.

2. *Approaches based on rights.*   Unlike utilitarian ethics, these emphasize the personal entitlements of individuals. Examples are a person's right to privacy, free speech, due process. Some rights have corresponding duties. For example, if a person has the right to be paid for an eight hour day, he or she is also obligated to contribute a "fair day's work" for a "fair day's pay." Business contracts reflect this approach, which is commonly used with occupational health and safety problems. A negative consequence of rights-based ethics is that it engenders a self-centered, legalistic focus on what is due the individual.

3. *Approaches based on justice.*   In these approaches, people are guided by fairness, equity, and impartiality when treating both individuals and groups. Fairness is the criteria for distributing the benefits and burdens of society, the administration of rules and regulations, and sanctions. This approach is appropriate for issues like employment discrimination. One disadvantage of a justice ethic is that it encourages a sense of entitlement.[24]

4. *Approaches based on caring.*   The focus in this approach is the well-being of another person. An ethical person is aware of the needs and feelings of others and takes the initiative to respond to that need. The criteria used to judge behavior is, "Who will be harmed and what will happen to existing relationships?"[25]

ETHICAL DECISION MAKING

How can managers ensure that they are taking an ethical approach to decision making? Nash devised twelve questions for examining the ethics of a business decision.[26]

1. Have you defined the problem accurately? What are the factual implications of the situation, rather than a biased perspective that reflects your loyalties?

2. How would you define the problem if you stood on the other side of the fence?

3. How did this situation occur in the first place? What is the historical background of events leading up to this situation?

4. To whom and to what do you give your loyalty as a person and as a member of the corporation?

5. What do you want to accomplish in making this decision?

6. How does this intention compare with the probable results?

7. Whom could your decision or action injure?

8. Can you discuss the problem with the affected parties before you make your decision?

9. Are you confident that your position will be as valid over a long period of time as it seems now?

10. Could you disclose without qualm your decision or action to your boss, your CEO, the board of directors, your family, society as a whole?

11. What would this decision symbolize for others if they interpret it correctly? What could it symbolize if the decision is misinterpreted by others?

12. Under what conditions would you allow exceptions to your stand?

The difficulty of making ethical decisions is exacerbated in international business due to different value systems and practices. Bribery, which is frowned upon in many cultures, is a daily way of life in others. It is illegal for American businesses to give bribes and kick-back payments in order to win contracts in other countries. However, this prohibition does not apply to competitors from countries who view bribery as a normal aspect of doing business.

One of the common dilemmas in international business is whether or not to subscribe to cultural relativism. Does one accept the values of the local culture (When in Rome, do as the Romans) or continue to observe or even impose one's own values? Do you promote women and minorities in international subsidiaries where there is little or no concern for diversity issues? Do you sell the pesticide that has been banned in the U.S. as a hazardous product to a Third World country that has no environmental or consumer safety laws? Many of these issues and their legal ramifications are extremely complex. It's important to identify the cultural values, historical precedents, and legal requirements that are involved. It's also helpful to consult with people from the other culture to make sure you understand the foreign viewpoint.

 Learning Points

1. Ethics refers to standards of conduct that indicate how one should behave based on moral duties and virtues arising from principles about right and wrong.

2. Ethical practices pay off in the long-run since trusting relationships and well-satisfied customers are the basis of repeat business.

3. Companies create an environment in which unethical practices are more likely when they focus solely on profit and intense competition, when top management gives lip service only to ethical behavior and fails to establish clear policies and adequate controls, and when they are insensitive to the customer's best interests and public concerns about ethics.

4. Companies that want to encourage moral behavior 1) communicate their expectations that employees will behave ethically and define what that means; 2) hire top executives who set a good example; 3) reward ethical behavior and punish unethical behavior; 4) teach employees the basic tools of ethical decision making; and 5) encourage the discussion of ethical issues.

5. Values are core beliefs or desires that guide or motivate attitudes and actions.

6. Rokeach developed a list of the most common American values, which people hold to varying degrees.

7. Terminal values are desirable end states of existence or the goals people want to accomplish in their lifetime. Terminal values are either personal or social.

8. Instrumental values are preferable modes of behavior or the means to achieving one's terminal values. There are two types: moral and competence.

9. Ethical values directly relate to beliefs concerning what is right and proper and motivate a sense of moral duty (trustworthiness, respect, responsibility, justice and fairness, caring, and civic virtue). Non ethical values are things we like, desire or find important. Ethical values should always take precedence over non-ethical values.

10. Kohlberg's theory of moral development consists of three levels: self-centered, conformity, and principled. In these stages, individuals move from a self-centered conception of right and wrong to an understanding of social contracts and internalized principles of justice and rights.

11. The four ethical models are: utilitarian, rights, justice, and caring ethics.

12. The difficulty of making ethical decisions is intensified in international business due to different value systems and business practices.

 TIPS for Managers

- Know your own personal values and those of the organization. Can you articulate them? Are they compatible?

- The top management of an organization sets the moral tone of the company. If they consistently behave in an ethical manner and set clear expectations that their subordinates should behave ethically, it is less likely that violations will occur. Some of the standards of moral behavior that are commonly expected of employees are: 1) keeping one's promises; 2) not harming others; 3) helping others in need; 4) respecting others and not treating them merely as means to your own ends; and (5) not using company resources for one's own needs.

- Managers should encourage and promote the discussion of ethical dilemmas. Employees should not be punished for questioning a decision on moral grounds. However, one of the difficulties of discussing ethics at work is that some people take the "moral high road" and criticize those who do not share their values. This makes it difficult to have reasoned discussions and often results in polarized views. Work at identifying and understanding the different perspectives on an issue and discuss the consequences of alternative actions that might be taken.

- Use the Ethics Warning System when you make a decision:[27]

  - Golden Rule-Are you treating others as you would want to be treated?

  - Publicity-Would you be comfortable if your reasoning and decision were to be publicized (i.e., how would it look on the front page of tomorrow's papers?)

  - Kid on your shoulder-Would you be comfortable if your children were observing you? Is your behavior an example of ethical behavior?

- Whistle blowing is legitimate 1) when it would benefit the public interest, 2) when the revelation is of major importance and very specific, 3) the facts have been checked and rechecked for accuracy, 4) all other avenues within the organization have been exhausted, and 5) the whistle blower is above reproach and has no personal advantage to gain by revealing the information.[28]

- Some companies utilize peer review systems to analyze their own ethics programs and find out what other companies are doing.[29]

Personal Application Assignment

Think back over the last few years and try to recall a specific event or situation at school, work, home or family life when you were confronted with an ethical dilemma or a difficult situation that called for a socially responsible action. It might be something to do with taking something that did not belong to you and that was not freely offered, or observing someone else's dishonest behavior, or having to decide between taking care of yourself and possibly harming another person.

1. In writing, describe the situation in some detail. Who else was there besides yourself? What were they doing? What were you doing? If you were on the receiving end of an unethical act, how were you treated? What were the issues involved?

2. What were the conflicts or dilemmas for you in this situation?

3. Why were they conflicts?

4. What did you do?

5. Why did you do that? Were there extenuating circumstances that affected your decision?

6. What were the results of your actions?

7. At the time of the situation, did you think you did the right thing?

8. Now, looking back, what if anything would you do differently?

9. What conclusions or learnings can you draw from this reflection?

[1] This exercise was developed and copyrighted (1988) by James Weber, director of the Beard Center for Leadership in Ethics, Duquesne University. It is reprinted here with his permission.

[2] Paul Steidlmeir, *People and Profits: The Ethics of Capitalism* (Englewood Cliffs, NJ: Prentice-Hall, 1992).

[3] Michael Josephson, *Making Ethical Decisions*, (Marina Del Rey, CA: The Josephson Institute of Ethics, 1993) p. 4.

[4] Robert F. Hartley, *Business Ethics: Violations of the Public Trust* (New York: John Wiley & Sons, 1993). This book describes ethical scandals and how companies handled them.

[5] Hartley, *Business Ethics*, p. 1 and 323.

[6] Michael Josephson, *Ethical Obligations and Opportunities in Business: Ethical Decision Making in the Trenches*, (Marina Del Rey, CA: Josephson Institute of Ethics, 1990).

[7] *Hartley, Business Ethics*, p. 5; and Gerald F. Cavanagh, *American Business Values*, (Englewood Cliffs, NJ: Prentice-Hall, 1984) p. 159.

[8] Matthew J. Baasten and Bruce H. Drake, "Ethical Leadership," *Social Sciences Perspectives Journal*, March 1990.

[9] Frederick B. Bird and James A. Waters, "The Moral Muteness of Managers," *California Management Review*, Fall 1989, pp. 73-88

[10] Milton Rokeach, *The Nature of Values* (New York: The Free Press, 1973).

[11] James Weber, "Exploring the Relationship Between Personal Values and Moral Reasoning," *Human Relations*, Vol. 46 (4), 1993, pp. 435-463 and "Managerial Value Orientations: A Typology and Assessment," *International Journal of Value Based Management*, Vol. 3 (2), 1990, pp. 37-54; and Gerald F. Cavanagh, *American Business Values*.

[12] D.A. Clare and D.G. Sanford, "Mapping Personal Value Space: A Study of Managers in Four Organizations," *Human Relations*, Vol. 32, 1979, pp. 659-666.

[13] These core ethical values were developed by a diverse group of thirty national leaders. Michael Josephson, *Making Ethical Decisions*, (Marina Del Rey, CA: The Josephson Institute of Ethics, 1993) p. 9.

[14] Weber, *"Personal Values and Moral Development,"* p. 459.

[15] Linda K. Trevino and Stuart A. Youngblood. "Bad Apples in Bad Barrels: A Causal Analysis of Ethical Decision-Making Behavior," *Journal of Applied Psychology*, 75, 1990, pp. 378-385.

[16] Lawrence Kohlberg, "Stages of Moral Development as a Basis for Moral Education," in C.M. Beck, B.S. Crittenden, and E.V. Sullivan (Eds.), *Moral Education: Interdisciplinary Approaches*, New York: Newman Press, 1971; and Anne Colby and Lawrence Kohlberg, *The Measurement of Moral Judgment, Vol. 1: Theoretical Foundations and Research Validations*, (Cambridge, MA: University Press, 1987).

[17] These titles are taken from David A. Whetton and Kim S. Cameron, *Developing Managerial Skills*, (New York: Harper Collins, 1991) p. 60.

[18] The more descriptive stage names are taken from Linda K. Trevino, "A Cultural Perspective on Changing and Developing Organizational Ethics," in *Research in Organizational Change and Development* (eds.) William A. Pasmore and Richard W. Woodman. (Greenwich, CT: JAI Press, 1990) pp. 195-230.

[19] Lawrence Kohlberg, *Essays in Moral Development, Vol. I: The Philosophy of Moral Development* (New York: Harper & Row, 1981); and Ronald Duska and Michael Whalen, *Moral Development* (New York: Paulist Press, 1975).

[20] Weber, *"Personal Values and Moral Reasoning,"* p. 454.

[21] Weber, *"Personal Values and Moral Reasoning,"* p. 441

[22] Kohlberg conducted the original research only on males, a common practice before researchers came to appreciate gender differences. Carol Gilligan argued that women take a more caring ethical stance, which is explained in the Follow-up section. In addition to gender bias, there were also questions about culture bias, the sequencing of the stages, etc.

[23] This case was originally prepared by Professor LaRue Tone Hosmer as a basis for class discussion. The names of all individuals and names and locations of all firms have been disguised. The case is copyrighted (1978) by the Regents of University of Michigan and is reprinted here with the author's permission.

[24]The first three ethical models are described in Cavanagh, *American Business Values*, pp. 139-145 and Gerald F. Cavanagh, Dennis J. Moberg, & Manuel Velasquez, "The Ethics of Organizational Politics," *Academy of Management Review*, Vol. 6 (3), 1981, pp. 363-374.

[25]Carol Gilligan, *In a Different Voice* (Cambridge: Harvard University Press, 1982).

[26]Adapted from Laura L. Nash, "Ethics Without the Sermon," *Harvard Business Review*, November-December 1981, pp. 79-90.

[27]Josephson, *Making Ethical Decisions*, p. 40.

[28]Sissela Bok, "Whistleblowing and Professional Responsibilities," in *Ethics Teaching in Higher Education*, ed. Daniel Callahan and Sissela Bok (New York: Plenum Press, 1980), pp. 277-95.

[29]"Business Ethics: Generating Trust in the 1990s and Beyond," New York: The Conference Board, 1994, p. 8.

Chapter

6

PERSONAL GROWTH, CAREER DEVELOPMENT, AND WORK STRESS

OBJECTIVES   When this chapter is completed, you should be able to:

A. Describe the characteristics of adult development.

B. Explain Levinson's concept of life structures.

C. List the different career anchors and their significance.

D. Describe the functions that mentors perform.

E. Identify trends in career management and planning.

F. Explain the transactional model of career stress.

G. Assess your current life-career situation and develop a plan for the future.

*Y*our New Employment Contract

Walter Kiechel III

Fellow voyagers into the brave new world, let us face facts: Restructuring has put the final kibosh on traditional notions of corporate loyalty, whether of employee to employer ("As long as I do the work, my job will be secure, right?") or employer to employee ("As long as we take good, paternalistic care of you, you won't leave, right?"). The question now before our much thinned ranks is just what will replace the old understanding. What can a manager rightfully expect of his company these days, or it of him?

Source: *Fortune*, July 6, 1987.

As some historians of scientific revolutions might put it, have I got an emerging paradigm for you. Corporations, particularly those that have been, as they say, leaned down, stoutly maintain that the New Employment Contract already exists. Its terms, in the short form: Hereinafter, the employee will assume full responsibility for his own career–for keeping his qualifications up to date, for getting himself moved to the next position at the right time, for salting away funds for retirement, and, most daunting of all, for achieving job satisfaction. The company, while making no promises, will endeavor to provide a conducive environment, economic exigencies permitting.

Everybody got that? Not quite. Preliminary reports from corporations attempting to install the new regime–AT&T, for example–indicate that there are complexities involved that both sides are only beginning to grasp. Some surprises: To make the arrangement work, the company may actually end up having to pay more attention to individual employees. Worse, the boss himself may have to learn new skills.

Herewith, an Office Hours guide to the new rules, first for perplexed employee, then for equally befuddled employer:

> *Mr. or Ms. Employee, congratulations on your new responsibility. To discharge same, you're going to have to engage in career planning. At a minimum, this entails figuring out what and where you are now, what and where you want to be, and how you're going to get there. For starters, what will it take to provide you career satisfaction? Possible answers include money, promotion, security, and inherently interesting work. "All of the above" is not necessarily an available option; you should at least assign priorities.*

Now wait a minute, comes the angry reply, isn't this all just a little too . . . selfish? Ah, my friend, to paraphrase the Wizard of Oz, movie version, you are the victim of disorganized, or at least outmoded thinking. Wilbert Sykes, a psychiatrist and chief executive of the TriSource Group, a New York City firm that counsels so-called high-performance individuals, explains: According to the old model, loyalty was a zero-sum game. Whatever attention you devoted to yourself was subtracted from that available to your employer. The new model, by comparison, is win-win. Said employer will benefit more when an employee operates out of decent and open-eyed self-regard.

Employees must be particularly open-eyed in assessing what they have to offer an employer. The experts at Career Development Team, a Manhattan firm brought in by the likes of AT&T and GE, observe that too often a person thinks of himself simply as his job title. No, no, you are an inventory of skills, experiences, and interests. The trick is finding a job that allows you to use that inventory, and maybe even add to it.

All right, you know what you want from a job and what you bring to it. With these in mind, consider your current position. Does it fill the bill? Could it, with a bit of tinkering, be made to? If, say, you were to take a broader view of what you're trying to accomplish for the company, and if this led you to take more initiative and apply a wider range of your talents to the job, might you not be more content with where you are right now? Career Development Team consultants report that most people in their program decide not that they want another job, but that they can take steps to be happier in the one they have. A middle-aged manager may find, for example, that he can use his hitherto smothered interest in teaching to help subordinates. In the trendy phrase of the new deal's proponents, it empowers employees.

The career planning exercise doesn't end here, though. Even if you're content with your job now, will you still be satisfied with it in five years? Will it even exist then? Are you doing it well enough to keep it? For answers, look first to your employer. As the experts genteelly put it, attempt to open a dialogue with your boss. Indeed, press him a bit; such info is critical to any serious responsibility-taking. If your efforts fail, try someone in human resources.

Also start chatting up your peers throughout the organization and the industry. Suggest topics of conversation: Where is the company headed? What are its fastest growing areas? If you do have to move on, but want to stay in the organization, that's where you should go, even if it entails retraining or stepping down a rung or two. The best spots, or at least the ones most likely to endure, are those where you can make an identifiable contribution to the bottom line.

You may in all responsibility conclude that to attain your career objectives, you will have to seek another employer. This is perfectly acceptable under the new rules. Indeed, if you're stalled, it's admirable. The experts offer lots of advice. In negotiating with a prospective employer, try to get points of agreement made explicit that would have been left implicit under the old rules, advises Paul Hirsch, a University of Chicago Business School professor whose forthcoming book is entitled *Pack Your Own Parachute*. Push to have your new job responsibilities, perks, and benefits spelled out, for example. It's still a rare manager who can command a full-fledged employment contract–an agreement, say for x years at y salary. Headhunter William Gould observes, however, that an executive in the $100,000-a-year-or-more range can reasonably ask that the letter offering the job guarantee one year's pay if he's fired within the first three years.

Since your responsibilities now include making sure that you have enough squirreled away for retirement, look carefully at the state of your benefits. Have you been with your present employer long enough to be vested in the pension plan? If you stand to lose benefits by changing employers, will your prospective new organization make you whole, as the phrase goes?

Finally, in leaving one job and going on to another, be prepared to grieve a little. As psychologist Harry Levinson notes, "All change is loss, and all loss must be mourned." If you don't mourn, TriSource President Douglas Lind adds, you won't be prepared to commit yourself to the new job.

Now, as to Mr. or Ms. Employer: Believe it or not, you have some new responsibilities, too. You smirk. Don't. The much proclaimed reason for introducing the new rules was all the change out there–global competition, takeovers, deregulation, new technologies–and the promise of more change to come. But as Robert Gilbreath, an Atlanta management consultant for Theodore Barry & Associates, notes, good people are your single most adaptive resource with which to meet that change. Ignore the new rules and you won't be able to keep the good people you have, or hire replacements.

First off, you're going to have to tell your employees more. No bleating about the highly confidential nature of the corporate strategy, please; you want them to plan their careers at the company, so you have to give them the dope to do it with. William Morin, chairman of Drake Beam Morin, a big outplacement firm, takes the principle a step further: "If you don't know what's going to happen, you've got to tell them that too."

You also have to ensure that each employee knows how he or she is doing. This often represents the most critical piece of information for someone mulling his career; under the new rules, to withhold it is unethical, and lousy. Quick question for the top brass: How many of your managers can sit down with an employee and give him an honest performance appraisal? Troubling follow-up questions: How many can act as career counselors, or as coaches? Remedial training may be required, as well as incentives–including, in some refractory cases, a swift kick in the executive downside–to take the new managerial responsibilities seriously.

To hold on to your better performers, under the new regime you may well have to do a better job of keeping pay up to market rates. As good career custodians, your folks increasingly will be out there in the world finding out what people with their inventory of qualifications can make. Nor can you buy them off with promises of future glories; you aren't making any promises, remember.

When a valued subordinate comes in to tell you he's going somewhere else, hold the hysterics about how deeply hurt you are, the cheap talk about how much the company has invested in him, or the animadversion on his character. If you want him to stay, match the offer or raise the ante. Otherwise, smile, shake El Responsible's hand, and wish him good luck. If you do it right, he just may come back someday.

Perhaps most revolutionary, if you're serious about the new rules, you will have to give your newly empowered employees the opportunity to do their jobs differently, more the way they think the work can best be done. But don't expect this to go down easily with your old-line, I-am-the-boss-and-I'll-tell-you-how-to-do-it-managers. Outplacement consultant Morin, who is writing a book on the new regime, observes, perhaps a bit tongue in cheek, "It's the same stuff we were talking about back in the early Sixties. Back then, though, we called it participatory management."

Premeeting Preparation

A. Read "Your New Employment Contract."

B. Read the entire chapter.

C. Complete the Life Goal Inventory.

D. What are the significant learning points from the readings?

Life Goal Inventory

1. The purpose of The Life Goal Inventory is to give you an outline for looking at your life goals in a more systematic way. Your concern here should be to describe as fully as possible your aims and goals in all areas of your life. Consider goals that are important to you, whether they are relatively easy or difficult to attain. Be honest with yourself. Having fun and taking life easy are just as legitimate life goals as being president. You will have a chance to rate the relative importance of your goals later. Now you should try to just discover *all* the things that are important to you. To help make your inventory complete, we have listed general goal areas on the following pages. They are:

- Career satisfaction
- Status and respect
- Personal relationships
- Leisure satisfactions
- Learning and education
- Spiritual growth and religion
- Material rewards and possessions

These categories are only a general guide; feel free to change or redefine them in the way that best suits your own life. The unlabeled area is for whatever goals that do not seem to fit into the other categories.

First fill in your own goals in the various sections of this inventory, making any redefinitions of the goal areas you feel necessary. Ignore for the time being the three columns on the right-hand side of each page. Directions for filling out these columns are on page 137.

CAREER SATISFACTION

General Description: Your goals for your future job or career, including specific positions you want to hold.

Individual Redefinition:

SPECIFIC GOALS	IMPORTANCE (H,M,L)	EASE OF ATTAINMENT (H,M,L)	CONFLICT WITH OTHER GOALS (YES OR NO)
1.			
2.			
3.			

STATUS AND RESPECT

General Description: To what groups do you want to belong? What are your goals in these groups? To what extent do you want to be respected by others? From whom do you want respect?

Individual Redefinition:

SPECIFIC GOALS	IMPORTANCE (H,M,L)	EASE OF ATTAINMENT (H,M,L)	CONFLICT WITH OTHER GOALS (YES OR NO)
1.			
2.			
3.			

PERSONAL RELATIONSHIPS

General Description: Goals in your relationships with your colleagues, parents, friends, people in general.

Individual Redefinition:

SPECIFIC GOALS	IMPORTANCE (H,M,L)	EASE OF ATTAINMENT (H,M,L)	CONFLICT WITH OTHER GOALS (YES OR NO)
1.			
2.			
3.			

LEISURE SATISFACTIONS

General Description: Goals for your leisure time and pleasure activities–hobbies, sports, vacations; and interests you want to develop.

Individual Redefinition:

SPECIFIC GOALS	IMPORTANCE (H,M,L)	EASE OF ATTAINMENT (H,M,L)	CONFLICT WITH OTHER GOALS (YES OR NO)
1.			
2.			
3.			

LEARNING AND EDUCATION

General Description: What would you like to know more about? What skills do you want to develop? What formal education goals do you have?

Individual Redefinition:

SPECIFIC GOALS	IMPORTANCE (H,M,L)	EASE OF ATTAINMENT (H,M,L)	CONFLICT WITH OTHER GOALS (YES OR NO)
1.			
2.			
3.			

SPIRITUAL GROWTH AND RELIGION

General Description: Goals for peace of mind, your search for meaning, your relation to the larger universe, religious service, devotional life.

Individual Redefinition:

SPECIFIC GOALS	IMPORTANCE (H.M.L)	EASE OF ATTAINMENT (H.M.L)	CONFLICT WITH OTHER GOALS (YES OR NO)
1.			
2.			
3.			

MATERIAL REWARDS AND POSSESSIONS

General Description: What level of wealth is important to you? What possessions do you want?

Individual Redefinition:

	IMPORTANCE (H,M,L)	EASE OF ATTAINMENT (H,M,L)	CONFLICT WITH OTHER GOALS (YES OR NO)
SPECIFIC GOALS			
1.			
2.			
3.			

OPEN

Definition:

SPECIFIC GOALS	IMPORTANCE (H,M,L)	EASE OF ATTAINMENT (H,M,L)	CONFLICT WITH OTHER GOALS (YES OR NO)
1.			
2.			
3.			

DIRECTIONS FOR RATING GOALS

2. *Goal importance:* Now that you have completed the inventory, go back and rate the importance of each goal according to the following scheme:

H (High) – Compared with my other goals, this goal is very important.

M (Medium) – This goal is moderately important.

L (Low) – A lot of other goals are more important than this one.

Ease of goal attainment: According to the following scheme, rate each goal on the probability that you will reach and/or maintain the satisfaction derived from it.

H (High) – Compared with my other goals, I could easily reach and maintain this goal.

M (Medium) – I could reach and maintain this goal with moderate difficulty.

L (Low) – It would be very difficult to reach this goal.

Goal priorities: Select the goals from the inventory that seem most important to you at this time. Do not choose more than eight. Rank order them in terms of their importance. (1 = High, 8 = Low)

1.

2.

3.

4.

5.

6.

7.

8.

3. *Anticipating conflicts:* One of the major deterrents to goal accomplishment is the existence of conflict between goals. The person who ignores the potential conflicts between job and family, for instance, will probably end up abandoning goals because of the "either/or" nature of many decisions.

The cross-impact matrix is one method of anticipating possible conflicts. List your goals on both axes of the matrix in order of priority (goal 1 is first on both horizontal and vertical axes). The next step is to estimate the potential impact of the vertical goal statements on the horizontal, using the following symbols:

(+) for a helpful impact ("working on goal 1 will help me with goal 3")

(-) for a hindering impact ("working on goal 2 will make it more difficult to accomplish goal 5")

(0) for no impact of any kind

The Cross-Impact Matrix

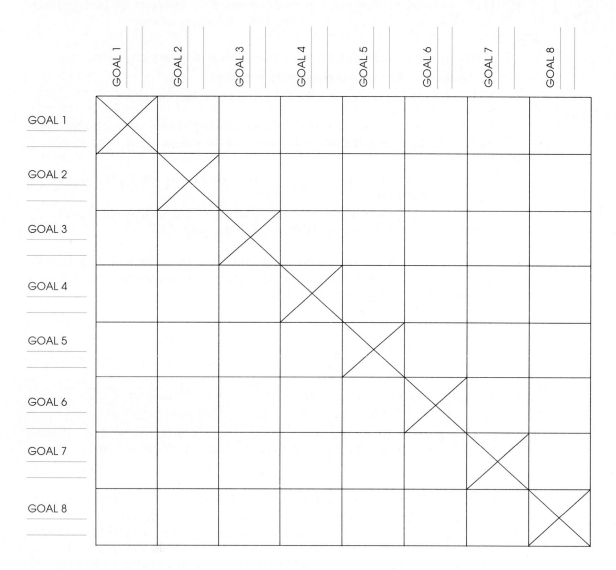

List conflicts in order of importance:

1.

2.

3.

4.

5.

Topic Introduction

One of managers' most important tasks concerns the personal growth and career development of their employees and themselves. To this end an understanding of the process of adult development helps us to realize that others are making the same journey through life and are experiencing similar challenges or hardships at certain points. In addition to providing insight into our personal experience, theories of adult development also help us to understand the developmental phases and challenges facing our colleagues at work.

Theorists generally agree upon the following characteristics of adult development.[1]

"**1.** Personality development throughout the life cycle occurs through a succession of relatively predictable phases.

2. Within each phase there is a cycle of intensity and quiescence–a disruption to the quasi-stationary equilibrium of one's former pattern of adaptation, leading to intense coping efforts and heightened activity (often involving significant changes in orientation and situational arrangements), followed by establishment of a new equilibrium.

3. The disequilibrium is generated, in each phase, by the emergence of a new focal conflict or dilemma created by new internal forces, environmental pressures and demands, or both.

4. One can cope with the focal conflict in defensive or developmental ways (i.e., the consequences may be positive or negative, growthful or regressive).

5. Growth involves the active engagement in a set of "developmental tasks" appropriate to resolving the focal conflicts and satisfying personal needs and social responsibilities."

Figure 6-1 portrays the stages three different researchers have identified. Gould[2] concentrates upon the inner subjective experiences of individuals forming each period; his view asserts that we grow up with a mythical idea of adulthood and that, as we age, we need to let go of the myth and accept ourselves and the reality of our lives. Levinson, on the other hand, describes the developmental tasks that must be mastered before one can successfully move on to the next stage of development.[3] Sheehy's stages are a synthesis of the preceding two.[4]

Levinson developed his theory of adult development from biographical interviews with forty men; he later expanded his research to include women. One of the gender differences Levinson found was that young men more easily formed a dream about what they would become than did young women. Another difference was that men were more likely to have a family and a career simultaneously if they so desired. In contrast, the women in the study made an either/or choice about family and career and had fewer cultural role models to guide them.

Other differences have been found between male and female development.[5] Male development focuses upon independence, self-sufficiency, and an emphasis upon work and career. In contrast, female development emphasizes interdependence and a struggle to combine relationships and accomplishments. Generally speaking, development for men signifies increased autonomy and separation from others so that they can concentrate fully on their work. Whereas men gain their primary identity from their work, women are more likely to define themselves in relation to others, so they focus more upon attachments than separation.

AGE	ROGER GOULD	GAIL SHEEHY	DANIEL LEVINSON
16	Escape from parental dominance	Pulling up roots	Leaving the family
18			
20	Substitute friends for family		
22		Provisional adulthood	
24	Aspiring builders of future		
26			Getting into the adult world
28			
30	What am I doing and why?	Age 30 transition	
32			
34			
36	A sense of urgency to make it	Major stabilization	Transition period
38			
40			Settling down and becoming one's own person
42		Midlife transition	
44	On terms with self as a stable personality		
46			
48			
50	Mellowing of friendships— valuing of emotions	Restabilization and flowering	
52			Midlife transition
54			
56			
58			Restabilization and entering into middle age
60			
			Another transition

Figure 6-1*   **Models of Adult Development**

Prepared by Dr. Eric Neilsen, Case Western Reserve University, Cleveland, Ohio.

Levinson and his colleagues[6] concluded that both men and women face a recurring developmental task at different stages of their lives. They must establish a "life structure," which refers to the pattern or design of a person's life, that is appropriate for each era of life. Life structures last approximately 6-8 years and constitute periods of stability. However, life structures become obsolete because no single structure could contain all aspects of the self or respond to the demands of different eras. For example, a man or woman who has been staying at home taking care of small children may no longer find this life fulfilling when the children become older and more independent. At this point, he or she may decide to return to work or develop an artistic side that was not possible given the previous child care demands. When a life structure no longer fits, people undergo a transition period that lasts 4-5 years. During this period, they reexamine their lives and eventually decide upon a new direction or life structure. The most widely recognized transition period is the mid-life crisis when people age 38-45 reevaluate what they have accomplished in comparison with their ambitions, and decide where they would like to place greater priority in the coming years. Transition periods are characterized by self-centeredness, introspection, and ambivalence about intimate relationships; during the periods of stability, people are more other-centered and dedicated to investing time and energy to key social relationships.[7]

The developmental challenge and dilemma facing people in their twenties (22 to 28) is to remain open enough to explore the world and stay committed enough to make something of themselves. Some people keep all their options open and make few commitments, while others marry young and/or invest in a serious career effort. Whatever options people build into their early adult life structure, they are likely to question these early decisions when they reach the age of 30 and have enough years of adult experience to reassess their dreams. Similar transitions occur around ages 40 and 50. It is during these transitions that people make changes in their lives and try to build a life structure that is more attuned to the person they have become and that allows them to place more priority on areas that are central to them and that they may have had to short-change in their earlier life structure. There is some evidence that people who do not resolve these issues during one transition will eventually be forced to confront them in a later transition.

Whether or not these life transitions turn into full-blown crises depends upon the individuals and their circumstances. For some people it's more a matter of reform than revolution. A crisis occurs when individuals find their current life structure intolerable but are not yet able to create a new one. How can managers help people through this process?

1. By expecting the phenomenon and seeing it as a normal stage of healthy adult development rather than a sign of instability.

2. By practicing active listening[8] or perhaps referring the individual to a professional counselor.

3. By being as flexible as possible regarding the changes the employee feels he or she needs to make.

Career Issues

In addition to a basic understanding of adult development, managers should also understand the key findings of career development research, which are presented in the following sections.

CAREER ANCHORS

In the beginning of one's career, the major psychological issue is figuring out a career direction that meets one's needs and interests. Schein developed one of the most helpful models for diagnosing career interests, which he termed "career anchors." As Schein states, "Certain motivational, attitudinal, and value syndromes formed early in the lives of individuals apparently function to guide and constrain their entire careers."[9] When people stray too far from these key interests, they serve as an anchor that pulls people back to their original interest. Different types of career anchors are 1) technical/functional competence, 2) managerial competence, 3) security and stability, 4) creativity/entrepreneurship, 5) autonomy and independence, 6) service, 7) pure challenge, and 8) life-style. These anchors, along with their characteristics and typical career paths appear in Figure 6-2.

Career Anchor	Characteristics	Typical Career Paths
1. Technical/functional competence	• Excited by work itself • Willing to forgo promotions • Dislikes management and corporate politics	• Research-oriented position • Functional department management job • Specialized consulting and project management
2. Managerial competence	• Likes to analyze and solve knotty business problems • Likes to influence and harness people to work together • Enjoys the exercise of power	• Vice-presidencies • Plant management and sales management • Large, prestigious firms
3. Security and stability	• Motivated by job security and long-term career with one firm • Dislikes travel and relocation • Tends to be conformist and compliant to the organization	• Government jobs • Small family-owned business • Large government-regulated industries
4. Creativity/entrepreneurship	• Enjoys launching own business • Restless; moves from project to project • Prefers small and up-and coming firms to well-established ones	• Entrepreneurial ventures • General management consulting
5. Autonomy and independence	• Desires freedom from organizational constraints • Wants to be on own and set own pace • Avoids large businesses and governmental agencies	• Academia • Writing and publishing • Small business proprietorships
6. Service	• Enjoys work that manifests own values • Having an impact, not money, is central • Expect management to share own values	• Consultants • Financial Analysists • Non-profit organizations • Socially responsible firms
7. Pure Challenge	• Prove self • Seeks ever greater challenges • Enjoys competition and winning	• Strategy/management consultants • Naval aviators
8. Life-style	• Integrates needs of individual, family and career • Desires flexibility (part-time work, sabbaticals, maternity/paternity leaves, etc.) • Common with dual career families	• Consultants • Socially progressive companies

Figure 6-2   **Career anchors**

Based upon the work of Edgar H. Schein, *Career Dynamics* (Reading, MA: Addison-Wesley, 1978), "Individuals and Careers," in Jay W. Lorsch (Ed.) *Handbook of Organizational Behavior*, (Englewood Cliffs: Prentice-Hall, 1987, pp. 155-171; and adapted by the authors and R. Dunham and J. Pierce, *Management* (Glenview, Ill: Scott, Foresman, 1989), p. 857.

BALANCING DUAL CAREERS

One of the most challenging aspects of modern life is balancing the demands of dual careers and raising a family. By 1995, the U.S. Department of Labor estimates that 81 percent of all marriages will be dual career couples. Although this results in higher income, stress is a common feature of many dual career marriages when couples run up against relocation issues, child-rearing responsibilities, and such demanding jobs that no one has time to take care of the home front. Working wives who still carry the major burden of household tasks experience a great deal of stress. Couples generally adopt one of the following strategies to manage dual careers.[10]

1. *Limiting the impact of family on work.* Parents can delay having children or sub-contract the child-rearing to day care centers or domestic help.
2. *Taking turns.* Spouses trade off career opportunities and child care at different times.
3. *Participating in joint ventures*—both spouses have the same career or different careers in the same organization.
4. *Choosing independent careers*—both partners pursue their careers as fully as possible and learn to cope with long separations or commuter marriages.
5. *Subordinating one career to the other.* One partner may leave the work force or accept a job that is less demanding so that the other partner can optimize his or her career opportunities.

All of these strategies have advantages and disadvantages. The disadvantages have to do with who pays the cost – the children, the marriage, or the partner who is sacrific-ing so that the other can maximize career opportunities, etc.? If couples can agree upon a strategy and align the rest of their lives accordingly, some of the stresses found in dual career marriages are more manageable.

MENTORING

A mentor is a senior person within the organization who assumes responsibility for a junior person. Mentors help socialize newcomers or junior members. Mentoring rela-tionships occur either naturally or as part of a company program to develop junior employees. AT&T Bell Laboratories assigns mentors to women and minority hires and "technical mentors" to help new employees master their jobs. Research has shown that having a mentor was one of the characteristics that differentiated female executives who made it to the top from those who did not.[11] A study of both men and women found that those who were extensively mentored received more promotions, were more highly paid, and reported higher job satisfaction than those who received little mentoring.[12]

What is it that mentors do for their protégés? Kram identified two functions: career and psychosocial functions.[13]

Career functions consist of:

1. *Sponsorship*—actively nominating a junior manager for promotions and desirable positions.
2. *Exposure and Visibility*—Matching the junior manager with senior executives who can provide opportunities and giving the junior person chances to demonstrate his or her ability (for example, letting the junior person make important presentations that are attended by key executives).

3. *Coaching*—Giving practical advice on how to accomplish objectives and achieve recognition.

4. *Protection*—Shielding a junior manager from potentially harmful situations or senior managers.

5. *Challenging Assignments*—Helping a junior manager develop necessary competencies through challenging job assignments and feedback.

The psychosocial functions are:

1. *Role modeling*—Giving a junior manager a pattern of values and behavior to imitate. (This is the most common of the psychosocial functions.)

2. *Acceptance and Confirmation* - Providing mutual support and encouragement.

3. *Counseling*—Helping a junior manager work out personal problems, thus enhancing his or her self-image.

4. *Friendship*—Engaging in mutually satisfying social interaction.

CAREER MANAGEMENT AND PLANNING

As shown in the opening vignette, there have been numerous changes in the area of career planning.[14] In career management[15] the necessity of tying strategic planning to human resource management has gained greater acceptance, along with the expectation that managers should be trained to provide career counseling to employees. Leaner management hierarchies and the baby boom cohort have made assessment of management potential and succession management more appealing. Flatter organizations have also focused attention on the need for nontraditional career paths that provide alternatives to promotion such as lateral or rotational moves, dual-career ladders, downward moves, and early retirement.

In terms of career management, there is more emphasis upon self-directed careers as a response to the economic recession. Midcareer choice points seem to be occurring earlier due to the bulge of baby boomers in managerial jobs and the need for balance in dual-career families. Today's employees are more likely to question and reject transfers and even promotions. Opting for self-initiated career plateauing (a cap to upward mobility) due to family considerations or lack of desire to assume the burdens of greater management responsibility is becoming more common although it is still seen as un-American in some companies. At the same time that some writers speak of a trend toward lowered career expectations and voluntary career plateauing, business magazines are full of articles about young MBAs who are single-mindedly pursuing careers at the cost of company loyalty and their private lives. Perhaps these seemingly contradictory trends represent life structures of different age groups as well as the diversity found in our society.

According to the Workforce 2000 report,[16] in the future people can expect to have ten or more different types of jobs and work for at least five different companies during their career. Since they will be responsible for managing their own career, they will need to invest in education and retraining and should plan on being continuous learners. This increasing pattern of career change has great implications for how organizations and educational systems manage career development. Although the career paths of many men and women may pass through two, three, or four distinct phases–each of which requires major new learning of knowledge, skills, and attitudes–education and training programs remain primarily oriented to the early stages of life. While some education and training programs are beginning to adapt more to service the market of older people who wish to make career changes or reenter the job market, other educational institutions still treat adult and continuing education as low-status, low-priority activities done half-heartedly in the name of community service. The provision of midcareer educational programs has been left primarily to private industry. This is, in some cases, as it should be, but all too often the implicit price for admission is a further commitment to the organization and to one's previous career path. Changing careers is made more difficult by selection criteria that demand previous experience in that career and tax laws that allow deductions for job-related training but not for changing jobs.

The failure to provide avenues for career change produces great losses in social productivity and in human satisfaction. Organizations do not benefit by locking their employees into careers that long ago ceased to be rewarding and challenging. Society loses the creativity and productivity of those who are barred from entry into new careers in midlife. This is particularly true for traditional females who devoted the first part of their adult lives to marriage and family. Although social norms are changing, entry into careers in midlife when family demands are less pressing still remains difficult for many women. Because of the glass ceiling which prevents both women and minorities from reaching senior positions, more and more women are forsaking the corporate career path to become entrepreneurs.

While organization and educational system changes are essential to ensure access to education and learning throughout our life span, it is equally important that men and women in our society gain a greater awareness and insight into the problems and possibilities of adult development. In earlier times, personal identity was maintained in relatively stable environments of expectation and demand. Once on a life path, personal choice was primarily a process of affirming expectations. People obtained a college degree or MBA, gained management experience, and worked their way up the organization. They were "managers" who also derived part of their identity from their employer ("I'm an IBMer."). However, in the last decade millions of managers have been fired, which is a real threat to one's sense of identity. In today's "future shock" world, environmental complexity and change have denied us the easy route to personal identity. Now, more than ever, identity is forged through personal choices. The challenge is to make the "right" choices and manage our careers wisely.

Goal setting is a critical aspect of personal growth and career development. The ability to conceptualize life goals and to imagine future alternatives for living can free us from the inertia of the past by providing future targets that serve as guides for planning and decision making. Research results from several areas–management, psychotherapy, and attitude change–all confirm the importance of goal setting for personal growth and achievement of one's goals.[17] The increased likelihood of change resulting from the setting and articulating of goals is illustrated, for example, by Kay, French, and Myer, who found that improvement needs among managers were accomplished only about one-fourth of the time when they were not translated into goals in performance appraisal interviews. When these needs were transformed into clearly stated goals, the likelihood of accomplishment increased to about two-thirds.[18] It is not enough just to think about how you would like to change. It is necessary to translate those visions into concrete goals.

The following exercises provide an opportunity to gain greater self-awareness and develop career planning skills.

My Life Line

Procedure for Group Meeting: The Life Line, Who Am I? and the Past Experience Inventory

SELF-ASSESSMENT AND LIFE PLANNING

(Time Allotted: 1 Hour, 15 Minutes)

Note: These are minimum times; you may want to take more time.

STEP 1. Form trios for life planning. (5 minutes) The total groups should divide into groups of three for the purpose of sharing the Life Goal Inventory prework and working together on the life planning activities that follow.

STEP 2. Life line exercise. (10 minutes) Each member of the trio should draw a line in the box on the preceding page to describe his or her view of his or her whole life from beginning to end.

Draw a line that corresponds to your own concept of your life line. Your life line can be any shape and can go in any direction. It could be a road, a river, a thread, a path, a graph line, or anything else you can imagine. Another way to think of it is as a route across a map. Place a mark on this line to show where you are right now. Discuss the feelings and thoughts you had in drawing the line and in placing your mark with others in your trio.

Notice that each life line has three distinct portions: your past, the place you are now (the "X"), and the portion of the line that represents your view of your future career path. These three portions represent the three basic perspectives for self-assessment and career planning.

The Past

Your unique experiences, acquired skills, and personal history.

- The past has happened; we cannot change it.
- Our past has a place in our current lives; we need to accept it and use it creatively but not be inhibited by it.
- The past, creatively used, yields insight about our unfulfilled potential.
- The past creates expectations for ourselves and can influence or limit the goals we set for the future.

The Present

The here-and-now of your life with all its joys and frustrations; your current priorities as they are embodied in your daily life situation and the way you spend your time.

- Individuals can consciously plan their lives by assessing themselves, their environments, and their resources in the present.
- You can choose where you would like to go on the basis of what satisfies you now.
- We need symmetry and wholeness in our lives. Often we make choices in the

present that lead to a lop-sided future (e.g., being too career oriented at the expense of a private life of fun, friends, and family).

- Each person has a reservoir of undeveloped potential in the present that suggests directions for future development.

The Future

Your fantasies, dreams, goals, hopes, and fears, as well as specific commitments and responsibilities you have undertaken.

- In large part, we can create our own future.
- Our future becomes self-determined to a large degree through the choices we make in the present.
- We can try to create the future by the process of:

By using the combination of these three perspectives on your life, it is possible to develop a more fulfilling life plan. By taking all three perspectives into account, a kind of triangulation occurs that identifies common themes from your past, your present, and your future.

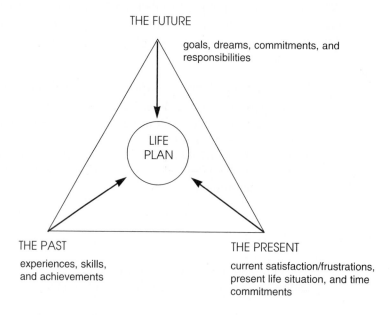

The next three exercises for your trio ask you to work together to assess yourselves from these three perspectives:

STEP 3.   Who am I *now*? (20 minutes)

- Write 10 separate short statements that answer the question, "Who am I?"

- Then rank these statements according to their importance to you.

- Discuss your answers and rankings with others in your trio.

RANK   WHO AM I?
ORDER

_____   **1.** I am _____

_____   **2.** I am _____

_____   **3.** I am _____

_____   **4.** I am _____

_____   **5.** I am _____

_____   **6.** I am _____

_____   **7.** I am _____

_____   **8.** I am _____

_____   **9.** I am _____

_____   **10.** I am _____

STEP 4.   Past experience inventory. (20 minutes) Complete the following questions and discuss them in your trio.

APPROXIMATE
DATES

1. Who have been the most influential people in your life, and in what way have they been influential?

_____   _____

_____   _____

_____   _____

2. What were the critical incidents (events) that made you who you are?

_____   _____

_____   _____

_____   _____

3. What have been the major interests in your past life?

_____ _____

_____ _____

_____ _____

4. What were your significant work experiences?

_____ _____

_____ _____

_____ _____

5. What were the most significant decisions in your life?

_____ _____

_____ _____

_____ _____

6. What role have family, societal, and gender expectations played in your life?

_____ _____

_____ _____

_____ _____

7. Where do you feel fully alive, excited, turned on? Under what conditions does this occur?*

_____ _____

_____ _____

_____ _____

8. Where do you feel dull, routine, turned off? What conditions produce that?

_____ _____

_____ _____

_____ _____

9. What are you really good at? What strengths do you have to build on?

_____ _____

_____ _____

_____ _____

10. What do you do poorly? What do you need to develop or correct?

_____ _____

_____ _____

_____ _____

11. What do you want to stop doing or do much less of?

_____   _____

_____   _____

_____   _____

12. What do you want to start doing or do much more of?

_____   _____

_____   _____

_____   _____

13. What do you want to learn or develop in myself?

_____   _____

_____   _____

_____   _____

* Questions 7–12 were adapted by Donald M. Wolfe from the work of Herbert Shepard.

STEP 5.   My future goals. (20 minutes) Share your Life Goal Inventory prework with each other. Your work on the previous exercise may suggest changes to you. If so, make them.

 Follow-Up

In cultures that believe in fate and destiny (e.g., Arab countries and Latin America), people are less proactive about planning their careers because "What will be will be." Cultures that believe people are the master of their own fate, (such as the United States) place more emphasis upon career planning. The disadvantage of this belief that humans control their destiny is that people blame themselves when they fail to achieve their career goals and ignore the role of luck. When economies undergo major restructuring, the careers of many people are disrupted through no fault of their own.

In recent years, the economy has been responsible for increased career-related stress. Obsolescence, mid-career transitions, job loss or threat of job loss, diminished upward mobility, forced early retirement, dual-career pressures,[19] increased workloads for the survivors in down-sized companies, and lack of balance between work and non-work are all sources of stress. _Stress is defined as the nonspecific response of an organism to demands that tax or exceed its resources._ There are three stages in the stress response: alarm, resistance, and finally, exhaustion.[20] Stress is positive when it motivates us to work harder and negative when the stress level is greater than our coping abilities. In the latter instance, stress interferes with our ability to perform at work and can result in illness.

The transactional model of career stress is portrayed in Figure 6-3. We begin with a _stressor situation_, which can be either external, such as a new job or job loss, or internal, like a mid-career transition resulting from a shift in personal values. Stressors take

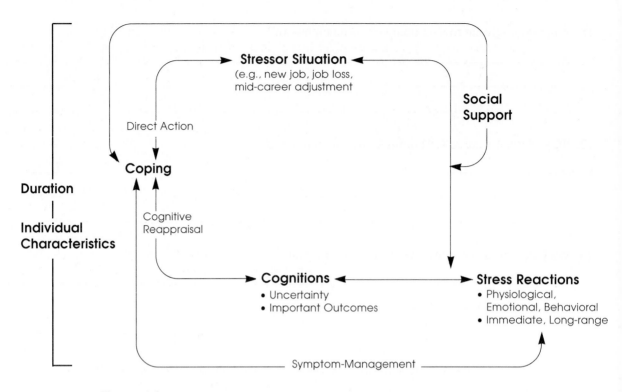

Figure 6-3.　**Transactional model of career stress**

the form of demands, constraints, or opportunities. A stressor does not result in a stress reaction unless it is first perceived as a stressor. What is stressful to one person may be merely challenging to another because people have different cognitions about stressor situations. *Cognitions* are "the individual's perceptions that the situation poses uncertainty about obtaining outcomes, and the perceived importance of those outcomes."[21] Thus, stress will be greater if people perceive that they have a lot at stake. For example, it is one thing to lose a job that you really enjoy with no other prospects in sight and no money in the bank. It is quite another to lose a job you dislike intensely when you have a sizable trust fund to fall back upon.

The next category in the model is *stress reactions*. These can be physiological (e.g., pulse rate, blood pressure), emotional (e.g., anxiety, irritability), or behavioral (e.g., loss of sleep, weight gain). There are both immediate (e.g., job dissatisfaction) and long-term stress reactions (e.g., illness or job change).

Coping is the means by which individuals and organizations manage external or internal demands that tax or exceed the individual's resources. Coping strategies focus on (1) changing the situation (direct action), (2) changing the way we think about the situation (cognitive reappraisal), or (3) focusing on the stress reaction (symptom management). Not all coping mechanisms that focus on symptom management are positive. For example, drinking and overeating are harmful whereas meditation and exercise are positive. Coping mechanisms are an attempt to establish some degree of control over the situation and prevent a stress reaction.

Social support is another factor that can prevent stress. It is defined as receiving information that tells people they are loved, respected, valued and part of a network of mutual obligations.[22] People who receive social support from their supervisors, coworkers, or families are somewhat buffered from the effects of stress.

The *duration* of the stressor situation also plays a role in this model. The longer the stressful situation lasts, the more likely that health problems will result. It is interesting that "daily hassles" may actually cause more stress than critical life events, such as divorce or the death of a loved one.[23] Stress is additive, which means that a seemingly innocuous stressor may be "the straw that breaks the camel's back" if the person has already been exposed to too many other stressors. This is another reason why the same stressful work event may impact individuals in different ways.

Individual characteristics also affect the stress process. For example, people who exhibit *Type A behavior who are quick to anger, mistrustful, and suspicious of other people* are more likely candidates for stress-related heart disease than both Type A personalities who are not hostile and people with Type B behavior.[24] The characteristics of Type A behavior are an obsession with achieving more and more in less and less time, inability to cope with leisure time, doing two or more things at once, impatience with the time it takes to make things happen, and constantly moving, walking and eating rapidly. Many workaholics exhibit this behavior, but only when it is accompanied by a hostile attitude is it harmful to the individual's health. Type B behavior is characterized by the absence of time urgency and impatience, no felt need to display or discuss achievements, and playing for fun and relaxation without an accompanying sense of guilt.

People with *external locus of control*, who believe that their lives are controlled by outside forces, also perceive situations to be more stressful than people who believe they control their own destiny. The latter condition is referred to as internal locus of control.[25]

Women and minorities in nontraditional careers, such as management, experience their own particular brand of work stress and career limitations like the glass ceiling. For example, African-American career stress is referred to as a "Black Tax" that results from 1) having to prove their competence by being workaholics, 2) mutual feelings of distrust between African-American executives, and 3) being involved with organizational policies that are not in the best interest of African Americans.[26]

Companies should be aware of the cost of excessive work stress, not only for minorities, but for all employees–decreased job satisfaction and performance, and increased absenteeism, alcohol and drug abuse, and illness.

 Learning Points

1. Adult development occurs in a succession of fairly predictable phases characterized by equilibrium and disequilibrium. The disequilibrium results from new psychological issues that arise from new internal forces and/or external demands or pressures.

2. Levinson's theory of adult development refers to life structures—the design or pattern of a person's life.

3. People go through both stable and transitional periods. During the latter, individuals reevaluate and re-create their life structures. Transitions occur about the ages 30, 40, and 50. If they are very turbulent, they are called crises.

4. Career anchors are motivational, attitudinal, and values syndromes formed early in life that function to guide and constrain people's careers.

5. The different career anchors are 1) technical/functional competence, 2) managerial competence, 3) security and stability, 4) creativity/entrepreneurship, 5) autonomy and independence, 6) service, 7) pure challenge, and 8) life-style.

6. The five strategies for managing dual careers are 1) limiting the impact of family on work, 2) taking turns, 3) participating in joint ventures, 4) choosing independent careers, and 5) subordinating one career to the other.

7. A mentor is a senior person within the organization who assumes responsibility for a junior person.

8. People who were extensively mentored received more promotions, were more highly paid, and reported higher job satisfaction than those who received little mentoring. Mentoring is especially helpful for women and minorities.

9. The career functions of mentoring are 1) sponsorship, 2) exposure and visibility, 3) coaching, 4) protection, and 5) challenging assignments.

10. The psychosocial functions of mentoring are 1) role modeling, 2) acceptance and confirmation, 3) counseling, and 4) friendship.

11. Current trends in career management include tying strategic planning to human resource management, training managers in career counseling, assessment of management potential, succession planning, and nontraditional career paths.

12. Current trends in career planning consist of self-directed careers, earlier mid-career status, more questioning/rejection of job moves and promotions, increased self-initiated career plateauing, and career planning as a mutual responsibility of the employee and organization resulting in greater employee need for information about company career opportunities.

13. People who set clearly stated career goals are more likely to achieve them.

14. Stress is defined as the nonspecific response of an organism to demands that tax or exceed its resources.

15. The transactional model of career stress consists of stressor situations, cognitions, and stress reactions. Social support and coping can prevent stress reactions. The stress process is also affected by the duration of the stressor and individual characteristics.

16. There are three types of coping mechanisms: direct action, cognitive reappraisal, and symptom management.

17. People who receive social support from their supervisors, coworkers, or families are somewhat buffered from the effects of stress.

18. Individual characteristics that are related to greater susceptibility to stress are hostile Type A behavior and external locus of control.

19. The cost of excessive work stress is decreased job satisfaction and performance, increased absenteeism, alcohol and drug abuse, and illness.

 for Managers

- Managers who sincerely try to help employees reach their career goals are usually rewarded with loyalty and commitment.
- Managers are more likely to provide effective counseling to employees if they themselves also receive it from their superiors. It has to be modeled for them.
- Organizations that evaluate their managers on their ability to develop employees will generally see more positive results in this area. It's not enough to state that career development is important; measuring and rewarding it provides a clearer message that career development is valued.
- Personal growth or change is not a steady progression but rather a series of fits and starts.
- Once again, managers need to recognize that employees will have unique career

goals and life situations. Too often managers who are single-mindedly pursuing a suite at the top find it difficult to value employees who are content to remain where they are. As long as employees perform their jobs well, lack of driving ambition should not be held against them.

- Managers need to bear in mind the different career stages of their employees. For example, a young "fast tracker" who may have many of the other skills needed for a managerial job may still be too involved in establishing his or her own career to mentor subordinates adequately. The best mentors are most likely to be found in the 40 to 60 age group because this coincides with a stage of adult development in which guiding the younger generation assumes greater importance.
- Ignore managers who drive their employees so hard that it is impossible for them to have a personal life usually have a higher degree of turnover.
- Take a careful look at workaholics. Sometimes working long hours is not a habit to admire but an indication of inefficient work habits and lack of social life outside of work. If this is the case, their need to socialize on the job may actually prevent other employees from getting their work done.
- Work schedules that change constantly do not allow employees to create a life outside of work. This is generally not healthy for an extended period. Most people need a balanced life to keep a perspective on problems and find a measure of contentment.
- Good time management skills can reduce stress.
- Make sure you are not a stress "carrier" who generates stress in subordinates by being disorganized, putting employees in double binds, making impossible demands, etc.

 # Personal Application Assignment

Eisenhower once said, "A plan is nothing; planning is everything." In career planning, too, the plan itself is not as valuable as the act of planning. Plans must give way to outside contingencies. But the process of planning–taking stock, devising objectives and possible means of reaching a goal, and then checking to see how one is faring and coming up with a new plan if necessary–is extremely valuable.

This assignment is "The Goal Achievement Plan and Achievement Progress Record." It is designed to help you create a plan for attaining a goal you select to work on in the immediate future. The steps in the plan are based on the factors that research has shown to be characteristic of successful goal achievers. Following these steps should help you improve your ability to achieve your goals.

A. From the Life Goal Inventory that you completed in the premeeting preparation, pick the goal you most want to work on in the *next six months*. In choosing this goal you should consider the following issues. (See the ratings you made of goals.)

   1. Importance of the goal

   2. Ease of attainment

   3. Whether the goal is in conflict with other goals

B. The goal you choose to work on may include two or three of the goals you listed in the inventory. The main thing is to be clear about the future state you are striving for. To do this, complete the following Goal Definition form.

Goal Definition

State as exactly as possible what goal you want to achieve *in the next six months*.

_____

_____

_____

_____

Now think about your goal in terms of the following questions.

How important is it that you achieve your goal?

_____

_____

_____

_____

What conflicts are there with other goals? How will you manage the conflicts?

_____

_____

_____

_____

How will you feel when you attain this goal? (Try to imagine yourself with the goal achieved. What are your feelings?)

_____

_____

_____

_____

How will you feel if you do not attain this goal? (Try to imagine again. What are your feelings?)

_____

_____

_____

_____

What do you think about your chances of succeeding? What will happen if you do succeed?

_____

_____

_____

_____

What will happen if you fail?

_____

_____

_____

_____

C. Now that you have defined your goal, the next step is to plan how to achieve it. There are four issues to be examined: two things that may prevent you from reaching your goal and things you and others can do to achieve your goal.

The questions on the accompanying Removing Obstacles and Planning Action form are designed to help you accomplish this.

Removing Obstacles and Planning Action

What personal shortcomings will keep me from achieving my goal?

1.

2.

3.

4.

What external obstacles will keep me from achieving my goal?

1.

2.

3.

4.

What can I do to eliminate or lessen the effect of any of these obstacles or shortcomings? (Note that you need not eliminate the block entirely. Anything you can do to lessen the force of the obstacle will start you moving toward your goal.)

OBSTACLE	WHAT I CAN DO ABOUT IT
_____	_____
_____	_____
_____	_____
_____	_____
_____	_____
_____	_____
_____	_____
_____	_____
_____	_____
_____	_____
_____	_____
_____	_____
_____	_____
_____	_____

What specific things can I do that will move me toward my goal?

1.

2.

3.

4.

5.

Circle the one that you are going to emphasize the most.

WHO CAN HELP ME ACHIEVE MY GOALS?	WHAT WILL I ASK OF THEM?
1. _____	_____
	_____
	_____
	_____
	_____
2. _____	_____
	_____
	_____
	_____
	_____
3. _____	_____
	_____
	_____
	_____
	_____
4. _____	_____
	_____
	_____
	_____
	_____
	_____

Progress Report

Now that you have made your plan, the next thing to do is to put it into effect. Figure out what steps you must take to reach your goal and how you will measure your progress. Plan out what you need to do each week and how long it will take to meet your goal. You may want to choose a partner who will help you monitor your progress. You can agree upon a contract that stipulates how often you will check in with each other and what kind of help you want from your partner.

[1]Donald M. Wolfe and David A. Kolb, "Career Development, Personal Growth, and Experiential Learning," *Reader*, 1991 edition, p. 147.

[2]Roger L. Gould, *Transformations* (New York: Simon and Schuster, 1979).

[3]Daniel J. Levinson, "A Conception of Adult Development," *American Psychologist*, Vol. 41, No. 1, January, 1986, pp. 3-13.

[4]Gail Sheehy, *Passages* (New York: Bantam Press, 1977).

[5]This section is taken from Joan V. Gallos, "Exploring Women's Development: Implications for Career Theory, Practice and Research." In Michael Arthur, Douglas T. Hall, and Barbara S. Lawrence (eds.) *Handbook of Career Theory* (Cambridge: Cambridge University Press, 1989), pp. 110-132.

[6]Daniel J. Levinson, in collaboration with C. N. Darrow, E. B. Klein, M. H. Levinson, and M. Braxton, *Seasons of a Man's Life* (New York: Ballantine, 1978), and ibid., 1986.

[7]Source: Daniel C. Feldman, "Career Stages and Life Stages: A Career-Development Perspective," The 1987 Annual: *Developing Human Resources*, (LaJolla, CA: University Associates, 1987), p.231.

[8]For more details on active listening, see Chapter 8, Interpersonal Communication, and Rogers and Farson's article entitled "Active Listening" in the Reader.

[9]Edgar Schein, *Career Dynamics: Matching Individual and Organizational Needs* (Reading, MA: Addison-Wesley, 1978), p. 133, and "Individuals and Career," in Jay W. Lorsch (Ed.) Handbook of *Organizational Behavior*, (Englewood Cliffs: Prentice-Hall, 1987), pp. 155-171.

[10]Edgar H. Schein, *Career Dynamics: Matching Individual and Organizational Needs* (Reading, MA: Addison-Wesley, 1978); and Lotte Bailyn, "Involvement and Accommodation in Technical Careers: An Inquiry into the Relation to Work at Mid-career." In John Van Maanen (Ed.), *Organizational Careers: Some New Perspectives* (New York: John Wiley, 1977).

[11]Ann M. Morrison, R.P. White, Ellen Van Velsor & the Center for Creative Leadership. *Breaking the Glass Ceiling: Can Women Reach the Top of America's Largest Corporations?* (Reading, MA: Addison-Wesley, 1987).

[12]George Dreher and Ronald A. Ash, "A Comparative Study of Mentoring among Men and Women in Managerial, Professional, and Technical Positions," *Journal of Applied Psychology*, October 1990, pp. 539-46.

[13]Kathy E. Kram, *Mentoring at Work: Developmental Relationships in Organizational Life* (Glenview, IL: Scott, Foresman, 1985), pp. 22-39.

[14] Michael B. Arthur, Douglas T. Hall, and Barbara S. Lawrence, *Handbook of Career Theory* (New York: Cambridge University Press, 1989).

[15]Douglas T. Hall, *Career Development in Organizations* (San Francisco: Jossey-Bass, 1986).

[16]William B. Johnston and Arnold E. Packer, *Workforce 2000: Work & Workers for the Twenty-First Century*. Hudson Institute, 1987 and William B. Johnston, "Global Workforce 2000: The New Labor Market." *Harvard Business Review*, March-April 1991, pp. 115-129.

[17]David A. Kolb and Richard E. Boyatzis, "Goal-Setting and Self-directed Behavior Change," *Reader,* 1984 edition.

[18]E. Kay, J. R. P. French, Jr., and H. H. Meyer, "A Study of the Performance Appraisal Interview" (Management Development and Employee Relations Services, General Electric Co., New York, 1962).

[19]Janina C. Latack, "Work, Stress, and Careers: A Preventive Approach to Maintaining Organizational Health," in Michael Arthur, Douglas T. Hall, and Barbara S. Lawrence (Eds.) *Handbook of Career Theory* (Cambridge: Cambridge University Press, 1989), p. 252.

[20]Hans Selye, *The Stress of Life* (New York: McGraw-Hill, 1956); and "The Stress Concept: Past, Present, and Future," in C. L. Cooper (ed.), *Stress Research: Issues for the 80's* (New York: Wiley, 1983).

[21]Latack, *Work Stress, and Careers*, p. 254.

[22]S. Cobb, "Social Support as a Moderator of Life Stress," *Psychosomatic Medicine*, 38, 1976, pp. 300-314.

[23]Richard S. Lazarus and Anita DeLongis, "Psychological Stress and Coping in Aging," *American Psychologist*, 38, 1983, pp. 245-254.

[24]Redford Williams, *The Trusting Heart: Great News about Type A Behavior* (New York: Times Books, 1989).

[25]Katherine R. Parks, "Locus of Control, Cognitive Appraisal and Coping in Stressful Episodes," *Journal of Personality and Social Psychology*, 46, p. 655-668.

[26]D. L. Ford, "Job-related Stress of the Minority Professional: An Exploratory Analysis and Suggestions for Future Research." In Terry A. Beehr and Rabi S. Bhagat (Eds.), *Human Stress and Cognition in Organizations* (New York: Wiley, 1985), pp. 287-324.

PART

2

CREATING EFFECTIVE WORK GROUPS

Chapter

INTERPERSONAL COMMUNICATION

OBJECTIVES By the end of this chapter, you should be able to:

A. Understand the model of communication.

B. List common sources of distortion.

C. Identify gender differences in communication.

D. Describe and identify the five response styles.

E. Explain how to create a climate that encourages nondefensive communication.

F. Recognize assertive communication and utilize I-statements.

G. Improve your active listening skills.

*D*o You Have What It Takes?

Kurt Sandholtz

Thumb through almost any high school yearbook, and among the homecoming queens and football stars you'll probably find a picture of some clean-cut kid with the caption "Most Likely to Succeed."

It's a curious designation.

On one level, no one takes it seriously. How can a bunch of high school seniors possibly select from their classmates the one destined to succeed? Succeed at what? On another level, everyone takes it seriously. However we define it, success is something we all pursue. And while the high school yearbook committee's pick is little more than a shot in the dark, researchers have spent years trying to pinpoint what makes a person "most likely to succeed."

Their efforts have produced reams of scientific and pseudo-scientific data. Perhaps the most comprehensive research to date comes from Stanford University and American Telephone & Telegraph Co. In separate long-term studies, research teams at these institutions have tracked managers from the college classroom to the executive suite. The basic question driving both inquiries was: Which characteristics of a student's background and personality are the best predictors of future business success, as measured by salary level and managerial rank 20 years after graduation?

Source: Reprinted from *Managing Your Career*, Fall 1987, p. 10 With permission of Dow Jones & Co., Inc.

The answers have been surprisingly consistent–and consistently surprising. "Some of the findings were totally unexpected," says Thomas Harrell, an emeritus professor of business and director of the Stanford study. "In retrospect, we shouldn't have been all that surprised. The results make a lot of sense."

Here, then, are summaries of key results from both studies. Like Prof. Harrell, you'll probably find much that stands to reason. But you may learn more from the surprises–those tidbits that prompt an "Aha!" or even a "No way!" Such reactions point to potential chinks in your armor.

COMMUNICATION SKILLS

"In our study, the single best question to predict high earnings was, "Do you like to make speeches?" says Prof. Harrell. "The correct answer, of course, is 'Yes'."

This is no startling revelation. Even our nation's chief executive is often referred to as "The Great Communicator." But like many executive traits, verbal ability is more important at the top than at the bottom. So in tailoring your college curriculum, look beyond the entry level; blowing off that "waste-of-time" writing course could come back to haunt you.

"The most sought-after skill, from the CEO on down is the ability to communicate with people," says John Callen, partner with executive recruiters Ward Howell International in New York. "The person who's comfortable with the press and public relations, who can make a speech on short notice–that person's always in demand."

INTERPERSONAL ABILITY

"The variable we found consistently related to management success was the personality trait of social extroversion or sociability," concludes one of Prof. Harrell's research papers.

That's academese for "successful executives like people." And because they like people, they're good at managing them. "Dale Carnegie had most of it right," says Prof. Harrell.

If this sounds patently obvious, then why do most business administration programs emphasize the analytical at the expense of the interpersonal? Good question, says Ann Howard, an industrial psychologist who directed the studies at AT&T.

"Research shows that administrative skills–planning, cost/benefit analysis, decision making–do get cultivated in business programs. Those are certainly functional skills," she says. "But when you're promoted into your first management job, it's unlikely you'll be doing much strategic planning." Instead, you'll be stuck with a bunch of people who you're supposed to supervise–a task few business schools teach you how to do, she says.

Meryl Lewis, a Boston University business professor, has noticed the same weakness in business school training. As part of a study entitled "The First Years Out," she asked more than 200 graduates of top M.B.A. programs, "What were your most and least valuable courses?" Response from graduating students was nearly unanimous. "They said they hated their O.B. (organizational behavior) classes," she says. When polled a year later, however, they'd done an about-face. "They said O.B. was among their most useful courses," says Prof. Lewis. "They were aware of a need for more of it than they got." In fact, organizational behavior was one of the few subjects the M.B.A.s were likely to brush up on, digging out old college notes and textbooks. "The bad rap that O.B gets is washed away by the first year on the job," she says.

If you distrust the research, take it from a seasoned executive recruiter. "There are lots of brilliant people who can't relate with others," says Robert LoPresto, a senior partner with Korn/Ferry International in Palo Alto, Calif. "We replace that kind of person every day."

Premeeting Preparation

A. Read "Do You Have What It Takes?"

B. Fill out the Communication Climate Inventory that follows.

C. Then answer these questions:

1. What communication skills would you like to learn or improve?

2. How do you plan on going about it? How can your learning group help you in this?

3. What are the significant learning points from the readings?

D. Read the Topic Introduction.

Communication Climate Inventory

James I. Costigan and Martha A. Schmeidler

The following statements relate to how your supervisor and you communicate on the job. There are no right or wrong answers. Respond honestly to the statement, using the following scale:

1. Strongly Agree
2. Agree
3. Uncertain
4. Disagree
5. Strongly Disagree

	Strongly Agree	Agree	Uncertain	Disagree	Strongly Disagree
1. My supervisor criticizes my work without allowing me to explain.	1	2	3	4	5
2. My supervisor allows me as much creativity as possible in my job.	1	2	3	4	5
3. My supervisor always judges the actions of his or her subordinates.	1	2	3	4	5
4. My supervisor allows flexibility on the job.	1	2	3	4	5
5. My supervisor criticizes my work in the presence of others.	1	2	3	4	5
6. My supervisor is willing to try new ideas and to accept other points of view.	1	2	3	4	5
7. My supervisor believes that he or she must control how I do my work.	1	2	3	4	5
8. My supervisor understands the problems that I encounter in my job.	1	2	3	4	5
9. My supervisor is always trying to change other people's attitudes and behaviors to suit his or her own.	1	2	3	4	5
10. My supervisor respects my feelings and values.	1	2	3	4	5
11. My supervisor always needs to be in charge of the situation.	1	2	3	4	5
12. My supervisor listens to my problems with interest.	1	2	3	4	5
13. My supervisor tries to manipulate subordinates to get what he or she wants or to make himself or herself look good.	1	2	3	4	5
14. My supervisor does not try to make me feel inferior.	1	2	3	4	5
15. I have to be careful when talking to my supervisor so that I will not be misinterpreted.	1	2	3	4	5
16. My supervisor participates in meetings with employees without projecting his or her higher status or power.	1	2	3	4	5
17. I seldom say what really is on my mind, because it might be twisted and distorted by my supervisor.	1	2	3	4	5
18. My supervisor treats me with respect.	1	2	3	4	5
19. My supervisor seldom becomes involved in employee conflicts.	1	2	3	4	5
20. My supervisor does not have hidden motives in dealing with me.	1	2	3	4	5
21. My supervisor is not interested in employee problems.	1	2	3	4	5

	Strongly Agree	Agree	Uncertain	Disagree	Strongly Disagree
22. I feel that I can be honest and straightforward with my supervisor.	1	2	3	4	5
23. My supervisor rarely offers moral support during a personal crisis.	1	2	3	4	5
24. I feel that I can express my opinions and ideas honestly to my supervisor.	1	2	3	4	5
25. My supervisor tries to make me feel inadequate.	1	2	3	4	5
26. My supervisor defines problems so that they can be understood but does not insist that his or her subordinates agree.	1	2	3	4	5
27. My supervisor makes it clear that he or she is in charge.	1	2	3	4	5
28. I feel free to talk to my supervisor.	1	2	3	4	5
29. My supervisor believes that if a job is to be done right, he or she must oversee it or do it.	1	2	3	4	5
30. My supervisor defines problems and makes his or her subordinates aware of them.	1	2	3	4	5
31. My supervisor cannot admit that he or she makes mistakes.	1	2	3	4	5
32. My supervisor tries to describe situations fairly without labeling them as good or bad.	1	2	3	4	5
33. My supervisor is dogmatic; it is useless for me to voice an opposing point of view.	1	2	3	4	5
34. My supervisor presents his or her feelings and perceptions without implying that a similar response is expected from me.	1	2	3	4	5
35. My supervisor thinks that he or she is always right.	1	2	3	4	5
36. My supervisor attempts to explain situations clearly and without personal bias.	1	2	3	4	5

Communication Climate Inventory
Scoring and Interpretation Sheet

Place the numbers that you assigned to each statement in the appropriate blanks. Now add them together to determine a subtotal for each climate descriptor. Place the subtotals in the proper blanks and add your scores. Place an X on the graph to indicate what your perception is of your organization or department's communication climate. Some descriptions of the terms follow. You may wish to discuss with others their own perceptions and interpretations.

PART I: DEFENSIVE SCORES

Evaluation

Question 1 _____

Question 3 _____

Question 5 _____

Subtotal _____

Neutrality

Question 19 _____

Question 21 _____

Question 23 _____

Subtotal _____

Control

Question 7 _____

Question 9 _____

Question 11 _____

Subtotal _____

Superiority

Question 25 _____

Question 27 _____

Question 29 _____

Subtotal _____

Strategy

Question 13 _____

Question 15 _____

Question 17 _____

Subtotal _____

Certainty

Question 31 _____

Question 33 _____

Question 35 _____

Subtotal _____

Subtotals for Defensive Scores

Evaluation	_____	Neutrality	_____
Control	_____	Superiority	_____
Strategy	_____	Certainty	_____

Total _____

18	25	30	35	40	45	50	55	60	65	70	75	80	85	90

Defensive   Defensive to Neutral   Neutral to Supportive   Supportive

PART II: SUPPORTIVE SCORES

Provisionalism

Question 2 _____

Question 4 _____

Question 6 _____

Subtotal _____

Spontaneity

Question 20 _____

Question 22 _____

Question 24 _____

Subtotal _____

Empathy

Question 8 _____

Question 10 _____

Question 12 _____

Subtotal _____

Problem Orientation

Question 26 _____

Question 28 _____

Question 30 _____

Subtotal _____

Equality

Question 14 _____

Question 16 _____

Question 18 _____

Subtotal _____

Description

Question 32 _____

Question 34 _____

Question 36 _____

Subtotal _____

Subtotals for Supportive Scores

Provisionalism _____

Empathy _____

Equality _____

Spontaneity _____

Problem Orientation _____

Description _____

Total _____

```
18   25   30   35   40   45   50   55   60   65   70   75   80   85   90
|  |  |  |  |  |  |  |  |  |  |  |  |  |  |  |  |  |  |  |  |  |  |
Supportive        Supportive to Neutral      Neutral to Defensive      Defensive
```

Topic Introduction

In a recent management development program after "listening" politely for 15 to 20 minutes to an exposition on the importance of interpersonal communications, one manager began grimacing and waving his hand actively and, even before being formally acknowledged, he blurted out, "I can't spend all of my time with this interpersonal communications stuff–there's work to be done!" True! There is work to be done, and for that very reason, effective interpersonal communications become crucial.

Let us examine a few examples.

Much of a manager's job centers on effective problem solving and decision making. The "goodness" of any decision can be assessed along two criteria.[1]   1) Is the decision logically sound (i.e., were all the appropriate and available facts brought to bear in a rational way)?   2) Do those who are affected by the decision and/or are responsible for implementing it accept the decision (i.e., are they committed to the decision)? The "right" decision from a logical viewpoint to which people feel uncommitted (i.e., drag their heels, "forget" to implement, or actively resist) is, indeed, not a particularly good decision at all.

Effective interpersonal communication is important in this regard in several ways. Thoughts, facts, and opinions that go unheard or are misunderstood may seriously reduce the logical soundness of the decision. Picture yourself in a meeting where your ideas and inputs seem to be ignored or not seriously considered by others. The *feelings* this would create in you could make it very hard for you to act committed to the decision–you feel left out ("they decided" versus "we decided").

Effective interpersonal communication is also very important in ensuring the acceptance of certain decisions in another way. Consider the situation in which it has been decided, for example, to install a new computerized record system. The decision makes sense from a logical viewpoint (i.e., the new system will be more efficient and productive). However, some people are concerned that they will have to develop new skills or that many jobs will be eliminated by the new system. If these feelings (irrational as they may or may not be) are not expressed, heard, and dealt with, the introduction of the new system may encounter several snags.

A similar set of dynamics has been uncovered with respect to the selling process. The buyer often appears to get cold feet just before the deal is to be completed. The seller had every rational reason to expect that things were going smoothly, but at the last minute, the sale is lost. The buyer usually gives the overt reason that the price is too high (in spite of the fact that the price seemed acceptable all along). Follow-up research in these situations has documented that the overt reason offered had little to do with losing the sale. Most often, the buyer had concerns or anxieties related to the personal consequences of the purchase (i.e., "If this machine will make my department as productive as you say, my boss will think I'm trying to build my empire and get his job!") Effective interpersonal communication skills are essential to building the trust necessary to bring out these concerns and deal with them effectively.

Spouses who claim that they have a communication problem, children who feel their parents "just don't understand them," bosses who cannot understand why their performance evaluations of subordinates seem to have no impact–the situations where effective interpersonal communication is important are infinite.

Mintzberg's ground-breaking study on the nature of managerial work identified communication as the most frequent and important of managerial activities.[2]

The manager's work is essentially that of communication and his (or her) tools are the five basic media–mail, telephone, unscheduled meetings, scheduled meetings, and tours. Managers clearly favor the three verbal media, many spending on the order of 80 percent of their time in verbal contact. Some managers, such as those of staff groups, spend relatively more time alone. But the greatest share of the time of almost all managers is spent in verbal communication.[3]

And even when managers are not trying to communicate, their actions (or lack thereof) are taken as messages. It's impossible to not communicate; rather the question for managers is, "Am I communicating effectively?" The definition of communication is *the process by which information is exchanged between a sender and receiver with the goal of achieving mutual understanding.*

To better understand this complex process of interpersonal communication, let's examine the basic model of communication

THE COMMUNICATION MODEL

The Greeks believed that the god Mercury plucked ideas from the brain of the speaker, impaled the ideas on the end of a spear, and plunged them into the listener's brain. Today most people think of communication as the following process:

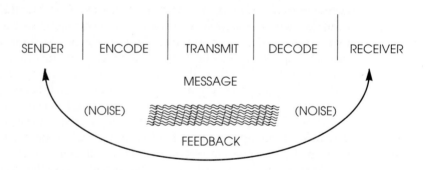

Very simply, senders think of what they want to convey to another person. The next step is to encode that message–to put it into verbal or nonverbal form and transmit it to the receiver. Receivers must then decode the message, that is, put it into a form that has meaning for them.

The potential for distortion in this process is very large. First, the way the sender encodes the message may not accurately reflect the message he or she wanted to transmit. "No, that's not what I meant," frequently accompanies communication attempts. Second, the form of transmitting the message may not succeed. For example, the new supervisor who tentatively touches upon an employee's habitual lateness may have failed to convey her displeasure with the employee's behavior and the consequences that lay in store.

Third, the way the receiver decodes the message is strongly related to the individual's background and personality. A feminist decodes a male boss' reference to "you girls" differently than a more traditional older woman. The recently hired low-level employee interprets a memo from the company president differently from a vice president. The most effective communicators are "receiver oriented" because they gear their messages to the receiver. They ask themselves, "If I were the receiver, how would this message strike me? How would I interpret it?"

Both encoding and decoding are heavily influenced by personal factors such as education, personality, socioeconomic level, family and child rearing, work history, culture, personal experience, and organizational role. It is a fact of communication that people perceive messages differently; thus, meaning lies in people, not in words. Chapter 8, Interpersonal Perception and Attribution, focuses more on the individualistic interpretations made in communication. The better one knows another person and understands their personal context, the easier it is to read their communications accurately.

Gender is another factor that influences how we encode and decode communication. According to Tannen[4], women are more concerned with maintaining the relationship with the person to whom they are speaking. They focus upon seeking and giving confirmation and support, and they try to gain consensus. Men are more concerned with status and trying to achieve or maintain the upper hand in a conversation. Whereas women try to create intimacy in conversations, men focus on establishing their independence.

Gender also affects the way we transmit messages and converse. Communication experts usually interpret gender differences in conversation as a reflection of power differences between men and women. For example, men and people with higher status speak more than women and people of lower status, invalidating a common stereotype that women are more talkative than men. Men are more likely to interrupt others who are talking, and women are interrupted more often than men. Men are more likely to control the topic and redefine what women say ("What you mean is..."). Some of the characteristics of female communication are attributed to their lower power status. For example, women are more likely than men to soften their statements by the use of *qualifiers* like "maybe, perhaps, sort of, I guess, kind of." When men use qualifiers, they are perceived as warm and polite; when women use qualifiers they are perceived as weak and unassertive. Women are also more likely to use *disclaimers* that weaken their position ("I'm not really sure about this, but..." "This probably doesn't mean anything, but..."). Because women are socialized to be more *polite* than males, they tend to phrase orders more politely ("Please finish the report" as opposed to "Get that report done"). Women are also more likely to frame orders as questions ("Can you meet me at my office?" rather than "Come to my office"). Compared to men, women use more *intensifiers*, adverbs that exaggerate the strength of an expression ("I am so-o-o-o hungry," "It was a *very*, very productive meeting"). As a result, female speech is sometimes perceived as overemotional in the workplace.[5]

Another likely source of distortion in the communication process is "noise," which is defined as interference with the intended message. There are three types of noise that prevent effective listening: 1) environmental (hot rooms, lawnmowers, etc.); 2) physiological (headaches or hunger pangs); and 3) emotional (worry, fear, anxiety). Emotional states create noise in the following manner: the employee who arrives late for an 8:30 meeting because of a domestic skirmish is unlikely to capture all the messages coming his or her way.

Because the communication process is fraught with potential for distortion, the feedback part of the model is crucial. In this case, feedback refers to the receiver's attempts to ensure that the message he or she decoded is what the sender really meant to convey. Asking for clarification and paraphrasing the sender's words ("Let me see if I have understood you correctly. Do you mean...?") are feedback methods. Senders can also check to see if their message got across. Managers often ask employees to paraphrase instructions to see if they are clear. The purpose of communication is *mutual understanding*. Unless we check with people, we may mistakenly assume that communication occurred when it did not.

The normal result of an attempt to communicate is a partial misunderstanding because of the uniqueness of the sender and receiver. Asking for clarification in the communication process is similar to the renegotiation of expectations in the pinch model (Chapter 1). Feedback is a way to avoid communication failures. When communication does break down, people often waste time and energy figuring out who is at fault, provoking a defensive reaction that further inhibits mutual understanding. However, if we accept misunderstandings as a basic reality of communication, we can stop looking for blame and start seeking better ways to communicate. A more effective response to breakdowns is, "How can we arrive at a level of mutual understanding that will allow us to accomplish our objectives?" and "How can we prevent a breakdown like this from happening again?"

Defensiveness is one of the most common barriers to good communication. Once people become defensive, they have difficulty hearing the sender's message because they are too caught up in protecting or justifying themselves. Defensiveness is usually caused by the sender's poor communication skills or by low self-concept of the receiver. The following section shows the relationship between different responding styles and defensiveness.

RESPONDING STYLES

A communication study revealed that 80 percent of all responses fell into five categories:

1. *Evaluative.* "What a great report!" "That idea will never work." An evaluative response indicates that the listener has made a judgment of the relative goodness, appropriateness, effectiveness, or rightness of the speaker's statement or problem. With this type of response, the listener implies what the sender should do.

2. *Interpretive.* "You're just saying that because you lost the account." The interpretive response indicates that the listener's intent is to teach, to tell the sender what his or her statement or problem really means, and how the sender really feels about the situation. With this type of response, the listener implies what the sender should think.

3. *Supportive.* "Don't worry, it'll work out." A supportive response indicates that the listener's intent is to reassure, to pacify, and to reduce the sender's intensity of feeling. The listener in some way implies that the sender need not feel as he or she does.

4. *Probing.* "Why do you think you're going to be fired?" A response that indicates the listener's intent is to seek further information, provoke further discussion along a certain line, and question the sender. With this response, a listener implies that the sender needs to develop or discuss a point further.

5. *Understanding.* So, you think your job's on the line and you're pretty upset about it?" An understanding response indicates that the listener's intent is only to ask the sender whether the listener correctly understands what the sender is saying, how the sender feels about the problem, and how the sender sees the problem. With this response, the listener implies nothing but concern that the sender's message is accurately received.

Our natural tendency as listeners is to evaluate and judge what others say to us. The most common responses are evaluative, but they are not always the most effective type of response to employ. Groups seeking creative solutions or resolution to a conflict are two examples of situations in which evaluative responses are clearly counterproductive.

Responses to messages communicate not only words but also a message about the relationship between the two people. By evaluating others, we place ourselves in a one-up position. The same is true when we interpret what others have said or try to pacify them and, even to some degree, when we use probing responses because they imply that the sender has not thought everything through. If our responses convey that we see ourselves in a one-up position with the sender, defensiveness results. Only the understanding response communicates that the listener has positioned himself or herself on the same level as the speaker. This is the type of response that is used in active listening, which is explained in the next section. It is not appropriate for all situations; none of the responses described are. No response style can be said to be innately good or bad, but there are times when a certain type of response would be more appropriate or effective than another. A good communicator is aware of the type of response that is called for in each situation.

Carl Rogers, the famous psychologist, found that defensive communication in therapy sessions could be avoided by being descriptive rather than evaluative and by assuming an egalitarian rather than a superior stance. Gibb contributed four more ways to avoid provoking defensive communication: 1) assuming a problem-solving orientation rather than trying to control the situation, 2) being spontaneous rather than strategic, 3) showing empathy rather than neutrality, and 4) being provisional rather than certain.[6]

An example of being certain rather than provisional is the manager who tears into employees when an error has been made before he or she has ascertained the facts of the situation. It's hard to repair the supervisor-employee relationship when this occurs, because it signifies a lack of trust and respect for the employee and an unwillingness to give the employee the benefit of the doubt. The Communication Climate Inventory you filled out as part of the premeeting preparation measures the behaviors that create defensive and non-defensive climates.

ASSERTIVENESS

Communication that is perceived as overly aggressive can also provoke a defensive reaction. An assertive style, neither too aggressive nor too passive, is most likely to produce the desired results when we need to stand up for ourselves, express honest feelings, or exercise our rights. Assertiveness is the ability to communicate clearly and directly what you need or want from another person in a way that does not deny or infringe upon the other's rights. New supervisors often have difficulty finding the right balance in the non-assertive-assertive-aggressive continuum. Figure 7-1 provides a helpful description of the differences among these three styles. One characteristic of an assertive style is the use of I-statements, which are described in the following paragraph.

An "I-statement" is a feedback format, designed to produce dialogue rather than defensiveness. I-statements have three components: 1) a specific and non-blaming description of the behavior exhibited by the other person, 2) the concrete effects of that behavior, and 3) the speaker's feelings about the behavior. Please look at the following examples of I-statements.

BEHAVIOR	EFFECTS	FEELINGS
When you come late to our project meetings	we have to use valuable time bringing you up to date, and others end up doing your share of the work,	and I resent that.
When you constantly interrupt me	I lose my train of thought and don't get to make my point,	and that makes me angry.

I-statements differ from "you-statements," such as "You are lazy and irresponsible," "You never pull your weight around here," or "You're rude and inconsiderate." More often than not, you-statements provoke a defensive response and an argument. I-statements are more likely to encourage an open dialogue because they are descriptive rather than evaluative, and they focus upon communicating the speaker's feelings and needs to the other person. In some cases, simply becoming aware of the effects of one's behavior and the feelings it provokes is enough to make people change negative behaviors.

Figure 7-1 A Comparison of Nonassertive, Assertive, and Aggressive Communication

	Nonassertive (No Influence)	Assertive (Positive Influence)	Aggressive (Negative Influence)
Verbal	Apologetic words. Veiled meanings. Hedging; failure to come to the point. Rambling; disconnected. At a loss for words. Failure to say what you really mean. Qualifying statements with "I mean," "you know."	Statement of wants. Honest statement of feelings. Objective works. Direct statements, which say what you mean. "I" statements.	"Loaded" words. Accusations. Descriptive, subjective terms. Imperious, superior words. "You" statements that blame or label.
Nonverbal General demeanor	Actions instead of words, hoping someone will guess what you want. Looking as if you don't mean what you say.	Attentive listening behavior. Generally assured manner, communicating caring and strength.	Exaggerated show of strength. Flippant, sarcastic style. Air of superiority.
Voice	Weak, hesitant, soft, sometimes wavering.	Firm, warm, well modulated, relaxed.	Tensed, shrill, loud, shaky; cold, "deadly quiet," demanding; superior, authoritarian.
Eyes	Averted, downcast, teary, pleading.	Open, frank, direct. Eye contact, but not staring.	Expressionless, narrowed, cold, staring; not really "seeing' others.
Stance and posture	Leaning for support, stooped, excessive head nodding.	Well balanced, straight on, erect, relaxed.	Hands on hips, feet apart. Stiff, rigid. Rude, imperious.
Hands	Fidgety, fluttery, clammy.	Relaxed motions.	Clenched. Abrupt gestures, fingerpointing, fist pounding.

THE WHAT (CONTENT) AND HOW (PROCESS)
OF COMMUNICATION

The content of what we communicate relates primarily to thoughts and/or feelings. *Thoughts* are the products of our minds. We imagine, muse about, remember, or reflect upon our thoughts. We experience thoughts as perceptions, ideas, reasons, rationales. We have thoughts about what we see, hear, touch, smell, and feel. *Feelings*, on the other hand, are the emotional reactions we have inside ourselves to our own or others thoughts, actions, and feelings. They are the "charge" or affect part of interpersonal communications.

Generally speaking, our facility to express, hear, and work with thoughts is much greater than our facility with feelings. What is rational, concrete, objective, and quantifiable seems easier and safer than emotions. Feelings are considered "touchy," "too personal," and something "we don't talk about, especially in business." Yet, feelings are the way we personalize our thoughts, ideas, and reactions. We can "make believe" we have no feelings about a given situation (disassociate our feelings from our thoughts) for a while. In the long run, such a strategy makes it difficult to communicate our thoughts clearly (it takes a lot of energy to communicate a thought dispassionately when you feel passionate!) and is not terribly good for personal health (stress, etc.).

Thoughts and feelings are clearly intertwined and the ability to differentiate between the two is an important communications skill. When we refer to the process of communication, the focus shifts from *what* (thoughts and feelings) to *how*–verbal and/or nonverbal. Many of our thoughts and our feelings are expressed via the words or phrases we speak. The words we express may be very concrete and direct, or they may be inferential and vague. This includes the tone, inflections, emphasis, and so on that we put on the words.

Much important communication is expressed via non-verbal means. A recent article on this topic concluded, "in spite of human garrulousness, perhaps as little as 20% of the communication among people is verbal....While people meander the earth through thickets of verbiage (theirs and others), many, perhaps most, do pay more attention to wordless signals and are more likely to be influenced and governed by non-verbal messages."[7] Generally speaking, our non-verbal signals relate to the feeling level of what (the content) is being communicated. And even when words are used, more meaning is taken from non-verbal signals. Mehrabian and Weiner found that words account for only 7 percent of the meaning we make out of communications; 55 percent of the meaning comes from facial expressions and posture, while 38 percent comes from vocal intonational and inflection.[8] Obviously, managers who continue doing paperwork while their employees are trying to talk to them are severely handicapping the communication process.

A second critical skill in enhancing the effectiveness of our interpersonal communications involves the concept of *congruence*. The verbal and non-verbal signals we send all need to be congruent with the thoughts and/or feelings we are experiencing inside ourselves and consistent with one another, so our verbal signals do not communicate a different message from our non-verbal signals (like the classic example of people who "say" verbally they are not angry while their face turns beet red and they are pounding on the table).

ACTIVE LISTENING: THE DYNAMIC SKILL IN INTERPERSONAL COMMUNICATIONS

Before we talk about specifics, you may find yourself wondering, "How can *active listening* improve interpersonal communications?" The key lies in the word "active." We are *not* referring to sitting quietly like a bump on a log just waiting patiently for the other person to finish (although frequent interruptions do hurt the communication process), rather, we are talking about taking *personal responsibility* to ensure that the messages sent are accurately decoded, and, if any distortions are uncovered, they are clarified before proceeding with the conversation.

We have a physiological excuse for being less than excellent listeners. The rate of speech is 100-150 words per minute, whereas our brains are capable of thinking at a rate of 400-500 words per minute. People often use this slack time to daydream, to judge what the sender is saying, or to prepare what they want to say next. In contrast, active listeners use this slack time to concentrate fully on the sender's message. Active listening involves a greater level of attending to the speaker.

The skills of active listening are demanding, but they can be learned using the guidelines in the paragraphs that follow. Some of the behaviors suggested may seem awkward and forced at first, but with practice, they will feel more natural. It is difficult to respond with patience, understanding, and empathy when the other person is expressing ideas that strike you as illogical, self-deceiving, or even morally wrong. However, the behaviors suggested will, if practiced faithfully, generate attitudes of tolerance and understanding that will make empathy and non-evaluative acceptance of the other person come more easily.

Being Nonevaluative

Active listening includes a variety of verbal and non-verbal behaviors that communicate to the speaker that he or she is heard and understood, that the feelings that underlie the words are appreciated and accepted, that regardless of what the individual says or thinks or feels, he or she is accepted as a person by the listener. The object is to communicate that whatever the qualities of the ideas, events, attitudes, and values of the person who is talking, the listener does not evaluate the person or his or her ideas or feelings. The listener accepts the person for what he or she is without making judgements of right or wrong, good or bad, logical or illogical.

Paraphrasing the Manifest or Presented Content (Thoughts and/or Feelings)

When we paraphrase, we put what the speaker has said in our own words and repeat it back to the speaker to test whether we have understood correctly. These phrases are used in paraphrasing.

"As I understand it, what you're saying is..."
"Do you mean that..."
"So your feeling is that..."

The key to paraphrasing is that one has to listen intently to what the other is saying. If we spend the time when the other is talking, thinking of what we are going to say next, or making mental evaluations and critical comments, we are likely not to hear enough of it to paraphrase it accurately.

The emphasis at this level is the *manifest or presented* content, that which is explicitly communicated verbally and/or nonverbally. The more indirect the content, the more important are the next two active listening skills.

Reflecting the Implications

This requires going a bit beyond the manifest content of what the other is saying, and indicating to the speaker your appreciation of where the content is leading. It may take the form of building on or extending the ideas of the speaker, using such phrases as

"I guess if you did that, you'd then be in a position to..."
"So that might lead to a situation in which..."
"Would that mean that...?"
"Are you suggesting that we might...?"
"Would that help with the problem of ...?"

It is important in reflecting the implications to leave the speaker in control of the discussion. When this technique is used to change the direction of the speaker's thinking or to show how much more clever the listener is by suggesting ideas the speaker has not thought of, it ceases to build trust and becomes a kind of skillful one-upmanship. When, however, this technique is genuinely used to help the speaker, it communicates very strongly that the listener has really heard and understood the drift of his or her thinking.

Reflecting the Underlying Feelings

This technique goes still farther beyond the overt feelings content of what is said and brings into the open some of the underlying feelings, attitudes, beliefs, or values that may be influencing the speaker to talk in this way. One tries to emphasize, to put oneself in the place of the speaker, to experience how it must feel to be in his or her situation. Then the listener *tentatively* expresses the feelings, using such phrases as

"I suppose that must make you rather anxious."
"If that happened to me, I'd be rather upset."
*"Times when I've been in that sort of situation, I've really felt
    I could use some help."*
"If I achieved that, I think I'd feel rather proud of myself."
"That must have been rather satisfying."

In reflecting the underlying feelings, delicacy is required so as not to overexpose the speaker or press him or her to admit to more than he or she would like to reveal. It is also important to avoid suggesting to the speaker that the feeling you reflect back is what he or she ought to feel in such a situation. This would tend to make the speaker feel evaluated, when what you are trying to do is to communicate acceptance of the underlying feelings. Often acceptance is communicated more by the manner and tone of the listener than by the words used.

Inviting Further Contributions

When one hasn't heard or understood enough yet to follow up with indications of understanding, empathy, and acceptance, one can at least communicate interest in hearing more. Phrases such as the following are useful.

"Tell me a bit more about that."
"How did you feel when...?"
"Help me understand..."
"What happened then?"

This differs from the probing response style described earlier because these questions are motivated solely by a desire to clearly understand what the speaker is trying to communicate. Specific requests for information may constitute a unilateral demand for openness on the part of the speaker. To maintain balance, questions should not be used exclusively, but should be followed after a bit by rephrasing or reflecting. And, generally, open-ended questions create a more supportive trusting climate than do pointed questions fired in machine-gunlike fashion.

Using Non-verbal Listening Responses[9]

Active listening is often communicated as much by one's posture and non-verbal movements as it is by what one says. The responses communicate interest and understanding: eye contact, body posture, leaning toward the speaker, head nodding, and receptive signals such as "um-hum."

Active listening skills, implemented in a climate of genuine concern and acceptance, help both parties in an interpersonal exchange understand, as fully as possible, the relevant content–facts and feelings–floating around on top and underneath the table.

Procedure for Group Meeting:
Active Listening Exercise

ACTIVE LISTENING: THE DYNAMIC SKILL
IN INTERPERSONAL COMMUNICATIONS

STEP 1.   In this exercise, everyone should have an opportunity to be an expresser, active listener, and observer who performs the following roles.

1. An *Expresser* gets a chance to enhance his or her ability to express thought and feelings in a congruent clear manner.

2. An *Active Listener* practices listening and paraphrases what the expresser states. It is particularly critical that the active listener resists the temptation to give advice or try to solve the problem for the expresser.

3. Two *Observers* watch the interaction silently, use the observer sheet on page 184 and provide feedback afterward. Each participant should have the opportunity to play each of the three roles. Participants can either choose a current topic that is controversial or one of the scenarios described on the following pages.

For each scenario there will be 1) a stage setting statement, 2) a scripted set of *words* to start the interaction, and 3) a suggested set of feeling states. The scenarios are listed from easy to hard as determined by the range and intensity of feelings associated with the scenario. Here's an example.

Setting the stage: You are speaking with an outside consultant, brought in by your boss. The consultant has just delivered a copy of his or her final report.

Script: I want to know why I wasn't consulted on that report! You were researching my territory and the decision will impact my people.

Suggested feeling states: bothered, insulted, left out, angry.

The roles needed in this scenario would be:

```
                          ( Observer )


( Consultant )                              ( You )


The Active                                  The
Listener            ( Observer )            Espresser
```

- "You" would communicate the first line as scripted, for example, "I want to know why...." In so doing, you would try to express some or all of the suggested feeling states (insulted, left out, etc.). "Consultant" would practice the *active listening* skills described in the introduction. "Observers" would watch the interaction carefully.

- As the "Consultant" (in the scenario) actively listens, "you" would carry on and add to the conversation in a manner consistent with the thought and feelings reflected in the original scripted opening. Carry on the communication at least five minutes.

Your first task is to read over the suggested scenarios and pick a scenario that, as the expresser (not the active listener),

a. Seems *real* to you (i.e., you have been or could imagine yourself actually being in that situation).

b. Involves some suggested feeling states that you would like to practice expressing that will stretch you but not immobilize you.

While this is meant to be a play-acting situation, it is also intended to be a serious opportunity to develop your interpersonal communication skills as *both* expressers and active listeners.

STEP 2.   Role plays. (10-15 minutes each round) Form groups of four. Each role play should take 10 to 15 minutes and consist of:

a. 5 to 8 minutes conducting the role-play scenario.

b. 8 to 10 minutes of feedback discussion initiated by the observers and then expanded by the expresser and the active listener.

During the feedback discussion, people should try to link insights gained from playing the different roles. For example, as an expresser, I *may* find out that I am more likely to give off mixed or confusing messages around high-intensity negative feelings than anything else. As the active listener, I *may* find that I am less likely to hear and pick up on high-intensity positive feelings.
Repeat this cycle until everyone has had an opportunity to play each role. If time permits, steps 1 and 2 can be repeated.

Suggested Scenarios

1. *Setting the stage:* You are speaking with an outside consultant, brought in by your boss. The consultant has just delivered a copy of his or her final report.

   Script: I want to know why I wasn't consulted on that report! You were researching my territory and the decision will impact on my people.

   Suggested feeling states: bothered, insulted, left out, angry.

2. *Setting the stage:* Linda and a colleague are talking in Linda's office. Linda is about to tell her colleague about an interaction she had with Ted, corporate vice president.

Script: After the meeting, I was walking down the hall and Ted stopped me and said, "Linda, you did a really great job on that account!" (smiling) I thought so too!

Suggested feeling states: proud, happy, contented, a sense of accomplishment.

3. *Setting the stage:* A subordinate is reporting to the boss on the status of his or her (the subordinate's) group. She or he knows, that in the boss' opinion, the group just has not been pulling its fair weight of late.

Script: We finally had a breakthrough in that contract. After all the hours I spent researching the market, I finally got an idea that he liked (longish sigh). For a while I thought that the group would lose another one.

Suggested feeling states: relieved, good, accomplished, productive, uncertain, scared.

4. *Setting the stage:* You are a secretary whose boss feels that you have more promise and can utilize your talents better and move ahead. You are about to speak to your boss.

Script: Last week you mentioned that I could read those articles and compose an annotated bibliography. I know that you want to make my job more interesting. Maybe you even think that I'm bored. But, really, I just don't want to be challenged any more. I guess that I like things as they are.

Suggested feeling states: embarrassed, scared, resentful, frustrated.

5. *Setting the stage:* Charlie has just been offered a middle management position of considerable prestige. He is talking to his boss about it.

Script: Frankly, I'm just not sure whether or not to accept the promotion. I should be overjoyed with the opportunity. It's a chance to influence some policy. Most people around here don't understand why I haven't left already. But parts of this job are very exciting. Marketing is always a challenge. So I just don't know.

Suggested feeling states: ambivalent, uncertain, frustrated, unfulfilled, afraid of success and/or failure.

6. *Setting the stage:* You are the first and only female member of your audit team. You had hoped the marked increase in travel would not be a problem because you love the work and do it very well. You are talking to your boss.

Script: I know I said I would have no problem with the travel aspects of the job. I thought I would enjoy it. But, I find that two to three weeks is too long. I'm not really happy when I'm traveling, and my husband is complaining.

Suggested feeling states: dissatisfied, concerned, uncomfortable, worried, nervous about relationship.

7. *Setting the stage:* You have just had an interaction with the division head, Mr. Samuels, who is your boss' boss. You are now telling your boss about it.

Script: What was I going to say to him anyway? Mr. Samuels–the division head!–pats me on the back and tells me how concerned he is for my image. I knew this place was pretty straight, but that's the most ridiculous thing that I ever heard–that I can't have my own painting in my office. Why does everything here have to be designer perfect?

Suggested feeling states: adamant, determined, angry, resistant, feeling pressured to fit into a mold.

8. *Setting the stage:* You and your boss have a lot of trouble agreeing on how things should be done and on priorities. Here we go again!

Script: No! This is not smoke screen for something else! Look, I really don't understand why I have to analyze the reports that way. I want to do an excellent job and I will. However, I'd like a little latitude in bringing some of my ideas into action.

Suggested feeling states: annoyed, confused, frustrated, unchallenged.

9. *Setting the stage:* Given the problems you and your spouse have been having, it has been amazing to you that you've been able to function at all. Your boss has just called you in and read you the riot act.

Script: Don't you think that I know that my work has been poor? Holy smokes, nobody is cooperating around here. I just...look...so I haven't been too pleasant. But I'm doing the best I can...under the circumstances.

Suggested feeling states: exasperated, strung out, as if the "bottom has dropped out," tense, as if you have to keep up a front.

10. *Setting the stage:* Your long-time friend and colleague, Todd, has come to chat about his future career plans and long-term growth with the company. Your own career has been very much on your mind for months, so you almost interrupt Todd in midstream.

Script: Todd, you sound like I did about 15 years ago. I'm 40 years old, Todd. I'm one of, maybe, a hundred middle managers. I've been working my ass off to become a CEO. Nothing was more important to me than my career. Yeah, I'm good, but my wife and kids–they're strangers to me–and I'm not going to become a CEO. Look at the years I wasted working for a goal I'll never reach.

Suggested feeling states: None–include whatever feelings you think you might have if you were this manager.

STEP 3.   Class Discussion. (15 minutes) Answer the following questions:

    a. What was it like to practice active listening?

    b. What did you learn about yourself and others by doing this exercise?

    c. When would it be a mistake to use active listening?

    d. What connections can you make between this exercise and the Readings?

Observer Sheet

Your role is an important one. You should silently observe the interaction and note specific examples of effective and ineffective communication as you see them. These data will be important in the feedback discussion.

ACTIVE LISTENING BEHAVIORS	EXAMPLES WHERE IT WAS EFFECTIVELY USED BY THE ACTIVE LISTENER	PLACES WHERE IT COULD HAVE BEEN USED AND/OR WAS USED INEFFECTIVELY*
1. Being nonevaluative		
2. Paraphrasing the content		
3. Reflecting possible implications		
4. Reflecting the underlying feelings		
5. Inviting further contributions		
6. Using non-verbal listening responses		

*The observations you note in this column will give you the chance to provide feedback to the person who was the *expresser*: 1) thoughts and feelings you heard them expressing that the listener did not hear or pick up on and 2) mixed messages you observed being expressed (incongruities between words and non-verbals).

Follow-Up

A rational mechanical view of the process of communication could be depicted in the following manner:

Person A ⟵————————————⟶ Person B

In other words, A says something to B and B hears what A said. Were it so simple, we would never experience what Bennis has labeled the "arc of distortion," which appears below.[10] A communicates something to B that was *not intended*. B reacts to this *unintended* communication, and this response confuses A, as well it would, since A is unaware of part of the message sent. *All behavior* conveys some message–it is a form of communication. In the broadest sense, therefore, when we study the concept of interpersonal communication, we are dealing with interpersonal relationships. The communication is the process vehicle through which relationships form, are managed, and, when necessary, dissolve.

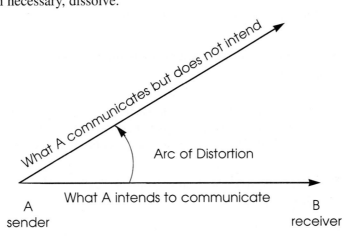

Communications must be understood within the context of the interpersonal relationship. If two people have been involved in an ongoing bitter argument over a business decision, it will be more difficult for them to hear the other's messages without distortion. We communicate in a different, more effective manner with people who are supportive than with people who are not. Poor relationships and poor communication go hand in hand when trust is lacking. Covey explains this in terms of an Emotional Bank Account that exists for each relationship.[11] We make deposits and build up a reserve when we are kind, courteous, honest, and dependable in our interactions with the other person. This results in a high level of trust that allows the other person to overlook our communication errors and give us the benefit of the doubt. However, when we treat the other person in ways that indicate a lack of consideration: discourtesy, ignoring them, being arbitrary, etc., our Emotional Bank Account with them becomes overdrawn. The level of trust is so low that each word must be chosen with great care so that the other person does not misinterpret the meaning and assume the worst. In reality, most people say many things that were better left unsaid or were better stated in a different manner. In the context of good relationships, such communications are tolerated and forgiven, and mutual understanding is much more likely to be achieved.

Learning Points

1. Communication is a major portion of a manager's job and an essential skill.

2. Communication is the process by which information is exchanged between sender and receiver with the goal of achieving mutual understanding.

3. There is much potential for distortion in the communication process. Therefore, it's best to assume that any communication also involves a partial misunderstanding. Requesting and giving feedback on the message is one way to ensure that the message received is the intended message. Active listening is another way to minimize the arc of distortion.

4. The arc of distortion is the difference between what the sender intended to convey and what the receiver understood the message to be.

5. Meaning lies in people, not in words.

6. Men and women communicate in different ways, primarily due to their different roles in society.

7. Defensiveness is a common barrier to communication because the energy devoted to defending oneself prevents attention to the message. Therefore, managers should learn to communicate in a manner that does not arouse defensiveness.

8. There are five common response styles:
   a. Evaluative
   b. Interpretive
   c. Supportive
   d. Probing
   e. Understanding

   Evaluative responses are most common. These styles also contain a message about the relationship between the two parties. Only the understanding response reflects an egalitarian stance rather than a one-up position.

9. A non-defensive climate is created when people are descriptive, egalitarian, focused on problem solving, spontaneous, empathic, and provisional.

10. Assertiveness is the ability to communicate clearly and directly what you need or want from another person in a way that does not deny or infringe upon the other's rights.

11. I-statements, (behavior, effects, feelings) are an effective way to provide feedback to others.

12. People have both thoughts and feelings. Both the sender and the receiver's feelings influence *what* thoughts get sent and received and *how* they get sent.

13. More meaning is taken from non-verbal signals and vocal intonation and inflection than from words themselves.

14. Both parties in an interpersonal exchange have the personal responsibility to use their active listening skills to ensure mutual understanding.

15. The components of active listening are:
   a. Being non-evaluative
   b. Paraphrasing
   c. Reflecting implications
   d. Reflecting underlying feelings
   e. Inviting further contributions
   f. Using non-verbal listening responses

 for Managers

- There are several principles of communication that are helpful to managers:[12]

  - Give other people confirmation or validation by acknowledging their presence and indicating acceptance of them and their ideas.

  - Do not exclude others or resort to in-group talk. Include everyone present in the interaction.

  - Avoid talking about yourself too much. Even if you see yourself as "the center of the universe," remember that it's hard for others to stay interested in monologues.

  - Avoid both excessive criticism and undeserved praise. Instead, give an honest appraisal in a gentle manner.

  - Use language that neither offends nor demeans other people.

- The nonverbal cues that signify that you are attending to what another person is saying are: facing them squarely with an open posture (no limbs crossed), leaning forward, and maintaining eye contact and a relaxed posture. Studies have shown that more information is shared when people come out from behind their desks and sit closer to their visitors.

- Take for granted that communication is a flawed process and try to eliminate as many pitfalls as possible. It's a good idea to ask employees to paraphrase your instructions (i.e., "Would you please put the instructions in your own words so that I can see if I communicated them clearly?") and to paraphrase for them the problems or requests that they bring to you (i.e., "Let me see if I've understood the problem correctly...").

- Some managers give written instructions along with verbal instructions to avoid both misunderstandings and later consultations.

- Before you communicate at work, ask yourself the following questions: What do I want to accomplish as a result of the following questions? Based on my knowledge of the receiver(s), how should I word this message and how should I transmit it? Am I the best person to send this message or does someone else have greater credibility or a better relationship with them? Will there be any likely resistance to the message that I need to take into consideration?

- Communication is a learned behavior, which means that people usually send messages that maximize rewards and minimize punishment. Managers who are guilty of the "kill the messenger" syndrome will be told only the "good news" even though the bad news may be crucial to the organization's survival.

- Self-concept serves as a filter through which we see all communication. People with low self-concepts present the greatest communication challenge because they can become defensive with little or no provocation. The specific content of your message is less important than what you are conveying to them about your relationship with them; if it's anything less than fully supportive, they become defensive.

- Active listening is the appropriate response to use with people in a conflict situation. It's difficult to maintain anger when the listener is making a concerted effort to understand both your point and your feelings.

- Some managers deplore the power of the grapevine, the informal communication network. However, all organizations have grapevines, and some managers use the grapevine for their own purposes, for example, floating trial balloons to see how people react. The power of the grapevine can be decreased by more open sharing of information through formal channels. In a bureaucracy, information is often synonymous with power. Providing greater access to information means that employees will devote less energy hoarding it or to ferreting it out.

- Most organizations are characterized by top-down information flows. Unless managers make a concerted effort to seek information from employees, they will remain in the dark on many issues. For senior managers, it is not always enough to talk only with the layer of people immediately beneath them because this group may have a vested interest in presenting only positive information or self-serving interpretations of situations. This is why the concept of "managing by walking around" is so important.

Personal Application Assignment

At the beginning of this chapter you filled out an inventory in which you evaluated the type of communication climate your supervisor established. That question was based upon Gibb's characteristics of defensive communication. This assignment is to gain insight into the type of communication climate you create. Choose one of the following ways to begin this assignment.

1. If you supervise employees, ask three of them to fill out a copy of the same questionnaire *anonymously*. If you're surprised at the results, discuss them and ask for clarification or examples from someone in your organization who you know will give you good, honest feedback. Take into consideration that your employees may be uncertain (or even terrified) about how you will accept feedback on your communication habits. Make sure they don't have to pay a price for their honesty.

2. Have a discussion on a controversial topic with someone (preferably someone difficult so you can test out the skills you practiced in this chapter). Try to create a supportive climate according to Gibb's framework. Afterward, evaluate the conversation. If it's possible, get the other person's evaluation of the conversation.

After you've completed (1) or (2), write up the experience in the usual format.

A. *Concrete Experience*
   1. *Objectively* describe the experience ("who," "what," "when," "where," "how" type information–up to 2 points).

   2. *Subjectively* describe your feelings, perceptions, and thoughts that occurred *during* (not after) the experience (up to 2 points). Does this section have too much detail? (If so, delete 1 point.)

B. *Reflective Observation*

    1. Look at the experience from different points of view. How many points of view did you include that are relevant (up to 2 points)?

    2. Use these perspectives to add more meaning to the incident (up to 2 points).

C. *Abstract Conceptualization*

    1. Relate concepts from the assigned readings and the lecture to the experience (i.e., What theories that you heard in the lecture or read in the *Reader* relate to your understanding of this incident?). Make reference to at least two sources. Use standard referencing format and include the page number to which you are referring. How many sources did you use and how clearly did you explain their theories (up to 4 points)?

    2. You can also create an original model or theory, but it should not replace course concepts.

D. *Active Experimentation*

   1. Write about what you will do in the future that will improve your effectiveness. Use rules of thumb or action resolutions.

   2. Are they described specifically, thoroughly, and in detail (up to 4 points)?

E. *Integration, Synthesis, and Writing*

   1. Did you write about something personally important to you (up to 1 point)?

   2. Was it well written (up to 2 points)?

   3. Did you integrate and synthesize the different sections (up to 1 point)?

[1]See Chapter 15, Leadership and Decision Making, for more detail on this point.

[2]Henry Mintzberg, *The Nature of Managerial Work* (New York: Harper & Row, 1973).

[3]Ibid., p.171.

[4]Deborah Tannen, *You Just Don't Understand: Women and Men in Conversation* (New York: Ballantine, 1990). Her previous book, *That's Not What I Meant*, presents ethnic and regional communication differences.

[5]The findings in this paragraph are reported in Laurie P. Arliss, *Gender Communication*, (Englewood Cliffs, NJ: Prentice-Hall, 1991); Judy Cornelia Pearson, "Language Usage of Women and Men," in John Stewart's *Bridges Not Walls*. (New York: Random House, 1986) pp. 283-300; Deborah Borisoff & Lisa Merrill, *The Power to Communicate: Gender Differences as Barriers*. (Prospect Heights, IL: Waveland Press, 1992).

[6]Jack Gibb, "Defensive Communication," *The Reader*.

[7]"Why So Much Is Beyond Words," *Time*, July 13, 1981, p. 74.

[8]A. Mehrabian and M. Weiner, "Decoding of Inconsistent Communications," *Journal of Personality and Social Psychology*, Vol. 6 (1967), pp. 109-114.

[9]The range of nonverbal behavior is clearly extensive and often culturally determined. Most important, this is not intended to help people learn "tricks" or "techniques" to be applied mechanistically. Incongruent *listening* behavior contributes to ineffective interpersonal communications.

[10]H. Baumgartel, Warren N. Bennis, and N. R. De, (eds.), *Reading in Group Development for Managers and Trainers* (New York: Asia Publishing House, 1967), pp. 151-156.

[11]Stephen R. Covey, *The 7 Habits of Highly Effective People*. (New York: Simon and Schuster, 1989). pp. 188-202.

[12]Joseph A. DeVito, *The Interpersonal Communication Book*. (New York: Harper & Row, 1989), p. 197.

Chapter 8

INTERPERSONAL PERCEPTION AND ATTRIBUTION

OBJECTIVES By the end of this chapter you should be able to:

A. Define perception and explain the perceptual process.

B. Identify the sources of misinterpretation in cross-cultural interactions.

C. Understand both the benefits and the drawbacks of the perceptual process.

D. Recognize common perceptual errors.

E. Describe the Johari window.

F. Explain attribution theory.

G. Understand the relevance of perception and attribution for managers.

The Blind Men and the Elephant

John Godfrey Saxe

It was six men of Indostan
To learning much inclined,
Who went to see the Elephant
(Though all of them were blind),
That each by observation
Might satisfy his mind.

The first approached the Elephant,
And happening to fall
Against his broad and sturdy side,
At once began to bawl:
"God bless me! but the Elephant
Is very like a WALL!"

The second, feeling of the tusk,
Cried, "Ho! what have we here
So very round and smooth and sharp?
To me 'tis mighty clear
This wonder of an Elephant
Is very like a SPEAR."

The third approached the animal,
And happening to take
The squirming trunk within his hands,
Thus boldly up and spake:
"I see," quoth he, "the Elephant
Is very like a SNAKE!"

The fourth reached out an eager hand,
And felt about the knee
"What most this wondrous beast is like
Is mighty plain," quoth he:
"'Tis clear enough the Elephant
Is very like a TREE!"

The fifth, who chanced to touch the ear,
Said: "E'en the blindest man
Can tell what this resembles most;
Deny the fact who can,
This marvel of an Elephant
Is very like a FAN!"

The sixth no sooner had begun
About the beast to grope,
Than seizing on the swinging tail
That fell within his scope,
"I see," quoth he, "the Elephant
Is very like a ROPE!"

And so these men of Indostan
Disputed loud and long,
Each in his own opinion
Exceeding stiff and strong,
Though each was partly in the right,
And all were in the wrong!

Premeeting Preparation

A. Read "The Blind Men and the Elephant."

B. Read the Topic Introduction.

C. What are the significant learning points from the readings?

Topic Introduction

So far we have studied individual differences in values, ethics, mental maps of management, learning styles, motivation, and communication. Yet another way in which people differ is the way we perceive the world. It is tempting to assume that human behavior is a response to an objective reality but, as the comedian Lily Tomlin noted, "Reality is nothing more than a collective hunch." The same stimuli may be present in our environment, but what we do with that stimuli is affected by individual differences. For example, if you talk with a rabid Republican and a fanatical Democrat the day after a U.S. Presidential debate, it may be difficult to believe they both watched the same debate. Each claims his or her candidate "won" and the other candidate was a disaster. This same thing can happen at work. We might see two managers with completely different impressions of an employee's performance; one manager wants to promote the employee while the other recommends firing. How do we end up with such diverse and even contradictory impressions? Chalk it up primarily to individual differences in perception.

Perception is the process by which we select, organize, and evaluate the stimuli in our environment to make it meaningful for ourselves. It serves as a filter or gate-keeper so that we are not overwhelmed by all the stimuli that bombard us. A key aspect of the perceptual process is selective attention. We simply do not see or hear everything that goes on around us. For example, when you live in another country and have reached a moderate level of fluency in that language, you occasionally stumble upon a new word that you have never heard before. Once you master the word, you realize to your chagrin that it is in fact a very common word–you just weren't "hearing" or attending to it before.

Both internal and external factors determine what sensory impressions we pay attention to. Internal factors that affect perception are motives, values, interests, attitudes, past experiences and expectations. For example, hungry people are more attuned to references to food than people not currently motivated by the hunger need. Hungry people may even "hear" the word "candy" when the speaker says "caddy" because we often hear what we want to hear. People tend to pick up only that stimuli that interests them or supports what they are looking for. Studies of both low-level supervisors and middle management executives revealed that these individuals perceived only those aspects of a situation that related to the goals and activities of their own departments.[1] Information that conflicts with what we believe is often ignored or distorted to conform to our preconceptions. Selective attention explains why two people can attend the same

meeting or event and have contradictory stories about what occurred. The diehard political supporters mentioned in the opening paragraph heard and saw only what they wanted to hear (great points made by their candidate, indications of strong leadership potential, etc.) and blocked out the strengths of the opposing candidate. In this way, their preconceived attitudes about the debate affected their perception and interpretation of the actual event.

The external factors that influence perception are characteristics of the target we perceive. Our attention is drawn by motion, intensity, size, novelty, and salience. Salience is the extent to which a given object or event stands out from the others around it. The salient object or event is the "figure" that dominates what we see; the rest is "ground" or background. What do you see in the picture on the left? What is figural to some people is merely background to others. Furthermore, our perceptions tend to remain constant; once a perceived object is fixed in our minds, it is difficult to reinterpret the stimuli.

The second stage in the perceptual process is the *organization* of the stimuli that has been perceived. Our thought processes automatically structure stimuli into patterns that make sense to the perceiver. One example of such patterns are cause-and-effect relationships. It is easier to see cause-and-effect relationships in the physical world than it is with social interactions and human behavior. Nevertheless, we organize stimuli in the same patterns. For example, if an organization is successful, people tend to attribute this success to the leader whether or not the leader really had an impact.[2]

According to social cognition theory, we organize stimuli into schemas.[3] Schemas are mental maps of different concepts, events or types of stimuli that contain both the attributes of the concept and the relationship among the attributes. Like geographical maps, schemas are representations of reality, but not reality itself. Everyone's maps are different. For example, each of us has a schema about "leadership" that includes the traits that we think describe a good leader. We tend to see these traits as a package deal; if someone has a few of these traits, we assume they also possess the other traits. Our leader schema might include attributes like trustworthy, directive, courageous, enthusiastic, and value-driven. If we see a leader who is trustworthy and directive, we may mistakenly assume he or she is also courageous, enthusiastic, and value-driven. Once schemas have been established, they affect how we handle future information because they determine what we attend to and what we remember. We are less likely to notice and remember free-floating stimuli than stimuli that fits into existing schemas.

The third step in the perceptual process is *evaluation* or inference. We interpret the stimuli in a subjective, rather than objective fashion. Our conclusions are biased by our individual attitudes, needs, experiences, expectations, goals, values, and physical condition at the time. Not only do interpretations differ from person to person, but the same person can have diverse perceptions of the same stimuli at different points in time. When large organizations are involved in major change efforts, it is easy to see examples of differential interpretations of the same stimuli in the diverse reactions to announcements about upcoming innovations. No matter how carefully such announcements are worded, employees reach vastly different conclusions, and harmful rumors are commonplace. People who are frightened about the changes are more likely to make negative inferences about the announcements than people who are looking forward to the innovation.

Nowhere is it more obvious that different groups see and interpret the world in different ways than when we deal with people from different cultures or ethnic groups. For example, there is a West African tribe that lives in round houses and, as a result, does not perceive perpendicular lines. The way the Japanese bow and present their business cards conveys meaningful cues that are not even perceived, much less correctly interpreted by most non-Japanese. Perceptual patterns are both learned and culturally determined.[4] They are also a barrier to effective cross-cultural communication when we fail to pay attention to cues that are important to another culture or when we misinterpret their behavior.

Adler has identified three sources of misinterpretation in cross cultural interaction:[5]

1. *Subconscious Cultural Blinders.* We use our own cultural assumptions to interpret the events and behavior of a foreign culture.

2. *Lack of Cultural Awareness.* We are unaware of our cultural values and norms and the way that other cultures perceive us. Without understanding our own culture, we cannot adapt our behavior so that it is perceived more accurately by others.

3. *Projected Similarity.* We assume that people from other cultures are more similar to us than they really are or that situations are similar when they are not. This is based on the ethnocentric view that there is only one way to be—like me.

A common danger that may result from our perception of people who are somehow different from us is stereotyping. *Stereotyping occurs when we attribute behavior or attitudes to a person on the basis of the group to which the person belongs.* Much of the cynicism in organizations is expressed in terms of stereotypes about other groups, such as "Top management cannot be trusted," or "You'll never get those employees to participate and work harder." The current emphasis upon managing diversity should cause people to challenge the incorrect stereotypes they hold about different groups in the work force. One fairly common stereotype is that older workers contribute less than younger workers. This stereotype is prevalent in Europe and Central America where older workers have no recourse or legal protection from discrimination. In reality, U.S. studies show that older workers are less likely to be absent, have half the accident rate of younger employees, and report higher job satisfaction.[6] Furthermore, researchers have found no evidence that older U.S. workers are less productive than younger workers.[7]

The drawbacks to perception are that it prevents us from taking in everything we should, makes our interpretations open to question, and promotes stereotypes. However, perception is an extremely useful process. It helps us to make sense of a world full of stimuli in three ways: first, by limiting the amount of information that enters our mind to prevent overload; second, by selecting what input we will attend to; and, third, by organizing and classifying the input we receive so we do not waste valuable time trying to make sense of behavior and situations that are in fact similar.

PERCEPTUAL DISTORTIONS

Stereotyping is one of several examples of distortion in the perceptual process. Another distortion, the *halo effect*, occurs when our evaluation of another person is dominated by only one of their traits. For example, a U.S. army study showed that officers who were liked were evaluated as being more intelligent than those who were disliked.[8] The halo effect does not always work to an employee's advantage. A perceived negative trait like sloppiness can prevent a boss from seeing the other positive characteristics an employee may have.

Central tendency is a perceptual distortion that occurs when a person avoids extreme judgements and rates everything as average. We see this when managers rate all their employees as "3's" on a five point scale, in spite of the fact that some employees really deserve a "5" or a "1". *Contrast effects* are present when our evaluations are affected by comparisons with other people we have recently encountered who are either better or worse in terms of this characteristic. For example, if a student has two of her university's best professors in the same semester, she may rate her other professors (who in reality are good professors) as only average or poor because she is comparing them with the excellent professors.

Another type of perceptual distortion is *projection*. This refers to the tendency to attribute one's own attitudes or feelings to another person, thereby relieving one's own sense of guilt or failure. Projection is a defense mechanism that protects people from confronting their own feelings. It is most common in people who have little insight into their own personalities.[9] Multinational enterprises have been reluctant to transfer female executives abroad on the grounds that a woman could not be effective in a traditional, male-dominated culture. In some cases, the MNC management is simply projecting upon the foreign culture its own feelings and prejudices about female managers. In reality, research has shown that female U.S. expatriates have been successful all over the world.[10]

The final source of perceptual distortion is known as the *perceptual defense*. These defenses act as a screen or filter, blocking out that which we do not want to see and letting through that which we wish to see.[11] The closer we get to schemas concerning our self-perceptions (self-image) and our relationships with important others, the more likely we are to call upon these defensive screens.[12] These defenses help to create self-fulfilling or circular perceptual processes, like the ones shown in the following examples.

**Example 1
The Stereotypical Female**

1. As a woman, I believe that men prefer women who are passive and unassertive.

2. Since I would like to develop meaningful relationships with men, I behave in a passive and unassertive manner.

3. I tend to develop relationships with men who themselves expect women to be passive and unassertive.

    or

3. I do not approach and/or am not approached by men who expect a woman to be active and assertive.

4. I am confirmed in my belief that men prefer women who are passive and unassertive.

    or

4. I do not have the opportunity to develop my own assertiveness.

Example 2
A Managerial
Dilemma

1. As a manager, I believe that subordinates are basically lazy and dislike work.

2. I assume, therefore, that to get the most out of subordinates, I must watch over their every move.

3. I behave in a strict manner, delegating little responsibility, and demanding that everything be cleared through me first.

4. My subordinates react to this parentlike stance by acting like rebellious teenagers. I have to lean on them all the time or they'll never do what I tell them.

5. Consequently, my original belief is confirmed; subordinates are basically lazy and dislike work.

The underlying pattern in these processes is one of 1) assumption or belief, 2) leading to behavior that is congruent with the assumption, followed by 3) observation of consequences, which, to the extent that selective perception is occurring, leads to 4) confirmation of the original assumption of belief. Testing the validity or desirability of this conceptual pattern is difficult, for several reasons.

One important reason is that normal social interaction is basically conservative–social norms operate to preserve existing interaction patterns and perceptions. Sociologist Erving Goffman[13] has described the tendency of people to preserve the "face" that others present to them. When people act "out of character," social pressures are mobilized to force them back into their role. In social situations we tend to act in such a way that we maintain our own self-image and the self-image we see others presenting. We resist telling someone that they have egg on their chin because we assume that this is not part of the image they want to present and we do not want them to "lose face" and be embarrassed. This conservative interaction norm tends to decrease the accuracy of interpersonal perception by relinquishing opportunities to test the accuracy of our perceptions of ourselves and others. The norm dictates that we cannot frankly tell others our impressions of them if these impressions differ from the face they are presenting. It also acts as an obstacle to our testing with others whether or not we are projecting the kind of self-image we think we are. "Do you see me the way I see myself?" When people present themselves as leaders, it is hard to tell them you do not feel like following. Thus, we are denied information about others' true thoughts and feelings by the face we present.

A theoretical conceptualization of this process is depicted in the following matrix, called the Johari window.[14] This is an information processing model that consists of four regions determined by whether information about oneself is known or unknown to oneself and others.

	KNOWN TO SELF	NOT KNOWN TO SELF
KNOWN TO OTHERS	Arena	Blindspot
NOT KNOWN TO OTHERS	Facade	Unknown

Arena	Open Self. This cell includes all the factors upon which I and others have mutually shared perceptions; that is, people see me the way I see myself (e.g., I feel confident and people see me as confident).
Facade	*Concealed Self.* In this cell are factors that I see in myself but that I hide from others (e.g., I feel insecure, but I strive to project the image of a very secure person); that is, people see a "false me," and I must always be on guard not to let them see the "real me."
Blindspot	*Blind Self.* In this cell are factors that other people perceive in me but that I do not see in myself (e.g., others see that my anxiety reduces my effectiveness but I do not see–or will not admit to myself–that I am anxious); that is, people know certain things about me, but they don't tell me ("Even your best friends won't tell you").
Unknown	*Unknown Self.* In this cell are factors that I do not see in myself nor do others see in me.

When a person's arena is very small, communication is greatly hindered. The more we know ourselves and allow others to know us, the greater the potential for effective communication. In a new group or new relationship, communication is less free and spontaneous. If trust is established, the arena expands as people feel it is safe to be themselves in the group and to perceive others as they really are.

It takes a good deal of energy to maintain a large facade because hiding or denying things is an effort. To move from the facade to the arena requires a sufficient level of trust and psychological safety to enable people to share their self-perceptions with others. To move from the blindspot to the arena requires that others give us feedback as to how they see us. The conditions of trust and psychological safety are again critical–so that people will risk telling us and so we will not react defensively to what they say. It is only as we move from the facade and blindspot into the arena that true sharing of perceptions and understanding between people can develop.

One of the basic competencies of effective managers is self-awareness. This requires an ability to both seek feedback from others and to disclose one's own feelings and thoughts. The following exercise is designed to help you develop these skills.

Procedure for Group Meeting: How I See Myself and Others

SELF-PERCEPTIONS: INDIVIDUAL WORK

(Time Allotted: 30 to 40 Minutes)

The first part of this unit is designed to help you sharpen your understanding of the image and perceptions you believe you communicate to others. During the second part, you will have the opportunity to explore how others believe they see you.

STEP 1.   As you think about the *image you have of yourself*, list, in the appropriate spaces provided in the first column of the perception matrix on page 203.

       a. The first five or six words that come to your mind
       b. An animal
       c. A musical instrument
       d. A food

It is important that you work quickly. Let your first thought be the one you record.

STEP 2.   The words you have just listed are, at best, simplified cues or indicators of how you see yourself–your self-image. It is your own interpretation of what these words mean to you that contributes to your self-image. In this step you are asked to a) interpret the meaning of those words and b) decide whether or not each element of your self-image (known to self) is a part of your arena or your facade. Use the space provided to record these points.

       a. Elements of my self-image that I believe are in my arena (i.e. known to me and known to others):

       b. Elements of my self-image that I believe are in my facade (i.e. known to me but not known to others):

STEP 3.   Each of us behaves in ways designed to allow various aspects of our self-image (known to self) to be known to others–an arena. Similarly, we behave in ways to keep various aspects of our self-image in our facade (not known to others).

   a. In the space provided, jot down examples of how you communicate to others important elements of your arena. (For example, if you feel confident and believe people see you as confident, how do you behave to communicate confidence?)

   b. In the space provided, jot down examples of how you behave to keep elements of your self-image (known to self) in the facade. (For example, if you feel insecure, but try to project an image of confidence, how do you behave to "cover" your feelings of insecurity?)

TESTING SELF-PERCEPTIONS: SMALL-GROUP SHARING

(Time Allotted: 60 to 90 minutes)

In this part of the unit, you will have the opportunity to get a glimpse of how others see you. This will be a real test of your interpersonal skills. Giving and receiving feedback in a productive manner is difficult but important.

STEP 1.   In your learning group, fill out the Perception Matrix form on page 203 for others in your group. It is important in filling out the Perception Matrix that you work quickly. Let your first thought be the one you record. It is helpful if there is no communication during this step.

STEP 2.   (Read this paragraph to yourself.) The sharing process you are about to begin may not be an easy task. As was pointed out in the Topic Introduction, normal social interaction is basically conservative–social norms operate to preserve existing interaction patterns and perceptions. During this sharing process, you are, in effect, being asked to operate with an atypical set of social norms to share and discuss your impressions of one another.

   In the discussions you have, it is important to remember that there is no one reality or truth. You have perceptions of yourself. Others have perceptions of you. Some of these perceptions will be shared–held in common. Others will be different. The issue is *not* whose perception is right or whose is wrong.

   If I have a perception of someone and they do not share that perception of themselves, this discrepancy can serve as an important learning opportunity for *both of us.*

a. If I am the one being perceived, I may learn something about my blindspot. I may learn about behavior that serves to move elements from my facade to my arena.

b. If I am the perceiver, I may learn something about the perceptual filters I use (e.g., I assume all big people are confident). I may learn that I tend to see in others elements of how I see myself.

All of us can learn something more about our own circular self-fulfilling perceptual processes. This awareness is only a first step. Whether or not a person chooses to alter these perceptual patterns is clearly a matter of individual choice.

STEP 3. People should share the perceptions they have of each other as recorded on their Perception Matrix. Go around the circle, sharing all the perceptions (words through food) for one person before moving on to the next person. You can record these on page 204.

STEP 4. Groups should now discuss their perceptions using the following suggestions to guide their discussions.

a. What can you infer about your schemas (the concepts or categories you most often use in perceiving other people) from the words you listed for each person in your group?

1. Did you list mostly adjectives (which tend to be evaluative or difference oriented, e.g., good versus bad, big versus small) or nouns (which tend to be neutral or non difference oriented, e.g., man, student) or verbs (which are behavior oriented as opposed to trait or characteristic oriented)?

2. Did your lists of words differ for each person or did your lists reflect similar concepts?

b. Was your perception of some people generally closer to the ways they saw themselves than was true of your perception of other people? To what do you attribute any differences? Do some people project clearer self-images? Length of time or context within which you knew the person? Similarity to yourself?

c. Where two or more people saw the same person in substantially different ways, they should try to understand how these differences arose.

d. Based on the individual work you did in the beginning of this unit, some of you may have found:

1. Elements that you thought were in your open arena were not known to others (i.e., they were in your facade).

2. Elements that you thought were in your facade were known to others (i.e., they are in your arena).

3. New perceptions from your blindspot.

In exploring these "surprises," it is most important that you listen to and understand others' descriptions of how you behave, which leads them to form the impressions they have.

e. It is very likely that you will uncover some typical circular perceptual defenses such as those discussed in the Topic Introduction. The group may want to outline a few of their own processes.

1. What does a person gain or achieve through the pattern?

2. What costs are incurred or opportunities forgone by maintaining the pattern?

3. What steps could be taken to change the nature of these circular patterns?

f. Finally, each of you chose, on some basis, to join this particular small group. What, if anything, have you learned during this exercise that might help to explain that choice process and its consequences?

g. What connections can you make between this exercise and the readings?

Perception Matrix
Own Perceptions

CATEGORY \ MEMBER	HOW YOU SEE YOUR-SELF	HOW YOU SEE A	HOW YOU SEE B	HOW YOU SEE C	HOW YOU SEE D	HOW YOU SEE E
5-6 Words						
Animal						
Musical Instrument						
Food						

*These are the self-perceptions you recorded in step 1 of your individual work.

Perception Matrix
Others' Perceptions*

MEMBER / CATEGORY	HOW I AM SEEN BY					
	A	B	C	D	E	F
5-6 Words						
Animal						
Musical Instrument						
Food						

* You may wish to use this space to record others' perceptions of yourself or themselves as people
  begin to share their matrices in the second part of this unit.

Follow-Up

The most pertinent aspect of perception in terms of organizational behavior is social perception–how we perceive and judge other people. Our behavioral responses to others are based upon our inferences about their behavior. According to attribution theory, when people observe behavior they attempt to determine whether it is internally or externally caused.[15] For example, if a male group member does not pull his weight on a project, other group members may attribute his behavior to internal reasons that are under his control, such as "he's irresponsible and lazy." Or they may attribute it to external reasons, like "he has too much other work to do a good job on this project." These attributions then determine the way peers and managers behave towards the person. If the employee is deemed irresponsible, his manager might take disciplinary measures or try coaching behavior. If the external cause is accepted, his manager might reorganize his work assignments, send him to time management courses, or negotiate with his other project leaders for more release time.

We use three types of information to help us make causal judgments about others:

1. Consensus refers to the extent to which others behave in the same manner.
2. Consistency is the extent to which the person acts in the same manner at other times.
3. Distinctiveness is the extent to which this person behaves in the same manner in other contexts.

Let's take the example of an HR manager who is trying to figure out whether an employee complaint about his boss' managerial style is valid. The HR manager will consider whether other employees have also complained about this particular manager (consensus). She will also consider whether the employee has complained about this same boss on previous occasions (consistency) and whether the employee has a habit of complaining about all his bosses (distinctiveness). If no one else has complained about the boss, and the employee's evaluation of the boss has been inconsistent (sometimes positive, sometimes negative), and if the employee is a habitual whiner, the HR manager will probably conclude that the problem lies within the employee (internal attribution) rather than the manager (external attribution). If other employees have also complained about the boss, the employee's complaints about this boss have been consistent over time, and the employee never complained about previous bosses, she is more likely to conclude that it is time to take steps to help the manager improve her style.

There are biases that distort our attributions about success and failure. The Chinese usually attribute personal success to luck and failures to personal failings.[16] In contrast, when Americans succeed they attribute it to personal, internal factors (for example, hard work, intelligence, initiative). However, when Americans fail they are more likely to blame it on external factors (such as tough competition, poor leadership, interdepartmental problems). This is called the *self-serving bias*. When U.S. managers evaluate their employees, the opposite occurs; they are more likely to attribute low performance to the subordinates' personal failings and they underestimate the influence of external factors upon subordinate performance. This is known as *fundamental attribution error.*[17]

Given these natural tendencies, managers should make an extra effort to ensure that their attributions about employees are accurate. Bertrand Russell, British scholar and mathematician, showed his understanding of human nature when he proposed the following conjugation of "irregular verbs."

I am firm.

You are obstinate.

He is a pig-headed fool.

Perception plays a major role in communication and decision-making in the workplace, particularly in the areas of hiring and firing, performance appraisals, promotions, and work assignments. Effective managers acknowledge that their own perceptions may be uniquely biased and work hard at gathering and understanding the perceptions of other people so there is a greater chance of approximating "reality."

It is as difficult for humans to understand the impact of their own perceptual schema as it is for a fish to understand the concept of water. Yet our perceptual maps and the fish's water are equally important for survival. Without a conceptual system to simplify and order our experiences, we would become overwhelmed by stimuli. Yet failure to recognize that our perceptions are to some extent our own creation can leave one closed, defensive, and unable to profit from new experiences. In the following analysis by an engineer of his reactions to the perception unit, we see one individual's struggle to understand his own way of perceiving others.

> Again it seems I am going to write a paper about myself rather than the suggested topic. Whenever I reflect on the subject matter we study, I can directly relate it to myself. I have always considered myself "free of hangups;" however, there are many things I do that I do not completely understand. Previously I have never taken the time to question myself, but now, being forced to think about a concept, I can see how I have been influenced by that concept and can attempt to explain, but not always justify, the way I feel toward many things. Well, here goes!

> I am the perfect example of a person blinded by his own perception of the world. Not all of the time, mind you, but mainly in one case–the case being when I become "snowed" by a girl. I'll begin by relating my current project in this area–at least I think the project is current, although I'm not sure as of this moment because of a possible misperception on my part. Being alone in a new city, I engaged in the well-known game of mixer this autumn in the hope of meeting someone interesting. I accomplished my goal without any difficulties, and here is where my problem began–I committed my unpardonable sin of becoming snowed.

> I do not have many difficulties with first perceptions. I think I am pretty objective and usually make good judgements. First impressions are almost solely objective! As long as I do not become emotionally involved, that is, as long as there is no filter between what I see and how I perceive what I have seen, I am quite able to understand what is communicated. However, once I am personally involved with the reason behind the attempted communication, my vision of what is actually happening is, I believe, distorted.

> This weekend, for example, I did not take Mary (a fictitious name) out because of our last date and a phone call I made after the date. Even though I wanted to take her out, I didn't; consequently, I have been asking myself all weekend what motivated me not to ask her out; and I do not have a specific answer–but I know it stems from how I perceived how she feels. However, this is what I think she feels, which just might not be what she does feel, and I do not let myself comprehend that there may be a difference between these two versions of the same feelings. I guess I feel that my logical reasoning of what a particular look or remark means necessarily is the correct idea. I completely leave out the possibility that everyone does not (thankfully) think about everything the same way I do.

Zalkind and Costello, in their article on perception, give five reasons of how a person misperceives.[18] These are:

1. You are influenced by cues below your own threshold (i.e., the cues you don't know you perceived).

2. You respond to irrelevant cues to arrive at a judgment.

3. You are influenced by emotional factors (i.e., what is liked is perceived as correct).

4. You weigh perceptual evidence heavily if it comes from a respectable source.

5. You are not able to identify all factors (i.e., not realizing how much weight is given to a single item).

I feel I am guilty, if one can be "guilty," of most of the mentioned means of misperception. However, I feel that rather than imposing a perceptual defense upon myself, I project a perceptual offense, and this greatly compounds my misperception. Rather than looking for favorable acts of communication and not allowing unfavorable perceptions, I am forever (when I become emotionally involved with a girl) on the lookout for any signs of displeasure. And at the slightest hint, my mind begins to work on such questions as "What if that means...?"

For example, to the question, "Did you have a good time?" I got the reply, "Yeah, I guess so." This was not perceived favorably. My perceptual offense was quickly in play and I have since been analyzing that statement. I don't know Mary well enough to say what anything she says really means, but because I was afraid the reply meant "I had a bad time," that is what I have convinced myself that she meant (although nothing else that was said even hinted at that idea; and to the friend who doubled with me, the opposite was obviously true). I didn't ask her out this weekend for reasons mainly based on this one perception of how she feels about dating me. Looking back on my action, I see I have committed three of the Zalkind-Costello means of misperception.

- no. 2–I may have responded to an irrelevant cue–her remark probably just came out and didn't really have any deep meaning behind it.

- no. 3–I was influenced by a (negative) emotional factor–I am so worried that she was not enjoying herself, with the repercussions that would have to my emotional happiness, that my perception might have been distorted.

- no. 5–I did not realize how heavily I weighted this single cue.

Being apprehensive of how she felt, I ended up analyzing every little remark made. I did not take time to think that my ways of comprehending a perception may be inaccurate–the thought never seems to enter my mind. The handout on perception states, "These defenses act like a screen or filter...blocking out that which we don't want to see and letting through that which we wish to see." I, however, feel that I block out that which I want to see and let in that which I don't want to see. This is a definite problem, but one that I never thought of before. And to compound matters, the perceptions I let in are my own personal version of what is perceived and may be the opposite of what is being communicated.

I do not have this problem until I begin to like a girl. Trained as an engineer, I think I am able to cope with objective matters; but when I try to understand another person, I seem to fail–especially when there are present emotional filters through which my perceptions are received. To take a statement out of context, Zalkind and Costello say, "A little learning encourages the perceiver to respond with increased sensitivity to individual differences without making it possible for him to gauge the real meaning of what he has seen." Well, I have had only a little learning about perception, and their statement applies to me perfectly. I try to play psychologist without knowing the first thing about what I am looking for. This is a habit I have gotten myself addicted to, and one I will have to break down in order to have a better understanding of the people around me. Right now the unknown (i.e., the human unknown–what people are thinking) confronts me and I am frustrated by it. In response to this frustration, I set up a perceptual defense (I guess my perceptual offense is nothing but a type of perceptual defense–there is an old football theory that the best offense is a good defense) which only adds to my frustration. Thus, to move from the unknown to perceptual understanding, I must first realize that I am reacting defensively to what is being communicated to me.

It seems I am now coming back to what seems to be a familiar theme in all the topics we have covered so far. Zalkind and Costello say, "The person who accepts himself is more likely to be able to see favorable aspects of other people." I feel this is especially true of myself. If I stop and realize that my date is probably thinking of the same things that I am (at the initial stages of human relations, most of the time is spent in the unconscious, hidden, and blind areas of perception), then I may prevent my perceptual defense from operating at the level it is now operating. If I continually look at weak points, and never strong points, and do not realize that I am doing such, I am not really aware of myself and therefore not aware of how others perceive me.

I feel I can improve myself in a number of ways. First, I must accept my own feelings and not worry or analyze them. As is stated in the pamphlet, "Each of us has both his tender and tough emotions." Second, I should stop analyzing logically–it's hard for me to accept the fact that all of my world is not logical. Third, I should experiment more in the giving and receiving of perceptual feedback. I spend too much time analyzing a date's behavior and not enough giving her feedback, thus blocking the understanding between us. Finally, the fourth area of improvement, and the factor that this paper has led me to explore, is increasing my own awareness and understanding of the causes of emotion. These steps of improvement exactly parallel those given in the pamphlet on how to use our emotional resources effectively. I hope I can put them to use and, once they are in use, build on them.

Learning Points

1. Perception is the process by which we select, organize, and evaluate the stimuli in our environment to make it meaningful for ourselves.

2. Selective attention means that people perceive only some of the stimuli that is actually present.

3. Both internal factors (motives, values, interests, attitudes, past experiences, and expectations) and external factors (motion, intensity, size, novelty, and salience) affect what we perceive.

4. Perceived stimuli is organized into patterns such as cause-and-effect relationships and schemas.

5. Schemas are cognitive frameworks that represent organized knowledge about a given concept, event or type of stimulus. Once established, they determine what stimuli we attend to and remember.

6. People interpret the stimuli they perceive in a subjective fashion.

7. Three sources of misinterpretation in cross-cultural interactions are 1) subconscious cultural blinders; 2) lack of cultural self-awareness; and 3) projected similarity.

8. Stereotyping occurs when we attribute behavior or attitudes to a person on the basis of the group or category to which the person belongs.

9. The drawbacks to perception are that it prevents us from taking in everything we should, makes our interpretations open to question, and promotes stereotypes.

10. On the positive side, the process of perception limits, selects, and organizes stimuli that would otherwise overwhelm us.

11. There are numerous perceptual distortions to avoid: stereotyping, the halo effect, central tendency, contrast effects, projection, and self-fulfilling perceptual defenses.

12. The Johari Window consists of four quadrants: the arena, blindspot, facade, and unknown. It refers to an information processing model that distinguishes among information about oneself that is either known or unknown to the self or the other in a social interaction. Good communication is most likely to occur when both parties are operating from their arena.

13. Attribution theory contends that when people observe other's behavior, they attempt to determine whether it is internally or externally caused. We look for information about consensus, consistency, and distinctiveness to decide on causation.

14. The self-serving bias occurs when people attribute their success to personal qualities while blaming their failure on external factors.

15. Fundamental attribution error is the tendency to overestimate the influence of personal failings and underestimate the influence of external factors when judging others.

for Managers

- As W.I. Thomas stated, situations that are perceived to be real are real in their consequences. Managers must deal with misperceptions, no matter how ridiculous they seem at times. It is not enough to ignore misperceptions with the comforting thought that they are untrue. For example, if employees perceive that their employer does not respect them or care about their welfare, there will be tangible consequences in the form of high absenteeism and low productivity.

- The most important lesson to be learned from perception is that no one's perceptions are ever totally accurate. Arguing about what different people really saw or heard is often futile. For this reason, it's best to take a provisional approach that allows for different perceptions:

  Not: "I know I'm right; I heard him with my own ears!"
  But: "I thought he said that, but perhaps I'm mistaken."

  Not: "I'm positive the staff decided to approve my budget just as it is."
  But: "Well, if we have different perceptions about the outcome of the decision, we'd better check it out with the rest of the staff. We both may have heard only what we wanted to hear."

- Rephrase what is said to you so you're sure you really understand the message.

- Question the validity of your conclusions about others and check your perceptions with other people.

- When people give you feedback, remember that their view of you may be distorted by their perceptions. It's a good idea to check feedback out with more than one person to make sure it is accurate.

- Once again, knowing yourself is useful in managing perceptions. If you suspect you have a bias in regards to certain people or issues, you can make a special effort to use active listening to keep your mind from leaping to conclusions and/or check out your perceptions with an objective person.

- People who have a greater degree of self-understanding are less likely to view the world in black and white terms and to make extreme judgements about others.[19]

- Our own characteristics affect the characteristics we are likely to see in others. Traits that are important to us are the ones we look for in others. The truism that we see in others, that which we most dislike in ourselves, applies to perception. People who are self-critical are more likely to criticize others.

- Make sure there are no promotional barriers for minorities in your organization that are based upon stereotypical assumptions.

- Trying to put yourself in the other person's shoes–empathizing with them – prevents distortion and improves communication.

- Self-disclosure is like a bell curve. Too much disclosure scares people off and makes them nervous. Too little disclosure doesn't give others enough information about the person to form a relationship with him or her.

Personal Application Assignment

The topic of this assignment is to write about an experience that involved perceptions or misperceptions. Choose an experience that was significant to you and one about which you are motivated to learn more.

A. *Concrete Experience*

1. *Objectively* describe the experience ("who," "what," "when," "where," "how" type information–up to 2 points).

2. *Subjectively* describe your feelings, perceptions, and thoughts that occurred during (not after) the experience (up to 2 points). Does this section have too much detail? (If so, delete 1 point.)

B. *Reflective Observation*

1. Look at the experience from different points of view. How many points of view did you include that are *relevant* (up to 2 points)?

2. Use these perspectives to add more meaning to the incident (up to 2 points).

C. *Abstract Conceptualization*

 1. Relate concepts from the assigned readings and the lecture to the experience (i.e., what theories that you heard in the lecture or read in the Reader relate to your understanding of this incident?). Make reference to at least two sources. Use standard referencing format and include the page number to which you are referring. How many sources did you use and how clearly did you explain their theories (up to 4 points)?

 2. You can also create an original model or theory, but it should not replace course concepts.

D. *Active Experimentation*

 1. Write about what you will do in the future that will improve your effectiveness. Use rules of thumb or action resolution.

 2. Are they described specifically, thoroughly, and in detail (up to 4 points)?

E. *Integration, Synthesis, and Writing*

 1. Did you write about something personally important to you (up to 1 point)?

 2. Was it well written (up to 2 points)?

 3. Did you integrate and synthesize the different sections (up to 1 point)?

[1]Dewitt Dearborn and Herbert Simon, "Selective Perception: A Note on the Departmental Identification of Executives," *Sociometry*, Vol. 21 (1958), p. 142, and Abraham Kofman, "Selective Perception Among First Line Supervisors," *Personnel Administrator*, Vol. 26 (September 1963).

[2]James R. Meindl & Sanford B. Ehrlich, "The Romance of Leadership and the Evaluation of Organizational Performance," *Academy of Management Journal*, 30, 1987, pp. 91-109.

[3]Susan T. Fiske and Shelley E. Taylor, *Social Cognition.* (Reading, MA: Addison-Wesley, 1984).

[4]Nancy Adler, *International Dimensions of Organizational Behavior.* (Boston: PWS-Kent, 1991).

[5]Adler, *International Dimensions*, pp. 75-82.

[6]Walter Keichel III, "How to Manage Older Workers," *Fortune.* November 15, 1990, pp. 183-186.

[7]Glenn M. McEvoy and Wayne F. Cascio, "Cumulative Evidence of Relationship Between Employee Age and Job Performance," *Journal of Applied Psychology*, February, 1989, pp. 11-17.

[8]Sheldon S. Zalkind and Timothy Costello, "Perception: Implications for Administration," *Administrative Science Quarterly* VII, September, 1962, pp. 218-235.

[9]Zalkind and Costello, "Perception," p. 226.

[10]Nancy Adler and Dafna N. Izraeli, *Women in Management Worldwide*, (Armonk, NY: M.E. Sharpe, 1988); and Mariann Jelinek and Nancy Adler, "Women: World Class Managers for Global Competition," *Academy of Management Executive*, Vol. 2, No. 1 (1988), pp. 11-19.

[11]Mason Haire and W. F. Grunes, "Perceptual Defenses: Processes Protecting an Organized Perception of Another Personality," Human Relations, Vol. 3 (1950), pp. 403-412; and M. Rokeach, *The Open and Closed Mind* (New York: Basic Books, 1960).

[12]For two excellent collections of material relevant to this point, see Warren G. Bennis et al, *Interpersonal Dynamics,* rev. ed. (Homewood, IL: Dorsey Press, 1968), and R. Wylie, *The Self Concept* (Lincoln: University of Nebraska Press, 1965).

[13]E. Goffman, "On Face Work: An Analysis of Ritual Elements in Social Interaction," *Psychiatry*, Vol. 18 (1955), pp. 213-231.

[14]Joseph Luft, "The Johari Window," *Human Relations and Training News* (January 1961), pp. 6-7.

[15]Harold H. Kelley, "Attribution in Social Interaction," in Edward E. Jones et al. (eds.) *Attribution: Perceiving the Causes of Behavior*, (Morristown, NJ: General Learning Press, 1972).

[16]Lucian Pye, *Chinese Negotiating Style* (Cambridge, MA: Oelgeschlager, Gunn, & Hain, 1982).

[17]Lee Ross, "The Intuitive Psychologist and His Shortcomings," in Leonard Berkowitz (ed.) *Advances in Experimental Social Psychology*, Vol. 10 (Orlando, FL: Academic Press, 1977) pp. 174-220; and Arthur G. Miller and Tim Lawson, "The Effect of an Informational Option on the Fundamental Attribution Error," *Personality and Social Psychology Bulletin*, June 1989, pp. 194-204.

[18]Zalkind and Costello, "Perception."

[19]E. Weingarten, "A Study of Selective Perception in Clinical Judgment," *Journal of Personality*, XVII (1949), pp. 369-400.

Chapter

GROUP DYNAMICS AND SELF-MANAGED WORK TEAMS

OBJECTIVES By the end of this chapter you should be able to:

A. Identify what organizational requirements must be in place to set the stage for successful work teams

B. Describe two models of group development

C. Distinguish between group content and group process

D. Explain and diagnose group process behaviors that either help or hinder group effectiveness

E. Describe and recognize group roles

F. Combine the role of a participant in task accomplishment with the role of an observer of group process

A Fair Day's Work

R. H. Richard and G. Ray Funkhouser

For 18 years Ginny had been doing about the same thing: packing expandrium fittings for shipment. She was so well practiced that she could do the job perfectly without paying the slightest attention. This, of course, left her free to socialize and observe the life of the company around her. Today Ginny was breaking in a new packer:

"No, not that way. Look, Jim, if you hold it that way, well, then you have to twist your arm when you pack this corner, see. This way it's easier."

"But that's the way Mr. Wolfe [the methods engineer] said we had to do it."

"Sure he did, Jim. But he's never had to do it eight hours a day like me. You just pay attention to what I say."

"But what if he comes around and says I should pack the other way?"

"Oh, that's easy. When he's here you do it his way. Anyway, after a couple weeks you won't see him again. Slow down. You'll wear yourself out. No one's going to expect you to do eighty pieces for a week anyway."

"But Mr. Wolfe said ninety."

Reprinted and adapted with permission from *The Ropes to Skip and the Ropes to Know* by R. H. Richard and G. Ray Funkhouser (New York: John Wiley, 1982), p. 189.

"Sure, he did. Let him do it. Look, here's how to pace yourself. It's the way I was taught, and it works. You know the 'Battle Hymn of the Republic'?" Ginny hummed a few bars. "Well, you just work to that, hum it to yourself, use the way I showed you, and you'll be doing eighty next week."

"But what if they make me do ninety?"

"They can't. Y'know, you start making mistakes when you go that fast. No, eighty is right. I always say, 'A fair day's work for a fair day's pay.'"

*P*laying Ball Without the Coach

Peter Burrows in Dallas

The machine shop where Judy Gravely works – at a Texas Instruments Inc. factory in Dallas–used to be a quiet, detached place. "We came in and put in our 40 hours, and were taught for years not to communicate," says Gravely, who machines parts for TI's missiles and bombs. All suggestions went up the ladder to a supervisor–often not to be heard of again.

No longer. Battered by defense cutbacks and vicious competition in its other high-tech markets, TI has turned to its grunts for answers on how to stay competitive. So Gravely and the other five members of her new work team now schedule their own jobs, order their own supplies, and track their own attendance. They also spend plenty of time communicating, often spotting problems before they happen. The results: The time to make a bail ring has dropped from 13.8 hours to just 5.5 hours.

Hoping to duplicate such enterprise in its other businesses, TI is adopting self-directed work teams in most parts of the company. It's difficult to quantify the collective impact on $7.4 billion TI, but sales per employee have improved–up from $88,300 in 1989 to $122,820 in 1992.

Most impressively, at the $2 billion Defense Systems & Electronics Group–where more than 80% of staffers are now on teams–profits have held steady, despite increased competition for scarce defense contracts. Fred Eintracht, team development chief for DSEG, explains that productivity gains for teams that have taken the reins range from 20% to 50%.

In part, this handing over of responsibility is an inevitable by-product of downsizing. For example, when 1,200 employees took an early-retirement package designed for only half that many, in October, 1991, DSEG executives suddenly found themselves with two fewer layers of management and more direct oversight than they could easily handle. DSEG President William "Hank" Hayes, for example, was left with 12 people reporting to him directly instead of four. "That tends to get rid of the urge to micro-manage," he explains.

That's a turnabout for TI, long known for an autocratic, top-down management style. Starting in the 1980s, increased competition in its key chip markets changed that cockiness. "We've finally started taking responsibility for what this all means for management–getting out of the way," says Hayes.

Change has not come easily or quickly, however. Even in the best cases, it takes about two years for a TI work team to take on its own day-to-day management, as the work process usually has to be completely redesigned. Supervisors have to recast themselves as facilitators–or be replaced. Information systems have to be changed to give the team members access to product cost data. And there's the up-front financial cost: TI boosted U. S. training spending 17% last year, to $35 million.

Still, some unexpected changes have sprung from the increased communication that has come to TI. In a move that would have been unthinkable a decade ago, for example, Hayes has already notified DSEG workers that half of them are likely to lose their jobs in coming months if new non-defense contracts aren't found. Workers don't like the news, but they appreciate the candor. Being taken seriously is the ultimate form of empowerment.

 # Premeeting Preparation

A. Read "A Fair Day's Work" and "Playing Ball Without the Coach."

B. Then read the Topic Introduction.

C. Answer the following questions.

1. Focus on an effective group to which you belong (or belonged).
   a. List the norms (unwritten rules of conduct) of this group.
   b. How do you think the group developed those norms?

2. Now think about a poorly functioning group to which you belong(ed).
   a. List its norms.
   b. How do you think they developed?

3. How would you go about changing the norms in a poorly functioning group?

4. What are the norms in your learning group or class? How do they hinder or promote learning?

5. What are the significant learning points from the readings?

 Topic Introduction

One of the most significant trends in business is the move towards teamwork. According to a recent study, 46% of Fortune 1000 companies are utilizing work teams.[1] The impetus for incorporating teams into organizational structures comes from the need for speed and flexibility. Downsizing strategies have eliminated supervisors and middle managers and delegated many of their functions to self-managed or self-directed teams. When they function well, such teams allow their members to make a greater contribution at work and constitute a significant competitive advantage for the organization. Research shows that self-managed teams were rated as more effective in terms of productivity, costs, customer service, quality and safety than traditionally managed teams. In addition to these benefits for the company, members of self-managed teams reported greater growth satisfaction, social satisfaction, and trust than did the members of traditionally managed groups.[2]

Self-managed work teams have the following characteristics. The teams determine how they will accomplish the goals they must achieve and how they will allocate the necessary tasks. Usually they are responsible for an entire product or process. The work teams take responsibility for planning, scheduling, organizing, directing, and controlling, and evaluating their own work process. Some teams also select their own members and evaluate members' performance. Leadership varies in these teams–some have no formal leader, others elect a leader, while still others have a formal leader assigned by management.

Even though there is currently a tendency to see work groups as a panacea, they are not appropriate for every organization. In order to succeed, teams require a common purpose and specific goals. They also need a supportive context–top management, an organizational culture, and policies that all promote and support teamwork.[3] Furthermore, team members and supervisors must be trained in the necessary skills. It is difficult for supervisors or managers to make the transition from a "boss" to a coach or facilitator. They too need to be taught skills to ensure that teams are taken seriously and allowed to succeed.

Team members require technical, administrative, and social skills. They are often cross-trained so that they possess all the technical skills needed by the team; in some companies, people are paid more when they learn new technical skills. Team members need administrative skills to run meetings and comply with whatever administrative or data-gathering requirements the team has. Team members also need interpersonal skills, such as communication, conflict resolution, problem solving, and decision making. One of the key requirements for work teams is an understanding of the group dynamics and skills presented in this chapter.

In an individualistic society like the U. S., working in groups does not come as naturally as it does in more collectivist societies where people feel a stronger sense of loyalty to groups. We have phrases like, "A camel is a horse put together by a committee," that reflect our reservations about group efforts. And in fact, Americans sometimes contribute less effort to group projects than when they work alone. This is known as "social loafing." This phenomenon was not observed in a comparison study with Chinese groups, presumably because this behavior is less likely in a collectivist society.[4] Nor do we find this behavior in "turned-on" U. S. groups and teams who work well together and find their work more productive and enjoyable as a team. Group experiences can be extremely rewarding when all goes well and extremely frustrating when members lack the proper skills. Some people believe that working in groups is inevitably less efficient, more time consuming and frustrating, and that it creates conformity in thinking. Many of these deeply held beliefs are simply unsubstantiated or found to be less generally true than was originally believed. Stoner's work,[5] for example, on the riskiness of group versus individual decisions is a case in point. It is clear that, contrary to popular belief, under certain conditions groups make more risky decisions than do individuals.[6]

All of us have participated in groups of various sorts–family, gang, team, work group–but rarely have we taken the time to observe what was going on in the group or why the members were behaving in the way they were.[7] One of the factors that affects behavior is the group's developmental age. We act differently in a brand new group than we do in a group that has been functioning for several years. Therefore, it is helpful to have an understanding of how groups typically develop, even though not all groups are exactly alike.

GROUP DEVELOPMENT

For many years, we believed that most groups evolved through the same sequence of stages. In each stage, members focus upon a specific issue that affects their behavior. The most famous model consist of these stages:[8]

1. *Forming* – a time of uncertainty when members are focused on each other, being accepted, and learning more about the group. By the end of this stage, members feel like they belong to the group.

2. *Storming* – members confront the issue of how much individuality they must relinquish to belong to the group. Conflict management is the focus of attention, and this stage is characterized by power struggles to see who will control the group.

3. *Norming* – members develop shared expectations about group roles and norms. Group cohesion and identity increases during this stage.

4. *Performing* – the group's energy is now devoted to achieving the group goals.

5. *Adjourning* – temporary groups disband and focus less on performing and more on closure.

Another way to understand group development is the punctuated equilibrium model (see Figure 9-1). According to this model, the productivity of some groups can be described as periods of inertia or equilibrium that are punctuated by a transition period of radical change that occurs at the midpoint of the group's calendar life.[9]

1. In the *first meeting*, the group sets its direction and does not reexamine it until the transition.

2. This is followed by *Phase I*, a period of inertia and equilibrium.

3. When the group has used up half its allotted time, a *transition* occurs that includes a burst of activity and a search for new ideas and perspectives. The group redefines its direction at this point.

4. A second phase of inertia and equilibrium, *Phase 2*, follows the transition.

5. Accelerated activity takes place during the group's last meeting in the *completion* phase.

Regardless of how long groups have to accomplish their task, some of them do not "get serious" until half of their time has been used up.

FIGURE 9-1   The Punctuated Equilibrium Model of Group Development

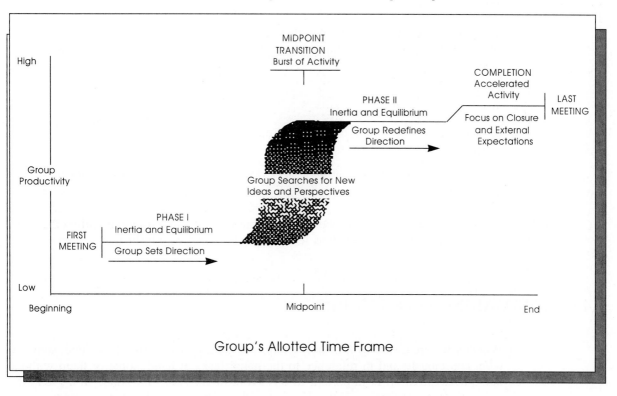

CONTENT VERSUS PROCESS

In any group there are at least two classes of issues operating at any given point. One is the reason for the group's existence in the first place (e.g., to solve a particular problem). When we observe *what* a group is talking about, we are focusing on the *content* or *task issues*.

When we try to observe *how* the group is functioning, we are talking about a second and equally important set of issues, group *process*. Group process concerns leadership, decision-making, communication, and how the group handles controversy. The content of the conversation is often a good clue as to what process issue may be on people's minds when they find it difficult to confront the issue directly. It often seems that groups spend considerable time talking about things that, on the surface, have nothing to do with the task at hand. Discussing the worthlessness of their previous Employee Involvement meetings may mean that members are not satisfied with the performance of their present group. The assumption is that it is less threatening to talk about how we feel about past EI meetings (there-and-then) than it is to talk about our feelings about the present meeting (here-and-now). The following sections focus on process issues that help us understand how groups function.

COMMUNICATION

One of the easiest aspects of group process to observe is the pattern of communication:

1. Who talks? for how long? how often?

2. Whom do people look at when they talk?
   a. Individuals, possibly potential supporters
   b. The group
   c. Nobody

3. Who talks after whom, or who interrupts whom?

4. What style of communication is used (assertions, questions, tone of voice, gesture, etc.)?

The kind of observations we make gives us clues to other important things that may be going on in the group, such as who leads whom and who influences whom.

DECISION-MAKING PROCEDURES[11]

Whether we are aware of it or not, groups are making decisions all the time, some of them consciously and in reference to the major tasks at hand, some of them without much awareness. It is important to observe how decisions are made in a group, to assess the appropriateness of the decision to the matter being decided on, and to assess whether the consequences of given–methods are really what the group members bargained for.

Group decisions are notoriously hard to undo. When someone says, "Well, we decided to do it, didn't we?" any budding opposition is quickly immobilized. We can undo the decision only if we reconstruct and understand how we made it and test whether this method was appropriate or not.

Some methods by which groups make decision are shown below.[12]

1. The *plop:* "I think we should appoint a chairperson."...Silence.

2. The *self-authorized agenda:* "I think we should introduce ourselves. My name is Jane Allen...".

3. The *handclasp:* Person A: "I wonder if it would be helpful to introduce ourselves?" Person B: "I think it would; my name is Pete Jones."

4. The *minority decision:* "Does anyone object?" or "We all agree, don't we?" Agreement or consensus may not be present, but it's difficult for others to object sometimes.

5. *Majority-minority voting:* "Let's vote and whoever has the most votes wins."

6. *Polling:* "Let's see where everyone stands. What do you think?"

7. *Consensus seeking:* Genuine exploration to test for opposition and to determine whether the opposition feels strongly enough to refuse to implement the decision; It's *not* necessarily unanimity but essential agreement by all. Consensus does *not* involve pseudo-"listening" ("Let's hear Joe out") and then doing what you were going to do in the first place ("OK, now that everyone has had a chance to talk, let's go ahead with the original decision").

TASK, MAINTENANCE, AND SELF-ORIENTED BEHAVIOR[13]

Behavior in the group can be viewed in terms of what its purpose or function seems to be. When a member says something, is the intent primarily to get the group task accomplished (task) or to improve or patch up some relationship among members (maintenance), or is the behavior primarily meeting a personal need or goal without regard to the group's problems (self-oriented)?

As the group grows and members' needs become integrated with group goals, there will be less self-oriented behavior and more task or maintenance behavior. Types of behavior relevant to the group's fulfillment of its *task* are the following:

1. *Initiating.* For any group to function, some person(s) must be willing to take some initiative. These can be seemingly trivial statements such as "Let's build an agenda" or "It's time we moved on to the next item," but without them, little task-related activity would occur in a group. People would either sit in silence and/or side conversations would develop.

2,3. *Seeking or giving information or opinions.* The clear and efficient flow of information, facts, and opinions is essential to any task accomplishment. Giving-type statements—"I have some information that may be relevant" or "My own opinion in this matter is..."—are important to ensure decisions based on full information. Information-seeking statements not only help the seeker but the entire group.

4. *Clarifying and elaborating.* Many useful inputs into group work get lost if this task-related behavior is missing. "Let me give an example that will clarify the point just made" and "Let me elaborate and build upon that idea" are examples of positive behaviors in this regard. They communicate a listening and collaborative stance.

5. *Summarizing.* At various points during a group's work, it is very helpful if some-one takes a moment to summarize the group's discussion. This gives the entire group an opportunity to pause for a moment, step back, see how far they have come, where they are, and how much farther they must go to complete their work.

Reprinted by permission of the Chicago Tribune-New York News Syndicate

6. *Consensus testing.* Many times a group's work must result in a consensus decision. At various points in the meeting, the statement "Have we made a decision on that point?" can be very helpful. Even if the group is not yet ready to commit itself to a decision, it serves to remind everyone that a decision needs to be made and, as such, it adds positive work tension into the group.

7. *Reality testing.* Groups can take off on a tangent that is very useful when cre-ativity is desired. However, there are times when it is important to analyze ideas critically and see whether they will hold up when compared to facts or reality. This helps the group get back on track.

8. *Orienting.* Another way of getting a group back on track is through orienting behavior that helps the group to define its position with respect to goals and points of departure from agreed-upon directions. When questions are raised about the direction the group is pursuing, everyone is reminded of the group goal and has an opportunity to reevaluate and/or recommit to meeting it.

The following behaviors keep a group in good working order, with a good climate for task work and good relationships that permit maximum use of member resources, namely, *group maintenance:*

1. *Gatekeeping.* Gatekeeping, directing the flow of conversation like a traffic cop, is an essential maintenance function in a group. Without it, information gets lost, multiple conversations develop, and less assertive people get cut off and drop out of the meeting. "Let's give Joe a chance to finish his thought" and "If people would talk one at a time, I'd find it easier to listen and add to our discussion" are examples of gatekeeping behavior.

2. *Encouraging.* Encouraging also ensures that all the potentially relevant information the group needs is shared, listened to, and considered. "I know you haven't had a chance to work it through in your mind, but keep thinking out loud and we'll try to help." "Before we close this off, Mary, do you have anything to add?"

3. *Harmonizing and compromising.* These two functions are very important but tricky because their overuse or inappropriate use can serve to reduce a group's effectiveness. If smoothing over issues (harmonizing) and each party's giving in a bit (compromise) serve to mask important underlying issues, creative solutions to problems will be fewer in number and commitment to decisions taken will be reduced.

4. *Standard setting and testing.* This category of behavior acts as a kind of overall maintenance function. Its focus is how well the group's needs for task-oriented behavior and maintenance-oriented behaviors are being met. All groups will reach a point where "something is going wrong" or "something doesn't feel right." At such points, effective groups stop the music, test their own process, and set new standards where they are required. "I'm losing track of the conversation. If other people are willing, maybe it would help if someone could summarize the last 10 minutes."

5. *Using humor.* The use of humor to put people at ease and reduce tension is an important maintenance function. However, the inappropriate use of humor can prevent groups from reaching their goals quickly and stop them from tackling uncomfortable issues that need to be resolved.

For a group to be effective, both task-oriented behavior and maintenance-oriented behavior are needed.

EMOTIONAL ISSUES: CAUSES OF SELF-ORIENTED EMOTIONAL BEHAVIOR[14]

The process described so far deals with the work-facilitating functions of task and maintenance. But there are many active forces in groups that disturb work, that represent a kind of emotional underground or undercurrent in the stream of group life. These underlying emotional issues produce a variety of self-oriented behaviors that interfere with or are destructive to effective group functioning. They cannot be ignored or wished away, however. Rather, they must be recognized, their causes must be understood, and as the group develops, conditions must be created that permit these same emotional energies to be channeled in the direction of group effort. What are these issues or basic causes?

1. The problem of identity: Who am I here? How am I to present myself to others? What role should I play in the group?"

2. The problem of control and power: Who has the power in the situation? How much power, control, and influence do I have in the situation? How much do I need?

3. The problem of goals: Which of my needs and goals can this group fulfill? Can any of my needs be met here? To which of the group's goals can I attach myself?

4. The problem of acceptance and intimacy: Am I accepted by the others? Do I accept them? Do they like me? Do I like them? How close to others do I want to become?

Self-oriented behaviors tend to be more prevalent in a group at certain points in the group's life. Early in the life of a new group one can expect to see many examples of self-oriented behaviors. Members are new to one another and a certain amount of "feeling out" is to be expected. Sometimes this takes place in after-hours social situations– "Why don't we get together after work for a drink?" On a less intense scale, the same phenomenon can be observed at the start of a group meeting with an old, established group. Side conversations and social chatter characterize the first few minutes while people catch up on where they have been since the last meeting.

A third point in a group's life when self-oriented behaviors can be observed is when a newcomer joins an already established group. It is not unlike the dynamics that develop when a new sibling arrives in a family. Everyone else may be sincerely happy with the newcomer ("We really need her resources"); nonetheless, this is now a "new" group. The old equilibrium has been changed and a new one must take its place.

None of the foregoing sounds particularly like an undercurrent, an emotional underground, that could be potentially destructive to effective group functioning. While all these issues can be observed in a group, their potential destructiveness is highest at that time when the group most needs to be maximally effective–under stress. In that sense, they are akin to regressive individual behaviors: in times of stress, individuals will regress to an earlier stage of development. Different individuals handle their anxiety in different ways, thus generating many different kinds of reactions in groups.

Types of emotional behavior that result from tension and from the attempt to resolve underlying problems appear below.[15]

1. Tough emotions: anger, hostility, self-assertiveness
    a. Fighting with others
    b. Punishing others
    c. Controlling others
    d. Counterdependency

2. Tender emotions: love, sympathy, desire to help, need for affiliation with others
    a. Supporting and helping others
    b. Depending on others
    c. Pairing up or affiliating with others

3. Denial of all emotion
    a. Withdrawing from others
    b. Falling back on logic or reason

Individuals have different styles of reducing tension and expressing emotion. Three "pure types" have been identified:

1. The "friendly helper" orientation: acceptance of tender emotions, denial of tough emotions–"Let's not fight, let's help each other;" —can give and receive affection but cannot tolerate hostility and fight.

2. The "tough battler" orientation: acceptance of tough emotions and denial of tender emotions–"Let's fight it out;" —can deal with hostility but not with love, support, and affiliation.

3. The "logical thinker" orientation: denial of all emotion–"Let's reason this thing out"; —cannot deal with tender or tough emotions; hence shuts eyes and ears to much going on around him or her.

BUT:

Friendly helpers *will* achieve their world of warmth and intimacy *only* by allowing conflicts and differences to be raised and resolved. They find that they can become close with people *only* if they can accept what is dissimilar as well as what is similar in their behavior.

Tough battlers will achieve their world of toughness and conflict *only* if they can create a climate of warmth and trust in which these will be allowed to develop.

Logical thinkers will achieve their world of understanding and logic *only* if they can accept that their feelings and the feelings of others (both tough and tender) are also facts and contribute importantly toward our ability to understand interpersonal situations. Table 9-1 portrays the different orientation and characteristics of each type. These three, as described, are clearly pure types; the average person has some elements of each. What differentiates people is their predisposition towards a particular type.

TABLE 9-1 Orientation of the "Pure Types"

1. FRIENDLY HELPER	2. TOUGH BATTLER	3. LOGICAL THINKER
Best of All Possible Worlds		
A world of mutual love, affection, tenderness, sympathy	A world of conflict, fight, power, assertiveness	A world of understanding, logic, systems, knowledge
Task-Maintenance Behavior		
Harmonizing Compromising Gatekeeping by concern Encouraging Expressing warmth	Initiating Coordinating Pressing for results Pressing for consensus Exploring differences Gatekeeping by command	Gathering information Clarifying ideas and words Systematizing Procedures Evaluating the logic of proposals
Constructs Used in Evaluating Others		
Who is warm and who is hostile? Who helps and who hurts others?	Who is strong and who is weak? Who is winning and who is losing?	Who is bright and who is stupid? Who is accurate and who is inaccurate? Who thinks clearly and who is fuzzy?
Methods of Influence		
Appeasing Appealing to pity	Giving orders Offering challenges Threatening	Appealing to rules and regulations Appealing to logic Referring to "facts" and overwhelming knowledge
Personal Threats		
That he or she will not be loved That he or she will be overwhelmed by feelings of hostility	That he or she will lose his or her ability to fight (power) That he or she will become "soft" and "sentimental"	That his or her world is not ordered That he or she will be overwhelmed by love or hate

We can learn to use emotional resources more appropriately by:

a. Accepting our own feelings and acknowledging that each of us has both tender and tough emotions.

b. Understanding group behavior at the feeling level as well as at the logical level, since feelings are also part of the group's reality.

c. Increasing our awareness through observation and analysis of the causes of emotions. By learning to recognize which events in the here-and-now trigger emotions, we can gain better control of ourselves in a given situation and behave more appropriately.

d. Experimenting with expressing emotion differently and asking for feedback.

Another issue that must be addressed with respect to group functioning is group norms. A norm is an unwritten, often implicit rule that defines what attitudes and behaviors characterize a "good" group member versus a "bad" group member. Norms are the group's shared beliefs about appropriate behavior, attitudes, and perceptions concerning matters that are important to the group. For example, in the opening vignette, "A Fair Day's Work," Ginny made sure Jim the newcomer learned the rules–that doing 80 pieces was good. Doing 90 would be bad because then the boss might pressure everyone to maintain that rate. Ginny was socializing Jim, teaching him the ropes. By doing so, she pointed out the difference between formal rules–those set by bosses and that may or may not be obeyed–and informal rules–norms that employees enforce among themselves. If a member does not comply with important group norms, the other members will pressure him or her to do so. If he or she still does not comply, the rest of the group may well ostracize the offending group member. If Jim were to insist on making 90 pieces, he would soon be labeled a rate buster and given the cold shoulder.

All groups create norms as they develop and mature. In and of themselves, norms are neither good nor bad. The important point is whether or not the norms that do exist support the group's work or act to reduce effectiveness. In this way, group norms control the behavior of members and make group life more predictable.

Let's take a real-world example. The president of a multimillion-dollar multinational corporation wanted to make a major change in the way he and his three vice presidents functioned. The general pattern of behavior was such that each vice president would argue for decisions that would benefit their particular department. Turf battles and tunnel vision were standard fare during group meetings.

It was the president's desire to create what he called "the Office of the Presidency." When he and his VPs met, he wanted everyone to look at the issues before them from an executive perspective. In other words, he wanted everyone to focus on the corporation as a whole, looking at decisions through the "eyes" of a president.

Clearly a host of group norms would have to change dramatically. Historically, no meeting ever began until the president arrived. After all, it was "his meeting." If the new philosophy was to be taken seriously, the "Office of the Presidency" had to function *irrespective* of who–as an individual–was present or absent.

One Monday morning the three VPs arrived for their normally scheduled meeting. But one "small" problem had arisen: a devastating weekend snowstorm caused the president to be stranded 1,000 miles away. Still, several critical topics were on the agenda. After considerable anxious grasping for solutions (conference calls, private jets, and even prayer) and much nervous laughter, they bit the bullet. The "Office of the Presidency" was called to order. An old norm had been changed.

The pinch point occurred Tuesday morning at 8:00 A M, only now it was the president who felt the anxiety. To his credit, he asked to be *informed* as to the decisions taken by the Office of the Presidency in his absence. Any other behavior on his part, such as reopening decisions he personally did not like, would have violated, and made a game of, the new normative expectations.

Many groups operate under the norm: "In this group, no one ever dares to question or suggest that we examine our norms." As a result, there is an absence of standard setting and testing and an implied punishment for anyone who engages in such behavior. Such a "Catch 22" norm is unlikely to facilitate the development of an effectively functioning group.

Procedure for Group Meeting:
The Inner-Outer Exercise

The purpose of this exercise is to provide an opportunity to experience and study group dynamics and discuss effective work groups.[16]

STEP 1.   Divide the class into pairs of subgroups of approximately eight to twelve members. There should be an equal number of members in the paired subgroups. Choose two observers for each pair of groups. The paired groups sit in two circles, a tight inner circle and an outer circle in which the chairs are placed behind those in the inner circle. The observers sit outside the second circle at opposite points so each has a clear view of a different part of the group.

The subgroups seated in the inner circle will be called Group A; the subgroups seated in the outer circle are Group B.

STEP 2.   Each subgroup has the same two tasks. The subgroups will also have the same amount of time to complete the tasks–4 periods of 4 minutes each for a total of 16 minutes (or whatever time periods your instructor chooses). You are allowed to work on the two tasks only when your subgroup is seated in the inner circle. At this time, you should act as if the other subgroup is not present. When your subgroup is seated in the outer circle, your role is to act as observers and potential consultants to the other subgroup. Therefore, you should observe carefully how the other subgroup functions. Try to identify what they are doing that either impedes or facilitates their accomplishment of the two tasks. Please write down your observations, *but do not talk with the other members of your subgroup while you are in the outer circle* because it will distract the other group.

The members of the first subgroup in the inner circle will have 4 minutes to work before time is called; then they will have 4 minutes to observe while the second subgroup sits inside the circle. The two subgroups may borrow ideas from each other, but the goal is for each subgroup to develop independent results.

The two tasks are:
1. Be the most effective group you can; and
2. Create a list of the ten characteristics of effective groups and rank order it.

To summarize, your subgroup has two roles: "problem-solvers" when you are seated inside the circle and "observers" when you are seated outside.

STEP 3.   Observers read the Observer Instructions on page 230.

STEP 4.   After the second round, members of the subgroup in the inner circle will turn around to face the members of the other subgroup who are seated directly behind them. Both people should act as consultants to the other subgroup. Tell the other person what you saw occurring in his or her group and give some advice about how the other subgroup could function more effectively. The idea is for everyone to listen carefully to someone who has observed his or her subgroup and take back to that group suggestions for improvement. Thus, members of both groups have the opportunity to both give and receive advice during a 4 minute period. Then complete the final rounds of the exercise.

STEP 5.   Each subgroup presents their list of the characteristics of effective groups or posts them on the wall if using flip charts. What are the similarities and differences? (5 minutes)

STEP 6.   Everyone counts off by four. Each group will have 20-30 minutes to discuss a different aspect of group process that has a major impact on the life of any group or team. Our goal is to figure out what behaviors either hindered or helped group effectiveness.

Group One's task (all the number 1's) is to explore the concept of "goals" as they have influenced the life of the two developing subgroups. You should look at goals from the perspective of those that were imposed on the group by the instructor, and those that evolved as the real group goals, which may or may not have anything to do with those established by the instructor. Did you see any individual goals that differed from the general goals of the group? Please develop specific examples of how individual and group goals influenced the life of the subgroups and helped determine their success. How can groups handle the problem of disparate goals?

Group Two's task (all the 2's) is to look carefully at the "membership" criteria that prevailed in the subgroups. Membership in this case is equivalent to what behaviors were acceptable or not acceptable in terms of gaining entry to the group. During this exercise, some individuals gained greater membership than others because of their behavior. What kinds of behavior or circumstances made some people less than "full" members? Why? The group must understand not only what these criteria were but also how they influenced the feelings, motivation, and morale of the group itself. Please give examples of each of the criteria that you develop and examples of how they influenced the life of the subgroups. What can a group do to make everyone feel like a full member?

Group Three's task is to take an in-depth look at the behavioral norms, the implicit or explicit "rules of the game," that influenced the life of each group. How did the groups handle conflict and stress, make decisions, listen, generate ideas, allow certain language to prevail, etc.? Be sure that with every norm that you identify you note specific examples and make comparisons among the subgroups when it is obvious that some of the norms differed radically. What can groups do to ensure that they develop norms that help rather than hinder group effectiveness?

Group Four's task is to explore the kinds of leadership that developed in the groups–who had it, who took it, to whom it was given, and who if anyone was able to establish and maintain a real presence of leadership? What different kinds of behaviors did leaders demonstrate? What behaviors resulted in either resistance or a loss of leadership? Decision-making is of specific importance here–how were decisions made, who made them, and how did this influence the group? The names of individuals are not important but specific behaviors are because we can then begin to understand how the life of each group was influenced. If you observe different types of leadership, what were the pros and cons of each leadership style? What can a group do to promote the type of leadership that is most effective for that group?

You will all have 20-30 minutes to develop an understanding of your particular concept and to provide specific examples of what occurred in the groups.

STEP 7.   Each of the four groups present their findings and examples.

STEP 8.   The observers present their communication feedback to the subgroup they observed. What are the implications of the communication pattern that emerged? What are the consequences of talking a lot in a new group and talking very little? (10 minutes)

1. Did your subgroup act out all the characteristics on your list? Why or why not?
2. How would you describe the relationships between the paired subgroups?
   Did you see any evidence of competition? If so, where did the competition come from?
   Did the subgroups learn from watching each other? Why or why not?
3. What was the result of the consultation period? Why did this result(s) occur?
4. What did you learn about the way you behave in groups?

OBSERVER INSTRUCTIONS

Your task is to unobtrusively chart the communication that takes place in one of the subgroups, using the Observer Chart on the following page. Please don't talk or distract the group in any way.

1. Write down the names of the people in your subgroup in the same order, both horizontally and vertically.

2. When a person speaks to another group member, please code who is speaking to whom and how often by putting a mark in the box that intersects the speaker's name on the side with the target of the communication, whose name is listed along the top. If it is a statement, write down a hatch mark. If it is a question, write down a question mark.

   The way to tell to whom a remark or question is addressed is to watch the eyes of the speaker. If the speaker is clearly making an effort to make eye contact with the whole group while talking (scanning) or is not looking at anyone when speaking, count the target as the "group" as a whole (the first column). Otherwise, count it as a communication directed at the person whom the speaker is looking at *when he or she finished talking*. That person is usually the one we are trying to influence or looking to for support. So even if the person has looked at other people while talking, code the communication in the box of the last person the speaker looked at.

3. Write down any observations you have about the way the subgroup is communicating or functioning on the bottom of the Observer Chart. Does anyone seem left out of the discussion and, if so, why? Is there a dominant person or subgroup that is controlling the communication? Is anyone exhibiting task behavior? Is anyone exhibiting process behaviors?

4. Add up the marks and prepare your feedback for the subgroup. Remember to deliver it in a non-evaluative and non-interpretive fashion so that no one becomes defensive.

Observer Chart – Who Speaks to Whom?

TARGET

Speaker	Group	Name 1	Name 2	Name 3	Name 4	Name 5	Name 6	Name 7	Name 8	Name 9	Name 10	Name 11	Name 12	TOTAL
Name 1														
Name 2														
Name 3														
Name 4														
Name 5														
Name 6														
Name 7														
Name 8														
Name 9														
Name 10														
Name 11														
Name 12														
TOTAL														

Code: Statements ⊬⊦⊤ Questions ???

Observations:

Follow-Up

As society becomes more complex and we continue to make major advances in our technological capability, more and more of organizational life will revolve around a team or group structure. The "information explosion" will guarantee that no one person can expect to have all the facts necessary to make many decisions. "Temporary systems" in which a group of people join for a short-term task and then disperse to form new and different task groups to tackle other problems have become more prevalent. Groups play an important role in organizational life today, and every indication points toward increased importance in the future.

The distinction made in this exercise between task issues and process issues can be important in understanding how groups function. Most of us assume that if a group of people is called together to perform a task, nothing but the task is important or relevant. This assumption rests upon the belief that it is not only feasible but essential that we separate our emotional self (needs, wants, motives) from our intellectual, rational, problem-solving self. This is impossible. When people enter a group situation, they bring their total selves, the emotional as well as the intellectual. In fact, certain aspects of our emotional selves will become more salient because we are in a group situation. Attempts to bury, wish away, or ignore the interpersonal aspects of group interaction is much like sweeping dirt under the rug–sooner or later the pile gets big enough that someone will trip over it.

In some ways, the appointment of a chairperson or moderator reflects recognition of the fact that groups do not always "stay on the track." While this is often useful, there are two potential problems with this approach. First, seldom do the group members spend any time discussing why they are "off the track." More often the chairperson will say something like "We're getting off the main track, let's get back to it!" and that's all that happens. It is extremely important to realize that if people are having difficulty staying on the track, there are reasons for the behavior and simply saying "Let's get back to it" does nothing to eliminate the basic causes. Worse than that, this kind of behavior ("Let's quit wasting time and get to the task") may further accelerate the underlying reasons for lack of involvement and may make the situation worse.

Second, there is no inherent reason that only one person in a group should have the responsibility for worrying about how the group is progressing. Everyone can and should share this responsibility. To delegate this function or role to one individual is in some situations a highly inefficient utilization of resources. People can learn to be effective participant-observers at one and the same time. In such a group, *anyone* who feels that something is not right can and should raise the issue for the total group to examine. Anyone who observes a need for a particular kind of task or maintenance behavior can help the group. In a well-functioning group (working on something other than a routine programmable task), an observer looking in from the outside might not be able to pick out the formal leadership. The "leadership function" passes around according to the group's need at a particular point. It is important, in other words, to distinguish between leaders as persons and leadership as a function. For example, summarizing or gatekeeping when the group needs it is performing an important act of leadership. To see the need and fail to respond can be viewed as a failure to fulfill one's membership responsibilities.

It is often argued that "We don't have the time to worry about people's feelings or to discuss how the group is working." Sometimes this is perfectly true, and under severe task pressure a different kind of process is necessary and legitimate. People can accept this, however, if they know from past experience that this situation is temporary. More often, however, lack of time is used as a defense mechanism to avoid the discussion completely. Furthermore, if a group is continually under severe time pressure, some time ought to be spent examining the effectiveness of the group's planning procedures.

A group that ignores individual members' needs and its own process may well find that it meets several times to make the same set of decisions. The reason for this is that the effectiveness of many decisions is based on two factors[17]–logical soundness and the level of psychological commitment among the members to the decision made. These two dimensions are not independent; in fact, some people who are uncommitted (often because of process issues) may withhold, on a logical basis, information necessary to make the soundest decision. In any event, the best decision (on a task or logical level) forged at the expense of individual commitment is indeed not a very good decision at all.

Finally, what can be done to learn to use self-oriented emotional resources more appropriately? As a first step, it is important to accept our own feelings and to realize that everyone has both tender and tough emotions. Within some American companies, managers (and particularly males) are expected to be tough, hard, and aggressive. Any sign of "tender emotions" (warmth, affection) may be perceived as a sign of weakness. However, feelings do not go away simply because we ignore them, and there is no question that emotions can affect group decisions. Given the opportunity to experiment with and get feedback on our emotional behavior (and a climate that supports such behavior), we can become more aware of when it is appropriate to be tough, tender, or neither.

It is foolhardy to assume that simply because a group of people assemble to perform a task, it will somehow automatically know how to work together effectively.[18] A comparison between the behavior of a football team and the behavior of a management team highlights the essence of this paradox. The football team spends untold hours practicing teamwork in preparation for the 60 minutes each week that its members' performance as a team really counts. In contrast, most management teams do not spend even 60 minutes per week practicing teamwork in spite of the fact that for 40 or more hours every week their behavior as a team really counts. For this reason, in recent years both management groups and work teams have undergone team-building training where they examine their goals, roles, procedures, and interpersonal relationships. Just as we did in the group exercise, team-building participants learn to diagnose what is occurring with their group and focus upon discovering more effective ways to work together.[19] Teams work better when they share common methods of problem-solving, decision-making and conflict management–topics that are addressed in following chapters.

INTERNATIONAL EXAMPLE OF GROUP NORMS – A CONCRETE EXPERIENCE AND REFLECTIVE OBSERVATION

As we saw in the exercise, norms vary from group to group. They also vary from culture to culture. The following vignette relates the "concrete experience" of one expatriate professor who taught overseas.

I sat back in my chair, glancing around the handsome room with its graduation photographs of faculty members in full academic regalia, including some remarkably fetching scarlet robes and exotic headgear from a Spanish university. Finding it difficult to break an unconscious habit of punctuality, I have spent many moments alone in this room, waiting for colleagues to arrive. As a result, I have learned to bring along small projects to occupy my time while waiting for those who live by a different internal clock. By now, other faculty members, all males except for myself, are dribbling in, responding to the external summons of a telephone call from on high, the Rector's (president's) secretary. They enter with a lot of good-natured greetings and jokes and, as always, it is a pleasure to see them.

In today's meeting, the Dean is trying to get faculty support and compliance with policies and procedures that will improve academic standards and quality. As usual, I am intrigued by the norms in these meetings. Even though there are only ten people present, the Dean jots down the names of the professors who wish to speak in the order in which they signal him. This order is respected in the beginning but becomes more difficult to maintain when people want to respond immediately to the comments. At this point they are reminded by the Dean or others that there are several people ahead of them in the queue. Occasionally, a senior faculty member is allowed to break in and make his comments without being reprimanded for being out of order. The result of the group's self-imposed structure is often a disjointed conversation with lots of looping back to previous points. There seems to be an unspoken expectation that everyone should speak at some point in the meeting, whether or not they are contributing a different opinion. The Dean fields and reacts to each comment or question, immediately judging its worth. I am always surprised that one person, rather than the group, is granted the power to dispose of ideas that could possibly be developed and honed by more group discussion. If the communication pattern were graphed, it would show that a large majority of the comments are directed to and returned from a central hub, the Dean. A much smaller percentage of the interactions occur laterally among the participants.

Since I agree with the policies and am already complying with the rules, my most fervent wish is to have the meeting end quickly so I can "return to work." I sense no similar urgency on the part of my colleagues; they are "at work." I decide to take advantage of the situation to clarify a practice I have never fully understood. I ask if students might not do better on future tests if their exams were returned to them. My suggestion is rapidly shot down with comments like, "This is the way it's always been done" and "Students would take advantage of the policy you are suggesting." Except for another expatriate, no one appears to find any merit in my suggestion and the discussion quickly moves on.

When the meeting ends, I head for yet another one with my departmental colleagues. I am immediately struck by the difference in atmosphere between the two meetings. Perhaps because we share many of the same values and because we have put in many hours and miles together, I feel more at ease, more listened to, and much more able to be myself in the second meeting. This group also has more experience working with women, so gender is not an issue. We are like a self-managed group in many ways. We begin a free-wheeling discussion in which everyone chimes in on a single topic until closure is reached, and then we move on to another point. We are tackling a topic that we chose ourselves–determining our regional strategy. Comments are directed to the entire group and everyone, including brand new employees, apparently feels free to respond with his or her opinions and even feelings. The group has a coordinator but not a formal leader. The coordinator helps keep the group on track at times, but does not make the decisions. After vigorous discussion with clear differences of opinion, the group makes consensus decisions. It never occurs to me that I am a minority or an outsider in this meeting, even though I do not always agree with what my colleagues do or say. I don't find myself glancing at my watch in this meeting, and when we leave to return to our individual offices, I have a smile on my face.

When I reflect on this situation, I see numerous cultural differences between myself, an American, and the other faculty members who are primarily Latin American. Although not all individuals or organizations fit these stereotypes, the following cultural differences are generally acknowledged and appear to influence the norms in the first meeting. A major difference is a polychronic versus monochronic orientation. People in monochronic cultures tend to be punctual and do one thing at a time in a linear fashion. In polychronic cultures, people pay attention to several things at once; punctuality is less important than finishing other activities. In this example the monochronic American arrives on time and is disconcerted when one topic is not discussed until it is completed. The polychronic Latins arrive when it is convenient and easily track the various topics being discussed at once. For them, speaking out in the meeting may serve to maintain relationships and promote a sense of collegiality; in contrast, the norm that everyone should speak runs counter to a U. S. value of not wasting time.

Other differences are that Latins tend to respect tradition and resist policy changes while many Americans value change, sometimes for its own sake. Decision-making is more centralized and leadership is more authoritarian in Latin America, which explains why people grant the Dean the right to pass judgement on suggestions. In comparison, Americans tend to be more participative and egalitarian. The take-a-number-to-speak norm is not found in all Latin groups; it may be somewhat unique to the dominant organizational culture. However, there is a greater emphasis upon control and rules in Latin cultures, accompanied by attempts to get around these rules. People with high status or connections are more successful at evading rules, which explains why senior faculty are not always obliged to respect the queue. In U. S. universities, senior faculty are also privileged. What varies from school to school and country to country is the particular form that privilege takes.

In both meetings, there are norms that promote friendly relations and an institutional concern for excellence. Beyond these similarities, the two meetings are characterized by very different norms even though the cultural composition is fairly similar in both groups. Cultural differences are less significant in the departmental group than in the more formal faculty meeting. The smaller group is part of a cultural subgroup with values that are closer to my own and norms that I have helped create. As a result, only in the second group do I feel like a full-fledged member.

Learning Points

1. In order to set the stage for successful work teams, organizations require supportive top management, an organizational climate and policies that promote teamwork, teams with a common purpose and specific goals, and supervisors and team members who have the necessary skills to make teams function.

2. Self managed work teams are not appropriate in all situations, but they can be more effective and satisfying than traditionally managed teams.

3. The Five-Stage Model of group development consists of forming, storming, norming, performing, and adjourning.

4. The Punctuated Equilibrium model describes group productivity as periods of inertia or equilibrium that are punctuated by a transition period of radical change that occurs at the midpoint of the group's calendar life. Productivity accelerates again right before the group's time is completed.

5. In any group there are two types of issues operating at any given time: content and process. Content issues refer to the task, "what" the group is working on. Process issues refer to "how" the group is going about achieving its task.

6. By observing communication patterns and decision-making procedures, we can understand better how a group functions.

7. Task behaviors contribute to accomplishing the group task or goal. They consist of initiating, seeking, or giving information or opinions, clarifying and elaborating, summarizing, consensus testing, and orienting.

8. Maintenance behaviors are geared toward creating a good climate for work and good relationships that permit maximum use of member resources. They are gatekeeping, encouraging, harmonizing and compromising, standard setting and testing, and using humor.

9. Groups need both maintenance and task behaviors to be effective. Groups that emphasize content and ignore their process are just as likely to fail as groups that emphasize process at the cost of task.

10. Self-oriented emotional behavior interferes with effective group functioning. Issues of identity, inclusion, power, acceptance, intimacy, and goal agreement occur and reoccur at various points in a group's development.

11. The "pure types" that represent the three different styles of reducing tension and expressing emotion are:
    a. The "friendly helper" (tender emotions)
    b. The "tough battler" (tough emotions)
    c. The "logical thinker" (denial of all emotions)
    However, each of these types can only create the type of climate in which they feel most comfortable by incorporating some of the perspectives of the other two types and accepting their dissimilarities.

12. We can learn to use our emotional resources better by
    a. Accepting our personal feelings.
    b. Trying to understand the feelings that occur in a group.
    c. Trying to identify what causes our emotions to be triggered in a group.
    d. Experimenting with expressing emotion differently and asking for feedback.

13. Group norms are unwritten, often implicit, rules that define the attitudes and behaviors that characterize good and bad group members. All groups have norms. By making them explicit, a group can determine whether their norms help or hinder their group's effectiveness.

14. Ideally, all members of a group should be participant-observers so everyone can contribute to keeping the group on track and bringing up the need to discuss process issues that may be hindering the group. Group leadership should be performed by more than just the designated leader.

15. Groups that ignore their process often take longer to resolve content issues because process problems prevent commitment and full sharing of information.

16. It takes practice and effort to transform a group into an effective team.

for Managers

- Groups of employees can have either positive or negative impact on productivity and the work environment, depending upon the norms and stances they have taken. The more cohesive the group, the more likely they are to take a unified position; cohesive groups aren't by definition more productive than cohesive groups.

- Informal leaders of employee work groups are important communication links for getting input, sending out trial balloons, and disseminating information about upcoming plans or events.

- Understanding group behavior is especially important at meetings. Heightening people's awareness of the roles they play is often helpful as is rotating the responsibility for chairing the meeting so everyone has an opportunity to develop leadership skills and see, at the same time, how difficult it is to run a good meeting.

- Asking a work group to help establish norms can be very effective. It can be done by asking them:

  What would be effective behaviors at work?
  How should we treat each other at work?
  How should we make decisions?
  How should we communicate?
  Do we have any norms that are keeping us from being effective?

- Teams need ready access to pertinent information if they are to succeed.

- If you want to avoid the problem of social loafing on a team, reward the team on the basis of their results and on the basis of individual contribution to those results.

- The characteristics of a productive team are:[20]
  - common agreement on high expectations for the team
  - a commitment to common goals
  - assumed responsibility for work that must be done
  - honest and open communication
  - common access to information
  - a climate of trust
  - a general feeling that one can influence what happens
  - support for decisions that are made
  - a win-win approach to conflict management
  - a focus on process as well as results.

Personal Application Assignment

The face-to-face group working on a problem is the meeting ground of individual personality and society. It is in the group that personality is modified and socialized; and it is through the workings of groups that society is changed and adapted to its times. (Herbert Thelen)

This assignment is to write about a group experience or incident about which you want to learn more. (You may wish to write about one of the exercises you did with your learning group in this course.)

A. *Concrete Experience*

   1. *Objectively* describe the experience ("who," "what," "when," "where," "how" type information–up to 2 points).

   2. *Subjectively* describe your feelings, perceptions, and thoughts that occurred during (not after) the experience (up to 2 points). Does this section have too much detail? (If so, delete 1 point.)

B. *Reflective Observation*

   1. Look at the experience from different points of view. How many points of view did you include that are *relevant* (up to 2 points)?

   2. Use these perspectives to add more meaning to the incident (up to 2 points).

C. *Abstract Conceptualization*

1. Relate concepts from the assigned readings and the lecture to the experience (i.e., what theories that you heard in the lecture or read in the Reader relate to your understanding of this incident?). Make reference to at least two sources. Use standard referencing format and include the page number to which you are referring. How many sources did you use and how clearly did you explain their theories (up to 4 points)?

2. You can also create an original model or theory, but it should not replace course concepts.

D. *Active Experimentation*

1. Write about what you will do in the future that will improve your effectiveness. Use rules of thumb or action resolutions.

2. Are they described specifically, thoroughly, and in detail (up to 4 points)?

E. *Integration, Synthesis, and Writing*

1. Did you write about something personally important to you (up to 2 points)?

2. Was it well written (up to 2 points)?

3. Did you integrate and synthesize the different sections (up to 1 points)?

[1]Edward E. Lawler, III, Susan A. Mohrman, and G. E. Ledford, Jr., *Employee Involvement and Total Quality Management: Practices and Results in Fortune 1000 Companies* (San Francisco: Jossey-Bass, 1992).

[2]Susan G. Cohen and Gerald E. Ledford, Jr., "The Effectiveness of Self-Managing Teams in Service and Support Functions: A Field Experiment." Paper presented at the Academy of Management annual meeting, San Francisco, August, 1990.

[3]Jon R. Katzenback & Douglas K. Smith, *The Wisdom of Teams* (Cambridge, MA: Harvard Business School Press, 1992).

[4]P. Christopher Earley, "Social Loafing and Collectivism: A Comparison of the United States and the People's Republic of China," *Administrative Science Quarterly,* December 1989, pp.565-81.

[5]James A. F. Stoner, "Risky and Cautious Shifts in Group Decisions: The Influence of Widely Held Values," *Journal of Experimental Social Psychology*, no. 4 (1968), pp. 442-459.

[6]Roger Brown, "Group Polarization," in *Social Psychology*, 2nd ed. (New York: Free Press, 1986).

[7]The literature on group dynamics has grown to enormous proportions. See J. Richard Hackman, (ed.), *Groups that Work (and Those that Don't)* (San Francisco: Jossey-Bass, 1990); Kimball Fisher, *Leading Self-Directed Work Teams* (New York: McGraw-Hill, 1993); and Alvin Zander, *Groups at Work* (San Francisco: Jossey-Bass, 1977, and *Making Groups Effective* (San Francisco: Jossey-Bass, 1982).

[8]B. W. Tuckman and M. C. Jensen, "Stages of Small Group Development Revisited," *Group and Organizational Studies*, December 1977, pp. 419-27; and M. F. Maples, "Group Development: Extending Tuckman's Theory," *Journal for Specialists in Group Work*, Fall 1988, pp. 17-23.

[9]Connie G. Gersick, "Time and Transition in Work Teams: Toward a New Model of Group Development," *Academy of Management Journal*, March 1988, pp. 9-41; and Connie G. Gersick, "Marking Time: Predictable Transitions in Task Groups," Academy of Management Journal, June 1989, pp. 274-309.

[10]For a discussion of the differences between content and process issues, see Edgar H. Schein, *Process Consultation: Its Role in Organizational Development* (Reading, MA: Addison-Wesley, 1988).

[11]Much of the following material has appeared in a variety of places and is a standard input into many training programs such as those conducted by the National Training Laboratory. This particular material was abridged with permission of the author from "What to Observe in Groups," From *Reading Book for Relation Training*, C. R. Mill and L. C. Porter, eds. (Arlington, VA: NTL Institute, 1982), pp. 28-30; and Barry E. Collins and Harold Guestzkow, *A Social Psychology of Group Processes for Decision Making* (New York: John Wiley, 1964).

[12]This typology was developed by Robert R. Blake.

[13]K. D. Benne and P. Sheats, "Functional Roles of Group Members," *Journal of Social Issues*, Vol. 2 (1948), pp. 42-47, and Edgar H. Schein, *Process Consultation*. (Reading, MA: Addison-Wesley, 1988).

[14]This section is based on Schein's *Process Consultation*.

[15]For another view of emotional behavior in groups, see William C. Schutz, "Interpersonal Underworld," *Harvard Business Review*, Vol. 36, no. 4 (July-August 1958), pp. 123-125, and W. W. Liddell and J. W. Slocum, Jr., "The Effects of Individual Role Compatibility upon Group Performance: An Extension of Schutz's FIRO Theory," *Academy of Management Journal*, Vol. 19 (1976), pp. 413-426.

[16]Adapted from Rodney W. Napier and Matti K. Gershenfeld, *Making Groups Work: A Guide for Group Leaders*, (Boston: Houghton Mifflin, 1983), pp. 114-120.

[17]This dichotomy of a decision's quality is analogous to issues raised during the discussion of the concept of psychological contract in the introduction of Chapter 1. In that case, the dichotomy was the decision to join versus the decision to participate. See also Chapter 15, Leadership and Decision Making, for more detail on effective decision-making styles.

[18]One such process for learning how to work more effectively in groups is called broadly "laboratory training." For a full discussion of this and related educational techniques, see Edgar H. Schein and Warren G. Bennis, *Personal and Organizational Change Through Group Methods: The Laboratory Approach* (New York: John Wiley, 1965).

[19]For good description of team building, see William G. Dyer, *Team Building: Issues and Alternatives* (Reading, MA: Addison-Wesley, 1987), and R. Fry, I. Rubin, and M. Plovnik, "Dynamics of Groups that Execute or Manage Policy," in *Groups at Work*, ed. by R. Payne and C. Cooper (New York: John Wiley, 1981), pp. 41-57.

[20]William D. Hitt, The Leader-Manager, (Columbus, OH: Batelle Press, 1988).

Chapter 10

MANAGERIAL PROBLEM SOLVING

OBJECTIVES By the end of this chapter, you should be able to:

A. Explain the four stages of managerial problem solving: situation analysis, problem analysis, solution analysis, and implementation analysis.

B. Describe the red/green modes of problem solving.

C. Explain the different roles a manager plays during problem solving.

D. Discuss the link between learning styles and problem-solving styles.

E. Identify what problem-solving stage a group is in and have some ideas about how to facilitate a group's progress.

The Pendulum Swings

Christopher M. Barlow

A group of construction specialists, attempting to reduce the cost of a new office building, proposed replacing a 10-story spiral staircase for the atrium with a 10-story brass pendulum. The architect was delighted. The owner was enthusiastic. Half a million dollars was saved!

This may give you visions of executives sliding down the brass pole, but it really made perfect sense. The function of the staircase was not to serve as a way to get from floor to floor. The building had elevators to do that. The spiral staircase was merely an architectural feature to convey an upsweeping dynamic vision to visitors.

The group realized that projecting an image was the key to the problem. They brainstormed a variety of different ways to project such an image. In the end they settled on the brass pendulum, partly because of the money it would save.

A group less skilled at problem solving would have proposed ways to build the spiral staircase more cheaply. This group got to the nub of the matter and focused on the function of the staircase. Groups need to manage their problem-solving and communication process to find the pendulums, not cheapen the staircase.

Used with permission from the author, Creativity and Value Consultant, Appleseed Associates, Cleveland, Ohio.

Premeeting Preparation

A. Read "The Pendulum Swings" and "The Cardiotronics, Inc. Case."

B. Read the Topic Introduction.

C. What were the significant learning points from the readings?

D. Make a plan to conduct tomorrow's meeting of Assembly Unit D as if you were Marion Andrews. Prepare a list of questions or statements that Marion could use during each stage of the problem-solving process described in the Topic Introduction. For example, what kinds of questions would facilitate good problem solving during the valuing stage, the priority-setting stage, and so on?

Role Play Preparation:
Questions/statements leaders can use during each stage of the problem solving process:

A. Valuing/Exploration

B. Priority Setting

C. Information Gathering

D. Problem Definition

E. Idea Getting

F. Decision Making

G. Participation

H. Planning

Cardiotronics, Inc.

Cardiotronics, Inc., was started 17 years ago in a small New Hampshire town by two biomedical engineers whose goal was to produce a quality cardiac monitor (a device that continuously displays the wave pattern of the heart's function). The company originally produced customized monitors on a small scale. After 5 years the owners had perfected a quality monitor that was significantly less expensive than custom monitors and they decided to mass produce it.

The company currently has just over 200 employees. It remains nonunionized, but the labor union in this old New England milltown has from time to time made efforts to win a union election.

For the past 11 years, the company has enjoyed a strong competitive edge and has gained a reputation for a quality product and prompt service. Recently, however, the company's top management team has been informed that a similar monitor, reputed to be of equal or better quality than Cardiotronic's, will soon be introduced into the U. S. market by a large Japanese electronics firm.

Monitor Assembly Process. The cardiac monitors (excluding cables) are produced in four stages. In the first stage, circuit boards are produced largely by machine process. During the second stage, the circuit boards are placed by hand on a "mother" board and are connected to one another. The final step in stage 2 is the attachment of the mother board to the base panel. In the third stage, the casing is mounted by hand onto the base panel and external hardware and cables are placed. In the final stage, the monitors are tested for a week before shipping.

The Second-Stage Assembly Task. Four assembly teams are responsible for the second stage of monitor assembly, the manual assembly and the wiring of the "mother" board. Each team consists of five workers operating in a U-shaped area. The mother board is started at station 1. Each worker adds their circuit, connects it to the others, and passes it to the next worker. The assembly process requires some manual dexterity but is relatively easy to do. Each job on the line is of equal difficulty as determined by a recent industrial engineering study. The assembly arrangement for one of these teams, Team D, is as follows.

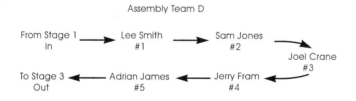

The following are the recently announced assembly team average daily production figures for the last month:

Team A = 40 boards
Team B = 32 boards
Team C = 43 boards
Team D = 35 boards

Your Problem as Marion Andrews, Supervisor of Team D. You are the new supervisor of Team D, Marion Andrews. You have been in the position for a month having recently been promoted from the quality control section where you worked for 5 years. During your second week you received a memo stating that to meet increased production requirements resulting from increased sales, all second-stage teams were to meet their minimum daily production rates. You informed the team in a brief meeting but had to leave for a week of supervisory training shortly thereafter. After returning from the training program you note that the daily production has increased to 36 but that your team is still 4 units below the daily minimum rate of 40 units. In looking into the problem you note the following:

- Work accumulates at the station of Joel Crane (station 3), and there are typically several "mother" boards waiting. Joel is 58 years old and has been with the company for 13 years. The supervisors of the other production teams do not consider Joel acceptable for transfer.

- Only one monitor from your team has been rejected in the past month by quality control.

- Assembly and test equipment is relatively new and in good working order.

Team D's assembly line will be closed for 30 minutes tomorrow, and you have decided to call a meeting for Team D.

How do you plan to conduct this meeting?

 # Topic Introduction

For many scholars who study organizations and management, the central characteristic of organizations is that they are problem-solving systems whose success is measured by how efficiently they solve the routine problems associated with accomplishing their primary mission, be it manufacturing automobiles or selling insurance, and how effectively they respond to the emergent problems and opportunities associated with survival and growth in a changing world.[1] Kilmann's view is representative of this perspective:

> *One might even define the essence of management as problem defining and problem solving, whether the problems are well structured, ill structured, technical, human, or even environmental. Managers of organizations would then be viewed as problem managers, regardless of the types of products and services they help their organizations provide. It should be noted that managers have often been considered as generic decision makers rather than as problem solvers or problem managers. Perhaps decision making is more akin to solving well-structured problems where the nature of the problem is so obvious that one can already begin the process of deciding among clear-cut alternatives. However, decisions cannot be made effectively if the problem is not yet defined and if it is not at all clear what the alternatives are, can, or should be.[2]*

In this view, the core task of management is problem solving. While experience, personality, and specific technical expertise are important, the primary skill of the successful manager is the ability to manage the problem-solving process in such a way that important problems are identified and solutions of high quality are found and carried out with the full commitment of organization members.

Problem solving has received more attention in recent years due to the emphasis upon employee involvement groups and total quality programs. As a result, the initiative and responsibility for problem solving has been pushed farther down in the organizational hierarchy. Problem solving techniques are being taught at all levels in companies that have a continuous improvement orientation.[3]

THE NATURE OF PROBLEM SOLVING

This chapter describes a model of the problem-solving process that defines the stages and tasks involved in such a way that managers can better manage their own and their organization's problem-solving activities. This model of problem solving is based on three premises: first, that problem solving is basically a process of learning from experience; second, that problem solving involves the manipulation and control of the external world through one's mental processes (mind over matter); and third, that problem solving is by its nature a social process.

A Process of Learning from Experience

The experiential learning process presented in Chapter 3 identifies four phases: concrete experience, reflective observation, abstract conceptualization, and active experimentation. Common sense notions of problem solving tend to focus on the phases of concrete experience and active experimentation–on the specific difficulties experienced in immediate situations and the actions taken to overcome them. Traditional educational ideas about learning, on the other hand, tend to focus on the phases of reflective observation and abstract conceptualization–emphasizing the gathering of information and development of general concepts. Just as it has been proposed that the process of traditional education is improved when the concrete and active emphasis of problem solving is added,[4] it can be suggested correspondingly that the effectiveness of problem solving is enhanced by the addition of the academic learning perspectives of reflection and conceptualization. In both cases, what results is a more holistic and integrated adaptive process. More specifically, by viewing problem solving as a process of experiential learning, more attention is given to finding the right problem to work on, problems are more adequately defined, better quality solutions are found, and the implementation process is more effective.

Mind over Matter

The ability to solve complex problems is uniquely human, resulting from the structure of the human mind, first, in its dialectic ability to perceive experiences in the world and to comprehend these experiences through words and other symbols. Second, human self-consciousness provides a perspective on and control over this process. We can choose which aspects of our experience to attend to and discipline ourselves to pursue a line of thought or action. As Kaplan described it, "The manager gives form to a problem in the way a potter sees and then shapes the possibilities in a lump of clay. The difference is that managers practice their craft using an intangible medium: information."[5] Thus, problem solving is the process of using our minds to control the world around us. It is literally the way we achieve the power of mind over matter. For centuries humans watched birds fly and dreamed that they, too, might fly. That vision of flight became a motivator of countless problem-solving efforts that have culminated today in flight achievements far beyond the dreams of our ancestors.

Problem solving is not just an activity of the mind; it is fundamentally a social process. Solutions to problems are inevitably combinations, new applications, or modifications of old solutions. From other people we get new dreams, new ideas, information, and help in getting things done. Language, communication, and conflict are central in problem solving. Particularly in organizations, it is difficult to conceive of a problem that does not in some way involve other people — in choosing the problem, supplying information about it, helping to solve it, or implementing the solutions. Given the social nature of problem solving, the effective management of problem solving involves four tasks:

1. The management of one's own and other's thinking processes to ensure an orderly and systematic process of analysis that determines the right problem or opportunity to work on, the most likely causes of the problem, the best solution given available alternatives and constraints, and a process for implementing the solution that ensures quality and commitment.

2. The proper organizational arrangements to promote cooperation among interdependent groups and assignment of problems to appropriate organizational units.

3. The management of relationships among people to ensure the appropriate involvement and participation of others.

4. The constructive use of conflict in an organization climate that removes interpersonal and group barriers to information sharing and collaborative problem solving.

A MODEL OF PROBLEM SOLVING BASED ON THE THEORY OF EXPERIENTIAL LEARNING

The model of problem solving derived from the theory of experiential learning describes an idealized problem-solving process that is characteristic of the fully functioning person in optimal circumstances. Ineffective problem solving is seen as the result of deviations from that normative process because of personal habits and skill limitations or because of situational constraints such as time pressure or the limited access to information that can result from one's position in the organization or from mistrusting relationships with subordinates. The model consists of four analytic stages that correspond to the four stages of the experiential learning cycle. Stage 1, situation analysis, corresponds to concrete experience; stage 2, problem analysis, to reflective observation; stage 3, solution analysis, to abstract conceptualization; and stage 4, implementation analysis, to active experimentation. These four stages form a nested sequence of analytical activities so that each stage requires the solution of a particular analytic task frame the succeeding stage properly.

The four stages of problem solving and the basic questions each answers are presented in the paragraphs that follow.

Situation Analysis: What's the Most Important Problem?

The task of *situation analysis* is to examine the immediate situational context to determine the right problem to work on. While problem-solving activity is often initiated by urgent symptomatic pressures, urgency alone is not a sufficient criterion for choosing which problems to work on. As every manager knows, the press of urgent problems can easily divert attention from more important but less pressing long-term problems and opportunities. Every concrete situation contains a range of problems and opportunities that vary in urgency and importance. Some of these are obvious, whereas others are hidden or disguised. Situation analysis requires exploration to identify the problem that takes precedence by criteria of both urgency and importance. This is what is meant by the popular saying, "Managers do things right; leaders do the right thing." Problem finding is equally as important as problem solving.

Problem Analysis: What are the Causes of the Problem?

Given the appropriate choice of a problem, the task of *problem analysis* is to define the problem properly in terms of the essential variables or factors that influence it. Here the task is to gather information about the nature of the problem and evaluate it by constructing a model of the factors that are influencing the problem. This model serves to sort relevant from irrelevant information and guides the search for further information to test its validity. The result of problem analysis is to define the problem so that the criteria to be met in solving it are identified.

Solution Analysis: What's the Best Solution?

Once the problem is analyzed correctly, the third stage, *solution analysis*, seeks to generate possible solutions and to test their feasibility for solving the problem against the criteria defined in stage 2. This is the most intensively studied stage of problem solving, best known through Osborns' early work on brainstorming.[6]

Implementation Analysis: How Do We Implement the Solution?

The solution chosen in solution analysis is next implemented in the fourth stage of problem solving: *implementation analysis*. Tasks essential for implementing the solution must be identified and organized into a coherent plan with appropriate time deadlines and follow-up evaluations. Responsibility for implementing the plan is developed through participation of those individuals and groups not already involved in the problem-solving activity who will be directly affected by the solution. Implementation activities from stage 4 are carried out in the situation identified in stage 1 and thus modify that situation, creating new opportunities, problems, and priorities. Effective problem solving is thus a continuing interactive cycle paralleling the experiential learning cycle. For example, when the participation of affected individuals is elicited in implementation analysis, new problems and opportunities may come to light as priorities for continuing problem-solving efforts. There is some evidence that the solution to one problem causes another.

THE DIALECTICS OF PROBLEM SOLVING

The process of problem solving does not proceed in a logical, linear fashion from beginning to end but rather is characterized by wavelike expansions and contractions alternatively moving outward to gather and consider alternatives, information, and ideas and inwardly to focus, evaluate, and decide. These expansions and contractions have been variously labeled green light/red light and divergence/convergence.

Elbow's[7] description of "doubting" and "believing" games is another way to conceptualize the two different mind sets required for problem solving. The doubting game focuses upon a reductive, structured, "objective" rationality. People with this orientation are constantly asking, "What's wrong with this?". As a result, they poke holes in ideas and arguments, torpedo assumptions, and probe in an analytical manner. In contrast, the first rule of the believing game is that people refrain from doubting or evaluating and instead focus on possibilities, how an idea *could* work. Thus, problem solving is not the result of a single mental function such as logical thinking. Effective problem solving involves the integration of dialectically opposed mental orientations—red and green mode mind sets.

The red mode mind set facilitates analysis, criticism, logical thinking, and active coping with the external environment. The green mode mind set facilitates creative imagination, sensitivity to the immediate situation, and empathy with other people. The red mode mind set is therefore most appropriate for the contraction phases of problem solving—priority setting in situation analysis, problem definition in problem analysis, decision making in solution analysis, and planning in implementation analysis. The green mode mind set, on the other hand, facilitates the expansion phases of problem solving—valuing, information gathering, idea getting, and participation. Effectiveness in problem solving is enhanced by approaching the expansion/contraction phases of each problem-solving stage in the appropriate mind set. For problem solvers to accomplish this matching of mind set and problem-solving task, they must first become aware of when they are in the red or green mode of consciousness and then learn to shift from one mode to another. With some practice, this can be accomplished quite easily, and usually, practice in identifying and separating the two mind sets has the effect of increasing the intensity of both. This purity of conscious mind set increases problem-solving effectiveness by enhancing the dialectics of each analytical stage. Similarly, managing the problem-solving process with groups of people requires the creation of a climate that stimulates and reinforces the appropriate mind set in participants.

The problem-solving process is further guided by four roles that focus the dialectic interplay of red and green mind sets on the relevant stage of the problem-solving process. In situation analysis, the problem solver adopts the role of a *leader,* focused on identifying goals and values in the situation in the green mode and setting priorities in the red mode. In problem analysis, the role is that of a *detective,* focused on gathering information in the green mode and building and evaluating models in the red mode. In solution analysis, the role is that of an *inventor*: generating ideas in the green mode and testing their feasibility in the red mode. In implementation analysis, the problem solver adopts the *coordinator* role: developing participation in the green mode and planning in the red mode. Conscious attention to these roles serves to focus attention on the priorities of each analytic stage and signals the transition from one stage to another. A diagram of this refined model is shown in Figure 10-1 and is described in the paragraphs that follow.

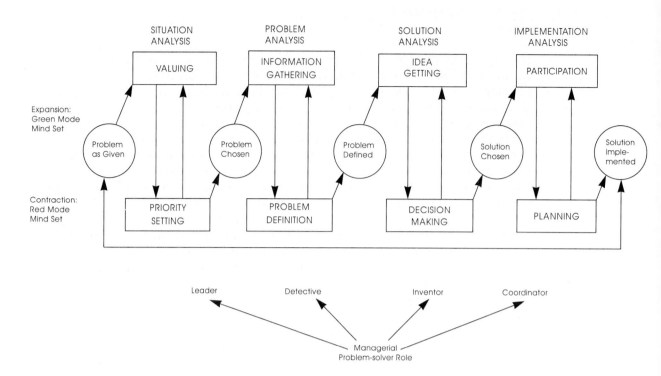

SITUATION   PROBLEM   SOLUTION   IMPLEMENTATION
ANALYSIS   ANALYSIS   ANALYSIS   ANALYSIS

VALUING   INFORMATION   IDEA   PARTICIPATION
                 GATHERING   GETTING

Expansion:
Green Mode
Mind Set

Problem   Problem   Problem   Solution   Solution
as Given   Chosen   Defined   Chosen   Imple-
                                                                    mented

Contraction:
Red Mode
Mind Set

PRIORITY   PROBLEM   DECISION   PLANNING
SETTING   DEFINITION   MAKING

Leader   Detective   Inventor   Coordinator

Managerial
Problem-solver Role

Figure 10-1   Problem Solving as a Dialectic Process

SITUATION ANALYSIS–VALUING AND PRIORITY SETTING

Most problem-solving activity begins with a problem as given–a specific circumstance, task, or assignment that demands attention. The task of situation analysis is to transform this problem as given into a problem that is consciously chosen to meet the dual criteria of urgency and importance. Urgent structured problems in organization are often the result of previous failure to address unstructured problems (e.g., the continued urgent need to replace bank tellers may result from the failure to address more unstructured problems of worker morale or career opportunities). Structured problems are repetitive and routine, and definite procedures are developed for dealing with them. Unstructured problems are novel and not covered by ready-made procedures because they occur infrequently or are very complex. In addition, for many organizations in rapidly changing environments, aggressive opportunity seeking is essential to maintain stability and growth. Careful situation analysis is therefore most critical in those cases where long-term adaptation to a changing environment takes precedent over expedient action.

When people discuss problems, they devote time to talking about how they would like the situation to be. For example, the technique of visioning involves asking people to close their eyes and imagine their ideal organization. This reflects the green mode, whereas the exploration of current realities represents the red mode. The result is a menu of problems and opportunities in the situation from which one can be chosen that satisfies the criteria of urgency and importance. The process of articulating desired goal states is called *valuing*. To be successful, the valuing process must overcome barriers that exist in most organizational settings to open sharing of values. Foremost among these barriers is the organizational press to be realistic. Wishing, wanting, and valuing must be explored independently of reality for them to develop fully. Two other barriers to the valuing process are the fear of conflict and the threat of isolation.

Charles Lindblom[8] noted some time ago that it is easier to find agreement on a course of action than it is to get agreement on the goals for the action. Discussion of values accentuates human individuality and emotional commitment with a resulting increase in conflict among viewpoints. In the dialectic view, such conflict is essential for the discovery of truth, although most managers shy away from conflict because it is unpleasant and they do not know how to use disagreement constructively. A related barrier to valuing is the threat of isolation that comes from holding values different from those of the majority. It is this barrier that gives rise to conformity and group-think in problem finding.[9] A worker, for example, may suppress his or her genuine values for achievement and excellence so as not to violate group norms of mediocrity. For this reason an effective valuing process requires an environment that gives security and support for individuality.

The contrasting pole to valuing in the situation analysis dialectic is *priority setting*. As with any dialectic, valuing and priority setting mutually enhance one another–valuing gives direction and energy to priority setting and priority setting gives substance and reality to valuing. Every managerial decision reflects values; choosing one problem as a priority reveals the values of the decision makers. Priority setting has three specific tasks: 1) to explore the current situation for those features that facilitate or hinder goal achievement, 2) to test the feasibility of changing those features, and 3) to articulate reality-based goal statements that give substance to values and allow them to be realized. Priority setting is not a rational, analytic process of reflective planning. It is an active, intuitive process of trial and error exploration of what is going on in the situation. It involves "knocking on doors," listening to people, trying things out, and taking risks.

Taken as a whole, the central issue in situation analysis is leadership, and the basic social role of the problem solver is that of a leader whose responsibility is to guide the problem-solving attention of the organization to those problems and opportunities whose solution will be of maximum benefit to the long-run effectiveness of the organization. Someone once said that the key to successful leadership is to find out which way people are going and then run out in front of them. There is an element of truth in this, for the successful leader in situation analysis identifies the values and goals of those in the situation and then holds up those that are most important as priorities for action.

PROBLEM ANALYSIS–
INFORMATION GATHERING AND PROBLEM DEFINITION

Problem analysis begins with the problem chosen in situation analysis and seeks to understand and define the problem in such a way that solutions to it can be developed. In the expansion mode, information about the concrete problem situation is gathered. The *information-gathering phase* of problem analysis is a receptive, open-minded phase in which all information associated with the problem is sought and accepted. This receptive stance has both a cognitive and interpersonal component. Cognitively, it is important in the information-gathering phase to avoid biases and preconception about the nature of the problem and its causes in favor of letting the data about the problem speak for themselves. Interpersonally, information gathering requires skills in the development of trusting relationships so that others do not hold back or modify information to say "what the boss wants to hear" or to avoid reprisals. In many organizations, these two components negatively interact with one another to produce a climate where the gathering of accurate information is very difficult. Mistrust and threat cause workers to withhold information, and this forces management to rely on its own prejudgments as to the nature of the problems. By acting on these prejudgments, they sometimes reinforce worker mistrust and perpetuate a cycle that restricts accurate information exchange.

In the contraction mode, *problem definition*, the task is to define the problem based on the information gathered. Problem definition is basically a process of building a model portraying how the problem works–factors that cause the problem, factors that influence its manifestation, and factors mediating the application of solutions. Two skills are critical in building a model that defines a problem: causal analysis and imagery. Causal analysis uses the inductive logic of experimental inquiry to evaluate data and identify those invariant causal relationships that define the problem. It is a means of sorting relevant from irrelevant information. Imaging is a way of refining the problem definition by imagining its dynamics and subjecting them to "thought experiments." Stated simply, imaging is the process of creating in one's mind a model or scenario of how the problem occurs and then subjecting that model to various transformations to understand how the model operates and how the problem might be solved. Prince describes this process nicely:

> *Imaging is our most important thinking skill because it accompanies and facilitates all other thinking operations. I find it useful to think of my imaging as my display system or readout of my thinking processes.*[10]

With practice, imaging can create richly detailed problem scenarios and can portray large amounts of information in complex interrelationships. When concrete information is juxtaposed against a conceptual model, it serves to evaluate that model. Furthermore, the model serves to guide the search for new relevant information. In a sense, the problem solver in the problem analysis is in the role of detective–gathering clues and information about how the "crime" was committed, organizing these clues into a scenario of "who done it," and using that scenario to gather more information to prove or disprove the original hunch. The dialectic between information gathering and the problem definition has a synergistic power over information or model alone. By combining them, one can learn from what does not occur or has not happened as well as from what has. As in Sherlock Holmes's famous case, "The Dog Who Didn't Bark," a model suggests events that should occur if the model is true and thus their nonoccurrence in reality can invalidate the model.

The output of the problem analysis phase is a model of the problem validated through the interplay of information gathering and problem definition–a problem as defined. The problem as defined describes the problem in terms of those essential variables that need to be managed to solve it.

SOLUTION ANALYSIS–
IDEA GETTING AND DECISION MAKING

Solution analysis is achieved through the interplay between getting ideas about how the problem can be solved and decision making about the feasibility of the ideas generated. This two-stage process has been highly developed in brainstorming. The first step of solution analysis focuses on creative imagination, the green light stage of brainstorming, where the aim is to generate as wide a range of potential solutions as possible in an atmosphere that is free from evaluation and supportive of all ideas. Research on both communication and meeting behavior reveals that most responses are evaluative. Obviously, this does not promote either creativity or participation.

The second substage, the red light stage of brainstorming, focuses on evaluation, sorting through the ideas generated in the first substage and evaluating them systematically against the criteria that an effective solution must meet. This substage ends with the selection of the best solution. In the solution phase, the problem solver takes the role of inventor, creatively searching for ideas and then carefully evaluating them against feasibility criteria.

IMPLEMENTATION ANALYSIS– PARTICIPATION AND PLANNING

Implementation analysis is accomplished through the interplay of planning and the process of carrying out plans. Since implementation of solutions in organizational settings is most often done by or with other people, the critical expansion task is *participation*, enlisting the appropriate involvement of those actors in the situation who are essential to carrying out the problem solution. Three subtasks are involved here:

1. The anticipation of the consequences that will result from implementing the solution and the involvement of those who will experience these consequences in developing ways to deal with them.

2. The identification of those key individuals who by virtue of expertise and/or motivation are best qualified to carry out the various tasks in implementation.

3. Sometimes in the process of accomplishing 1) and 2), it becomes necessary to ask these key individuals to recycle through the problem solving process to reevaluate whether the most important problem has been chosen, whether the problem is properly defined, and whether the best solution has been identified.

In the participation phase of implementation, the essential attitude to adopt is inclusion of others, receptivity, and openness to their concerns and ideas.

The *planning phase* of implementation analysis is an analytic process involving the definition of tasks to be accomplished in implementing the solution, the assignment of responsibility to qualified individuals, the setting of deadlines and planning for follow-up monitoring, and the evaluation of the implementation process. If the problem and its solution are very complex, planning may be quite complicated using network planning methods such as PERT (Program Evaluation Review Technique) or CPM (Critical Path Method) of analysis. Often, however, a simple chart listing key tasks, responsible individuals, and time deadlines is sufficient for planning and monitoring implementation.

As with the other three stages of our problem-solving model, there are two dialectically related processes involved in implementation analysis. The first involves developing plans for implementation and identifying the potential consequences of implementing these plans. An iterative process is often useful here–scout potential issues that may arise in implementation, develop a rough plan, share it with those involved in the situation to get reactions, and then modify the plan. The other dialectic can be termed the "who's" and the "what's." Managers appear to have distinct stylistic preferences about how they deal with this issue. Some prefer to define the "what's" first–the plan and tasks to be accomplished–and then assign these tasks to individuals to carry them out. Others begin with the "who's," seeking to identify qualified and interested individuals and then developing plans with them. While the best approach probably varies with the situation and task, beginning with the "who's" has the advantages of giving priority to often-scarce human resources and maximizing participation and delegation. In synthesizing these dialectics, the problem solver in implementation analysis adopts the role of coordinator, working to accomplish tasks with other people.

Reprinted by permission of Tribune Company Syndicate, Inc.

Cultural differences can be seen in the way problems are solved in different countries.[11] Some cultures (for example, Thailand, Indonesia, and Malaysia) are more likely to accept situations as they are; therefore they are slower to identify and resolve problems. In other cultures, like the U.S., managers are more likely to take a problem-solving approach to most situations and perceive problems as an opportunity to make improvements. Fixing problems is part of the American orientation towards action.

The alternative solutions developed in problem solving are also affected by cultural orientations toward time. Cultures that are oriented towards the past (England, Italy) tend to look for historical patterns and lessons. Future-oriented cultures (U.S., Australia) are more likely to generate new alternatives because they are less bound to the past.

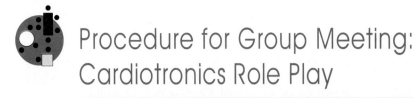

Procedure for Group Meeting: Cardiotronics Role Play

PART 1. ASSEMBLY TEAM D MEETING

(Time Allotted: 45 Minutes)

During the meeting, groups will have the opportunity to practice problem solving on a real work problem by means of a role play.

STEP 1. In this role play each group of six class members will be Assembly Team D with individuals in your group assuming the role of Marion Andrews, Lee Smith, and so on. (In groups of five, combine the Lee Smith role with that of Sam, i.e., "Sam can speak for his friend Lee who is sick today." Groups larger than six should have observers. Observers should take notes on the group's problem-solving process during the role play using the Cardiotronics Case Review form on page 257.)

STEP 2. Group members should choose roles. One person should play Marion Andrews and prepare to conduct the meeting. Role descriptions for the other team members are on the pages cited.

Lee Smith	page	267
Sam Jones		269
Joel Crane		271
Jerry Fram		273
Adrian James		275

Tear out the page describing your role and make a "name tent."

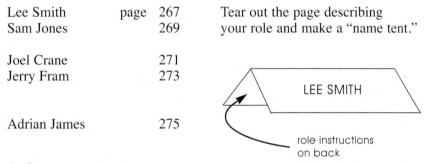

role instructions on back

STEP 3. Action.

Instructions for Team D workers

Place your name tent in front of you after you have read the role descriptions and prepare to be the person described.

FOUR TIPS ON ROLE PLAYING:
- Be *yourself* as much as you can.
- Imagine yourself in that person's life.
- Don't "ham it up."
- Talk loudly enough for the observers to hear.

Instructions for Marion Andrews

The assembly line just closed and the five workers from Assembly Team D have gathered in your office. You have 30 minutes to conduct the problem-solving meeting before everyone goes back to work.

PART II. ANALYSIS

(Time Allotted: 1 Hour, 15 Minutes)

STEP 1. After finishing the role play, write down the decision that was reached. (5 minutes)

In our group it was decided to:

STEP 2. The group should prepare a group review of its problem-solving process by completing the Cardiotronics Case Review on page 257 (30 minutes).

STEP 3. Results from each group should be summarized for discussion on a chalkboard or flip chart so the whole group can compare subgroup results. The "Summary of Role-Play Results" on page 266 give one format for preparing this summary. The last row in this chart gives results for 10 groups of business executives for comparison purposes. (5 minutes)

STEP 4. Everyone should read the summary. (5 minutes)

STEP 5. Total group discussion. (30 minutes) Each group should share the solution it decided on and describe the highlights of the problem-solving process. Consider the following questions:

a. What differences were there in the problem-solving process followed in each group?

b. Were these differences related to the adequacy of the solutions arrived at (e.g., firing or removing Joel is not a particularly good solution since work would only pile up at Jerry's position; realizing this requires green mode-information getting so that Jerry feels free to share his role information)?

c. What common obstacles to effective group problem solving came up? How were these dealt with by Marion Andrews? By other Team D members?

d. What connections can you make between this exercise and the readings?

Cardiotronics Case Review

DESCRIBE HOW THE FOLLOWING PROBLEM-SOLVING ACTIVITIES TOOK PLACE	APPROXIMATE % OF TOTAL PROBLEM-SOLVING TIME SPENT IN THIS ACTIVITY	SEQUENCE IN WHICH ACTIVITY TOOK PLACE IN MEETING (1 = FIRST, 2 = SECOND, ETC.)
Valuing Examining the situation for opportunities and problems:		
Priority Setting Agreeing on the most important problem:		
Information Gathering Getting information on possible causes:		
Problem Definition Choosing most likely cause:		
Idea Getting Generating possible solutions:		
Decision-Making Selection of the best idea:		
Participation Deciding how/when to involve others:		
Planning Constructing a plan:		

Follow-Up

Most experienced managers tend naturally to follow a problem-solving sequence that is close to that described in the four-phase model of situation analysis, problem analysis, solution analysis, and implementation analysis. There are however, significant differences in the amounts of energy devoted to each of these phases, which sometimes inhibits effective problem solving. Perhaps the most significant of these is the tendency to spend too little time defining the problem at hand before generating possible solutions. This tendency to be solution oriented often results in the treatment of symptoms, rather than causes of the problem, and time is wasted working on solutions before relevant information is known. If this process is widely typical of an organization's problem solving, a crisis fire-fighting atmosphere develops where symptom-oriented solutions fail to resolve basic problems that recur over and over. This further reduces the time available for thoughtful situation and problem analysis.

Effective problem solving requires balanced attention to each phase of the problem solving process and equal emphasis on the expansion/green mode and contraction/red mode mind sets. We learned in Chapter 3, Individual and Organizational Learning, that individual learning styles emphasize different aspects of the experiential learning cycle. There is a strong correlation between people's learning styles and the way they approach problem solving.

USING THE EXPERIENTIAL LEARNING MODEL TO ANALYZE PERSONAL APPROACHES TO PROBLEM SOLVING

Figure 10-2 overlays a model of the problem-finding and problem-solving process on the experiential learning cycle and identifies problem-solving activities that characterize different stages of the cycle. In this figure we can see that the stages in a problem-solving sequence generally correspond with the learning style strengths of the four major learning styles described earlier. The accommodator's problem-solving strengths lie in executing solutions and in initiating problem finding based on some goal or model about how things should be. The diverger's problem-solving strengths lie in identifying the multitude of possible problems and opportunities that exist in reality ("compare model with reality" and "identify differences"). The assimilator excels in the abstract model building that is necessary to choose a priority problem and create alternative solutions. The converger's strengths lie in the evaluation of solution consequences and solution selection.

Let us briefly examine two organizational studies to illustrate the practical implications of this theoretical model. The first study[12] was conducted in the Trust Department of a large U.S. bank. One aim of this study was to discover how the learning styles of investment portfolio managers affected their problem solving and decision making in the management of the assets in their portfolios. While the study involved only 31 managers, there was a strong correspondence between the type of decisions these managers faced and their learning styles. More specifically, nearly all the managers in the Investment Advisory section of the department, a high-risk, high-pressure job (as indicated by a large percentage of holdings in commons stock, a large percentage of discretionary accounts, and a high performance and risk orientation on the part

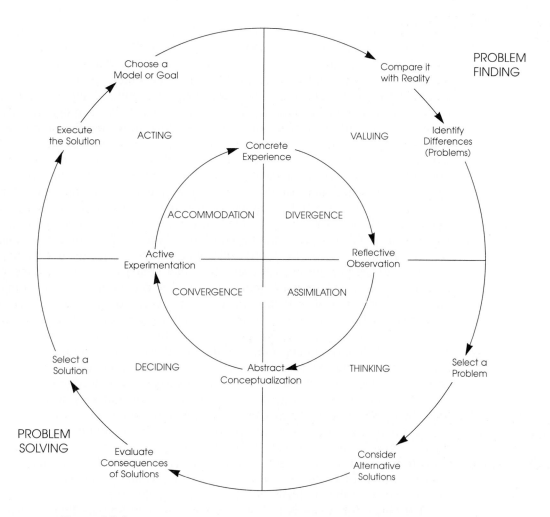

Figure 10-2   Comparison of the Experiential Learning Model and the Problem-Solving Process

of clients), had accommodative learning styles (scoring very high on the AE and CE LSI scales). On the other hand, the people in the Personal Trust section, where risk and performance orientation were low and where there were few discretionary accounts and fewer holdings in common stock, scored highest on reflective observation. This finding supports the view that high-pressure management jobs select and develop active experimentation learning skills and inhibit reflective observation learning skills.

The study also attempted to study differences on the basis of their LSI scores, in the way managers went about making investment decisions. The research focused on differences between managers with concrete experience (CE) learning skills and abstract conceptualization (AC) learning skills. Managers were asked to evaluate the importance of the information sources that they used in making decisions. CE managers cited more people as important sources (e.g., colleagues, brokers, and traders), while the AC managers listed more analytically oriented printed material as important sources (e.g., economic analyses, industry and company reviews). In addition, it seemed that CE managers sought services that would give them a specific recommendation that they could accept or reject (e.g., a potential list), while the AC managers sought information that they could analyze themselves to choose an investment. This analytic orientation of the AC managers is further illustrated by the fact that they tended to use more information sources in their decisions than the CE managers. These data fit well with the learning/problem-solving model. The concrete managers prefer go/no-go implementation decisions based on personal recommendations, while the abstract managers prefer to consider and evaluate alternative solutions themselves.

The second study of the relationship between learning styles and managerial problem solving was a laboratory computer simulation of a production "trouble-shooting" problem where the problem solver had to determine which specific type of "widget" was failure-prone.[13] This experiment was conducted with 22 middle-level managers at the Massachusetts Institute of Technology's Sloan Fellows program. The study focused on the different types of problem-solving strategies that assimilators and accommodators would use to solve this problem. It was predicted that the accommodators would use a strategy that called for little complexity in use and interpretation, little inference from the data, and little cognitive strain in assimilating information, whereas assimilators would prefer a strategy that had the opposite characteristics–more complex use and interpretation and more assimilation strain and required inference. The former strategy, called successive scanning, was simply a process whereby the problem solver scans the data base of widgets for a direct test of his or her current hypothesis. It requires little conceptual analysis, since the current hypothesis is either validated or not in each trial. The latter strategy, called simultaneous scanning, is in a sense an "optimal" strategy in that each data point is used to eliminate the maximum number of data points still possible. This strategy requires considerable conceptual analysis since the problem solver must retain several hypotheses mentally at the same time and deduce the optimal widget to examine to test these hypotheses. The results of the experiment confirmed the hypothesis that accommodators would use successive scanning, while assimilators would use the more analytical simultaneous scanning strategy. It was further found that managers with accommodative learning styles tended to show more inconsistency in their use of strategies, while the assimilative managers were quite consistent in their use of the simultaneous scanning strategy. The accommodative managers seemed to be taking a more intuitive approach, switching strategies as they gathered more data during the experiment. Interestingly, the study found no differences between accommodative and assimilative managers in the amount of time it took them to solve the problem. Although the two groups used very different styles in this problem, they performed equally well.

The Guide for Analysis of Your Personal Problem-Solving Process that follows identifies more specifically the types of problem-solving activities that characterize the different phases of the learning/problem-solving process. Its purpose is to assist you in the analysis of problem situations and how you approach them in a manner similar to that used in the experiments just described. Activities that characterize the four learning style types are grouped together around the learning cycle so you can assist your stylistic emphasis in the problem-solving processes you reported.

Guide for Analysis
of Your Personal Problem-Solving Process

Describe the problem briefly. _____

_____

_____

Rate on a scale of 1 to 7 how much each of the following activities were a part of your approach to the problem you were trying to solve. Record the consensus score of your group.

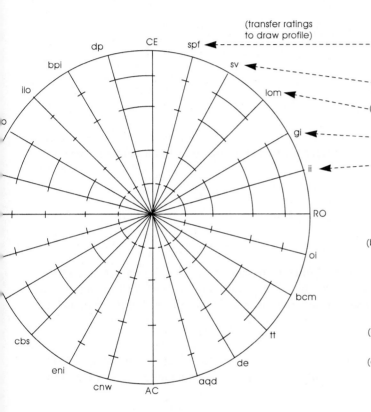

(transfer ratings to draw profile)

		Very Little	Moderate	Very Much	
(spf)	Being sensitive to people's feelings	1 2	3 4 5	6 7	DIVERGER
(sv)	Being sensitive to values	1 2	3 4 5	6 7	
(lom)	Listening with an open mind	1 2	3 4 5	6 7	
(gi)	Gathering information	1 2	3 4 5	6 7	
(ii)	Imagining implications of ambiguous situations	1 2	3 4 5	6 7	
(oi)	Organizing information	1 2	3 4 5	6 7	ASSIMILATOR
(bcm)	Building conceptual models	1 2	3 4 5	6 7	
(tt)	Testing theories and ideas	1 2	3 4 5	6 7	
(de)	Designing experiments	1 2	3 4 5	6 7	
(aqd)	Analyzing quantitative data	1 2	3 4 5	6 7	
(cnw)	Creating the new ways of thinking and doing	1 2	3 4 5	6 7	
(eni)	Experimenting with new ideas	1 2	3 4 5	6 7	CONVERGER
(cbs)	Choosing the best solution	1 2	3 4 5	6 7	
(sg)	Setting goals	1 2	3 4 5	6 7	
(md)	Making decisions	1 2	3 4 5	6 7	
(co)	Committing yourself to objectives	1 2	3 4 5	6 7	
(seo)	Seeking and exploiting opportunities	1 2	3 4 5	6 7	ACCOMMODATOR
(ilo)	Influencing and leading others	1 2	3 4 5	6 7	
(bpi)	Being personally involved	1 2	3 4 5	6 7	
(dp)	Dealing with people	1 2	3 4 5	6 7	

Learning Points

1. Some scholars characterize organizations as problem-solving systems whose success depends upon how well they perform that process.

2. The problem-solving model presented is based upon three premises:
   a. Learning from experience.
   b. Mind over matter.
   c. Problem solving as a social process.

3. The problem-solving model consists of four stages:
   a. Situation analysis.
   b. Problem analysis.
   c. Solution analysis.
   d. Implementation analysis.

4. The role of the manager is different for each stage and can be characterized as:
   a. Leader.
   b. Detective.
   c. Inventor.
   d. Coordinator.

5. Problem solving is not a logical, linear process. Instead, it is characterized by wavelike expansions and contractions alternately moving outward to gather and consider alternatives, information, and ideas and inwardly to focus, evaluate and decide.

6. Each of the stages in the problem-solving model possesses two substages that reflect the two dialectics of problem solving: the expansion/green mode and the contraction/red mode.

7. Effective problem solving requires balanced attention to each phase of the problem-solving process and equal emphasis on the expansion/green and contraction/red mode mind sets.

8. There is a correlation between individual learning styles and the way people solve problems.

- The management of group problem solving can be enhanced by avoidance of the following common obstacles to effective group problem solving:

  - *Preparation for the Meeting*
    Little or no preplanning.
    Low expectations.
    Failure to include the right people or inclusion of irrelevant people.
    Group's goal and function are ambiguous (e.g., is it advisory, information sharing, decision making?).

  - *Managing the Meeting*
    Lack of clarity about procedures and ground rules:
      Goals and agenda.
      How decisions get made (by voting or by consensus, etc.).
      Time.
      Structure (chairperson, recorder, etc.).
    Group members do not follow an orderly problem-solving sequence together.
    Failure to balance the discussion–dominance by high-status or aggressive members.
    Conflict is either avoided or allowed to become personalized as opposed to problem focused.
    Members do not understand what is being said but think they do.

  - *Situation Analysis*
    Urgent and structured problems take priority over important problems.
    Symptoms are treated as the problem (e.g., often people as opposed to situations are seen as the problem).
    Problems are accepted as given–reluctance to express hopes and dreams and to search for opportunities.

  - *Problem Analysis*
    Premature discussion of solutions.
    Critical facts are not made known to all.
    No distinction is made between facts and opinions.
    Problem situations are defined as choice situations.

  - *Solution Analysis*
    Generation and evaluation of ideas not kept separate.
    Premature focusing.
    Unproductive conflict and competition in evaluation.
    Undue weight given to secondary decision criteria–the primary criterion is–Does the solution solve the problem? Secondary criteria such as cost should not be allowed to overshadow the primary criterion.

  - *Implementation Analysis*
    Failure to gain commitment of those who will implement solutions.
    Failure to assign clear responsibility to individuals for tasks.
    Failure to follow up and monitor.

- Try to include people with different learning styles in problem-solving groups and see that their disparate skills are both valued and utilized.

- Feelings and perceptual biases influence the problem-solving process as do the mental ruts that prevent us from generating creative solutions. Discussing the situation with neutral outsiders or objective insiders is often helpful.

- Remember that problems are embedded within a system. For example, a scheduling problem can be related to a turf fight between department heads. It's important to consider all the system links, both to define the problem and to make sure that implementation obstacles don't arise.

- The successes of Employee Involvement Groups has shown that employees are capable of solving problems that management either did not recognize or had not been able to resolve.

Personal Application Assignment

In this assignment you will write about an experience involving problem management. Choose an experience about which you want to learn more.

A. *Concrete Experience*

1. *Objectively* describe the experience ("who," "what," "when," "where," "how" type information–up to 2 points).

2. *Subjectively* describe your feelings, perceptions, and thoughts that occurred during (not after) the experience (up to 2 points). Does this section have too much detail? (If so, delete 1 point.)

B. *Reflective Observation*

1. Look at the experience from different points of view. How many points of view did you include that are *relevant* (up to 2 points)?

2. Use these perspectives to add more meaning to the incident (up to 2 points).

C. *Abstract Conceptualization*

    1. Relate concepts from the assigned readings and the lecture to the experience (i.e., what theories that you heard in the lecture or read in the *Reader* relate to your understanding of this incident?). Make reference to at least two sources. Use standard referencing format and include the page number to which you are referring. How many sources did you use and how clearly did you explain their theories (up to 4 points)?

    2. You can also create an original model or theory, but it should not replace course concepts.

D. *Active Experimentation*

    1. Write about what you will do in the future that will improve your effectiveness. Use rules of thumb or action resolutions.

    2. Are they described specifically, thoroughly, and in detail (up to 4 points)?

E. *Integration, Synthesis, and Writing*

    1. Did you write about something personally important to you (up to 1 point)?

    2. Was it well written (up to 2 points)?

    3. Did you integrate and synthesize the different sections (up to 1 point)?

Summary of Role-Play Results

GROUP NO.		SITUATION ANALYSIS		PROBLEM ANALYSIS		SOLUTION ANALYSIS		IMPLEMENTATION ANALYSIS		Solution Decided on by Assembly Team D
		Valuing "Examine Solution"	Priority Setting "Agree on Problem"	Information Getting "Information on Causes"	Problem Definition "Choosing Cause"	Getting ideas "Generate Ideas"	Decision Making "Select Idea"	Participation "Involve Others"	Planning "Construct Plan"	
1	Sequence									
	% Time									
2	Sequence									
	% Time									
3	Sequence									
	% Time									
4	Sequence									
	% Time									
Averages for 60 managers (1/2 female; 1/2 male; 10 Groups) (av. rank)	Sequence (av. rank)	1	3	2	4	5	7	6	8	
	% Time	5.2%	6.2%	7.7%	5.2%	43.0%	12.9%	6.2%	14.0%	

STATION 1
LEE SMITH

You find you can easily do more work, but you have to slow down because Joel gets behind. So as not to make Joel feel bad, you hold back. You don't want to get Joel into trouble. Right now, the job lacks challenge and is boring.

STATION 2
SAM JONES

You and Lee work closely together, and you are usually waiting for the board from Lee. Waiting for the board is more prevalent in the latter part of the day than in the beginning. To keep busy, you often help out Joel who can't keep up. However, you are careful not to let the supervisor catch you helping Joel because Joel might be let go. Joel is a bit old for the pace set and feels the strain. For you, the job is easy, and you feel the whole job is slowed down too much because of Joel. "Why couldn't Joel be given less to do?" you ask yourself.

STATION 3
JOEL CRANE

You work hard, but you just aren't as fast as the others. You know you are holding things up, but no matter how you try, you get behind. The faster you try to go, the more difficult it is to make correct connections. You feel quality is important, and you don't want to make mistakes. The rest of the workers are fine people and have more energy than you do at your age.

STATION 4
JERRY FRAM

You are able to keep up with the pace, but on your last assembly job, you were pressed. Fortunately Joel is slower than you are, and this keeps that pressure off you. You are determined that Joel will not be moved off the job. Somebody has to protect people from speed-up tactics.

From this study and others, we know that there are certain behaviors that are typical of conflict situations: stereotyping, overvaluation of one's own group, devaluation of the other group, polarization on the issues, distortion of perceptions, and escalation. "Escalation is reflected in such changes as increasing the number and size of the issues disputed, increasing hostility, increasingly competitiveness, pursuing increasingly extreme demands or objectives, using increasing coercive tactics, decreasing trust, and enlisting other parties to take sides in the conflict."[4] Conflict is characterized by an unwillingness to give the other party the benefit of the doubt regarding their motives or actions.

In the opening vignette, "Joe D'Amico's Better Idea," union and management certainly exhibited these conflict behaviors. While the cause of this particular conflict was not solely related to competition over scarce resources, it was resolved in the same manner as in the Robbers Cave study. An overarching goal was established–keeping the plant open and retaining their jobs. To achieve this goal, they had to give up an ingrained adversarial relationship and perceive themselves as members of the same team.

The distinctive nature of group conflict is related to the effects of group membership on individual behavior. Many other studies[5] have since confirmed and added to the body of knowledge about the effects of group membership on individual behavior. Researchers have noted strong tendencies to believe whatever others in a strong reference group believe, even when it contradicts one's visual perceptions. Groups to which we belong, particularly the ones we value most, tend to affirm us in ways we cannot always do for ourselves. By accepting us, they let us know that we are "okay" and erase a lot of the doubts we may have about our identity. But with that acceptance often comes a series of pressures, subtle or overt, to conform to a set of values or behaviors that the group deems acceptable.

In organizations there are different functional groups, professional specialties, geographical groupings, hierarchical levels, ethnic groups, sexes, and social class distinctions. Any or all of these can serve as focal points for the creation of strong reference groups that provide their members with a sense of acceptance and identity in exchange for group loyalty and commitment. To the individual, these reference groups are often the most immediate and tangible sources of a sense of belonging to the organization. As a result, these groups are a vehicle for gaining commitment to organizational goals and motivation to work.

Yet group loyalty and commitment lead group members to value their own priorities, goals, and points of view more highly than those of "out" groups. This often leads to a competitive we–they atmosphere between groups, which further strengthens internal group loyalty and outgroup hostility in a cycle of increasing intensity. Organizations may find this to be a major stumbling block in optimizing productivity and reaching the organization's goals. For example, the people in production see the marketing department as making inordinate demands on them for changes in products with insufficient lead time. Marketing, on the other hand, may see production as intractable, a group that does not understand the necessity of meeting the competition from other companies. As a result of the conflict, the energy of both groups is being expended in defense of their own position as well as attacking the position of the other group, all at the expense of organizational goals. Furthermore, in many cases, conflict is a major source of stress for the individuals involved.

Is competition between groups always dysfunctional? Not necessarily. There are numerous examples in our society of the advantages of intergroup competition. In the sports world one team is always competing against another. This phenomenon produces much excitement for audiences since they have an emotional identification with one or the other team and feel actively involved in the battle. The competitive nature of the encounter produces excitement for the players and motivates or induces them to exert maximum effort to reap the rewards of winning. In the business world, companies compete with one another for a larger share of the consumer dollar.

Competition between organizations often increases the excellence of the product and customer service.

Situations in which competition between groups is productive have several distinguishing characteristics. First, they usually involve entities (groups) that are not part of the same formal organizational structure. The Giants and the Colts are a part of the NFL, but they represent independent and autonomous operating organizations. Deliberate intergroup competition has been used by many government contracting agencies within the framework of parallel projects. The same task (usually a feasibility study) is given to two or more different companies with the understanding that the best proposal will win the follow-up contract. The assumption underlying the strategy is that the higher quality of the final product resulting from such a competitive structure will justify the duplication of effort and expenditure of funds. A second distinguishing characteristic is that seldom do any of these competing organizations (groups) find it necessary to work together to solve a common problem or to reach a common goal. For example, when a group of baseball owners tries to elect a new commissioner, the competitive element that proved so beneficial in their other activities often gets in the way when they must collaborate. Disparate units of the same organization can compete without harming the overall organization only when there is no interdependence or need for collaboration between them.

In sum, competition is both functional and the essence of the marketplace when it results in greater team spirit and effort. It is dysfunctional when it siphons energy away from the overall mission of the organization.

Conflict within organizations is inevitable and comes from several sources. In addition to we-they situations resulting from group membership, conflict is likely to occur anywhere in the organization where there are "joints" or interfaces between different functions. The current move towards "horizontal corporations" that organize themselves around core processes rather than functions is, in part, an attempt to avoid conflict between the "silos" of functional departments.[6] Other common causes of conflict are differences in values, interests, personalities, education, culture, perceptions, goals, and expectations. Conflict may also result from deficient information that causes misunderstandings. Ambiguity can cause conflict when people battle over power or turf that has not been clearly assigned. Competition over scarce resources in whatever form–recognition, money, or even offices with windows–is also a source of conflict. Whenever the work is structured in such a way that groups are interdependent and their output depends upon that of another department, there is a potential for conflict.

To some degree the human factor determines whether conflict will actually occur at some of these interfaces. Individuals and different ethnic groups are comfortable with varying levels of conflict. In our culture we receive two somewhat contradictory messages: 1) fight and stand up for yourself, but 2) only when it is acceptable. Part of being politically savvy is understanding when conflict is appropriate. Some people thrive upon conflict and create it wherever they go; others go to great lengths to avoid it. Managers at either end of this continuum are likely to be less than effective in their jobs and in their ability to create a positive work environment for their employees.

PROMOTING FUNCTIONAL CONFLICT

In addition to blocking the achievement of organizational goals, dysfunctional conflict reduces productivity, morale, and job satisfaction and can cause heightened anxiety, absenteeism, turnover. Functional conflict, however, plays an important role in organizations. Conflict forces us to articulate our views and positions which usually results in greater clarification and understanding. It makes the values and belief system of the organization more visible and makes it easier to see organizational priorities. Conflict helps preserve groups when it serves as a safety valve that allows people to blow off steam and still maintain the relationship. When people band together in a conflict,

Procedure for Group Meeting:
The Nadir Corporation Negotiation[13]

THE TASK

Throughout its 40-year history, the Nadir Corporation has been run by George Nadir, founder, president, and majority stockholder. Nadir rules with a heavy hand and takes part in all company decisions. He adjudicates disputes between the two major divisions of the company, marketing and manufacturing, insisting at all times that the divisions communicate through him on major issues. Nadir corporation has been a very successful consumer-oriented manufacturing organization over the last 12 years, growing at an average annual rate of 8 percent in sales. It is an above-average performer in terms of profits in its industry. Further details about Nadir products and financial performance are not essential for this exercise.

Nadir's surprise sale of his stock to Apogee, Inc., has made Nadir Corp. a wholly owned subsidiary that must now operate without "the old man." Not being willing to impose a new president on Nadir without first finding out what the company's needs and executive resources are, Apogee has sent its executive vice president for acquisitions, Pat Cleary, to meet with Nadir personnel to get a clearer picture of what should be done–whether, for instance, a new president should come from the outside or from within and just what kind of manager he or she should be. Pat Cleary has sent a memo (below) to members of the manufacturing and marketing departments.

Half of you will represent manufacturing (group A). The manufacturing division is divided about evenly between managers who began their careers as engineers and managers who operated the facilities starting as hourly workers. Marketing (group B) is managed totally by college graduates, with about half having started as engineers, the other half coming to the company from liberal arts backgrounds.

APOGEE CORPORATION
INTEROFFICE MEMO

TO: Manufacturing Department
           Marketing Department
FROM: Pat Cleary, Executive Vice President
RE: Criteria for Choosing New President, Nadir Corporation

You are requested to hold a department meeting for the purpose of establishing criteria for choosing a new president for Nadir Corporation. Please prepare a brief report listing five criteria, in short phrases, that you think should be used in the choice. Please rank order them in terms of their importance to the Nadir Corporation.

When you have prepared your reports, we will have a joint meeting of the two departments to evaluate them.

STEP 1. The total group will be the Nadir Corporation, with half the learning groups representing marketing and the other half representing manufacturing. Assign or divide into the groups on whatever basis seems most appropriate, keeping the same number of members in each group. The group leader or instructor will act as Pat Cleary and will coordinate the simulation and discussion. (*Note:* If your total group size exceeds 18 people, you may want to run two separate, but simultaneous, sessions.) (10 minutes)

STEP 2. Marketing and manufacturing meet separately to prepare their response to Cleary's memo, listing their criteria for choosing a new president of the Nadir Corporation. In preparing these reports, you should take your role as members of marketing and manufacturing into account but rely primarily on your own personal judgments about what kind of person would make the best president of Nadir. Short phrases should be used, and there should be no more than five criteria listed by each group. They should be rank ordered in terms of importance to the company. *Each group member should make a clear, legible copy of the group report for use in the next step.* (30 minutes)

STEP 3. To evaluate the two reports, Cleary has asked individuals in marketing to pair off with someone in manufacturing. During this period you will be paired with a member of the other team. The pairing may be done as you wish. You will be expected to provide a copy of your group's criteria report for your discussion partner to review. (20 minutes)

Your task as a two-person team will be to decide which set of criteria is better in its entirety and by how much. You must allot 100 points between the two, but cannot allot 50 to each under the assumption that no two reports are ever exactly alike. Even if the wording is identical the thoughts behind them will not be. There must be a preference indicated, whether by 52:48 or by 90:10. Concentrate on the content of the list rather than on peripheral things such as style or elegance of wording.

At the end of 20 minutes (the instructor or leader should let you know when the time is up), return to your original group and total the number of points each member brought back to get the total group score. Give your numerical results to the instructor who will tabulate them and announce which is the better report.

STEP 4. Back in your original groups, discuss the preceding hour's events (20 minutes), focusing on

  a. What occurred between you and the representatives of the other group?

  b. How did your original group operate during the time in which you were generating the criteria report?

   1. What was the predominant leadership style? What were its effects?

   2. What were the effects of time and task pressures on group interaction?

   3. How were conflicts handled? Decisions made?

  c. What is the state of this group now?

   1. What is the climate in this group right now? Is it different from when you were doing the task?

   2. How willing would you be to give or receive help from someone in the other group right now? How easy would it be for you to work with the other group now (e.g., to implement the winning criteria list)?

   3. What effect did winning or losing have on your group?

STEP 5.   Reconvene as a class. (30 minutes) Read the Follow-up in this chapter, and, using it as a guide, discuss:

   a. What happened within the groups during the task? Were the summary predictions in the Follow-Up correct? How did they vary from the reality?

   b. What happened between the two groups?

   c. In the group discussion (step 4), what was the winning group's discussion like? Were the summary predictions valid?

   d. What was the climate like in the losing group? Were the summary predictions valid for them?

   e. What conclusions can you draw about the effect of intergroup competition on group behavior? On your behavior as an individual group member?

   f. How might Pat Cleary's memo be rewritten to reduce conflict?

   g. What connections can you make between this exercise and the readings?

STEP 6.   Meet once again with your partner from the other group to analyze your negotiation process and provide feedback on your conflict handling mode or style.

   a. What conflict style(s) did you and your partner use? What effect did your style have on the other person?

   b. What type of negotiation occurred during the role play?

   Distributive   1   2   3   4   5   Integrative

   Why?

   c. Were you able to separate the people from the problem?

   Yes _____ No _____

   Examples of where this occurred or didn't occur:

   d. Did you focus on interests or positions? Examples?

   e. Did you invent options for mutual gain? Examples?

   f. Did you insist on objective criteria? Examples?

   g. If you had to repeat this negotiation session, how would you improve it?

Follow-Up

Schein, in *Organizational Psychology*,[14] provides a brief but lucid description of inter-group problems in organizations. This summary draws heavily upon his ideas. The simulation you have just experienced has been replicated many times with a variety of groups.[15] Because the results have been surprisingly constant, it is now possible to predict what will generally happen as a consequence of intergroup competition. These predictions are summarized here.

What Happens *Within* Groups?

The members of each of two competing groups begin to close ranks and quickly experience increased feelings of group loyalty and pride. Each group sees itself as the best and the other group as the enemy. Under the pressure of time and task deadlines, the group willingly accepts more structure and autocratic leadership. The group climate is characterized by work, as opposed to play or fight; task, as opposed to maintenance. Conformity is stressed and there is little tolerance for individual deviation.

What Happens *Between* Groups?

Whatever interaction there was between the members of the two groups before the competition decreases and becomes more hostile. Whatever communication there is becomes very selective, each group hearing only comments that confirm its stereotype of the other and support its own position.

What Happens to the *Winners*?

The winning group climate can be called "fat and happy." Tension is released; there is little desire to get on to work. People would prefer to play and rest on their laurels. There is little desire to explore earlier conflicts and possibly learn from them.

Generally, the winners not only retain their prior cohesion, but become more cohesive. The exception is when the group really does not feel as if it won or when the decision is close and they did not win decisively. Under these conditions, winners often act like losers.

What Happens to the *Losers*?

The members deal initially with having lost in one of two ways. Some groups deny reality– "We didn't really lose. It was a moral victory." Other groups seek a scapegoat, someone other than themselves to blame for the defeat. The rules, for instance, are often blamed.

A losing group is, however, also a "lean and hungry" group. Tension increases, old conflicts are reexamined, and the group really digs in and learns a lot about itself in preparation for the next task.

What Happens to *Negotiators* Between Groups?

The negotiator often experiences significant role conflict between being a good judge and a good group member. Judges often find it difficult to ignore loyalties to their own groups and be completely neutral. If theirs happens to be a loser, they experience much difficulty reentering, and often bear the brunt of much of the scapegoating behavior (often in a jocular fashion).

People seldom realize how much responsibility a person feels when asked to represent a group and the tension that results from being put in such a position. In addition, it is often unclear just how free a representative really is to be himself or herself as opposed to being what the group expects him or her to be. How flexible is the person to deviate from the group's mandate in response to changes in the situation? Finally, if the group loses, the representative often feels guilty and responsible.

Most of us have seen instances where too much conflict has paralyzed groups. However, too little expressed conflict between groups can be just as dysfunctional.[16] Brown maintains that conflict will exist between groups by their very nature and that the task of the manager is not necessarily to eliminate conflict but to maintain it at a level appropriate to the task. Too much conflict can lead to defensiveness and an inability to work collaboratively toward organization goals. Too little conflict can stifle ideas and innovation. Conflict is often repressed when there are relative differences in power between groups because the "low-power" group finds that expressing their views to the "high-power" group is much too risky.

The manager who wishes to manage conflict productively needs to develop skills in diagnosing dysfunctional situations at both extremes. Many conflicts in society (race, sex, age) require the effective manager to be aware of those larger conflicts, assessing as clearly as possible the extent to which his or her organization reinforces them, and working to change those attitudes, behaviors, and structures that institutionalize them.

As we have seen in the exercise, intergroup conflict is easy to induce. Getting the conflicts in the open and managing them effectively is another matter. Generally, it has been found that intergroup conflict, once it begins, is extremely hard to reduce.[17] The strategy of locating a common enemy or a superordinate goal is useful, but much work must be done to overcome the negative consequences that have already developed before such strategies become feasible. Educational techniques exist and are being used with considerable success to help organizations deal with intergroup conflict that has dysfunctional consequences.

Given the difficulties of reducing intergroup competition, Schein's strategies for eliminating it in the first place are very important. Schein suggests four steps that have proved to be effective in helping organizations avoid the dysfunctional consequences of intergroup conflict.

1. Relatively *greater emphasis is given to total organizational effectiveness* and the role of departments in contributing to it; departments are measured and rewarded on the basis of their *contribution to the total effort* rather than on their individual effectiveness.

2. *High interaction and frequent communication* are stimulated between groups to work on problems of intergroup coordination and collaboration; organizational *rewards are given partly on the basis of help* that groups give each other.

3. There is frequent *rotation of members* among groups or departments to stimulate high degrees of mutual understanding and empathy for one another's problems.

4. *Win-lose situations are avoided.* Groups should never be put into the position of competing for the same organizational reward. Emphasis is always placed on pooling resources to maximize organizational effectiveness; rewards are shared equally with all the groups or departments.

Learning Points

1. Conflict is a form of interaction among parties that differ in interests, perceptions, and preferences.

2. Groups in conflict tend to stereotype the other party, see their own group as ideal, and overvalue the contributions of their own members, while devaluing those of the other group. Their perceptions of one another become distorted and hostilities tend to escalate.

3. Sherif's Robbers Cave experiment revealed that conflict behavior was induced by having two groups of boys compete for scarce resource–limited prizes. The hostility that resulted decreased greatly when the researchers introduced super-ordinate goals that were important to all the boys and required collaboration.

4. Two ways to resolve intergroup conflict are: a) noncompetitive contact in which the groups have equal status; and b) establishing a superordinate goal that can only be attained through joint cooperation.

5. Organizations are full of reference groups that provide individuals with a sense of belonging and identity in exchange for loyalty and commitment. However, a we-they attitude often develops when these groups come into contact with each other.

6. We-they attitudes between internal groups can foster competition and a lack of collaboration that hinders productivity and achievement of the overall goals of the organization. In contrast, competition with external groups can be very productive.

7. Common causes of group conflict in organizations are we-they attitudes of reference groups, competition for scarce resources, ambiguous authority, inter-dependence, deficient information, and differences in values, interests, personali-ties, education, culture, perceptions, goals, and expectations.

8. While dysfunctional conflict siphons energy away from organizational goals, functional conflict plays an important role in organizations. One way to ensure that conflict is functional is to train employees in conflict management skills.

9. The five conflict handling modes are based upon a person's strategic intentions along two axes:.
   a. Assertiveness—desire to satisfy one's own concerns
   b. Cooperativeness— desire to satisfy the concerns of the other party

10. The five conflict handling modes are:
    a. Competition.
    b. Accommodation.
    c. Compromise.
    d. Collaboration.
    e. Avoidance.

11. Effective managers use the mode that is appropriate to the situation.

12. There are two types of bargaining: distributive (win–lose) and integrative (win–win).

13. Fisher and Ury's scheme of principled negotiation consists of:
    a. Separate the people from the problem
    b. Focus on interests not positions
    c. Invent options for mutual gain
    d. Insist on objective criteria.

14. Too much or too little conflict are both dysfunctional states.

15. It is easier to create conflict than resolve it.

 for Managers

- One way to avoid conflict is by clearly determining both authority and responsibility.

- Try to reframe conflict situations from a "we-they" position to a "we versus the problem" approach. For example, the manager of an auditing department realized her efforts to incorporate the auditing department of a recently merged smaller bank were not succeeding. In fact, hostility between the two groups was increasing. Rather than fighting over whose procedures were best, the manager wisely reframed the situation and asked the entire group to start from scratch and use the merger as an opportunity to devise the best possible procedures. Their final product was "ours," and in the process, the two departments became a cohesive unit.

- Look for mutual goals and values, or even a common enemy. Make sure common enemies are outside the company and not a person or group with whom it is important to have a collaborative relationship.

- Managing conflict may appear to be too time consuming in the short run, but conflicts that are allowed to fester can cause great harm and take up more time in the long run.

- Managers can sometimes decrease conflict by the use of a liaison or a buffer. Liaisons or boundary spanners absorb heat from both sides and try to interpret the actions of both groups to each other. Buffers can also be inanimate objects that prevent two groups from having to interact, for example, the order wheel in restaurants and automatic reordering systems in warehouses.

- Managers can set the stage for collaboration between departments or divisions by having a clear understanding of the contribution each group makes and passing that on to others.

- They can also show an interest in all groups and insist that they work together. The manager's attention is often one of the scarce resources in an organization. Therefore, managers who share their attention as equally as possible (or at least explain to the others why they are focusing upon a certain area) are more likely to have a collaborative climate.

- Managers can make it clear that they welcome the existence of differences within the organization.

- When conflicts are brought to managers to be settled, they should:

   a. Listen with understanding rather than evaluation and recognize and accept the feelings of the people involved without judging them.

   b. Analyze the source of the conflict and make sure all parties understand the nature of the conflict from everyone's perspective.

c. Suggest procedures and ground rules for discussing and resolving the differences:

- Everyone will be treated with respect

- Although groups may be committed to their own position, they should still be open to other perspectives

- Avoid unproductive conflict strategies such as blaming, forcing, threatening, manipulating

- Seek a win-win solution

- Give all parties equal opportunity to present their views and arguments and ensure fair treatment

- Keep the focus on the current situation rather than past history that has no relevance.

d. Suggest problem-solving procedures, such as brainstorming and agreement on objective criteria, to judge solutions.

e. Teach problem-solving skills so employees can resolve conflicts themselves in the future.

Personal Application Assignment

This assignment is to write about a situation involving intergroup conflict. Choose an experience about which you want to learn more. When you address the "Reflective Observation" section, answer these questions: How does the other group see you? How do you think you see them?

A. *Concrete Experience*

1. *Objectively* describe the experience ("who," "what," "when," "where," "how" type information–up to 2 points).

2. *Subjectively* describe your feelings, perceptions, and thoughts that occurred *during* (not after) the experience (up to 2 points). Does this section have too much detail? (If so, delete 1 point.)

B. *Reflective Observation*

1. Look at the experience from different points of view. How many points of view did you include that are *relevant* (up to 2 points)?

2. Use these perspectives to add more meaning to the incident (up to 2 points).

C. *Abstract Conceptualization*

    1. Relate concepts from the assigned readings and the lecture to the experience (i.e., What theories that you heard in the lecture or read in the Reader relate to your understanding of this incident?). Make reference to at least two sources. Use standard referencing format and include the page number to which you are referring. How many sources did you use and how clearly did you explain their theories (up to 4 points)?

    2. You can also create an original model or theory, but it should not replace course concepts.

D. *Active Experimentation*

    1. Write about what you will do in the future that will improve your effectiveness. Use rules of thumb or action resolutions.

    2. Are they described specifically, thoroughly, and in detail (up to 4 points)?

E. *Integration, Synthesis, and Writing*

    1. Did you write about something personally important to you (up to 1 point)?

    2. Was it well written (up to 2 points)?

    3. Did you integrate and synthesize the different sections (up to 1 point)?

[1]Kenneth W. Thomas, "Conflict and Negotiation Processes in Organizations," in M. D. Dunnette and L. M. Hough (eds.), *Handbook of Industrial and Organizational Psychology,* 2nd ed., (Palo Alto, CA: Consulting Psychologists Press) Vol. 3 1991, p. 653.

[2]M. Sherif, *Intergroup Relations and Leadership* (New York: John Wiley, 1962).

[3]M. Deutsch, "An Experimental Study of the Effects of Cooperation and Competition upon Group Process," *Human Relations,* Vol. 2 (1949), pp. 199-231, and G. W. Allport, *The Nature of Prejudice* (Reading, MA: Addison-Wesley, 1954).

[4]Thomas, "Conflict and Negotiation," p. 697.

[5]For example, D. Cartwright and A. Zander, *Group Dynamics Research and Theory* (New York: Harper & Row, 1968); M. Deutsch, The Resolution of Conflict (New Haven, CT: Yale University Press, 1973); Clayton Alderfer and Ken K. Smith, "Studying Intergroups Relation Embedded in Organizations," *Administrative Science Quarterly* (March 1982), pp. 35-64; and Stephen P. Robbins, *Managing Organizational Conflict* (Englewood Cliffs, NJ: Prentice Hall, 1974).

[6]John A. Byrne, "The Horizontal Corporation," *Business Week*, December 20, 1993, pp. 76-81.

[7]K. W. Thomas, "Conflict and Conflict Management," in *Handbook of Industrial and Organizational Psychology,* edited by M. D. Dunnette (Chicago: Rand McNally, 1976), pp. 889-935.

[8]Roy J. Lewicki and Joseph A. Litterer, *Negotiation,* (Homewood, IL: Irwin, 1985) p. 280.

[9]Kenneth Thomas, "Conflict and Conflict Management," *Journal of Organizational Behavior,* 13 (1992), pp. 265-274.

[10]Roger Fisher and William Ury. *Getting to Yes: Negotiating Agreement Without Giving In.* Boston: Houghton Mifflin, 1981.

[11]Fisher & Ury, *Getting to Yes,* p. 4

[12]For information on international negotiations, see Nancy J. Adler, *International Dimensions of Organizational Behavior* (Boston: PWS-Kent, 1991); and Lennie Copeland and Lewis Griggs, *Going International* (New York: Random House, 1985).

[13]The intergroup exercise used in this unit is similar to many that have been developed previously. The original concept should probably be credited to Sherif, *Intergroup Relations and Leadership,* but has been further developed by many others, notably, Robert Blake.

[14]Edgar H. Schein, *Organizational Psychology* (Englewood Cliffs, NJ: Prentice Hall, 1965), pp. 80-86.

[15]The most systematic research in organizational settings is reported in Robert R. Blake, H. A. Shepard, and Jane S. Mouton, *Managing Intergroup Conflict in Industry* (Houston: Gulf, 1964).

[16]L. Dave Brown, "Managing Conflict Among Groups," *Reader.*

[17]The reality of this is nowhere clearer than in our efforts to combat years of racial prejudice and discrimination.

Chapter

12

MANAGING DIVERSITY[*]

*This chapter was partially developed and written by David Akinnusi, Lyda Detterman, Rafael Estevez, Elizabeth Fisher, Mary Ann Hazen, David Kolb, Dennis O'Connor, and Michelle Spain, a diverse group if there ever was one.

OBJECTIVES By the end of this chapter you should be able to:

A. Explain the advantages and disadvantages of culture.

B. Define ethnocentrism and stereotyping.

C. Describe four dimensions of cultural differences.

D. List the positive aspects of managing diversity well.

E. Explain what happens to tokens in organizations.

F. Understand how to manage diversity in organizations.

What's Your Eccentricity Quotient?

Joyce S. Osland

How weird can you be in a major corporation and still keep your job? Kathleen McDonald, organization development team leader who was responsible for a project on managing diversity at Exxon, devised an eccentricity model to help employees answer that very question.

According to McDonald, the employees' goal is to balance their *perceived competence* with their *perceived eccentricity* (PC=PE). She defines perceived competence as how you and your job performance are seen by others in your organization. But note that this perception can be different from reality; perceived competence is how good others in the organization "think" you are.

Perceived eccentricity refers to those parts of you or your actions which do not fit neatly into the "ideal organization person" as defined by your organization. As McDonald describes it, perceived eccentricity is the corners of the square peg as you work in an environment that rewards round pegs. Obviously, some of those corners can be worn down, while others are difficult if not impossible, to remove. In most *Fortune 500* companies, anyone who is female, foreign born, or a person of color is likely to have a higher perceived eccentricity score than a WASP male. Likewise, people with different lifestyles, vocal religious beliefs, or a unique style of dress, mannerisms, or

Adapted with permission from an unpublished document by Kathleen McDonald.

speech may also be perceived as eccentric in some organizations. In technical environments, perceived eccentricity can also relate to the degree of risk and innovation you display.

How you manage the perceived eccentricity side of your equation has to do with how much acceptance you seek and what that acceptance represents. How much of an insider can you be? How much of an insider do you want to be? How much of yourself are you willing to leave at home or to censor at work? These can be tough issues, especially for minorities who feel the strain of struggling to fit an "ideal type" that bears little resemblance to them.

McDonald described the experience of a white woman who moved from a plant to a technical service position. At the plant she and just about everyone else wore pants. For her new job she upgraded her wardrobe to slack suits. Eventually word drifted back to her that the sales people did not want to take her with them on customer calls because of her "eccentric" dress. She had a choice to make: she could work at raising her perceived competence so that her new colleagues would see her as an invaluable resource even in a burlap sack, or she could invest in a new wardrobe and decrease her perceived eccentricity. She went out and bought skirts—a quicker if more expensive route to correcting an imbalance in the eccentricity model.

However, it's easier to change clothes than skin color. The African-American male who entered a predominantly white company and was assigned to a supervisor who was also brand new, had more difficulty in overcoming the perceived eccentricity of his race. Because the new supervisor couldn't inform him about the company's norms early on or interpret his competence to others in the organization, it took longer for the African-American to establish his perceived competence.

McDonald says that you can be as eccentric as you are competent. And it's usually a good idea to establish your competence before you test the company's tolerance of eccentricity. How do you scope out your perceived competence and eccentricity? From performance appraisals, the rewards that come your way and from feedback. And you may have to take an active role in seeking out feedback so you can decide how to manage yourself in the workplace. McDonald's eccentricity model is a good barometer for figuring out the consequences of your choices.

Examples of employees whose perceived eccentricity far outweighed their perceived competence come readily to mind. These are folks who are no longer around to tell their tale or who are continuously passed over for promotion. The danger of that kind of imbalance is clear. However, McDonald sees no advantage in the opposite kind of imbalance, even though there are typically many people in organizations who are perceived to be more competent than they are eccentric. The danger here is that employees will lose valuable opportunities to grow, both personally and professionally, by playing it safe. And organizations won't learn how to live with and profit from the diversity of their employees. So if your organization perceives you as more competent than eccentric, even up the equation and break out a little. Let those at work know how wonderfully weird or innovative you can be. You'll be doing everyone a favor.

Premeeting Preparation

A. Read "What's Your Eccentricity Quotient?"

B. Read the entire chapter to become familiar with the topic and prepare for the group meeting. Do this first.

C. Complete the:

    1. Analysis of a Personal Experience of Being Different.

    2. Intensity of Differentness Rating.

D. What are the significant learning points from the readings?

Analysis of a Personal Experience of Being Different

The experience of being different from others can be frustrating, isolating, and even painful. In our desire to avoid these feelings of difference, we are often tempted to deny our individual uniqueness and to "fit in" — to adopt the superficial characteristics of the majority. But doing so is not good for us as individuals for we are denying part of ourselves, which can result in feelings of alienation. It is ineffective as well, for our skills lie with who we are, not who we pretend to be. Nor is this denial of differences good for the organization, for without a variety of perspectives and alternatives for action, organizations become rigid and less effective.

Think of a recent experience you have had where you felt you were being treated as though you were "different," where others were not recognizing you as a unique person. It could be an experience in this course, at work, or anywhere. (Use another page if you need more space.)

1. Describe what happened in the situation.

2. How did you feel, think, and act?

3. How did others feel, think, and act?

4. What was the outcome of the situation?

When you have finished, score your experience for its intensity of differentness.

Intensity of Differentness Rating

We are all unique individuals with unique cultural and subcultural backgrounds and identities. As a result, we all have experiences of being different, of being stereotyped and discriminated against. These feelings are most pronounced and intense:

- When the situation is very important (e.g., where a job is at stake, in personal relationships, or where physical safety is concerned).
- When our own cultural experiences are markedly different from the dominant culture around us.
- When these differences are visible to others (e.g., skin color, sex, age, language, manner of dress).
- When there are power differences between ourselves and the dominant culture (i.e., when we are "one-down" in influence or rank).
- When we are alone or isolated from others who share our culture or subculture.
- When others are stereotyping us in a way that we and others notice.
- When we have strong emotional reactions of frustration, anger, or humiliation.

Look back over your description of the situation where you felt "different." Score it on the following issues.

		0	1	2
1.	How important was the situation to you?	Relatively unimportant	Important	Very critical
2.	How different were you?	Very little difference	Some difference	Great difference
3.	Were these differences visible to others?	No	A little	Obvious
4.	Were there power differences?	I was one-up, in charge	Equal	I was one-down
5.	Were you isolated from others similar to you?	I had several others like me for support	One other supportive	I was alone
6.	Were you stereotyped?	I was treated as a unique individual	I felt stereo-typed	There was direct evidence of stereotyping
7.	Did the situation cause you to react emotionally?	No emotional reaction	I felt slightly upset	I had strong emotional reaction

Add the numbers circled to get your total intensity of differentness score: _____ .

Topic Introduction

As companies become more global and the workforce becomes more diverse, we find ourselves increasingly involved with coworkers who differ from us in their cultural or subcultural identities. Neither trend is likely to diminish. The markets with the most potential for growth, as well as the cheapest labor supply, are located in other parts of the world. Without some degree of cross-cultural understanding and sensitivity, international business cannot succeed. As we mentioned in Chapter 1, according to predictions about the year 2000, white males will comprise only 39% of the total workforce.[1] By the end of the century only 15% of new hires will be white males; the remaining 85% of new hires will be composed of women, African-Americans, Hispanics, Asians, and Native Americans.[2] Many companies are already trying to take advantage of a diverse workgroup by learning to 1) appreciate and understand differences, 2) communicate and work with diverse groups, and 3) develop an organizational culture that welcomes all groups and their unique contributions. The purpose of this chapter is to focus upon both cross-cultural and domestic diversity issues.

CULTURE

But while he gains so much from culture, man is also brainwashed, to some extent by the culture to which he is exposed from birth. Equipped with a collection of stereotypes with which to face the world, man is apt to lose sight of possible alternative modes of behavior and understanding. (V. Barnow)[3]

Culture causes humans to see the world differently through their cultural lenses and is also a major determinant of behavior. We accept Lewin's[4] theory that behavior is a function of personality and environment, but too often the cultural context of the person's environment is overlooked. People are usually introduced to their own culture in the act of confronting another. One learns what it means to be an American, Japanese, or South African, etc. by rubbing up against other nationalities. And even then, one discerns mainly those aspects of one's own culture that come into conflict with those of the other culture. "What the observer notices about the culture he visits will depend not only on the society he chooses to study, but also his (or her) own cultural background."[5] We don't notice similarities as quickly because our eyes are drawn first to differences. Another way to explain this phenomenon is to cast it into the Gestalt scheme of figure and ground. What is ground in one's own culture and country becomes figural when thrown up against the relief provided by another culture. Figure 12-1 presents a list of American cultural values.

Hofstede[6] states that culture is to human collectivity what personality is to the individual. The way humans react to the basic issues that confront all humankind is determined by culture. For example, old age and dying represent an inescapable problem for all societies, but the manner of approaching and resolving this problem derives primarily from particular cultural values and beliefs: the prestige and respect given to the elderly, beliefs about the afterlife, and economic values determine how a culture will handle the problem of old age and death.

Culture provides us with both ready-made solutions to basic human issues and a sense of identity. However, we must also acknowledge the price we pay for these provisions. The concept of trade-offs is a useful one when studying different cultures. Traditional cultures with clear norms may be more confining and slower to change, but their members usually possess a strong sense of identity. Creativity and adaptability are often identified as by-products of American culture; however, the price we pay for allowing people the freedom to go their own way in our polyglot and highly mobile society is insecurity and rootlessness. All cultures have advantages and disadvantages when considered objectively. Human nature sometimes prevents us from appreciating the advantages or the good points of other cultures. This quality is referred to as ethnocentrism.

Ethnocentrism is defined as the "exaggerated tendency to think the characteristics of one's own group or races are superior to those of other groups or races."[7] Humans are preoccupied with the differences between their "own" kind and outsiders. Anthropologists have encountered many tribes whose name is literally translated as "the human beings;" this implies that those outside their tribe are not human and, therefore, not worthy of the same consideration.

Ethnocentrism is very obvious in the epithets used by countries at war, but it is not triggered only by military conflict. Within the United States our ethnocentrism is reflected in race issues, the deterioration of our neighborhoods, and complaints about promoting minorities at work—all of which represent threats to the economic and social dominance of the white majority.[8] Because ethnocentrism in this country seldom results in all-out warfare, we should not be lulled into overlooking its existence. Everyone possesses some degree of ethnocentrism. For anyone who deals with people who are different, the first step is to acknowledge one's ethnocentrism and try to curb the natural thought that one's own group/culture/sex is, by definition, better than others.

---

1. **Action is good.**
   Change can be induced through individual or group action. "Getting things done" is commendable. Problems, once identified, can be solved.

2. **Man's environment can be controlled.**
   Nature is to be conquered and made over to suit man's needs.

3. **Progress is straight-lined and upward, not spiral.**
   Change is inevitable and Utopia is the result of achievement and progress.

4. **The material is more real than the spiritual.**
   The concrete and observable are relevant. Material comfort and convenience are emphasized.

5. **A person's success is self-made.**
   Social status accrues to one who succeeds in the face of competition.

6. **The individual is the keystone of society.**
   Individual responsibility is important, and "the greatest good for the greatest number" leads to a successful society. Minority rights must be protected.

7. **Man is a moral creature.**
   Personal conduct can be evaluated in universal moral terms.
   Clear-cut ethical distinctions can be made that affect all people equally.

8. **Time is money.**
   Time is a material thing. It should be actively mastered or manipulated to one's advantage.

9. **The world is rational**
   Scientific reasoning is the unquestioned way of understanding the physical world.

10. **The American is open and friendly and so are other people when dealt with in an open and friendly way.**
    People of traditional, formal cultures often view as ill-mannered the openness, use of first names, personal questions, display of enthusiasm in public, and open displays of affection that are characteristics of Americans. Americans tend to overlook this disapproval.

Figure 12-1   **Concepts Shaping the American Way of Life**

CULTURAL DIFFERENCES

The next step in cross-cultural relations is gaining an understanding of your own culture and that of the people from another culture or subculture. Until we understand the rules of another culture, we can only interpret their behavior using our own cultural norms and assumptions. This leads to misperceptions and false attributions about their behavior. One dimension of cultural differences, the concept of individualism versus collectivism, provides us with a clue to some of the major differences we see both abroad and in our own country.[9]

Individualism is a cultural pattern found in most northern and western regions of Europe and in North America. It is defined as the extent to which people are responsible for taking care of themselves and giving priority to their own interests. Collectivism is characterized by individuals who subordinate their personal goals to the goals of some collective. Individuals give their loyalty to a group and in return the group takes responsibility for the individual. Collectivism is common in Asia, Africa, South America, and the Pacific.

In individualistic cultures, people define themselves as an entity that is separate from the group. There is an emphasis upon personal goals and less concern and emotional attachment to groups. Successes are individual successes whereas in collectivist cultures, successes are group successes. Competition is interpersonal in individualistic cultures; in collectivist cultures, it occurs between groups. People in collectivist cultures define themselves as part of a group. They are concerned for the integrity of the group and have an intense emotional attachment to the group. For example, the bond between a mother and son (Indo-European collectivist cultures) or father and son (East Asian collectivist cultures) will be stronger than the bond between a wife and a husband because the family group is the most important. Vertical relationships (parent-child, boss-subordinate) are more important in collectivist cultures, whereas horizontal relationships (spouse-spouse, friend-friend) are more important in individualistic cultures.

In-groups are also very important in collectivist cultures. In the previous family example, the extended family is the in-group. In-group members in collectivist cultures warrant very different treatment than out-group members who are often treated with hostility and distrust. In contrast, people in individualistic cultures tend to treat people more consistently because they see themselves as belonging to more and larger in-groups, for example, Texans, people like us in terms of social class, race, beliefs, attitudes, and values. The difference is that the individualists' ties are not as strong with all these groups.

There is an emphasis upon harmony and face saving in collectivist cultures. In contrast, people in individualistic cultures are more likely to value confrontation and "clearing the air." Individualistic cultures have more short term relationships and use contracts in business dealings. Collectivistic cultures think in terms of long term relationships, which makes the use of contracts less important.

Not everyone in an individualistic culture is individualistic; the same is true for collectivist cultures. In both types of cultures, one can find "allocentric" people who value social support and "idiocentric" people who value achievement. Individualistic cultures have higher GNP's, but they also have more social ills and higher heart attack rates. Collectivist cultures report lower degrees of loneliness, alienation and social problems. However, they have more government corruption because in-group loyalty dictates that those in power will try to enrich their in-group rather than concern themselves for the country as a whole.

Individualism and collectivism affect how we structure organizations and how we expect people to act in the work place. Hofstede concluded that American management techniques are not universally applicable because they reflect U.S. values (like individualism). He administered surveys to 166,000 employees of a multinational corporation to see whether or not there were cultural differences among them. Even though they worked for the same company and held similar positions, they varied along four different dimensions:

1. Power distance: the extent to which a society accepts the fact that power in institutions and organizations is distributed unequally.

2. Uncertainty avoidance: the extent to which a society accepts or avoids uncertain and ambiguous situations.

3. Individualism: the extent to which people are responsible for taking care of themselves and give priority to their own interests. Its opposite is collectivism in which individuals give their loyalty to a group and in return the group takes responsibility for the individual.

4. Masculinity: the extent to which the dominant cultural values are assertiveness, the acquisition of money and things as opposed to its opposite, femininity, which refers to dominant values of caring for others, quality of life, and people.

Americans, he found, value equality (low power distance), are individualists (extremely high individualism) who willingly tolerate uncertainty (low uncertainty avoidance) and value achievement and striving more than nurturance and support (above average masculinity). American management techniques, he argues, are largely based on these values. As a result, they do not work as well in a culture, for example, that values the collective over the individual, emphasizes feminine values, or desires great power distance. The practical implication of this research is that management practices need to be adjusted to the values and attitudes of the culture or subculture in question. This is true not only in cross-cultural management in other nations but in our day-to-day relationships with those who identify with different subcultures within one's own country. The focus of this chapter is managing diversity in multicultural organizations. It underscores the importance of individual differences and seeks to develop skills in managing these differences.

STEREOTYPING

People entering organizations bring with them their own assumptions and preconceptions, and they use these ideas to form new impressions about other groups in the organization. When we act toward individual members of a group based on our assumptions about the group to which they belong, we are engaging in a stereotypic behavior. Aronson[10] describes this as follows: "To stereotype is to assign identical characteristics to any people in a group regardless of the actual variation among members of the group."

A stereotypic perception of individual differences is called a prejudice. Stereotypes abound in organizations. The common ones are based on sex, race, age, and professional groups. For example, as stated in the chapter on perception, there is no empirical evidence to support the stereotype that older workers are less productive.[11] In fact, research shows that job satisfaction, job involvement, internal work motivation, and organizational commitment increases with age.[12]

Another example of stereotyped perceptions pertains to female managers. Of the adult Americans in a recent study who preferred a boss of a particular gender (almost 50%), 85% of the men and 65% of the women would rather work for a man.[13] Professional workers are least likely to say that a boss' gender makes a difference to them. Yet, studies of actual boss-subordinate relationships fail to indicate any differences in satisfaction with male or female bosses.[14]

Stereotypes about both women and minorities can be seen in the glass ceiling that prevents them from attaining high-level positions in some organizations and, in some cases, lower salaries. In a comparative study of 814 white and 814 African-American managers, the latter group felt less accepted by their peers, perceived themselves as having less managerial discretion, reached career plateaus more frequently, had lower levels of career satisfaction, and received lower performance ratings.[15] On the positive side, another study of almost 40,000 pairs of African-American and white employees found no systematic race or sex bias in performance appraisals.[16]

Workplace stereotypes prevent people who are different from feeling accepted and living up to their full potential. They also deny individual uniqueness. A person is often responded to only as a member of a group instead of as an individual with his or her own unique characteristics. This often creates difficulties in interpersonal communication and cooperation at work. Such differences are even more pronounced in decision-making and problem-solving situations where participants approach problems with different values, dispositions, and perspectives.

Another effect of stereotyping is that it blocks learning in organizations. If we view individuals and organizations as learning systems, then individual differences need to be fostered rather than suppressed if learning is to occur. Friedlander[17] asserts that "for an organism to learn, it must be sufficiently heterogenous to contain differences. These are differences in perception, value, preferences, time orientations, plans, expectations, etc." Therefore, the multicultural organization learning provides an excellent opportunity for individual and organizational learning because it accommodates people with unique differences and perspectives. For example, one occasionally sees references to the "feminine" values that are found in the management practices of certain successful companies. Presumably these companies tolerated the "deviance" of individual female managers and, in the process, discovered or learned that such practices had value. We know that culture constrains our ability to conceive of alternative behavior; therefore, seeking out different cultural and individual perspectives is a way of ensuring that we are not blindly pursuing solutions that would be better served by diverse views. Lumping together minority group members and overlooking their unique perspectives diminishes the opportunity to learn from them, as does treating minorities as groups that have little to contribute to the workplace.

Customers are themselves a diverse group. Minority employees can help companies understand and better serve their diverse customers if the company is willing to listen. Furthermore, organizations that have a reputation for managing diversity well will have a competitive advantage in attracting and retaining well-qualified employees.

THE MINORITY EXPERIENCE

Organizations exist in a multicultural environment and cannot avoid this reality. People in organizations bring with them aspects of their cultural experience, and thus, organizations come to mirror issues facing society and the world. Brown,[18] for example, reminds us that the minorities in a society that allow discrimination tend to be particularly sensitive to discriminatory behaviors within the organization that employ them. They perceive discriminatory intent in behaviors that may seem appropriate and nondiscriminatory to members of the dominant culture. As a result, members of the majority may feel insulted if accused of discrimination. They do not recognize that they are "beneficiaries" of institutional discrimination and do not understand why minorities are so sensitive about discrimination. People from different cultures or groups are likely to put outsiders through a testing period. Minorities who have had negative experiences with majority members or institutions are especially likely to watch for possible signs of discrimination or untrustworthiness in new relationships or settings and take longer to form relationships with majority members. This is sometimes mistakenly interpreted as standoffishness; in fact, it's merely a different timetable for forming relationships.

PART

LEADERSHIP AND MANAGEMENT

Chapter

13

LEADERSHIP

OBJECTIVES By the end of this chapter, you should be able to:

A. Define leadership.

B. Describe what followers expect of leaders.

C. Differentiate between leadership and management.

D. Identify the traits related to leader success.

E. Define initiating structure and consideration behavior.

F. Explain what we mean by a contingency theory of leadership.

G. Describe the behavior of effective transformational leaders.

H. Describe how charismatic leaders function.

*A*rrogance: The Executive Achille's Heel

Brian S. Moskal

What makes potential management superstars fail to live up to their advance billing or not make the most of their careers? Wayne D. Calloway, chairman and CEO of PepsiCo Inc. and one of the nation's most admired corporate leaders, thinks he has some answers–at least why would-be superstars fell short of their mark in his $17.8 billion organization based in Purchase, N.Y. PepsiCo recently conducted an internal study to determine why executives and managers failed, and if the company was at fault. The study focused on young recruits, a lot of them M.B.A.s–all bright and full of potential.

"By failure, I don't mean skid row," says Mr. Calloway. "I'm talking about the young gifted manager who is capable of being a division president but somehow doesn't get there–tops out as a vice president or director. Nothing to be ashamed of, but not up to his or her potential."

Source: adapted from *Industry Week*, June 3, 1991, p. 19.

The results surprised him. The three major reasons why bright young people failed had nothing to do with intelligence, or where they went to school, or even how well they knew their jobs. All three reasons for failure were traceable to one core area–flawed values.

"To be specific, the single biggest reason for failure at PepsiCo was **arrogance**. There's nothing wrong with confidence, but arrogance is something else. Arrogance is the illegitimate child of confidence and pride. Arrogance is the idea that not only can you never miss (shooting) a duck, but no one else can ever hit one," explains Mr. Calloway.

Arrogance is an insurmountable roadblock to success in a business where the "team" is what counts. The flip side of arrogance is teamwork–the ability to shine, to star, while working within the group, believes Mr. Calloway.

Lack of commitment was the second biggest reason why executives failed at PepsiCo. "I don't mean they're not willing to work long hours or make personal sacrifices. I mean an unwillingness to commit to a goal that's bigger than they are–to keep coming at a problem even after failing, until they finally come up with a solution," observes Mr. Calloway.

"The failed superstars at PepsiCo were not willing to commit themselves in the (manner of) Thomas Edison, who tried an experiment 128 different ways (before finding success). Instead, our failed superstars gave up after one frustration and they never moved ahead. They somehow failed to really commit themselves to a bigger idea, a bigger notion. They eventually quit," recalls Mr. Calloway.

PepsiCo found the third biggest reason for failure had (and has) to do with another human value–**[lack of] loyalty**. "In these days of mixed allegiance, loyalty has gone the way of poodle skirts and bobby socks in terms of publicity. But not in reality. I don't mean an unwillingness to question authority. I mean an unwillingness to put a larger cause–like the company or team performance–above your own interests. If an executive doesn't have this concept of loyalty, what eventually starts to (creep) through is pettiness, constant complaints and excuses, cutting down co-workers, and, finally, acrobatics to cover his (or her) backside so he (or she) doesn't get blamed for mistakes. It all adds up to mediocre performance at best–destructive behavior at worst."

The flip side of failure is success, and it turns out that winners at PepsiCo demonstrate teamwork, commitment, and loyalty in pretty large doses. "Keep in mind, we're not talking about a 'go-along-to-get-along environment' but a success-driven atmosphere packed with some of the most aggressive business people you'll ever meet," observes Mr. Calloway.

The PepsiCo CEO contends that truly successful businesses are never dominated by arrogant, dishonest types for long. "They may succeed for a short time or in a specific situation, but over (a long) time victory goes to people who work hard, are consistent, fair, open, and candid," believes Mr. Calloway.

Premeeting Preparation

A. Read "Arrogance: The Executive Achille's Heel."

B. Think of four leaders that you have had occasion to observe or read about. If you have not observed a leader in a work setting, choose leaders from clubs, teams, neighborhoods, etc.

_____ LEADER 1's INITIALS   _____ LEADER 2

_____   _____

_____   _____

_____   _____

_____   _____

_____   _____

_____ LEADER 3   _____ LEADER 4

_____   _____

_____   _____

_____   _____

_____   _____

_____   _____

C. Now write down the ways these leaders behave differently from each other. Be specific. For example, if one leader strikes you as being a better communicator than another, don't stop with "M.G. communicates well; B.D. communicates poorly." Write down the specific behavior that is different, for example, "M.G. makes expectations clear; B.D. doesn't explain what she wants us to do."

D. Return to the list of adjectives you generated for C. Rank the adjectives according to how important they are in terms of a leader's effectiveness. The most important characteristics should be number one, the second most important should be number two, etc.

E. What are your own strengths as a leader?

F. Is there anything you could improve that would make you a better leader?

Topic Introduction

Thumb through U.S. business magazines and you'll find a great deal of print devoted towards corporate leaders. Some people think we tend to romanticize leadership and either give leaders more credit than they deserve or expect them to work miracles when their hands are fairly well tied.[1] However, there is also strong evidence that leaders do in fact make a notable difference in organizations,[2] particularly those undergoing crisis, growth, and change. Not only do companies with effective leaders report higher net profits, but in times of increased competitive pressures and widespread demands for change, good leadership is not just a competitive advantage but an essential survival factor. The increased demand for leadership skills is not limited to people in executive suites. Given the flattened hierarchies in companies that have terminated middle managers and the move towards empowerment, total quality, and networks, companies are looking for leadership from people at all levels.

Leaders are "individuals 1) who establish direction for a group, 2) gain their commitment, and 3) motivate them to achieve goals to move in that direction."[3] An important aspect of this definition is that leaders make others "want" to follow them voluntarily. Leadership is generally held to be in the eye of the beholder since there are no leaders without followers. We develop a schema concerning leaders that determines whether or not we perceive someone as a leader.[4] The adjectives you listed in the pre-meeting preparation should give you a better idea about your own leadership schema.

FOLLOWER EXPECTATIONS OF LEADERS

According to U.S. research, followers expect four characteristics of their leaders, in descending order of importance.[5]

1. Integrity (truthful, trustworthy, consistency in word and deed, has character, has convictions)
2. Competence (capable, productive, efficient)
3. Forward-looking (sense of direction and concern for the future)
4. Inspiring (enthusiastic, energetic, positive about the future)

In combination, these characteristics determine a leader's credibility. When employees perceive management to have high credibility and a strong philosophy, employees are more likely to:[6]

- Be proud to tell others they are part of the organization
- Talk up the organization with friends
- See their own values as similar to those of the organization
- Feel a sense of ownership about the organization.

In contrast, those who do not perceive management to be credible work primarily for money, produce only when watched, bad-mouth the organization in private, and would consider leaving the organization in rough times. In other words, there is a positive pay-off for leaders and management teams that work hard at building and preserving their credibility with subordinates.

Our schemas of what constitutes good leadership vary from one culture to another. In the U.S. people value charisma in their leaders; in West Germany, charisma is distrusted because it reminds people of Hitler. We find more participative leadership and shared governance in cultures with small power distance (e.g., Scandinavia). In contrast, cultures characterized by large power distance tend to have autocratic leaders (e.g., the Philippines).[7] Latin Americans have historically preferred authoritarian leaders and centralized decision-making.[8]

Therefore, expatriate managers who work abroad and have a more participative style may find that Latin American subordinates are, at least initially, uncomfortable when the leader does not call all the shots. Asking for advice may be interpreted as incompetence or weakness in cultures where leaders are supposed to be omnipotent experts.

Villages in French West Africa have a different tradition of leadership. Each village has a "palaver" tree where the entire village meets to discuss important issues. Representatives from the elders, the young men, and the women express their opinions and talk until a consensus opinion is reached. When working with people from other cultures or ethnic groups, it is very important to understand their accustomed leadership style and to adapt one's own style accordingly.

At present in the U.S., we expect our leaders to provide or help us create a vision that encompasses both environmental threats and opportunities and an appropriate response to the situation. Some political pundits maintain that George Bush lost the 1992 presidential election primarily because he did not grasp the importance of what he called "the vision thing."

MANAGERS VERSUS LEADERS

Managers are in danger of making a similar mistake if they do not understand that being a good manager and a good leader are not necessarily synonymous. Much has been written about the differences between managers and leaders. Whereas leaders establish a vision, managers do planning and budgeting. While leaders focus on imaginative ideas, managers focus on processes and systems. Leaders spend time and effort aligning people so that they understand and accept their vision and strategies, while managers focus upon organizing and staffing. While leaders motivate and inspire others, managers take a control and problem-solving approach. As a result, leaders tend to produce change while manages tend to produce order, predictability, and the key results expected by stakeholders.[9]

Obviously both leadership and management are important. Leaders should not ignore the organization's core competencies (a Japanese concept that refers to well-developed operating capabilities) to focus solely upon an abstract vision.[10] And managers should not get so caught up in pushing the organization along that they lose sight of the broader picture or overlook the importance of providing a vision that motivates people. In recent years, the following phrase caught our attention, "managers do things right and leaders do the right thing." For most of us, it makes more sense to aim for both–to develop ourselves as leaders who also strive to be good managers with a thorough understanding of organizational functions.

When effective leadership is absent in an organization, it is more difficult to adapt to changes, the superordinate goals and values that take priority over individual interests may be missing, and it is more difficult to take pride in being part of something bigger than we are.[11]

The way we conceive of leadership and the theories we use to explain it have evolved over time. Although there are 5000 studies on leadership, no one theory is universally accepted. The rest of the chapter presents the practical highlights of leadership research: 1) leader traits; 2) behavior styles; 3) contingency theory; 4) transformational and charismatic leadership; and 5) self-leaders.[12]

The first leadership studies focused on the question of why some people become leaders and others do not. Years ago common wisdom held that leaders were born, not made, so researchers began by looking at leader traits. This attempt to figure out what characteristics distinguished leaders from non-leaders yielded limited results. However, a recent study of successful business leaders found they shared the following traits: drive, honesty and integrity, leadership motivation, self-confidence, cognitive ability, knowledge of the business, creativity, and flexibility.[13] There are two leader traits, intelligence and high energy, that are inherited, which means there is at least some truth to the statement that leaders are born. One's childhood experiences play a more important role than genes in determining leadership potential.[14] Furthermore, leaders can be developed, primarily through work experiences, challenging job assignments, role models, mentors, and training. Opportunity, luck, and the motivation to lead also determine who will become leaders. The Kotter article in the *Reader*, "Firms With a Superior Leadership Capacity; Practices That Create Better-Than-Average Management Teams" explains what companies can do to cultivate leadership in their employees.

Once researchers gave up on the idea that leaders were born, they started observing differences in behavior between leaders and non-leaders. Much of the early research identified two principle dimensions of leader behavior—a concern for task/production and a concern for people, defined below.

1. *Initiating structure*—leader behavior that organizes and defines what group members should be doing to maximize output.

2. *Consideration*—leader behavior associated with creating mutual respect or trust and that focuses on a concern for group members' needs and desires.

Although research programs (The Ohio State studies, University of Michigan studies, the Managerial Grid) reported that leaders who were rated as high on both these dimensions were generally more likely to have high subordinate performance and satisfaction, the results were not conclusive because these studies did not take situational factors into consideration. Not every situation requires leaders who employ a high degree of both initiating structure and consideration. For example, highly skilled employees who are self-motivating require neither of these behaviors on the part of a leader.[15]

Once again, researchers and practitioners came to the conclusion that there is no "one best way" to lead; it depends upon the situation. Effective leaders analyze the factors pertaining to the situation, task, followers, and the organization, and then choose the appropriate style.

Contingency theories of management employ various leadership styles. One continuum which appears in Figure 13-1 ranges from one extreme at which the manager has total freedom to make decisions to the other extreme where managers and employees make joint decisions. In Chapter 15, the Vroom model of leadership and decision-making is another example of a contingency theory of leadership that includes an autocratic-consultative-participative-delegative continuum of leader styles. Other theories go beyond decision-making behavior styles to include concepts like initiating structure and consideration behavior. For example, House's Path Goal theory of leadership[16] (See Figure 13-2) maintains that leaders motivate higher performance by helping subordinates attain individual goals that are aligned with organizational goals. It is based upon expectancy theory (effort→performance→outcome) and the effect leaders have

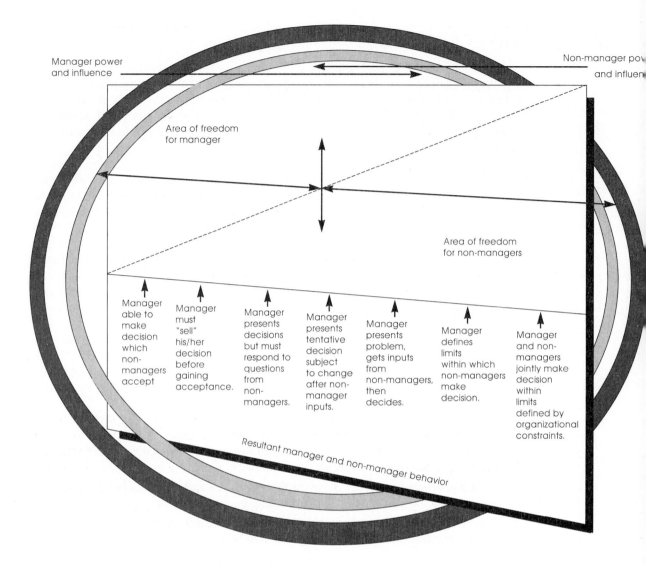

Manager power
and influence

Non-manager power
and influence

Area of freedom
for manager

Area of freedom
for non-managers

Manager able to make decision which non-managers accept

Manager must "sell" his/her decision before gaining acceptance.

Manager presents decisions but must respond to questions from non-managers.

Manager presents tentative decision subject to change after non-manager inputs.

Manager presents problem, gets inputs from non-managers, then decides.

Manager defines limits within which non-managers make decision.

Manager and non-managers jointly make decision within limits defined by organizational constraints.

Resultant manager and non-manager behavior

FIGURE 13-1 Continuum of Manager-Non-manager Behavior
Reprinted by permission of *Harvard Business Review*. An exhibit from "How to Choose a Leadership Pattern" by Robert Tannenbaum and Warren H. Schmidt, (May-June 1973). Copyright © 1973 by the President and Fellows of Harvard College; all rights reserved.

upon subordinate expectations.[17] Leaders motivate employees when they 1) clarify the path that will result in employee achievement, 2) provide the necessary guidance and support to get the job done, 3) remove the obstacles that block the path to goal achievement, and 4) link rewards to goal accomplishment. Leader behavior is acceptable if subordinates perceive it as a source of either immediate or future satisfaction. Depending upon both *subordinate contingency factors* (locus of control, experience, perceived ability) and *environmental contingency factors* (task structure, formal authority system, and work group), the leader employs one of four leadership styles which should result in employee performance and satisfaction.[18]

Directive. The leader informs subordinates what is expected of them, sets performance standards, schedules activities, and provides specific guidance as to what should be done and how to do it. This is essentially the same as the "initiating structure" concept mentioned before.

Supportive. The leader is friendly and approachable and shows concern for the needs, status, and well-being of subordinates. He or she treats subordinates as equals. This is essentially the same as the "consideration" concept found in behavior theories of leadership.

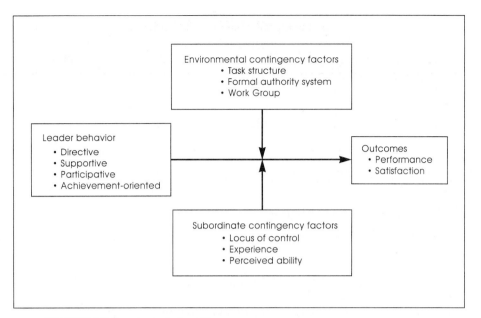

FIGURE 13-2 The Path Goal Theory

Participative. The leader consults with subordinates, solicits their suggestions, and takes suggestions into consideration before making a decision.

Achievement-oriented. The leader sets challenging goals, emphasizes excellence, expects subordinates to perform at their highest level, continuously seeks improvement in performance, and shows a high degree of confidence in the employee's abilities.

Although there is widespread acceptance of a contingency approach to leadership, no one theory contains all the possible contingencies. Some of the proven connections between specific situational factors and leadership styles appear below.

- Subordinates benefit from a directive style when they are working with an unstructured or stressful task. When they know how to do a routine job, further instruction not only wastes time but may be perceived as insulting.

- When subordinates perform boring, repetitive, unsatisfying tasks, leaders should consider restructuring the job (see Chapter 21 on Job Design and Job Involvement) so it would meet more of the employees' needs. If that proves impossible, leaders should use a supportive style that allows employees to meet their social needs on the job.

- In highly formalized organizations where everything is standardized, there is little need for a task-oriented leader. Cohesive work groups with norms that heavily influence employees make both consideration and initiating structure leader behavior redundant.

- Subordinates who do not want to take responsibility at work prefer autocratic, rather than participative leaders.

- Leaders behave differently with different followers. Highly motivated, skilled and trustworthy subordinates are sometimes given preferential treatment and constitute an in-group.[19] Although it is very natural for leaders to treat their in-group members differently, this practice usually results in jealousy and resentment among out-group members, and reduced cooperation and communication between the two groups.

One contingency factor that has generated a good deal of controversy in recent years is gender. Are there differences in the way U.S. women and men lead? According to a meta-analysis or comparison of all the research done on this subject, the only significant difference in male and female management styles is that women were found to utilize a more participative decision-making style.[20]

The following exercise allows us to look at the relationship between emergent leader behavior and the particular contingencies in a given situation.

Procedure for Group Meeting:
The Perfect Square

The purpose of this exercise is to provide an opportunity in which we can observe different types of leadership and to examine the linkage with situational contingencies.

STEP 1.   Form a circle with 8-18 people in a large area of empty space where you can spread out without running into chairs or walls.

STEP 2.   Ask for a volunteer(s) to be an observer. If your group is small, one observer will do. If your group has 18 people, you can have up to three observers. The observers should withdraw from the circle. The observer instructions are found on page 336. Please read them carefully.

STEP 3.   The members of the circle should blindfold themselves. If you wear glasses, place them in your pocket or give them to an observer to hold.

STEP 4.   The instructor (or student facilitator) will read you the instructions for the exercise. The blindfolded group has 20 minutes to complete the assigned task. (25 minutes)

STEP 5.   Individual Reflection. Please answer the following questions without talking in the next ten minutes. (10 minutes)

1. What different types of leadership emerged in this exercise? In your opinion, who were the leaders and why? What leader behaviors did they exhibit?

2. What occurred in the group to help you solve the problem?

3. What occurred in the group that hindered you from solving the problem or from solving it quickly?

4. What did you learn about leadership from this exercise?

5. What did you learn about yourself as a leader in this exercise?

STEP 6.   Group Discussion. Discuss these questions with your group. Ask the observers what they observed. Choose a representative to report to the entire class a summary of questions 1-4. (20-30 minutes)

STEP 7. Plenary debriefing session (20 minutes)

1. Have an observer from each group briefly and objectively describe what happened when their group did the blindfolded exercise. Next, the group representative presents their report.

2. Can you see any relationships between this exercise and the "real world" you experience at work or in other organizational settings?

3. What are the important contingencies in this particular situation? What type of leadership works best in a situation like this? What leader behaviors are needed? What's the difference between a leader and a facilitator?

4. There are no leaders without followers. In this exercise, what were the characteristics of a good follower?

5. What did you learn about yourself as a leader in this exercise?

6. If you were to repeat this exercise, what would you do differently to be a better leader?

Follow-Up

In recent years, attention has shifted somewhat from contingency theories of leadership to *transformational*[21] and *charismatic* leadership. Transformational leaders are value-driven change agents who make followers more conscious of the importance and value of task outcomes. They provide followers with a vision and motivate them to go beyond self-interest for the good of the organization. Given the difficult challenges currently facing business, the need for leaders who can transform organizations is understandable. In several studies, researchers have listened to effective transformational leaders describe how they lead others. The Bennis and Nanus article in the *Reader, "The 4 Competencies of Leadership,"* found that highly effective and charismatic leaders manage four areas: attention, meaning, trust, and self. They manage attention by being highly committed to a compelling vision or outcome. They manage meaning by making ideas seem real and tangible for others, by means of both words and symbols. They manage trust by being reliable and congruent so that people know what they stand for. And, finally, they manage self by knowing and using their skills effectively, learning from mistakes, and focusing on success rather than failure. Kouzes and Posner[22] asked leaders to describe their "personal best" leadership experience, a time when they accomplished something extraordinary in their organization. From these critical incidents, they identified five leadership practices.

1. Challenging the Process (questioning the status quo, seeking new opportunities to improve and grow, taking risks)
2. Inspiring a Shared Vision

3. Enabling Others to Act (fostering collaboration and empowerment)

4. Modeling the Way (setting a good example and planning small wins)

5. Encouraging the Heart (recognizing individual contributions and celebrating team accomplishments)

While charismatic leaders share some behaviors with transformational leaders, the former are seen as extraordinary or heroic leaders. Charismatic leaders have special relationships with their followers and elicit high levels of performance, loyalty, sacrifice and enthusiasm. They develop a vision to which they are strongly committed that touches the emotions of their followers. Charismatic leaders take risks and act in unconventional ways. Such leaders are very self-confident and good at communicating.[23]

There are two types of charismatic leaders. *Ethical charismatic leaders* use power to serve others, align their vision with their follower's needs and aspirations, accept and learn from criticism, encourage followers to think independently, work to develop followers into leaders, and rely upon internal moral standards. In contrast, *unethical charismatic leaders* are motivated by personalized power, pursue their own vision and goals, censure critical or opposing views, encourage blind obedience, dependency, and submission in their followers, and lack an internal moral compass.[24]

An opposing view to charismatic leaders as an answer to the challenges of today's business world is the concept of "superleadership." [25] Sims and his colleagues contend that it is time to move beyond the notion of leaders as heroes to leaders as hero-makers who empower subordinates and teach them to be self-leaders. We find the same normative trend in Block's[26] argument that leaders should be stewards who choose service over self-interest. In doing so, they are willing to be accountable for the well-being of the larger organization by operating to serve, rather than control those around them. Looking for strong leaders to "save us" localizes the responsibility, power, ownership and privilege at the top of the organization. Instead, organizations should move from patriarchy to partnership. Thus, the organizational vision is not simply created and passed down from the top; each employee is responsible for articulating a vision for his or her own area of responsibility.

The concept of a leader as servant or coach is a far cry from the arrogance that tripped up the PepsiCo fast-trackers described in the opening vignette. MBA's are often accused of arrogance, a trait that produces little except resentment. It is a characteristic that we associate less and less with effective leadership and good work relationships.

Theories about leadership have evolved from the original emphasis upon traits, to behavior styles theory and situational theories, to fairly recent research on transformational and charismatic leadership, self-leadership, and leaders as stewards. This evolution reflects both the progress that has been made in understanding a complex concept and our changing expectations and conceptions about leaders.

Learning Points

1. Although Americans tend to romanticize leadership, there is evidence that leaders do make a notable difference in organizations, particularly when they are undergoing crisis, growth, and change.

2. Leaders are individuals a) who establish direction for a group, b) gain their commitment, and c) motivate them to achieve goals to move in that direction.

3. There are no leaders without followers.

4. Followers expect the following characteristics from their leaders: a) integrity; b) competence: c) forward-looking; and d) inspiring.

5. Our schemas of what constitutes good leadership vary from one culture to another and from one era to another.

6. Not all managers are leaders because the functions they perform are different. Leaders tend to produce change while managers tend to produce order, predictability, and the key results expected by stakeholders.

7. Successful business leaders possess the following traits: drive, honesty and integrity, leadership motivation, self-confidence, cognitive ability, knowledge of the business, creativity, and flexibility.

8. Intelligence and high energy are inherited traits, but it is possible to develop and train people to become leaders.

9. Leadership styles are differentiated by leader behavior, such as initiating structure or consideration behavior, and the way the leader makes decisions (e.g., the autocratic-delegative continuum).

10. The leadership styles found in House's Path Goal Theory of Leadership are: directive, supportive, participative, and achievement-oriented. The effectiveness of the style depends upon both employee and environmental contingency factors.

11. Effective leaders analyze the factors pertaining to the situation, task, followers, and the organization, and then choose the appropriate style.

12. Other than preferring a more participative decision-making style, the managerial style of female managers does not differ significantly from that of males.

13. Transformational leaders are value-driven change agents who make followers more conscious of the importance and value of task outcomes. They provide followers with a vision and motivate them to go beyond self-interest for the good of the organization.

14. Effective leaders: a) challenge the process; b) inspire a shared vision; c) enable others to act; d) model the way; and e) encourage the heart.

15. Charismatic leaders develop a special relationship with their followers that includes high levels of performance, loyalty, sacrifice, and enthusiasm. They are adept at communicating an inspiring vision.

16. Instead of relying upon hero-leaders, superleadership focuses on empowerment and turning employees into self-leaders. Another new leadership schema that is supposedly more appropriate for today's business environment is the idea of leaders as servants.

for Managers

- Think of followers as volunteers who contribute their efforts not because they are paid, but because their needs are met in the process. This prevents leaders from taking their followers for granted.

- Leaders need to have an in-depth and up-to-date understanding of what makes both their followers (including ones from diverse backgrounds) and their organization tick.

- Many initially successful leaders let power go to their heads. A measure of humility and the ability to accept negative feedback and admit mistakes can prevent this common occurrence.

- Consistency, honesty, and fairness all contribute to a leader's respect and credibility. When followers perceive that they are being manipulated by a leader or that the leader is motivated by self-interest rather than the good of the organization, it may be impossible for the leader to regain his or her credibility.

- The leadership function is shared in many effective groups. Leaders rise to the occasion but return to follower status once their contribution is made. Such groups do not require a leader so much as a facilitator (rotating or fixed) who helps the group stay on track and allows people to be heard.

- Lessons from Korean parables of leadership are:[27]
  a. Listen to the unheard–the hearts of followers, their uncommunicated feelings, unexpressed pains, and unspoken complaints–rather than listening only to superficial words of followers.
  b. Humble rulers with deep-reaching inner strength who bring well-being to their followers are more effective than vain rulers.
  c. A leader's commitment and willingness to work alongside his or her followers is a strong determinant of success.
  d. The wise leader earns the devotion of followers by placing them in positions that fully realize their potential and secures harmony among them by giving all of them credit for their distinctive achievements.

Personal Application Assignment

Your assignment is to write about a leadership experience or incident about which you want to learn more. (You may wish to write about one of the exercises you did with your learning group in this course.)

A. *Concrete Experience*

   1. *Objectively* describe the experience ("who," "what," "when," "where," "how" type information–up to 2 points).

   2. *Subjectively* describe your feelings, perceptions, and thoughts that occurred during (not after) the experience (up to 2 points). Does this section have too much detail? (If so, delete 1 point.)

B. *Reflective Observation*

   1. Look at the experience from different points of view. How many points of view did you include that are *relevant* (up to 2 points)?

   2. Use these perspectives to add more meaning to the incident (up to 2 points).

C. *Abstract Conceptualization*

1. Relate concepts from the assigned readings and the lecture to the experience (i.e., what theories that you heard in the lecture or read in the *Reader* relate to your understanding of this incident?). Make reference to at least two sources. Use standard referencing format and include the page number to which you are referring. How many sources did you use and how clearly did you explain their theories (up to 4 points)?

2. You can also create an original model or theory, but it should not replace course concepts.

D. *Active Experimentation*

1. Write about what you will do in the future that will improve your effectiveness. Use rules of thumb or action resolutions.

2. Are they described specifically, thoroughly, and in detail (up to 4 points)?

E. *Integration, Synthesis, and Writing*

1. Did you write about something personally important to you (up to 2 points)?

2. Was it well written (up to 2 points)?

3. Did you integrate and synthesize the different sections (up to 1 point)?

[1]James R. Meindl & Sanford B. Ehrlich, "The Romance of Leadership and the Evaluation of Organizational Performance," *Academy of Management Journal*, 30 (1987), pp. 91-109; Jeffrey Pfeffer, "The Ambiguity of Leadership," *Academy of Management Review*, January 1977, pp. 104-111; and Alan B. Thomas, "Does Leadership Make a Difference to Organizational Performance?", *Administrative Science Quarterly*, September 1988, pp. 388-400. Pfeffer's position is that leaders have limited power within their organizations and even less control over external factors. When something occurs within an organization, we attribute the cause to the leader regardless of his or her actual contribution.

[2]Stephen Motowidlo, "Leadership and Leadership Processes," in *Handbook of Industrial Organizational Psychology*, 2nd ed., ed. M.D. Dunnette (Palo Alto, CA: Consulting Psychologists Press, 1992).

[3]Adapted from Jay Conger, *Learning to Lead* (San Francisco: Jossey-Bass, 1992), pp. 18-19.

[4]James G. Hunt, *Leadership: A New Synthesis*. London: Sage, 1991.

[5]James M. Kouzes and Barry Z. Posner, *The Leadership Challenge*. (San Francisco: Jossey-Bass, 1987), p. 16. See also the latest book by these authors, *Credibility Factor: How Leaders Gain and Lose It, Why People Demand It*. (San Francisco: Jossey-Bass, 1993).

[6]Charles O'Reilly, "Charisma as Communication: The Impact of Top Management Credibility and Philosophy on Employee Involvement." Paper presented at the annual meeting of the Academy of Management, Boston, 1984.

[7]Geert Hofstede, "Motivation, Leadership, and Organization: Do American Theories Apply Abroad?" *Reader*.

[8]Fernando Quezada and James E. Boyce, "Latin America," in *Comparative Management*, ed. Raghu Nath (Cambridge, MA: Ballinger, 1988), pp. 247-269.

[9]John P. Kotter, *A Force for Change: How Leadership Differs from Management*. (New York: Free Press, 1990)

[10]Leonard R. Sayles, "Doing Things Right: A New Imperative for Middle Mangers," *Organizational Dynamics*, Spring 1993, pp. 5-14.

[11]Abraham Zeleznik, "The Leadership Gap," *Organizational Dynamics*. Vol. 4:1, February, 1990.

[12]See Gary Yukl's book, *Leadership in Organizations*, (Englewood Cliffs, N.J.: Prentice-Hall, 1994) for a comprehensive, reader-friendly treatise geared for both academics and practitioners. Camilla Stiver's *Gender Images in Public Administration*, (London: Sage, 1993) looks at leadership theory from a feminist perspective.

[13]Shelley A. Kirkpatrick and Edwin A. Locke, "Leadership: Do Traits Matter?," *Academy of Management Executive*, 5(2), (1991), pp. 48-60.

[14]Conger, *Learning to Lead*, pp. 22-24.

[15]Jon P. Howell, David E. Bowen, Peter W. Dorfman, Steven Kerr, Philip M. Podsakoff, "Substitutes for Leadership: Effective Alternatives to Ineffective Leadership," *Organizational Dynamics*, Summer 1990, pp. 21-38.

[16]Robert J. House, "A Path-Goal Theory of Leader Effectiveness," *Administrative Science Quarterly*, September 1971, pp. 321-38.

[17]See "Motivation: A Diagnostic Approach" by Nadler and Lawler, *Reader*, for an explanation of this theory.

[18]Adapted from Robert J. House and Terence R. Mitchell, "Path-Goal Theory of Leadership," *Journal of Contemporary Business*, Autumn 1974, p. 83.

[19]Robert C. Liden & George Graen, "Generalizability of the Vertical Dyad Linkage Model of Leadership". *Academy of Management Journal*, 1980, 23, pp. 451-465.

[20]Alice H. Eagly & Blair T. Johnson, (1990). "Gender and Leadership Style: A Meta-analysis". *Psychological Bulletin*, 108, pp. 233-256. See also the article by Gary Powell in the *Reader*.

[21]See the article by Noel M. Tichy and Mary A. Devanna, "The Leadership Challenge–A Call for the Transformational Leader," *Reader*.

[22]Kouzes and Posner, *The Leadership Challenge*, p. 14.

[23]Jay Conger and Rabindra N. Kanungo, *Charismatic Leadership*. (San Francisco: Jossey-Bass, 1988); and in a chapter in the same book by Bernard Bass, "Evolving Perspectives on Charismatic Leadership," pp. 40-77.

[24]Jane Howell, "Two Faces of Charisma: Socialized and Personalized Leadership in Organizations." In J. Conger and R. Kanungo (eds.) *Charismatic Leadership*. (San Francisco: Jossey-Bass, 1988), pp. 213-236 and Jay Conger, "The Dark Side of Leadership," *Organizational Dynamics*, (Autumn 1990), pp. 44-55.

[25]Charles C. Manz and Henry P. Sims, "Superleadership: Beyond the Myth of Heroic Leadership," *Organizational Dynamics*, 1991, Vol. 19, pp. 18-35.

[26]Peter Block. *Stewardship: Choosing Service Over Self-Interest*. (San Francisco: Berrett-Koehler, 1993).

[27]W. Chan Kim & Renee A. Mauborgne: "Parables of Leadership," *Harvard Business Review,* July-August, 1992, pp. 123-128.

Chapter 14

LEADERSHIP AND ORGANIZATIONAL CULTURE

OBJECTIVES By the end of this chapter you should be able to:

A. Define organizational culture and explain its function.

B. Explain how it evolves and is maintained.

C. Describe the characteristics of a strong culture.

D. Explain the relationship between strong cultures and high performance.

E. Identify the four stages in the organizational life cycle.

F. Describe how leaders can manage culture.

*B*est Corporate Culture is a Melting Pot

Jack Falvey

Promoting from within has been a policy of misguided company loyalty that has damaged the foundations of organizations it seeks to build.

Because of promote-from-within policies, many companies are headed today by organization men of the 1940s. Many of these inmates-turned-wardens have never worked outside of the corporations they head. Is it any wonder they are having difficulty adjusting to a world marketplace? Take this example.

A major company introduced a new consumer product. The market for a product accelerated, and soon a foreign competitor entered the arena. As the company's share began to erode, top management met to determine strategy. The competitor's clever advertising was to be countered with trade deals and deep price cuts. The decision was unanimous. Why? Because everyone in the meeting was with the company 15 years before when a similar foreign product threatened another segment of the business. Everyone's experience was exactly the same. "We were successful before, so we will do the same thing again."

Unfortunately, the foreign challenge was slightly different this time and so were the results. There were layoffs, then several plant closings, and, finally, sale of the product, or what was left of it, to another company.

When I speak to management groups of established companies, the view from the podium is sometimes frightening. They look alike; they dress alike; unfortunately, they think alike. They are the products of a success profile. They are plain vanilla. But strength comes from diversity. When you face a problem, isn't it better to have five or six options, rather than just one?

When, on the other hand, there is "cross-pollution," some wondrous things begin to happen. A consumer goods president took over as chief executive officer of a computer company. He insisted that stock be available before a new product was launched, knowing that advertising backed by empty shelves was a waste. Consumer electronics companies usually had announced first, promoted and sold second, and delivered third. He reversed the order and filled the distribution pipeline first. He single-handedly caused a major shakeout of his competition by his product's success.

To compound the promote-from-within syndrome, companies have established traditional areas of the business from which all top managers will come. Organizations are headed by finance businessmen 20 years after they are no longer in the finance business. Engineers have computer companies that have consistently driven down prices and increased performance of their products with technical breakthroughs but that have failed to make the products usable in the marketplace. Family ownership imposes similar limitations when it gives each son a small division or sees to it that every cousin has an office somewhere.

Is it any wonder our industrial giants become targets of opportunity for anyone who chooses to pose a serious challenge to their products, services, or marketplace? (In some cases the challenge is directly to those companies' management teams in the form of takeover bids or green mail.)

One of the major moves in our business environment is the formation of ventures by talented, aggressive, well-trained managers who have left their companies. Most could not survive or contribute within an in-bred organization. The proliferation of prospering companies that have been spun off should tell us something about the company men who were unable to make a success of those subsidiaries.

Between 20 and 30 percent of all openings should be filled from outside. The broader the mix, the better. Every position should have outside talent included in the selection process. If inside people are not competitive, how can your organization be competitive in the marketplace?

Consultants who work across industry lines will confirm that the fundamentals in every industry are almost identical. There are no real barriers to mobility. Junior managers especially should be valued if they have three or four different work experiences because they have found that managing their own careers produces far better returns than delegating that responsibility to a single organization.

The mobile manager of the 1960s who did duty in six cities and then returned to the home office should now be replaced by the mobile manager of the 1980s who has worked across six different industries and deals comfortably in business on three different continents. The time of the generalized top manager is coming, and none too soon. Narrow specialists have always had difficulty with the big picture.

The rules of business have been shifting dramatically and rapidly for the past decade. Stable, secure management teams are remnants of the past. Dynamic, diverse management is needed for the present and the future. The rigid rules of reorganization construction must be broken.

The process of regenerating cannot be done overnight. Broaden your view and bring in more talent from nontraditional sources. Its addition will add new strength. It may already be long overdue.

Premeeting Preparation

A. Read "Best Corporate Culture is a Melting Pot."

B. Fill out the accompanying Organizational Culture Questionnaire for an organization to which you belong(ed).

C. Read the Topic Introduction.

D. Complete The G.B.A. Construction Company, Part I, and prepare your individual analysis.

Note: For your individual and collective learning, *do not* read Part II of the case in advance.

Organization Culture Questionnaire

For each of the seven organization culture dimensions described, place an (a) above the number that indicates your assessment of the organization's <u>actual</u> position on that dimension and an (i) above the number that indicates your choice of where the organization should <u>ideally</u> be on this dimension.

1. *Conformity.* The feeling that there are many externally imposed constraints in the organization; the degree to which members feel that there are many rules, procedures, policies, and practices to which they have to conform rather than being able to do their work as they see fit.

   Conformity is not
   characteristic
   of this organization.

   1 2 3 4 5 6 7 8 9 10

   Conformity is very
   characteristic
   of this organization.

2. *Responsibility.* Members of the organization are given personal responsibility to achieve their part of the organization's goals; the degree to which members feel that they can make decisions and solve problems without checking with superiors each step of the way.

   No responsibility is
   given in the
   organization.

   1 2 3 4 5 6 7 8 9 10

   There is a great emphasis on
   personal responsibility in the
   organization.

3. *Standards.* The emphasis the organization places on quality performance and outstanding production, including the degree to which the member feels the organization is setting challenging goals for itself and communicating these goal commitments to members.

   Standards are very
   low or nonexistent in
   the organization.

   1 2 3 4 5 6 7 8 9 10

   High challenging standards are
   set in the organization.

4. *Rewards.* The degree to which members feel that they are being recognized and rewarded for good work rather than being ignored, criticized, or punished when something goes wrong.

   Members are ignored,
   punished, or criticized.

   1 2 3 4 5 6 7 8 9 10

   Members are recognized and
   rewarded positively.

5. *Organizational clarity.* The feeling among members that things are well organized and that goals are clearly defined rather than being disorderly, confused, or chaotic.

   The organization is
   disorderly, confused,
   and chaotic.

   1 2 3 4 5 6 7 8 9 10

   The organization is well organized
   with clearly defined goals.

6. *Warmth and support.* The feeling that friendliness is a valued norm in the organization, that members trust one another and offer support to one another. The feeling that good relationships prevail in the work environment.

There is no warmth
and support in the
organization.

1 2 3 4 5 6 7 8 9 10

Warmth and support are
very characteristic of the
organization.

7. *Leadership.* The willingness of organization members to accept leadership and direction from qualified others. As needs for leadership arise, members feel free to take leadership roles and are rewarded for successful leadership. Leadership is based on expertise. The organization is not dominated by, or dependent on, one or two individuals.

Leadership is not
rewarded; members are
dominated or dependent
and resist leadership
attempts.

1 2 3 4 5 6 7 8 9 10

Members accept and reward leadership based on expertise.

8. What are the dominant values of this organization?

9. What are some of the behavioral norms of the organization that an outsider or a newcomer would quickly notice?

10. How do the leaders of the organization reinforce these values and norms?

11. How are newcomers socialized in this organization?

12. Does this culture help or hinder the organization in terms of performance?

13. What do you want to learn about organizational culture and socialization?

14. What are the significant learning points from the readings?

The G.B.A. Construction Company, Part I[1]

INTRODUCTION

The G.B.A. Construction Company was started in the early 1930s by G.B.A., Sr. His son, G.B.A., Jr., took over as president in 1946. G.B.A., Sr., passed away a few years later. There are two major stockholders at present: G.B.A., Jr., who owns 65 percent of the stock, and A.H., who owns 35 percent. A.H. started the business with G.B.A., Sr., but in recent years has been relatively inactive in the business.

The following sketches provide a brief view of G.B.A., Jr., and the business history of the G.B.A. Company.

G.B.A., JR.–A SNAPSHOT

G.B.A Jr., took over as president of the company in 1946. He is a tireless worker and through his many years of experience has become a consummate businessman.

Under his leadership the company has developed a reputation for excellence–highest-quality work, on-time delivery, and within-budget estimates. G.B.A., Jr.'s personal reputation has done much to build the company. While very knowledgeable in all aspects of the construction business, he is particularly skilled in financial matters.

His managerial style can best be described as that of a benevolent autocrat. He is used to making most, if not all, of the major decisions by himself. As he put it, "It's my company, so why shouldn't I make the decisions?"

The benevolent part of his style manifests itself in a somewhat paternal attitude toward employees. For example, he recently instituted a program wherein key employees received company pins with diamonds to signify their length of service to the organization. G.B.A., Jr., felt that rewarding people in this manner would motivate employees. According to the grapevine, however, many recipients felt these pins (and other similar awards) were "Mickey Mouse."

His relationships with his key officers are rather aloof: "He's not the kind of guy you can get very close to." The climate of the organization is very much influenced by his personal style. Secrecy is high (lots of closed files), and people maintain J/C files (just in case the boss asks). As is characteristic of benevolent autocrats, people fear and respect him at the same time.

He is presently in his mid-fifties and in good health. While not concerned overtly with his own personal health, he is somewhat concerned that his partner and other colleagues in the industry are increasingly suffering heart attacks.

He and his wife do some traveling and he looks forward to the time when he can relax more and travel, play tennis, and so on. His son has just entered an Ivy League school but shows few signs of interest in coming into the business. G.B.A., Jr.'s daughter is a budding commercial artist and is presently unmarried.

BUSINESS HISTORY

The history of the company has been solid and profitable. When the entire construction industry had lean years, the G.B.A. Co. continued to do as well as or better than comparable companies in the field. Its main business is in the area of shopping centers, office buildings, hotels, motels, and the like. Several recent trends are important.

Volume in 1973 was $200 million and is predicted to be $300 million in 1974 and $400 million to $500 million in 1975. Although no one expects this rapid rate of growth to continue at its present or projected pace, the long-range goal is to grow at about 15 to 20 percent per year in both volume and profit.

Job or project size has increased to the point at which the "average" job is now about $5 million per job. The company expects this trend to continue. The company expects, in other words, to be in a position to take on and successfully manage larger projects of longer duration rather than many small projects. Changes in the structure and functioning of the organization will be necessary to cope with this change in the nature of their business.

Increasingly, the company was finding itself in the position, and indeed was seeking such situations, in which it was brought in at the early planning stages of a project. In this way, the company worked directly with architects and planners, under a negotiated overall cost and fee, and was in a position to significantly influence design and specification.

Although the company is always looking for ways to improve and grow, there is no expectation that the nature of its basic business will change substantially in the future (e.g., to go into the construction of nuclear power plants). G.B.A. Co. knows its business, knows that it can do it well, and plans to continue in this vein. Geographically, most of the business is in the South, Southeast, Midwest, and West of the United States. Division II is located in the same city as the corporate central offices. There are increasing opportunities coming across Mr. G.B.A.'s desk for expansion into new areas overseas, particularly in developing nations such as Saudi Arabia.

ORGANIZATION STRUCTURE

The company is organized into four divisions and a central office as follows:

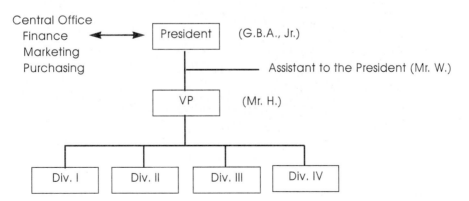

THE PROBLEM

Early in 1973, G.B.A., Jr., contacted a Boston-based consulting firm. He had seen a seminar flyer that described this consulting company's capability as being in the general area of the "human side of enterprise." He believed this group might be able to help him with some of his concerns. Discussions with G.B.A., Jr., and his top management group led to the specification of two major problem areas–succession and continuity of management.

G.B.A., Jr., recognized that the time would soon come when he could not or would not want to be as involved in the day-to-day problems of the company. The G.B.A. Co. would need a new president sometime soon, and he ought to be planning for it now.

From his viewpoint and that of his top management group as well, it was very undesirable to go outside for a new president. Most felt that this would be taken as a sign in the industry that the G.B.A. Co. did not have the backup strength or the internal capability to "grow its own new chief executive." An outsider, in addition, would find it hard to break into the organization and develop the necessary relationships with other key executives.

The candidates from within the organization were essentially four: the assistant to the president, division manager I, division manager II, and division manager III. (Division manager IV was very new and young and, therefore, not a candidate.) A sketch of each of these men follows.

ASSISTANT TO THE PRESIDENT–J.W.

J.W. is a man in his mid-forties who has worked for the company about ten years. He holds a B.S in engineering. Prior to coming to work for G.B.A. Co., he worked as the equivalent of a division manager with a comparable company.

His main responsibilities have been to work with G.B.A., Jr., in the design and implementation of corporate policies and procedures. In this capacity he has become exposed to some of the modern thinking in the areas of recruitment, executive compensation, and so on. His technical skills in construction and his prior experiences have enabled him to be a "backup division manager." In other words, when the need arose, he has been more than able to step in and manage business just like the existing division managers.

He is very soft spoken, less overtly aggressive than his officer colleagues, and believes very strongly in loyalty as a motivating factor. He is very loyal to G.B.A., Jr., and the company– "They have treated me very well and I'll do anything I'm asked to do." His willingness to stay in the very difficult position of assistant to the president, with all its attendant home office and field office conflicts, is an example of his loyalty. His compensation is lower than that of the division managers because he is not as directly tied in to profits as they are.

In spite of the conflicts of his job, he gets along reasonably well with the key officers. They and he recognize that the problems encountered are a function of the role and not a function of J.W.'s personality.

MANAGER I

Manager I, in his late thirties, is the youngest of the division managers–late thirties. He graduated from a prestigious southern engineering school and came into the company about six years ago. He was hired to start a new division in the Southeast and worked closely with A.H., the vice president, to build this new division.

The first four to five years of this effort were very disappointing. His division was consistently the big loser. At officers' meetings when financial figures were reviewed, Manger I was always the target of digs and barbs from the others. That situation has changed dramatically and his division is now the biggest winner. In 1973, his division will account for a substantial portion of the total volume and profits.

Manager I is, in some ways, like Mr. G.B.A., Jr. He is hard-driving and level-headed and has a quiet charm and confidence that appeals to clients. He has a reputation of letting some details fall through the cracks; for example, he never answers phone messages, misses planes, and is often the last to arrive (often late) at an officers' meeting. His rationale is that selling new business and taking care of clients are his primary jobs–anything else comes second. This, of course, is consistent with the climate Mr. G.B.A., Jr., has set for the company.

MANAGER II

Manager II is in his early forties and a college graduate. He was hired eight years ago by G.B.A., Jr., to take over as manager of the Central Division. Prior to coming to the G.B.A. Co., he held a high-level position with a competitor.

His division has been a solid producer under his leadership–not outstanding but clearly adequate. The fact that he is physically located in the same building as the corporate offices is, in the minds of some people, the reason for his success. In other words, some people believe that G.B.A., Jr. is responsible for a large percentage of the business that Manager II gets for the company. From his point of view, his physical proximity to G.B.A., Jr., does not interfere with his ability to "be his own man."

Of all the division managers, Manager II's style is the most participative. He is a good group builder and has the reputation for developing his younger people very well. He is more willing and able to delegate responsibility. He demonstrates, in much that he does, a concern for the human side of issues. During officers' meetings, for example, he would be most likely to support someone who was under attack.

MANAGER III

Manager III is the senior man in the manager group (25 years with the company), just a few years younger than G.B.A., Jr., himself. He is the only one of the division managers without a formal college education, having learned the business from the University of Hardknocks. His knowledge of the business is unquestioned, and he is respected by all.

His division, the Western Division, has always been a high-variance division in terms of profit performance. From a volume perspective, it has always been high–"He'll take any job" according to the others. Profits, however, have never been as high as expected, and others attribute this in large measure to Manager III's style.

"He does everything his own way by himself" is the comment most often made. He calls every site several times a day, issues orders, and makes all the decisions by himself. Not one of his subordinates does anything without checking with him first. As could be expected, this style creates many home and field office problems and conflicts. He resists most corporate policies and procedures and yields grudgingly only after direct intervention by G.B.A., Jr.,; even then there are some "special rules" for him (i.e., he is often allowed to ignore company policy).

These profiles of the candidates were constructed by the behavioral science consultants on the basis of interviews in the company. In addition, the consultants assessed the motivational patterns of the candidates using the McClelland framework (see Chapter 4 for a description of these motive patterns). Achievement, power, and affiliation motivation have considerable relevance for issues of leadership style, organizational climate, and organizational growth. The consultants prepared the following table indicating how each of the key people rank in terms of McClelland's three motives. (For example, G.B.A., Jr. is equally high in his power and achievement needs and lowest in his affiliation needs.)

	PRESIDENT	MANAGER I	MANAGER II	MANAGER III	ASSISTANT TO THE PRESIDENT
n-Achievement	High	High	High	High	Moderate
n-Power	High	Moderate	Low	High	Low
n-Affiliation	Low	Low	Moderate	Low	High

As a group the candidates were "a bunch of supreme primadonnas," by their own admission. Each believed that he could handle the job of president. While they all "said" they could work under the others, it was very clear that the choice of one would have to be handled delicately. Whoever among them was chosen might have a period of some tension, jealousy, and covert (if not overt) conflict until he "proved his mettle."

In spite of this dilemma, it was not considered desirable, unless no other alternative existed, to bring in someone from the outside. However, G.B.A., Jr., was smart enough to realize that some other changes might also be necessary to deal with the second of his concerns–continuity of management. Simply selecting a new president might not be enough. The company might also need a new management strategy and climate.

The concern over continuity of management comes from several sources. G.B.A., Jr., recognized that each of his key executives was in high demand. None of them would find it hard to switch jobs quickly and beneficially. Their individual compensations (with the exception of J.W., his assistant) were tied directly and heavily into their individual profit performance. In terms of both salary and bonus, they all did well, but they wanted "something" more.

The key executives had several concerns regarding continuity. What would happen to the company if or when G.B.A., Jr., died? How could they get security? What would happen to them? As they put it, "We, too, have put our sweat and blood into this company. Do we fall to the whims of some trustees? Your wife?"

G.B.A., Jr., recognized that he had been the central, dominant figure in the life of the company during the past 25 years. It was not clear whether, even if he remained president, the company could continue to be managed in the same way and cope with all the normal problems of rapid and continued growth. So, in addition to succession, he was concerned with making any changes required to ensure continuity of management.

YOUR TASK

The concerns of succession and continuity are complex problems, and many factors are involved in successfully dealing with such problems. In preparation for the upcoming group meeting, you should answer these questions:

1. What do you see as the major strengths and weaknesses of the four main candidates?

2. Which candidate would you recommend as the new president of the G.B.A. Company?

3. What is your rationale for the choice? What kind of leadership style does the company need now?

4. How would you rank the other candidates?

5. In addition to a new president, what other changes should the G.B.A. Company consider to provide for the continuity of management and the organizational culture it will need in the future? New structures? New procedures? New reward systems? Why?

Topic Introduction

Organizational culture has become an exceedingly popular topic in the last fifteen years. The publicity given to successful companies with strong cultures[2] has had several results. Many companies have put more effort into developing strong cultures while others have paid more attention to maintaining a high-performance culture. Managers have also come to realize that cultural values sometimes impede the organizational changes they would like to make. Thus, we have seen an increased focus on the leader's role in creating, maintaining, and changing organizational culture.[3]

Schein defines organizational culture as:

"Organizational culture is the pattern of basic assumptions that a given group has invented, discovered, or developed in learning to cope with its problems of external adaptation and internal integration, and that have worked well enough to be considered valid, and, therefore, to be taught to new members as the correct way to perceive, think, and feel in relation to those problems."[4]

In simple terms, organizational culture is the pattern of shared values and beliefs that lead to certain norms of behavior,[5] in other words, "the way we do things around here." The sources of an organizational culture are the values of the founders or strong leaders of the organization and the solutions to problems which other members have learned over time. Industry, environment, and national culture also influence the culture of an organization.

A discussion of organizational culture raises once again the issue of "fit," both internally and externally. Two important aspects of culture are external adaptation and internal integration of new members. One of the functions of a culture is to ensure that its members "fit" the culture. This is very common with "strong cultures," which have the following characteristics.[6] People in the organization can easily identify the dominant values. The selection processes target people who are likely to fit into the culture and find it satisfying. Socialization and training convey to newcomers the "ropes" they need to learn. Employees who do not fit the culture or produce in accordance with its values are sometimes fired. People within the company are rewarded for acting in accordance with the dominant values of the organization. By their behavior, leaders and managers send clear, consistent signals about desired values and norms. Managers measure and control what is important to the culture.

The distinction between strong and weak cultures is that strong cultures are "thicker." They have more values and beliefs that are more widely shared and more "ordered." By "ordered," we mean that cultural members know which values are more important relative to other values. For example, the value of customer service trumps (is given priority over) a value like informality.[7]

Because of the intensity and consensus of shared values in a strong culture, the individual-culture fit is important. However, there are other important aspects of "fit" to be considered. When choosing a management system and organization structure:

1. The *people* in the organization, their abilities, and motives.

2. The *organization's tasks* and the kinds of behavior needed to accomplish those tasks most effectively.

3. The *organization's external environment* and the demands it makes on the organization for creativity, flexibility, quality, and so on.

4. The *strategy* which dictates how an organization attempts to position itself in relation to its competitors.

5. The *organization's culture* as determined by the leadership styles of management and the organization's structure and values.

Stated simply, the goal of organization design is to match people with tasks that require and inspire their motives and abilities and to design tasks and a strategy that can cope with environmental demands and opportunities. The organizational culture should reinforce these efforts. Culture serves as the glue that holds the organization together. Culture also provides members with a sense of identity, generates commitment to something larger than self-interest, and helps people make sense of what occurs in the organization and the environment. Furthermore, strong organizational cultures serve the same control function as the cultural rules we learn in childhood. When groups of people share the same behavioral norms, there is less need for external controls and close supervision.

Although organizational cultures result in control, alignment, and motivation, these contributions do not yield high performance unless there is a fit with the environment. This brings us to the second aspect of culture, external adaptation. Lack of external adaptation or "fit" was the impetus for some of the widespread restructuring that U.S. industry has undergone in recent years. In addition to outdated strategies, structures, technology, and employee skills, many companies had cultures that did not fit a rapidly changing global economy.

Because so many excellent companies had strong organizational cultures, there seemed to be a relationship between strong culture and high performance. One study supports this assumption when leadership is also present. Kotter and Keskett found that corporate culture can in fact have a significant impact on a firm's long-term economic performance. Firms with strong cultures that focused on all the key constituencies (customers, stockholder, and employees) and that had leadership from managers at all levels outperformed other firms without these characteristics. "Over an 11 year period, the former increased revenues by an average of 682 percent versus 166 percent for the latter, expanded their work forces by 282 percent versus 36 percent, grew their stock prices by 901 percent versus 74 percent, and improved their net incomes by 756 percent versus 1 percent." They predict that corporate culture will probably be an even more important factor in determining company success or failure in the next decade. Cultures, even strong ones, that are not adaptive or change-oriented may not survive.[8] Thus, the culture-environment fit warrants a good deal of attention.

Many companies with strong cultures that were successful in the past failed to adapt as the environment changed. Their cultures became arrogant, inwardly focused, politicized, and bureaucratic. Managerial self-interest took precedence over concern for customers, stockholders, employees and companies failed to emphasize good leadership. Previous success often led the companies to resist innovation and continue with strategies and policies that were no longer viable.[9] Employees who wanted to change such companies often became discouraged and quit because they did not fit the culture: thus, the situation perpetuate itself.

Both AT&T and the banking industry had strong cultures. But when their external environments changed, these stable and inbred cultures became a threat to their survival. The survivors learned to play a different game and developed more competitive and innovative organizational cultures. At present, IBM is fighting to modify what has always been a very strong culture, complete with an extensive language all its own. IBM culture was seen as an advantage in the past but is currently criticized for its slowness and arrogance. Therefore, the company broke with tradition and hired an outsider as CEO, Lou Gerstner. He had the following reaction to IBM culture, "I have never seen a company that is so introspective, caught up in its own underwear, so preoccupied with internal processes...People in this company tell me it's easier doing business with people outside the company than inside. I would call that an indictment."[10] Gerstner and others are trying to make the culture more cooperative and customer-oriented.

Two disadvantages of strong cultures are their pressure for conformity and resistance to change.[11] If the culture is self-sealing and refuses to consider new assumptions, its very strength can become a weakness.

> *"Many outstanding organizations have followed...paths of deadly momentum–time-bomb trajectories of attitudes, policies, and events that lead to falling sales, plummeting profits, even bankruptcy...Productive attention to detail, for instance, turns into an obsession with minutia; rewarding innovation escalates into gratuitous invention; and measured growth becomes unbridled expansion."[12]*

Organizations need people who question cultural values and suggest different assumptions. For this reason, it comes as no surprise that one study found that companies with well-organized workplaces and strong participative cultures performed better than did other firms.[13] Presumably, the value placed upon participation would allow for the expression of different opinions and assumptions about the external environment. One of the dilemmas in organizations is finding the right degree of stability and flexibility. Managers need to understand and respect past history while simultaneously ensuring that organizational learning and adaptation is taking place.

Leaders can affect an organizational culture, but they cannot unilaterally determine what that culture should be.[14] Culture emerges from a consensus held by people in a social system. Cultures take time to develop and are slow to change because cultural values are internalized and provide us with part of our identity. Thus, managers should not see cultural change as a quick fix. Nevertheless, it is possible to instill certain values and reward certain behaviors. Consistency is essential in managing culture. Too many companies have an official set of cultural values that does not represent the real values that are acted out in the organization. Employees quickly spot the hypocrisy when managers do not "walk the talk."

STAGES OF ORGANIZATIONAL GROWTH

The leader's role in managing culture varies according to the stages of organizational growth that are explained in the following paragraphs. Organizations (like people) go through stages of growth and development.[15] Although the time spent in each stage varies, most organizations evolve in a predictable sequence. The typical stages in the organizational life cycle are inception, high-growth, maturity, decline or renewal. Stage I, *Inception*, is the start-up phase in which we find an entrepreneur with vision, energy and a strong desire to succeed. At this point, the organization seldom has a formal structure; people pitch in to help wherever they are needed. Communication is informal and face-to-face. The entrepreneur makes most of the decisions and there is little formal planning. In this stage, creativity and morale are often high because people enjoy the challenge of being in on the ground floor of a new venture.

If the organization survives this stage (and many do not), it moves to stage II, *High-Growth*. In this stage, the organizational structure becomes more centralized and formal. Rapid growth requires more formal budgeting processes. The management style is less entrepreneurial and more professional, relying on analytical tools. The moral and excitement, so high in Stage I, begin to show the signs of stress. That old feeling of personal contact, easy access to the boss, and so on begins to wane as the organization grows in size. During this period of rapid growth the following problems are common.

1. Lower morale due to loss of close family feeling.
2. Lack of coordination among functional departments (now the organization structure has become more complex).
3. Missed deadlines, overrun budgets, poor or uneven quality control (things are falling through the cracks.)
4. Chief executive officer overload– "I'd like to let go but I don't dare."
5. Frequent reorganization (about every six months).

If these normal stresses and strains are not managed effectively, the organization may find itself on a sharp downward spiral While the forces are undoubtedly many and complex, a critical variable appears to be the organization's ability to reorganize and accept the fact that at different points in its life it needs different kinds of top management motivation and leadership and a different organizational culture. These transitional issues are particularly disconcerting to the entrepreneur-owner. The organization is his or her "baby" and letting go in certain areas and recognizing the need for more teamwork and group problem solving and conflict resolution, for example, is by no means simple.

In the third stage, *Maturity*, the organization usually reacts to the rapid growth of the second stage by decentralizing its structure. By this point, communication has become very formal, and there are numerous rules and regulations concerning the planning process. Long term planning is common. Managerial decisions are made by bargaining with different functions. This is a stage of slow or declining growth.

The fourth stage, *Decline*, is characterized by rigid, top-heavy, and overly complex organizational structures. Communication breakdowns are common. There is often blind adherence to a "success formula," regardless of environmental changes that make this formula obsolete. Decision making emphasizes form rather than substance, and self-serving politics are the norm. There is an excess of conformity and compromise. There are nine early warning signals of organizational decline:[16]

1. Excess personnel
2. Tolerance of incompetence
3. Cumbersome administrative procedures
4. Disproportionate staff power
5. Replacement of substance with form (planning process more important than results)
6. Scarcity of clear goals and decision benchmarks
7. Fear of embarrassment and conflict prevents problem identification
8. Loss of effective communication
9. Outdated organizational structure

Experts say decline is almost inevitable unless management takes steps to avoid it. This is best done before the organization finds itself in difficulty. Some organizations manage to halt a decline and enter a renewal stage that allows the organization to shift itself back to a previous stage.

Each stage requires a different type of leadership that is capable of tackling the major growth challenges. Leaders should also manage organizational culture differently in each stage.[17] In the inception stage, an organizational culture is often the glue that holds the organization together and makes growth possible. The leader should elaborate, develop and articulate the cultural values. In the high-growth stage, culture tends to be taken for granted. The culture often becomes more diverse as subcultures form in the different areas of the organization. Leaders can reward the subcultures whose values are in the organization's best interests. In the maturity and decline stages, the culture often becomes dysfunctional and the leader's task is to change the culture and make it more adaptive.

Procedure for Group Meeting: The G.B.A. Construction Company Case

STEP 1. The class should divide up into learning groups (approximately five to six persons per group.)

STEP 2. Each group should prepare a 5-minute summary analysis of the G.B.A. case to share with the total class. (20 minutes) Use the accompanying G.B.A. Co. Case Summary form to write down your conclusions. This summary should touch on the following points:

a. What do you see as the major strengths and weaknesses of the four candidates?

b. Which candidate would you recommend as the new president of the G.B.A. Co.?

c. What is your rationale for this choice?

d. What other changes would you recommend to help the new president create the kind of organizational culture needed by the G.B.A. Co. over the next five to eight years?

STEP 3 When the subgroups have completed their work in step 2, the entire class should reconvene for a summary discussion and analysis. (40 minutes)

a. Each of the subgroups should share its analysis with the total class. Others should ask clarification questions during the process to ensure understanding. (20 minutes)

STEP 3 *After* sharing these analyses, the class should take a few moments to read over the G.B.A. Construction Company—Part II, and discuss the additional questions raised at the end of the case. (20 minutes)

	ASSISTANT TO THE PRESIDENT (J.W.)	MANAGER I	MANAGER II	MANAGER III
MAJOR STRENGTHS				
MAJOR WEAKNESSES				

a. GROUP CHOICE FOR THE NEW G.B.A. PRESIDENT	b. RATIONALE FOR CHOICE

c. CHANGES RECOMMENDED TO HELP THE NEW PRESIDENT CREATE THE ORGANIZATIONAL CULTURE NEEDED.

The G.B.A. Construction Company, Part II

THE IMMEDIATE RESULTS

Late in 1973, manager II was selected to be the new president of the G.B.A. Co. The major points in his favor, at the time, were as follows:

1. A high n-Achievement, combined with a moderate n-Affiliation, was felt to be critical in developing the teamwork needed among the top management group.

2. His ability and commitment to developing younger people would set a tone for the company that would help it develop the human resources needed to continue its rapid growth.

3. He seemed strong enough and had enough of a history with G.B.A., Jr., to "help" him keep his fingers out of the daily operations.

Manager I was also a strong candidate. His age and lack of experience were his major drawbacks. There was an underlying feeling that with more experience and "polish," he could be a strong candidate the next time around. For now, his strengths were best utilized as a division manager.

Manager III was not a serious contender. In a nutshell, he was too much like G.B.A., Jr.

The assistant to the president, J.W., was a hard candidate to exclude for a variety of reasons. Chief among these was a concern that if his loyalty were not rewarded, he might subsequently leave the company. These fears proved valid and he left a year later.

THE LONGER TERM*

So, it is late 1973, and manager II has taken over as president. Very shortly thereafter, as pointed out, the assistant to the president left the company. Manager III retired when manager II took over, and the Western Division was managed out of the home office for a while. A. H. also retired as had been expected.

Businesswise, the next 18 months were very favorable. Then, as the general economy took a downturn, so, too, did the construction business. Falling sales volume and reduced profits impacted all the senior managers, including the new president, for their compensation was still closely tied to bottom-line results.

This downturn was mitigated somewhat by the increasing business opportunities in Saudi Arabia. The new president had personally spearheaded this move overseas, and while this drained energy from other matters, it did keep sales volume and profits from dropping even further.

Stylistically, the new president appeared not to be working out as expected. His participative style was most reflective in his dealing one-on-one with people informally, as peers. This was his forte. For whatever reasons, he had considerable discomfort

*G.B.A., Jr., was interviewed during April 1981 and graciously provided this current update.

with the more formal group settings. G.B.A., Jr., commented, "He seemed to behave in an inferior way" (as if he felt very insecure). Consequently, he could not get the top team together much as it had appeared he might.

So, one day late in 1975, upon returning from one of his frequent trips to Saudi Arabia, he said almost in desperation to G.B.A., Jr., "I'm not sure I want to be the head of a big company!" He and G.B.A., Jr., subsequently negotiated an agreement wherein he would run the Saudi Arabian business on a contract basis for one year. G.B.A., Jr., thus took over again as president.

At the end of this one-year contract, they agreed to part company completely. So manager II left the G.B.A. Construction Company to start his own construction business in the same city as the G.B.A. Company's home office. According to G.B.A., Jr., he has taken on a lot of big jobs (although not as big as those taken by the G.B.A. Co., he is quick to point out) and has had dramatic turnover in staff. The causes of his dramatic turnover are unknown. What is clearer is the implication that "He deserves whatever he gets for being disloyal."

THE NEW AND CURRENT PRESIDENT

So, in the fall of 1976, G.B.A., Jr., turned over the reins of his company to manager I. Four and one-half years later, G.B.A., Jr., talks glowingly and proudly of "his new president's" accomplishments. He has proven to be a very solid long-range planner and organizer...in spite of the fact that he is "much more intellectual" than anyone else in top management.

In comparison with the previous president (manager II, not G.B.A., Jr.), he finds it harder to communicate informally with peers on a one-to-one basis. On the other hand, he has proven to be very good in formal group settings. While the maturity of a few more years to develop undoubtedly helped manager I develop into presidential timber, it is important to examine briefly several other changes.

With respect to G.B.A., Jr., by his own reports, he is still working hard. He is, however, much less involved now than he was during manager II's reign.

Several critical structural changes have also taken place that have had a very positive impact on the culture and behavior. Flowing in part from his relative discomfort in informal one-on-one situations and relative comfort in formal group settings, the new president has instituted two important group structures. One, an operations committee of key managers from each of the divisions, was formed to focus on company-wide (versus division specific) issues such as contracting, cost cutting, and policy. A similar Human Resource Committee was formed to focus on issues of personnel (benefits, recruitment, etc.) and training. The new president serves as formal chairperson for both committees.

Finally, a way was found in the last three years, to, in effect, create two companies. The new one is structured on a partnership format that is owned by G.B.A., Jr., and his senior top management team of officers and provides a trust for G.B.A., Jr.'s family. Ultimately, this new corporation will develop a solid equity base. When this happens, the family trust portion (and ultimately G.B.A., Jr.'s portion) will be bought out. While he was appropriately reticent to share the details, G.B.A., Jr., was clear that this new structure had virtually eliminated the previous concern among his officers about continuity and their long-run futures.

A POSTSCRIPT: THE 20:20 VISION OF HINDSIGHT

Several points about the concepts of motivation and organizational culture are highlighted-with the clarity afforded by 20:20 hindsight.

Let us begin by reexamining the original choice of manager II. The underlying question is: "Was he the right or the wrong candidate?" and there is no absolute answer to this question. Several explanatory clues can be traced, however.

It is important to realize that a prime reason for the company's success under G.B.A., Jr.'s leadership was the fit or match between the elements that make up organization culture. G.B.A., Jr.'s personal skills and his personal style were matched to the types of people he gathered around himself as part of his executive team. These human factors were furthermore aligned and matched with key elements of the management operation systems, organizational structure, and strategy.* The combination and alignment or matching among all these elements created a coherent environment or climate that shaped and channeled individual behavior.

Manager II's personal style may well have been the one needed to carry the company through its next stage of development. We'll never know for sure. It is reasonably clear, however, that manager II did not have the time, skill, or support from G.B.A., Jr., to design and implement other environmental changes. These changes potentially could have created the alignment and matching that gives the concept of organizational culture such power in influencing behavior. A new president with a new style cannot function in an environment (e.g., executive team, organizational systems, structures, strategies, reward systems, and the like) designed to fit a very different presidential style (G.B.A., Jr's). The totality of culture variables, taken together, seem to far outweigh the power of a given personality in influencing the behavior of people in organizations.

This line of argument gains further support when we review the characteristics of manager I. While not identical to G.B.A., Jr., manager I was nonetheless like him in many ways. It is not surprising, therefore, that after a few years of seasoning, he should emerge as the replacement for manager II. The resulting stress on the organization-including very importantly the top executive team-was much less severe. The fit between manager I's style and the existing environmental variables was guaranteed to be closer since G.B.A., Jr., and manager I were more similar. Add to this the fact that important structural changes concerning equity (referred to earlier) did not get implemented until after manager II was relieved and manager I took over.

Pascale and Athos sum up these issues well:[18] "There is no quick fix in sight. Rather, each company's CEO and other top executives need to recognize that is takes time, discomfort, stamina, and commitment to strengthen what is weak in their organizational development. Moreover, there is no sure blueprint for success. Every firm has to be good at (the elements of culture or environment) and their fit to one another... And each company, like each individual, has to develop in its own way."

The entire group should now discuss the following points in light of what actually happened:

1. Knowing how clear things can appear in hindsight, what additional clues were there—*if any*—that manager II *may* have been an inappropriate choice?
2. Could manager I have handled the job in late 1973? Why or why not?
3. How might manager II have fared if comparable structural changes (i.e., operations committee, human resources committee, the creation of two companies) had been instituted during his reign? How might manager I have fared in the absence of these structural changes?
4. What happens to managers who take over from the founder of a company?
5. What connections can you make between this exercise and the readings?

* For more detail on this concept of fit or alignment, see Pascale and Athos, *The Art of Japanese Management*.

ASSESSING THE ORGANIZATIONAL CULTURE OF THE CLASSROOM

(Time Allotted: 1 1/2 Hours)

This exercise utilizes a technique known as the *nominal group technique*. It is designed to gather ideas or data quickly in a democratic fashion. The round-robin nature of this technique prevents influential people from controlling the air time or the vote. Once ideas are mentioned, they become the property of the group, not ideas advocated by specific individuals.

STEP 1.   Write down three to five statements that describe

       a. The current state of the organizational culture of your learning organization— this course.

       b. The ideal state of this learning organization.

       c. The current state of your learning group.

       d. The ideal state of your learning group.

Note: 1) It's not necessary to write complete sentences as long as your words or phrases will be understood by others. 2) For the "current state" questions, try to think of both positives and negatives to "cover the waterfront." 3) For the "ideal state" questions, don't limit yourself by merely reversing negative characteristics you may have identified for the current state. Give yourself free rein here to be creative and think beyond the constraints of the current situation. (15 minutes)

STEP 2.   The instructor will go around the room asking each participant to read out loud one statement from their list and write it on a flipchart or blackboard. Participants can "pass" when all the statements on their list have been recorded. (15 minutes)

STEP 3.   The class will examine the statements to see if all are comprehensible and that there are no duplicates. Some statements may need to be combined. (10 minutes)

STEP 4.   Participants mark the three statements that are most significant to them as individuals with a marker or chalk mark. Put a hatchmark beside or beneath the three statements. This is a way of quickly prioritizing group opinion. (10 minutes)

STEP 5.   The marks will be counted, identifying the major issues regarding the organizational culture in the course.

STEP 6.   The class as a whole can discuss the results, using the discussion questions that follow. (30 minutes)

DISCUSSION QUESTIONS ABOUT ORGANIZATION CULTURE

1. Does the culture of the learning organization fit your values and needs?
2. Is there a fit between the task of our learning organization and the other aspects of our organizational culture?
3. During the unit on psychological contracts, a contract was formulated. To what extent is the culture supporting or inhibiting this contract?
4. What steps can be taken to change the culture in this classroom to enhance the realization of the psychological contract or to bring the reality closer to the ideal state?

Follow-Up

Changing an organizational culture is not a quick process because of all the "fits" within the organization. Often the first step in changing a culture involves a change to a more participative management style. This allows people to openly discuss the culture and its impact.

How do leaders create and transmit organizational culture? There are two types of mechanisms that managers can use to create or modify culture.[19] The primary mechanisms are shown below.

1. **What leaders pay attention to, measure and control on a regular basis** – If managers talk about the importance of continuous improvement (TQM) but show no interest in the improvements suggested by employee groups, employees correctly discern that quality is not a value of this organizational culture. In contrast, if managers monitor and evaluate quality improvements, this sends out the opposite message and reinforces the value of producing quality products. Similarly, when the CEO visits the R&D lab the first thing every morning, this is a clear signal that innovation is a value of the organizational culture.

2. **The reactions of leaders to critical incidents and organizational crises** – What happens, for example when the company faces a downturn in business or a cash flow problem? Does upper management immediately start firing lower-level employees or does everyone make sacrifices (e.g., four-day work weeks or across-the-board pay cuts for everyone) and start looking for creative solutions? The response shows employees what the company values.

3. **Observed criteria by which leaders allocate scarce resources** – How does the organization create its budgets? What gets funded? What are acceptable levels of financial risk? Budget decisions and the budget process itself reflect cultural values and beliefs. For example, a company that utilizes bottom-up budgets may do so because they value entrepreneurial managers.

4. **Deliberate role modeling, teaching, and coaching by leaders** – One international manager was a master at recreating the organizational culture in new overseas offices. Since he was the only person in the office with in-depth

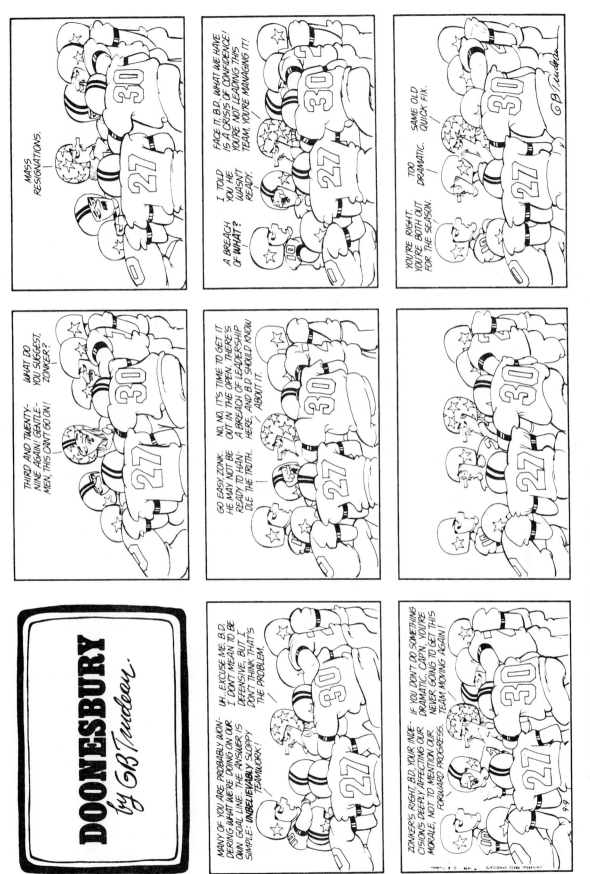

knowledge of how the organization functioned, he had new employees come to his office to review their work during the first month. He used this opportunity to correct their mistakes, teach them the finer points of their jobs, answer their questions, hear their suggestions, and explain how their work fit into the broader picture of the local office and the international organization. He told them stories about the organization's heroes and success stories from other countries. At the same time, he developed a personal relationship with them and gained their loyalty and commitment. As a result, they felt comfortable going to him in the future with their concerns and ideas, even after the office had grown much larger and he no longer supervised their work directly. By doing this, he transmitted to them the values of the international headquarters and created a strong culture.

5. **Criteria for allocating rewards and status** – We can analyze what behavior is rewarded to determine what the organization values. Are whistleblowers who point out unethical practices congratulated and promoted, or are they shunned or even fired? Those who enact the key values of the organizational culture should be rewarded and respected. Otherwise, we cannot tell who are the cultural heroes that we should try to emulate.

6. **Criteria for recruitment, selection, promotion, retirement and excommunication** – The question of who fits and does not fit the organizational culture and who deserves to play a key role figures either consciously or unconsciously in these personnel decisions. Companies that are concerned with creating a strong culture devote time and energy to hiring and promoting only those people whose values are compatible with those of the company. It is very difficult, if not impossible and unethical, to change people's personalities. Service companies in particular find it easier to hire people who already have a service ethic. There is, however, a danger in trying to obtain a perfect person-culture fit with every employee. Cultural deviants often keep organizations "honest" by questioning the culture's dominant assumptions and behaviors. Too much conformity is not healthy, so organizations are wise to pay attention to deviant views. Excommunication takes the form of either firing or being given a less important job (perhaps kicked upstairs) and isolated.

The *secondary mechanisms* that managers have at their disposal appear below.

1. **The way in which the organization is structured and designed** (decision-making, coordination, reporting structure)

2. **Systems and procedures** (performance appraisal, information, control, decision support systems, etc.)

3. **Rites and rituals**

4. **The design of physical space, facades, and buildings**

5. **Anecdotes, legends, myths, and parables about people and events**

6. **Formal statements of philosophy, creeds, and values**

Managers can utilize many of these same mechanisms to change an organizational culture. It is not impossible to change a culture, but it is a difficult task and one that is not accomplished overnight. Some experts claim it is a 7 to 10 year process. Successful cultural changes usually involve effective leaders with an outsider's perspective who take advantage of a propitious moment or crisis to mobilize support for a cultural change. Leaders create a new vision that they communicate with optimism and enthusiasm.[20] However, it is also important to "honor the past" and maintain some aspects of a culture for the sake of continuity.[21] According to Trice and Beyer, all cultural change is partial, and we cannot expect to completely eradicate a previous culture.[22]

We usually associate cultural change with a strong, visionary leader. However, cultural changes have also occurred from the bottom-up, when management has planted the seed and allowed workers the autonomy to make the necessary changes. Ford's focus on quality and customer service is an example of a bottom-up change effort.[23] Other change efforts, like Corning Glass Works' switch to a total quality culture, have used widespread education and training programs as the catalyst.[24]

Learning Points

1. Organizational culture is defined as a pattern of shared values and beliefs that produce certain norms of behavior.

2. Strong cultures have the following characteristics:
   a. People in the organization can easily identify the dominant values.
   b. The selection processes target people who are likely to fit into the culture and find it satisfying.
   c. Socialization and training convey to newcomers the "ropes" they need to learn.
   d. Employees who do not fit the culture or produce in accordance with its values are sometimes fired.
   e. People within the company are rewarded for acting in accordance with the dominant values of the organization.
   f. By their behavior, leaders and managers send clear, consistent signals about desired values and norms.
   g. Managers measure and control what is important to the culture.

3. Organizational culture is formed by 1) the values of the founder or strong leaders and 2) learned solutions to problems over time.

4. Compared to weak cultures, strong cultures have more values and beliefs that are more widely shared and more ordered.

5. There should be a fit between the people, the organization's task, environment, strategy, and culture.

6. Organizational culture provides members with a sense of identity, generates commitment, helps people make sense of what occurs in the organization and the environment, and serves as a control mechanism.

7. A strong culture does not guarantee good performance unless it focuses on all its key constituencies (customers, stockholder, and employees) and has leadership from managers at all levels.

8. Two disadvantages of strong cultures are their pressure for conformity and resistance to change.

9. Most organizations go through predictable stages of growth—inception, high-growth, maturity, decline, and sometimes renewal. Each stage requires a different type of leadership.

10. Leaders can affect an organizational culture, but they cannot unilaterally determine what that culture should be. It is not impossible to change a culture, but it is a slow, difficult task.

11. The primary mechanisms a leader can use to create, transmit, or change culture are:
    a. what leaders pay attention to, measure and control on a regular basis
    b. the reactions of leaders to critical incidents and organizational crises
    c. observed criteria by which leaders allocate scarce resources
    d. deliberate role modeling, teaching and coaching
    e. criteria for allocating rewards and status
    f. criteria for recruitment, selection, promotion, retirement and excommunication

 # for Managers

- Before you join an organization, try to read its culture and determine whether or not your values are compatible with those of the organization.

- Figure out your organization's cultural characteristics and use that understanding when making analyses and decisions. Awareness of the history of the organization can keep new managers from making errors.

- Respect the past, but make sure the culture is adapting and learning in the present.

- Establishing an effective organizational culture requires consistency. What managers do to reinforce culture is stronger than what they say.

- Don't assume that continuity will naturally occur in an organizational culture; it must be nurtured. If you don't need to change the organizational culture, work to maintain and strengthen the existing culture. Whenever decisions are made, people should ask the question, "Is this decision in keeping with our cultural values?".

- Encourage a certain degree of nonconformity. While it is more difficult to handle people who don't fit the culture very well, they are often valuable in pointing out the assumptions that are guiding the dominant culture. Sometimes, they see the need for change more clearly than others.

- One of the disadvantages of culture is that it blinds us to other values and other ways of doing things. Strategy decisions are affected, sometimes adversely, by the organizational culture.

- Helping a work group or organization to make their norms explicit identifies what values need to be reinforced or changed.

- Creating traditions and events that emphasize the cultural values you deem important help form a culture (e.g., the Glorious Booboo Award in the R&D lab, roasts for people who get promoted or retire, and Friday afternoon TGIF parties).

- Some companies utilize stories rather than policy manuals to transmit culture to employees. Stories and parables are easy to remember and help guide employee behavior. Managers can also analyze what's going on in the company by listening to the stories that are commonly told.

- The organization's culture must be taken into consideration whenever changes are planned because culture can be a major impediment to change. Changes that utilize the culture, rather than fight against it, are more likely to succeed. Even so, cultural change is a slow, evolutionary process that requires patience.

- Cultures that promote ethical behavior were found to be high in both risk and conflict tolerance and have members who identify with the professional standards of their job.[25]

 # Personal Application Assignment

Your assignment is to analyze the culture of an organization you know well (a work setting, church, club or even the school where you are taking this course).

1. What is the background of the founders?

2. What explains the organization's growth and survival?

3. What does the organization stand for? What is its motto?

4. What values does the organization talk about?

5. What values does the organization act out?

6. How do people get ahead? What does it take to do well in this organization? To stay out of trouble?

7. What kind of mistakes are not forgiven?

8. Who is considered deviant in the culture and why? How does the organization treat them?

9. How are good employees rewarded?

10. What are the main rules that everyone has to follow in this organization?

11. How does the company respond to crises?

12. What message is conveyed by the physical setting?

13. How do things get done in this organization?

14. How do people spend their time at work?

15. How does the company take in new members?

16. What kinds of stories are told about the organization?

17. Who are the heroes and why?

18. Is there anything that cannot be talked about?

19. How do people exercise power?

20. What is the organization's code of ethics?

Based upon the answers to these questions, what is your analysis of this organizational culture?

[1]Part I of this case was prepared early in 1974. Part II, which follows later, covers the period 1974 to 1981.

[2]Richard T. Pascale and Anthony G. Athos, *The Art of Japanese Management: Applications for American Executives* (New York: Simon and Schuster, 1981);Tom Peters and Robert H. Waterman, *In Search of Excellence* (New York: Harper and Row, 1982); Tom Peters and Nancy A. Austin, *A Passion for Excellence* (New York: Random House, 1985); and T.E. Deal and A.A. Kennedy, *Corporate Cultures: The Rites and Rituals of Corporate Life* (Reading, MA: Addison-Wesley, 1982); and John P. Kotter and James L. Heskett, *Corporate Culture and Performance*, (Toronto: The Free Press, 1992).

[3]Harrison M. Trice & Janice M Beyer, *The Cultures of Work Organizations* (Englewood Cliffs: Prentice Hall, 1993). This book is a compendium of what is known about organizational culture to date. See also *Gaining Control of the Corporate Culture,* Ed. by Ralph H. Kilmann, Mary J. Saxton, and Roy Serpa and Associates (San Francisco: Jossey-Bass, 1986).

[4]Edgar H. Schein, "Coming to a New Awareness of Organizational Culture," *Sloan Management Review* (Winter 1984), pp. 3-16.

[5]Linda Smircich, "Concepts of Culture and Organizational Analysis," *Administrative Science Quarterly* (September 1983), p. 342.

[6]Edgar Schein, *Organizational Culture and Leadership* (San Francisco: Jossey-Bass, 1985).

[7]Vijay Sathe, "Implications of Corporate Culture: A Manager's Guide to Action," *Organizational Dynamics*, Autumn 1983, pp. 5-23.

[8]Kotter and Heskett, *Corporate Culture and Performance*, p. 11.

[9]Kotter and Heskett, Ibid., p. 142.

[10]Judith H. Dobrzynski, "Rethinking IBM," *Business Week*, October 4, 1993, pp. 88. See also Geoff Lewis, "One Fresh Face May Not Be Enough," *Business Week*, April 12, 1993.

[11]Richard Pascale, "The Paradox of 'Corporate Culture': Reconciling Ourselves to Socialization," *California Management Review* (Winter 1985), *Reader*.

[12]Danny Miller, *"The Icarus Paradox,"* (New York: Harper Business, 1990) p. 3.

[13]R.D. Denison, "Bringing Corporate Culture to the Bottom Line," *Organizational Dynamics* (Autumn 1984), pp. 5-22.

[14]Trice and Beyer, *Culture of Work Organizations*, p. 356-57.

[15]Ken G. Smith, Terence R. Mitchell, and Charles E. Summer, "Top Level Management Priorities in Different Stages of the Organizational Life Cycle," *Academy of Management Journal,* December 1985, pp. 799-820; Peter Lorange and Robert T. Nelson, "How to Recognize and Avoid Organizational Decline," *Sloan Management Review*, Spring 1987, pp. 41-48.

[16]Lorange and Nelson, Ibid., pp. 43-45.

[17]Edgar H. Schein, *Organizational Culture and Leaders* (San Francisco: Jossey-Bass, 1992).

[18]Pascale and Athos, *The Art of Japanese Management*, p. 206.

[19]Schein, *Organizational Culture and Leadership*, pp. 228-253.

[20]Kotter and Heskett, *Corporate Culture*, p. 147; and Trice and Beyer, Cultures of Work Organizations, pp. 399-413.

[21]Alan L. Wilkins, *Developing Corporate Character* (San Francisco: Jossey-Bass, 1989). See John Thorbeck's "The Turnaround Value of Values," *Harvard Business Review*, January-February, 1991, pp. 52-62 for a first hand account by a manager who took company history into account and successfully revived company values.

[22]Trice and Beyer, *Culture of Work Organizations*.

[23]Richard Tanner Pascale. *Managing on the Edge: How the Smartest Companies Use Conflict to Stay Ahead* (New York: Simon and Schuster, 1990).

[24]Lawrence Schein, "A Manager's Guide to Corporate Culture," Research Report from The Conference Board.

[25]Victor and John B. Cullen, "The Organizational Bases of Ethical Work Climates," *Administrative Science Quarterly*, March 1988, pp. 101-125.

Chapter

LEADERSHIP AND DECISION MAKING

This unit is based on the research of Victor Vroom and his colleagues. Cases used with permission of the University of Pittsburgh Press and the American Institute for Decision Sciences. Further information about training programs based on the model can be obtained from Kepner-Trego Associates, Inc.

OBJECTIVES By the end of this chapter you should be able to:

A. Explain why decision making is a social process.

B. Identify your personal approach to organizational decision making.

C. Describe and apply the Vroom-Yetton model of decision making.

D. List the five leadership styles included in the Vroom-Yetton model.

Pajama Talk

The Sleepytime Pajama factory was going great guns. Sales were up. The work force was expanding. There was only one hitch. To remain competitive, factory managers were constantly adapting both work techniques and products. Workers were often transferred to different jobs or had parts of their job modified, either in the name of progress or as a result of high turnover and absenteeism. The biggest problem facing Sleepytime was worker resistance to these changes. As soon as they became proficient at one job, they'd be switched to another. They worked on a piece-rate incentive system, and it wasn't easy to work their way up to producing 60 units per hour, the standard efficiency rate. Some suspicious souls thought management just switched workers to new jobs when they had finally mastered their tasks and could begin to earn bonuses for producing more than 60 units. Even though workers received a transfer bonus that made up for the money lost learning new jobs, it didn't make up for the loss in status of being a "greenhorn" on a new task. Workers still hated to be transferred to a new job, and some quit rather than change. Others complained bitterly about management and fought with their supervisors and the time-study engineers. Statistics showed that experienced workers took longer to relearn new jobs and get up to speed than did new employees with no work experience! This convinced the company that the problem was really a question of motivation and resistance to change.

Based on Lester Coch and John R. French, Jr.,"Overcoming Resistance to Change," *Human Relations*, Vol. 1 (1947), pp. 512-531.

Mr. Sleepytime himself, Joe Berg, had the production people organize the output figures in relation to the changes that had been introduced during the last year. He was surprised to find that the work groups supervised by Kathy Johnson seemed to have fewer problems with changes. Her groups got back to speed quicker after the changes and had a higher level of output than the others. She also had fewer terminations, even after the job transfers. So Berg sent his industrial relations expert out on the floor to figure out what was going on.

After observation, the expert discovered that the difference lay in how the supervisors handled the changes. Supervisors of the low-productivity groups simply announced to their employees that a job had to be changed, explained the new piece rate, and answered questions.

In contrast, Johnson used physical demonstrations with her workers in which she showed them samples of pajamas made using new and old techniques, explained the cost differential, and asked them if they could tell the difference between them. Or she'd bring in pajamas made by a competitor who was underselling them and show them why changes had to be made to respond to this challenge. Next, she'd ask the group how the new jobs should be designed. They'd come up with a blitz of ideas for improving the job, and then they worked with the time-study engineer to test out the innovations. Johnson let the workers do most of the talking and planning. She didn't have in her head a "one best way" to make the changes; she let them figure it out for themselves. As a result, they bought into the changes and became committed to making them work. Johnson made the factory workers participants in the change process rather than victims of it. And so it was that Berg learned that the sooner people are brought into a change effort and allowed to participate in the decision making, the better.

 # Premeeting Preparation

(Time allotted: 30 minutes)

A. Read "Pajama Talk."

B. Read the descriptions of decision-making alternatives for individual and group problems in Table 15-1 and describe how you would handle each of the five decision-making cases that follow.
Indicate whether the case describes an individual or group problem and which decision-making approach you would use. Choose your approach based on what you would do in each case. This will allow a comparison between your decision-making style and the recommendations of the decision-making model described in this chapter.

C. After completing B, read the Topic Introduction and the Procedure for Group Meeting.

D. What are the significant learning points from the readings?

TABLE 15-1 Decision Styles for Leadership: Individuals and Groups

INDIVIDUAL PROBLEMS*	GROUP PROBLEMS†
AI. You solve the problem or make the decision yourself, using information available to you at that time.	AI. You solve the problem or make the decision yourself, using information available to you at that time.
AII. You obtain any necessary information from the subordinate and then decide on the solution to the problem yourself. You may or may not tell the subordinate the purpose of your questions or give information about the problem or decision on which you are working. The person's input is clearly in response to your request for specific information. He or she does not play a role in the definition of the problem or in generating or evaluating alternative solutions.	AII. You obtain any necessary information from subordinates and then decide on the solution to the problem yourself. You may or may not tell the subordinates what the problem is in getting the information from them. The role played by your subordinates in making the decision is clearly one of providing specific information that you request rather than generating or evaluating solutions.
CI. You share the problem with the relevant subordinate, getting ideas and suggestions. Then *you* make the decision. This decision may or may not reflect your subordinate's influence.	CI. You share the problem with the relevant subordinates individually, getting their ideas and suggestions without bringing them together as a group. Then *you* make the decision. This decision may or may not reflect your subordinates' influence.
GI. You share the problem with one of your subordinates, and together you analyze the problem and arrive at a mutually satisfactory solution in an atmosphere of free and open exchange of information and ideas. You both contribute to the resolution of the problem, with the relative contribution of each being dependent on knowledge rather than formal authority.	CII. You share the problem with your subordinates in a group meeting. In this meeting you obtain their ideas and suggestions. Then *you* make the decision, which may or may not reflect your subordinates' influence.
DI. You delegate the problem to one of your subordinates, providing the person with any relevant information that you possess, but giving the person full responsibility for solving the problem alone. Any solution that the person reaches will receive your support.	GII. You share the problem with your subordinates as a group. Together you generate and evaluate alternatives and attempt to reach agreement (consensus) on a solution. Your role is much like that of chairperson, coordinating the discussion, keeping it focused on the problem, and making sure that the critical issues are discussed. You can provide the group with information or ideas that you have, but you do not try to "press" them to adopt "your" solution, and you are willing to accept and implement any solution that has the support of the entire group. You can also delegate the decision to the group and let them solve it alone.

*INDIVIDUAL PROBLEMS = have potential effects on only one person. The problem is confined to that manager's area of responsibility.

†GROUP PROBLEMS = have potential effects on all or some subgroup of immediate subordinates.

A = AUTOCRATIC   C = CONSULTATIVE
G = GROUP DECISION   D = DELEGATION

Case 1: The Finance Case

You are the head of a staff unit reporting to the vice president of finance. The vice president has asked you to provide a report on the firm's current portfolio to include recommendations for changes in the selection criteria currently employed. Doubts have been raised about the efficiency of the existing system in the current market conditions, and there is considerable dissatisfaction with prevailing rates of return.

You plan to write the report, but at the moment you are quite perplexed about the approach to take. Your own speciality is the bond market, and it is clear to you that detailed knowledge of the equity market, which you lack, would greatly enhance the value of the report. Fortunately, four members of your staff are specialists in different segments of the equity market. Together, they possess a vast amount of knowledge about the intricacies of investment. However, they seldom agree on the best way to achieve anything when it comes to investment philosophy and strategy.

You have six weeks before the report is due. You have already begun to familiarize yourself with the firm's current portfolio and have been provided by management with a specific set of constraints that any portfolio must satisfy. Your immediate problem is to come up with some alternatives to the firm's present practices and select the most promising for detailed analysis in your report.

How would you go about doing this?

Is it an individual or a group problem?

What decision-making method would you use?

Circle the box that indicates the approach you would use in this case.

Individual	A1	A11	C1	G1	D1
Group	A1	A11	C1	C11	G11

Case 2: International Consulting Company

You are regional manager of an international management consulting company. You have a staff of six consultants reporting to you, each of whom enjoys a considerable amount of autonomy with clients in the field.

Yesterday you received a complaint from one of your major clients to the effect that the consultant whom you assigned to work on the contract with them was not doing his job effectively. They were not very explicit as to the nature of the problem, but it was clear that they were dissatisfied and that something would have to be done if you were to restore the client's faith in your company.

The consultant assigned to work on that contract has been with the company for six years. He is a systems analyst and is one of the best in that profession. For the first four or five years his performance was superb, and he was a model for the more junior consultants. However, recently he has seemed to have a "chip on his shoulder" and his previous identification with the company and its objectives has been replaced with indifference. His negative attitude has been noticed by other consultants, as well as by clients. This is not the first such complaint that you have had from a client this year about his performance. A previous client even reported to you that the consultant reported to work several times obviously suffering from a hangover.

It is important to get to the root of this problem quickly if that client is to be retained. The consultant obviously has the skill necessary to work with the clients effectively. If only he were willing to use it!

Is it an individual or a group problem?

How would you as regional manager deal with this problem?

Circle the box that indicates the approach you would use in this case.

Individual	A1	A11	C1	G1	D1
Group	A1	A11	C1	C11	G11

Case 3: The Engineering Work Assignment

You are supervising the work of 12 civil engineers. Their formal training and work experience are very similar, permitting you to use them interchangeably on projects. Yesterday your manager informed you that a request had been received from an overseas affiliate for 4 engineers to go abroad on extended loan for a period of six to eight months. For a number of reasons, he argued and you agreed, this request should be met from your group.

All your engineers are experienced in and are capable of handling assignments such as this. From the standpoint of present and future work projects, there is no particular reason why any one should be chosen over any other. The problem is somewhat complicated by the fact that the overseas assignment is in what is generally regarded in the company as an undesirable location.

Is it an individual or a group problem?

How would you deal with this problem?

Circle the box that indicates the approach you would use in this case.

Individual	A1	A11	C1	G1	D1
Group	A1	A11	C1	C11	G11

Case 4: The Pharmaceutical Company

You are executive vice president for a small pharmaceutical manufacturer. You have the opportunity to bid on a contract for the Defense Department pertaining to biological warfare. The contract is outside the mainstream of your business; however, it could make economic sense, since you do have unused capacity in one of your plants, and the manufacturing processes are not dissimilar.

You have written the document to accompany the bid and now have the problem of determining the dollar value of the quotation that you think will win the job for your company. If the bid is too high, you will undoubtedly lose to one of your competitors; if it is too low, you would stand to lose money on the program.

There are many factors to be considered in making this decision, including the cost of the new raw materials and the additional administrative burden of relationships with a new client, not to speak of factors that are likely to influence the bids of your competitors, such as how much they need this particular contract. You have been busy assembling the necessary data to make this decision, but there remain several "unknowns," one of which involves the manager of the plant in which the products will be manufactured. Of all your subordinates, only she is in the position to estimate the costs of adapting the present equipment to its new purpose, and her cooperation and support will be necessary in ensuring that the specifications of the contract will be met. However, in an initial discussion with her when you first learned of the possibility of the contract, she seemed adamantly opposed to the idea. Although she has been an effective and dedicated plant manager over the past several years, her previous experience has not particularly equipped her to evaluate the overall merits of projects like this one. From the nature of her arguments, you inferred that her opposition was ideological rather than economic. You recall in this context that she is involved in the local nuclear freeze movement.

Is it an individual or a group problem?

How would you go about determining the amount of the bid?

Circle the box that indicates the approach you would use in this case.

Individual	A1	A11	C1	G1	D1
Group	A1	A11	C1	C11	G11

Case 5: The Oil Pipeline

You are general supervisor in charge of a large gang laying an oil pipeline. It is now necessary to estimate your expected rate of progress to schedule material deliveries to the next field site.

You know the nature of the terrain you will be traveling and have in your records the historical data needed to compute the mean and variance in the rate of speed over that type of terrain. Given these two variables it is a simple matter to calculate the earliest and latest times at which materials and support facilities will be needed at the next site. It is important that your estimate be reasonably accurate. Underestimates result in idle supervisors and workers, and an overestimate results in tying up materials for a period of time before they are to be used.

Progress has been good, and your five supervisors and other members of the gang stand to receive substantial bonuses if the project is completed ahead of schedule.

Is it an individual or a group problem?

How would you go about scheduling material deliveries?

Circle the box that indicates the approach you would use in this case.

Individual	A1	A11	C1	G1	D1
Group	A1	A11	C1	C11	G11

Topic Introduction

To a manager, executive, or administrator, no other job function encapsulates the frustrations and joys of leadership more dramatically than decision making.[1] It is in making decisions that managers most acutely feel the responsibilities, the power, and the vulnerability of their jobs. This central focus of decision making in the experience of leadership is illustrated in the autobiographies of political leaders, who characteristically organize their life stories around major decision points they faced, the dilemmas and pressures they experienced, and how in the end the "buck" stopped on their desks. Harry Truman described his decision to fire General MacArthur and his decision to drop the atomic bomb in this way. Richard Nixon's "six crises" were phrased as major decision points that called for lonely soul searching and personal commitment to the right course of action. Most of us in our life and work face decisions of less than presidential magnitude; nonetheless, from time to time we share the existential loneliness of making an important decision.

Yet there are two things wrong with using this admittedly powerful subjective experience of decision making as the focus for analyzing and improving the decision-making process in organizations. First, these experiences suggest that decisions can be thought of as independent solitary events that are relatively unconnected to other decisions and the process that brought the decision point to a head. If there is anything to be learned from the Bay of Pigs fiasco or the Vietnam experience, it is that the organizational process of problem identification, information sharing, and problem solving, if mishandled, can undo the work of the finest, most logical, and experienced individual decision maker.

Second, these political memoirs suggest that decision making is an individual process and therefore the skills of logical analysis and problem solving (described in Chapter 10) should be sufficient to produce high-quality decisions. In reality, decision making in organizations is also a social process. Organizational functioning requires an unending stream of decisions great and small. These decisions are identified, made, and communicated by individuals and groups throughout the organization. As a manager you depend on the decisions of others and the information they bring you. You also delegate decisions and share information about them with others. Part of a manager's role is determining who in the organization has the information, experience, and wisdom needed to make a particular decision. Another part is understanding who are the stakeholders in each issue who need to be involved because their acceptance of the outcome is crucial. Seeing decision making as a social process means that the manager is responsible for determining how the problem is to be solved, but not necessarily the solution. The sense that any decision is made alone in an organization is an illusion. There are those who feel that Richard Nixon's greatest failure was falling prey to this illusion. Those who knew him say that he was a brilliant analyst and individual problem solver. Yet his Achilles' heel was his inability to develop an effective social process of decision making that involved others in appropriate ways.

The focus of this unit is on managing the process of decision making, as opposed to the problem-solving skills of making a specific decision. It underscores the social aspects of that process and the alternative ways of making decisions with other people: the costs and benefits and the appropriate application of these decision-making methods in different situations.

The decision-making alternatives you used in the premeeting section reflect a contingency theory of leadership. The continuum ranges from autocratic decision-making behavior, (in which the leader decides alone) to participative styles, ranging from consultation to joint decision-making and, at the far end of the continuum, delegation (subordinates decide alone). The choice of style depends upon the problem at hand. Once again, managerial effectiveness depends upon having the skills required to analyze the problem in question and the ability to vary one's leadership behavior accordingly.

To understand the decision-making process, we must first examine the nature of effective organizational decisions and the components of decision effectiveness. The effectiveness of a decision can be judged in terms of three outcomes:

1. The *quality or rationality* of the decision, which is defined as the extent to which decisions influence employee performance and further the attainment of organizational goals.
2. The *acceptance* of the decision, defined as the degree of employee commitment to executing the decision effectively.
3. The amount of *time* available to make the decision, in other words, *efficiency*.

The extent to which these three criteria of quality, acceptance, and efficiency are critical varies from one decision to another. For some decisions, particularly those you will implement yourself, acceptance is not critical, but high quality may be absolutely essential, as for example, in decisions about how to program the computer for inventory control. Other decisions have very little quality requirement but involve great acceptance. The decision about how the secretarial pool will cover the phones at lunch time is an example of this type of decision. The solution devised has little in the way of a logical requirement because any one of the secretaries can do the job, but it must be acceptable to the people involved. Efficiency is usually an important consideration in everything we do in organizations, but other objectives, such as developing subordinates or encouraging organizational learning, sometimes take priority.

It is therefore important to be able to diagnose decision situations to determine the quality, acceptance, and efficiency requirements and the method of decision making that will best meet these criteria. No single decision-making method or management style is appropriate for all jobs or even all decisions in a single job.

One of the situational contingencies that determines the appropriate leadership style concerns whether or not the problem is structured or unstructured. A problem is well structured if we know the current state of the problem, the desired state, and the alternative courses of action that can remedy it. Structured problems are repetitive and routine problems for which a definite procedure has been developed. In contrast, unstructured problems are novel, and no procedures have been developed to handle them because they occur infrequently and/or are very complex. For example, repairing an airplane is a structured problem; designing a completely new spaceship is an unstructured problem. Since a situation involving an unstructured problem require more ideas and brains, a more participative leadership style is required.

Victor Vroom and his associates[2] have developed a formal model that helps us to analyze specific decision situations and to determine the decision-making approach that is likely to be most effective. The model is constructed in the form of a decision tree based on seven rules (shown in Table 15-2) that were derived from research on problem solving and decision making. It poses eight questions for managers to ask about a decision:

A. Is there a quality requirement such that one solution is likely to be more rational than another? Does the technical quality of the decision matter?
B. Do I have sufficient information to make a high-quality decision?
C. Is the problem structured?
D. Is my subordinate's commitment to the decision critical to effective implementation?
E. If I were to make the decision by myself, is it reasonably certain that subordinates would be committed to the decision?

TABLE 15-2 Rules Underlying the Vroom-Yetton Model

RULES TO PROTECT THE QUALITY OF THE DECISION

1. **The leader information rule.** If the quality of the decision is important and the leader does not possess enough information or expertise to solve the problem by himself or herself, then AI is eliminated from the feasible set.

2. **The goal congruence rule.** If the quality of the decision is important and subordinates are not likely to pursue the organization goals in their efforts to solve the problem, then GII is eliminated from the feasible set.

3. **The unstructured problem rule.** In decisions in which the quality of the decision is important, if the leader lacks the necessary information or expertise to solve the problem by himself or herself and if the problem is unstructured, the method of solving the problem should provide for interaction among subordinates likely to possess relevant information. Accordingly, AI, AII, and CI are eliminated from the feasible set.

RULES TO PROTECT THE ACCEPTANCE OF THE DECISION

4. **The acceptance rule.** If the acceptance of the decision by subordinates is critical to effective implementation and if it is not certain that an autocratic decision will be accepted, AI and AII are eliminated from the feasible set.

5. **The conflict rule.** If the acceptance of the decision is critical, an autocratic decision is not certain to be accepted, and disagreement among subordinates in methods of attaining the organizational goal is likely, the methods used in solving the problem should enable those in disagreement to resolve their differences with full knowledge of the problem. Accordingly, under these conditions, AI, AII, and CI, which permit no interaction among subordinates and therefore provide no opportunity for those in conflict to resolve their differences, are eliminated from the feasible set. Their use runs the risk of leaving some of the subordinates with less than the needed commitment to the final decision.

6. **The fairness rule.** If the quality of the decision is unimportant but acceptance of the decision is critical and not certain to result from an autocratic decision, it is important that the decision process used generate the needed acceptance. The decision process used should permit the subordinates to interact with one another and negotiate over the fair method of resolving any differences, with full responsibility on them for determining what is fair and equitable. Accordingly, under these circumstances, AI, AII, CI, and CII are eliminated from the feasible set.

7. **The acceptance priority rule.** If acceptance is critical and not certain to result from an autocratic decision, and if subordinates are motivated to pursue the organizational goals represented in the problem, then methods that provide equal partnership in the decision-making process can provide greater acceptance without risking decision quality. Accordingly, AI, AII, CI, and CII are eliminated from the feasible set.

Source: Victor A. Vroom, "A New Look at Managerial Decision Making," *Organizational Dynamics*, Vol. 2 (Spring 1973), p. 67.

F. Do subordinates share the organizational goals to be attained in solving this problem?

G. Is conflict among subordinates likely in preferred solutions? (This is irrelevant to individual problems.)

H. Do subordinates have sufficient information to make a high-quality decision? (This applies only to individual problems.)

By answering these questions sequentially and tracing the answers through the model's decision tree (see Figure 15-1), the manager is led to a set of effective decision alternatives for the problem. There are eighteen effective decision sets, one at the end of each branch of the decision tree. The decision-making methods listed in the effective decision sets are those described at the beginning of the chapter.

The method listed first in a set indicates the approach that minimizes person-hours (i.e., is most efficient given quality and acceptance constraints). For example, an automatic decision or delegation takes less time than a group decision. With the exception of delegation, the method listed last is the approach that maximizes participation, given quality and acceptance constraints. The decision tree eliminates those decision-making methods that would jeopardize the quality and acceptance requirements of a given problem. The manager can then choose from the methods remaining in the effective decision set depending on whether he or she aims to maximize efficiency or participation.

To summarize and understand how the model works, let us analyze an actual case problem using the Vroom-Yetton model. You are on the division manager's staff and work on a wide variety of problems of both an administrative and a technical nature. You have been given the assignment of developing a universal method to be used in each of the five plants in the division for manually reading equipment registers, recording the readings, and transmitting the data to a centralized information system. All plants are located in a relatively small geographical region. Until now there has been a high error rate in the reading and/or transmittal of the data. Some locations have considerably higher error rates than others, and the methods used to record and transmit the data vary between plants. It is probable, therefore, that part of the error variance is a function of specific local conditions rather than anything else, and this will complicate the establishment of any system common to all plants. You have the information on error rates but no information on the local practices that generate these errors or on the local conditions that necessitate the different practices.

Everyone would benefit from an improvement in the quality of data as it is used in a number of important decisions. Your contacts with the plants are through the quality control supervisors, who are responsible for collecting the data. They are a conscientious group committed to doing their jobs well but are highly sensitive to interference on the part of higher management in their own operations. Any solution that does not receive the active support of the various plant supervisors is unlikely to reduce the error rate significantly.

QR	Quality Requirement	Is there a quality requirement such that one solution is likely to be more rational than another? Does it really matter which solution is chosen?
LI	Leader's Information	Do I have sufficient info to make a high-quality decision?
ST	Problem Structure	Is the problem structured?
AR	Acceptance Requirement	Is subordinate commitment to the decision critical to effective implementation?
AP	Acceptance Probability	If I were to make the decision by myself, is it reasonably certain that my subordinates would be committed to the decision?
GC	Goal Congruence	Do subordinates share the organizational goals to be attained in solving this problem?
CO	Subordinate Conflict	Is conflict among subordinates likely in preferred solutions? (This is irrelevant to individual problems.)
SI	Subordinate Information	Do subordinates have sufficient info to make a high quality decision? (This applies only to the individual problems.)

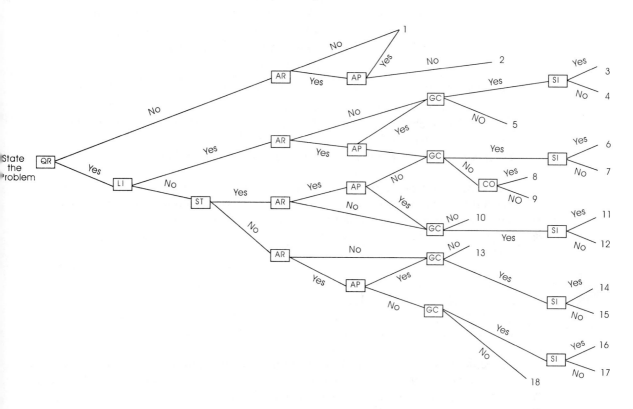

The feasible set is shown for each problem type for group (G) and individual (I) problems.

1	G: AI, AII, CI, CII, GII		7	G: GII		13	G: CII
	I: AI, OI, AII, CI,			I: GI			I: CI
2	G: GII		8	G: CII		14	G: CII, GII
	I: DI, GI			I: CI, GI			I: DI, CI, GI
3	G: AI, AII, CI, CII, GII		9	G: CI, CII		15	G: CII, GII
	I: AI, DI, AII, CI, GI			I: CI, GI			I: CI, GI
4	G: AI, AII, CI, CII, GII		10	G: AII, CI, CII		16	G: GII
	I: AI, AII, CI, GI			I: AII, CI			I: DI, GI
5	G: AI, AII, CI, CII		11	G: AII, CI, CII, GII		17	G: GII
	I: AI, AII, CI			I: DI, AII, CI, GI			I: GI
6	G: GII		12	G: AII, CI, CII, GII		18	G: CII
	I: DI, GI			I: AII, CI, GI			I: CI, GI

Figure 15-1   Decision-Process Flow Chart for Both Individual and Group Problems
Adapted from Victor H. Vroom and Arthur G. Jago, "Decision Making as a Social Process: Normative and Descriptive Models of Leader Behavior," *Decision Sciences*, Vol. 5 (1974); *by permission of the American Institute for Decision Sciences.*

First, we can see that this is a group problem, since it potentially affects all the plants. Answering the eight diagnostic questions and tracing them through the decision tree, works as follows:

A– *quality requirement?*	Yes, since a system that accurately records and transmits data is necessary.
B– *leader's information?*	No, since error variance seems to depend on local conditions that you don't know about.
C– *structured problem?*	No, you don't know what is causing the errors.
D– *acceptance necessary?*	Yes, a solution that does not receive active support of the various plant supervisors is unlikely to reduce error.
E– *unilateral decision accepted?*	No, QC supervisors are highly sensitive to interference on the part of higher management.
F– *goal congruence?*	Yes, they are a conscientious group committed to doing their jobs well.
H– *subordinate information?*	Irrelevant to a group problem.

This leads then to feasible decision sets 16 or 17, which have only one decision method for a group problem—GII. Thus, the model recommends a group consensus decision in deciding how to develop a universal data system for all the plants.

Procedure for Group Meeting

The purpose of the group exercise is to provide an opportunity to practice using the decision tree and identify and discuss reasons for differences between what the model recommends and your own decision-making style.

STEP 1. Each learning group should record its answers to the five cases on the chalkboard or flipchart so that all members can view one another's approach to the cases. The following Case Analysis Record Form provides a format for recording the data.

STEP 2. The learning groups should work through the decision tree on the preceding page for each case and arrive at a group recommendation (30 minutes). Trace your decision steps with a different color for each case or utilize a different tree for each one.

STEP 3. The instructor takes the class through the cases using the Vroom-Yetton model, answering the eight questions for each case (30 minutes).

STEP 4. The class discussion should focus upon the comparison between the class and Vroom's recommendations made by the groups and Vroom (see page 394). Answer the following questions:
a. Did your recommendations differ from Vroom's? If so, how and why do they differ?
b. What assumptions did you make with the cases?
c. What assumptions does the model make?
d. What factors are missing from this model?

Case Analysis Record Form

PARTICIPANT NAMES	CASE 1	CASE 2	CASE 3	CASE 4	CASE 5
Group recommendation after using the decision tree					
Vroom-Yetton model recommendation					

 Follow-Up

A normative model, like the Vroom-Yetton model, raises three questions: 1) When managers utilize this model, how likely are their decisions to be effective? 2) Do managers really make decisions like this? and 3) If not, why not?

First, research has shown that when managers choose one of the alternatives within the feasible set, a greater percentage of their decisions were found to be effective. In six studies, when managers used the leadership style indicated by the model, 62 percent of their decisions were effective; when they did not, only 37 percent of their decisions were successful[3]. Another study of 45 retail cleaning franchises revealed that managers whose leadership behaviors conformed to the Vroom-Yetton model had more satisfied employees and more profitable operations than other managers[4].

Second, research comparing the Vroom-Yetton model with the actual behavior of managers has shown that there is a general correspondence between the model recommendations for a specific situation and a manager's behavior in that situation. Vroom and Jago report, "In approximately two-thirds of the problems, nevertheless, the behavior which the manager reported was within the feasible set of methods prescribed for that problem, and in about 40 percent of the cases it corresponded exactly to the minimum man-hours solution"[5]. Thus, managers seem to be using an intuitive notion something like the Vroom-Yetton model to manage the decision-making process in their organizations. In some ways, however, the *differences* between model recommendations and managerial behavior are more interesting, in that they shed light on the assumptions on which the model is based and on particularly difficult issues in managing the decision-making process.

For example, when we have asked managers how they would solve the engineering work assignment case described in the prework for this unit, many of them chose an AI or AII decision. Most resisted strongly the idea of bringing the group together for decision making either in the CII or GII modes. Vroom's GII solution brought cries of "No way!" or "It will never work!" Further discussion of differences between individual styles and the Vroom GII decision recommendations raised some interesting comments:

- "The group wouldn't be able to deal with a difficult problem like this."
- "I wouldn't know how to control the conflict this situation creates if it were made a group decision."
- "In most groups the members would expect the manager to make this decision, and they would have to live with it."

These comments bring out some of the assumptions underlying the Vroom-Yetton model and hence define some of the problems in its application. These assumptions are:

1 Managers are equally skilled in using the different decision-making alternatives.

2. Groups are equally skilled in their adaptation to these decision-making alternatives.

3. Organizational history and the resulting organizational culture have no impact on a single decision analyzed by the model.

What the model does is analyze a specific decision dispassionately in terms of its quality, acceptance, and efficiency requirements without regard to the preceding assumptions about managerial and group skill or organization culture. Yet in any specific situation, these issues must be considered to ensure that decisions are effective.

In conclusion, we suggest the following considerations in applying the Vroom-Yetton model to actual managerial situations:

1. Intuitive managerial decision-making models are more simplified than the Vroom-Yetton model. They do not account for some of the interactions among decision rules portrayed in Figure 15-1. This is supported by Vroom and Jago's research.

2. Managers tend to underemphasize the importance of the acceptance and commitment components of decision effectiveness. This is also supported by Vroom and Jago's research.

3. Managers tend to use decision-making styles they are skilled at and avoid styles they feel uncomfortable with. For many, this means avoiding the more difficult group decision-making procedures.

4. Organization history and culture will affect the decision-making method chosen, independent of the logical dictates of the situation. Organization culture affects decision making in several ways:

   a. Group members will adjust to norms about "the way things are decided around here" and may have little experience or skill in other methods, such as group consensus.

   b. Managers may use a particular decision-making method because their boss uses it and be constrained in their flexibility of decision making by the style dictated from above. If your boss is AI with you, you have nothing to be GII with your subordinates about.

   c. Answers to the eight diagnostic questions may be influenced inaccurately by organizational norms. For example, in the military, where obeying orders is a pivotal norm, managers may tend to believe incorrectly that their authoritative decision will be accepted (question E).

These considerations suggest that the Vroom-Yetton model is useful in determining how the decision-making process should be conducted, but the application of this ideal requires managerial skill training in all of the decision-making methods, team development in the various forms of group decision making, and organizational development to create norms that value quality, acceptance, and efficiency as the primary criteria for effective decision making.

UPDATED VERSION

Vroom and Jago[6] developed a more sophisticated version of this theory that includes four new contingencies: time constraints, geographical dispersion (which acknowledges the difficulty of getting people together for a discussion), motivation to minimize the time needed to make the decision (so that it can be devoted to something more pressing), and motivation to develop subordinates. The new version utilizes a continuum ranging from 1 to 5 rather than a simple yes or no response to each question. It has four decision trees, two for group decisions and two for individual decisions. At the individual and group level there are separate trees for use when decisions must be made quickly and when time is not such an important consideration.

The new model allows for greater situational complexity and is designed to be used with a computer program. Neither the leadership styles nor the premises underlying the original questions have changed, but the increased sophistication of the model makes it too complex for our teaching purposes in this course.

The Vroom model gives us a partial answer to the question, "What are the pros and cons of group decisions?". The advantages are more complete information and knowledge, diverse views, increased commitment to the decision, and the increased legitimacy of a democratic decision. However, group decisions can also be time-consuming and overly influenced by conformity pressures or a dominant person or subgroup.

TABLE 15-3 Some Apparent Realities of Decision Making in Complex Organizations

SOME THINGS INDIVIDUAL MANAGERS CANNOT EXPECT TO DO MUCH ABOUT	SOME THINGS INDIVIDUAL MANAGERS CAN DO	SOME THINGS THE ORGANIZATION CAN DO
The fact that decision making in organizations is not a totally rational, orderly process	Exercise choices in the problems to work on, which battles to fight and where, and when to cut losses.	Set values and tone to support problem solving and risk
The nature of managerial work: the juggling of problems and conflicting demands	Develop intimate knowledge of the business and good working relationships with the people in it	Design organizational structure, reward, and control systems to support action rather than bureaucracy
People are flawed: they are limited information processors, have biases and emotions, and develop vested interests	Know yourself: know your strengths, weaknesses, and hot-buttons, and when to ask for help	Provide assignments where decision-making skills can be developed
Fundamental forces in the business environment	Develop the diverse set of skills necessary to act in different situations	Keep business strategy focused on things about which management is knowledgeable
Basic organizational components determined largely by the business one is in		

Morgan M. McCall, / Robert E. Kaplan, *Whatever It Takes: The Realities of Managerial Decision Making, 2e* © 1990, p. 120. Reprinted by permission of Prentice Hall, Englewood Cliffs, NJ.

DIFFERENCES IN DECISION MAKING

There is evidence that women tend to utilize a more participative decision making style than men.[7] Cultural values are another contingency that affects decision making[8]. In countries with high power distance, decisions will be made by top management; participative decisions will be rare. The speed with which decisions are made also varies from culture to culture. One of the most interesting cultural differences concerns the value we place upon rationality. Rationality refers to decision-making that is based upon logical analysis. In the U.S., where rationality is highly revered, even intuitive decisions may be couched in rational terms. Other cultures (Sweden, Israel) are more comfortable with intuitive decision making.

 # Learning Points

1. Individual decisions are not independent, solitary events. Instead they are closely connected to previous decisions and are influenced by the process that brought the decision point to a head.

2. Although decision making at very high levels is frequently characterized as a lonely individual struggle, decision making is also a social process. Decision making involves information sharing and interdependence among organization members. The manager's job is to manage the decision process by assessing what information and what players need to be involved.

3. The Vroom-Yetton model is a contingency theory of leadership. The continuum of leadership styles includes autocratic, consultative, group decisions, and delegation.

4. The effectiveness of a decision can be judged in terms of three outcomes:
   a. The quality or rationality of the decision.
   b. The acceptance or commitment on the part of subordinates to execute the decision effectively.
   c. The amount of time required to make the decision.

5. Utilizing groups to make decisions involves more time but results in greater acceptance of the decision and more likelihood of successful implementation.

6. Structured problems are repetitive and routine problems for which a definite procedure has been developed. Unstructured problems are novel, with no procedures to handle them because they are infrequent and/or complex.

7. The Vroom-Yetton model helps managers analyze specific decision situations and determine which approach will be most effective.

8. The Vroom-Yetton model utilizes the following factors in determining the appropriate approach: quality requirements, source of necessary information, goal congruence, type of problem (structured or unstructured), and potential acceptance and conflict by subordinates.

9. Managers whose leadership behavior approximates the model are more likely to make effective decisions than managers whose behavior does not conform to the model.

10. The Vroom-Yetton model is a normative model (i.e., a "one best way" to figure out which decision making alternative to use). In reality,

   a. managers' intuitive models for making decisions are simpler than Vroom's.

   b. managers tend to underemphasize the importance of employee acceptance and commitment.

   c. managers tend to use the decision-making procedure with which they feel most skilled and comfortable instead of the one that would be most effective.

   d. the organizational history and culture strongly affects the choice of decision-making style.

for Managers

- One of the most important factors for a manager to bear in mind when decisions are being made is the concept of setting precedents. With individual problems, solutions for one person or group often serve as a precedent for others. If you want to establish a reputation for fairness, it's worthwhile to consider whether you would want a given decision to be a guide for future ones. With both group and individual problems, the criteria used for making the decision should reflect the cultural values you are trying to promote within the organization.

- Some decisions eventually become obvious with time. The trick lies in knowing which decisions (or which parts of them) can be postponed and which need to be made immediately. This is learned by experience.

- Since decision making is learned by experience, it's desirable to start employees out making decisions at the lowest possible level. Too often the first decisions employees get to make are when they are promoted to supervisor and find themselves overwhelmed. Teaching employees good decision-making techniques, explaining why you made the decision you did, asking what decision they would make in your shoes, and delegating as many decisions as possible are all ways to develop good decision makers before they find themselves in the hot seat.

- Decisions are only as good as the information upon which they are based. Therefore it's important to have reliable and accurate information sources. In some organizations the higher one goes, the more difficult it is to have accurate information because people are busy telling you either what they think you want to hear or information that reflects well upon them. Kotter found that the aggressiveness with which managers sought out information distinguished effective managers from less effective ones.[10]

- Test the water about possible solutions with carefully chosen people (i.e., informal opinion leaders, graybeards, powerful people who are interested in the issue). Yes-men and -women or people with a narrow perspective or a self-serving approach are obviously not good choices.

- It is not uncommon to have second thoughts about decisions. Indeed, it's a natural cognitive phenomenon called cognitive dissonance. Knowing this can help you be more patient when employees (or even you) have second thoughts, even when a decision seemed to be final and everyone was in agreement.

- People can only process so much information because our brains have limited capacity. Furthermore, it is sometimes impossible to have all the information that is needed to make a good decision. Thus, there is often an element of ambiguity involved with decision making. People have different tolerance levels for ambiguity, which affects their decision-making process.

- Part of the psychological contract regarding employee input on decisions concerns the manager's response. When managers request input from employees, they "owe" them the courtesy of explaining what the final decisions were and why the employee suggestion was or was not used. When managers do not do this, employees are likely to say, "I don't know why I bothered; they just went ahead and did what they wanted to anyway." In the future, such employees may be less forthcoming with their suggestions. However, when managers do explain how decisions were made and why an employee suggestion could not be used, they are both recognizing the employee's contribution and training him or her to make decisions in the future. Employees are not always aware of the broader contingencies their managers face. Sharing the rationale behind decisions is a way to develop employees.

- Chester Barnard, one of the first writers about management, introduced the "zone of indifference." Within that zone, employees will accept directives without questioning their boss' power, but ask them to do a task that lies outside that zone and they will resist[10]. We can adapt this concept to employee participation in decision making. Answering "yes" to Vroom and Yetton's question, "If I were to make the decision by myself, it is reasonably certain that it would be accepted?" implies that this problem falls within the employees' zone of indifference. Asking for participation on such issues wastes time and can even frustrate employees. The wise manager understands when employee involvement in decisions is important and when it is not.

- Table 15-3 presents a realistic approach to decision making.

Personal Application Assignment

This decision is to choose a decision-making experience to write about. If you have trouble deciding, you can always use the Vroom model to analyze a decision with which you were involved.

A. *Concrete Experience*
    1. *Objectively* describe the experience ("who," "what," "when," "where," "how" type information - up to 2 points).
    2. *Subjectively* describe your feelings, perceptions, and thoughts that occurred during (not after) the experience (up to 2 points). Does this section have too much detail? (If so, delete 1 point).

B. *Reflective Observation*
    1. Look at the experience from different points of view. How many points of view did you include that are relevant (up to 2 points)?
    2. Use these perspectives to add more meaning to the incident (up to 2 points).

C. *Abstract Conceptualization*
   1. Relate concepts from the assigned readings and the lecture to the experience (i.e., what theories have you heard in the lecture or read in the *Reader* that relate to your understanding of this incident?). Make reference to at least two sources. Use standard referencing format and include the page number to which you are referring. How many sources did you use and how clearly did you explain their theories (up to 4 points)?
   2. You can also create an original model or theory, but it should not replace course concepts.

D. *Active Experimentation*
   1. Write about what you will do in the future that will improve your effectiveness. Use rules of thumb or action resolutions.
   2. Are they described specifically, thoroughly, and in detail (up to 4 points).

E. *Integration, Synthesis, and Writing*
   1. Did you write about something personally important to you (up to 1 point)?
   2. Was it well written (up to 2 points)?
   3. Did you integrate and synthesize the different sections (up to 1 point)?

Leadership and Decision-Making Case Answers

(Do Not Read Until You Have Completed Chapter 15)

	ANALYSIS								PROBLEM TYPE	FEASIBLE SET
	A	B	C	D	E	F	G	H		
Case	Quality?	Leader's Information?	Structured?	Acceptance?	Prior Prob-ability of Acceptance?	Goal Congru-ence?	Subordi-nate Conflict?	Subordi-nate Informa-tion?		
1	Yes	No	No	No	—	Yes	—	Yes*	14, Group	C11, G11
2	Yes	No	No	Yes	No	No	—	—	18, Individual	C1, G1
3	No	—	—	Yes	No	—	—	—	2, Group	G11
4	Yes	No	Yes	Yes	No	No	Not ap-plicable	—	8 or 9, Individual	C1, G1
5	Yes	Yes	—	No	—	Yes	—	No*	4, Group	A1, A11 C1, C11 G11

*The question pertaining to this attribute is asked in the decision tree, but it is irrelevant to the decision outcome in these group cases because it applies to the individual DI alternative only.

[1]For an interesting discussion of decision making, see Morgan McCall and Robert Kaplan's book, *Whatever It Takes: Decision Makers at Work* (Englewood Cliffs, NJ: Prentice Hall, 1985).

[2]Victor H. Vroom and P. Yetton, *Leadership and Decision Making* (Pittsburgh, PA: University of Pittsburgh Press, 1973; and Victor H. Vroom and Arthur G. Jago, *The New Leadership: Managing Participation in Organizations* (Englewood Cliffs, NJ: Prentice-Hall, 1988). The latest version of their model is too complex for our teaching purposes in this chapter. Therefore, the questions shown here are a slightly modified version of those found in their original model.

[3]Vroom and Jago, *The New Leadership*, p.79

[4]C. Margerison and R. Glube, "Leadership Decision Making: An Empirical Test of the Vroom and Yetton Model," *Journal of Management Studies*, Vol. 16, pp. 45-55.

[5]Vroom and Jago, "Decision Making as a Social Process: Normative and Descriptive Models of Leader Behavior," *Decision Sciences*, Vol. 5 (1974)," p. 754.

[6]Vroom and Jago, *The New Leadership*.

[7]Alice H. Eagly & Blair T. Johnson, (1990). "Gender and Leadership Style: A Meta-analysis." *Psychological Bulletin*, 108, pp. 223-256. See also the article by Gary Powell in the *Reader*.

[8]Nancy J. Adler, *International Dimensions of Organizational Behavior* (Boston, MA: PSW-Kent, 1991).

[9]John Kotter, *The General Managers* (New York: Free Press, 1982).

[10]Chester Barnard, *The Functions of the Executive* (Cambridge, MA: Harvard University Press, 1938).

Chapter

16

LEADERSHIP: THE EFFECTIVE EXERCISE OF POWER AND INFLUENCE

OBJECTIVES By the end of this chapter, you should be able to:

A. Identify the three possible outcomes of an influence attempt.

B. Describe the various sources of power.

C. Identify the influence tactics people use at work.

D. Describe and recognize the four influence styles.

E. Identify four behaviors that foster win-win outcomes.

F. Identify ways that managers maintain their influence.

*H*ow to Manage the Boss

Peter F. Drucker

Most managers, including of course most chief executives, have a boss. Few people are as important to the performance and success of a manager as the boss. Yet while management books and courses abound in advice on how to manage subordinates, few if any even mention managing the boss.

Few managers seem to realize how important it is to manage the boss or, worse, believe that it can be done at all. They bellyache about the boss but do not even try to manage him (or her). Yet managing the boss is fairly simple–indeed generally quite a bit simpler than managing subordinates. There are only a few Dos, and even fewer Don'ts.

The Wall Street Journal, August 1, 1986. Reprinted with permission of *The Wall Street Journal* © 1989 Dow Jones Co., Inc. All rights reserved.

The first Do is to realize that it is both the subordinate's duty and in the subordinate's self-interest to make the boss as effective and as achieving as possible. The best prescription for one's own success is, after all, still to work for a boss who is going places. Thus the first Do is to go to the boss—at least once a year—and ask: "What do I do and what do my people do that helps you do your job? And what do we do that hampers you and makes life more difficult for you?"

THE CORRECT DEFINITION

This sounds obvious—but it is rarely done. For even effective executives tend to mis-define a "manager" as someone who is responsible for the work of subordinates—the definition of 50 years ago—and thus tend not to perceive that they have any responsibility for the boss's performance and effectiveness. But the correct definition of a manager—as we have known it for at least 40 years—is someone who is responsible for the performance of all the people on whom his or her own performance depends.

The first person on whom a manager's performance depends is the boss, and the boss is thus the first person for whose performance a manager has to take responsibility. But only by asking, "what do I do to help you or to hamper you?"—the best way to ask is without beating about the bush—can you find out what the boss needs and what gets in the boss's way.

Closely related is the need for awareness that your boss is a human being and an individual; no two persons work alike, perform alike or behave alike. The subordinate's job is not to re-educate the boss, not to make the boss conform to what the business schools and the management books say bosses should be like. It is to enable a particular boss to perform as a unique individual. And being an individual, every boss has idiosyncrasies, has "good words" and "bad words," and, like the rest of us, needs his own security blanket.

To manage the boss requires thinking through such questions as: Does this individual who is my boss want me to come in once every month—but no more often—and spend 30 minutes presenting the performance, the plans and the problems of my department? Or does this individual want me to come in every time there is anything to report or to discuss, every time there is the slightest change, every time we make a move? Does this individual want me to send the stuff in as a written report, in a nice folder, complete with tabs and a table of contents? Or does this individual want an oral presentation? Is this individual, in other words, a reader or a listener? And does this boss require (as do for instance most financial executives) 30 pages of figures with everything as his security blanket—and should it be tables or graphs?

Does this individual need the information to be there when he or she gets to the office in the morning, or does this boss (as do a good many operating people) want it at the end of the day, say around 3:30 on Friday afternoon? And if there is disagreement among the management group, how does this boss want to have it handled? To have us iron it out and report our consensus (as did Gen. Eisenhower and President Reagan)? Or for us to report our disagreements in full detail and with complete documentation (as did both Gens. George Marshall and MacArthur)?

What are the things the boss does well? What are his strengths? And what are the boss's limitations and weaknesses—the areas in which the subordinate needs to support, to buttress and to supplement the boss? A manager's task is to make the strengths of people effective and their weaknesses irrelevant—and that applies fully as much to the manager's boss as it applies to the manager's subordinates. If for instance the boss is good at marketing but uncomfortable with financial figures and analysis, managing the boss means to bring him into the marketing decision but to prepare the financial analysis beforehand and in depth.

Managing the boss means, above all, creating a relationship of trust. This requires confidence on the part of the superior that the subordinate manager will play to the boss's strengths and safeguard the boss against his or her limitations and weaknesses.

KEEP THE BOSS AWARE

The final Do: Make sure the boss understands what can be expected of you, what the objectives and goals are on which your own energies and those of your people will be concentrated, what your priorities are, and, equally important, what they are not. It is by no means always necessary that the boss approve–it is sometimes not even desirable. But the boss must understand what you are up to, must know what to expect and what not to expect. Bosses, after all, are held responsible by their bosses for the performance of their subordinates. They must be able to say: "I know what Anne (or Joe) is trying to do." Only if they can say this will they be able to delegate to their subordinate managers.

And now two Don'ts:

Never expose the boss to surprises. It is the job of the subordinate to protect the boss against surprises–even pleasant ones (if any such exist). To be exposed to a surprise in the organization one is responsible for is humiliation, and usually public humiliation. Different bosses want very different warnings of possible surprises. Some–again , Ike is a good example–want no more than a warning that things may turn out differently. Other bosses–President Kennedy for example–demand a full, detailed report even if there is only a slight chance of a surprise. But all bosses need to be protected against surprises. Otherwise they will not trust a subordinate–and with good reason.

Never underrate the boss! The boss may look illiterate; he may look stupid–and looks are not always deceptive. But there is no risk at all in overrating the boss. The worst that could happen is for the boss to feel flattered. But you underrate the boss he will either see through your little game and will bitterly resent it. Or the boss will impute to you the deficiency in brains or knowledge you imputed to the boss and will consider you ignorant, dumb, or lacking in imagination.

But the most important thing is not what to do or what not to do. It is to accept that managing the boss is the responsibility of the subordinate manager and a key–maybe the most important one–to his or her own effectiveness as an executive.

 # Premeeting Preparation

A. Read "How to Manage the Boss."

B. Answer the following questions:

1. Think about someone who handles power very well. How does he or she do it?

2. What differences in behavior have you observed between someone who has power and influence and someone who does not?

3. What do you want to learn about power?

4. What are the significant learning points from the *Reader?*

C. Complete the Influence Style Self-Diagnosis.

D. Read the Topic Introduction.

Personal Influence Style Diagnosis

The focus of this chapter is the effective exercise of power and influence. Before reading the topic introduction, do a simple self-assessment of your style of influencing others. Generally speaking, how descriptive is each of the following styles of your typical influence behavior? Using the key provided, record your rating (from 1 = not descriptive to 5 = very descriptive) in the space to the left of each paragraph. Then read the topic introduction.

1	2	3	4	5
Not at All Descriptive of Me		Somewhat Descriptive		Very Descriptive of Me

Influence Style Self-Diagnosis

_____ I am direct and positive in asserting my own wishes and requirements. I let others know what I want from them, and I am quick to tell others when I am pleased or dissatisfied with their performance. I am willing to use my influence and authority to get others to do what I want. I skillfully use a combination of pressures and incentives to get others to agree with my plans and proposals, and I follow up to make sure they carry out agreements and commitments. I readily engage in bargaining and negotiation to achieve my objectives, using both tough and conciliatory styles according to the realities of power and position in each situation.

_____ I am open and nondefensive, being quick to admit when I do not have the answer, or when I have made a mistake. I listen attentively to the ideas and feelings of others, actively communicating my interest in their contributions, and my understanding of their points of view. I am willing to be influenced by others. I give credit for others' ideas and accomplishments. I make sure that everyone has a chance to be heard before decisions are taken, even when I do not agree with their position. I show trust in others, and I help them to bring out and develop their strengths and abilities.

_____ I appeal to the emotions and ideals of others through the use of forceful and colorful words and images. My enthusiasm is contagious and carries others along with me. I bring others to believe in their ability to accomplish and succeed by working together. I see and can communicate my vision of the exciting possibilities in an idea or situation. I get others to see the values, hopes, and aspirations that they have in common, and I build these common values into a shared sense of group loyalty and commitment.

_____ I produce detailed and comprehensive proposals for dealings with problems. I am persistent and energetic in finding and presenting the logic behind my ideas and in marshalling facts, arguments, and opinion in support of my position. I am quick to grasp the strengths and weaknesses in an argument and to see and articulate the logical connections between various aspects of a complex situation. I am a vigorous and determined seller of ideas.

Topic Introduction

Power and influence have negative connotations for many people. They conjure up unpleasant images such as the misuse of power by politicians, the high-pressure tactics of some salespeople, and the destructive behavior exhibited by military dictators. On the other hand, the ability to get things done is a crucial requirement for both personal and organizational success. Managers need a certain degree of power and influence to obtain the necessary resources for their units, to ensure that good ideas are heard and decisions are implemented, and to place competent people in key positions. Another advantage of having power is having access to top decision makers and receiving early information on decisions and policy shifts. Therefore, understanding and knowing how to manage power is a key skill for employees and managers alike.

In one comparative study of successful and unsuccessful executives, all the characteristics of the unsuccessful executives can be traced to an abuse or misuse of power. Their personal inadequacies were: 1) insensitive, abrasive, and intimidating; 2) cold, aloof, and arrogant; 3) betrayed other's trust; 4) overly ambitious and political; 5) unable to delegate or build a team; and 6) overdependent upon others (a mentor, for example).[1]

In contrast, the personal characteristics of people who obtain and exercise a great deal of power are: 1) energy, endurance and physical stamina; 2) the ability to focus their energy and avoid wasted effort; 3) sensitivity so they can read and understand others; 4) flexibility–the ability to consider different means to achieve goals; 5) personal toughness–a willingness to engage, when necessary, in conflict and confrontation; 6) the ability to submerge one's ego and be a good subordinate or team player to enlist the help and support of others.[2]

The power and status differences that exist between supervisors and subordinates are real and natural. They cannot be ignored or wished away. Indeed, in its simplest, most basic form, your role as a manager is to *make a difference* in the behavior of your subordinates. Your responsibility as a manager is to behave in ways that add to your subordinates' ability to do their jobs effectively and efficiently. The issue is not, therefore, whether or not managers have power, but how they choose to exercise the power demanded by the role and with what consequences. One does not "make a difference" without exercising power and influence.

Power is defined as the capacity to influence the behavior of others. Influence is the process by which people successfully persuade others to follow their advice, suggestions, or orders. In general, there are three possible outcomes to an influence attempt–*commitment, compliance,* or *resistance.* Whereas commitment implies internal agreement, compliance is merely going along with a request or demand without believing in it. Resistance occurs when a person's influence attempt is rejected. This can take the form of a flat refusal, passive-aggressive tactics (making excuses or pretending to agree while resorting to delaying actions or sabotage), or seeking out a third party or superior who has the power to overrule the request.

SOURCES OF POWER

Traditionally, managers have relied almost exclusively upon the power inherent in their position. An extreme form of this sounds like "I'm the boss. I have the right and responsibility to tell you what to do, and if you don't perform, I retain the ultimate power of reward and punishment." Increasingly, managers are being forced to develop other influence skills. The greater need for different forms of influence is due to 1) a shifting value structure among younger generations who have less respect for traditional authority, 2) rapid organizational change, 3) the diversity of people, goals, and values, and 4) increased interdependence.[3] Many managers spend the majority of their time on interdependent lateral relationships with people who are neither subordinates nor superiors.[4] In the lateral relationships that we find in staff positions, self-directed work teams, and network organizations (see Chapter 20), power comes from *expertise, effort,* and *relationships (referent power)*, rather than one's position or the ability to *reward* or punish others (*coercive power*). *Charisma* is a personal attribute that is another source of power. Power also comes from "being in the right place." A good location is one that provides 1) *control over resources*, 2) *control and access to information*, in addition to 3) formal authority (*position*).[5] Units that cope with the critical uncertainties facing an organization also acquire a measure of power that they would not otherwise have. This is termed the *strategic contingency model* of power.[6] For example, when a business school in a developing country faced a cash flow problem, the financial director became the most powerful person in the organization. People deferred to his opinion, even on academic issues that clearly fell outside his expertise. Once the school regained its financial footing, the power he and his subordinates held was diminished.

INFLUENCE TACTICS

In addition to understanding the sources of power, we need to know what influence behavior looks like. When people were asked to describe incidents in which they had influenced others at work, researchers identified eight generic influence tactics that appear in Figure 16-1.[7] American managers prefer consultation, rational persuasion, and inspirational appeals over more coercive tactics. They often begin with the softer influence tactics and, if they are not successful, move to harder tactics, like threats. Managers who use a variety of tactics tend to be more successful that those who rely upon a single tactic.

Complex and vital influence attempts, such as those required for major strategies or new projects, always require multiple influence tactics. A successful attempt is likely to begin with gathering facts, citing parallel examples (who is doing this?), marshalling the support of others (perhaps insured by an effective web of influence), precise timing and packaging of a presentation, and, in the case of initial resistance, persistence and repetition over weeks or even months. Less frequently, but sometimes successfully, managers may resort to manipulation, threats, or pulling rank.[8]

In the group exercise, we will focus upon the influence styles that readily lend themselves to skill-based training and practice.[9] Effective managers need to develop the capacity to analyze a situation and determine which influence tactic will be most effective. Although people often use a combination of influence tactics, we tend to be predisposed to certain styles that feel more natural. In the premeeting preparation, you were asked to determine how much each style describes your influence behavior. These styles are described more fully in the following paragraphs. Two of the styles rely upon "pushing" energy while the others utilize "pulling" energy.

Figure 16-1   Definition of Influence Tactics

Rational Persuasion: The agent uses logical arguments and factual evidence to persuade the target that a proposal or request is viable and likely to result in the attainment of task objectives.

Inspirational Appeals: The agent makes a request or proposal that arouses target enthusiasm by appealing to target values, ideals, and aspirations, or by increasing target self-confidence.

Consultation: The agent seeks target participation in planning a strategy, activity, or change for which target support and assistance are desired, or is willing to modify a proposal to deal with target concerns and suggestions.

Ingratiation: The agent uses praise, flattery, friendly behavior, or helpful behavior to get the target in a good mood or to think favorably of him or her before asking for something.

Personal Appeals: The agent appeals to target feelings of loyalty and friendship toward him or her when asking for something.

Exchange: The agent offers an exchange of favors, indicates willingness to reciprocate at a later time, or promises a share of the benefits if the target helps accomplish a task.

Coalition Tactics: The agent seeks the aid of others to persuade the target to do something, or uses the support of others as a reason for the target to agree also.

Legitimating Tactics: The agent seeks to establish the legitimacy of a request by claiming the authority or right to make it, or by verifying that it is consistent with organizational policies, rules, practices, or traditions.

Pressure: The agent uses demands, threats, frequent checking, or persistent reminders to influence the target to do what he or she wants.

Source: Adapted from Gary Yukl, *Leadership in Organizations* (Englewood Cliffs, NJ: Prentice Hall, 1994) p. 225.

ASSERTIVE PERSUASION

In the *assertive persuasion* style, we "push" others with our intellect. Assertive persuasion is considered the bread and butter of the business world. The essential quality of assertive persuasion as an influence style is the use of facts, logic, rational argument, and persuasive reasoning. While the influencer may argue forcefully with great élan and spirit, the power of assertive persuasion does not come from an emotional source. Facts and logic are, by definition, emotionally neutral. A person may react to a fact emotionally and thereby be persuaded to behave in a certain way. However, the feelings of the person using assertive persuasion are meant to be kept out of their argument. The facts are supposed to speak for themselves.

People using assertive persuasion to persuade others are usually highly verbal and articulate. They confidently present their ideas, proposals, and suggestions and can support their proposals with rational reasons.

People using this style structure their arguments and enumerate the points they want to make so their listeners can follow their logic. Sometimes they are guilty of selectively listening to others' attempts at assertive persuasion, hoping to find a weak spot so that they can effectively reason against others' proposals.

This style is most appropriate when the issue in question is suited to a logical approach, which is not the case with emotional or value-laden issues. Assertive persuasion also works best when the person exerting influence is already respected and enjoys a certain prestige.

REWARD AND PUNISHMENT

The second "pushing" style is *reward and punishment*, in which we are "pushing our will" onto other people. Reward and punishment involves the use of bargaining, incentives and pressures, and demanding certain behavior from other people. People who use this style state their expectations for how others will behave and also evaluate that behavior.

Rewards may be offered for compliance, and punishment or deprivation may be threatened for noncompliance. Naked power may be used, or more indirect and veiled pressures may be exerted through the use of status, prestige, and formal authority.

This influence style is characterized by "contingency management": letting others know clearly what they must do to get what they want and /or to avoid negative consequences through your use of bargaining, negotiating, making offers, and threats. The use of the word "if" often signals the use of this style: "If you do X, I'll do Y." Very often, however, the consequence–the "then" part of the "if" statement–is left implicit or vaguely defined.

Both reward and punishment and assertive persuasion (discussed shortly) involve agreeing and disagreeing with others. The difference is that in assertive persuasion, one agrees or disagrees with another's proposal because it is more or less effective, correct, accurate, or true. In using reward and punishment, on the other hand, the judgment of right or wrong is an evaluation based on a moral or social standard, a regulation, or an arbitrary performance standard. The person making the evaluation sets himself or herself up as the judge instead of appealing to a common and shared standard of rationality.

People using reward and punishment are very comfortable, generally, in conflict situations. They are comfortable giving clear feedback–both positive and negative–and are very direct about prescribing their goals and expectations. They are comfortable evaluating the work of others and saying what they like and don't like about it.

As you reflect on the description just given, it will be clear that any individual, regardless of formal position, can effectively utilize many reward and punishment behaviors. Anyone, theoretically, can make evaluative statements involving praise and criticism. Similarly, if a meeting were dragging, anyone could prescribe a goal and expectation ("We've got to finish our work by six o'clock"). However, not everyone can utilize incentives and pressures. The ability to follow through on 1) an evaluation and/or 2) a prescribed goal or expectation is dependent on one's access to and control of meaningful rewards and punishments (incentives and pressures). Many managers recognize that subordinates can and do exercise significant incentives and pressures. By withholding support, dragging their heels, carrying out orders they know to be inappropriate (I'm safe because I'm doing exactly what my boss told me to do!"), and other forms of subtle "sabotage," subordinates are demonstrating that bosses are not the only ones who have reward and punishment power. This style is not appropriate with individuals or groups who have a strong need to be in control or not be controlled by others.

People who use this style should state their expectations clearly in a direct manner. They must be assertive rather than wishy-washy or tentative, so that it is clear what will happen if the other party does not do what the influencer is demanding.

PARTICIPATION AND TRUST

Unlike the first two styles that involve pushing energy, the use of the *participation and trust* influence style *pulls* others toward what is desired or required by *involving them*. By actively listening to and involving others, an influencer using participation and trust increases the commitment of others to the target objective or task. This is in sharp contrast to the reward and punishment style in which compliance (not commitment) must be monitored frequently.

People who use participation and trust are generally rather patient and have developed the capacity to be very effective listeners. They are very good at reflecting back to people (paraphrasing) both the content and feelings of what the person has said. They build on others' ideas and are quick to credit others for their contributions.

People who use participation and trust as an influence style also effectively use personal disclosure. By sharing personal information about themselves, others are encouraged to reciprocate, which is one of the first steps in developing a trusting relationship. People who use this style readily admit their own areas of uncertainty and mistakes. By openly acknowledging their own limitations and taking a nondefensive attitude toward feedback, they help others to feel more accepted for what they are.

On the surface, participation and trust may appear to some to be a weak and wishy-washy style of influence in contrast, for example, to the toughness of assertive persuasion or reward and punishment. It is not. It can be very powerful by building the trust and commitment needed to implement actions and with it a willingness to be influenced. As with the other influence styles, participation and trust can be misused to manipulate others. The manager who tries to involve subordinates in a consensus decision-making process when the manager has already chosen a solution is treading on thin ice. When there is no other acceptable option, the assertive persuasion or reward and punishment mode of influence is probably more appropriate.

COMMON VISION

Another influence style that pulls rather than pushes is the *common vision* style. It aims to identify a common vision for the future and to strengthen the group members' belief that through their collective efforts, the vision can become a reality. The appeals are to the emotions and values of others, activating their personal commitment to private hopes and ideals and channeling that energy into working toward a common purpose. People using this style clearly articulate goals and the means to achieve them. The well-known speeches of Martin Luther King, Jr. and John F. Kennedy are classic examples of the effective use of common vision, although it is by no means a style that is useful only in large-group or political settings. This style is especially important in organizations undergoing major change efforts, as is seen in the article in the *Reader* by Tichy and Ulrich on transformational leadership.

Within the everyday world of organizations, there are numerous opportunities for the effective use of common vision. Many organizational meetings become an exercise in competing assertions. In such situations, the ability to help the group to pull together around a common goal can provide a much needed spirit of collaboration and inspiration: "What we can accomplish *if* we work together."

People who use common vision are generally very emotionally expressive. They are enthusiastic and are willing and able to project and communicate their feelings in an articulate manner. They talk in emotionally vivid imagery and metaphors. People using this style look for common ground and the synergy that can result from working together. Oftentimes, people who use this style well are described as charismatic leaders.

Please return to the Influence Style Self Diagnosis and determine which style is described in each paragraph.

THE VALUE ISSUES–POSITIVE VERSUS NEGATIVE POWER

None of the styles described here are inherently right or wrong, good or bad. All are important and relevant and can be used in a variety of ways. Think about a time when you felt really powerful. While the exact words will differ, most probably you felt strong, perhaps even on top of the world. What were the stimuli of those feelings? Were you uplifted by a moving speech? Did someone else recognize, comment upon, and reward you by acknowledging your competence? Maybe you were asked to become involved in solving a sticky organizational problem or given the resources and latitude to spearhead a project.

"It is not always that way. . . . There are times when we feel powerless . . . weak, turned off, at the bottom of a pile of garbage. Perhaps you felt put down by someone else's exercise of power: an autocratic boss, pushy friend, power hungry political leader or whatever. There are, indeed, two faces of power."[10]

The important distinction, therefore, has to do with how the exercise of power and influence is experienced: What is its impact? Assertive persuasion, reward and punishment, participation and trust, and common vision can be used in a way that results in other people feeling stronger. They can also be used to make people feel weaker–to feel like pawns in the hands of someone else. Common vision, for example, will result in people feeling weaker if it is used only to raise people's hopes and expectations without anything ever being realized or gained. People will thus feel "had" and become cynical to further influence attempts. On the other hand, we recognize that there are some situations (i.e., terminations) in which it is extremely difficult to exercise needed influence and leave people stronger.

We learned in Chapter 4 that McClelland identified a need for power as a basic motivator, even though it is difficult in our society to acknowledge this need because we are often suspicious of power. McClelland[11] resolved this dilemma by referring to the two faces of power. While a need for power always refers to a desire to have a strong impact upon others, one face of power, personal power, is an unsocialized concern for personal dominance. It is characterized by an I win–you lose perspective and a need to dominate others. The second face of power is socialized. People who are high in the motive need show a concern for group goals, empowering others and a win-win approach. This second face of power, the socialized version, is required for long-term success in organizations. In our society we often say that "power corrupts," and we believe that even people who started out with a need for socialized power degenerate into a selfish concern for personal dominance. While this may not always be the case, it is essential to examine one's personal need for power. This is another instance where it is important to know oneself. What is your need for power? What has been your experience with power and influence, and how does this affect the way you use power and influence with other people?

WIN-WIN BEHAVIORS

When people are utilizing socialized power and seeking a win-win outcome, we can observe the following behaviors during influence interactions, no matter what influence style the person is utilizing.[12]

1. *Attending* – When we attend to the other party, we give them our undivided attention which is conveyed by direct eye contact and verbal and non-verbal signs that we are paying close attention. This conveys the message that their thoughts, feelings, and ideas are important and worth listening to. Attending behavior on our part also sets the expectation that the other party will give our ideas equal respect.

2. *Asking* – Asking questions in a non-judgmental manner allows us to gain greater insight into the other party's thoughts and feelings. This increased knowledge can contribute to the influence process, much like the focus on interests rather than positions in Principled Negotiation (Chapter 11).

   Asking behavior is evidenced by questions such as, "How can I support you?", "Could you give me a few examples to help me understand?", "What do you think about _____?", and "What do you have in mind?".

3. *Understanding* – Understanding behavior indicates to the other party that we comprehend their meaning and can reflect back to them the gist of what they have said to us. By correctly paraphrasing their messages, we show the other party that we have been paying close attention to their opinions. This is also an opportunity to obtain feedback on whether or not we have understood their position correctly. In addition to paraphrasing, people also summarize the facts or information given by the other party to verify their understanding.

   Understanding behavior can be observed in questions like, "If I have heard you correctly, you are saying. . . ." "The heart of what you have just said is. . . ." and "So you are saying. . . ."

4. *Empathizing* – Empathizing behavior acknowledges the other party's feelings, as opposed to the content they have communicated. This indicates that the other party is entitled to feel a certain way and, by providing time for those feelings to be expressed, that we care about them.

   Empathizing behavior can be seen in phrases like, "It sounds like you are feeling . . . ," "In your shoes, I'd feel . . ."

THE WIZARD OF ID reprinted by permission of Johnny Hart and Field Enterprises, Inc.

All of these behaviors involve pulling ideas, thoughts, or feelings from the other party so that we can better understand them. To do this, we must temporarily set aside our own agenda (to either influence or not be influenced) and focus upon the agenda of the other party.

It is important to remember that influence attempts have both content and relationship outcomes. You may be successful at winning what you want (content) from the other party, but if they resent being coerced or manipulated, you have harmed your relationship with them. These win-win behaviors help protect your relationship with the other party. In order to balance the content and relationship outcomes, it is helpful to plan out beforehand what it is that you want from the other party (content objective) and secondly, what impression you want the other party to have of you as a result of this influence attempt (relationship objective).

The need to exercise power and influence is an inherent part of the managerial role. Effective managers develop the skills needed to have win-win outcomes versus win-lose outcomes whenever the situation allows that potential. During the upcoming group exercise, you will have an opportunity to practice both the influence styles and win-win behaviors.

Procedure for Group Meeting:
Influence Role Play

The purpose of this exercise is to allow you to practice each influence style and increase your own behavioral flexibility.

STEP 1. Divide into four-person groups and discuss the following. (20 minutes)
   a. Self-assessments - Which style(s) do you use most frequently? Do the descriptions in the Influence Style Self Diagnosis accurately describe how you try to influence others?

   b. Which styles have you seen the other members in your four-person group use most often throughout this course?

   c. Which style(s) are you most likely to be influenced by?
   Which style(s) are you most inclined to resist or not be influenced by?

STEP 2. Preparing for role plays: individual work. (10 minutes)
On the pages that follow you will find six potentially stressful influence situations. Individuals should read these situations carefully and select one (to start) that best meets the following criteria:
   a. It seems real to you (i.e., you have been in that situation and/or could easily imagine yourself being in that situation).
   b. You would expect yourself to experience at least a moderate level of stress in dealing with that situation.
   c. Pick a situation that calls for an influence style that you would like to develop.

Jot down your response to questions a) through d) in each situation in the space provided following the situation you have chosen to work on.

STEP 3. Conducting and critiquing the role plays. (minimum 1 hour)
The basic structure will be as follows:

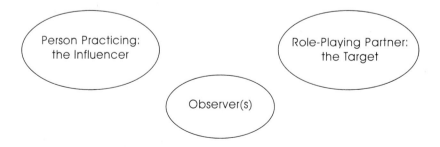

Person Practicing: the Influencer

Role-Playing Partner: the Target

Observer(s)

The sequence will be as follows:

a. One person volunteers to go first. That person (the influencer) selects a partner (the target). The others are to be silent observers who can use the observation forms following each situation.

Very briefly (2-4 minutes), the influencer tells his or her partner what the other person (boss, coworker, etc.)–the target–is like and how they are likely to act. Partners should, within reason, behave in a way to produce the moderate stress level desired.

b. Enact the situation. (5-6 minutes)

c. Feedback discussion. (8-10 minutes)

1) The influencer begins by stating:
   a) Which response style he or she was planning to use and which one(s) was actually used.
   b) His or her content and relationship objectives. Were they achieved?

2) The observers and the target person relate:
   a) Which styles they thought the influencer was using based upon the specific behavior they observed (e.g., "It looked like you were using trust and participation when you began talking about your previous personal experiences" – personal disclosure.)
   b) What influencer behaviors made the target feel stronger? Weaker?
   c) What win-win behaviors did you observe? (Attend, ask, understand, empathize?)
   d) What two or three specific suggestions would you offer the influencer to enhance his or her impact in a situation like this?

The influencer should focus on listening to and understanding this feedback (i.e., use of participation and trust style) and *not* try to convince the others why their observations are wrong or misinformed (i.e., use of reward and punishment and/or assertive persuasion.)

Then repeat the procedure so that each person has at least one practice opportunity. (If time permits, the entire small group can select a second stressful influence situation and repeat the entire practice process, Steps 2 and 3.)

STEP 4.   General Debriefing (15 minutes)
   a. What did you learn about influencing other people from doing these role plays?
   b. What connections can you make between this exercise and the readings?

Observations Category	INFLUENCE STYLES			
	Assertive Persuasion Logic, Facts, Rationality, Ideas, Proposals, Reasons For and Against	Reward and Punishment Evaluations, Use of Incentives and Pressures, Bargains, Stating Own Personal Goals and Expectations	Participation and Trust Active Listening, Recognizing Others' Contributions, Involving Others and Getting Their Contributions, Disclosing Own Areas of Uncertainty	Common Vision Building a Sense of Group Spirit, a We Feeling, Creating a Superordinate Group Goal, Shared Identity
Which styles did the influencer use most frequently? 1 = most frequently 4 = least frequently				
Examples of influence behavior that strength-ened the other person (positive power)				
Examples of influence behaviors that weak-ened the other person (negative power)				
Missed opportunities (i.e., example of where the style might have had a positive impact but was not used)				
Which style did the influencer use most effectively? 1 = most effective 4 = least effective				
	Win-Win Behaviors			
Which of these behaviors did the influencer use?	Attend	Ask	Understand	Empathize

SITUATION 4

You are one of five department heads in a software company. As the person in charge of production, you have no authority over the other department heads. However, you are worried that lack of collaboration between departments is costing the company business. Therefore, you have scheduled lunch with the head of marketing and sales because you think his/her department promises customers things that your department cannot produce.

Planning Questions:

a. Which style(s) do you think would be most effective in this situation? Do you require compliance or commitment in a situation like this?

b. What is it that you want the person you are trying to influence (the target) to do, i.e., what is your content objective?

c. What kind of an outcome are you looking for, in terms of your relationship with the other party, i.e., what is your relationship objective?

d. Plan out how you will handle this influence attempt.

After the Role Play:

e. What were the content and relationship outcomes?

f. Is there any way this influence attempt might have been improved?

Observations Category	INFLUENCE STYLES			
	Assertive Persuasion Logic, Facts, Rationality, Ideas, Proposals, Reasons For and Against	Reward and Punishment Evaluations, Use of Incentives and Pressures, Bargains, Stating Own Personal Goals and Expectations	Participation and Trust Active Listening, Recognizing Others' Contributions, Involving Others and Getting Their Contributions, Disclosing Own Areas of Uncertainty	Common Vision Building a Sense of Group Spirit, a We Feeling, Creating a Superordinate Group Goal, Shared Identity
Which styles did the influencer use most frequently? 1 = most frequently 4 = least frequently				
Examples of influence behavior that strength-ened the other person (positive power)				
Examples of influence behaviors that weak-ened the other person (negative power)				
Missed opportunities (i.e., example of where the style might have had a positive impact but was not used)				
Which style did the influencer use most effectively? 1 = most effective 4 = least effective				
	Win-Win Behaviors			
Which of these behaviors did the influencer use?	Attend	Ask	Understand	Empathize

SITUATION 5

One of your subordinates has been promising to finish a report now for three weeks. Every time you inquire as to how it's going, what you get back is, "Oh, it's coming along. It's more complicated than either one of us imagined." The grapevine has informed you that your subordinate's marriage is going through some rocky spots. While you want to be fair, your boss is putting the screws on you to get the report in. The pressure on you is really mounting and something has to give. The "last straw" meeting you called is about to begin.

Planning Questions:

a. Which style(s) do you think would be most effective in this situation? Do you require compliance or commitment in a situation like this?

b. What is it that you want the person you are trying to influence (the target) to do, i.e., what is your content objective?

c. What kind of an outcome are you looking for, in terms of your relationship with the other party, i.e., what is your relationship objective?

d. Plan out how you will handle this influence attempt.

After the Role Play:

e. What were the content and relationship outcomes?

f. Is there any way this influence attempt might have been improved?

Observations Category	INFLUENCE STYLES			
	Assertive Persuasion Logic, Facts, Rationality, Ideas, Proposals, Reasons For and Against	Reward and Punishment Evaluations, Use of Incentives and Pressures, Bargains, Stating Own Personal Goals and Expectations	Participation and Trust Active Listening, Recognizing Others' Contributions, Involving Others and Getting Their Contributions, Disclosing Own Areas of Uncertainty	Common Vision Building a Sense of Group Spirit, a We Feeling, Creating a Superordinate Group Goal, Shared Identity
Which styles did the influencer use most frequently? 1 = most frequently 4 = least frequently				
Examples of influence behavior that strength-ened the other person (positive power)				
Examples of influence behaviors that weak-ened the other person (negative power)				
Missed opportunities (i.e., example of where the style might have had a positive impact but was not used)				
Which style did the influencer use most effectively? 1 = most effective 4 = least effective				
	Win-Win Behaviors			
Which of these behaviors did the influencer use?	Attend	Ask	Understand	Empathize

SITUATION 6

You have heard several accounts from reliable sources that one of your top performers, a man in his fifties, has been sexually harassing the young women in his department. You would hate to lose this employee, but you strongly disapprove of people who abuse their power in this fashion. You want him to stop this behavior before the company loses the young women as employees or is slapped with a lawsuit.

Planning Questions:

a. Which style(s) do you think would be most effective in this situation? Do you require compliance or commitment in a situation like this?

b. What is it that you want the person you are trying to influence (the target) to do, i.e., what is your content objective?

c. What kind of an outcome are you looking for, in terms of your relationship with the other party, i.e., what is your relationship objective?

d. Plan out how you will handle this influence attempt.

After the Role Play:

e. What were the content and relationship outcomes?

f. Is there any way this influence attempt might have been improved?

Follow-Up

In their day-to-day work, managers are continually faced with a host of questions about the process of leadership. How can I get the job done most effectively? What is the "best" leadership style? How can I build commitment and loyalty among the members of my work team to me and to the company and its objectives? When should I listen and when should I give orders? If I become too friendly with my subordinates, will I lose their respect? How can I get others to do their work well? These are all contingency questions–there is no one right or wrong answer for every occasion.

Some managers mistakenly believe that the more power they give to their employees, the less power they have for themselves. This is true only if you impose a win-lose framework on the situation and see power as a limited commodity. In fact, power is often paradoxical–the more one gives away, the more one has for oneself. Managers who work hard to develop and empower their employees are examples of people who accrue power by giving it to others. McClelland stated it well when he wrote, "This expresses the ultimate paradox of social leadership and social power: to be an effective leader, you have to turn all your so-called followers into leaders."

Researchers have identified the steps that practicing managers use to establish sustained managerial influence:[13]

1. **Develop a reputation as a knowledgeable person or an expert. This is the most commonly reported form of gaining influence.** This requires keeping up-to-date in one's field or area. However, it is not sufficient to be knowledgeable; others must also be aware of this fact so it is sometimes necessary to market oneself.

2. **Balance the time spent in each critical relationship according to the needs of the work rather than on the basis of habit or social preference.** Managers should spend their time where it will do the most good in advancing organizational goals. This may necessitate switching from a narrow focus upon subordinates or technical areas to developing both lateral and upward relationships and external relationships in order to have greater influence.

There are two interesting findings related to building relationships and personal advancement. First, women are more likely to assume that hard work will result in promotion whereas men tend to believe that political contacts within the organization are essential to their advancement.[14] Secondly, there is some research evidence, which is not gender-related, that managers who spend time networking and trying to "look like a star" are more likely to win promotions in U.S. companies than effective, competent managers who devote their energies to their jobs and subordinates.[15] In organizations that allow this to happen, impression management and political skills, rather than merit and performance, are rewarded and the people who make it to the top will be more dedicated to their personal career than to the company and, in some cases, less competent than others. Once again, the concept of the two faces of power helps us determine what type of networking and relationship building we want to encourage–networking for the good of the organization or unit (social power) as opposed to networking that only benefits the individual (personal power).

3. **Develop a network of resource persons who can be called upon for assistance.** In many cultures in Latin America and Africa, things get done in organizations because of personal relationships. People who take the time to cultivate good relationships within the organization usually receive better service and cooperation than those who do not. Although this phenomenon is less striking in the U.S., relationships are still extremely important. Luthan and his colleagues

observed managers at work and identified networking as one of four key behavioral categories that emerged. He defined networking as "socializing/politicking and interacting with outsiders."[16] The other three categories were communication, traditional management behavior, and human resource management.

4. **Implement influence tactics with sensitivity, flexibility, and adequate levels of communication.** As with any strategy, it is necessary to understand one's audience and do no harm to the long-term relationship with the other party–in this case, the target one wishes to influence. Therefore, good influencers analyze the target and use the communication style that will be most effective with them. Managers who are good at influencing others are also good listeners who can adapt their tactics to the responses they hear from the target.

There are contradictory findings concerning gender differences in the use of influence tactics; some studies find no differences between men and women[17] while others find that the only difference is that women are less assertive with their superiors[18] and more likely to appeal to altruism and rationale-based strategies than threats of punishment with their subordinates.[19]

 # Learning Points

1. Power often has negative connotations for people, but it is a crucial part of leading and managing. A manager cannot "make a difference" without exerting power and influence over employees.

2. Power is defined as the capacity to influence the behavior of others.

3. Influence is the process by which people successfully persuade others to follow their advice, suggestions, or orders.

4. In general, there are three possible outcomes to an influence attempt: commitment, compliance, or resistance.

5. Managers traditionally relied upon the power inherent in their position. Changes in both society and the workplace demand that managers be proficient in several influence styles.

6. Other sources of power are expertise, effort, and relationships (referent power), the ability to reward or punish others (coercive power), position, and charisma. People also gain power when they have control over resources, control and have access to information, and work in units that cope with the critical uncertainties facing the organization.

7. Eight commonly used influence tactics are: 1) consultation, 2) rational persuasion, 3) inspirational appeals, 4) ingratiating tactics, 5) coalition tactics, 6) pressure tactics, 7) upward appeals, and 8) exchange tactics.

8. American managers prefer consultation, rational persuasion, and inspirational appeals over more coercive tactics.

9. Managers who use a variety of influence tactics tend to be more successful than those who rely upon a single tactic.

10. Berlew and Harrison identified four influence styles:
    a. Reward and punishment
    b. Participation and trust
    c. Common vision
    d. Assertive persuasion

11. Power has two faces: a negative, unsocialized need to dominate others and a socialized concern for group goals and empowering others.

12. Behaviors that can be used with any influence style to foster a win-win outcome are: attending, asking, understanding, and empathizing.

13. Effective managers diagnose the situation and determine which style would be most effective. This reflects a contingency approach to power and influence.

14. Power is paradoxical in that the more a leader empowers others, the more power he or she receives.

 TIPS for Managers

- Naked ambition often generates distrust. Others sense that ambitious people will not let human considerations stand in the way of their quest for success.

- Some political behavior occurs when there is too much uncertainty in the organization. Managers can reduce political jockeying by establishing clear evaluation criteria that distinguish between high and low performers and reward them accordingly. Managers will be less likely to resort to political influence when organizational goals are clearly specified and when they do not have to compete for scarce resources.[20]

- Managers can deal with existing political fiefdoms by removing or splitting the most dysfunctional subgroups and warning individuals who are motivated by personal power. Top management should identify "an apolitical attitude that puts organizational ends ahead of personal power ends" as an important promotion criteria.[21]

- Another way to gain power is by ingratiating yourself with the boss. While this tactic may do wonders for your vertical power quotient, it accomplishes less with peers and, from their point of view, throws into question both your competence and trustworthiness.

- There are several ways to acquire power that are unrelated to one's position in the hierarchy within a system. Possessing a scarce expertise, serving as a liaison between two groups who have difficulty getting along, having access to information or people with hierarchical power, having a personal network that facilitates both tasks and information gathering, as well as being seen as an objective source of sound judgment are all ways to accrue power.

- People who are skilled at influencing others take pains to reduce the status gap that may exist between them. They communicate in ways that do not put the other person in a one-down position.

- Managers should convey orders or requests in a polite, but confident manner.

- Don't give orders when you don't have the power to back them up. Instead, try another influence style.

Personal Application Assignment

This week's assignment is to write about a situation involving leadership and influence (or the lack thereof). Choose an experience about which you want to learn more. You could try out a different influence style than you normally use and write about that experience.

A. *Concrete Experience*
   1. *Objectively* describe the experience ("who," "what," "when," "where," "how" type information–up to 2 points).
   2. *Subjectively* describe your feelings, perceptions, and thoughts that occurred during (not after) the experience (up to 2 points). Does this section have too much detail? (If so, delete 1 point.)

B. *Reflective Observation*
   1. Look at the experience from different points of view. How many points of view did you include that are *relevant* (up to 2 points)?
   2. Use these perspectives to add more meaning to the incident (up to 2 points).

C. *Abstract Conceptualization*
   1. Relate concepts from the assigned readings and the lecture to the experience (i.e., what theories that you heard in the lecture or read in the *Reader* relate to your understanding of this incident?). Make reference to at least two sources. Use standard referencing format and include the page number to which you are referring. How many sources did you use and how clearly did you explain their theories (up to 4 points)?
   2. You can also create an original model or theory, but it should not replace course concepts.

D. *Active Experimentation*
   1. Write about what you will do in the future that will improve your effectiveness. Use rules of thumb or action resolutions.
   2. Are they described specifically, thoroughly, and in detail (up to 4 points)?

E. *Integration, Synthesis, and Writing*
    1. Did you write about something personally important to you (up to 1 point)?
    2. Was it well written (up to 2 points)?
    3. Did you integrate and synthesize the different sections (up to 1 point)?

[1]Morgan W. McCall, Jr. and Michael M. Lombardo, "What Makes a Top Executive?" *Psychology Today*, February 1983, pp. 26-31.

[2]Jeffrey Pfeffer, *Managing with Power: Politics and Influence in Organizations* (Boston, MA: Harvard Business School Press, 1992, p. 166).

[3]Bernard Keys & Thomas Case, "How to Become an Influential Manager," *Academy of Management Executive*, Vol.. 4 (4), 1990 pp. 38-51.

[4]Leonard Sayles. *Leadership: Managing in Real Organizations*. (New York: McGraw-Hill, 1989). See the Bradford and Cohen article in the *Reader* for advice on influencing people over whom one has no authority.

[5]Pfeffer, *Managing with Power*, p. 69. See also David Mechanic's "Source of Power of Lower Participants in Complex Organizations," *Administrative Science Quarterly*, 7, 1962, pp. 349-364.

[6]See Salancik and Pfeffer's "Who Gets Power–and How They Hold Onto It: A Strategic Contingency Model of Power," *Reader*.

[7]Gary Yukl, *Leadership in Organizations* (Englewood Cliffs, NJ: Prentice Hall, 1994) p. 225. These tactics are a modification of the exploratory work described in David Kipnis, Stuart M. Schmidt, & Ian Wilkinson, "Intraorganizational Influence Tactics: Explorations in Getting One's Way." *Journal of Applied Psychology*, 65, 1980, pp. 440-452.

[8]Keys and Case, *"Influential Manager"* p. 47.

[9]The ideas and materials here (with permission of Situation Management Systems, Inc.) are part of a series of training programs originally developed by David Berlew and Roger Harrison on positive power and influence. For more detail on the actual program, contact Situation Management Systems, Inc., Box 476, Center Station, Plymouth, MA 02361.

[10]David C. McClelland, "The Two Faces of Power," D. A. Kolb, I. M. Rubin, and J. McIntyre, *Organizational Psychology: Readings on Human Behavior in Organizations*, 4th ed. (Englewood Cliffs, NJ: Prentice Hall, 1984), pp. 59-72.

[11]David McClelland, Ibid.

[12]The ideas presented here are part of a training program originally developed by Irv Rubin and Robert Inguagiato on Win-Win Relationships. They are used with the permission of the Temenos Foundation. For more detail on the actual program, contact Temenos Foundation, 37 Kawananakoa Place, Honolulu, Hawaii, 96817.

[13]Keys and Case, *"Influential Manager,"* p. 43.

[14]Margaret Henning and Ann Jardim, *The Managerial Woman* (New York: Anchor Press/Doubleday, 1977).

[15]Fred Luthans, "Successful vs. Effective Real Managers," *Academy of Management Executive*, May 1988, pp. 127-132; and Fred Luthans, Richard M. Hodgetts, and Stuart Rosenkrantz, *Real Managers* (Cambridge, MA: Ballinger, 1988).

[16]Luthans, *"Successful vs. Effective Real Managers,"* p. 129

[17]George F. Dreher, Thomas W. Doughtery, & William Whitely, "Influence Tactics and Salary Attainment: a Gender-Specific Analysis" *Sex Roles*, May 1989, pp. 535-50.

[18]Anne-Marie Rizzo & Carmen Mendez, "Making Things Happen in Organizations: Does Gender Make a Difference?", *Public Personnel Management*, 17 (1), Spring 1988, pp. 9-20.

[19] Nancy L. Harper & Randy Y. Hirokawa. "A Comparison of Persuasive Strategies Used by Female and Male Managers: An Examination of Downward Influence" *Communication Quarterly*, 36 (2), Spring 1988, pp. 157-168.

[20]Don R. Beeman and Thomas W. Sharkey, "The Use and Abuse of Corporate Politics," *Business Horizons*, March-April 1987, p. 30.

[21] Ibid, p. 30.

Chapter 17

EMPOWERMENT AND COACHING

OBJECTIVES By the end of this chapter you should be able to:

A. Describe the characteristics of high-performance organizations.

B. Define empowerment.

C. Explain the four aspects of empowerment.

D. Describe how managers can empower employees.

E. Identify four different types of coaching.

F. Distinguish between effective and ineffective feedback.

Leader as Developer

David Bradford and Allen R. Cohen

During the conference when we were discussing difficult subordinates, I realized that I had completely written Mike off and had stopped any effective communication with him. Mike was a 53-year-old sales representative who had been with the company for over 12 years. He was well liked by the central office staff but had not met his sales plan for five of the last six years. Furthermore, I was starting to hear complaints about him from some of our clients.

I first tried to put myself in Mike's shoes. What must it be like to be near the end of one's career and starting to go downhill? If I were Mike, how receptive would I be to criticism? I might then be able to understand one of his habitual behaviors that had been particularly annoying to me: his tendency to look only to external factors for his failures, to blame "bad luck," the market, competitors who used unfair tactics, and the like.

Still, before meeting with Mike, I did two things. I considered what would be a reasonable goal for him in six months–what exactly did I expect of him in terms of sales level, generating new business, and the like. Then I thought, "What is it in Mike's behavior that would cause him trouble in making sales? Is it something in his style or is some knowledge lacking?"

Excerpted from *Managing for Excellence* by David Bradford and Allen R. Cohen (N.Y.: John Wiley, 1984), pp.157-158.

I then sat down with Mike and began by acknowledging that our relationship had deteriorated, that I had been dissatisfied with him but hadn't confronted him before, and also that I probably hadn't helped him as much as I could have. Mike immediately blamed me for everything that had gone wrong. It was fortunate that I had thought this out before, because my first response was defensive, to attack back. What helped was that I had already thought about why Mike must be hurting–clearly his pain was greater than anything I was now feeling about his comments.

After Mike had vented his feelings, I repeated that I wanted to change our relationship so that I could be more helpful. In return, we needed to get agreement on some specific goals for Mike. Although I would help him, it would be his responsibility to meet certain objectives. He was to be accountable for them, and if he failed to meet or substantially reach them in six months, he would be placed on probation. We mutually negotiated these goals. When I felt he was setting them too low, I pointed out what other sales personnel would do. We ended up with my original list modified, but in a way both of us could live with.

I then asked Mike what he thought might cause him difficulty in going about reaching his goals. In what areas did he need more training, and were there ways he behaved that caused problems? (I also asked him to discuss what he thought was easy for him–what his especially strong areas were.) As he shared his self-perception, I also shared my perception. I tried to point to specific behaviors at specific times that illustrated the problem areas I saw. At one point, he got very defensive and offered external reasons why the problems I identified were not his fault. I used his response as an illustration of what I was pointing out in his behavior.

In this discussion, we agreed to specific areas in which he could benefit from training. I sent him to a training program to work on his time-management problem. Also, we set up regular meetings (every two weeks) when we would review progress. I said that I was always available if he had a question, but that the initiative was up to him.

Mike did not meet the goals at the end of six months. I placed him on probation, with notice of termination in three months. I again met with him on a regular basis to offer assistance and coaching. Seven days before the end of his probation, Mike came in and said that the fit between him and the job was not right and quit.

As a result of this process, there was minimal reaction by the office staff (who had very much liked Mike). There was neither a decrease in morale nor a rise in paranoia among the others. Mike found another job in an area both of us had discussed as being more in line with his skills. Perhaps most gratifying to me, he expressly thanked me for my concern. He is doing well in his new position and is much happier.

# Premeeting Preparation

---

A. Read "Leader as Developer."

B. Fill out the Empowerment Questionnaire on the following page.

C. Read the Topic Introduction.

D. Practice building the spaceship Enterprise following the blueprints on pages 444-448.

The following questionnaire consists of managerial behaviors that promote empowerment. How frequently does your manager do each of the following? Please mark the response that best describes your manager's behavior.

My Manager	Very Infrequently	Infrequently	Sometimes	Frequently	Very Frequently
1. Lets me do my job without interfering					
2. Makes an effort to locate and remove barriers that reduce efficiency					
3. Encourages all of us to work as a team					
4. Clearly defines what is expected of me					
5. Provides me with honest feedback on my performance					
6. Openly recognizes work well done					
7. Keeps us focused on customer needs					
8. Encourages me to monitor my own efforts					
9. Encourages all of us to work as a team					
10. Allows me to make decisions about my own work					
11. Listens to me before making decisions affecting my area					
12. Provides me with an environment conducive to teamwork					
13. Rewards me for meeting company goals					
14. Informs me regularly about the state of the business					
15. Encourages me to make suggestions					
16. Makes sure I have all the information I need to do my work					
17. Behaves in ways that demonstrate respect for others					
18. Explains how my job fits into the company objectives					

Topic Introduction

Companies that survive and flourish in today's business environment are those that focus upon high performance, which translates into the cost competitiveness, high-quality products and services, innovation, and speed that is necessary to gain a competitive advantage. Harris reported the following characteristics of high-performing companies.[1]

- Joint goal-setting by managers and workers with objectives and targets that are always a bit beyond current levels to promote greater achievement.
- Employees reach a consensus upon norms of competence and high performance and standards of excellence that are incorporated into the corporate culture by means of logos and slogans.
- Continual reinforcement of positive behavior and accomplishment.
- Constructive feedback to redirect worker energies from ineffective to effective work habits and activities so that people learn from failure.
- Capitalizing on human assets and potential by giving individuals and work groups more flexibility, responsibility, and autonomy–while maintaining accountability.
- Encouraging and modeling a spirit of innovation and entrepreneurialism.
- Recruiting, selecting, promoting, and rewarding top performers, and identifying them as role models.
- Fostering synergy and collaboration so that individual competition is replaced by teamwork and group achievement.
- Using training, education sessions, and self-learning methods to develop people's potential for success and high performance.
- Eliminating underachievers who do not respond positively to demands for high performance.
- Altering organizational structure so that it is more decentralized, mission-oriented, and responsive.
- Making work meaningful and fun by cultivating informality and fellowship in a context of achievement and accomplishment.
- Leading by staying close to personnel, suppliers, and customers so that managers respond quickly to market and employee needs.
- Providing a mix of benefits, rewards, and incentives to encourage talented performance.

Creating organizations like this, where people see themselves as business people rather than employees,[2] requires a different style of management. There has been a gradual shift from a command-and-control model to an involvement-oriented approach centered upon employee commitment and empowerment. The command-and-control model is based upon the assumption that hierarchy and vertical relationships are the best way to organize. Managers working with a command-and-control mentality perceive their job as making decisions, giving orders, and ensuring that subordinates obey. The limited role of subordinates in this model ("Do what you're told") can result in passive workers with little commitment to organizational goals. When this occurs, management often finds itself shouldering the lion's share of the responsibility and prodding employees to get the work done. People talk in terms of "we and they" (workers versus management) rather than "us."

The involvement-oriented approach[3] is based upon the belief that the best way to organize is to give employees the freedom and responsibility to manage their own work as much as possible. In addition to the work itself, employees also do the thinking and controlling aspects that only supervisors and managers do in the command-

and-control model. In the involvement-oriented approach, employees are given both the information and the power to influence decisions about their work. Not surprisingly, high involvement organizations require a special breed of employee–people who are capable and skilled at basic problem solving, communication, and quantitative techniques. They must also be responsible and willing to make a commitment to learning, to developing themselves, and to being a productive member of an organization. For their part, supervisors and managers in high involvement organizations must be willing to share both power and information and listen to employees.

The command-and-control model worked fairly well for many years, but it is less appropriate for highly competitive, rapidly-changing global businesses. There are many U.S. companies that still operate in the command-and-control fashion, but it is harder for them to compete against companies that utilize their human resources more fully.[4] With a command-and-control approach, one can obtain satisfactory performance, but high performance only results when employees are truly committed to the success of the organization. Although the research has some limitations, the involvement approach is more productive than a control-oriented approach, except for companies who produce simple products or services in a stable environment.[5] High involvement organizations also have less turnover because employees find them a more attractive place to work.[6] Listen to the differences in how these two employees talk about their managers.[7]

> Down on the floor (in a GM plant), you can see the operation, and you know how it's supposed to be done. Up there, upper management's saying, 'Nah, nah, we can do it cheaper and more efficient if we do it our way.' So these people up there that are calling all the shots are not experiencing what really needs to take place on the floor. And they don't really care, because they're thinking, 'Short-term dollars and cents, it looks real good' and we're here down on the floor thinking, 'Long-term, it's our job.' Plus we want to give a person exactly what they bought: a perfect vehicle for the price. Any auto worker would tell you that. . . . They should not concentrate so much on quantity–and let us work on the quality. (GM worker)

> Honda's thing is, the guy on the line is the gut professional on his job, and he knows what is best for that process at that time. He knows best how to make it better. You give us an opportunity to have a say-so, and we can do a good job. (Honda worker)

Management can be either a competitive advantage for a company or an obstacle to high performance. Most experts agree that to succeed in the current business environment, companies need managers who see themselves less as bosses and more as facilitators and coaches.

Rather than calling all the shots, the new breed of manager or supervisor focuses on developing subordinates and encouraging them to become involved and take responsibility for their own output. "The key assumption in the involvement-oriented approach is that if individuals are given challenging work that gives them a customer to serve and a business to operate they can and will control their own behavior."[8] The new managers talk about "working themselves out of a job" as subordinates are trained to take over duties formerly done by supervisors or middle managers. The involvement approach to managers relies heavily upon self-control and self-management. This frees up management time to concentrate on areas that are more likely to ensure the organization's survival. For example, managers can utilize the time they formerly spent checking up on employees to focus on obtaining the resources subordinates need to do their jobs, adding value to the product, looking for and learning from problems, and creating the best possible environment for employees.[9]

Empowerment

"Empowerment" is the term that describes a large part of what the new breed of managers actually do. *Empowerment is defined as granting employees the autonomy to assume more responsibility within an organization and strengthening their sense of effectiveness.* We have known for many years that certain types of charismatic leaders, like John F. Kennedy, empower their followers by making them feel stronger and more capable of taking action.[10] The term "empowerment," however, has become popular only within the last ten years and refers to an enabling process that increases the intrinsic task motivation for employees[11] and increases their self-efficacy, which is the individual's belief that he or she is capable of performing a task.[12] Managers empower employees by influencing these four factors:[13]

1. *Meaning* – Employees see their jobs as having meaning when they care about their work and perceive it as important and meaningful.
2. *Competence* – Employees are capable of performing all the work that must be done.
3. *Self-Determination* – Employees have significant autonomy, considerable freedom and independence, and are able to use personal initiative in carrying out their work.
4. *Impact* – Impact refers to feeling that one has some control and influence over what happens in one's department.

Empowerment is predicated upon the beliefs reflected in both Theory Y (Chapter 2) and Hackman's Job Characteristics model (Chapter 21), that people want to make a contribution and desire greater autonomy and meaning at work. Herbert Simon, Nobel Laureate, states that many people are motivated by a sense of altruism that translates into organizational commitment. However, not everyone shares these values or can break the old habits of the command-and-control model. Thus, it comes as no surprise that some employees and managers have found the transition to an "empowered" workplace exceedingly difficult. Of the managers who have made the shift, some did so because empowerment fits their own value system; others use empowerment simply because it is a more effective management technique.[14]

In addition to personal values and habits, another barrier to empowerment can be organizational cultures with norms that work against employee involvement. For example, at one university new faculty members are cautioned by senior faculty not to jeopardize their chances for tenure by making suggestions to the administration or getting involved in controversial topics. They are also told stories about professors who have been fired in the past for disagreeing with the administration on topics that fell within the professors' area of expertise. This perception of a closed-minded administration may no longer be true, but faculty members are still fearful of rocking the boat. Even when they believe the administration is making a serious mistake, they muzzle themselves and narrow their focus to their individual job or department. "I'll just teach my classes and let them stew in their own juices." Thus, the norms of silence and centralized decision making are perpetuated in the organizational culture. Faculty perceive themselves as a relatively powerless group. They complain about the administration, but they are not proactive about making improvements. This is an example of *learned helplessness*, which is, in many ways, the exact opposite of empowerment.

Contrast this example with the five characteristics of high performance-high commitment work cultures: delegation, teamwork across boundaries, empowerment, integration of people and technology, and a shared sense of purpose.[15] Employees who have the most relevant information or the most appropriate work skills are delegated the responsibility for completing the work. Integrating people with technology signifies that employees control the technology, rather than being controlled by it. A shared sense of purpose implies a common vision of the organization's purpose and the methods for accomplishing this purpose.

When organizations introduce the idea of an empowered work force, they are changing the psychological contract that exists between management and employees. New behavior and expectations are required of both groups, but not everyone can adapt to these changes. Middle managers, who feel the pinch most personally in change efforts, sometimes find it difficult to relinquish their traditional ways of dealing with subordinates and carve out a new role for themselves. One tactic that has been used to prevent managers from micro-managing subordinates is to give them more direct reports than one person could ever supervise. Eventually, they realize that the only way to survive is to allow subordinates and teams greater autonomy.

Among the suggested strategies for empowering one's staff are:[16]

1. Solicit input from employees on a regular basis.

2. Ask for their help in solving problems.

3. Teach employees to make sound decisions by allowing them to gain experience with carefully selected decisions. As their judgement improves, let them make progressively more complex decisions.

4. Remove any bureaucratic obstacles that stop employees from taking initiative and responsibility. In many organizations, people feel powerless to fix things because both procedures and management practices promote the status quo and get in the way of positive changes.

5. Rather than supplying answers to employees, ask questions that encourage them to come up with answers. "What would you do if you had to make this decision?" "What factors do we need to consider here?"

6. Provide workers with all the information they need to make decisions about the business.

7. Let people know it's up to them to do whatever is necessary to serve the customer, without having to request permission.

8. Provide a positive emotional atmosphere that promotes self esteem and self-development.

9. Reward achievements in visible and personal ways.

10. Serve as a role model for employees.

11. Coach people so they can successfully master tasks.

One of the common concerns supervisors and managers have about employee empowerment is whether it means relinquishing all their own authority. When managers share power with subordinates, their own power does not diminish as it would if power were a zero sum commodity. When power is shared, it expands. Managers who practice empowerment are still responsible for setting the direction for their subordinates, or for seeing that a direction is set in a participative fashion. Furthermore, wise managers do not simply turn over power to subordinates without first ensuring that they have the necessary information and skills to make wise decisions. Managers who empower their employees still have to:

- know what is going on
- set or communicate the direction for the department or unit
- make decisions subordinates cannot make
- ensure that people are on course
- offer a guiding hand and open doors to clear the way

- make sure that employees have the necessary skills to assume greater autonomy and responsibility
- ensure that employees have the necessary information to make good decisions
- assess performance[17]

Mary Parker Follett[18] first proposed the idea of depersonalizing authority and adopting the law of the situation in which "the situation is the boss." She observed that workers react to receiving orders by becoming more passive and taking less and less responsibility. However, by examining the situation, it becomes evident to almost everyone, regardless of their hierarchical position, what needs to be done, In this way, the situation becomes the boss. It is much easier to examine situations when employees have access to both information and data-analysis skills. When employees and managers engage in a "data-based dialogue," the inherent tensions of a superior-subordinate relationship are reduced.[19]

Coaching

Empowerment implies a strong commitment to employee development. Managers see themselves as resource people who are responsible for developing their subordinates. One of the primary skills managers need for this task is coaching. *Coaching is defined as a conversation that follows a predictable process and leads to superior performance, commitment to sustained improvement, and positive relationships.* [20] Coaching generally takes place in a one-on-one conversation. Although it is usually performed by managers with subordinates, coaching can also be initiated by skilled coworkers or subordinates (e.g., the case of the young manager who is taught the ropes by an older subordinate).

There are four types of coaching. [21]

1. *Tutoring*. Tutoring is used to teach employees necessary job skills they have not yet learned. For example, when employees do not know how to run a team meeting, they must be taught the specific steps in the process, and given both practice and feedback.

2. *Counseling*. In counseling sessions, the purpose is to help employees gain personal insight into their feelings and behavior. Counseling is appropriate for employees with attitude problems they themselves do not recognize. The focus in counseling is on problem recognition and solution.

3. *Mentoring*. In mentoring sessions, the objective is to help employees gain a better understanding of the organization, its goals, and advancement criteria. This approach is used, for example, when employees ask why another employee has been promoted and they have not. In such sessions, managers try to make employees more politically savvy and warn them of possible traps. They also help employees live up to their full potential and encourage them to be more proactive in managing their careers.

4. *Confronting*. The purpose of confronting is to improve employee performance. Confronting is used, for example, with an employee who is consistently late to work. Performance standards are clarified, the discrepancy between the standard and the employee's performance is pointed out, the cause of the discrepancy is identified, and both parties problem-solve to find a solution.

STEPS IN THE COACHING PROCESS

The tutoring process for teaching new skills consists of the following steps.[22]

1. Explain the purpose and importance of what you are trying to teach.
2. Explain the process to be used.
3. Demonstrate how it is done.
4. Observe while the person practices the process.
5. Provide immediate and specific feedback (coach again or reinforce success).
6. Express confidence in the person's ability to be successful.
7. Agree on follow-up actions.

The correct approach to take with employees who are not performing well depends upon the cause. Unsatisfactory performance often has multiple causes, some of which lie within the control of the employee and some that do not. Fournies suggested that managers use the following guidelines to determine what action they should take. [23] When employees are unaware that their performance is unsatisfactory, the manager (or team) provides feedback. When poor performance occurs because employees are not really sure what is expected of them at work, the manager (or team) provides clear expectations. When employee performance is hampered by obstacles that are beyond their control, the manager removes the obstacles. When the employee simply does not know how to do a task, the manager provides training. The manager should also make sure that good performance is followed by positive, rather than negative consequences, and that poor performance is not rewarded by positive consequences. If all these steps have been taken to ensure good performance, and the employee is still not able or willing to perform well, it is time for the type of confrontation coaching shown in the vignette. Although there are differences in counseling, mentoring, and confronting sessions,[24] the following steps can be used as a general guideline for all three.

Prior to the coaching session:
- Does the supervisor/manager have all the facts about the situation?
- What type of coaching does the situation require?
- How might the employee react and feel about the discussion?
- Think about the best way to present what you want to say to the employee.

During the session:
- Discuss the purpose of the session.
- Try to make the employee comfortable.
- Establish a non-defensive climate characterized by open communication and trust.
- Praise the employee for the positive aspects of their performance.
- Mutually define the problem (performance or attitude).
- Mutually determine the causes. Do not interpret or psychoanalyze the employee's behavior; instead, ask questions, "What's causing the lack of motivation you describe?"
- Help the employee establish an action plan that includes specific goals and dates.
- Make sure the employee clearly understands what is expected of him or her.
- Summarize what has been agreed upon in the session.
- Affirm your confidence in the employee's ability to make needed changes based upon his or her strengths or past history.

After the session:
- Follow up to see how the employee is progressing.
- Modify the action plan if necessary.

Procedure for Group Meeting:
The Enterprise Spacecraft Game

The Enterprise Game is designed to simulate the dynamics that occur between self-directed work teams and facilitative management teams. During the exercise, the group will divide into two groups—the Enterprise Teams, which manufacture spacecraft, and the Facilitator Teams, teams of managers whose role is to increase effectiveness and empower the work teams. Both work for a company that is implementing a continuous improvement approach. The exercise focuses upon a visit by the Facilitator Teams to the Enterprise production facility. The teams have agreed that the Facilitator Team should visit Enterprise, observe their production process, and help Enterprise improve their operations by implementing new production systems.

STEP 1. Choose a game coordinator. The group should first choose someone to act as game coordinator. This person will act as a leader and timekeeper for the exercise, the government inspector and buyer of Enterprise's products, and the postgame discussion leader. (The instructor often plays this role.)

STEP 2. Form the Enterprise and Facilitator Teams. The group should divide itself approximately in half to form two corporations. (If there are more than 20 people in the total group, it will be easier if the group subdivides so that the game is run in two parallel sections with two game coordinators, two Facilitator Teams, and so on.) The game coordinator should flip a coin to determine which group is the Facilitator Team and which is the Enterprise Team.

STEP 3. Go over the timetable and game procedure shown in Table 17-1. The game coordinator may want to copy this summary on a blackboard so that the procedure is visible to everyone.

STEP 4. Each team reads their instructions on the following page.

STEP 5. Instructions for the game coordinator. While the two corporations are preparing for the first production period, you should read the instructions for the entire exercise. Your most important tasks are to
   a. Keep to the time schedule described in Table 17-1.
   b. Sell materials to Enterprise Teams during production periods 1 and 2.
   c. Inspect and buy acceptable spacecraft materials from Enterprise Teams during production periods 1 and 2 (see quality criteria on blueprints).
   d. Ask the Enterprise Teams to post the number of material sets bought and sold and their profit and loss for each round on the blackboard.
   e. Have the teams average their numerical responses on the scale that analyzes the facilitation process.
   f. Record the two teams averages for each pair of facilitator-Enterprise Teams on the blackboard and lead the discussion which follows.

10. Make a fold (up direction) about 1 inch from the bottom along OP.

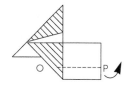

It should now look like this:

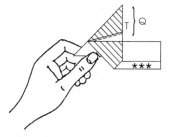

Read all of step 11 and then go back and do it part by part.

11. a. Hold spaceship in hand.

   b. Open up Q with finger and flatten the lined area (/ / / / /) by bringing central point R toward the main body of the plane.

   c. Fold along ST to keep it flat.

   d. Make wings level so that plane can fly.

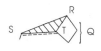

Finished plane should look like this:

side view

top view

front view

QUALITY CRITERIA

1. Printed lines should be in the position shown on the diagram.
2. The wingtip must be turned up enough to let the stars show completely.
3. The "pilot's cabin" (step 11) must be puffed out noticeably. Skinny cabins crowd the astronauts. Cabin folds must be creased on printed lines wherever possible.
4. The two wings must be even with each other (i.e., the entire wing deck should be at the same level).
5. The nose of the spaceship should be pointed.

The game coordinator will buy only those spacecraft that meet these quality control points.

Follow-Up

Effective coaching utilizes the communication skills we have studied in previous chapters—active listening, empathy, creating a non-defensive climate, response styles, assertive communication, the use of I-statements, and understanding the role of perception in communication. Communication has to be supportive so that the employee can absorb the message.

Another crucial coaching communication skill that we have not yet studied is providing effective feedback. Feedback helps individuals to keep behavior "on target" and thus better achieve their goals. Achievement-oriented people, in particular, want and need frequent and specific feedback to continue performing at optimal levels. The purpose of feedback is to provide people with information that they may or may not choose to utilize. In a work setting there may well be consequences for not utilizing the information, but feedback offered in the spirit of helpful data is less likely to arouse defensiveness. Before offering feedback, check with others to make sure your perceptions are valid and unbiased. Effective feedback has the following characteristics:

1. Effective feedback is descriptive as opposed to evaluative. For example, to tell a person "When you interrupt and don't let me finish my statements (description), it makes me feel as if you don't value my ideas (personal reactions)" it has a very different impact from the evaluative statement, "Boy, you sure are a power-hungry s.o.b." The latter is bound to cause a defensive reaction. While the former may not be totally pleasant, it is nonetheless easier to hear because it is more descriptive than evaluative.
2. Effective feedback is specific rather than general. To be told that one is "not per forming well" will not be as useful as being told "your last three shipments were sent without the proper paperwork." Vague feedback based on fuzzy impressions is generally very hard to translate into the specific developmental goals that are so important to improvement.
3. Effective feedback is directed toward behavior that the receiver can control. To be told that "short people don't get ahead very fast in this company" is frustrating (as well as of questionable legality!)

4. To the extent possible, it is better for feedback to be solicited rather than imposed. If people can formulate the questions they feel a need to explore, their motivation to listen carefully is significantly enhanced. While this is an "ideal" to be reached, there are still times when you, as a manager, will see a need to give an employee some unsolicited feedback. Even under these circumstance, you can share the control and provide the employee with an opportunity to participate by saying, for example, "I've noticed a few things I think it would be good for us to talk about. Is now a good time to talk? If not, when would be a good time for you?"

5. As seen in the preceding example, effective feedback is well timed. Feedback must be offered when the receiver can best accept it. For example, the end of a hectic day or when an employee is worried about a family-related problem are not the most propitious times to give feedback.

6. Feedback should be immediate and continual rather than delayed and sporadic. It does the receiver little good to find out that six months ago he or she did something "wrong." Feedback is generally most effective at the earliest opportunity after the behavior in question has occurred.

7. Good feedback suggests rather than prescribes avenues for improvement. If we demand that other people change their behavior in a certain way, we fall into the control-oriented communication that provokes a defensive reaction [25] and disempowers people. Furthermore, we lose sight of the crucial role of self-determination in behavioral change. This means that people must decide for themselves what they want to do and take responsibility for their own actions.

8. Effective feedback is intended to help. Feedback is ineffective when the person giving feedback seems driven to do so for his or her own needs (for example, venting one's personal frustration on an employee). Feedback is not punishment, although ineffective feedback may feel that way. It simply provides information that the receiver's behavior is off target.

In summary, the eight rules of thumb for giving effective feedback in a way that increases productive discussion and decreases defensiveness are:

- Descriptive rather than evaluative.
- Specific and data-based rather than general.
- Directed toward controllable behaviors rather than personality traits or characteristics.
- Solicited rather than imposed.
- Close to the event under discussion rather than delayed for several months.
- Occurs when the receiver is most ready to accept it.
- Suggests rather than prescribes avenues for improvements.
- Is intended to help, not punish.

There are also guidelines for receiving feedback. The most important is to take feedback as helpful information that warrants serious consideration. If the feedback is not clear, request more information or examples. If the feedback does not seem accurate, and we know that the perceptions of others may be invalid, get a second opinion by asking others how they perceive your behavior. Feedback is worthless if: 1) we automatically deny its validity; 2) rationalize our behavior; or 3) assume the manager is only telling us this because he or she does not like us or is trying to manipulate us.

POSITIVE REGARD

Coaching and developing employees is a type of helping relationship. Carl Rogers, the famous psychologist, discovered the importance of unconditional positive regard in his own helping relationships.[26] "I feel that the more acceptance and liking I feel toward this individual, the more I will be creating a relationship which he can use. By acceptance I mean a warm regard for him as a person of unconditional self-worth–of value no matter what his condition, or his feelings....This acceptance of each fluctuating aspect of this other person makes it for him a relationship of warmth and safety, and the safety of being liked and prized as a person seems a highly important element in a helping relationship." Positive regard for employees is also one of the competencies of high-performing managers.[27] Assuming that employees mean well, rather than assuming the worst about them, creates a self-fulfilling prophecy when they try to live up to their boss' good opinion.

 # Learning Points

1. Companies that survive and flourish in today's business environment are high-performance companies characterized by cost competiveness, high-quality products and services, innovation, and speed.

2. The command-and-control model is giving way to an involvement-oriented management approach in high performance organizations because committed workers are more productive.

3. In the command-and-control model, managers make decisions, give orders, and make sure they are obeyed.

4. In the involvement-oriented approach, managers develop employee commitment by sharing both power and information, and developing the employee skills needed to plan and control their own work.

5. Empowerment is defined as granting employees the autonomy to assume more responsibility within an organization and strengthening their sense of effectiveness.

6. The four aspects of empowerment are meaning, competence, self-determination, and impact.

7. The characteristics of high performance-high commitment work cultures are delegation, teamwork across boundaries, empowerment, integration of people and technology, and a shared sense of purpose.

8. Empowerment does not imply that managers and supervisors relinquish all their own authority. They are still responsible for setting the direction, knowing what is going on, removing obstacles, ensuring that employees are on course, ensuring that employees have the necessary skills and information, and assessing performance.

9. Coaching is a conversation that follows a predictable process and leads to superior performance, commitment to sustained improvement, and positive relationships.

10. There are four types of coaching: tutoring, counseling, mentoring, and confronting.

11. Effective feedback is objective rather than judgmental, descriptive rather than vague, directed toward controllable behavior, solicited rather than imposed, and well timed. It is immediate rather than delayed, suggests rather than prescribes avenues for improvements, and is intended to help, not punish.

12. Positive regard for others is a characteristic of both effective helper/coaches and high-performing managers.

for Managers

- Some organizations (such as Cadillac) have turned their organizational chart upside down to form an inverted pyramid to communicate that management's primary purpose is to serve the people who serve the customer.
- Federal Express not only has an inverted organizational structure, they reinforce it by having employees fill out yearly Survey/Feedback/Action (SFA) forms on their managers that include items such as:
  - Feel free to tell my manager what I think.
  - My manager let's me know what's expected of me.
  - Favoritism is not a problem in my work group.
  - My manager helps us find ways to do our jobs easier.
  - My manager is willing to listen to my concerns.
  - My manager asks for my ideas about things affecting our work.
  - My manager lets me know when I've done a good job.
  - My manager treats me with respect and dignity.
  - My manager keeps me informed about things I need to know.
  - My manager lets me do my job without interfering.
  - My manager's boss gives us the support we need.
  - Were the concerns identified by my work group during last year's SFA feedback session satisfactorily addressed?
- Upper management is also evaluated on their openness to ideas and suggestions, their fairness, and whether or not they keep employees informed. The survey results affect the managers' bonuses and future with the company. Thus, Federal Express has modified their structure, evaluation system, and rewards to encourage managers to empower employees.
- If turning the organizational chart upside down is too radical a move, companies can flatten it out and give middle managers so many people to supervise that they can no longer micro-manage.[28]
- Encourage subordinates to call meetings.[29]
- Avoid being the source of all wisdom, satisfying though it is to your ego. Instead, use the Socratic method and ask questions that model for employees the thought processes needed to make good decisions.
- Manager-employee relationships can be mutually helpful. Managers model the receiving end of coaching when they themselves are open to feedback and coaching from subordinates.
- Developing employees sometimes means giving up tasks that one enjoys and does very well (at least in your own eyes) and turning it over to someone who will perhaps do a worse job with it until they have mastered it. Or the employee may do it differently, which can also be hard to accept. Letting go of tasks and delegating is an investment that should pay off in the future with competent employees who free up your time to look at the broader picture.
- Many new managers are shocked by the amount of time they must spend counseling or developing employees. It is an important part of the job, but employees with serious personal problems should be referred to professional counselors.
- Active listening is a key part of coaching because people often determine what is bothering them or what decision they want to take by talking things out with another person. In presenting their story to a listener, many people imagine how the listener is reacting and this provides the speaker with another perspective.

Personal Application Assignment

The topic of this assignment is to write about an experience that involved coaching or empowerment, or the lack thereof. Choose an experience that was significAnt to you and about which you are motivated to learn more. Alternatively, you may want to experiment with the skills taught in this unit and write about the outcome.

A. *Concrete Experience*
   1. *Objectively* describe the experience ("who," "what," "when," "where," "how" type information—up to 2 points).

   2. *Subjectively* describe your feelings, perceptions, and thoughts that occurred during (not after) the experience (up to 2 points). Does this section have too much detail? (If so, delete 1 point.)

B. *Reflective Observation*
   1. Look at the experience from different points of view. How many points of view did you include that are relevant (up to 2 points)?
   2. Use these perspectives to add more meaning to the incident (up to 2 points).

C. *Abstract Conceptualization*

1. Relate concepts from the assigned readings and the lecture to the experience (i.e., what theories that you heard in the lecture or read in the *Reader* relate to your understanding of this incident?). Make reference to at least two sources. Use standard referencing format and include the page number to which you are referring. How many sources did you use and how clearly did you explain their theories (up to 4 points)?

2. You can create an original model or theory, but it should not replace course concepts.

D. *Active Experimentation*

1. Write about what you will do in the future that will improve your effectiveness. Use rule of thumb or action resolutions.

2. Are they described specifically, thoroughly, and in detail (up to 4 points)?

E. *Integration, Synthesis, and Writing*

1. Did you write about something personally important to you (up to 1 point)?

2. Was it well written (up to 2 points)?

3. Did you integrate and synthesize the different sections (up to 1 point)?

[1] This list is paraphrased from Philip R. Harris, *High Performance Leadership* (Glenview, IL: Scott, Foresman and Company, 1989) pp. 14-15.

[2] Tom Peters, *Liberation Management* (New York: Alfred A. Knopf, 1992).

[3] Edward E. Lawler III, *The Ultimate Advantage* (San Francisco, CA: Jossey-Bass, 1992) pp. 28-9.

[4] Richard E. Walton, "From Control to Commitment in the Workplace," *Harvard Business Review*, March-April, 1985, pp. 76-84.

[5] Lawler, *Ultimate Advantage*, p. 44.

[6] Lawler, Ibid, p. 41.

[7] Myron Magnet, "The Truth about the American Worker," *Fortune*, May 4, 1992, p. 58 and 64.

[8] Lawler, Ibid, p.29

[9] Warren H. Schmidt and Jerome P. Finnigan, *The Race Without a Finish Line* (San Francisco: Jossey-Bass, 1992), p. 46. Although these authors are writing about managers in TQM programs, which are not synonymous with high-involvement companies, this statement holds true for any manager who has empowered workers.

[10] David C. McClelland, *Power: The Inner Experience* (New York: Irvington, 1975) and Jay A.Conger and Rabindra N. Kanugo, "The Empowerment Process: Integrating Theory and Practice," *Academy of Management Review*, 13, 1988, pp. 471-482.

[11] Kenneth W. Thomas and Betty A. Velthouse, "Cognitive Elements of Empowerment: An Interpretative Model of Intrinsic Task Motivation," *Academy of Management Review*, October 1990, pp. 666-81.

[12] Albert Bandura, "Self-efficacy: Toward a Unifying Theory of Behavioral Change," *Psychological Review,* 84, 1977, pp. 191-215.

[13] Gretchen M. Spreitzer. *"When Organizations Dare: The Dynamics of Individual Empowerment in the Workplace."* Unpublished dissertation, University of Michigan, Ann Arbor, 1992.

[14] See Robert Frey's "Empowerment or Else," *Harvard Business Review*, September-October 1993, pp.80-94, for a vivid description of one manager's experience in empowering his workers.

[15] John J. Sherwood, "Creating Work Cultures with Competitive Advantage," *Organizational Dynamics*, Winter 1988, pp. 5-27.

[16] These suggestions come from a variety of sources including Bandura, *"Self-efficacy;"* and William C. Byham with Jeff Cox, *Zapp! The Lightning of Empowerment* (Pittsburgh, PA: DDI Press, 1989).

[17] Adapted from Byham, *Zapp*, p. 108.

[18] Elliot M. Fox and L. Urwick (eds.). *Dynamic Administration: The Collected Papers of Mary Parker Follett* (New York: Hippocrene Books, 1982).

[19] Asbjorn Osland, *Total Quality Management in Central America: A Case Study in Leadership and Data-Based Dialogue*. Unpublished dissertation, Cleveland, OH: Case Western Reserve University, 1994.

[20] Dennis C. Kinlaw, *Coaching for Commitment* (San Diego, CA: Pfeiffer & Company, 1993), p. 31.

[21] Kinlaw, Ibid.

[22] Byham, *Zapp*, p. 129

[23] Ferdinand Fournies. *Coaching for Improved Work Performance*. (New York: Van Nostrand Reinhold, 1978).

[24] Kinlaw provides more detailed instructions for each type of coaching in *Coaching for Commitment*.

[25] Jack Gibb, "Defensive Communication," *Reader*

[26] Carl Rogers, *On Becoming a Person* (Boston: Houghton Mifflin, 1961) p. 34.

[27] Richard E. Boyatzis, *The Competent Manager: A Model for Effective Performance* (New York: John Wiley, 1982).

[28] Peter Block, *The Empowered Manager* (San Francisco: Jossey-Bass, 1990). pp. 66-71.

[29] Block, Ibid, p. 70.

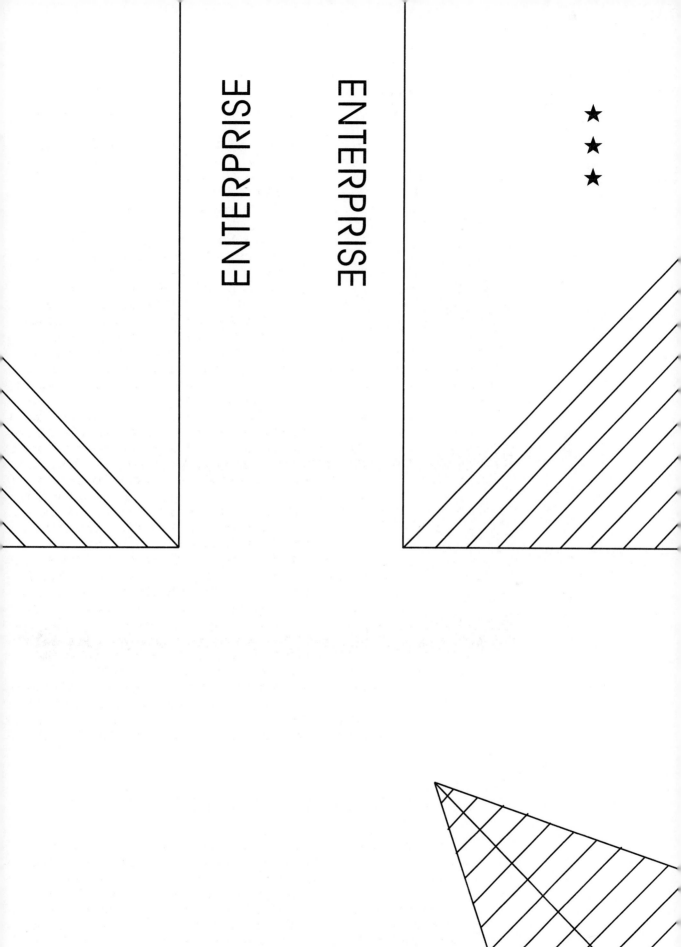

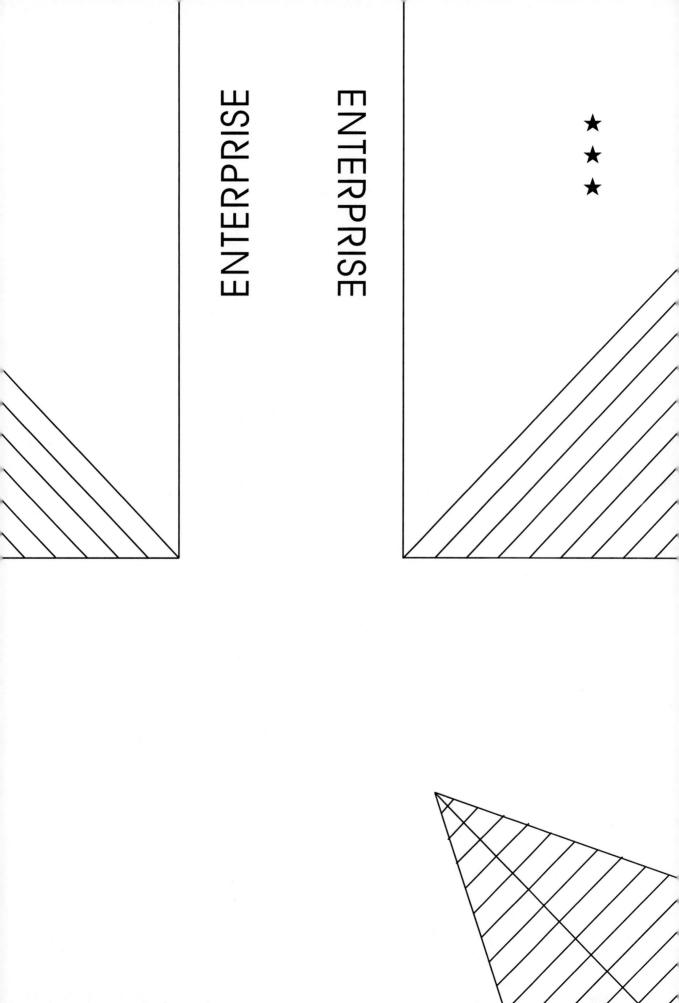

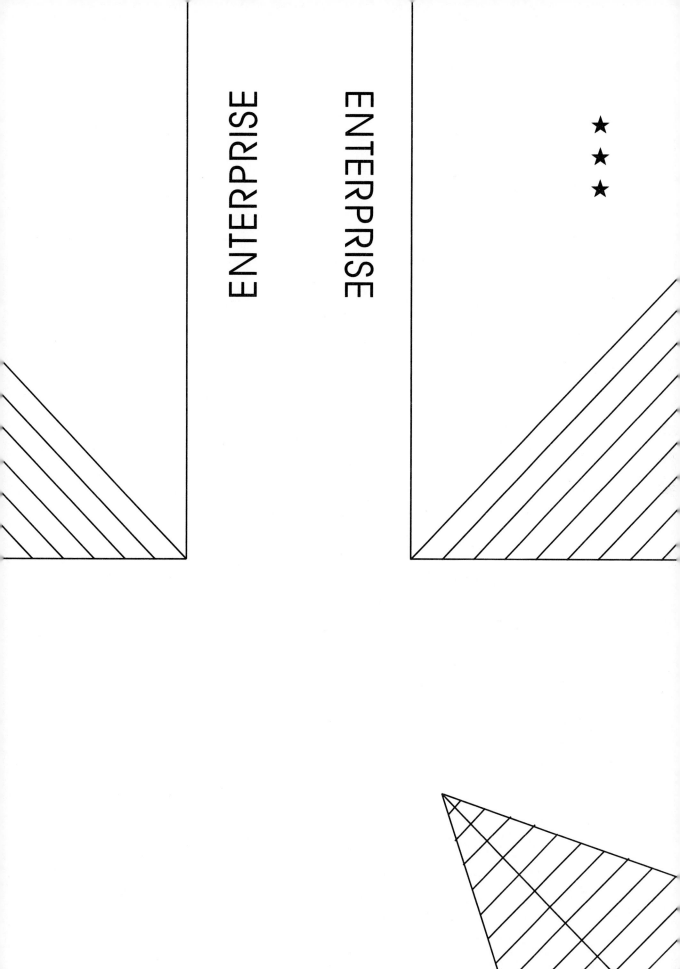

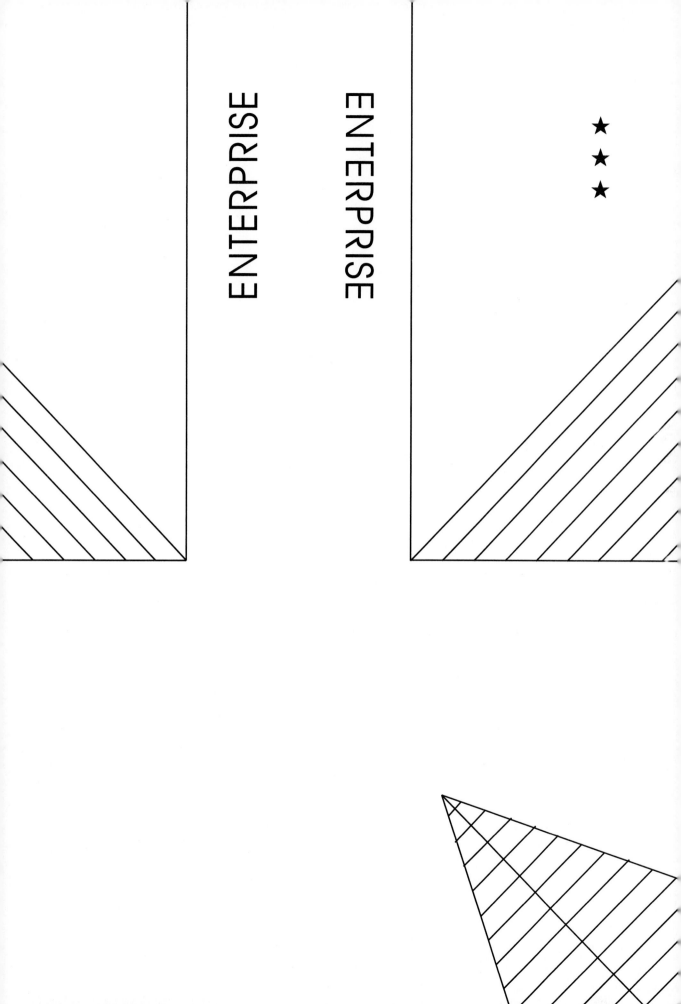

PART 3   LEADERSHIP AND MANAGEMENT

ENTERPRISE

ENTERPRISE

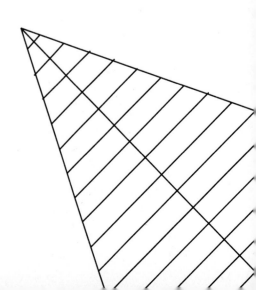
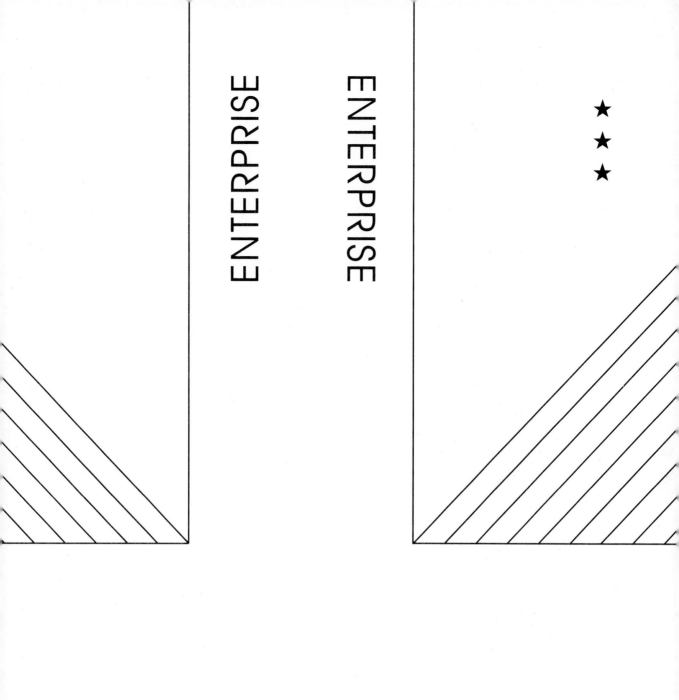

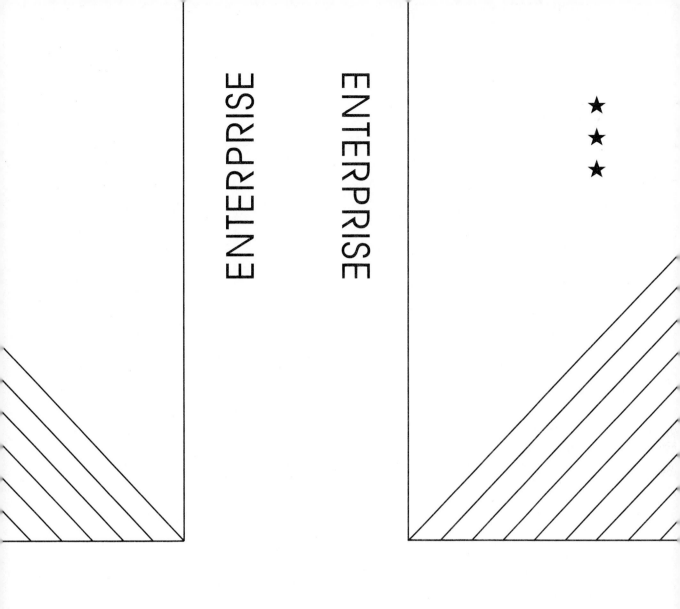

ENTERPRISE

ENTERPRISE

★
★
★

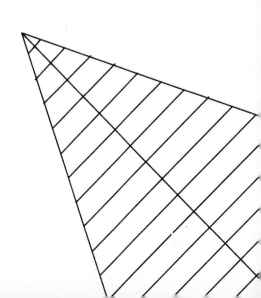

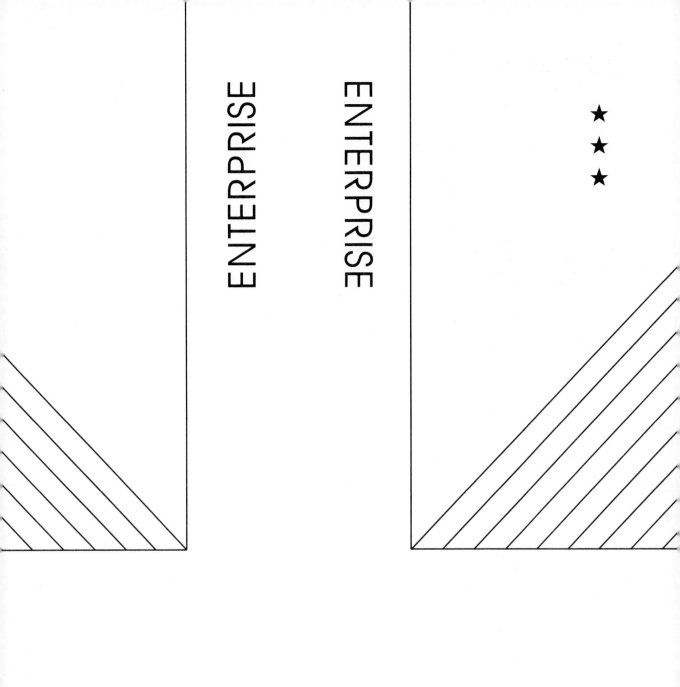

ENTERPRISE

ENTERPRISE

★
★
★

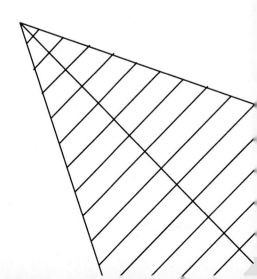

ENTERPRISE

ENTERPRISE

★
★
★

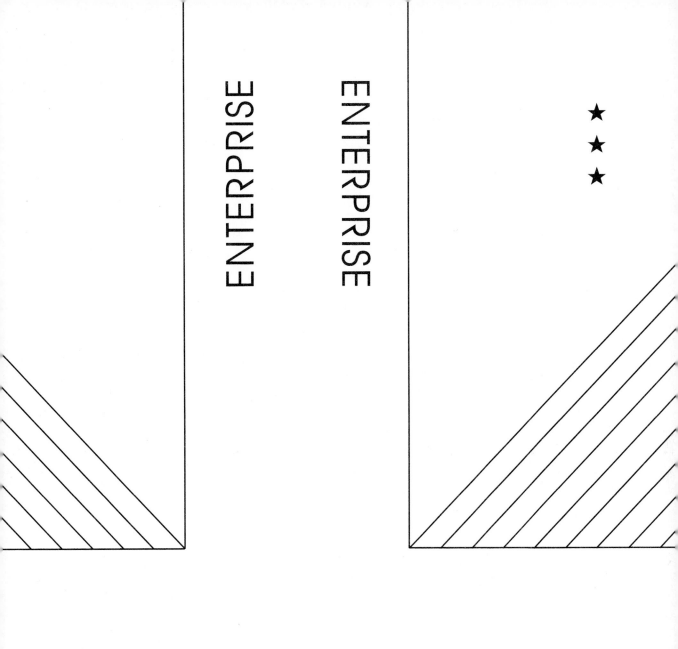

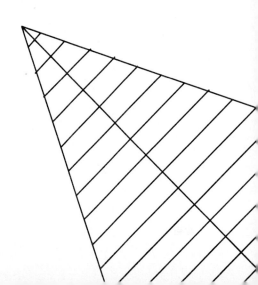

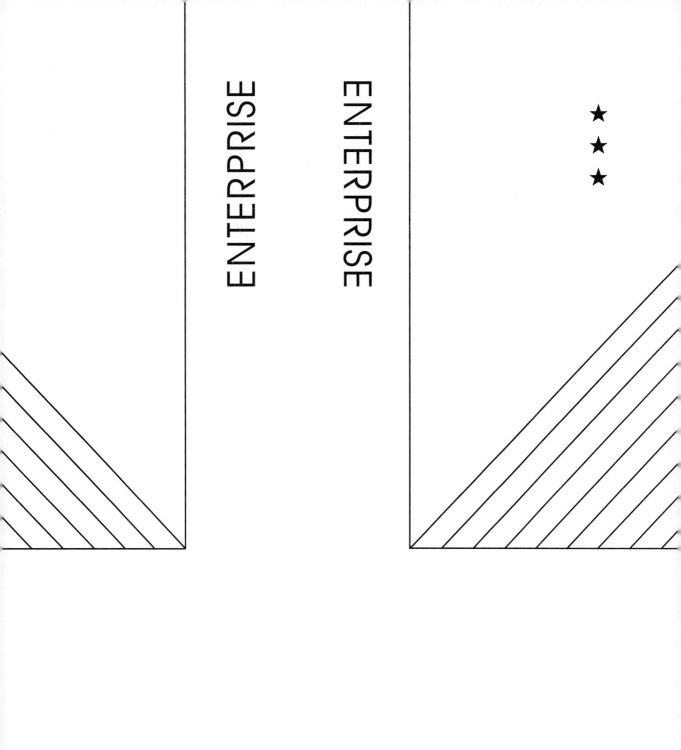

ENTERPRISE

ENTERPRISE

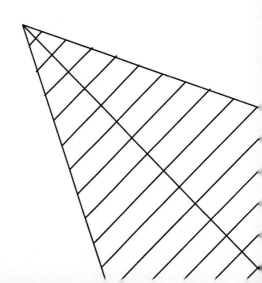

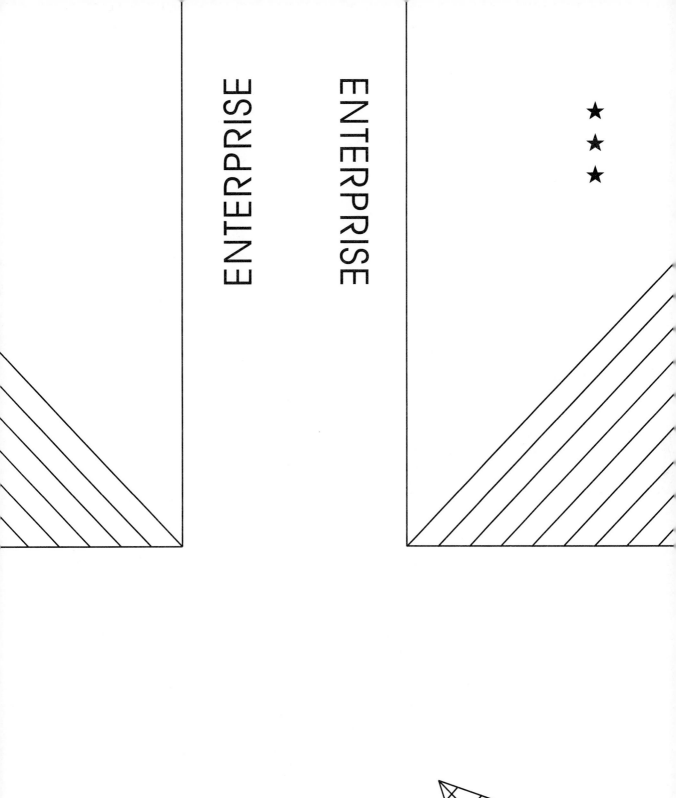

ENTERPRISE

ENTERPRISE

★
★
★

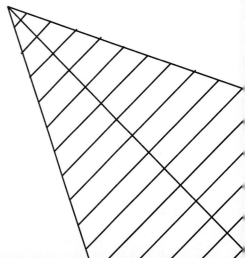

Chapter 18

PERFORMANCE APPRAISAL

OBJECTIVES By the end of this chapter, you should be able to:

A. Explain the importance of performance feedback.

B. Describe the process of performance appraisal.

C. Identify the components of effective appraisals.

D. Demonstrate some of the skills required for a good appraisal.

E. Explain the opposition to appraisal systems.

A Description of Rejection

Ellen Goodman

She was brilliant. Everyone involved in the case agreed about that. She was unattractive. Everyone agreed about that, too. She was overweight, whiny, argumentative, unkempt (the list goes on) sloppy, hypercritical, unpopular.

The life of Charlotte Horowitz, whose dismissal from a Missouri medical school became a Supreme Court case this week, has become painfully public. A description of rejection.

From all reports, she interacted with the world like a fingernail on a blackboard. She was punished for the crime of being socially unacceptable.

Charlotte Horowitz was older than most of the other students when she was admitted to the University of Missouri, Kansas City, Medical School in 1972. She was also brighter, a misfit from New York who won her place despite the admission officer's report that read, "The candidate's personal appearance is against her... ."

By the school's "merit system," she was tops in her medical school class. As her advisor wrote: "Her past record is the best in the school. She has functioned at a high level and has had no problems with a patient at any time." Yet she was dismissed by the dean on the verge of graduation. The grounds were tardiness, bad grooming, and abrasive personal style.

Of course, the case in front of the Supreme Court won't judge those grounds. It will deal with the issue of due process: whether she was given proper notice and a fair hearing; whether universities and professional schools have to extend certain legal rights to their students.

But the theme of this difficult, emotional story is prejudice. The most deeply rooted way in which we pre-judge each other. The sort of discrimination which is universal, almost unrootable. Prejudice toward appearance. Discrimination against what we "see."

The most unattractive children in the classrooms of our youth had their lives and personalities warped by that fact. Their painful experiences of rejection nurtured in them an expectation of rejection. That expectation, like some paranoia, was almost always fulfilled.

It is a mystery why some "unattractive people" wear it in their souls and others don't; why one becomes a Barbra Streisand and another a reject. But often, along the way, some people give up being accepted and become defensively nonconforming. They stop letting themselves care. They become "unkempt, argumentative, abrasive." And the list goes on.

Everyone's self-image is formed in some measure by the way they are seen; the way they see themselves being seen. As their image deteriorates, their personality often shatters along with it. At that point, the rest of us smugly avoid them, stamping them "unacceptable," not because of their "looks" but because of their behavior.

It happens all the time.

There is no law that can protect children from this sort of discrimination. We are all, in that sense, the products as well as the survivors of our childhood. But the cumulative, spiraling effect of appearance on personality is worse for women than for men. If Charlotte Horowitz had been a man, surely her brains would have alleviated her physical attractiveness. As a woman, her unattractiveness was further handicapped by brains.

As Dr. Estelle Ramey, a professor at Georgetown Medical School and former head of the Association of Women In Science said, "If the bad fairy ends up the last one at your crib, you'll be cursed as a brilliant unattractive woman."

But this case isn't a question of the curse, the birth penalty, the "life isn't fair" sort of discrimination. It's a story of a university so "blinded" that its officials felt that they had the right to throw away a life and mind because it was housed in a body that was "overweight, sloppy, and hypercritical."

"What's been lost in all this," says Dr. Ramey, "is the contribution a brilliant human being might have made in a field which needs all the fine minds we have."

You see, Charlotte Horowitz was brilliant. Everyone involved in the case could, at least, see that.

Premeeting Preparation

A. Read "A Description of Rejection."

B. Think back on the best performance appraisal you ever received whether it occurred in a work setting, school, or extracurricular activity. Write down what was good about it.

C. Think about the worst performance appraisal you ever received or gave. What made it so ineffective?

D. Write a list of the conditions you think are necessary for an effective performance appraisal.

E. What were the significant learning points from the readings?

F. Consider your performance in this course:
  1. What have you done so far that has contributed to your own learning and that of your learning group?
  2. What have you contributed to the general atmosphere of the class?
  3. Are there extenuating circumstances that have affected your performance in the course?
  4. What have your weaknesses and strengths been so far?
  5. What would you like to improve in your performance?
  6. How do you plan to do it?

G. Read the Topic Introduction.

Performance appraisals are often one of the least favorite activities of managers. Yet they can be a valuable managerial tool for maintaining and improving performance and reinforcing what's important in an organization. An analogy is sometimes made between performance appraisal systems and seat belts-people believe in them but do not want to use them personally. Without such systems, however, personal decisions about promotions, raises, and terminations might have little objective basis.

Performance appraisal systems attempt to evaluate employees fairly using a standardized model, but because humans operate these systems we cannot guarantee total objectivity. Given what we know about the correlation between feedback and high performance,[1] it is surprising how many organizations do not evaluate employees in a systematic fashion. Even when organizations have systems in place, many managers fail to comply. In such instances employees often interpret skipped or late reviews as an indication that their manger is not concerned about them and does not appreciate their work. It is not uncommon to find organizations in which reviews hold great significance for employees but are perceived as little more than a waste of time by their managers.

Why the difference in opinion about performance reviews? At the organizational level, some appraisal systems are outdated and cumbersome and seem to measure only that which can be qualified. It's difficult for managers to take such systems seriously and see how they have any positive results. On the personal level, some managers resent the time consumed by appraisals and feel uncomfortable sitting in judgement upon another person. McGregor argued that the conventional approach to performance appraisal:

> *unless handled with consummate skill and delicacy, constitutes something dangerously close to a violation of the integrity of the personality. Managers are uncomfortable when they are put in the position of "playing God." The respect we hold for the inherent value of the individual leaves us distressed when we must take responsibility for judging the personal worth of a fellow man. Yet the conventional approach to performance appraisals forces us, not only to make such judgements and to see them acted upon, but also to communicate them to those we have judged. Small wonders we resist!*[2]

Those systems that force managers to compare and rank all their employees goes against the values some hold about the importance of valuing people in their own right and not creating "losers" merely to comply with a bureaucratic requirement . Many people are uncomfortable giving negative feedback to people and fear that doing so may make a bad situation even worse.

In contrast to these reasons why managers tend to avoid appraisals, we know that managers who see appraisals as a useful tool can utilize their human resources more effectively. Research has shown that monitoring and providing feedback on performance is one of the most effective ways to improve performance.[3] Appraisals allow managers the opportunity to give feedback on performance and set goals for future performance which, as we learned earlier, are effective ways to motivate employees.

In addition, performance feedback serves a variety of functions for the employee.[4]

1. Contributing to the development of one's self-concept.
2. Reducing uncertainty about whether their behavior is on track and how it is perceived by others.
3. Signaling which organizational goals are most important in relation to others.
4. Helping individuals to master their environment and feel competent.

An awareness of these functions may help managers to realize that a performance appraisal session means more to employees than just finding out what their salary will be for the next year.

Let's return to McGregor's statement that managers feel uncomfortable when they are put in the position of "playing God." To an extent, this is determined by the attitude the manager has toward appraisal. If the manager's underlying approach is to help the employee develop, his or her feedback is more likely to be effective and well received. The theory-in-use that underlies this approach is one that acknowledges the role of enlightened self-interest. In other words, if employees understand what is required of them and what they need to do or stop doing to be promoted or receive good performance ratings, they will do it. Managers utilizing this approach see their function as presenting employees with objective feedback about their performance and career plans. A less successful managerial approach to appraisal is the judgmental "gotcha," which is more likely to result in defensiveness than in the behavioral changes the manager desires. The performance appraisal activity requires leaders and managers to switch into a coaching role.

While the specific mechanics of implementation will vary across organizations, the "ideal" performance appraisal system is designed to achieve five basic objectives:

1. Provide feedback to subordinates to facilitate their ability to achieve organizational (and personal) goals.
2. Provide management with data to make salary and promotional decisions.
3. Identify needed professional development.
4. Motivate employees to be more effective workers.
5. Comply with equal opportunity regulations and ensure fairness.

Depending on how this process gets implemented, managers often find themselves in a role conflict. On the one hand, they are asked to be helper-coaches in the feedback process; on the other hand, they serve as judges, linking performance assessment to salary and promotion decisions. Some research on the performance appraisal process points strongly to the need to separate these roles.[5] In addition to mastering the coaching skills described in the last chapter, it's important for managers to understand the unique aspects of the performance appraisal process, which are presented in the next section.

PERFORMANCE APPRAISAL PROCESS

Too often managers see appraisals as a once-a-year event. In reality, appraisal is a process that begins long before the appraisal interview and consists of the following steps:

1. Reviewing legal requirements.
2. Translating organizational goals into individual job objectives or requirements.
3. Setting clear expectations for job performance and communicating both expectations and instructions clearly.
4. Providing employees with the job training or coaching that they require to meet the expectations.
5. Supplying adequate supervision, feedback, and coaching throughout the year.
6. Acknowledging employee accomplishments and diagnosing employees' relative strengths and weaknesses and presenting all of these objectively during the appraisal interview.
7. Using the appraisal interview to establish performance goals and a development plan with the employee, which includes an action plan for improved performance or further education and the efficient future use of the employee's abilities.

Framing performance appraisal as a process rather than an annual interview means that appraisal is better integrated with the rest of the organization's functions. For example, if promotions are closely tied to appraisals, managers are more likely to give them the attention they require to have an impact upon performance morale. We know that people generally focus their energies on that which is evaluated. If the leaders measure only tangible factors (such as financial and output figures), the intangibles (like service orientation, ability to get along with coworkers, etc.) are given less importance. The same phenomena can be observed with performance appraisal systems. Organizations that evaluate managers on how well they develop and evaluate their subordinates are more likely to give the appraisal process the attention it requires to be effective.

There are four common responses to appraisals that wise managers seek to avoid:

1. "I never knew that's what the boss expected me to do!"
2. "Why didn't they tell me before they weren't happy with my work?"
3. "I wish I had known all along that they liked my work. I wouldn't have wasted so much time worrying about it or looking for other jobs!"
4. "I got a poor review because my boss doesn't like me."

By clarifying expectations carefully, giving immediate feedback throughout the year, and demonstrating a concern for fairness, managers can avoid some of these reactions. Providing immediate feedback has several advantages. First, it offers an opportunity to improve performance. Second, it gives employees an idea about how their supervisor sees them so that the appraisal does not come as a shock. Third, it can keep the channel of communication open between managers and employees. Often new supervisors see an employee doing something incorrectly but are not sure how to give feedback. Instead, they become more and more angry with the employee and either "dump" the feedback when they can no longer contain themselves or save it for the appraisal interview. This is sometimes referred to as "gunny-sacking." In the meantime, their relationship with the employee usually suffers, and they may have rounded out the employee's character with negative attributions that are inaccurate. The feedback given during the appraisal interview, be it positive or negative, should never come as a total surprise to employees.

The fairness issue with appraisals relates to the necessity for managers to know themselves and their personal tendencies. The research on similarity and attraction indicates that people prefer those who are similar to themselves. They also tend to give higher ratings to subordinates who are similar to them.[6] The result can be what Moore termed a "bureaucratic kinship system" based upon "homosexual reproduction," in which men with the power to hire and promote, reproduce themselves.[7] It is not uncommon to look around a table of senior managers and discover that they resemble one another, either physically or socially. Thus, it is easy for managers to perceive an employee they like more positively than the person that really deserves. The opposite can occur with employees that managers either dislike or perceive as different than themselves. This is what occurred in the opening vignette, "A Description of Rejection," in which a medical student was not judged upon her outstanding test scores and patient care, but upon her "differentness," which was apparently unacceptable.

When certain appraisal conditions are met, the potential sources of bias such as age, race, sex, and being different are less likely to have a negative effect on performance appraisals. These conditions are:

1. when employees make their work visible to appraiser;

2. when appraisers and appraisees together clarify objectives and task responsibilities; and

3. when the appraiser uses the behaviorally based appraisal scales,[8] described later in the chapter.

Attributions theory maintains that we make attributions about the causes of behavior of both others and ourselves to understand what we see occurring.[9] We guess or infer the causes of people's behavior and base our reactions to their behaviors on these inferences rather than on the way they really behave. A practical example of attribution theory might be the 'golden boys or girls" who surface, to the puzzlement of their peers, in some organizations. While such people usually possess a certain degree of talent, they are seldom as outstanding as their superiors apparently need to believe.

Perhaps this is explained by the finding that managers are more likely to attribute excellent performance to internal causes (effort, ability) in the case of people who are members of their "in group" than if they are members of their outgroup.[10] Attributions, like perceptions, sometimes have more to do with the observer than with the person being observed. Appraisals are yet another instance when managers have to step back and ensure that their decisions and evaluations are not overly biased, either positively or negatively, by their personal values and preferences. If you recall, the chapter on Interpersonal Perception and Attribution contains examples of perceptual biases that can affect performance evaluation (central tendency, projection, halo effect, etc.).

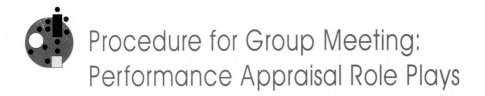

Procedure for Group Meeting:
Performance Appraisal Role Plays

CLASS PERFORMANCE APPRAISALS

(Time allotted: 1 to 1 1/2 Hours)

This exercise provides you with an opportunity to practice the "consummate skill and delicacy" required in a performance appraisal. The class should divide into four-person teams. The exercise stimulates a performance appraisal interview between two team members who will take on the roles of supervisor and employee, while the other two members act as observers. Roles will be rotated so each person has a chance to perform every role. The performance to be evaluated is performance in this course. Class participants prepared for the Employee role by doing the Premeeting Preparation.

STEP 1.   Decide whom each person will evaluate so that everyone has an opportunity to both evaluate and be evaluated once in the four rounds of the exercise.

STEP 2.   Take 10 minutes to plan the appraisal interview for the person you will evaluate.
Use the following questions to help you prepare for the supervisor role.

a. What has the employee done so far that has contributed to his or her own learning and that of your learning group?

b. What has the employee contributed to the general atmosphere of the class?

c. Are there any extenuating circumstances that have affected the employee's performance in the course?

d. Is there anything you are doing that has hindered the employee's performance in the class? What could you do to help the employee improve his or her performance? Is there anything that you could suggest that might utilize the employee's talents better in the classroom or learning group?

e. What are the employee's weaknesses and strengths so far?

f. Choose at least one strength and one weakness that you have observed in the employee's performance in class to discuss during the 5-minute interview. Base your choice on which behaviors could make a significant difference if they were to be changed. Write down how you could phrase the employee's weak point to him or her in case it's not brought out in his or her self-evaluation.

STEP 3. Read the Performance Appraisal Interview Guidelines below.[11]

STEP 4. The supervisors should conduct a 5-minute performance appraisal interview with the employee while the two other observers watch and fill out the Observers' Worksheet on page 485.

STEP 5. After each interview all four participants should talk about how it went and what, if anything, could have been done differently.

STEP 6. Perform the interviews with the other three dyads and critique them.

STEP 7. Class debriefing session:

a. What did you learn about performance appraisal interviews from this exercise?

b. What did you learn about yourself in this process?

c. Will the appraisal affect your future performance in this course? Why?

d. What connections can you make between this exercise and the readings?

PERFORMANCE APPRAISAL INTERVIEW GUIDELINES

Prior to the interview

1. Fix a time and date for the interview that allows the employee enough time to prepare the self-appraisal.
2. Ask the employee to prepare the self-appraisal and provide an outline for doing so.
3. Don't postpone the interview or come late to it. Employees interpret these actions as a lack of interest in them and the appraisal process. To do any good, appraisals have to be taken seriously by managers.
4. Choose a private location where you will not be interrupted.
5. Set aside enough time (1-2 hours) so that you will have time to complete your discussion.
6. Gather all the materials and relevant information about the employee's performance. Some managers also give copies of this information to the employee.
7. Choose which parts of the employee's performance should be included in the interview. Decide how to phrase these points.

During the interview

8. Explain the format and purpose of the performance appraisal interview:
   a. To discover the employee's opinions regarding their performance, problems, motivations, and career goals.
   b. To provide your appraisal of the employee's performance.
   c. To problem solve together about performance.
   d. To plan for the next period.
9. Ask the employee to present their self-appraisal.
10. Respond to the employee's self-appraisal and convey feedback. First, tell the employee the parts of the self-appraisal with which you agree and then identify parts with which you disagree. Next, provide other feedback that would impact performance. In doing this,
    a. Be appreciative of the person's accomplishments.
    b. Support the person even when you are criticizing his or her behavior.
    c. Avoid defensiveness (on both your parts).
    d. Encourage participation.
11. Ask if there are any conditions or problems that have been hindering the employee's work.
12. Problem solve with the employee regarding what both of you could do to improve the employee's performance.
13. Together set objectives and design a plan for the next period.
14. Discuss the employee's long-term career goals and the training and experience needed to reach them.

After the interview

15. Fill out the performance appraisal form *after* the interview so the employee sees that his or her input was included.
16. Follow up on training and coaching needs identified in the interview.

Observers' Worksheet

1. Did the supervisor explain the purpose of the appraisal interview?

2. Did the supervisor give the employee sufficient time to present his or her self-appraisal?

3. Did the supervisor do a good job of presenting his or her feedback?

4. Did the supervisor use active listening, or did he or she do most of the talking?

5. Did the supervisor create a nondefensive climate and refrain from becoming defensive himself or herself?

6. Did the supervisor take a problem-solving approach, or did he or she spend too much time giving advice or orders to the employee?

7. Did the supervisor jointly set goals and an action plan for the future with the employee?

8. Other comments:

Follow-Up

Doing appraisal interviews may be uncomfortable in the beginning, but it is a skill that can be mastered with practice. The opening vignette in Chapter 17 is an example of a successful performance appraisal process with a problem employee. Managers who use performance appraisals well can utilize their human resources more fully. It is a mechanism for increasing the communication and dialogue so essential to effectiveness.

One of the truisms that is repeatedly mentioned when we discuss this topic is that the appraisal instrument itself is only as good as the people who use it. Therefore, it is important that supervisors be trained in appraisal techniques.

There are different ways to measure performance; some of the more common forms are described below. Early appraisal instruments often focused upon employee *traits* (diligence, appearance, initiative). Compared with other forms of appraisal, this approach has proved to be less effective and less likely to stand up in a court of law. Trait measures are often vague and lead managers into a murky ethical quagmire–what right do managers have to ask employees to change their personality? The answer is no. However, managers do have the right to demand performance; more effective appraisal systems measure performance outcomes.

Another type of instrument measures *results* or outcomes. MBO programs (management by objectives) is an example of this type of system. Under this system, supervisors validate whether employee goals were completed satisfactorily and on time. While this type of appraisal system has the advantages of clarifying goals and often motivates employees, it has been subjected to many criticisms. For example, results-oriented systems usually focus only on factors that can be easily quantified, they encourage a "results at all costs" mentality that may work against other company values, they fail to take into consideration factors that may be outside the person's control, and they fail to tell the employee how to improve performance.[12]

Other systems measure *behavioral* criteria (e.g.,"distributes overtime equally," "explains job requirements to new employees in a clear manner"). Behaviorally Anchored Rating scales (BARS) describe the specific behavior that managers observe in subordinates in an effort to clarify expectations for employees and make the instrument as objective as possible. Each point on a continuum is a different behavior rather than the Likert scale numbers (Low 1 to 5 High) used to measure traits. Instruments that utilize some form of behavioral criteria lend themselves more to coaching and developing employees because they focus upon specific behaviors.

Appraisals can be made by any combination of the following appraisers: supervisors or managers, peers, subordinates, customers, and employees themselves. Peer reviews are becoming more common in companies that are moving to a team approach. They have to make sure their appraisal systems do in fact reward teamwork.

CRITICISM OF PERFORMANCE APPRAISAL SYSTEMS

New ways of doing business and managing people require appraisal systems that fit and complement new organizational goals. Two practices have received a good deal of criticism because they sometimes make good employees feel like losers. Forced ranking systems (every employee in a unit is compared to the others and ranked accordingly) and forced distribution in performance categories (e.g., only 20% can be superior performers, 30-40% good performers, etc.) encourage competition, require difficult judgement calls that may or may not be accurate, and can demotivate the employees who don't come out on top. Eastman Chemical Company, winner of the 1993 Malcolm Baldrige National Quality Award, decided that its old appraisal system no longer fit an organizational culture that emphasized teamwork and more open and trustworthy communications. Therefore, a team designed a system that responded to these employee suggestions: eliminate forced distributions, eliminate performance categories, obtain performance input from sources other than the supervisor, enhance coaching and development, minimize individual performance and teamwork conflicts, identify only extremes in performance (the superstars and the below-average employees), and separate the systems for handling selection (promotion, transfer, and layoffs), compensation and coaching. The design team concluded that self esteem is critical to motivation and that employees like to believe, not only that they are above average performers, but that they are growing and improving from year to year.[13]

Deming, the Total Quality guru, was very opposed to performance appraisals and referred to them as one of the seven deadly diseases plaguing American management. He and his disciples[14] criticize appraisal systems for the following reasons. Appraisals usually lack objectivity and attribute variations in performance to employees rather than crucial factors that are outside their control. Appraisals encourage an individual focus rather than a team orientation. When appraisals are based upon measurable goals, they promote both short-sightedness and a short-term focus. Furthermore, employees come to see the boss as their "customer," rather than the real customer (the next person in the process, be they external or internal). When the main goal of employees is to gain the approval of their superior, fear, rivalry and politics can result. Deming criticized merit rewards for rewarding people for doing well "in the system" rather than rewarding attempts to improve the system.

So how do we measure performance in a total quality program? TQM writers suggest that outstanding performers should receive recognition and poor performers should be coached. Groups should gather continuous data on their own performance and should receive coaching whenever necessary. Companies should base compensation on market rate, seniority or the company's prosperity. However, U.S. companies that are switching over to total quality programs have been slow to relinquish their performance appraisal systems.

Deming's opposition to performance appraisal may stem from his exposure to the Japanese system which is very different from the U.S. approach. Japanese reviews tend to be informal, ad hoc, and based upon continuous feedback. Their objective is to find out why the employee's performance is not in harmony with that of the group. In Arab cultures, appraisals are also generally informal and held on an ad hoc basis. Their purpose is to set employees on track or reprimand them for bad performance.[15] We cannot assume that an appraisal system that functions well in one culture (or one company) can be easily transferred to another.

Learning Points

1. Performance appraisals are used to improve performance and motivate employees.

2. Feedback serves the following functions for employees:

   a. Helps to form their self-concept.

   b. Reduces uncertainty about whether their behavior is on track.

   c. Signals which organizational goals are most important.

   d. Helps them to master their environment and feel competent.

3. The attitude managers bring to performance appraisal determines the effectiveness of that appraisal. Managers who are sincerely trying to develop their employees and provide them with objective feedback are more successful than those who take a judgmental approach.

4. Performance appraisal requires that managers take on the role of coaches.

5. The "ideal" performance appraisal system is designed to achieve four basic objectives:

   a. Provide feedback to employees to facilitate their ability to achieve organizational and personal goals.

   b. Provide management with data to make salary and promotional decisions.

   c. Identify areas for improvement to facilitate employee career development.

   d. Motivate employees to be more effective workers.

6. Performance appraisal is a process that begins with translating organizational goals into clear expectations for each individual, training people to do their jobs, providing effective supervision and coaching, determining strengths and weaknesses, and developing plans for the employee. It is not a once-a-year event but an ongoing activity.

7. Providing immediate feedback gives the employee an opportunity to improve, ensures that the appraisal is not a surprise, and keeps the employee-manager channel of communication open. Saving up negative feedback and "dumping" can cause a defensive reaction.

8. Fairness is always a matter of concern with appraisals, because people tend to rate those who are similar to themselves more highly than those who are different.

9. Attributions or inferences about why people behave the way they do can also bias the appraisal process.

10. Appraisal instruments measure either traits, results, or behavioral criteria.

11. Total Quality experts suggest that companies stop doing performance appraisals and focus more on continuous feedback and coaching.

patterned activities of production are the transformation of matter/energy, and the finished product is the output. Maintaining the system requires continued inputs, which in social systems depend in turn on the product or output. Thus, in a successful system, the outputs furnish new matter/energy for the initiation of a new cycle. The auto manufacturer sells the firm's products and by doing so obtains the means of securing new raw materials, compensating the labor force, and refining production technology. This assures the continuation and growth of the organization. In addition, systems require an information return in the form of negative feedback, which allows the system to correct deviations from its goals. For the manufacturer this information takes the form of sales figures, return of poor-quality products, return of investment, and so on.

With this overview of open systems theory, let us now examine the basic components of an open system (see Figure 19-1).

1. *Definition of system.* First, we must understand what is meant by the concept "system." Basically, a system is a set of units or elements actively interrelated and operating in a regular fashion as a total entity. The importance of this definition is that it focuses on processes of relationship and interdependence among structural components rather than on their constant attributes.

2. *Closed versus open systems.* Theoretically, a closed system has totally impermeable boundaries and receives no matter/energy or information from the environment and exports no matter/energy or information to the environment. No such systems exist in nature. Thus, systems are only relatively open or closed, depending on the extent of a continuing flow of matter/energy and information between the system and the environment.

3. *Inputs.* Inputs in organizational systems are matter/energy in the form of raw materials, human labor, power, and so on and information in the form of data about the environment, knowledge of production techniques, and so on. Organizational systems have input subsystems to cope with the input process (e.g., personnel departments to hire and train workers, supply departments for production materials, and market research groups for analyzing market data).

Figure 19-1   Components of an Open System

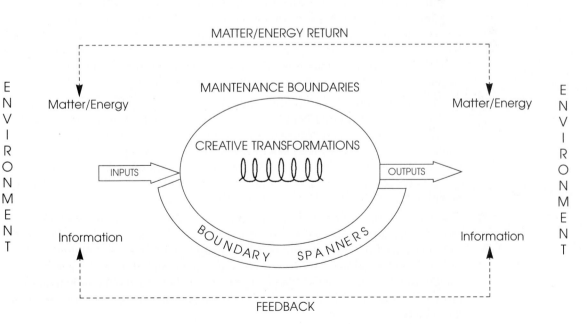

4. *Creative Transformation*. Through work processes of various kinds, inputs are transformed into outputs by means of transformation subsystems—energy is transformed, products are created and produced, information is analyzed, people are trained and managed, and services are organized. The basic tendency in systems is for these transformation subsystems (as well as input and output subsystems) to become more differentiated and specialized, requiring successively higher levels of integration and coordination to hold the system together.

5. *Outputs*. System outputs include products, knowledge, or services useful to the system's survival and waste. In organizations, these outputs are managed by output subsystems, such as sales or pollution control.

6. *Maintenance boundaries*. Systems develop maintenance boundaries to control input and output processes and define the system's identity. In some cases, these boundaries are physical, such as a fence around a plant to keep out unauthorized personnel or to prevent pilferage. Boundaries are also symbolic, as in the case of bookkeeping systems for transferring money into and out of the organization. More intangible are cultural and psychological boundaries, such as norms for membership and inclusion in the system. Systems vary as to how permeable their boundaries are— how open or closed they are. Prisons, for example, are relatively closed organizational systems physically, symbolically, and culturally, whereas a community organization such as the YMCA is more open.

7. *Boundary spanners*. Systems create units that handle transactions with external entities. For example, public relations departments deal with the media and community groups. Organizations appoint people, such as Equal Opportunity specialists and safety officers, to deal with government regulatory agencies. Customer service departments deal with both clients and internal departments as they span the boundary between the people who produce the outputs and those who consume them.

8. *Matter/energy returns*. According to the second law of thermodynamics, all systems have a tendency toward entropy or maximum disorganization and disorder. Thus, to survive, systems must achieve a steady state by generating outputs that are of greater value than the inputs. In this way, the system acquires energy for the transformation process, for internal repair, and for reserves to ensure a comfortable survival margin. For example, an organization buys coal, transforms it to ashes, and uses the energy released to produce products that are sold, thus providing resources for the acquisition of other resources the systems needs and profits for the organization.

9. *Feedback*. To control its activities and maintain a steady state, a system needs feedback from its environment to alert it to deviations from its course (called negative feedback). A thermostat controlling room temperature is a simple example of this negative feedback process. In complex organizations and environments, identifying and analyzing the information needed to control systems processes is much more multifaceted and complex. Without adequate negative feedback controls, no system will survive.

10. *The environment*. In general systems theory the environment of a system includes the suprasystem of larger systems of which it is a part. The body is the suprasystem of the heart, defining relationships among the heart and other organs. Organizational suprasystems include the community and the wider society to which it belongs. These suprasystems help define the organization's physical, economic, political, and social relationships with other subsystems of the society.

The open systems view of organizations is not so much a theory as it is a perspective or a vantage point from which one can build a theory of how particular organizations function. Since general systems theory is of necessity formulated at a high level of abstraction to encompass living systems at all levels from single cells to society, it needs to be translated to a more concrete level to be useful for a particular manager in a particular organization. The value of the open systems approach is that its perspective rises above that of a particular job or function to encompass a systematic framework for interrelating specific components of an organization. That is, it can help managers to see beyond the tasks and priorities of their own department and understand how their work fits into the total picture of the organization's interaction with the environment.

All managers have a personal theory of organizations that they use to make sense of their organizational lives. For some it is very explicit and systematic; for others it is more implicit or "intuitive." No theory is absolutely more correct or better than any other theory. The value of a theory depends on the user's style and what the theory is used for. Theories are guides to perception and action. It is important, therefore, that we understand our personal theories and how they influence our behavior. Many people, for example, do not realize how situation-specific their theories are. When they enter a new situation, they apply their old theory and are chagrined to find out that something is wrong. The more firmly entrenched their theory is, the more likely they are to blame others for their failure ("They just don't accept my leadership") rather than modify their theory.

Atari is an example of a company whose organizational theories have affected its behavior and performance. In the late 1980's, Atari was known as a company that managed "to snatch defeat from the jaws of victory." They developed a computer (520T) in 1985 that could outperform and undersell the Macintosh. However, Atari's management practices prevented them from cashing in on what looked like a sure winner. They tightened the company's boundaries and endangered its external relationships with both dealers and customers. First, they made it too expensive for software developers to gain access to the new computers, which limited software development. Next, they squeezed out and antagonized loyal dealers by deciding to distribute through manufacturer's representatives who had to qualify as new dealers. They also sold through mass merchandisers and discount mail-order houses. However, these vendors did not do the quality control and shipping repairs that experienced dealers were used to providing, so the machines' reputation for quality suffered in the beginning. Rather than offer certain upgrades, Atari lowered prices. The minimal amount of advertising they did appeared in Atari magazines. Thus, their marketing was geared to people who were already customers. The company was more successful in Europe where it does 85% of its business. However, this has been at the expense of the local market and the company is criticized for turning its back on loyal U.S. dealers and customers. Its answer to declining sales was always to cut prices, but Atari could never match its competitors' features or prices in the AT clone market. At the time, these decisions must have appeared correct to Atari's management, but their perceptions of how the company should operate led to the company's decline.

In spite of this, Atari has continued to design interesting, innovative products.[2] Whether or not they parlay this design strength into success depends in part on Atari's ability to learn from past mistakes and devise new organizational theories.

Just as our perceptions of other individuals are subject to a series of potential biases or limiting filters, our theory of organization is subject to a similar set of potential distortions. The basic dilemma is that we all must have a theory to organize our experience and action. In the absence of some theory, however narrow or implicit, the world becomes a jumble of chaotic possibilities. Kuhn points out with respect to scientific theories:

In the absence of a paradigm (theory) or some candidate for a paradigm, all the facts that could possibly pertain to the development of a given science are likely to seem equally relevant. As a result, early fact gathering is a far more nearly random activity than the one that subsequent scientific development makes familiar.[3]

Thus, the presence of a theory provides greater focus and efficiency in problem solving. As soon as a theory becomes formalized and accepted, however, we bump into another problem. Important information, events, or changes in the environment that are outside the boundary of the theory are either not examined at all or are examined with a biased eye. The basic theory, in other words, becomes very resistant to change.

Argyris and Schön describe this phenomenon as the "self-sealing" nature of most theories.[4] In part to reduce uncertainty and anxiety, our personal theories are often designed to create a self-fulfilling prophecy. They are untestable. We need, therefore, to build into our theories what Argyris and Schön call a "double-loop learning" capacity. We need to act and at the same time test the appropriateness of our actions to revise our personal theories when experience dictates a need for such revision.

This is by no means an easy task. In the upcoming class session you will have an opportunity to sharpen your understanding of your own personal theory of organizational functioning. By sharing and discussing your view with others, you can gain a better grasp of the assumptions and values on which it is based.

 # Premeeting Preparation Assignment

Your task before the class meeting is to analyze the particular organization that your subgroup decided to focus on in step A of the premeeting preparation. The forms provided in this assignment will help you construct your own personal theory or model of how the organization you choose functions. A personal organizational theory is simply a representation or picture of the components of an organization and how they function together. This "picture" can be crude and simple or very detailed and complex. It can be accurate or inaccurate. The purpose of the exercise is to help you refine and increase the accuracy of your organizational model by systematically analyzing the organization using the general framework provided by open systems theory. Sharing your analysis with others should broaden your view and correct misperceptions you may have about the organization you selected.

The preparation assignment has three main parts: 1) defining the boundaries of the organization you are examining, 2) analyzing the organization's environment, and 3) analyzing the organization's internal functioning.

PART I: DEFINING THE BOUNDARIES OF THE ORGANIZATION

The first step in creating your organizational theory is to focus sharply on the organizational entity you want your theory to describe. For many individuals, this represents the single organization in which they are currently working and living. For some, their focus is on the immediate locale or departmental environment. For others, the focus includes a broad network of organizations. The important task here is to define just what portion of your organizational experience you want your theory to explain. It may be useful to pick an organization of moderate size to avoid making the analysis too complex and time consuming. (You may want to create this description with other members of the subgroup you formed in step A of the premeeting preparation.)

Complete the following:
The organization my theory seeks to explain is:

_____

_____

_____

_____

What is the organization's mission (its primary function or long-term goal)?

_____

_____

_____

_____

Is the organization a part of a larger system? (For example, a company may be owned by a larger corporation, or a state university will be a part of state government and the looser system of higher education in the United States.) List the larger system or systems of which your organization is a part.

_____

_____

_____

_____

PART II: ANALYZING THE ORGANIZATION'S ENVIRONMENT

This step involves identifying the environmental entities that interact with the organization and are critical to its survival. These entities can be organized groups or organizations (e.g., unions), clusters of people (e.g., customers or the labor market), individuals; bodies of knowledge (e.g., the body of research on chemistry), governments, or even more abstract entities (e.g., changing values of young people). They can be loosely grouped into three types: those that provide *inputs* to the organization (e.g., suppliers), those that consume *outputs* from the organization (e.g., customers), and those that *maintain* the boundaries of the organization by defining what it can and cannot do (e.g., regulatory agencies). These are somewhat arbitrary categories, however, since the organization will engage in transactions with each of the entities critical to its survival that involve both *giving* something and *getting* something in return. For example, a manufacturer will give money to get coal from a supplier (input) and get money from customers for giving them its products (output). The form on page 506 provides space for you to list each significant entity and the nature of the transaction the organization makes with that entity—what the organization gives and what it gets in return

PART III: ANALYZING THE ORGANIZATION'S INTERNAL FUNCTIONING

In this portion of the analysis of your organization, you will be building a model of how the organization functions internally to transform inputs into outputs and maintain its boundaries. The forms provided will assist you in examining three aspects of internal organizational functioning.

1. The way in which the organization is *differentiated*—that is, how the organization divides itself into specialized subgroups to accomplish its major tasks.

2. The way in which the organization is *integrated*—that is, how the organization draws together and coordinates the work of various specialized subgroups.

3. The important *creative transformations* that the organization must perform to survive and be effective—that is, the tasks and processes that the organization must manage and control to cope with its environment and achieve its mission.

Organizational Differentiation

The form on page 507 provides space to list the major formal and informal groups in the organization. Formal groups are often easy to identify because they appear on organizational charts and are often clearly defined by physical location, task, and so on. As anyone who has looked at an organization knows, formal groups can often be identified at several levels of detail (e.g., division, department, section, work groups, etc.) For this analysis, it is best to use major groupings without going into subsections of those groups.

Informal groups are more difficult to identify and require a more intimate knowledge of the organization you are analyzing. Nonetheless, in many organizations informal groups such as an African-American caucus, a regular luncheon meeting of key executives, or a group of friends often perform significant functions for the organization.

When you have completed your list of major groups, list each group's major task or tasks and the major environmental entities that the group transacts with (if any).

Organizational Integration

The next step is to analyze how the work of these different groups gets coordinated to make the organization function smoothly as a unit. The form on page 508 is designed to assist you in this analysis. In the circles provided, put the name of the major formal and informal groups you identified in the differentiation analysis. Then draw lines connecting groups that coordinate their activities with one another. Write on the line *how* that coordination takes place. For example, if marketing and sales coordinate their work via the formal hierarchy with a common supervisor, you might write on the line connecting marketing and sales "common boss." On the other hand, marketing might coordinate with research via new product teams, task forces, committees, or an informal liaison; some groups may not coordinate with others at all.

The last task in building your model is to identify the key processes that the other organization must manage to survive and be effective. To do this you will need to examine the model you have created thus far and examine your own experience with the organization to identify those aspects of the organization's operation that are central to its operation—either because they are necessary for its survival or because they are problematical for the organization at this time. To assist in this examination, we have listed on pages 509-10 a variety of factors that can be important to an organization's functioning. On these pages circle those issues that are critical management issues for your organization, and briefly note in each circled box why it it crucial. For example, in a rapidly growing organization size may be a critical issue to manage. You will circle box 48 and write "to manage rapid growth" to explain why this is important. If you identify key management issues not listed on these pages, relabel an unused box, circle it, and note why it is critical.

Analyzing the Organization's Environment

SIGNIFICANT EXTERNAL GROUPS OR ENTITIES	Nature of Transactions	
	WHAT THE OTHER ENTITIES GIVE THE ORGANIZATION	WHAT THE ORGANIZATION GIVES THEM
Input Entities		
Output Entities		
Maintenance Entities		

Analysis of Organizational Differentiation

MAJOR ORGANIZATIONAL GROUPS	PRIMARY TASK(S)	ENVIRONMENTAL RELATIONSHIP(S)
Formal 1		
2		
3		
4		
5		
6		
7		
8		
9		
10		
Informal 11		
12		
13		
14		
15		
16		

Analysis of Organizational Integration

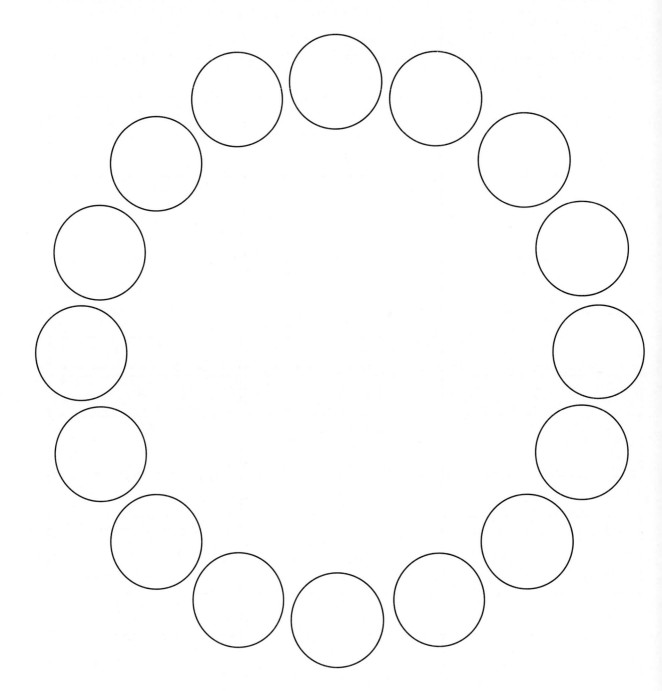

Key Creative Transformations

1 Architectural/ Physical Facilities	2 Capital	3 Career Development
4 Cliques and Interest Groups	5 Community Relationships	6 Compensation/ Benefits
7 Conflict	8 Control Process	9 Costs
10 Shared Values/Beliefs	11 Decision-Making Methods	12 Efficiency, Waste
13 Formal Authority Structure	14 Formal Information System	15 Formal Reward System
16 Government Relationships	17 Influence Styles	18 Informal Communication
19 Informal Rewards	20 Strategy	21 Interpersonal Relationships
22 Job/Role Definitions	23 Job Satisfaction of Employees	24 Management Style

25 Market Relationships	26 Morale/Employee Attitudes	27 Motivation
28 Systems	29 Organizational Culture/ Norms	30 Performance Appraisal
31 Employee Skills	32 Planning Process	33 Policy and Procedures
34 Problem/Opportunity Identification Process	35 Problem Solution Process	36 Profits
37 Return on Investment	38 Scheduling	39 Selection Procedures
40 System Goals	41 Team Functioning	42 Technology
43 Time Demands	44 Training/ Education	45 Turnover/ Absenteeism
46 Unions/Worker Organizations	47 Work Flow	48 Size

Procedure for Group Meeting: Building Theories of Organization

STEP 1.   Subgroups meet to compare and refine individual models. (30 minutes) The groups formed in step A of the premeeting preparation should meet together to share the models they created in the prework assignments. Each person in turn should share his or her model with the others and solicit their reactions. The group may want to pool the individual models to form a consensus model of how their common organization or type of organization functions. This will facilitate discussion and evaluation of the organization's health and effectiveness in Step 2.

STEP 2.   Each subgroup joins with another subgroup to compare models and evaluate the organization's health and effectiveness. (1 hour, 15 minutes) Before beginning, everyone should read the Follow-up with special emphasis on the ten criteria for organizational health and effectiveness described at the end of the Follow-up. There are two tasks for the combined subgroups. First, they should briefly describe to one another the models they have built for their respective organizations. And, in this sharing process, they should explore how their organizations are different and what seems to account for these differences (different missions, environments, technologies, for example).

STEP 3.   Use your analysis to evaluate the health and effectiveness of the organizations using the ten criteria outlined in the Follow-up. Your first clue about an organization's health and effectiveness may well come from how difficult you found it to build the organizational models. Some organizations have clear missions, clear structures, and well defined key management issues. Others seem disorganized and confusing; the organization itself lacks a clear model of how it functions or should function to be as effective as possible. The group should examine each criterion in turn, rating their organizations on how well it meets these criteria. For example in criteria 1, does the organization recognize and deal effectively with the important entities in its environment or does it have a more closed view that focuses only on customers or financial returns?

DEBRIEFING QUESTIONS

1. What personal values seem to underlie your own personal theory of organizations, for example, "Organizations should/should not..."

2. What implicit assumptions, if any, are you making about human nature? About human motivation? About the purpose of your organization?

3. In the study of organizations there are a series of what we might call continuing dilemmas, such as

   a. The relationship between a "people orientation" versus a "productivity/task orientation."

   b. Organization profit versus social responsibility.

   c. Individual goals/needs versus organizational goals/needs.

   What dilemmas seem inherent in your own personal theory? What is your own personal position on these dilemmas?

4. How generalizable is your theory? Does it apply only to your organization? Or is it useful in understanding other organizations as well?

5. Does your managerial action flow directly from your theory as described here? Or is your "theory in action" different than this expressed theory?

6. Given your theory, what would you be likely to overlook? Where might you be biased?

7. Is your theory "self-sealing"? Do you have feedback that would allow "double-loop learning"?

8. What connections can you make between this exercise and the readings?

 Follow-Up

THE OPEN SYSTEMS APPROACH TO ORGANIZATIONS

It is increasingly clear that there is no longer "one best way" to organize and manage. The appropriate organization structure and management depends on the demands of the organization's environment, the tasks it must accomplish, and the people who are its members. Modern organizations must, in other words, be viewed as open systems. In this view, organization effectiveness is governed by four major factors: the individuals who make up the organization, groups within the organization, the organization itself, and the environment in which the organization exists. Effective management of the interfaces between these factors is central to organizational success. Figure 19-2 illustrates this model of organizations.

Figure 19-2 The Open System View of Organizations

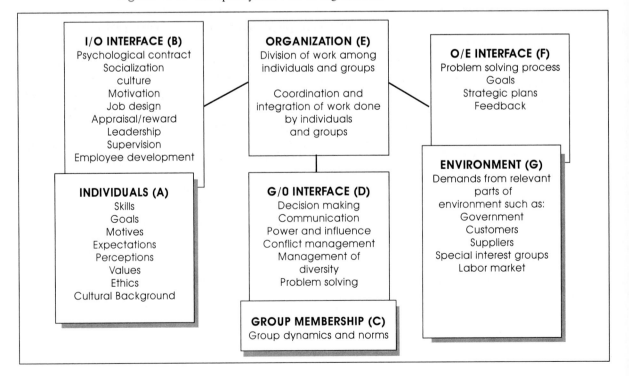

A. The major input resources to an organization are its human resources. Individuals bring to their jobs diverse skills, goals, needs, expectations, perceptions, values, ethics and cultural backgrounds.

B. The interface between the individual and the organization is critical to the full utilization of human resources. The individual and the organization establish a "psychological contract." The individual member expects to make certain contributions to the organization and to receive certain rewards in return. In like manner, the organization expects to provide certain rewards to the individual in return for certain contributions. Individuals are socialized into the organization through its personnel recruitment, hiring procedures, job experience, and training programs. It is at this interface between the individual and the organization that management practices such as leadership, supervision, employee development, job motivation, job design, organizational culture, and the appraisal-reward process become important.

C. People within an organization are formed into formal or informal groups that develop their own norms and dynamics.

D. At the organization-group interface, we find management practices such as decision-making, communication, power and influence, conflict management, the management of diversity, and problem solving that relates to internal matters.

E. The organization itself provides the major transformation or throughput function. Individual and group tasks are identified and assigned according to the demands of the organization's technology; this leads to division of labor or specialization. However, specialization creates an equally important requirement to integrate the work of individuals and the various groups in which they work. It is here that such variables as job clarity and delegation of work and responsibility assume importance.

F. An organization exists to act upon the environment; to have certain transactions with the environment. The desired nature or effect of these transactions defines the mission and goals of the organization. Feedback from the environment is required to determine the quality of these transactions, or how effectively it is performing its mission. This critical interface between the organization and its environment is defined by the problem solving process that determines the organization's goals and strategic plans and the feedback procedures that the organization uses to measure its impact on the environment.

G. The environment has an impact on the organization in many ways. For example, within many organizations today, governmental agencies are demanding changes in employment practices. This demand clearly has an influence on the individuals who are brought into the organization (A), on the way in which individuals respond to leadership and the organizational culture (B), and on the appropriate form of organization (E). Special interest groups (e.g., environmental protectionists) can and do have an impact on organizational goals (F) and the human resources available to the organization (A).

ORGANIZATIONAL HEALTH AND EFFECTIVENESS

The open systems model helps to describe an *effective* organization. An effective organization is one that is able to accomplish the following functions. It attracts skilled and motivated individuals (A) and manages them in such a way as to increase their skills and motivation (B). It separates tasks and allocates them to appropriate individuals and groups (E) without producing gaps and overlaps (i.e., the authority structure produces clear assignment of authority and responsibility). It develops effective formal and informal work units (C). It effectively coordinates the work of different individuals and groups (E). It has an effective problem-solving procedure for setting and reviewing goals and plans (F). It has clearly defined and well-communicated goals and plans that reflect the organization's basic mission and that are based on a careful analysis of the demands of relevant parts of the environment (G), and it obtains and uses feedback from the environment to evaluate effectiveness (F). More specifically, the following characteristics of organizational health or effectiveness can be identified.[5] These dimensions are much like the "vital signs" (e.g., temperature, pulse rate, blood pressure) that a physician would diagnose. Their main value is that they can signal a potential problem somewhere in the system, although they do not, in and of themselves, represent a complete diagnosis of specific organization problems.

1. The organization and its parts see themselves as interacting with each other *and* with a *larger* environment. The organization is an "open system."

2. The total organization, the significant subparts, and individuals manage their work against *goals* and *plans* for achievement of these goals.

3. Form follows function (the problem, or task, or project determines how the human resources are organized.)

4. Decisions are made by and near the sources of information regardless of where these sources are located on the organizational chart.

5. There are minimum inappropriate win-lose activities between individuals and groups. Constant effort exists at all levels to treat conflict and conflict situations as *problems* subject to problem solving methods.

6. There is a shared value, and management strategy to support it, of trying to help each person (or unit) in the organization maintain his or her integrity and uniqueness in an interdependent environment.

7. Communication laterally and vertically is *relatively* undistorted. People are generally open and confronting. They share all the relevant facts, including feelings.

8. There is constructive "conflict" (clash of ideas) about tasks and projects, and relatively little energy is spent in clashing over *interpersonal* difficulties, because they have been generally worked through.

9. The reward system is such that managers and supervisors are rewarded (and punished) comparably for all of the following:
   a. Profit or production performance
   b. Growth and development of their subordinates
   c. Creating a viable working group

10. The organization and it members have the capacity to learn quickly. General practice is to build in *feedback mechanisms* so that individuals and groups can learn from their own experience.

THE 7-S FRAMEWORK

The 7-S framework described in the opening vignette is another popular model for analyzing organizations. It emphasizes the importance of "fit" among the internal components of an organization. However, the strategy component must still be in line with the external environment. Table 19-1 portrays the seven S's and their definitions. The "hard" S's are strategy, structure, and systems. The "soft" S's are style, skill, staff, and superordinate goals. This last category is also referred to as "shared values." The 7-S framework is a summary checklist that highlights the complexity of organizations, but in a manageable way. Within each of the S's, the analysis can be expanded into great detail. The crucial learning from this model is that all seven areas are important and must complement one another.

In their ground-breaking book, *The Art of Japanese Management*, Pascale and Athos accused U.S. companies of devoting less time than the Japanese to the four "soft" S's. They maintain that companies must focus on all seven areas to be successful, like the Matsushita company described in the vignette.[6] Look again at the theory you created. Do all the 7 S's figure in your theory?

BOUNDARYLESS ORGANIZATIONS

A fairly recent development concerns the way we perceive organizational boundaries. Boundaryless organizations work at eliminating or diminishing the boundaries between both internal and external entities in order to be more effective.[7] For example, Chrysler used cross-disciplinary teams that included designers, engineers, plant managers, and people from finance, marketing and human resources. In the past, the plans for a new car would have been passed sequentially and bumpily from department to department, taking much more time. Some companies also include customers in the product phase. Others, like Johnson and Johnson, have computers located within their customers' facilities that keep them abreast of inventory. Honda believes that helping their suppliers become better companies makes Honda a better company. To this end, Honda assigned a team of engineers to work with and train employees at Parker-Hannifin. The benefits to Parker-Hannifin were cost savings and faster production time.

Table 19-1　The Seven S's

Component	Definition
Strategy	Plan or course of action leading to the allocation of a firm's scarce resources, over time, to reach identified goals and create unique value.
Structure	Characterization of the organization chart (functional, decentralized, etc.) and how separate entities are tied together.
Systems	Procedural reports, routine processes, and systems.
Staff	"Demographic" description of important personnel categories within the firm (engineers, entrepreneurs, MBAs, etc.) "Staff" is not meant in line-staff terms. Employee socialization and development.
Style	Characterization of how key managers behave in achieving the organization's goals; also the cultural style of the organization.
Superordinate goals/ shared values	The significant meanings or guiding concepts that an organization imbues in its members.
Skills	Distinctive capabilities of key personnel or the firm as a whole.

Adapted from Richard T. Pascale and Anthony G. Athos, *The Art of Japanese Management* (New York: Simon & Schuster, 1981) p.81. Copyright © 1981 by Richard Tanner Pascale and Anthony G. Athos. Reprinted by permission of Simon & Schuster, Inc.

Learning Points

1. Today's managers are confronted with increasing complexity both within and without their organizations.

2. Open systems theory highlights the necessity of maintaining the basic elements of the input-creative transformation-output process and for adapting to the larger environment surrounding the organization.

3. All managers have their personal theory of organizations.

4. These theories are guides to perception and action, bringing order to what would otherwise be chaotic stimuli; however, they also determine what we see. When theories prevent us from perceiving important information, events or changes in the environment, we call them "self-sealing."

5. Successful managers recognize that theories may not always be transferred from one situation to another. Therefore, managers should build "double-loop learning" into their theories.

6. Healthy, effective organizations have the following characteristics:
   a. Acknowledgment of interdependence among subparts and the larger environment.
   b. A unified approach to common goals.
   c. Form following function.
   d. Decisions being made closest to the source of information.
   e. Conflicts viewed as problems to be solved, not as win-lose situations.
   f. A high level of personal integrity.
   g. Relatively undistorted communication.
   h. Constructive conflict over tasks, not over interpersonal difficulties.
   i. Managers rewarded for profit or performance, growth and development of subordinates, and creating a variable work group.
   j. Feedback mechanisms that enable learning from experience.

7. The 7-S framework consists of three "hard" S's—strategy, structure, and systems—and four "soft" S's—staff, style, shared values, and skills. Organizations must pay attention to each of these areas and ensure that they complement one another.

8. Boundaryless organizations work at eliminating or diminishing the boundaries between both internal and external entities to increase their effectiveness.

 # for Managers

- List all the stakeholders that operate in your system. Identify what each entity wants and needs from you and your unit. Are you meeting their expectations?
- Changes in one part of the system will reverberate throughout the system.
- Always build feedback loops into work processes and units.
- Managers sometimes pay attention to and analyze only those organizational aspects that interest them. The open systems model and the 7-S framework encourage managers to broaden the scope of their attention and take their analyses to greater depth.

Personal Application Assignment

This assignment is to analyze your own organization using the 7-S model, which is described in the article by Waterman, Peters, and Phillips entitled, "Structure is not Organization." This article is found in Kolb et al.'s *Organizational Behavior* reader (1990,1994) or in *Business Horizons*, June 1984 (pp.14-26).

Write about each of the seven aspects of your organization. If you are not currently employed, try the model with another organization you know well (your church, academic department or school, athletic team, orchestra, etc.).

Strategy:

Structure:

Systems:

Staff:

Style:

Skills:

Superordinate Goals/Shared Values:

Is there a "fit" among these seven components? Why or why not? Is there too much fit or too little?

[1]The 7-S's, a framework for analyzing organizations, are: strategy, structure, systems, staff, style, skills, and shared values.

[2]Stan Veit, "What Ever Happened to Power Without the Price? The Atari Story," *Computer Shopper*, October 1992, Vol.12 (10), p.836.

[3]T. S. Kuhn *The Structure of Scientific Revolutions* (Chicago: University of Chicago Press, 1970), p. 15.

[4]C. Argyris and D. Schön, *Theory in Practice: Increasing Professional Effectiveness* (San Francisco: Jossey-Bass, 1974), and C. Argyris, "Double Loop Learning Organizations." *Harvard Business Review* (September-October 1977).

[5]Adapted from Richard Beckhard, *Organization Development: Strategies and Models* (Reading, MA: Addison-Wesley, 1969), pp. 10-11.

[6]Richard T. Pascale and Anthony G. Athos, *Art of Japanese Management* (New York: Simon & Schuster, 1981). Pascale also uses the 7S model in *Managing on the Edge: How the Smartest Companies Use Conflict to Stay Ahead* (New York: Simon & Schuster, 1990).

[7]For an introduction to this topic, see Stewart R, Clegg, *Modern Organizations: Organization Studies in the Postmodern World* (London: Sage, 1990) and James B. Quinn, *Intelligent Enterprise* (New York: The Free Press, 1992).

Chapter

20

ORGANIZATION DESIGN

OBJECTIVES By the end of this chapter you should be able to:

A. Distinguish between mechanistic and organic structures.

B. Distinguish between formal and informal organizational structure.

C. Describe the three pure types of organizational structures and their advantages and disadvantages.

D. Describe horizontal and network organizations.

E. Explain the differentiation-integration issue in organization design.

*D*ownsizing and the Horizontal Corporation

The most striking trend in organizational design in recent years has been widespread downsizing. In addition to lower-level employees who got the ax, over 5 million white-collar workers in Fortune 1000 companies lost their jobs between 1987 and 1991 as companies scrambled to eliminate superfluous levels of hierarchy and become lean and mean enough to survive global competition. As a result, the pyramids that characterize most company structures are flatter, and many companies are taking a serious look at innovative structures that bear no resemblance to pyramids at all.

There's no question that U.S. companies were guilty of adding on excess white-collar workers in recent decades. In 1950, 23% of manufacturing workers were non-production workers compared to 47% in 1988. Global competition and shrinking productivity rates made this group a natural target for reducing costs. However, downsizing hasn't always been a sure bet. Many of the companies who downsized did not show significant improvement afterwards. Downsizing sets off waves of anxiety in companies as people wonder who will be the next to go and what they can do to guarantee their own job security. This type of worry and the political machinations that often result have a way of distracting people from focusing on productivity. Many times, the really outstanding performers the company can least afford to lose opt to

Based upon John A. Byrne, "The Horizontal Corporation," *Business Week*, December 20, 1993. pp. 76-81.

accept a job somewhere else or take an early retirement package rather than risk being fired. Morale, commitment, and loyalty all take a nosedive if downsizing is not handled well. Even those who manage to survive often make the unhappy discovery that they are now expected to do the work of their fired colleagues whose departure they are still mourning.

What lessons have we learned from years of downsizing? Cameron, Freeman, and Mishra* identified the best practices found in a four-year longitudinal study of white-collar downsizing and redesign in thirty organizations in the U.S. automobile industry. Companies that used downsizing to improve their effectiveness demonstrated all of the following practices.

1. Downsizing was implemented by command from the top down, but it was also initiated from the bottom up. Teams or task forces analyzed and identified redundant jobs, studied other organizations that had already undergone downsizing, and helped plan the changes.

2. Downsizing was short-term and across-the-board to get people's attention, but it was also long-term and selective in emphasis so that valuable employees were not lost. Successful companies didn't just cut people, they also changed the organizational design and the organizational culture so that everyone began to question whether their tasks were really adding value to their product or service.

3. Companies paid special attention both to those employees who lost their jobs (via outplacement, counselling, relocation expenses, sponsoring) and those who didn't (confronting survivor guilt and changed conditions by providing more information, recognition, and training for new roles).

4. The same downsizing approach was directed at the firm's external network. Companies reduced the number of their suppliers formed partnership relationships with the remaining suppliers and targeted customer groups to reduce costs and inefficiencies.

5. The result of successful downsizing was small, semi-autonomous organizations that cooperated well with centralized functions so that the larger organization was integrated.

6. Downsizing was not just a means to an end, but its focus on continuous improvement and quality is also an end in itself.

One of the most important lessons we've learned is that downsizing doesn't do much good unless we also change the way the work is done. It's not so much a matter of laying off people as getting rid of unnecessary work. For this reason, some companies are looking at different ways of organizing themselves, and one of these ways is the horizontal corporation.† There are two key ideas behind the horizontal corporation—the necessity of managing across rather than up and down the more traditional hierarchy and the elimination of functional boundaries. If a company were to adopt the pure horizontal design, it would consist of a group of senior managers in the traditional support functions. However, everyone else in the company would be a member of multidisciplinary teams working on core processes. According to the companies that are experimenting with this organizational form, AT&T, DuPont, GE, and Motorola, productivity increases because the effort previously exerted on sending information and coordinating up and down the hierarchy is now directed solely at serving the customer.

An article by John Byrne in *Business Week* identified seven key elements of the horizontal corporation.

*Kim S. Cameron, Sarah J. Freeman, and Aneil K. Mishra, "Best Practices in White-Collar Downsizing: Managing Contradictions," *Academy of Management Executive*, Vol. 5, (3), 1991, pp. 57-73.
†The remainder of this vignette is based upon John A. Byrne, "The Horizontal Corporation," *Business Week*, December 20, 1993, pp.76-81.

SEVEN OF THE KEY ELEMENTS OF THE HORIZONTAL CORPORATION

1. Organize Around Process, Not Task

Forget about functions and departments and create the structure around core processes which have distinct performance goals.

2. Flatten Hierarchy

Eliminate any work that does not add value, combine tasks, and use a limited number of teams to supervise a complete process.

3. Use Teams to Manage Everything

Teams are the central organizational building block, and to reduce the need for supervisors, they should manage themselves.

4. Let Customers Drive Performance

Customer satisfaction, rather than stock appreciation or profitability, should be the key success factor used to measure performance.

5. Reward Team Performance

Modify appraisal and compensation systems to reward skill acquisition and team results.

6. Maximize Supplier & Customer Contact

Maintain a high degree of direct contact with suppliers and customers.

7. Inform & Train All Employees

Train employees to make their own analyses and decisions and then share the raw data.

The first challenge in moving to a horizontal corporation is identifying the core processes that serve customers and eliminating the chaff. One AT&T division assigns both an "owner" and a "champion" to the multidisciplinary teams that take responsibility for one core process. The owner is accountable for daily operations while the champion oversees the linkage between the process and the overall business strategy and goals.

The use of multidisciplinary teams means that companies can decrease the number of "disconnects" and "handoffs" that occur whenever work is passed from one functional area or department to another. While this should pay off in improved efficiency and customer service, it involves a wrenching change for employees who have grown up in functional departments with the goals of climbing to the top of a vertical hierarchy. Horizontal corporations are a whole new ball game. Employees will be rewarded for their ability to take a broader perspective and work with a team of people from other functional areas. Managers will be expected to manage processes and think in systematic terms rather than technical terms. In addition to demanding new skills, a switch to a horizontal corporation also requires a different organizational culture that is less bureaucratic, more change-oriented, and more customer-oriented.

So far, we are more likely to see horizontal structures at the lower levels of companies. The companies that have implemented this type of structure have called it a success. For example, Chrysler used this approach with the Neon car and found that it reduced both development time and costs. John F. Welch Jr., chairman of GE, was one of the first to push the idea of a "boundaryless" company. GE replaced a traditional structure in their lighting business with 100 processes or programs worldwide. The horizontal approach has speeded up their cycle times and responses to customers as well as reduced costs. No companies, however, are making a total transition to a horizontal corporation, probably because there will always be a need for some managers with functional expertise. In the future, we can expect to see more hybrid organizations who, whenever possible, organize multifunctional teams around core processes.

Premeeting Preparation

A. Read *Downsizing and the Horizontal Corporation.*

B. Can you draw the organizational chart for your employer?

If you have never worked, see if you can get an organizational chart of your university or college.

C. How does this structure either help or hinder people in doing an effective job?

D. Read "The Family Hotel," page 534. How would you redesign this organization? Answer the questions on page 537.

E. What are the significant learning points from the readings?

Topic Introduction

One of the largest challenges organizations face is to determine what type of structure best meets their needs. Once again, we run into the concept of "fit" because organizations are most effective when their structure fits the particular demands that confront the organization. The difficulty of adapting to the rapid rate of change and complexity of the current business environment is reflected in numerous corporate reorganizations and new types of structures.[1]

In general, we can categorize organizational structures as either mechanistic or organic. *Mechanistic organizations* are rigid bureaucracies with strict rules, narrowly defined tasks, top-down communication, and centralized decision making. They are best suited to routine functions within stable environments. A banana plantation is mechanistic because everyone has assigned jobs, and the work is very predictable. McDonald's is another example of a mechanistic organization. There are rules to ensure that customers receive a more or less standardized product all over the world, and the work is broken down into specific, standardized tasks. Walk into any McDonald's, and you will find employees performing the same tasks in the same way.

In contrast, *organic organizations* are flexible, decentralized networks, with broadly defined tasks. One example of an organic structure is a new start-up firm in which employees do whatever needs to be done at a given moment, rather than follow a fixed job description. They also communicate directly with anyone in the company rather than limiting their communication to their direct superior or subordinates, and unit co-workers. Organic structures are most appropriate for complex, changing environments that require flexibility. A "skunkworks" where a relatively small, multidisciplinary group of employees sequesters itself until it comes up with a new computer design is another example of an organic organization. One seldom finds organizations that are totally mechanistic or totally organic. For example, although a skunkworks is organic, other parts of the same company may be more mechanistic.

Organization structure refers to the pattern of roles, authority, and communication that determines the coordination of the technology and people within an organization. The formal structure of an organization consists of what is typically depicted in an organization chart. The boxes and the lines that connect them are important elements of the organization's role, authority, and communication structures. The boxes themselves reflect the functions that have been identified to accomplish organizational tasks. The "line functions" are those directly involved in task accomplishments (i.e., marketing, finance, production). Equally important are those "staff functions" designed to provide administrative or support services to the line functions. The lines connecting the boxes reflect two phenomena. One involves authority: who has control over whom. This hierarchy often corresponds very directly to one person being able to hire and /or fire others in lower positions, a key element of positional power. In addition, these lines reflect the formal communication network: the chain of command to be followed for certain forms of communication.

Some Typical Pictures: Three Pure Models of Organization Structures

While no organization chart will look exactly like any other of the three examples offered here, the basic ideas behind these three pure forms can be presented by using a hospital as our example.

Functional Form— In this model the organization is differentiated primarily by the functional specialties (e.g., nurses, physicians) required to accomplish the organization's mission. Each organization member, throughout the chain of command, reports to his or her functional superior (e.g., a nurse reports to a head nurse who reports to a nursing director). A health care delivery system may be functionally organized as show in Figure 20-1.

Product or Service Form— In this model the organization is differentiated primarily by the products it manufactures or the services it dispenses (see Figure 20-2). Each organization member in this system reports directly or indirectly to a manager in charge of a particular product or service (e.g., a pediatric nurse reports to the director of the pediatric clinics). Large enterprises sometimes organize by geographical units (the Northwest region, the Southwest region, etc.), which are similar to product or service structures.

Matrix Form— In this model the organization is differentiated both by function and product, and most members have two or more reporting relationships, or bosses (see Figure 20-3). For example, a nurse working in the pediatric ward would report to the pediatric clinic director and to a nursing director for the hospital in general.

ADVANTAGES AND PROBLEMS

One way of thinking about the differences in these three models is to consider who has the authority to hire and fire and prescribe the duties of organization members. In the functional model, it is the functional supervisor; in the product service model, it is the product service director; and in the matrix model, it is a joint decision of some kind. Each form has some pros and cons.

Functional models of organizations enable the system to develop and maintain higher levels of expertise in the various functional areas or specialties. Organization members' loyalties are to the function, or specialty, and its standards of performance. In addition, each functional department can maintain subspecialists in various areas and allocate their time across the various services (e.g., inpatients, outpatients) being performed by the organization. If the system is organized by product or service, it becomes very expensive to maintain all the same subspecialists in each service area. In other words, in functional structures-one cardiologist, for example-could serve inpatients, outpatients, and the operating room; under a product management structure, however, maintaining the equivalent expertise in each area would require hiring several cardiologists who may not even be fully utilized. Often this same duplication of resources in product-oriented structures extends to support services and equipment as when each product-service area requires its own clerical system, data processing system, records systems, and so on.

On the other hand, under a functional structure, it is often very difficult to perform the integration and coordination of services and inputs required by the organization. Problems in the various services areas become difficult to manage since the various functional representatives in that department often do not have a strong direct reporting relationship to the service director. For example, pediatricians in the outpatient department under a functional structure may see themselves more responsible to the chief of pediatrics than to the outpatient director. If coordination of doctors, nurses, and social workers is important in the outpatient department, and each health professional is responding to a different functional director, then the coordination becomes difficult and problems may develop. These problems can be in the form of inability to agree on schedules to ensure proper coverage, difficulty in developing work responsibilities for each function in a given service, problems in developing procedures for

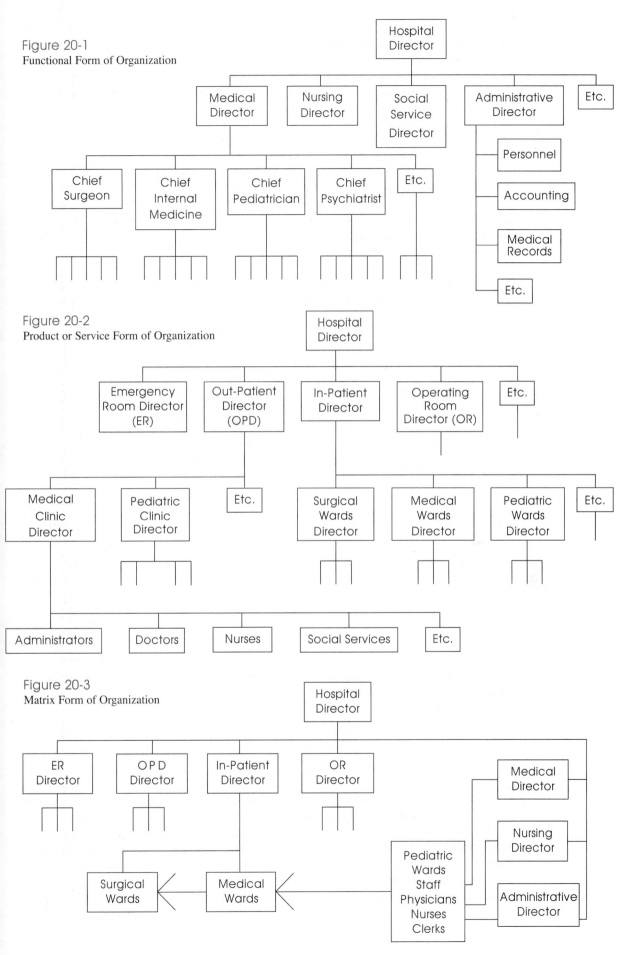

Figure 20-1
Functional Form of Organization

Figure 20-2
Product or Service Form of Organization

Figure 20-3
Matrix Form of Organization

coordinating activities in the service, or even trouble agreeing on the goals and objectives of the service. The product or service structure reduces these coordination problems by placing everyone in a given service area under one coordinating authority, although as indicated, it sometimes does so at the expense of duplication of resources in the total organization.

Also, in dealing with professionals in organizations, it is often important to maintain high levels of collegial interaction for the purpose of maintaining professional standards, creativity, and morale. The product or service structure sometimes reduces opportunities for this type of interaction because people are physically separated into different organizational groups.

The matrix form of organization evolved out of the need to provide both the advantages of functional specialization and the coordination of products or service activity. By maintaining the functional organization, the subspecialists can be retained and allocated where needed in the organization, and the functional director can provide for in-service education and screening to maintain professional standards. At the same time, the product or service managers having authority over the functional representatives when they are in their service areas enables the managers to carry out their coordinative functions. Unfortunately, the existence of two or more bosses for the various organization members involved can often lead to situations of role conflict. The matrix structure, then, requires functional and product or service directors to develop skills in managing these conflict areas.

This requires skills in allocating decision-making responsibility (who has authority over organization members under various situations), managing role conflicts, and so on. Thus matrix management can provide the advantages of both other systems of organization, but it does so at the cost of increasing complexity and management skills required. Therefore, matrix organization structures should be used only where the nature of the organization's tasks requires high degrees of both functional expertise and coordination of services. To make matrix organization succeed, people have to change the way they perceive organizations and focus less on trying to find the ideal structure and more on achieving interdependent goals. As one manager described it, "The challenge is not so much to create a matrix structure as it is to create a matrix in the minds of our managers." [2]

New Organizational Forms—Horizontal and Network Organizations

Galbraith, one of the foremost experts on organizational design, contends that organizations need to develop lateral capability in today's environment.[3] This term refers to the coordination of different functions without communicating through the hierarchy. He identifies three types of lateral capability:

1. coordination across functions
2. coordination across business units in a diversified corporation
3. international coordination of activities across countries and regions

Two organic structures that develop lateral capability are becoming increasingly popular. One is described in the opening vignette on *horizontal corporations*, which are flat structures with minimal layers of management and self-managing multidisciplinary teams organized around core process. Their primary goal and benefit is customer satisfaction, which is attained by reducing the boundaries with suppliers and customers alike and empowering employees. Other benefits that have been claimed for leaner, flatter, structures are lower management costs, more widely shared communications and decision making, and greater employee involvement. We do not have enough research either horizontal corporations or the network structures described in the following section to claim a complete understanding of their advantages and disadvantages.

NETWORK ORGANIZATIONS

The second new type of structure are network organizations, shown in Figure 20-4, which appeared in the 1980's. *Network organizations consist of brokers who subcontract needed services to designers, suppliers, producers, and distributors linked by full-disclosure information systems and coordinated by market mechanisms.* These organizations are also referred to as hollow corporations because some activities are farmed out to other companies that form the network. For example, Nike, Apple Computer, Reebok, and Benneton do virtually no manufacturing. Instead, they form relationships with other companies who are responsible for manufacturing, selling, and transportation of their products. Their contribution, as the center of the network, is the design, marketing, advertising, and integration of the network.[4]

Figure 20-4   Network Organization Structure

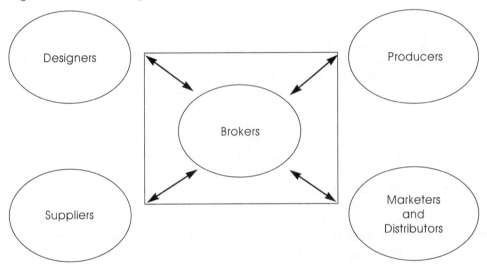

The characteristics of networks are:

1. Vertical disaggregation- Functions normally performed within the organization are carried out by independent organizations.
2. Brokers-Networks of designers, suppliers, producers, and distributors are assembled by brokers.
3. Market Mechanisms-The key functions are tied together by market mechanisms rather than plans and controls.
4. Full-Disclosure Information Systems-Broad access computerized information systems substitute for extensive trust-building processes based on experience.[5]

Benneton, one of the most successful clothing companies in Europe, has 2,500 national and international retail franchise outlets and 200 small firms that manufacture clothes. Benneton's core is modern information technology that tracks each purchase from the cash registers in every franchise, so they can reportedly respond to market changes in ten days time. Benneton is relieved of the headaches of the manufacturing work that is subcontracted out to subcontractors that work exclusively for Benneton and are guaranteed both demand and a set of profit margin.[6]

Network organizations have given rise to new ways of collaborating with other companies.[7] Network partners must agree to ground rules that result in trustworthy relationships and transactions. Companies develop close and helpful relationships with several suppliers and customers so they do not become overdependent upon one particular relationship.

The primary benefit of network structures is that they allow organizations to concentrate on what they do well and subcontract activities that lie outside their specialty. Network structures help companies deal with complex relationships both within and outside the organization in rapidly changing environments. For example, when labor costs become too high in a developing country, Nike simply looks for subcontractors in countries with lower labor costs. This highlights the need for subcontractors to stay abreast of environmental changes and remain flexible.

Organizational Design: The Issues and Principles

These three forms and the numerous possible variations can be viewed as choices available for designing the fiber and structure of an organization. The issue becomes, "How does one choose among these options?" There are several crucial principles involved in this choice.

First, it is important to recognize that there is no "one best way" to structure an organization. The overriding design principle is that *form follows function*. The contingency approach, therefore, dictates a focus on the appropriateness of the structure (the *form*) to the job or task at hand (the *function*). It is immediately clear, using just this principle, that the appropriate structure for an R&D department may well look very different from the appropriate structure for the production department. R&D departments often have organic structures whereas production departments have historically been more mechanistic. Both the entire organization and various subparts need to be designed with this principle in mind.

Second, there is the basic differentiation-integration issue of organization design. All complex organizations must somehow subdivide their total task (differentiation). Indeed, the driving force behind the need for an organization in the first place had to do with the job being more than one person could handle alone. Once the differentiation is made, the organization's designers must then confront the second design decision-integration. Differentiated elements must be coordinated. The pieces must be put back together and kept moving in a particular direction to achieve the organization's basic purpose.

The level of differentiation is contingent upon the nature of the environment and the task. Stable environments require less differentiation than dynamic environments characterized by high degrees of uncertainty. Simple tasks require less differentiation than complex tasks. The greater the level of differentiation, the stronger the need for integration mechanisms that will coordinate the efforts of the entire organization.

Let us examine some of the more typical integrative mechanisms or choices.

Formal Integration Mechanisms

1. *Formal rules.* All organizations have formal rules and procedures, operating manuals, or policy books. The purpose of these, from an organizational structure and design point of view, is to eliminate the need for ad hoc information processing and decision making. When a situation or problem comes up, the individual employee refers to the policy book and finds the right answer. Carried to an inappropriate extreme, use of formal rules and procedures as a way of coping with needed integration results in our stereotyped image of the ossified bureaucracy. Rules proliferate, policy manuals abound and are continuously updated, and "nothing happens unless it is written in the rules."

2. *Formal hierarchy.* From an organization structure and design point of view, a major reason for the existence of the formal hierarchy is to deal with exceptions. Since it is not possible to develop rules for every task situation, people (bosses) are needed to process certain information and make certain decisions about exceptions to the rules. If the same exception occurs frequently enough, it may result in a new rule or policy.

As task complexity increases, the hierarchy also tends to become overloaded. "I'm overloaded with day-to-day fires and have no time for longer-range issues such as employee development and planning," is a common lament of the "overexceptioned" manager. When this condition develops, the organization must look to a third integrative mechanism.

3. *Formal targets or goals.* Through the use of specific subunit goals, budget limits, completion dates, and so on, subunits are able to work on their differentiated tasks with less continuous information processing and decision making. The pieces come together-assuming that everyone meets his or her agreed-upon targets as expected without the need for ongoing communication. Some tasks, however, do not lend themselves easily to such mechanisms. It is harder for the R&D department, for example, to agree to "be creative" by X date than it is for the production department to agree to Y units by X date.

4. *Liaison positions.* Liaisons are individuals who have the responsibility for ensuring that communication and coordination takes place between different departments or units. To perform this job well, they must be seen as impartial facilitators who look out for the best interests of both parties.

5. *Representative groups.* These are task forces or standing committees that coordinate their activities by sharing information and looking for ways to resolve intergroup differences.

6. *Integrating managers.* At times, organizations appoint a manager who has authority over interdependent groups and can thereby ensure coordination and resolve conflicts by issuing orders.

Organization design is buttressed by appropriate reward systems. No matter how well designed an organization appears on paper, if the desired behaviors that will reinforce or implement the design are not rewarded, the design will fail. There is a very close relationship between rewards and punishment and organization design issues. For example, in an organization that severely punishes mistakes and deviation from the rules, one can expect many exceptions to rules that will be bumped upstairs. The hierarchy is likely to become overloaded with exceptions, and as a result, rules and procedures grow like Topsy. In contrast, if mistakes are tolerated and managers are encouraged to exercise discretion in interpreting the rules, there is no need to create a rule for every conceivable situation. As a result, much more decision making will be handled at lower levels in the hierarchy. These examples show that the behaviors that are rewarded and punished, that is, the reward system, affect the integration mechanisms and the organizational design.

In many organizations you can hear "Always ask for twice what you need because they will cut your budget in half anyway" or "If we set a realistic goal and met it, they'd expect us to do it faster next time." or "I know it can't be done that fast, but if that's what they want to hear, that's what I'll tell them, and then I'll try to blame the other shift for the delay." Such comments are a sign that the use of formal targets as an integration mechanism is being subverted by the reward system. When people are penalized for setting accurate goals and targets, they resort to deception.

The Informal Organizational Structure

The points just discussed focus upon the formal organizational structures. An organizational chart, as we have noted, specifies the nature of the formal organizational authority and communication patterns. However, these charts do not always reflect the reality of life within an organization. For example, a young boss may not have the necessary technical expertise so employees turn to an older employee as the real source of authority in their department. Employees and managers typically leave people out of the communication loop who are not respected or powerful. The in-groups in companies in collective cultures (e.g., Latin America) often call the shots and share information, regardless of where these members appear on the organizational chart. All these examples of variations from the formal structure reflect the organization's social system. Thus, organizations have both formal structures and an informal structure that determines how both authority and communication really function.

The importance of understanding the distinctions between formal versus informal organizations and the problems that can arise if the two are not understood is at no time clearer than when one attempts to introduce a technical change into an organization and encounters great resistance. Such as was the case in Trist's study of an attempt to change the process by which coal was mined.[8] The anticipated production increases from the new method were not being realized, and upon investigation it was observed that the new technology substantially altered the social system that had developed within this mine. The men were used to working in close-knit teams characterized by loyalty and mutual help. The new technology involved factorylike, individualized work stations that disrupted the informal group patterns that made their jobs satisfying. The point here is that, whereas a formal organization chart can be redrawn to account for the effects of a technological change, the informal social system, which does not appear on an organization chart, is also influenced by the technological change. Both must be taken into account.

Informal Integrative Mechanisms

We have already discussed several integrative mechanisms that are a part of the formal organizational structure. At this point, we need to explore the integrative mechanisms that are a part of the informal organizational structure.

1. *Informal rules—norms.* The informal counterpart to the formal use of rules in an organization is the enforcement of norms. A norm is an unwritten, informal "rule" that governs individual behavior in an organization. All social systems develop norms; they are an inherent consequence of social interaction. Consequently, the existence of norms is neither inherently good nor bad. The diagnostic question is whether or not the norms that arise function to support or reinforce or to inhibit the organization's primary formal mission or function.

   Imagine an R&D group whose primary function is the generation of new, creative ideas. This group has a formal leader, a boss. One might observe in such a group that ideas are freely exchanged and critically examined, with one exception. The boss's ideas tend to go unchallenged. When the boss states an opinion, the group behaves as if it were a decision, a fact. Now, if the boss possesses a unique technical expertise, one could argue that this is a functional norm. However, it is possible that, for a variety of reasons, people have come to believe that some form of punishment will befall anyone who does not agree with the boss-the "yes-man" syndrome. This norm would be potentially dysfunctional to the group's efforts to fulfill its primary formal function.

"And so you just threw everything together? ...
Mathews, a posse is something
you have to *organize*."

Let us carry the example one step farther. A new person joins the group. As the "New kid on the block," he or she does not yet know all the rules of the game—the norms. The person, at some point, may vigorously try to persuade the boss that his or her idea has some serious flaws. A norm has been violated. There is some anxious laughter in the group, some uneasy shuffling around in the chairs. After the meeting, an old-timer pulls the newcomer aside for a "Dutch uncle" talk. "Look, friend, let me tell you something for your own benefit. In this group, you never take on the boss the way you did today. It's no-no, a taboo." Unless an organization is willing to consciously examine its norms—a norm in itself—it runs the risk of having this element of the informal structure act counter to the organization's primary formal unction. Norms will develop in all social systems. The issue is one of diagnosing their appropriateness to the task of the organization and instituting new norms where necessary.

2. *The informal hierarchy—status differentials.* An important source of status in any organization is one's position in the formal hierarchy. Bosses are differentiated from subordinates in terms of the formal power associated with their position-power to control rewards, to make certain decisions, to resolve certain expectations to formal rule, and so on. In many organizations, one finds other less formal dimensions along which people differentiate one another. Any element of difference can be a source of status and power. For example, in some organizations, a comment made by a male would be treated much more seriously than if the comment were made by a female—a sex differentiation. Age seniority or educated-non-educated differentiations are also common: "These young turks are really something. They think a college education gives them all answers!" Many organizations find themselves to be heavily dependent on a particular task or function: "We're a marketing-oriented company" or "We're an R&D-oriented

company." The perceived consequence may be "When push comes to shove, the top positions always go to people from Marketing." The impact of these status differences can be positive or negative in terms of the organization's primary formal function. Differentiated subunit tasks must be integrated-coordination is essential. Age-seniority, sex, educational background may have little to do with the issue at hand. Integrative decisions influenced by the informal hierarchy may, therefore, ultimately be dysfunctional to the accomplishment of the organization's mission.

3. *Informal goals—individuals needs and goals.* The degree to which goals and organizational goals can be integrated has and will continue to be a major source of concern to organizational theorists and practicing managers. Many approaches exist and are being implemented to maximize the degree of overlap, such as goal-setting procedures, management by objectives, participative performance appraisal systems, and flexible and adaptive formal reward systems. The less the agreement between formal targets and goals and individual needs and goals, the more difficult it will be to achieve the needed integration of formally differentiated subtasks.

Examples of these informal goals are not easy to see because they tend to be defined as "antiorganizational" and therefore operate under the table. Such comments as "She always has a hidden agenda" or "He's always trying to build his own little empire" are indicative of the tension between formal organizational goals and informal individual goals. In the specific context of group decision making, this tension has been discussed more fully as an example of self-oriented behaviors in Chapter 9.

A typical example of this tension can be seen operating on many assembly lines. A formal goal or target has been set of X units per hour per employee. This becomes the group norm or standard. Along comes a capable individual who wants to get ahead (perhaps someone with a high achievement need). Efforts on this person's part to better the formal standard are met with group pressures to get back in line; the group punishes rate busters. Here individual needs to belong to the group (an affiliative need) may take precedence over the formal goal of increasing productivity.

MAPPING ORGANIZATIONAL STRUCTURES

The usefulness of mapping the formal and informal aspects of an organizational structure is demonstrated in several research studies. Allen,[9] for example, finds that, in addition to the formal organization structure, the informal structure, as represented by patterns of friendship and extraorganizational social encounters, has an important effect on the flow of technical ideas. Scientists were found to discuss technical ideas with many of the same people with whom they interacted on a social basis.

Allen's research also uncovered the existence within research and development laboratories of people he called "technological gatekeepers." These few people were mentioned very frequently as informal sources of critical information. These gatekeepers act as a link between the organization and the outside environment, as evidenced by their attendance at professional meetings and reading of professional and technical periodicals. Knowledge of who these gatekeepers are and of the nature of the existing sociotechnical and social networks within an organization can serve as important inputs into many organizational decisions. One would not, for example, want to redesign the office and break up an effective informal communication group by moving its members apart from one another and these gatekeepers. [10]

A second important set of insights into organizational structure comes from research on the impact of different communication networks.[11] Mechanistic pyramid structures often have closed, one way communication networks, like the one shown below in Figure 20-5.

Figure 20-5

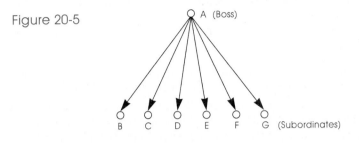

This has been called the closed, one-way communication network. A can communicate with B, C, D and the rest, who "cannot" communicate with each other and seldom communicate with A (short of saying "yes").

A different type of network is typically found in organic structures, which is shown in Figure 20-6. This has been called the open, two-way communication network. Full, open communication is encouraged between each and every group member.

Figure 20-6

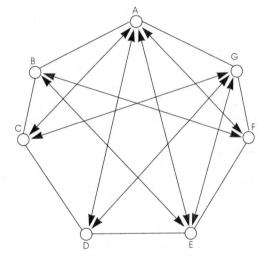

In experimental investigations with these two (pure and extreme) networks, the following effects have been observed. For a given task, the closed network is considerably faster than the open network—the boss finishes sending the message sooner in the closed network. The closed network is considerably less efficient, however, in terms of accuracy—more of the members get the wrong message. In a series of related experiments, the open network has been found to be more adaptable to changes in task requirements.

With respect to morale, the members of the open network are most satisfied and feel more involved in the task. In the closed network, only A (the boss) feels satisfied and involved. In the open network, every member has the opportunity to assume a position of leadership. The open network, therefore, provides a training ground for the development of future managerial talent. There are clear relationships between the structure of a group (or organization) and the content of the communication. The process by which information is communicated influences people's feelings of satisfaction, involvement, commitment, and future capability to assume leadership positions.

The interdependence of formal and informal structures is often complex and difficult to map. However, in the process one may gain surprising insights into the real communications process of a group or organization.

THE FAMILY HOTEL

The Schmidt family started out with one hotel. Through judicious investment, they gradually grew to a corporation that owned six upscale hotel properties and a food distribution business. The father and three sons were extremely active in running the hotels. The father was the president of the company. Each son was in charge of a different functional area at the corporate level—vice presidents of finance, food and beverage, and sales and marketing. The other two vice presidents, in personnel and accounting, were new hires who were not family members. Although each of the properties had a general manager (GM), most employees considered the family members to be the real bosses in the organization. The family occasionally countermanded the order of the GM's, and older employees contacted the owners directly when there were problems. The corporate vice presidents sometimes came to the properties and visited the hotel staff in their functional areas without notifying the GM of their presence. Sometimes the GM's were first informed of new corporate policies and changes by their own subordinates. In their defense, the turnover rate at the properties was so high that the family felt they had to intervene, and the family members were all fairly competent and knew the business. But the GM's dissatisfaction with their intervention resulted in even more turnover.

In 1985, the business reached a turning point. Because of their success, the family decided to expand their hotel ventures to different parts of the country. But this decision caused dissension within the family. One of the sons disagreed with this strategy and opted to leave the family business for awhile to see if he could succeed on his own. Another son, who was tired of his father's authoritarian style, chose to return to school and complete his graduate education. The third son wanted to focus solely on the expansion and his father wanted to do what he enjoyed most—making deals and pursuing new ventures. Since the family was no longer capable of overseeing the operations themselves, they hired an operations manager to run the business.

The formal organizational chart for the company is shown in Figure 20-7. But the new operating manager, Glen Chase, suspected that this chart did not reflect reality. He found himself in a delicate situation. From working with other family businesses, he knew that it was difficult for founders to relinquish authority and control to others. However, after talking with the staff comprising the executive committee at one of the properties, Chase also knew the organizational structure had to be modified and it had to be done quickly before the positions at corporate were filled.

Jack Wilson had been a general manager (GM) for ten years, although many of those years were spent working for other hotel chains. Jack said that he didn't feel he could really do his job because so many directives came from corporate headquarters that he spent all his time responding to them. Furthermore, policies and procedures that were appropriate for another hotel in a different geographic area were inappropriate for him. He felt his hotel's problems were somewhat unique and resented being told how to run his property. He also said that in the past the family and the different staff people who came from headquarters had given him conflicting advice. He handled that by always doing what the family said, since they had the power to fire him. However, his relations with other staff members had suffered as a result and he worried about his reputation at headquarters. He also felt he had to walk a narrow line with the employees. If they didn't like something, they called headquarters, and a family member would come swooping down to investigate. Sometimes he would not be informed of the complaint until that time. Because of the cronies who were friends of the family, Jack wasn't sure how far he could go in making changes in the hotel or even talking about problems openly with anyone in the organization.

Donna Novak was the personnel director. She had previously worked in manufacturing firms that had formalized HR programs. She was still a bit shocked by the comparatively unsophisticated personnel practices that are common in much of the hotel industry. She complained that she felt she had to hire whomever the family referred, whether or not they were qualified for the job. However, her main problem was keeping the hotel staffed. Turnover was high, and unskilled workers were at a premium in this community. She was convinced that some of the hotel's policies, like the lack of retirement benefits, were causing turnover. She also feared that the autocratic and arbitrary management practices of some of the department heads were responsible for high turnover. The hotel chain had a reward system that gave bonuses to department heads based upon their productivity. However, the salaried and hourly employees received no bonuses, and some of them felt they were being taken advantage of by the department heads just so their bonuses would be earned. For example, some of the department heads were slow to put in requests for people to fill positions; the employees assumed these managers were saving money on salaries, while the employees had to do the work of two people.

Sam Sloan was the food and beverage director, a position that is usually second in prestige only to the general manager of the property. Sam complained that he spent all his time preparing profit and loss statements for headquarters by hand since the hotel operations were not computerized. He said he understood the importance of keeping records and was very interested in the food and beverage figures but had no time left to check out trends in the industry. He was afraid he was falling behind in his field. The only opportunity he had to keep up came with the visits of the F&B vice president who did a good job passing on the new ideas he had collected in his travels.

Jill Smith, the banquets manager, stated flat out that she had the most stressful job in the hotel. She said the salespeople promised the moon to prospective customers but

FIGURE 20-7   The Family Hotel Formal Organizational Chart

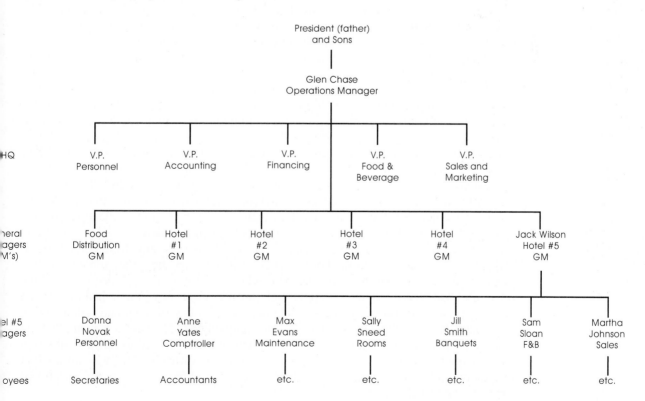

often failed to tell her specifically what the clients had requested. Her waiters and waitresses had to fight over tableware with the restaurant servers. Furthermore, the chef gave her a hard time because she could not give him the exact count of meals needed until everyone showed up for their banquet. All day long and most nights she raced from meeting room to meeting room, handling irate customers and upset employees, until she did not have time for anything else in her life.

Anne Yates, the comptroller, was fairly satisfied with her job and the company with the exception of the financial control system. She said that the figures from the departments were sent directly to headquarters and they weren't sent back to the hotel until it was too late to use them for either controlling or forecasting. As a result, budgeting was a nightmare, and when the GM or the department heads looked bad as a result, they tended to blame her. Anne was hoping that automation would help the situation.

Martha Johnson, the sales director, had worked her way up in the organization from the banquet department. She talked at length about the difficulties between sales and the other departments in the hotel. Since the salespeople are the only ones who go home at five o'clock, they are not taken seriously by the others. They have to maintain their reputation and credibility with customers, but they depend heavily upon other departments to satisfy the customers. Martha says she has to check many things herself to make sure banquets or the kitchen are following the customer's request form, but the other departments resent her checking up on them. If she doesn't, however, mistakes happen. Martha said she has a running feud with the F&B director because he tries to bury some of his costs in her budget. Martha also wishes she had more sales expertise. She was grateful to move up within the company but suspects there is more she should be doing to modernize the sales office.

Sally Sneed is one of the few college graduates on the property. She studied education but found she disliked classroom teaching. She is the rooms manager and is responsible for the reservations and rooms functions. She gets along well with the other departments and, other than the occasional communication problems with sales, has no major problems. She was, however, very concerned about the competition that the hotel faces. Room occupancy had dropped since two new hotels were constructed in the vicinity. Sally felt that the hotel had to offer something unique so it could keep its clientele. She thought one of the biggest problems was lack of renovation. The property was getting a little shabby, but all the capital expenditures were determined at headquarters and renovation requests took a long time to approve.

Sally's concerns about capital expenditures were shared by Max Evans, the maintenance department head. He'd worked at the property for two years and had recently been promoted. His crew was tired of patching carpets and trying to make old kitchen equipment hold together a while longer. He wished the kitchen people were trained to take better care of the equipment, because he thought they might cut down on some of their repair jobs. His major problem though was keeping all the department heads happy. Some of them expected him to stop whatever work was in progress and do their jobs first. He felt as if he were being pulled in several directions at once. Sometimes he just gave up and had his men go to whatever department was yelling the loudest.

After talking with the managers on the property, Glen also learned that the department heads met with Jack once a week in their executive committee meeting. At this time Jack just read them the latest directives from headquarters. There were few attempts at problem solving, presumably because all answers came from corporate and everyone knew Jack had limited power. Glen was worried about the problems he had uncovered and also felt the hotels needed to be more innovative. Since many of the managers had worked their way up through the system, some of them had never seen alternative ways of doing business. Glen thought of a few of them had fallen behind the times. He himself wanted to try out some innovations. He was very aware that the certain properties were losing out to the competition and wanted to turn the situation around quickly. As the organization was currently structured, he was afraid that wasn't possible. So he dug out his OB textbook, reread the chapter on organizational structure and tried to come up with a new design.

Answer these questions before coming to class:

1. What type of formal structure does the company currently have?

2. Describe the company's informal structure.

3. What are the strengths and weaknesses of the informal structure?

4. What can you figure out about the communication networks that exist? Draw dashed lines on the chart in Figure 20-7 to show the communication patterns.

5. What are the issues for each of the participants?

PERSON	ISSUES
Jack, general manager	
Donna, personnel	
Sam, food and beverage	
Jill, banquets	
Anne, comptroller	
Martha, sales	
Sally, rooms	
Max, maintenance	
Glen, operations manager	

6. What changes in the structure could best address these issues?

7. **a.** How would you resolve the integration problems between the property and the headquarters?

   b. How would you resolve the integration problems between departments in Hotel #5?

We left Glen Chase, the operations manager, rereading his OB textbook. He'd figured out some ideas about a better organizational design and had flipped to the chapter on implementing change. There he read that changes are more likely to be implemented when the people involved have a chance to participate in the decision. He decided to test this out and called a meeting of all the department heads at the property he'd visited.

Prepare to run the following role-play session as Glen Chase. You may wish to refer back to the problem solving chapter to refresh your memory about what to consider in such a meeting.

Procedure for Group Meeting: The Family Hotel Role Play

(Time Allotted: 30 Minutes)

STEP 1.   Choose volunteers to play each of the managers. The volunteers should be seated around a table. Leave an empty chair for people from the rest of the class who may want to join in for a few minutes.

STEP 2.   Glen Chase starts the meeting off in his or her best problem-solving style and asks other managers for their input on creating a new organizational design. The group should draw a new organizational chart that includes their suggested changes.

STEP 3.   Debriefing (20 minutes)

a. What kind of organizational design did the role players devise?

b. What was the rationale behind their choices?

c. What are the strengths and weaknesses of this design?

d. What integration mechanisms did they suggest? Why?

e. What connections can you make between this exercise and the readings?

Follow-Up

Glen Chase convinced the Schmidt family to decentralize and allow the properties to have more autonomy. He decided that the informal structure they'd been operating with was really a functional structure or a matrix that refused to acknowledge itself. He tried to strengthen the general managers' position by developing a GM's council and encouraging them to make decisions with him rather than merely trying to figure out what the family wanted. A bonus system was set up for each property which rewarded the GM's for innovations in their hotels. The executive committees on the properties were encouraged to solve problems and work as teams. However, so many of the managers were young and lacking in managerial skills that integration problems still occurred.

Chase's tactic with the vice presidents at headquarters was to have them do project work on system problems and/or innovations. This kept them too busy to do the daily monitoring that occurred in the past and caused them to be seen more as special resources by the staff on the properties. The system evolved into a modified matrix form in which the GM's became the primary authority on the properties and the corporate staff were secondary functional bosses who provided technical resources and back-up support for the hotel employees.

The design of an organizational structure depends upon the environment, the technology, the people, organizational size, and strategy. Far from being a negligible factor, the design of the organization has a direct influence upon effectiveness. As the opening vignette showed, design issues can be crucial to an organization's ability to compete.

An aspect of the environment that affects the choice of structure is national culture. High-power-distance cultures tend towards organizational structures with centralized decision-making. Low-power distance cultures prefer decentralized decision making. The uncertainty avoidance dimension relates to the degree of formalization—the need for formal rules and specialization. High uncertainty avoidance cultures will prefer formalized structures. Based upon European MBA students' diagnoses and solutions for business cases, Stevens concludes that the "implicit model" of the organization for most French was a pyramid (both centralized and formal); for most Germans, a well-oiled machine (formalized but not centralized); and for most British, a village market (neither formalized nor centralized).[12] Matrix structures were not widely accepted in France because they go against the French respect for the hierarchy and unity of command.[13]

Learning Points

1. Mechanistic organizations are rigid bureaucracies with strict rules, narrowly defined tasks, top-down communication, and centralized decision-making. They are best suited to routine functions within stable environments.

2. Organic organizations are flexible, decentralized networks, with broadly defined tasks. They are most appropriate for complex, changing environments that require flexibility.

3. Organization structure refers to the pattern of roles, authority, and communication that determines the coordination of the technology and people within an organization.

4. The functional form of organizational structure is organized around the functional specialties required to accomplish the organization's mission. It allows for greater development of functional expertise but may make organizational coordination more difficult.

5. The product or service form is organized around the products or services offered by the organization. Coordination problems are reduced in this structure, but it runs the risk of having duplicated resources and decreased opportunity for collegial interaction among people of the same function.

6. The matrix form is organized around both functions and products. It is an attempt to profit from the advantages of both functional and product structures. However, having both a product and a functional boss can cause confusion and conflict.

7. Horizontal corporations are flat structures with minimal layers of management and self-managing multidisciplinary teams organized around core processes.

8. Network organizations consist of brokers who subcontract needed services to designers, suppliers, producers, and distributors linked by full-disclosure information systems and coordinated by market mechanisms.

9. A guiding rule is "form follows function." Therefore, different patterns of the organization may well be designed very differently.

10. A basic problem faced by any organization structure is that of differentiation-integration. Complex organizations have to divide the work (differentiation), but how then do they coordinate (integrate) the different parts to achieve the organization's goals?

11. Formal integration mechanisms are:
    a. Formal rules.
    b. Formal hierarchy.
    c. Formal targets or goals.
    d. Liaison positions.
    e. Representative groups.
    f. Integrating managers.

12. Informal integration mechanisms are:
    a. Informal norms.
    b. Informal hierarchy.
    c. Informal individual needs and goals.

13. Organization design is reinforced or weakened by the reward system. Whether or not individuals are rewarded for cooperating will help determine the success of integration efforts.

14. Both formal and informal aspects of organization design are important. The informal aspects refer to social behavior and relationships.

15. Closed, one-way communication networks are quicker, but less accurate and more dissatisfying for members other than the boss.

16. Open, two-way communication networks, while slower, have the advantage of greater accuracy, higher morale and satisfaction, and increased adaptability to changes in task requirements. These networks are better for developing future managers because they provide shared opportunities for leadership.

17. Organization design is determined by strategy, environment, technology, organizational size, and people.

- Looking at a problem, it's important to ask, "What is the problem, not who?" Unless managers are sophisticated about design issues, they are likely to see individuals, rather than structure, as the problem.
- When a succession of people fail in a position, it is often a signal that the position or the organization design is at fault. Some jobs and even departments are simply doomed to failure by poor designs, and it's a manager's job to determine that and rectify it.
- There is a saying, "When in doubt, reorganize." Don't reorganize unless you have undertaken a thorough analysis and are positive that the design issues are really the culprit.
- Make sure the informal structure is well understood before any changes are made. Some organizations succeed in spite of their structure because the informal structure is stronger than the formal structure.
- It's difficult to forecast the unanticipated consequences that will result from new structures. Without doubt there will be some. Therefore, it makes sense to brainstorm possible consequences and leave some room for later modifications.
- A change in organizational design will often result in resistance. It is upsetting to most people to participate in reorganization. Getting employee participation in the process of developing a new design is one way to reduce resistance. See the contents of Chapter 22 regarding change.
- Advice for managing network partnerships is 1) don't be the first to play games by taking advantage of the other party, 2) reciprocate with both cooperation and lack of it when the other party demonstrates it; 3) don't be too greedy; and 4) don't be too clever and try to outsmart your partner.[14]

Personal Application Assignment

In this assignment you are to write about the design of an organization you know well by answering the following questions:

1. How would you diagram the formal structure of your organization?

2. How would you describe its communication networks?

3. How would you diagram the informal structure of your organization?

4. How does your organization deal with the differentiation-integration issue?

5. What are the strengths and weaknesses of your organization's design?

6. What improvements could you suggest?

[1] Charles Handy, *The Age of Unreason* (London: Hutchinson, 1988).

[2] Christopher A. Bartlett and Sumantra Ghoshal, "Matrix Management: Not a Structure, a Frame of Mind," *Harvard Business Review*, Vol. 68(4), 1990, pp. 138-145.

[3] Jay R. Galbraith, *Competing with Flexible Lateral Organizations* (Reading, MA: Addison Wesley, 1994).

[4] Edward E. Lawler, III, *The Ultimate Advantage* (San Francisco: Jossey-Bass, 1992) pp. 69-70.

[5] Raymond E. Miles and Charles Snow, "Organizations: New Concepts for New Forms," *California Management Review*, Vol. 28, 1986, pp. 62-73; and Russell Johnston and Paul R. Lawrence, "Beyond Vertical Integration—The Rise of the Value-Adding Partnership," *Harvard Business Review*, Vol. 66(4), 1988, pp. 94-101. Charles C. Snow, Raymond E. Miles, and Henry J. Coleman, jr., "Managing 21st Century Network Organizations," *Organizational Dynamics*, 20(3), 1992, pp. 5-19.

[6] Stewart R. Clegg, *Modern Organizations* (London: Sage, 1990).

[7] Russell Johnston and Paul R. Lawrence, "*Beyond Vertical Integration*"

[8] Eric Trist as reported in Warren G. Bennis et al., *The Planning of Change*, 2nd ed. (New York: Holt, Rinehart and Winston, 1969), pp. 269-281.

[9] T. Allen, "Communications in the Research and Development Laboratory," *Technology Review*, Vol. 70 (1967), pp. 31-37.

[10] The architecture of an organization is an important element of its formal structure. For more detail on this element see Fred I. Steele, *Physical Settings and Organization Development* (Reading, MA: Addison-Wesley, 1973).

[11] See, for example, Paul Lawrence and Jay Lorsch, *Developing Organizations: Diagnosis and Action* (Reading, MA: Addison-Wesley, 1969).

[12] Geert Hofstede, "Motivation, Leadership, and Organization: Do American Theories Apply Abroad?" the *Reader.*

[13] Andre Laurent, "The Cultural Diversity of Western Conceptions of Management," *International Studies of Management and Organizations*, Vol. 13, no. 1-2 (1983) pp. 75-76.

[14] Robert Axelrod, *The Evolution of Cooperation* (New York: Basic Books, 1985).

Chapter

21

JOB DESIGN

OBJECTIVES By the end of this chapter, you should be able to:

A. Define and describe the historical roots of work alienation.

B. Describe the impact of technology on job design.

C. Identify characteristics of job situations that motivate people.

D. List and describe six methods for increasing job involvement.

*B*enchmarking At Xerox

When Xerox realized in 1983 that they would have to become more competitive, they adopted a quality program entitled, "Leadership through Quality." Their objective was to increase the quality of goods and services and decrease costs. The behaviors that Xerox was trying to foster in a new organizational culture were:

1. Use of a systematic approach to understand and satisfy both internal and external customer requirements.
2. A shift from a predominantly short-term orientation to the deliberate balance of long-term goals with successive short-term objectives.
3. Striving for continuous improvement in meeting customer requirements, rather than accepting a certain margin of error. Doing things right the first time.
4. Participative and disciplined problem solving and decision making using a common approach.
5. An open style with clear and consistent objectives which encourages problem solving and group-derived solutions.*

Their program now consists of three processes: quality, problem-solving, and benchmarking. Xerox has trained over 100,000 employees in the quality process and problem solving in order to improve performance. Their employee involvement groups were institutionalized after they proved their worth by out-performing other areas. The third process, benchmarking, was developed when Xerox realized that the

---

*This list is taken from a case entitled, "Xerox Corporation: Leadership Through Quality," by Amy B. Johnson and Lori Ann MacIssac. In Todd D. Jick, *Managing Change*, (Homewood, IL: Irwin, 1993) p. 216.

first two programs did not provide enough guidance to employees about where they should direct their improvement activities. For Xerox, benchmarking means sending out a team to look at and learn from "best practices." Their findings are then turned over first to their quality teams and then to the employee involvement teams to see how they can implement these practices. The following section is excerpted from "A Bible for Benchmarking, by Xerox," by Robert C. Camp in *Financial Executive*, July/August, 1993, pp. 23-27.

"The formal definition of benchmarking is the continuous process of measuring our products, services and practices against those of our toughest competitors or companies renowned as leaders. We have never changed this definition, because it embodies some very tough lessons we learned while introducing benchmarking.

The first lesson concerns the competition. Although you must focus strongly on the competition, if that's the sole objective, playing catch-up is the best you can do. Watching the competition doesn't tell you how to outdistance them. The mix of our benchmarking activities has changed 180 degrees. In the early days, we spent 80 percent of our benchmarking time looking at the competition. Today, we spend 80 percent of that time outside our industry, because we have found innovative ideas from business in other industries.

The four major types of benchmarking are internal, functional, generic and competitive. *Internal benchmarking* holds that large organizations have multiples of the same unit set up to do the same thing, such as similar marketing offices, districts, multiple distribution centers and order-taking points. The company can compare practices among internal areas and determine which one is the benchmark, bringing the others up to the same performance level. Quickly answering customer inquiries and complaints makes customers happy, so we set up a customer problem resolution process as the benchmark, derived from our sister affiliate, Xerox Canada. We did not have to leave the Xerox family to find benchmarks in this case.

Functional benchmarking is the story of L.L. Bean. In the early 1980's, when most managers were transfixed with competitive benchmarking, the Xerox review team members asked, "Who's the benchmark?" They expected to hear names like Kodak, IBM, Cannon or Minolta. We said no: The benchmark is L.L. Bean. Now imagine the surprised faces in that audience. "Wait a minute-we're a copying company. How could we possibly compare ourselves to this little outdoor specialty company up in Freeport, Maine?"

But all companies take their customers' orders and, provided we maintain some common characteristics, we can compare ourselves to companies in other industries. L.L. Bean's products, like ours, don't come in nice little standard packages, as you might guess about a company that sells ax handles, red flannel shirts, boots and canoes. And the company picked its orders manually (employees put together the orders by hand) as we did, but the similarities stopped there: L.L. Bean picked its orders three times faster!

The first rule of running an efficient warehouse is ensuring that the fast-moving merchandise is closest to the main aisle, a principle called velocity sequencing. The employee can push a cart with customer order boxes and pick the necessary items. In fact, L.L. Bean uses the number of feet that a picker travels daily as a productivity indicator.

But L.L. Bean did something else. The company recognized that orders came in randomly and were unlikely to coincide with the locations of the items, so it changed the order fulfillment system. Within a set time period, employees sorted the orders and put like items together, enabling the picker to make one trip and pick all the red flannel shirts necessary for that batch of orders. Xerox did not have a comparable system, which accounted for the productivity differences. For functional benchmarking, the practices are the most important consideration.

Today *generic benchmarking* is one of our most important focal points. After benchmarking with several other prominent firms and conducting some studies, we recognized that we would get the greatest return by improving basic business processes. We identified 67 processes for one unit and assembled a plan to revamp all of those steps. Process owners are designated who document their processes and ensure that they are benchmarked.

Competitive benchmarking for us meant streamlining without compromising service. Before benchmarking, Xerox had four layers-four places where we stored and handled material, and we were 30 percent off the mark. Our competitor had two layers, at manufacturing and the service person. The cost and asset levels affecting the profits and losses or the balance sheet were almost directly proportionate to the number of layers. Since then, we have changed our structure to look more like our competitor's, without any loss of service quality.

With the help of benchmarking, we have cut unit manufacturing costs in half since the early 1980s, and parts acceptance is nearly 100 percent. In-process inventory has been reduced by two-thirds.

The best way to accomplish positive change is to believe in a need for improvement, determine what to improve and give people a vision of the goal. Benchmarking achieves all those objectives by bridging the gap between internal and external practices. However, it is not an isolated quick fix, but a continuous practice that must harmonize with other company initiatives."

 Premeeting Preparation

A. Read "Benchmarking At Xerox."

B. Read the Topic Introduction.

C. Using the instructions provided at the end of this chapter, learn to fold the moon tent and the shallow water cargo carrier (see instructions, pages 552–555 and 559–562).

D. What are significant learning points from the readings?

Topic Introduction

Without work, all life goes rotten, but when work is soulless, life stifles and dies.
—Camus

Ever since people ceased working for themselves as farmers and craftsmen and cast their fate with organizations, worker motivation and involvement has been a matter of both interest and concern. The Industrial Revolution and its effect upon the nature of manual work and the social structure focused greater attention on the concept of alienation.[1] Karl Marx[2] put an inflammatory finger on part of this concept when he stated that the separation of labor from ownership and the means of production resulted in powerlessness among the laboring class. Durkheim stated that the reduction of work into small, repetitive segments led people to see their jobs as meaningless.[3] He also applied the term "anomie" to describe a social system in which normative standards are weak. Anomie conveys a sense of disorientation, anxiety, and isolation in individuals; Durkheim maintained that the switch from an agrarian to an industrial society created anomie because there were fewer norms or rules to regulate the urban industrial society that evolved in the 1800's in Europe. Mayo,[4] who researched the Hawthorne experiment described in Chapter 2, claimed that factories that prevented social interaction resulted in worker isolation and affected productivity. Mayo disagreed with the prevailing assumptions of economic theory and industrial practice that he called the "rabble hypothesis." There were three tenets to that hypothesis, said Mayo, and he took exception to all three: society consists of unorganized individuals—discrete atoms rather than natural social groups; each individual acts according to calculations of his or her own self-interest rather than being swayed by group norms; and each individual thinks logically, rather than being swayed by emotions and sentiments.[5]

As a result of the Industrial Revolution, workers found themselves performing small, simple, boring repetitive jobs that had limited meaning and challenge for them. Precisely because jobs were so simple, workers were easily replaced, giving further justification for the belief that workers were merely cogs in the industrial machine. The cost of this efficiency was alienation, defined as self-estrangement, on the part of workers.

Alienation has been studied in connection with various aspects of modern life, such as politics and religion, and with certain members of society, women, ethnic groups, youth, drug-users, youth gangs, and so on. In 1968 a Louis Harris survey proclaimed that 33 million Americans felt alienated.[6] While alienation was once seen as the consequence of an unjust economic system, it is also seen as a basic reaction to society.[7] This reaction is characterized by estrangement, noninvolvement, aggressive anxiety, and lack of commitment.

Seeman[8] developed a definition of alienation that is composed of six aspects:

1. Powerlessness: the sense of low control versus mastery of events.

2. Meaninglessness: the sense of incomprehensibility versus understanding of personal and social affairs.

3. Normlessness: high expectancies for (or commitment to) socially approved means versus conventional means for the achievement of given goals.

4. Cultural estrangement: the individual's rejection of commonly held values in the society (or subsector) versus commitment to the prevalent group standards.

5. Self-estrangement: the individual's engagement in activities that are not intrinsically rewarding versus involvement in a task or activity for its own sake.

6. Social isolation: the sense of exclusion or rejection versus social acceptance.

Work alienation is an area of particular interest to the field of organizational behavior. Many causes have been identified, but most of them are related to one of the following trends.[9]

1. The Industrial Revolution
2. The urbanization of workers
3. The division of labor and resultant narrowed job scope
4. The bureaucratic reorganization with its emphasis upon formalized and centralized authority
5. The changing technology that produced mechanization and automation

CHARACTERISTICS AND MANIFESTATIONS OF WORK ALIENATION

Characteristics of a typical alienated worker are "lack of communication, poorly defined self-concept, apathy, lack of goals, resistance to change, and limited exercise of alternatives, choices, and decisions"[10] The "blue-collar blues" are perhaps the most common manifestation of worker alienation and are described as "general dissatisfaction with life, blunted aspiration, aggressive feelings toward other kinds of people, low political efficacy, mild but debilitating health reactions" [11] Labor distrust and strife, union grievances, reduced productivity, tardiness, absenteeism, and subversion signal the presence of alienated workers in the workplace.

Individuals react differently to their alienation. Responses include fatalism, withdrawal, revolutionary impulses to reorder either work or society, involvement in orderly change, subversion, or sabotage. A common response to work alienation is to compartmentalize one's life and focus upon leisure and/or consumption.

Robert Blauner's book, entitled *Alienation and Freedom: The Factory Worker and His Industry*,[12] is considered a classic in the field of worker alienation. He looked at four industries characterized by varying degrees of technology: craft, machine tending, assembly line, and continuous process automation. Blauner studied the printing, textile, auto, and chemical industries to determine which types of alienation were present using four of Seeman's categories (powerlessness, meaninglessness, isolation, and self-estrangement). He discovered that workers in the printing field were the least alienated, due primarily to the control they had over their work and the pride they showed in both their work and profession. The most alienated group were the auto workers who evidenced each of the four types of alienation. They had no control over their work on the assembly line, worked on only a small percentage of the finished product, lacked informal social structure and status structures, and viewed their jobs only as a means to further other ends.

The textile workers were the next most alienated group because they, too, had limited control and were even more powerless than autoworkers due to the lack of strong union representation. However, because most textile workers lived in milltowns with a strong social structure where kinship ties and religion played a major role, isolation alienation was not found in this group. While some of the male textile workers experienced self-estrangement, the women, immigrants, and rural southerners who worked in the mills did not manifest the same needs for self-expression as northern textile workers or workers in the other industries.

Blauner found the chemical workers were more alienated than the printers but less alienated than the auto and textile workers. Unlike the two latter groups who were at the beck and call of their machines, the chemical workers were responsible for monitoring machines. Like printers, chemical workers had freedom to control various aspects of their work and could easily see its meaningfulness. The technology allowed them to have social contacts and work in teams. Chemical workers appeared to be loyal to their employer and enjoyed the opportunity to master the work and troubleshoot when a machine broke down.

Blauner concluded that the type of technology determines the degree of worker alienation. He also predicted that automation was a positive improvement over mechanized technology and heralded a less alienated future for factory workers.

Although the assembly line is the most efficient design when one considers only the task, few companies have succeeded in ameliorating the mind-numbing quality of assembly line work. As Garson wrote after observing life in an auto factory: "The underlying assumption in an auto plant is that no worker wants to work. The plant is arranged so that employees can be controlled, checked, and supervised at every point. The efficiency of an assembly line is not only in its speed but in the fact that the workers are easily replaced. This allows the employer to cope with high turnover. But it's a vicious cycle. The job is so unpleasantly subdivided that men are constantly quitting and absenteeism is common. Even an accident is a welcome diversion. Because of the high turnover, management further simplifies the job, and more men quit. But the company has learned to cope with high turnover. So they don't have to worry if men quit or go crazy before they're forty."[13]

Some auto plants have worked hard to make assembly work more satisfying, usually by forming work teams that are responsible for one section of a car or an entire car. Nevertheless, managers still face the challenge of making repetitive work interesting. Blauner was certainly correct in his assumption that technology has an impact on the way that work is designed and the way it affects the social system—the people using the technology. Technology helps or hinders the development of relationships and determines how much latitude employees have in decision making.

For example, groupware computer networks provide rank-and-file employees with information that was previously seen only by senior managers, and electronic mail allows them to communicate with anyone they please. As a result, this technology is breaking down the hierarchical nature of some companies.[14] Technology also dictates how meaningful a job appears to an employee. Therefore, the crucial factors in work motivation are often limited by the "sociotechnical" system operating in the organization. Successful changes in work design must address both the technology and the social system.

The exercise that follows is designed to allow you to experiment with different sociotechnical systems. You will be asked to consider your learning group as manufacturing companies. During the first round you will work in assembly-line fashion; in the second round you may organize as you wish. By using a questionnaire to keep both productivity records as well as satisfaction indices, you will be able to examine the factors that influence work motivation and productivity.

Procedure for Group Meeting:
Moon Tents and Shallow Water
Cargo Carriers Simulation

Step 1.   Company formation and organization. Each learning group will form a company that will make moon tents and shallow water carriers.

Step 2.   Choice of manager. The instructor will choose a person to play the role of general manager (GM) from each learning group. The GM will be in charge of making purchases and production decisions. The GM will then choose an assistant general manager (AGM) who will be in charge of organizing the assembly line, quality control, and sales. The rest of the group will be assembly-line workers. The GM's instructions are found on page 551, as are the AGM's and the workers' instructions. WORKERS SHOULD SIT QUIETLY— NO TALKING ALLOWED—WHILE THE GM AND THE AGM READ THEIR INSTRUCTIONS.

Step 3.   Preparation for production of the moon tent. (10 minutes) After reading the GM's instructions, the GM should make decisions about production goals and materials purchasing, following the steps in moon tent production forms beginning on page 552.

Meanwhile, the AGM should be setting up the assembly line and assigning tasks to workers. Workers should sit in a row and perform one or more steps in the construction and then pass the moon tent on to the next person. WORKERS ARE NOT ALLOWED TO TALK TO EACH OTHER; THEY MAY ONLY ADDRESS THE GM OR AGM. Workers should practice their step of the production under the direction of the AGM, who should also establish quality control procedures.

Step 4.   Production of the moon tent. (15 minutes) The GM should conduct the 6-minute production run as specified on the moon tent form. Following production, the instructor should buy those products of acceptable quality from each company's AGM. The GM or the AGM should compute the company's profit and loss and each person should complete the Moon Tent Questionnaire on pages 557-558.

Step 5.   Production of shallow water cargo carriers. (40 minutes) There are two major modifications in your instructions for the production of the shallow water cargo carriers:

a. In this round the production steps have been expanded. Your company will be allowed to make an initial bid, do a time trial, and rebid before making the final production run.

b. Also, *your company may organize in any way and establish whatever work procedures it wishes.* Workers may talk whenever they like. Managers are freed from the authoritarian role they were asked to play during the last round. You may find the data from the Moon Test Questionnaire useful in planning your production of the shallow water cargo carrier.

Instructions for the General Manager (GM)

Your task is to be an authoritative manager of an assembly line. There's no need to exaggerate your role, but you and your AGM are the only ones who understand what needs to be done. Just tell the workers what to do; they're probably not interested in the details. You've had trouble with them in the past because they sometimes loaf on the job. Your success, however, depends upon their producing lots of moon tents. Don't waste time establishing a relationship with these workers because turnover is high at this plant.

1. Don't let the workers do much talking. Remember time is money and your bonus is at stake here. The more moon tents they make, the more money you make.

2. Make sure your AGM is carrying out his or her task of lining the workers up correctly and assigning them to their "Steps in the Assembly Production Line" found on pages 552-555.

3. Read the "Steps in Moon Tent Production" on page 556 so you understand your responsibility for setting production and profit levels for your unit. Make these decisions by yourself so everyone knows you have real managerial potential.

4. Make your production level decisions, tell the workers what their quota levels are, and carry out the production run.

5. Figure out your profit statistics or ask your AGM to do so.

Instructions for the Assistant General Manager

Your job is to supervise the work of the assembly-line workers. *Don't let them talk on the the line or valuable seconds will be lost.* Don't let them give you any advice or you'll look weak. Try to make all the decisions so your boss will be impressed by your authoritative manner.

1. Arrange the workers in a straight line.

2. Divide the number of steps (14) in the assembly-line production (see page 552) by the number of workers you have to find out how many steps each one must perform. For example, if you have five workers and 14 job steps, four workers should do 3 steps each and one should do 2 steps.

3. Assign each worker the steps for which he or she is responsible. Don't have any duplication of effort.

4. Inspect each moon tent when it is done. Use the Quality Control Points on page 556 to guide you.

5. Do whatever else your GM tells you to do.

Instructions for Workers

Guess what? Two more college-educated people have been brought in to run your production unit. You wonder how much they know about making moon tents, but you're smart enough to know it doesn't pay to talk on the assembly line. Just keep your mouth shut and do what you're told. Last time you made a suggestion, they called you a troublemaker.

Steps in Moon Tent Assembly Production Line

The following are directions for making a moon tent. For each step there is a picture telling you what to do and another picture showing how it should then look. Check this before going on to the next step. There are 14 steps.

1. You should have a piece of paper that is blank on one side and looks like this on the other side:

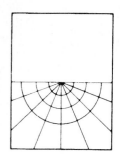

2. Turn the paper over so that the blank side is facing up and the pattern is nearest you.

printed pattern at this end   YOU

3. Fold AB to CD.

A ———————————— B

C ———————————— D

It should look like this:

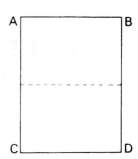

4. Fold G to F

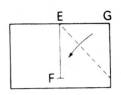

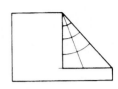

It should look like this

5. Bend down H to F

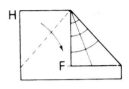

It should now look like this:

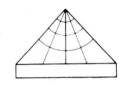

6. Fold one layer of paper (up direction) along JK.

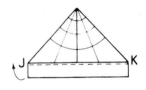

It should now look like this:

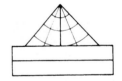

7. Turn the moon tent over to the other side.
It should now look like this:

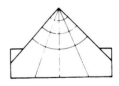

8. Fold (up direction) along LM.

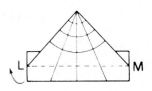

It should now look like this:

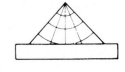

9. Tuck section N (just the top layer of paper) back around the edge of the tent, so it is between the back of the tent and the back layer of paper.

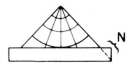

Fold section O (back piece) toward you over the edge of the tent and press flat.

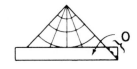

It should now look like this:

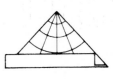

10. Do the same thing to the left end (don't turn over). It should look like this:

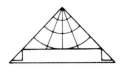

11. Pick up the tent and hold it in your hands with open side (P) down.

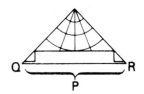

Open up P with your fingers and keep pulling it apart until points Q and R meet.

Turn the paper so that Q is facing up and R is underneath. It should look like this:

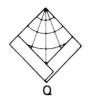

12. Fold up Q along ST.

It should now look like this:

13. Turn over so that R is facing up. Fold up on UV.

It should now look like this:

14. Open up W and stand up your Moon Tent!

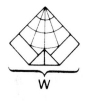

For "quality control," make sure Q and R
stay up along the tent.

Passes Quality Control →

Not Good →

QUALITY CONTROL POINTS FOR THE MOON TENT

1. The top of the tent must come to a point.
2. The printing must be on the outside of the tent.
3. The turned-up points at the base of the tent must lie flat against the tent sides.

Steps in the Moon Tent Production

Cost and profit information for the moon tent as well as typical assembly times for one unit are shown below. The instructor or a nonparticipant should record the number of sets purchased, number of sets sold, and the profit or loss on a chalkboard or newsprint so that everyone can see the other teams' bids. The instructor should also act as the buyer and final approver of product quality.

1. Cost and Profit for the Moon Tent

NUMBER OF SETS PURCHASED	TOTAL COST	TOTAL SELLING PRICE	TOTAL PROFIT
3	$147,900	$150,000	$ 2,100
4	195,000	200,000	5,000
5	240,000	250,000	10,000
6	279,000	300,000	20,100
7	319,000	350,000	30,100
8	360,000	400,000	40,000
9	400,000	450,000	50,000
10	440,000	500,000	60,000
11	474,000	550,000	76,000
12	519,600	600,000	80,400
13	559,650	650,000	90,350
14	599,900	700,000	100,100
$14+n$	$599,900+ 40,250n$	$700,000+ 50,000n$	$100,100+ 9,750n$

2. Assembly Times for One Moon Tent
   This table gives assembly times for one moon tent based on the actual performance of people who have assembled them.

   - Fast assembly time (top 10%)   35-45 seconds
   - Average assembly time   45-55 seconds
   - Slow assembly time (bottom 10%)   over 55 seconds

3. Production Decision
   Record the number of moon tent sets you decided to purchase and produce:

   _____

4. Maximum Potential Profit

Your maximum potential profit can be computed in the following manner: From the information provided in the cost and profit table (item 1), you can determine the potential profit associated with reaching your final production decision (item 3).

Enter the maximum potential profit here:_____

Production of the Moon Tent: You now have 6 minutes to produce the number of Moon Tents for which you purchased materials. Only units that meet quality control specifications will be accepted for sale.

5. Postproduction Inspection-Products Sold

Carefully inspect the units you have produced for quality and record the acceptable number of completed products here:_____ (Wait for the leader or inspector to inspect your products.)

6. Actual Profit Earned

To determine the actual amount of your net profit (or loss, if negative):

a. Enter here the total selling price (see cost and profit table) for the number of products of satisfactory quality you have completed: $a =$ _____ Note: You cannot sell more products than your final production decision (item 3).

b. Enter here the total costs (item 1) for the final number of products you decided to produce (item 3): $b =$ _____

c. Your actual net profit or loss can be computed in the following manner: Net profit or loss = $a - b =$ _____

7. Possible Profit Ratio

Your percentage of possible profit is the ratio between net profit (6c) and maximum potential profit (4a). Enter that ratio here_____

8. Each person should fill out the Moon Tent Questionnaire.

Moon Tent Questionnaire

1. How satisfied were you with your group?

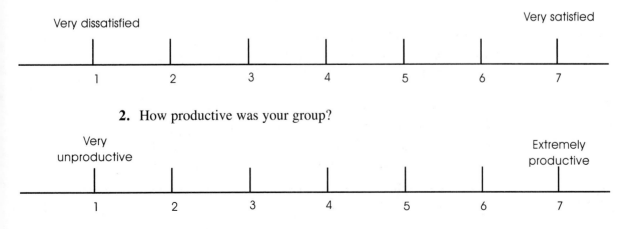

3. What did you like about your work?

4. What did you dislike?

Directions for Making the Shallow Water Cargo Carrier

These are directions for making a shallow water cargo carrier. The first 9 steps are the same as for the moon tent. For each step there is a picture showing what to do, and another picture showing what it should then look like. There are 14 steps.

1. Hold the sheet of paper so the printing on it is facing up, the letters SWCC nearest you are upside down (ƆƆMS).

   It should look like this:

   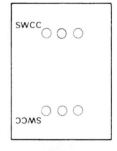

2. **Fold AB to CD.**

   It should now look like this:

   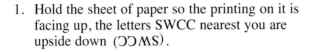

3. **Fold in along JG and JH so that E and F meet at point K.**

   It should now look like this:

   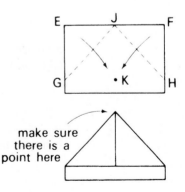

4. Fold one layer of paper (up direction) along LM.

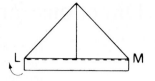

It should now look like this:

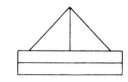

5. Turn your shallow water cargo carrier over to the other side. It should now look like this:

6. Fold (up direction) along NP.

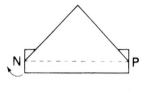

It should now look like this:

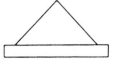

7. Tuck section Q (just the top layer of paper) back around the edge of the carrier, so it is between the back of the carrier and the back layer of paper.

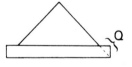

Fold section Q (back piece) toward you over the edge of the carrier and press flat.

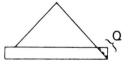

It should now look like this:

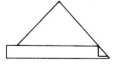

8. Do the same thing to the left end (don't turn it over). It should now look like this:

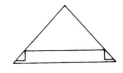

9. Pick up the shallow water cargo carrier and hold it in your hands with the open side (R) down. Open up R with your fingers and keep pulling it apart until points S and T meet.

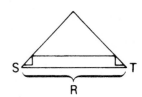

Turn the paper and fold so that S is facing up and T is underneath. It should now look like like this:

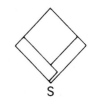

10. Fold up S to U.

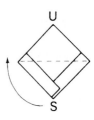

It should now look like this:

11. Turn over so that T is facing up (side without printing on it). Fold up T to U.

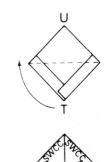

It should now look like this:

12. Pick up the carrier and hold it in your hands, with the open side, V, down. Open V with your fingers and keep pulling it apart until points W and X meet. Turn the paper so that W is facing up and X is underneath. It should look like the diagram shown here:

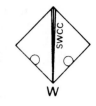

13. Fold W to A and then bring W back down again to its original position. There should now be a crease at BC.

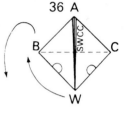

Turn over so that X is facing up. Fold X to A and then bring X down again to its original position. There should now be a crease at DE

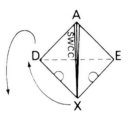

Grab Y (front and back at the top left point) with left hand, and Z (front and back at the top right poi with right hand and pull apart as far as it will go.

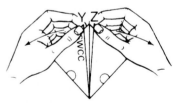

It should now look like this:

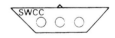

14. Stand it up. You have finished making your shallow water cargo carrier!

QUALITY CONTROL POINTS FOR THE SHALLOW WATER CARGO CARRIER

1. The lettering SWCC must appear on the outside of the boat.
2. The middle point must be a point, not a curve.
3. The middle point must come even with or above the sides of the boat.

STEPS IN SHALLOW WATER CARGO CARRIER PRODUCTION

Cost and profit information for the shallow water cargo carrier, as well as typical assembly times for one unit, are given as follows.

1. Cost and Profit Information for the Shallow Water Cargo Carrier

NUMBER OF SETS PURCHASED	TOTAL COST	TOTAL SELLING PRICE	TOTAL PROFIT
3	$267,000	$270,000	$ 3,000
4	352,000	360,000	8,000
5	420,000	450,000	30,000
6	450,000	540,000	90,000
7	483,000	630,000	147,000
8	512,000	720,000	208,000
9	540,000	810,000	270,000
10	570,000	900,000	330,000
11	605,000	990,000	385,000
12	636,000	1,080,000	444,000
13	663,000	1,170,000	507,000
14	700,000	1,260,000	560,000
$14+n$	$700,000 + 37,000n$	$1,260,000 + 90,000n$	$560,000 + 53,000n$

2. Assembly Times for One Shallow Water Cargo Carrier

This table gives assembly times for one WCC based on the actual performance of people who have produced them.

- Fast assembly time (top 10%)   40-50 seconds
- Average assembly time   50-60 seconds
- Slow assembly time (bottom 10%)   over 60 seconds

3. Tentative Decision

After building your model and inspecting the information given, make a tentative decision about the number of units you wish to buy for production in a 6-minute period. Record that number here_____.

4. Timed Trial Run

Now that you have made your tentative production decision, prepare for a timed practice trial. When you are ready, take a timed practice assembly. Record the construction time it took to complete one unit here_____.

5. Profit Reduction Resulting from Change of Decision

Having taken the time trial, you may wish to change your decision about the number of SWCCs you produce in 6 minutes. Production decision changes invariably cost money. The following table tells how much this change will cost.

CHANGE	PROFIT REDUCTION
1 more or 1 less	$12,000
2 more or 2 less	19,000
3 more or 3 less	27,000
4 more or 4 less	36,000
5 more or 5 less	46,000
6 more or 6 less	57,000

6. Production Decision

   After making your final decision, record here the number of sets you decided to produce_____.

7. Maximum Potential Profit

   Your maximum potential profit can be computed in the following manner.
   a. From the information provided in the cost and profit table (item 1), you can determine the profit associated with reaching your final production decision (item 6). Enter that maximum potential profit here:

      $a =$ _____
   b. If your final production decision (item 6) is different from your tentative production decision (item 3), you must subtract from the profit entered in a the correct profit reduction indicated in the table provided in item 5. Enter that number amount here.

      $b =$ _____
   c. Enter your maximum potential profit here; subtract b from a:

      $c =$ _____

   Production of the shallow water cargo carrier: You now have 6 minutes to produce the number of SWCCs for which you purchased materials. Only units that meet quality control specifications will be accepted for sale.

8. Postproduction Inspection-Products Sold

   Carefully inspect the units you have produced for quality and record the acceptable number of completed products here_____. (Wait for the leader or inspector to inspect your products.)

9. Actual Profit Earned

   To determine the actual amount of your net profit (or loss, if negative):
   a. Enter here the total selling price (see table, item 1) for the number of products of satisfactory quality you have completed:

      $a =$ _____

      Note: You cannot sell more products than your final production decision (step 6).
   b. Enter here the total costs (item 1) for the final number of products you decided to produce (item 6):

      $b =$ _____
   c. If your final production decision (item 6) was different from your tentative production decision (item 3), enter here the correct profit reduction as indicated in the table provided in item 5:

      $c =$ _____
   d. Your actual net profit or loss can then be computed in the following manner:

      Net profit or loss $= a - (b + c) =$ _____

10. Possible Profit Ratio
    Your percentage of possible profit earned is the ratio between net profit (9d) and maximum potential profit (7c). Enter that ratio here_____.

11. Each person should fill out the Shallow Water Cargo Carrier Questionnaire.

Shallow Water Cargo Questionnaire

1. How satisfied were you with your group?

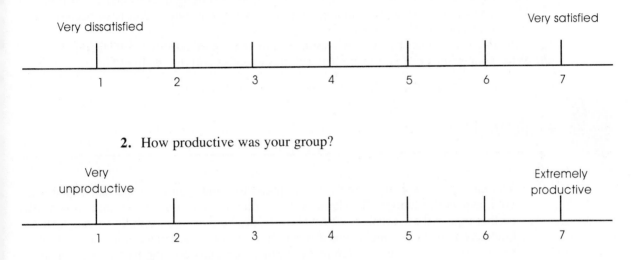

2. How productive was your group?

3. What did you like about your work?

4. What did you dislike?

STEP 6.   Work and motivation discussion. (30 minutes, entire group) Tabulate the data from the two questionnaires by teams and display them on a chalkboard or newsprint. The discussion should explore the following questions:

a. What were the most dramatic data differences between the first and second rounds? In which teams did they occur?

b. Have the teams with the greatest differences discussed the reasons for them? Did similar things happen in other teams? List them.

c. In general, what were the factors that led to satisfaction and productivity in the first round? In the second round?

d. If you had to continue working in this kind of production, what arrangement of work would you prefer? Why?

e. What conclusions can you now come to about improving the quality of work life in organizations? What kinds of things are helpful in sustaining interest and motivation?

f. Had there been a different technology and task, what would the effect have been on the way you went about the work?

g. How might you redesign the jobs you had to increase productivity? Satisfaction?

h. What connections can you make between this exercise and the readings?

 Follow-Up

You have just finished a simulation designed to allow you to create and experience your own work situation. You have probably drawn some conclusions about how work of this type is best organized to maximize productivity and employee satisfaction. Quite probably your conclusions differ from those of some others in the class. In that regard you are not much different from other managers and the behavioral scientists who have worked in the area of motivation. Just about everything conceivable has been tried to improve employee motivation and productivity, from incentive plans to piped-in music, with mixed results.[15]

The term "alienation" is not as popular as it once was; we are more likely to hear about the other side of the coin, "job involvement or commitment." However, we still hear some managers complain that their workers are not motivated. In general, productivity has increased in the U.S. particularly in the high involvement organizations described in Chapter 17. When managers say their workers are unmotivated, they really mean that they are not motivated to do the tasks assigned to them. These same workers are likely to show great motivation in other areas of their life: at home, in hobbies, in community affairs, and so on. The practical implication of this distinction for worker satisfaction and productivity is that the time and effort spent lamenting lazy workers might be better spent in examination of the nature of the work itself and in the redesign of these tasks and jobs to add the personal autonomy, need satisfaction, and challenge that stimulate the motivation to work. The intrinsic motivation of the employee is very important, but job motivation is also affected by the situations in which workers find themselves, and, in particular, the way in which their jobs are designed.

Based upon what we know about alienation and motivation, job situations that motivate people have the following characteristics:

1. *Skill variety*—the degree to which a job requires a range of personal competencies and abilities in carrying out the work.

2. *Task identity*—the degree to which a job requires completion of a "whole" and identifiable piece of work, that is, doing a good job from beginning to end with a visible outcome.

3. *Task significance*—the degree to which the job is perceived by the employee as having a substantial impact on the lives of other people, whether those people are within or outside of the organization.

4. *Autonomy*—the degree to which the job provides freedom, independence, and discretion to the employee in scheduling the tasks and in determining the procedure to be used in carrying out the task.

5. *Job feedback*—the degree to which carrying out the job related tasks provides the individual with direct and clear information about the effectiveness of his or her performance.[16]

Skill variety, task identity, and task significance are geared towards replacing the sense of meaningfulness that was lessened by dividing jobs into small, repetitive segments. Granting employees autonomy over their jobs encourages them to feel responsible (powerful and in control) for the outcome of their work and reduces legalistic approaches to work, for example, "That's not my job" or "If they're gonna give me a robot's job to do, I'm gonna do it like a robot! Anyway, it just lowers my production record to get up and point out someone else's error."[17] Job feedback allows employees to receive immediate feedback from the work itself, not from a supervisor. This relates to one of the conditions Mc Clelland found to be most favorable for people with high needs for achievement—immediate concrete feedback that allows them to adjust their performance to meet their personal and/or organizational goals. Jobs that involve dealing with others and have friendship opportunities are ways of encouraging social belonging and combating the social isolation that Mayo reported.

In their Job Characteristics Enrichment Model, which appears in Figure 21-1. Hackman and Oldham[18] show that the positive outcomes of job enrichment characteristics are high internal work motivation, high-quality work performance, high satisfaction with the work, and low absenteeism and turnover. However, these outcomes occur at maximum level only when all three of the critical psychological states are experienced: 1) experienced meaningfulness of the work, 2) experienced responsibility for the work outcomes, and 3) knowledge of the actual results of the work. Hackman and Oldham also note that there are three types of individual differences that must be taken into consideration when planning job redesign projects. The first is the *knowledge and skill of the employee*—is the employee capable of performing an enriched job? The second is *growth-needs strength*, which refers to the individual's personal need for learning, self-development, and challenge. People with low growth needs may well prefer repetitive jobs to enriched ones? The final individual difference is *satisfaction with contextual factors*. Job redesign efforts are unlikely to be successful if employees are dissatisfied with contextual factors.

Ensuring that the work situation is one that employees find motivating and involving is a major, ongoing task of managers. Because of the close relationship between well-designed jobs and productivity, it is an area that managers and organizations cannot afford to overlook. It is possible to design jobs that are more congruent with human needs and motivation. The major ways of doing so are briefly described as follows:

1. *Job rotation programs* that move people from one job to another to decrease their boredom and allow them to learn different skills.

2. *Job enlargement policies* increase the number of tasks performed by an individual. In an assembly-line example, a worker would perhaps install an entire door panel rather than securing only one part of the door. Herzberg called the addition of interrelated tasks "horizontal job loading." [19]

Job enlargement can meet employees' motivational needs because it allows more ownership over a product or process and decreases monotony. It also provides an opportunity for workers to feel more competent, since they may get to use more of their skills. Being responsible for a larger task may increase the meaningfulness of the job in the worker's eyes. However, remember the comment of one critic, "You combine seven boring jobs and what do you get?"

3. *Job enrichment* methods attempt to change the nature of the job by broadening responsibilities, giving more autonomy for decision making, creating client systems and direct feedback systems, and generally enlarging the scope of jobs. Herzberg called this type of job design "vertical job loading" because it also includes tasks formerly performed by someone at a higher level—planning and control functions.[20] For example, a sales support clerk who formerly handled only one piece of the paperwork for the entire sales staff is now given responsibility for all paperwork in one district. He is encouraged to deal directly with the sales staff and quickly becomes an important resource for them. He also has discretionary control over the scheduling of his work and the responsibility for making sure he has made no errors. A feedback system is established so he can gauge both the quality and quantity of his output. Both contact with the sales staff and the monitoring of his work were formerly performed by his supervisor.

Figure 21-1 Job Characteristics Enrichment Model

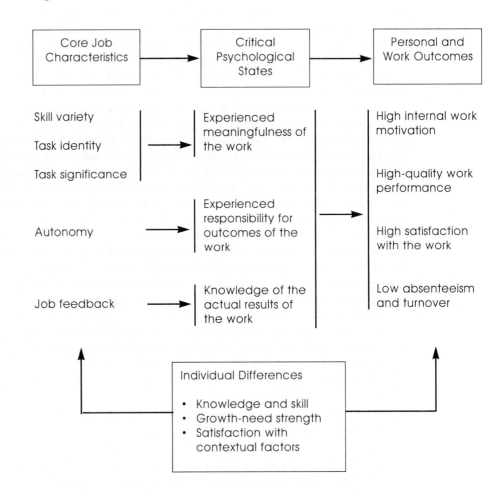

J.R. Hackman and G.R. Oldham, *Work Redesign* © 1980, Addison Wesley Publishing Co., Inc. Reading, MA. Adapted from p. 90. Reprinted with permission of the publisher.

What is motivating about job enrichment? It resolves the problems of meaninglessness, powerlessness, and isolation. Job enrichment not only has the same motivational advantages as job enlargement, but the effects with job enrichment are stronger and enrichment has the added benefit of granting workers autonomy. With all the publicity about entrepreneurs who want to run their own show, we can see how important autonomy is to many employees. Autonomy allows people to utilize even more skills and to exercise their creativity and capacity to learn and develop. Research on work redesign programs indicates that they do reduce absenteeism and turnover; however, there are mixed results on productivity. Some job enrichment efforts result in higher productivity, while others do not.[21]

4. *Sociotechnical system* interventions attempt to match the necessary technology of the job with the social needs of the employees. Their goal is to produce a fit or integration of these two components. It's noteworthy that the basic unit of work design here is usually the group rather than the individual. Job rotation, enlargement, and enrichment focus upon individual rather than group needs.[22]

The most common example of sociotechnical systems are autonomous work teams. Such teams are totally responsible for assigning the work, determining the work schedule, work process, quality control procedures, reward structure, and so on. One of the most famous examples of autonomous work teams was found in the Volvo plant in Uddevalla, Sweden.[23] Instead of using an assembly line, the cars remained stationary while teams of eight to ten workers assembled three entire cars a day. This job design reduced tedium because the workers did a variety of jobs that required expanded skills. Furthermore, the workers experienced both greater task identity and control over their work.

The team approach at Uddevalla resulted in increased quality and satisfaction, but productivity and absenteeism were still a problem.[24] The teams required fifty labor hours to build a car which is twice the hours needed at Volvo's Belgium plant. The Japanese can build a car in less than twenty hours. Volvo decided to shut down the Uddevalla plant and their Kalmar plant, which also used autonomous work teams, in order to cut costs. Many car manufacturers are utilizing some form of work teams, but they vary in terms of how many tasks they are responsible for and how much autonomy is granted to the teams.

Sociotechnical systems have the advantages of all the previous design systems plus the added benefit of group membership. Interdependent work teams anchor people firmly within a social system, thus avoiding isolation and normlessness. Furthermore, groups are more creative and productive than are individuals when it comes to complex technology.

5. *Self-managed work teams*, highlighted in Chapter 9, share many similarities with sociotechnical systems. Both emphasize skill variety, task identity, task significance, autonomy, job feedback, and the social belonging that comes from group membership. In sociotechnical systems, however, more attention is specifically concentrated on balancing technical and human systems. Self-managed work teams decide how they will accomplish the goals for which they are responsible and allocate the necessary tasks. They are responsible for planning, scheduling, organizing, directing, controlling, and evaluating their own work process, which is usually an entire process or product. Some teams select and evaluate their own members.

6. The *quality movement* was started by Edward Deming,[25] an American Management consultant who taught his famous fourteen principles to the Japanese in the 1950's, at the time the "Made in Japan" label was synonymous with poor quality. Japan's current reputation for producing goods of extremely high quality is credited in large part to Deming.

In addition to improving quality, other basic goals of quality programs are to lower costs, speed up the flow of information, materials and products, increase flexibility, reduce inventory, and improve customer satisfaction. Quality programs focus on managing the process of the work rather than people and give workers the challenge of constantly trying to improve the quality of the work processes and placing primary emphasis upon the customer. This provides workers with a sense of meaning. Such programs teach statistics as a common language that is used to measure variances from the perfect quality standard. Each employee is taught to inspect his or her own work so that defects and reworks are reduced or even eliminated. This emphasis on immediate feedback on quality stimulates needs for achievement. Quality programs generally involve group problem-solving efforts, which meet people's need for affiliation. Quality programs focus on the requirements of the task, but their manner of doing so also meets the motivational needs of employees.[26]

Continuous improvement, "kaizen" in Japanese, is a key factor in Total Quality programs. This term is sometimes used interchangeably by companies to describe their total quality effort. Continuous improvement programs are designed to take advantage of employee experience and commitment to improving the products, services, and the work practices of the organization.[27] In recognition of the importance of quality in global competition, the U.S. government initiated the Malcolm Baldridge Quality Award to honor organizations that attain "world-class" quality in their products, services, and operations. The competition criteria are:

- A plan to keep improving all operations continuously
- A system for measuring these improvements accurately
- A strategic plan based on benchmarks that compare the company's performance with the world's best
- A close partnership with suppliers and customers that feeds improvements back into the operation
- A deep understanding of the customers so that their wants can be translated into products
- A long-lasting relationship with customers, going beyond the delivery of the products to include sales, service, and ease of maintenance
- A focus on preventing mistakes, rather than merely correcting them
- A commitment to improving quality that runs from the top of the organization to the bottom[28]

None of the work redesign programs described in this chapter should be seen as a quick fix for organizations. Some programs succeed while other do not. The reasons for failure sometimes have more to do with the way programs are implemented than with the particular merits of the program in question. The following chapter focuses on how to successfully manage the change process.

1. The changes in the nature of work and the social system brought about by the Industrial Revolution resulted in feelings of
   a. Powerlessness (Marx).
   b. Meaninglessness (Durkheim).
   c. Social isolation (Mayo).

2. These feelings came to be known as "alienation," which is simply defined as self-estrangement.

3. The cause of work alienation is usually traced to the Industrial Revolution, urbanization of workers, the division of labor that led to narrowed job scope, bureaucracy, and the switch to mechanized and automated technology.

4. Characteristics of work alienation are lack of communication, poorly defined self-concept, apathy, lack of goals, resistance to change, and limited exercise of alternatives, choices, and decisions.

5. Blauner found that the type of technology affected the degree of alienation found within four different industries. Workers in craft technologies and automated technologies had less alienation than did workers in mechanized technologies such as assembly lines.

6. Motivation is an internal state. However, it is also affected by work situations that encourage or discourage its expression.

7. Jobs that are motivating have the following characteristics:
   a. Skill variety
   b. Task identity
   c. Task significance
   d. Autonomy
   e. Job feedback

8. Methods of job redesign and motivating employees are
   a. Job rotation-switching different jobs.
   b. Job enlargement-horizontal job loading, which combines related tasks.
   c. Job enrichment-vertical job loading, which increases job scope by including planning and control functions formerly held by supervisors. It also includes client contact and direct output feedback.
   d. Sociotechnical systems-integration of the needs of both people and technology. The basic work unit is usually the group rather than the individual. Autonomous work teams are an example.
   e. Self-managed work teams decide how they will accomplish the goals for which they are responsible and allocate the necessary tasks. They are responsible for planning, scheduling, organizing, directing, controlling, and evaluating their own work process, which is usually an entire process or product.
   f. Quality movement- employees are motivated by the constant challenge to improve quality and processes.

9. Job redesign efforts have been found to improve both satisfaction and productivity in some cases. However, job enrichment programs are also contingent upon the individual worker's 1) knowledge and skill; 2) need for growth, self-development and challenge, and 3) satisfaction with contextual factors.

for Managers

- The key to success in redesigning work often lies in the way changes are implemented. Therefore, it's important to pay attention to implementation and the "fit" between the new design and other aspects of the organization.

- Whenever a new system of work design is implemented, it's realistic to expect that production may drop until employees master the new system and work their way up the learning curve.

- Job enrichment cannot take the place of decent pay and job security. Bear in mind Maslow's hierarchy, which states that pay and security are lower-level needs that must be satisfied before the higher-level needs met by job enrichment come into play.

- One way of checking up on job design is to do a flowchart on each work process. Find out how many different people need to "touch" a piece of paperwork before it is completed. Any time a paper is passed to other people for handling, it must then compete for their attention with all the other papers in their in-basket. If speed is important, it makes more sense to have as few people as possible touching a document.

- What value does each job add? Some activities add only costs and should be eliminated, (e.g.,writing reports to impress superiors).

- Focus on providing motivating situations for those who desire it, within the organization's capabilities. There may well be people whose ambition or need to grow outstrips the opportunities an organization can provide. Rather than go overboard (remember Quinn's positive and negative circles in Chapter 2 and the danger of emphasizing employee needs at the cost of productivity?), counsel such employees to look for work elsewhere. Once again, managers have to exhibit good judgment and a knack for balance. If a manager ignores the motivational needs of employees, low productivity, alienation, and high turnover and absenteeism may result. On the other hand, too much attention to employee needs without equal emphasis upon the needs of the organization encourages people to fixate on themselves and lose sight of the greater good. Redesign programs have to be closely tied to the success of the organization.

- Statistics show that a greater number of Americans are now living alone and that the majority of households are not traditional nuclear families. This may mean that more employees are seeking to meet their social needs at work than was true when family and community ties were stronger.

- Conditions that affect the success of work design interventions are organizational culture, technology, union support or lack thereof, and the nature of the work force itself.

- Gain-sharing is another way to motivate employees that is receiving a good deal of attention. In gain-sharing, the organization establishes a base period of performance. When performance gains occur, a formula is used to share the financial gains with all employees. Gain-sharing focuses attention on cost savings, continuous improvement, and higher performance from everyone, including managers.

Personal Application Assignment

The assignment for this chapter is to focus upon an experience you've had with job involvement and design in an organization. Choose a significant incident or situation related to the concepts discussed in the chapter that occurred at work or elsewhere.

A. *Concrete Experience*

1. *Objectively* describe the experience ("who," "what," "when," "where," "how" type information—up to 2 points).

2. *Subjectively* describe your feelings, perceptions, and thoughts that occurred during (not after) the experience (up to 2 points). Does this section have too much detail? (If so, delete 1 point.)

B. *Reflective Observation*

1. Look at the experience from different points of view. How many points of view did you include that are *relevant* (up to 2 points)?

2. Use these perspectives to add more meaning to the incident (up to 2 points).

C. *Abstract Conceptualization*

1. Relate concepts from the assigned readings and the lecture to the experience (i.e., what theories that you heard in the lecture or read in the *Reader* relate to your understanding of this incident?). Make reference to at least two sources. Use standard referencing format and include the page number to which you are referring. How many sources did you use and how clearly did you explain their theories (up to 4 points)?

2. You can also create an original model or theory, but it should not replace course concepts.

D. *Active Experimentation*

    1. Write about what you will do in the future that will improve your effectiveness. Use rules of thumb or action resolutions.

    2. Are they described specifically, thoroughly, and in detail (up to 4 points)?

E. *Integration, Synthesis and Writing*

    1. Did you write about something personally important to you (up to 1 point)?

    2. Was it well written (up to 2 points)?

    3. Did you integrate and synthesize the different sections (up to 1 point)?

[1]For an interesting history and summary of the research done on both work alienation and job involvement, see Rabindra Kanungo's *Work Alienation: An Integrative Approach* (New York: Praeger, 1982).

[2]Karl Marx, *Economic and Philosophical Manuscripts* (Moscow: Foreign Languages Publishing House, 1844/1961).

[3]Emile Durkheim, *The Division of Labor in Society*, trans. G. Simpson (New York: Free Press, 1956), and *Suicide* (New York: Free Press, 1951)

[4]Elton Mayo, *The Human Problems of an Industrial Civilization* (New York: Macmillan, 1933), or see *The Social Problems of an Industrial Civilization* (Cambridge, MA: Harvard University Press, 1945) for a better summary of Mayo's theory.

[5]Charles Perrow, *Complex Organizations: A Critical Essay* (New York: Random House, 1986), p. 59.

[6] Louis Harris, "Harris Survey: 33 Million Americans Feel Alienated," *The Washington Post*, December 16, 1968, Section A, p. 21.

[7]Kenneth Kenniston, "Alienation and the Decline of Utopia," *The America Scholar*, Vol. 39 (1960), pp. 161-200.

[8]Melvin Seeman, "On the Meaning of Alienation," *American Sociological Review*, Vol. 24 (1959), pp. 783-791, and "Alienation Studies" *Annual Review of Sociology*, Vol. 1 (1975), pp. 91-123.

[9]Robert Blauner, *Alienation and Freedom*: *The Factory Worker and His Industry* (Chicago: University of Chicago Press, 1964).

[10]Robert Cooper, "Alienation from Work," *New Society*, January 30, 1969, pp. 161-163.

[11]Stanley E. Seashore and J. T. Barnowe, "Behind the Averages: A Closer Look at America's Lower-Middle Income Workers," *Proceedings of the 24th Annual Winter Meeting, Industrial Relations Research Association* (December 1971), pp. 358-370.

[12]Blauner, *Alienation and Freedom*.

[13]Barbara Garson, "Luddites in Lordstown," in *Life in Organizations*, by Rosabeth Moss Kantor and Barry A. Stein, eds. (New York: Basic Books, 1979), pp. 216-217.

[14]John R. Wilke, "Computer Links Erode Hierarchical Nature of Workplace Culture," *The Wall Street Journal*, Thursday, December 9, 1993, p. 1, col. 1. See also Shoshana Zuboff, *In the Age of the Smart Machine* (New York: Basic Books, 1988) for a description of how advanced computer technology changed the nature of work and power.

[15]See William Pasmore, "Turning People on to Work," in *Organizational Psychology: Reading on Human Behavior in Organizations,* ed. by Kolb, Rubin, and McIntyre (Englewood Cliffs, NJ: Prentice Hall, 1984).

[16]This list is composed of factors identified by J. Richard Hackman and Greg Oldham, *Work Redesign* (Reading, MA: Addison-Wesley, 1980), pp. 77-80; J.R. Hackman, G.R. Oldham, R. Janson, and K. Pardy, "A New Strategy for Job Enrichment," *Reader*.

[17]Garson, *Luddites in Lordtown*, p. 235.

[18]J. Richard Hackman and Greg R. Oldham, "Development of the Job Diagnostic Survey," *Journal of Applied Psychology*, Vol. 60 (1975), pp. 159-170.

[19]Frederic Herzberg, "One More Time: How Do You Motivate Employees?" *Harvard Business Review* (January-February 1968).

[20]Ibid.

[21]Ricky W. Griffin, "Effects of Work Redesign on Employee Perceptions, Attitudes, and Behaviors: A Long-term Investigation," *Academy of Management Journal*, June 1991, pp. 425-435.

[22]An entire issue of the *Journal of Applied Behavioral Science*, Vol. 22, no. 3 (1986), edited by W. Pasmore and W. Barko, is devoted to sociotechnical systems and includes information about autonomous work teams. See also the article by Scheonhoven on "The Sociotechnical considerations for the Development of the Space Station: Autonomy and the Human Element in Space" in D.A. Kolb, I.M. Rubin, and J.S. Osland, *The Organizational Behavior Reader* (Englewood Cliffs, NJ: Prentice Hall, 1990).

[23]Jonathan Kapstein, "Volvo's Radical New Plant: The Death of the Assembly Line'?" *Business Week*, August 28, 1989, pp. 92-93.

[24]S. Prokesch, "Edges Fray on Volvo's Brave New Humanistic World," *New York Times*, July 7, 1991, p. C5.

[25]See Myron Tribus' article, "Deming's Redefinition of Management" in the *Reader*.

[26]David A. Garvin's book, *Managing Quality: The Strategic and Competitive Edge* (New York: Free Press, 1988) and Warren H. Schmidt and Jerome Finnigan, *The Race Without a Finish Line* (San Francisco: Jossey-Bass, 1992) provide a good starting place for reading about the quality movement.

[27]Dean M. Scrodoeder and Alan G. Robinson, "America's Most Successful Export to Japan: Continuos Improvement Programs," *Sloan Management Review*, Spring 1991, pp. 67-81; L.S. Vansina, "Total Quality Control: An Overall Organizational Improvement Strategy," *National Productivity Review,* Winter 1989/1990, pp. 59-73.

[28]See Warren H. Schmidt and Jerome P. Finnigan, *The Race Without a Finish Line* (San Francisco: Jossey-Bass, 1992) for lessons from the Baldrige Award winners.

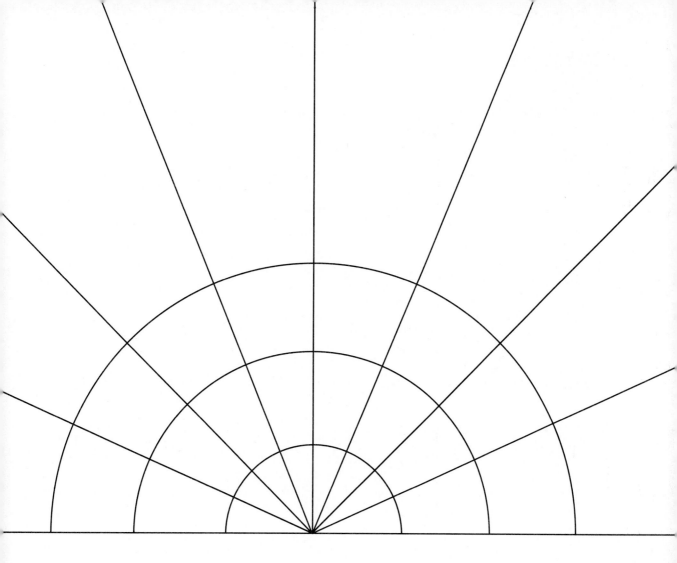

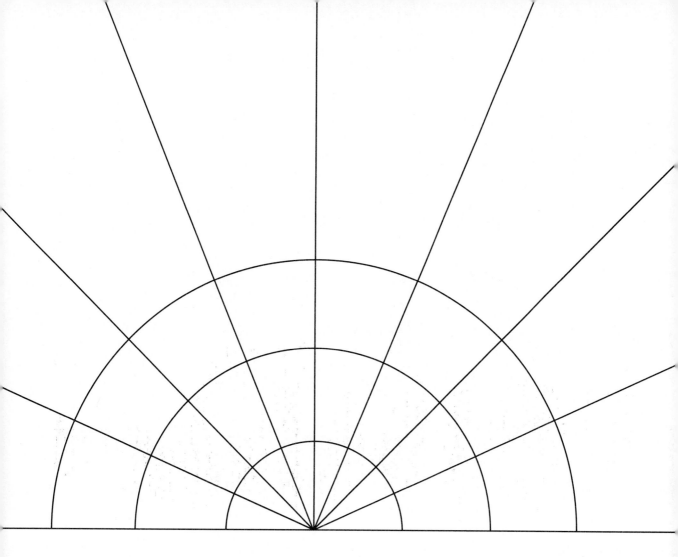

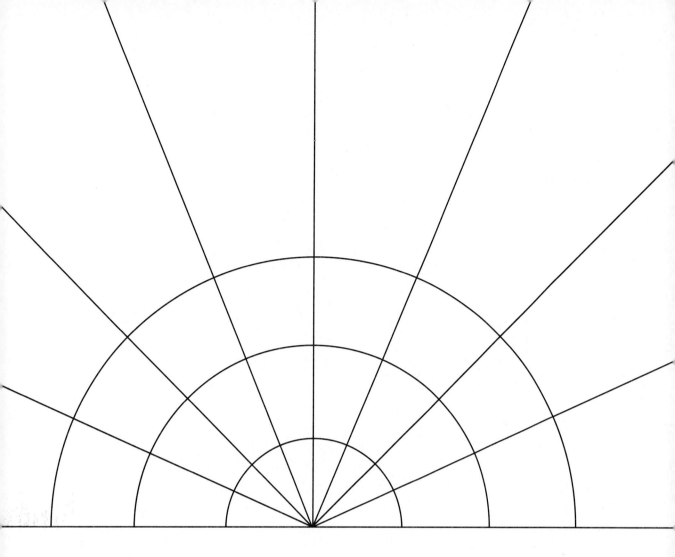

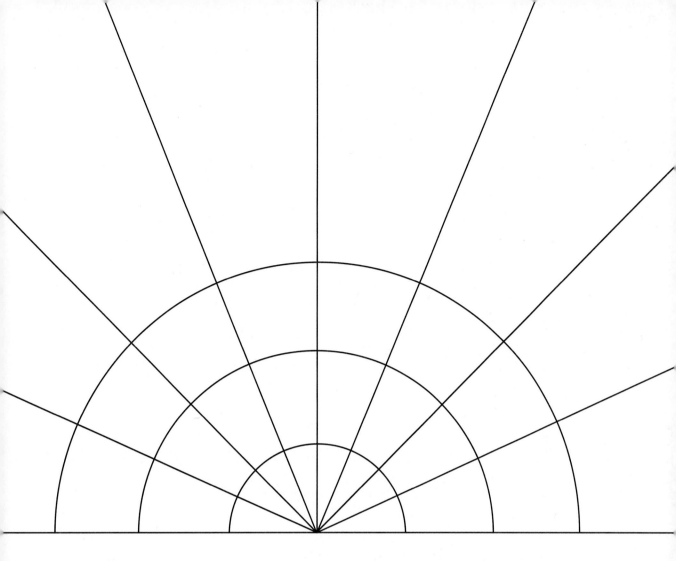

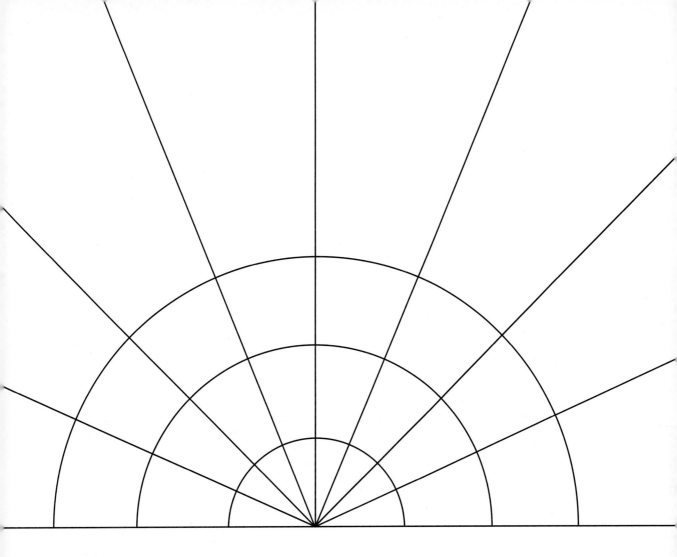

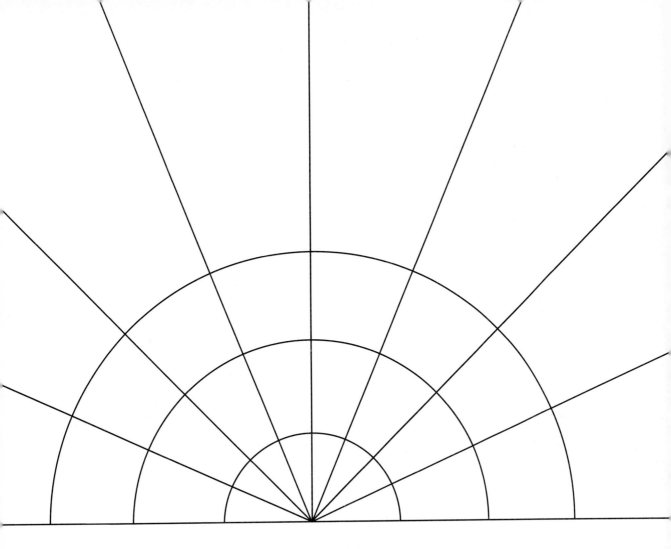

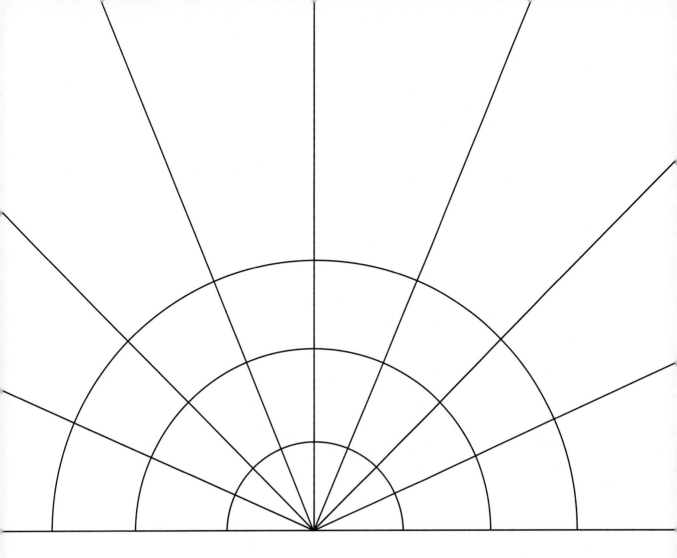

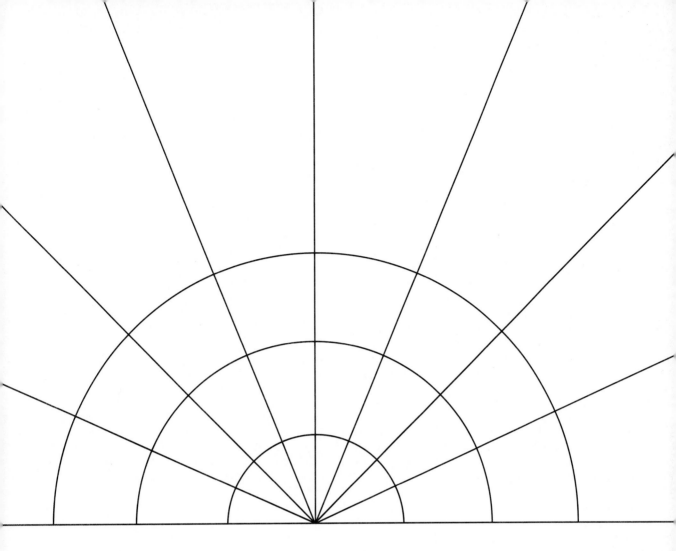

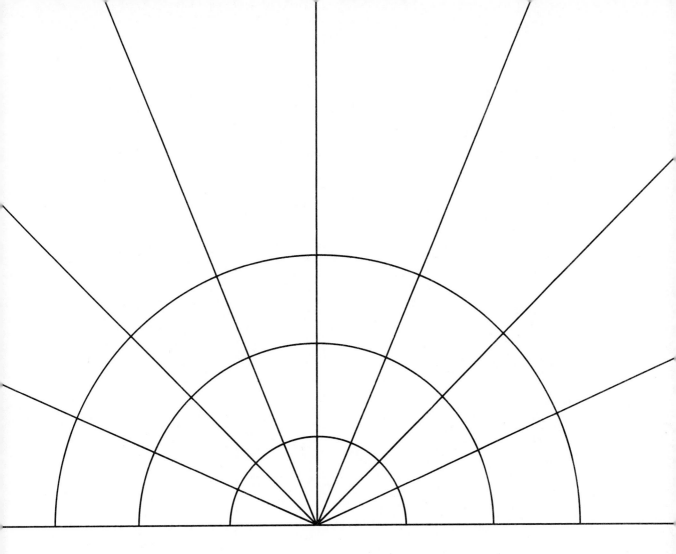

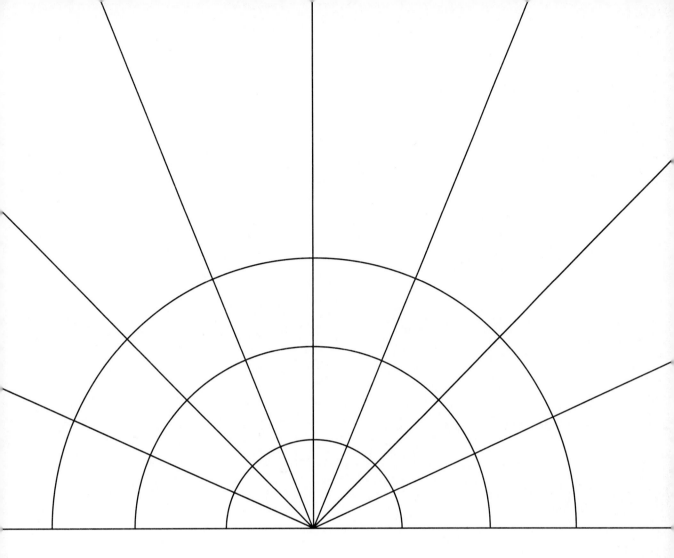

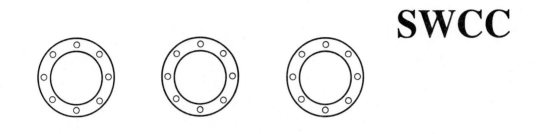

SWCC

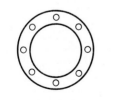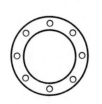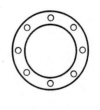

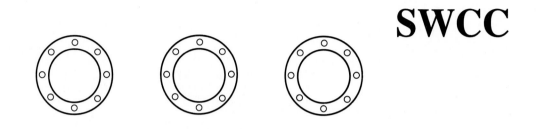

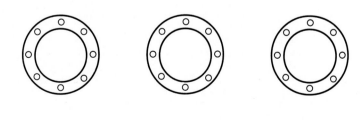

ЭЭМS

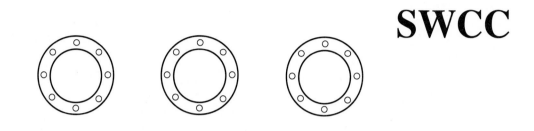

SWCC

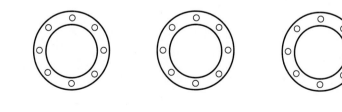

SWCC

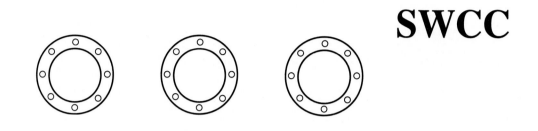

SWCC

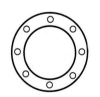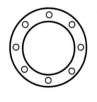

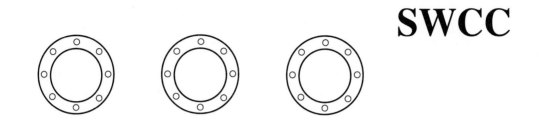

SWCC

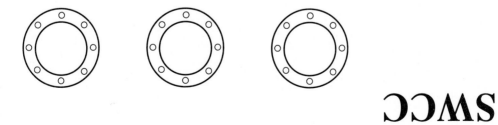

SWCC

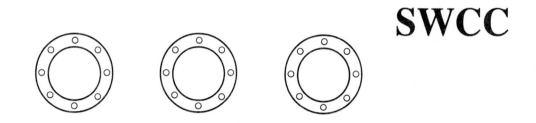

SWCC

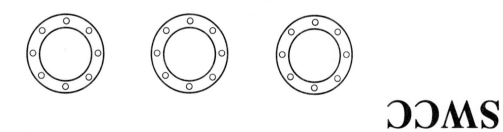

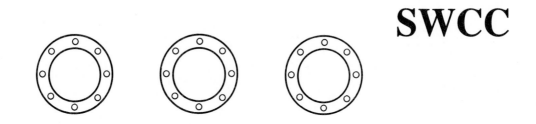

SWCC

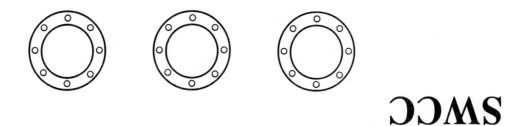

SWCC

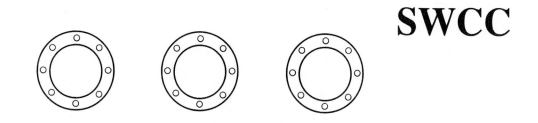

SWCC

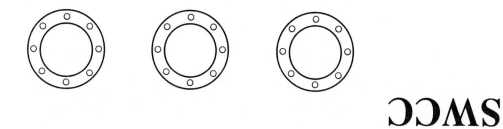

SWCC

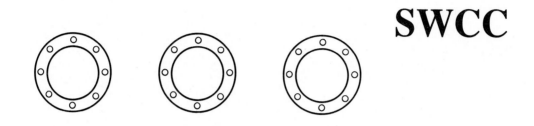 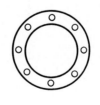

SWCC

SWCC

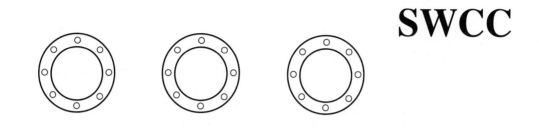

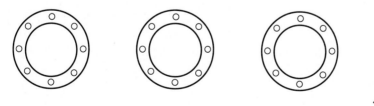

SWCC

Chapter

22

MANAGING CHANGE

OBJECTIVES By the end of the chapter you should be able to:

A. Describe the nature of change.

B. Explain the process of planned change.

C. Describe the characteristics of successful change efforts.

D. Understand the manager's role in the change process.

E. Define resistance to change and its function.

F. List tactics for dealing with resistance to change.

How to Live in a Fad Culture

Stanley Bing

Every so often a guy like Kip Breen descends from corporate Mecca, all teeth and gray twill, to spread ultrasenior management's latest instant credo with beamish zeal and a steel fist. That year it was something called Negative Task Evaluation, and it made us dance like Saint Vitus before it disappeared into the mists of corporate time, as fads do.

"It's pretty simple," Kip said benignly, easing a glossy, user-friendly packet across my blotter. "We want each manager to break down his ongoing activities, then derive the amount of time each chore requires as a percentage of the total workweek. Then you just work out a couple of simple graphs to see who is spending an inappropriate amount of time on matters of minor importance."

And then fire them, I thought.

In the coming months, I filled out more graphs than an infertile couple. People were evaluating one another all over the place, and relationships grew formal. We needn't have worried, though, because while middle management was diddling with its new Tinkertoy, the big guys were seized by a more terrible trend then careening around the horn: decentralization. Out of the window went the assiduously kept charts. With them flew 400 nice folks, willy-nilly. Nothing has been heard of Kip since, except over booze, when we survivors haul out his memory just for a hoot. Then we get back to work.

Reprinted from Esquire, Aug., 1986. With permission of publisher and author.

You'll have to excuse us guys on the inside if we get a little giggly each time the next new dogma comes along. We've been converted before, after all. We've managed in a minute and Theory Z'd, spotted megatrends, spun matrices, woven grids; we've hammered ourselves into hard-networking intrapreneurs, and sat in stupefaction before lanky preachers nagging us to Be Excellent! Some of us, thank God, have even found Wellness. We're willing to give each new creed a chance, until its hasty priests begin torturing the innocent into false confessions. The damned thing is, when the right idea is given the chance to mellow, spread, and ooze deep into the culture, it can actually do some good. But don't hold your breath.

Even when the idea is right—which it rarely is—most corporations still get it wrong. "You can go back to Management-by-Objective, Son of Management-by-Objective, Management-by-Objective meets Appraisal-and-Counseling," says E. Kirby Warren, professor at Columbia University's Graduate School of Business. "Most of these fads would have some real value if senior management took the time to ask themselves: 1) How do I adapt the idea to our culture and business? 2) What has to be changed to reinforce that thing we're talking about? and 3) Are we committed to staying with it long enough to make it work?"

But in today's overheated environment, most firms are too desperate to wait for results. "When we're facing intense competition from Asia, and money is relatively expensive, and technology is available and moves rapidly, it's not surprising that people reach out for what you call fads," says Joseph Bower, professor at Harvard Business School. "If you take almost any of them and discuss it with the author, it's a perfectly qualified view of how a set of ideas can run a company. But if it's treated as a kind of cookbook, as a single tool carried to an extreme, you get nonsense."

Still, when the guys with liver spots get that nutsy gleam in their eyes, you may have to snap to. Here are some pointers on how to survive.

It must be an autocracy, because democracy doesn't squeeze like that. The guys put in charge of forging the new culture aren't usually the Mother Teresa type. They take things personally, and they're not long on patience. Don't be fooled by warm and fuzzy verbiage designed to win your heart. This is a full blown drill. Get out on deck and run around.

Keep your mouth shut. Yes, the anal graphs and rah-rah lingo may seem absurd, but develop some instant naivete—I've seen more than one astute critic mailed overnight to the Elmira office for being a party pooper. "It's a religion," says a friend currently being strangled in the noose of a Quality circle. "To openly question or be cynical about it—you're more than grumpy, you're an apostate."

Charts are not enough. The need to play with neat fad gewgaws doesn't call off your actual job. "I had this subordinate who insisted on spending six months doing a PERT chart, while completely ignoring his other duties," recalls Wes, strategic-planning director at a multinational. "I love the memory of Frank pouring over a chart as big as a barn door that was supposed to govern our actions for the next year. He finally finished it, and we never looked at it again." Frank is out on the Coast now, by the way, teaching people how to do PERT charts.

General Pinochet! I had no idea you were dropping by. There's a healthy whiff of authoritarian zealotry in many fads, and some big boosters may think they've been named Ayatollah. Push them gently off your back. Unostentatious resistance to excess—even excess orthodoxy—is rarely questioned. "One of the darker moments last year was when the Productivity Czar asked everyone to sign a *Petition of Commitment*," recalls my friend Andy, a marketing manager at a retail firm. "It was invasive and ridiculous. I tried to kid him out of it. It turns out a lot of other people did, too. He was even advised against it by some of his peers, who felt it was sort of like reading the Bible in the office." The loathed petition now resides on the czar's wall, half full. Not one of the missing was punished.

Dare to be sold. A little credulity can be a beautiful thing. Several years ago I worked for a manufacturing company that decided to dedicate itself to Excellence. The propaganda campaign we inflicted on our workers was fierce. Management spent actual money to improve service. Worker initiative was rewarded. And, unbelievably, the elephantine organism began to lumber forth, to feel pride and a determination to succeed. It was corny and inspirational. We were a team, suddenly, and felt it. I wouldn't have missed it for the world.

A year into the program, the corporation was abruptly sold to a group of midwestern investors who broke it down and resold its body parts for cash. So long, Excellence. Hello, Leverage. What the hell: One good fad deserves another.

Premeeting Preparation

A. Read "How to Live in a Fad Culture."

B. Please answer the following questions:

1. Think back on a time when a major change effort took place within your organization or group. What was the change? What preceded it? What happened when the change occurred? How did people react to it? Was it successful?

2. What theories do you have about organizational change? What factors might determine success or failure?

3. What skills are necessary for instituting change?

4. What do you want to learn about organizational change and development?

5. What are the significant learning points from the readings?

C. Read the entire unit.

 Topic Introduction

Change is a way of life in today's business environment. The ability to manage change is a key factor in organizational survival, as witnessed by the title of the introductory section of Business Week's annual report on the top 1000 companies, "The Nimble Giants: Hard-Learned Lessons in the Art of Change Are Paying Off at Last."[1] Organizations are restructuring, re-engineering and rethinking how they do business in an effort to keep pace with changes in technology, economic conditions, global competition, world politics, and social and demographic change. Therefore, managers and employees alike need to understand the nature of organizational change.

There are several common roadblocks to organizational change. 1) Changes often upset the political system in organizations and come into conflict with the vested interests of people who prefer the status quo. 2) Managers are limited in their power to make changes, in part because complex systems resist change. 3) It is difficult for changes to endure. Some innovations succeed initially, but conditions eventually revert to their previous state. 4) What works in one part of an organization does not always transfer successfully to another area, so it is difficult to develop standardized change programs. 5) Oftentimes when organizations most need to change, they are least able to do so. For example, the demoralized employees of failing companies usually lack the energy, trust, and optimism that is required to make changes.[2]

In spite of these inherent difficulties, we have learned the following lessons from numerous successful change efforts. Change is usually neither easy nor fast, except when there exists a strong consensus about what the organization needs to change and a pent-up demand for change among employees. Although a successful change effort generally requires top management support, that alone is not sufficient to change a large system. There must be a critical mass of people who support the change. *Critical mass is defined as the smallest number of people and/or groups who must be committed to a change for it to occur.* Successful changes often begin at the periphery of the organization with dedicated general managers who focus energy upon work improvements rather than abstract principles like participation or organizational culture.[3] Their success then moves to the core of the organization as other units imitate their example.

Another requirement for successful change efforts is a sufficient level of trust within the organization so that people are willing to give up the known for the unknown and question some of their basic assumptions. Change almost always requires examining and rethinking the assumptions people hold about the environment, the way the organization functions, and their working relationship with other people.

People often undergo a mourning period before they can let go of previous ways of behaving, psychological contracts, conceptions of their organization, and relationships. Change requires both new behaviors and organizational learning, which must eventually be institutionalized so that the change can endure. Previously, it was assumed that changes in attitudes led to changes in individual behavior. In reality, the opposite is true. Behavior is shaped by the roles people are expected to play within organizations. Therefore, new roles, responsibilities, and relationships force people to develop new attitudes and behaviors.[4]

The study of human behavior reveals that people do not easily change long-term behaviors. Anyone who has tried to give up a cherished "bad habit" understands that behavioral change can be tricky, if not downright difficult or impossible. Lewin[5] described the process of change as unfreezing, moving, and refreezing. *Unfreezing* is accompanied by stress, tension, and a strong felt need for change. The *moving* stage refers to relinquishing old ways of behavior and testing out new behaviors, values, and attitudes that have usually been proposed by a respected source. *Refreezing* occurs when the new behavior is either reinforced, internalized, and institutionalized or rejected and abandoned.

Based upon the preceding lessons, it should be obvious that change is a process, rather than an event or a managerial edict. Furthermore, it is a process that is somewhat unpredictable since it is difficult to foresee how all the actors and interconnected parts of a system will react. Once we start tweaking a system, there are usually unanticipated consequences that require some modification in the change plans. Although there may always be a few surprises in a change effort, managers can avoid many problems if they are careful not to move immediately from a superficial diagnosis of a problem to the action steps. There will be more effective results and fewer tensions if a more thorough diagnosis is made of the situation to be changed and if the change process is managed systematically. Kolb and Frohman have developed a sequence for initiating and managing change that is a simple, seven-stage process (see Figure 22-1).[6]

The model emphasizes two important facets in the management of change:

1. It is a sequential process and each step is equally important.

2. Much of the success of the change effort will depend on the manager's relationship to those who will be affected most by the change and the appropriate participation of those people in the change process.

As with most models of behavior, the steps may blur into one another, but the articulation and recognition of them can help steer a clearer course through a change effort. The central issues for the change manager are summarized next for each stage of the change process.

SCOUTING

Although many managers feel they have an adequate knowledge of their own systems, it is beneficial in the beginning to test that assumption. At this stage, the manager is determining readiness for change, identifying obvious obstacles, and observing what is going on. This stage involves a passive diagnosis of the situation to size up costs and benefits of intervention (Is it worth "rocking the boat"?). The key task is to find the entry points for initiating a change, those individuals whose permission is needed, and key informal leaders in the system. The scouting phase of change is important because the choice of an incorrect entry point may doom an improvement to failure before it ever begins. For example, individuals who are most receptive to new ideas are sometimes "deviants" in their own group, while the group's leaders will be more cautious and conservative. To align oneself with the less respected "deviants" may cause difficulties in gaining the wider acceptance and legitimacy necessary to carry out the change.

FIGURE 22-1   The Process of Planned Change

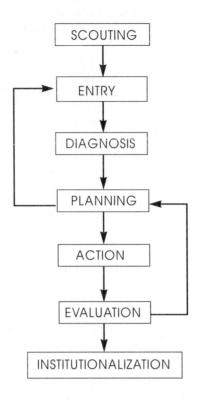

ENTRY

Once the entry point(s) has (have) been chosen, the manager and the system to be changed begin to negotiate a "contract" through the entry point representative(s) that will define if and how the succeeding stages of the planned change process will be carried out. The term "contract" is set in quotation marks because this process implies more than a legal document agreed upon at the outset of a project. The emphasis here is on a continuing process of sharing the expectations of the change manager and the system and agreeing on the contributions to be made by both parties. It is important to emphasize the continuing process of contract renegotiation, because as the planned change process enters succeeding stages, the nature of the problem may change and the resources needed for its solution may increase or decrease. Another aspect of the continuing negotiation process is represented by the feedback loop that reenters the entry stage from the planning stage (see Figure 22-1). As the diagnosis and planning stages proceed, the entry point into the system may have to shift or expand to include those parts of the system that are affected by and/or are responsible for the problem. For example, the personnel department of a company might begin work on the problem of high turnover among first-level management. Diagnosis of the problem may well reveal that the reasons for this turnover lie in poor morale in the line operations. Since responsibility for the ultimate solution of this problem lies with the line managers, the entry contract must be expanded to include these managers in the change process.

The main issue around which the contract negotiation process centers is power—gaining the influence necessary to implement the new program or method of operating. There are five primary sources of this power as shown on the next page.

1. The legitimately constituted authority of the system (e.g., the president says one should do this)

2. Expert power (e.g., the prestige of a consultant, or the compelling logic of a solution)

3. Coercive power (e.g., go along or you may lose your job)

4. Trust-based power (the informal influence that flows from collaborative problem definition and solutions)

5. Common vision power (which taps into a common vision that many people share for the future).

In most change projects power from all five of these sources is brought to bear in implementation of the change. However, the trust-based power derived from collaborative problem definition is often especially critical to the success of those planned change efforts where the system's formal power structure and experts are seen as part of the problem that needs to be solved.

DIAGNOSIS

Diagnosis, as much as possible, should be a collaborative effort involving as many of the affected parts of the system as possible. It focuses on four elements: the perceived problem, a force field analysis, the goals of the group or organization, and the available resources.

1. *Problem definition:* The first step in defining the specific problem is to identify the subpart(s) of the system where the problem is located and identify the relationship between that subpart and other parts of the system. This is necessary to anticipate the effect of change in one part of the system on other aspects of the system's functioning. If more and/or different problems surface as the diagnosis progresses, the group can assign priorities and focus attention on the most important problem or the problem that must be solved before other problems can be attacked.

2. *Identification of forces that promote and resist change:* Lewin[7] saw change as a dynamic balance of forces working in opposite directions. He devised the "force field analysis," which assigns pressures for change and resistance to change to opposite sides of an equilibrium state. For example, several years back Ford found itself pressured by foreign competition, declining market share, and stakeholder complaints to change the company. These were some of the forces that promoted change at that time. However, within Ford there were also forces that inhibited change such as an entrenched adversarial union-management relationship, and both managers and workers who were accustomed to a way of working that was less efficient and innovative than much of their competition. Eventually a critical mass of employees became convinced of the need to change in order to keep their jobs. The pressures for change were stronger than the resistance, allowing the company to make major innovations in a fairly short period of time. Identifying the major forces for and against change is a useful aid in diagnosing the situation. Managers have three choices: to increase the strength of a pressure(s) to change, to decrease or neutralize the strength of a resistance(s) to change, or to try to convert a resistance into a pressure for change. The key point here is the conception of change as a dynamic process in which a state of equilibrium is reached.

3. *Goal definition:* At this point goals do not need to be as precise and measurable as they should be later. It is usually sufficient to articulate the state you would like the organization or group to reach as a result of the change effort. Broadly stated, goals can give direction to the planning effort without overly constraining it.

4. *Resource identification:* Since people in the system will be involved in implementing the change (indeed, they are the major resources in many cases), their abilities, motivation, and commitment must be used if the change effort is to proceed properly. As these are identified, the manager will also want to ask, "What resources from outside our system do we need to use to reach our goal?"

PLANNING

The result of the diagnostic phase form the starting point for the planning phase. Depending on the findings, these results may require a renegotiation of the entry contract. During the planning phase, the entry contract should be expanded to include those members of the system who will be responsible for implementing the change and/or those who will be immediately affected by it.

The first planning step is to define the objectives to be achieved by the change. Once clear-cut objectives have been established, alternative solutions or change strategies should be generated. Following this, some attempt should be made to simulate the consequences of each of the intervention alternatives. Often this is done simply by thinking through the implications of each change strategy, but more sophisticated simulation methods, such as computer simulation, can be used. The final change strategy is then chosen from the available alternatives.

Intervention plans can be classified on two dimensions: the source of power used to implement the intervention (formal power, expert power, coercive power, trust-based power, and common vision power) and the organizational subsystem to which the intervention is addressed. The six organizational subsystems are as follows:

1. *The people subsystem.* Two general types of interventions can be used in this subsystem: personnel flow interventions and education. The personnel flow interventions affect the selection, placement, rotation, and retention of organization members. Educational programs have been designed to change motives, skills, and values. Some common educational interventions include seminars, university programs, data collection and feedback, role playing, and on-the-job training.

2. *The authority subsystem.* The authority subsystem has a formal and an informal aspect. Changes can be made in formal authority relationships—in job titles and responsibilities, in the span of control, in the number of organizational levels, and in the location of decision points. In addition, informal leadership patterns can be the object of change interventions. For example, a team-building program may be designed to base leadership more on team members' expertise than on organization titles.

3. *The information subsystem.* This subsystem also has a formal and an informal aspect. The formal information system of the organization can be redesigned to give priority and visibility to the most important information and to provide mechanisms for getting information to the right place at the right time. Much of the organization's information, however, is carried by the informal system, which is often faster than the formal system. Many work team development programs focus in part on this process, using interventions designed to improve the quality of communications among organization members.

4. *The task subsystem.* The two identifiable parts of this subsystem are the human satisfactions offered by the job and the technology on which the job is based. Job enlargement, an important area of organizational development, has done much to redesign jobs to obtain a better match between the job holder's motives and the satisfactions provided by the job. Several schemes have been developed for classifying technology and exploring the implications of each classification for the organization of the firm and for the individual holding the job.[8] Likewise, the impact of technological change on the organization has been studied in detail, although little has been done to plan systematic technological changes with a consideration for their impact on other organizational subsystems or on the total development of the organization.

5. *The policy/culture subsystem.* As the name implies, this subsystem has a formal, explicit aspect and an informal, implicit aspect. The policy subsystem is made up of rules concerning working hours, promotion, the formal reward system, and work procedures. The culture subsystem consists of the norms and values of the organization—what type of behavior is rewarded, how conflict is handled, what is expected among peers. Perhaps the most common focus of organization change is on the formal policy system. Attempts to change the culture of an organization are more difficult.

TABLE 22-1 Planning Checklist

SUBSYSTEM	PROBLEM DEFINITION	PROPOSED SOLUTIONS	POSSIBLE EFFECTS ON OTHER SUBSYSTEMS
1. People		1. 2. 3.	1. 2. 3.
2. Authority		1. 2. 3.	1. 2. 3.
3. Information		1. 2. 3.	1. 2. 3.
4. Task		1. 2. 3.	1. 2. 3.
5. Policy/culture		1. 2. 3.	1. 2. 3.
6. Environmental		1. 2. 3.	1. 2. 3.

The Grid OD program is one example of a systematic and comprehensive approach to culture change.[9]

6. *The environmental subsystem.* The environment can be divided, somewhat arbitrarily, into the internal physical environment and the external environment. One important component of the internal environment is architecture. The spatial relationships of organization members, for example, can have a great impact on the information system.[10] The external environment has many characteristics that affect the organization: rapidity of change, uncertainty, quality and quantity of labor supply, financial and material resources, political and legal structures, market, and so on. An organization chooses its environment when it begins operation. It can subsequently redefine certain elements of its environment. For example, an organization initially conceived to serve a specific market can redefine its objective and self-image to that of a growth company in a wider market, thereby relating more to uncertain rather than stable aspects of its environment. This redefinition will have implications for all the other organizational subsystems

The six organizational subsystems can form a checklist to be used by the manager when planning or executing any action intervention. An example of such a checklist is shown here as Table 22-1. The primary purpose of the checklist is to remind the manager that a change in one subsystem will affect other organizational subsystems. The list can be useful for selecting the best leverage point and for identifying the other subsystems most likely to be affected by the intervention. It may be easier, for example, to redefine jobs than to change motives, an indication that the manager should at least start with the task subsystem rather than the people subsystem. In addition, the manager must plan the intervention in such a way that both aspects of the subsystems are kept in harmony: educational programs and personnel flow interventions must be compatible, the formal and informal authority systems must be mutually supportive, the design of a formal information system must take into account the existing informal flow of information, a program that will redesign jobs must consider the human satisfaction factor as well as the existing technology, policy changes are doomed to subversion if they are not supported by cultural changes, and a close relationship must be maintained between the internal and the external environment.

The checklist can also be useful in identifying the sources of power available for bringing about change and for determining which source, or combination of sources, is the most appropriate for the type of intervention planned. Certain combinations may not be enough to implement even the best plan. The lack of trust-based power, for example, could doom the intervention to failure, as in the case of one consultant who was hired by the head office to do work in the field offices. Perceived as a representative of the head office, with which most of the field offices had great difficulty working, the consultant was unable to develop trust-based power. The intervention in the people subsystem of the field offices therefore met with little success. The consultant's own "postmortem" noted that it was the inability to establish trust with each field office that prevented acceptance of the change program.

ACTION

The action phase of a planned change effort can encompass a wide range of activities from management training to creation of new information systems, to changes in organization structure, to changes in architectural and spatial relationships. No matter what the changes are, there is likely to be some resistance to change. *Resistance to change is a natural reaction to change and part of the process of adaptation.* This resistance, when it occurs, is often treated as an irrational negative force to be overcome by whatever means necessary; yet, in some cases, resistance to change can be functional for the survival of a system if it helps us perceive the potential problems of a planned change. If an organization tried every new scheme, product, or process that came along, it would soon wander aimlessly, flounder, and die. The positive function of resistance to change is to ensure that plans for change and their ultimate consequences are thought through carefully. The failure of most plans for change lies in the change's unanticipated consequences. In industry, these failures often take the form of technical changes (e.g., a new information system, a new production process) that fail to anticipate and plan for the social changes that the technical changes cause (e.g., increases and decreases in power at different levels of the organization in the information system example on new working relationships and/or more or less meaningful work in the new production process example). The result is that managers and administrators are annoyed at the stupidity of those subordinates who resent these logical improvements. Yet the subordinates often are not resisting the logic of the improvement (and hence logical arguments for the change do not help) but, rather, the social changes or threats to core organizational values that management has not recognized.

Another cause of resistance to change can be the sudden imposition of changes in someone's environment without that person's prior knowledge of, or participation in, the change. To have an important part of one's environment suddenly changed by forces outside one's knowledge and control can cause great anxiety, even panic. The human response to this experience is hostility toward the source of change and resistance to the new method. The process of growth and maturation consists of gaining mastery over one's environment. Management, by imposing change, serves to arrest this process by denying subordinates the opportunity to live in an environment they can understand and control. People who spend their lives in organizations managed by imposed change can become helpless, passive victims of the system, cursed by management for their stupidity and lack of initiative. We will discuss tactics for dealing with resistance to change more fully later on in the chapter, but some of the dysfunctional aspects of resistance to change can be alleviated by careful preparation for the action phase. If system members can be involved at the appropriate stages for the scouting, entry, diagnosis, and planning phases, the plan for change can be made more intelligent and more appropriate to the technological and social needs of the system.

EVALUATION

The tradition in the scientific evaluation of change projects has been to separate the evaluation phase from the action phase. To ensure unbiased results, an independent researcher is often hired to evaluate the change efforts. While this approach has some benefit from the standpoint of scientific objectivity , it has some cost in terms of the effective implementation of change. It should be clear in this model that the evaluation phase is an integrated part of the change process.

The evaluation of the action strategy is conducted in terms of the specific objectives defined during the planning phase as well as interim task goals designed to determine if the change is progressing as desired. Members of the system therefore know on what dimensions they are being evaluated. The potential bias created by this knowledge can be overcome by careful choice of objective evaluation indices that cannot be manipulated. For example, the goal of an action intervention may be to increase the quantity of patentable products produced by a research group. The validity of the results obtained from using the number of patents as the evaluation index will not be affected by the group's knowledge of the intervention goal, whereas the use of self-evaluation ratings of creativity might.

To develop within the system the ability to use the information generated for self-analysis, the group or organization should monitor the progress of the action phase and evaluate the data itself. The results of the evaluation stage determine whether the change project moves to the institutionalization stage or returns to the planning stage for further action planning and perhaps to the entry stage for further contract negotiation among the participants.

INSTITUTIONALIZATION

If the steps so far outlined have been followed, a great deal of effort will have gone into the change, excitement about reaching change goals will have been high, and the natural tendency will be to experience a letdown once the change has been implemented. Institutionalization should not mean a rehardening of the organization's arteries, but a new way of working that combines stability and flexibility. If the change is seen as "complete," those arteries will harden. If it is seen as "continuous," there will be mechanisms in place for continuing to flex and change as situations demand. Some of these conditions necessary for the maintenance of the change are as follows:[11]

1. Management must pay conscious attention to the "continuous transition."
2. Explicit process or procedures for setting priorities for improvement should be instituted.
3. There should be systematic and continual processes of feedback.
4. The reward system should reward people for time and energy spent on these processes.

Procedure for Group Meeting:
The Hollow Square Exercise[12]

Materials: Each group should bring one pair of scissors and four envelopes.

This exercise is designed to simulate the stage in the change process when the planners of a change must communicate the change to the people who will implement it.

STEP 1. The class divides into groups of 8 people. This group is then further subdivided into four planners and four implementers. If there is an odd number of students, place 3-5 people on the planning team. However, the implementation teams should always consist of exactly four people.

STEP 2. Once the groups have decided who will be planners and implementers, the implementers will wait in a separate area until the instructor has given the planners their instructions. Please do not read the instructions for the planning team.

STEP 3. The instructor reads the planning teams their instructions (page 640) and provides them with the materials they need to perform the exercise. Please do not read the instructions for the implementation teams. (Materials to photocopy are also included on page 643-646.)

STEP 4. The planning teams have 30 minutes to plan how they will communicate the instructions to their implementation team.

STEP 5. The instructor reads the implementation teams their instructions (page 633).

STEP 6. All implementation teams begin the 15 minute assembly period at the signal of the instructor. The first team to complete the assembly wins. During this time, the planning team can only observe and refrain from making any noises that might distract or influence the implementing team.

STEP 7. When the assembly period is completed, each participant should complete both sections of the evaluation that follows. Then each subgroup should average their scores for each question (i.e., the implementation team comes up with their own team average and the planning team does likewise).

EVALUATION OF THE IMPLEMENTATION TEAM

a.   How well was the puzzle completed?

       1   2   3   4   5   6   7

Not at
all well

Very
well

b.   How faithfully did the implementers follow the planning team's
instructions?

       1   2   3   4   5   6   7

Not at
all well

Very
well

c.   How well organized was the implementation team?

       1   2   3   4   5   6   7

Not at
all well

Very
well

d.   How well did the implementation team understand the planning
team's instructions?

       1   2   3   4   5   6   7

Not at
all well

Very
well

e.   To what extent did the implementation team try to clarify the
planning team's instructions (e.g., asking questions, paraphrasing
instructions, etc.)?

       1   2   3   4   5   6   7

Not at
all well

Very
well

EVALUATION OF THE PLANNING TEAM

a. How clear (explicit, unequivocal) were the instructions given by the planning team?

	1	2	3	4	5	6	7

Not at
all clear

Completely
clear

b. How well organized was the planning team?

	1	2	3	4	5	6	7

Not at
all well

Very
well

c. To what extent did the planning team involve the implementation team in their strategies?

	1	2	3	4	5	6	7

Not at
all

To a
large degree

STEP 8. *Group Discussion.* The two subgroups that worked together compare their evaluation scores. Discuss the following questions and choose a representative to present your answers to the class during the plenary session.

1. Are there any differences in the way the panning and implementation teams perceived each other? Why or why not?

2. What did the planning team do that helped the implementation team? Did they do anything that hindered the implementers? Use the chart below to record these factors.

3. What did the implementation team do that helped them succeed in this exercise? Did they do anything that hindered their success?

4. What can you learn about organizational changes from this exercise?

STEP 9. *Plenary Session.* Each group presents their findings.

ANALYSIS OF COMMUNICATING CHANGE	
PLANNING TEAM ACTIONS THAT Helped Hindered	IMPLEMENTATION TEAM ACTIONS THAT Helped Hindered

The class as a whole discusses the following questions.

1. What feelings and thoughts did the implementation teams experience while awaiting the instructions for an unknown task?

2. How did the implementation teams organize to accomplish this task?

3. How much time did the planning teams devote to figuring out how to transmit the message to the implementation teams?

4. Did the time at which the planners brought the implementers into the process (early on or just before the assembly period) have an effect upon the proceedings? If so, what was the effect and why did it occur?

5. What parallels can you draw between this simulation and organizational change efforts you have observed or experienced?

6. Look at Figure 22-2 for lessons about communicating changes.

INSTRUCTIONS FOR THE IMPLEMENTATION TEAMS

1. You have the responsibility for carrying out a task for four people in accordance with the instructions given to you by your planning team. Your planning team can call you back to the classroom to receive these instructions at any time during their thirty minute preparation period. However, if they have not called you by _____ (five minutes before you are scheduled to carry out your task), you should report to them. Your task is programmed to start exactly at _____. Once you begin, your planning team cannot provide you with any more instructions.

2. Your mission is to complete the assigned task as quickly as possible.

3. While you are waiting for the planning team to call you in to receive your instructions, please discuss and take notes on the following questions. Your notes will be useful during the debriefing session.

   a. What feelings and thoughts are you experiencing as you await the instructions for an unknown task?

   b. How can the four of you organize yourselves as a team to accomplish this task?

Follow-Up

One of the key success factors in the hollow squares exercise is the presence of a shared, communicated vision. If the planning group does not communicate the overall goal, it is difficult for the implementation team to fill in the gap between the instructions they have received and what they must do to complete the puzzle.

Vision is also an important factor in determining an organization's readiness for change. David Gleicher of Arthur D. Little developed the following formula to help gauge when it is worthwhile to undertake a change effort.

$$C = (abd) > x$$

In this formula, C = change, a = level of dissatisfaction with the status quo, b = clear or understood desired state, d = practical, first steps toward a desired state, and x = cost of changing. As Beckhard states: "For change to be possible and for commitment to occur, there has to be enough dissatisfaction with the current state of affairs to mobilize energy toward change. There also has to be some fairly clear conception of what the state of affairs would be if and when the change were successful. Of course, a desired state needs to be consistent with the values and priorities of the client system. There also needs to be some client awareness of practical first steps or starting points toward the desired state."[13]

It is possible to increase the level of dissatisfaction with the status quo by sharing productivity information about competitors with employees or by survey-feedback techniques that present employees with the aggregated results of their individual opinions. In this manner, more people perceive the need for change and form the necessary critical mass.

According to Beer and his colleagues[14], the manager's role in the change process is a series of six steps which they call the critical path. The steps are sequential and their exact timing is of critical importance:

1. Mobilize commitment to change through joint diagnosis of business problems
2. Develop a shared vision of how to organize and manage for competitiveness
3. Foster consensus for the new vision, competence to enact it, and cohesion to move it along
4. Spread revitalization to all departments without pushing it from the top
5. Institutionalize revitalization through formal policies, systems, and structures
6. Monitor and adjust strategies in response to problems in the revitalization process.

RESISTANCE TO CHANGE

Once readiness has been determined, a successful change must 1) have a *high-quality solution* to the system's problem in terms of its technical and logical soundness and 2) must be *acceptable* to the members of the system. The acceptability of a change is often determined less by the quality of the problem solution and more by the *process* through which the change is introduced.[15] For example, changes that are imposed by administrative decree are often actively or passively resisted because the members of the system are not aware of the problem that the change is intended to solve.

An adequate process is one of four common sources of resistance to change. The other three are 1) inadequate solution, 2) individual resistance, and 3) systematic resistance. At times, decision makers show poor judgment and select a change target or intervention that is inappropriate. In this case, resistance occurs because people perceive that the *solution is inadequate* and a real threat to the organization and/or its core values.

Another form, *individual resistance,* results not from a considered opinion that the proposed change is incorrect, but from personal discomfort with any kind of change. Some individuals, as well as national cultures, value tradition and the status quo more than change and the risk-taking it implies.

Systemic resistance occurs when one aspect of the system is changed without adjusting the other parts. To implement most changes, we also need to modify the performance review system, recruiting, compensation policies and systems, and career planning and manpower planning systems.[16] For example, when one chemical producer decided to adopt a global strategy, it was not enough to change their production standards and capacity. They also started recruiting employees with international backgrounds and foreign language skills. They established a policy that overseas experience was a prerequisite for senior management positions. These complementary changes in the system removed any obstacles that may have prevented employees from adopting an international focus.

Kanter identified the following sources of resistance that occur when the change process is inadequately managed: 1) feeling out of control, 2) excess uncertainty from not knowing where the change will lead, 3) lack of time to mentally adjust to changes, 4) stress caused by too many changes and forced attention to issues that were formerly routine, 5) feeling compelled to defend the status quo because doing otherwise would involve a loss of face, 6) concerns about future competence when the ground rules seem to be changing, 7) ripple effects to personal plans that will be affected by the change, 8) greater work and energy demands necessitated by the change, 9) past resentments, and 10) the real threat posed by a change in which some people will be winners and others will be losers. [17] She concludes that all resistance to change is certainly not irrational and managers who understand the reasons for resistance are better able to deal with it constructively. Managers often resent and become angry with employees who resist change. However, this reaction does nothing to reduce the resistance and often exacerbates an already difficult situation. More effective tactics for dealing with resistance to change are:[18]

1. *Education and Communication*. Help people understand the reasons for the
   change, the form it will take, and the likely consequences. This clears up
   misunderstandings that often cause resistance.

2. *Participation and Involvement*. Encourage others to help with the design and
   implementation of the changes. This creates commitment to the change and
   usually improves the quality of the change decisions. The disadvantages of this
   tactic are the time it consumes and, if the participants lack the necessary expertise,
   their solutions may be inadequate.

3. *Facilitation and Support*. Provide encouragement, support, training, counseling,
   and resources to help the people who are affected by the change.

4. *Negotiation and Agreement*. Offer incentives in return for decreased resistance to
   the change.

5. *Manipulation and Co-optation*. Manipulation usually takes the form of distorting
   or withholding information or starting false rumors so that employees agree to a
   change. For example, one multinational wanted their employees to switch to a
   less expensive retirement plan. HR staff presented only the attractive features of
   the new plan and suppressed the information that employees would fare worse

under the new plan. Co-optation occurs when the leaders of the resistance are "bought off" by allowing them a role in the change process. If people realize they have been manipulated or co-opted, they lose the trust that is so essential to the change process and can become even more resistant.

6. *Coercion.* When people are threatened with negative incentives (e.g., unwanted transfers, denial of promotion and pay raises, negative performance evaluations, etc.) if they do not accept a change, this is called coercion. Most people resent coercion, and its use may irreparably harm relationships. However, at times there is no other alternative to reduce resistance.

The first three tactics, while more time-consuming, are more likely to result in commitment to the change. The last three tactics may yield compliance with the change, but not commitment.

It is generally accepted that the best way to allow Americans to feel some sense of ownership of the change process is through participation. However, this is not true in cultures, like the Philippines and Mexico, where people expect leaders to make the decisions. Cultures have varying orientations to change itself. While change is a key American value, many other cultures, like Great Britain and China, place greater emphasis upon tradition. In such cultures, managers will tend to be less proactive about making changes, and change processes are likely to take more time. The same is true of cultures that believe more in fate than in human control of one's destiny. Managers in cross-cultural settings need to understand the various cultural values about change and recognize that change interventions that work in one country may not be successful elsewhere.[19]

 # Learning Points

1. Managing change has become a crucial skill for both managers and employees.

2. Critical mass is defined as the smallest number of people and/or groups who must be committed to a change for it to occur.

3. Successful changes often begin at the periphery of the organization with dedicated general managers who focus energy upon work improvements rather than abstract principles.

4. Much of the success of the change effort depends on the manager's relationship to those who will be affected most by the change and by the appropriate participation of these people in the change process.

5. Change is a sequential process and each step is equally important.

6. Kolb and Frohman's process of planned change consists of seven steps: 1) scouting, 2) entry, 3) diagnosis, 4) planning, 5) action, 6) evaluation, and 7) institutionalization.

7. Scouting involves a discrete diagnosis of the situation to determine whether change is feasible and worthwhile and to identify the appropriate entry point, that is, the people who have the necessary power and interest in the change.

8. The entry phase involves negotiating a contract about the expectations of the manager and the system regarding the change.

9. The diagnosis stage consists of problem definition, identification of pressures for and against change, goal definition, and resource identification.

10. The planning phase establishes the objective of the change and the alternative change strategies. It is also necessary to identify the possible consequences of each strategy upon the other subsystems that will also be affected by any change.

11. The action phase can consist of a number of change interventions. Resistance to change should be viewed, not as an obstacle, but as a natural reaction that can improve the final result.

12. In the evaluation phase the group or organization monitors the progress of the action phase and determines whether the change should be institutionalized or returned to the planning stage.

13. Institutionalization refers to the maintenance of the change effort that implies continuous attention to feedback on its progress and ensuring that policies and reward systems reinforce the change.

 # for Managers

- Don't make changes just for the sake of making change. Too much change in a system is just as frustrating to employees as the feeling that any change is impossible. Think through the pros and cons of any change very carefully before taking action. For some people, making changes has more to do with their own need to impact the system than the needs of the system.

- As a manager leading a major change effort, the best analogy is that of a surfer riding the crest of a big wave. If few others see the need for change, it probably won't happen.

- Almost all organizations should focus a good bit of energy on innovation and change on a regular basis. But not everyone in the organization needs to be involved in this. Some organizations utilize parallel or collateral organization structures. Parallel organizations have the freedom and flexibility to do the innovating and problem solving, while the "maintenance organization" carries on with business as usual. People who dislike uncertainty and who cherish a fondness for the status quo are more satisfied in maintenance organizations, while the creative, entrepreneurial types prefer the parallel organization. Managers who point out that both of these structures and types of employees are equally valuable to the organization can avoid potential conflict between these groups.[20]

- Trust is an important aspect of any change project. Often clients do not make significant movement until they begin to trust the consultant(s) involved. Employees do not believe management's new visions for the future unless their trust has been won. Trust allows people to unfreeze and move. Therefore, it's very important that managers do not make promises they cannot keep.

- Successful change efforts seem to be characterized more by a desire to capitalize on some identified potential or strengths than by a focus solely to the negative aspects of the organization. Moving toward a desired state seems to produce more of the energy needed for change than merely moving away form a negative state.

- The more people have been allowed to participate in the change effort, the more commitment there will be to its success.

- New programs require careful attention and nurturing. Having the head of a new program report directly to the CEO until the program is well established is one way of ensuring its survival.

- Change is not always a rational, linear process. Where major organizational transformation is required, change involves a leap of faith to move the organization to another plane which cannot always be seen from the point of departure. For this reason, such changes require shared values and symbolic gestures by managers.

- People sometimes go through a period of "mourning" in large-scale change projects. Accepting this difficulty, acknowledging it with employees, allowing them to vent their feelings, and even planning ritual celebrations like farewell parties help people to get through this period more easily.

 # Personal Application Assignment

This assignment is to write about a change effort or a consulting project you were part of or observed. Choose one about which you are motivated to learn more.

A. *Concrete Experience*
1. *Objectively describe the experience* ("who," "what," "when," "where," "how" type information—up to 2 points).
2. *Subjectively* describe your feelings, perceptions, and thoughts that occurred during (not after) the experience (up to 2 points). Does this section have too much detail? (If so, delete 1 point.)

B. *Reflective Observation*
1. Look at the experience from different points of view, How many points of view did you include that are relevant (up to 2 points)?
2. Use these perspectives to add more meaning to the incident (up to 2 points).

C. *Abstract Conceptualization*

    1. Relate concepts from the assigned readings and the lecture to the experience (i.e., what theories that you heard in the lecture or read in the *Reader* relate to your understanding of this incident?). Make reference to at least two sources. Use standard referencing format and include the page number to which you are referring. How many sources did you use and how clearly did you explain their theories (up to 4 points)?

    2. You can also create an original model or theory, but it should not replace course concepts.

D. *Active Experimentation*

    1. Write about what you will do in the future that will improve your effectiveness. Use rules of thumb or action resolutions.

    2. Are they described specifically, thoroughly, and in detail (up to 4 points)?

E. *Integration, Synthesis, and Writing*

    1. Did you write about something personally important to you (up to 1 point)?

    2. Was it well written (up to 2 points)?

    3. Did you integrate and synthesize the different sections (up to 1 point)?

INSTRUCTIONS FOR THE PLANNING TEAMS

Each individual on the team (unless the team has five members) will be given an envelope containing four pieces which, when properly assembled with pieces from other participants, will make a hollow square design.

During the next thirty minutes, your task is to:

1. Plan how these pieces, distributed among you, should be assembled to make the design shown below in Figure 22-1.
2. Instruct your operating team on how to implement your plan so as to complete your task ahead of the other teams. (You may begin instructing your operating team at any time during the thirty minute planning period—but no later than 5 minutes before they are to begin the assembly process.)

GENERAL RULES

1. You must keep all four pieces that you have in front of you at all times.
2. You may not touch the pieces of other planning team members or trade pieces with other members of your team during the planning or instructing phase.
3. You may not show Figure 22-1 to the implementation team at any time. Nor may you provide them with written instructions or drawings.
4. You may not actually assemble the entire square at any time (this is to be left to your operating team at the moment the assembly period begins).
5. You may not number or otherwise mark the pieces.
6. **Members of your operating team must also observe the above rules until the signal is given to begin the assembling.**
7. When time is called for your operating team to begin assembling the pieces, you may give no further instructions. Just step back and observe the implementation team at work without making any noises that might distract or influence the executors.

FIGURE 22-1   Hollow Square Exercise

A. Overall Pattern

B. Detailed Assembly Guide

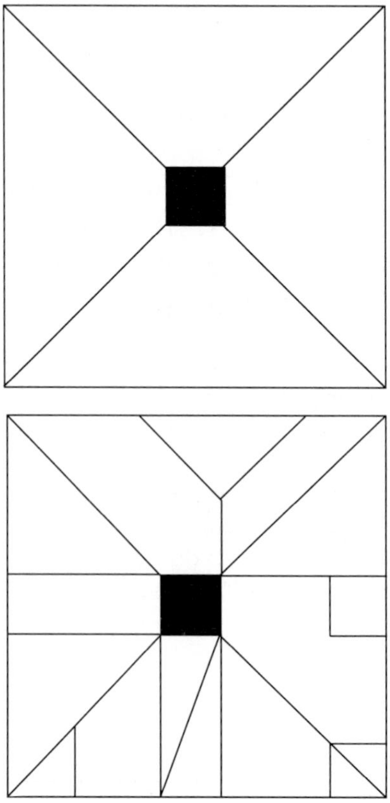

FIGURE 22-2   Lessons About Communicating Changes[21]

Problems that may occur when one group makes plans that another group is to carry out:

1. Planners sometimes impose restrictions on themselves that are unnecessary.
2. It is sometimes difficult for planners to see the task from the point of view of the implementers.
3. Sometimes in planning, more attention is given to details while the larger clues and possibilities go unnoticed.
4. Planners sometimes fail to apportion their time wisely because they plunge into the act of planning before they think through their entire task and the amount of time available to them.
5. Planners sometimes have different understandings of their task and the boundaries in which they must operate.
6. When members of a planning team fail to listen to one another, time is lost in subsequent efforts to clarify what each party meant.
7. Sometimes planners fail to prepare a proper physical setup for the implementation team.
8. Sometimes planners become so involved in the planning process that they do not plan their method of instructing the implementers.

Common problems when planners instruct implementers:

1. Sometimes the planners do not consider the implementers' anxieties when they orient them to the environment and task.
2. Planners may not allow enough time for instruction and fail to help the operators feel prepared and comfortable about doing their job.
3. Planners may not encourage questions from the implementers and therefore assume greater understanding on the part of the implementers than really exists.
4. The planners' own feelings of anxiety or security are likely to be transmitted to the implementers.
5. Planners sometimes give detailed instructions before giving the implementers an "overall" feel for the task.
6. Planners sometimes stress minute problems instead of more important points.
7. The instructions may be given in a way that discourages members of an operating group from working as a team.

Common problems when operators carry out the plans of others:

1. If instructions are confusing, implementers tend to display irritation toward each other and the planners.
2. If instructions are unclear, considerable time will be spent in clarification.
3. Members of an operating team will often have different perceptions of their instructions.
4. The factor of pressure will influence different implementers in different ways—the efficiency of some will go up and the efficiency of others will decline.
5. If members of an operating group do not feel themselves to be a team, they will usually perform less efficiently.

[1]"The Nimble Giants: Hard-Learned Lessons in the Art of Change are Paying off at Last." *Business Week*, March 28, 1994, pp. 64-69.

[2]Some of these roadblocks are mentioned Rosabeth M. Kanter, Barry A. Stein, and Todd D. Jick, *The Challenge of Organizational Change* (New York: The Free Press, 1992) pp. 5-8.

[3]Michael Beer, Russell A. Eisenstat, and Bert Spector, "Why Change Programs Don't Produce Change," *Harvard Business Review*, November-December 1990, pp. 158-166.

[4]Beer et al, *"Why Change Programs Don't Produce Change,"* p. 159.

[5]Kurt Lewin, "Frontiers in Group Dynamics," *Human Relations*, Vol.1 (1947), pp.5-41.

[6]This model of the planned change process was generated through the collaborative efforts of Frohman and Kolb. For a more detailed description, see David A. Kolb and Alan L. Frohman, "An Organization Development Approach to Consulting, " *Sloan Management Review*, Vol. 12 (1970), pp. 51-65.

[7]Kurt Lewin, *Field Theory in Social Science* (New York: Harper & Row, 1951).

[8]See Jay R. Galbraith, "Organization Design." In J. Lorsch (Ed.) *Handbook of Organizational Behavior* (Englewood Cliffs, NJ: Prentice-Hall, 1987) pp. 343-357; J. Thompson, *Organizations in Action* (New York: McGraw-Hill, 1967), and J. Woodward, *Industrial Organization: Theory and Practice* (New York: Oxford University Press, 1965).

[9]Robert R. Blake and Jane Mouton, *Building a Dynamic Corporation Through Grid Organization Development* (Reading, MA: Addison-Wesley, 1969).

[10]For a systematic treatment of the impact of architectural and physical settings, see Fred I. Steele, *Physical Settings and Organization Development* (Reading, MA: Addison-Wesley, 1973).

[11]Richard Beckhard and Reuben Harris, *Organizational Transitions: Managing Complex Change* (Reading, MA: Addison-Wesley, 1987).

[12]This exercise was developed by Dr. Bernard Bass, Director, the Center for Leadership Studies, SUNY Binghamton, and is used with his permission.

[13]Richard Beckhard, "Strategies for Large System Change," in D. A. Kolb, I. M. Rubin, and J. S. Osland, *The Organizational Behavior Reader* (Englewood Cliffs, NJ: Prentice Hall, 1990).

[14]Beer et al, *"Why Change Programs Don't Produce Change,"* pp.161-165.

[15]Alfred J. Marrow, David G. Bowers, and Stanley E. Seashore, *Management by Participation* (New York: Harper & Row, 1967).

[16]Richard Beckhard and Wendy Pritchard, *Changing the Essence* (San Francisco: Jossey-Bass, 1992).

[17]For an interesting account of managing organizational change in today's environment, read Rosabeth Moss Kanter's *The Change Masters* (New York: Simon & Schuster, 1983), or an excerpt, "Managing the Human Side of Change," in the *Reader*.

[18]John P. Kotter and Leonard A. Schlesinger, "Choosing Strategies for Change," *Harvard Business Review*, March-April 1979, pp. 106-14.

[19]This article describes the various forms of organizational change efforts that emerge in different cultures—Claude Faucheux, Gilles Amado, and Andre Laurent, "Organizational Development and Change," *Annual Reviews of Psychology*, 33, 1982, pp. 343-370.

[20]For more information on parallel organizations, see B. A. Stein and R. M. Kanter, "Building the Parallel Organization: Creating Mechanisms for Permanent Quality of Work Life," *Journal of Applied Behavioral Science,* Vol. 16 (1980), pp. 371-388; and Gervase R. Bushe and A. B. (Rami) Shani, *Parallel Learning Structures* (Reading, MA: Addison-Wesley, 1991).

[21]Adapted from Bernard Bass, "When Planning for Others," *Journal of Applied Behavioral Science*, 6 (2), 1970, pp. 151-171 and used with permission.

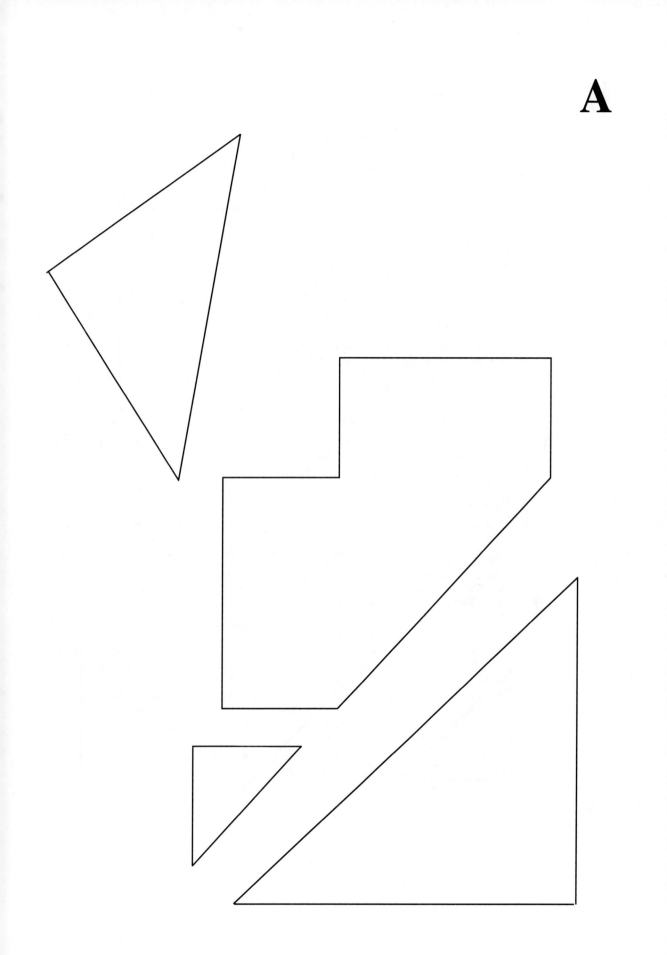

B

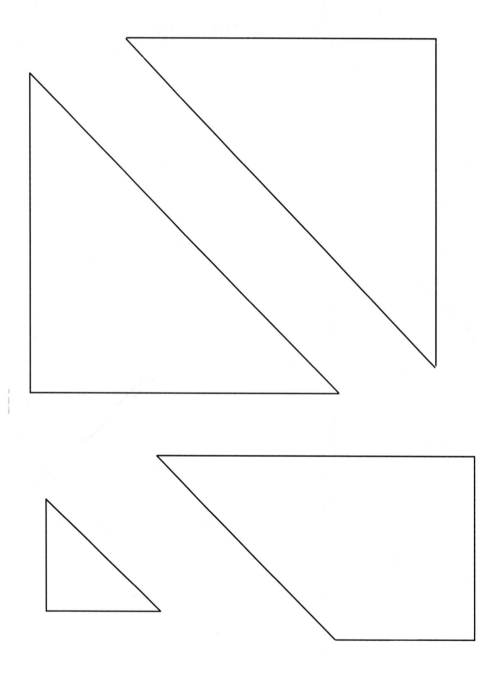

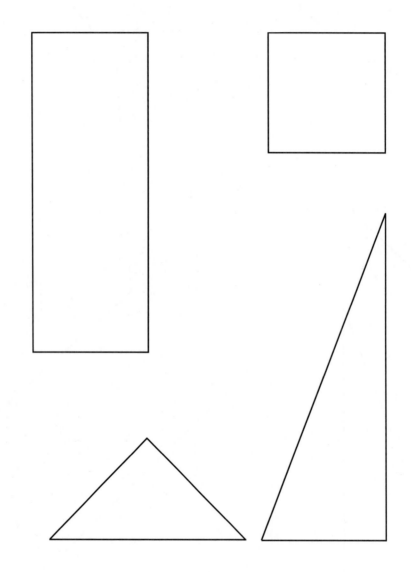